"One must first be a human being. All true art grows out of that which is distinctively human."

Edvard Grieg

By Finn Benestad and Dag Schjelderup-Ebbe

TRANSLATED BY WILLIAM H. HALVERSON AND LELAND B. SATEREN

University of Nebraska Press: Lincoln and London

Edvard Grieg

The Man and

the Artist

Originally published as *Edvard Grieg: mennesket og
kunstneren,* © 1980 H. Aschehoug & Co. (W. Nygaard),
Finn Benestad and Dag Schjelderup-Ebbe

The paper in this book meets the minimum requirements of the American National Standard
for Information Sciences – Permanence of Paper for
Printed Library Materials, ANSI Z39.48-1984.

Publication of the English translation was supported by a generous grant from the American-
Scandinavian Foundation.

Library of Congress Cataloging in Publication Data
Benestad, Finn.
[Edvard Grieg. English]
Edvard Grieg: the man and the artist / by Finn
Benestad and Dag Schjelderup-Ebbe; translated by
William H. Halverson and Leland B. Sateren.
p. cm.
Translation of: Edvard Grieg: mennesket og kunstneren.
Bibliography: p.
Includes indexes.
ISBN 0-8032-1202-X (alkaline paper)
1. Grieg, Edvard, 1843-1907. 2. Composers – Norway –
Biography. I. Schjelderup-Ebbe, Dag. II. Title.
ML410.G9B413 1988   780'.92'4—dc19   87-20608
[B]   CIP   MN

The picture on the dust jacket is a detail from a
famous painting of Edvard and Nina Grieg by P. S.
Kröyer. (Nationalmuséet, Stockholm)

The frontispiece is a reproduction of an 1890 portrait
of Grieg by Eilif Peterssen. The original belongs to
Mr. Egil Monn-Iversen, Oslo.

Contents

LIST OF ILLUSTRATIONS

Illustrations are listed in the order in which they appear in the book. All items listed are photographs unless otherwise noted.

To the Reader

In 1897, regarding a proposed biography that was to be written by his friend Iver Holter, Grieg wrote: "If you will permit me to give you a word of advice, it is this: write without regard for me or anyone else. Simply allow your entirely independent self to speak." This frank counsel from Grieg himself has served as our guiding principle in the writing of this book. We have attempted to give an unvarnished picture of Norway's greatest son in the realm of music—to present him as he truly was both as a man and as an artist.

This has proved to be a fascinating task, both because of Grieg's exceptional versatility and because so much of his music is of such sterling quality. There is, of course, no denying that Grieg and his music have a particularly strong hold on the affection of Norwegians, and for this reason the temptation to eulogize is strong. Some readers may feel that we have occasionally fallen prey to this temptation. We can only say that we have indeed given free rein to our enthusiasm whenever, on the basis of careful appraisal, we have judged a composition to be particularly valuable. However, Grieg's production was uneven, and we have made no attempt to conceal this fact.

There cannot be the slightest doubt that Grieg was a musical genius. His works bear such an original and marked individual stamp that his authorship is immediately recognizable. His lasting influence can be traced in both the Norwegian and the international context, thanks not least to his pioneering work in the field of harmony. Moreover, as one of the leading representatives of national Romanticism, he was recognized abroad, almost from the outset, as a symbol of authentic Norwegian music.

Grieg was a man of many outstanding talents. As a writer he may be ranked with Schumann and Berlioz. As a public speaker he was considered by many people to be the near equal of Björnstjerne Björnson, Norway's great national poet. He had charisma, this spiritual radiation that one sometimes encounters in truly great personalities. And he had a special knack of putting his message across, whether in words or in music.

There was always great excitement at the Peters publishing firm in Leipzig when a new collection of *Lyric Pieces* composed by Grieg was received. His music was extremely popular in concert halls the world over while managing to speak directly to millions of musical amateurs as well.

With the aid of descriptions and analyses, we hope to demonstrate that Grieg was a master not only of the smaller musical forms but of the larger forms as well. However, we also want to stress the fact that the musical miniature should in no way be underestimated, for genius is just as likely to find expression in a small poetical piece for the piano as in a grandly conceived sonata movement.

We have made every effort to use language that will be readily understood by all music lovers. Nonetheless, from time to time—especially in connection with the detailed analysis of musical examples—we have had to use words and phrases drawn from the specialized vocabulary of music theory.

The book presents a great deal of previously unexplored material regarding both Grieg's life and his compositions. In order to avoid a polemical approach and the use of numerous footnotes, however, we have deliberately refrained from commenting on inaccuracies that have occurred in other books and articles on Grieg.

The Catalog of Works on pp. 409–29 is based on Dan Fog's *Grieg-Katalog* (1980), a comprehensive bibliography of Grieg's published works. We express our sincere thanks to Mr. Fog for giving us permission to use his material. Our Catalog of Works also includes Grieg's unpublished compositions. Moreover, for the first time in Grieg literature *incipits* are used, i.e., brief musical excerpts indicating the initial notes or principal themes of each piece.

The book also contains an alphabetical Index of Compositions and a General Index.

Throughout the time that we have been preparing this book for publication we have received invaluable assistance from the music division of the Bergen Public Library, the main center of Grieg research. We should like to thank its personnel for their willing and friendly cooperation. We also extend our thanks to the management of the Troldhaugen Trust for the kindness they have shown us, and to the respective staffs of the photo archive divisions of the University of Oslo Library, the University of Bergen Library, and the Royal Library in Copenhagen. The sources of our illustrations are usually listed following the picture captions.

Our thanks are also due to others who have lent us letters and pictures and provided valuable information on Grieg and his contemporaries. We are especially indebted to Inge Bergliot Benestad, teacher of music, and Öivind Eckhoff, university lecturer, both for their critical perusal of our manuscript and for much valuable advice.

As the book is now presented in an English version, we wish to express our deep gratitude to the translators, Dr. William H. Halverson of The Ohio State University and Dr. Leland B. Sateren of Augsburg College, for the exceptional competence and care with which they have fulfilled their arduous task.

FINN BENESTAD
DAG SCHJELDERUP-EBBE

Translators' Preface

It is with great pleasure that we present to the English-speaking world this translation of *Edvard Grieg: Mennesket og Kunstneren*, the definitive biography of Edvard Grieg by Professors Finn Benestad and Dag Schjelderup-Ebbe of the University of Oslo. The authors have for many years been at the forefront of Grieg research and have written many articles and books on various aspects of Grieg's life and works. *Edvard Grieg: The Man and the Artist* is, therefore, the rich product of many years of intensive and devoted study. It is authoritative and thoroughly up-to-date, and will undoubtedly serve as a major reference work on Grieg for many years to come.

Edvard Grieg: The Man and the Artist should properly be regarded as a new edition of the book rather than simply a translation, for the authors have worked closely with us in the preparation of the manuscript and have used the opportunity to bring their book up to date. And—surprisingly perhaps – there have been many important developments bearing upon our knowledge of Grieg since the publication of the Norwegian edition in 1980. The most astonishing development, certainly, was the release for public performance (1981) and subsequent publication (1984) of Grieg's only symphony, which in accordance with the composer's explicit instructions had not been performed since 1867. The intriguing story of how this came about is related in the chapter entitled "Formative Years in Copenhagen."

Of even greater interest to musicologists, however, was the discovery in New York City in 1984 of a collection of twenty-nine holograph manuscripts and 371 letters in Grieg's own hand. Among the items discovered were autograph scores of some of Grieg's most important compositions, including both *Peer Gynt* suites, several selections from *Sigurd Jorsalfar*, six complete volumes of *Lyric Pieces, Bergliot, Symphonic Dances*, and much more—over 400 manuscript pages in all. The letters—mostly to Dr. Max Abraham, director of the C. F. Peters publishing firm (Leipzig) until his death in 1900—contain Grieg's instructions for changes that were to be made in certain scores, comments regarding business details, and observations on music, current events, other composers, and many other topics. All of these materials were originally in the possession of the C. F. Peters firm, which published most of Grieg's compositions after 1888. It was long assumed that they had been lost during World War II, but happily they had been removed from Germany before the war by the sons of Henri Hinrichsen—Dr. Abraham's nephew, who in 1900 had succeeded him as director of C. F. Peters—and eventually came into the possession of Mrs. Walter Hinrichsen of New York City. Mrs. Hinrichsen, realizing the importance of these materials to Grieg scholars and to the Norwegian people, entered into negotiations that resulted in the purchase of the entire collection by the Norwegian government in 1986. It is now housed in the Bergen Public Library, which is also the repository for all the "music, . . . books, manuscripts, autographs, and letters from artists" bequeathed to the library by Grieg upon his death in 1907.

A third development that has further enriched this translation is the continued march toward completion of the C. F. Peters edition of *Edvard Grieg's Complete Works* (hereafter GGA, an acronym derived from the German title of this publication). Fourteen volumes of this definitive work (which will eventually comprise twenty volumes) have been published as of this writing, and professors Benestad and Schjelderup-Ebbe—both members of the editorial committee responsible for GGA—have also had access to materials in preparation for all of the remaining volumes. Thus we have, for example, been able to use throughout this book the English titles used or planned for use in GGA. Since the latter will certainly be normative for the foreseeable future, it is our hope that the present book will contribute to the standardization of English titles of Grieg's compositions.

GGA will also contain new English translations of the texts of many of Grieg's songs. Whenever the authors quote a song text for which a new translation has been prepared, we have used that translation. In the remaining cases we have provided our own translations of these texts.

The Norwegian alphabet contains three vowels for which there are no exact equivalents in English: æ (pronounced like the "a" in "man"), ø (pronounced like the "u" in "fur"), and å (pronounced like the "o" in "more"). When these vowels occur in proper names, we transliterate as follows: æ = ae, ø = ö (the German *umlaut,* which we assume is more familiar to most readers), and å = aa.

Norway's capital city acquired its present name—Oslo—in 1925. It was called "Christiania" from 1624 to 1877, at which latter date the spelling was changed to "Kristiania." Because this change occurred during his lifetime, Grieg sometimes uses one spelling and sometimes the other, as do other writers quoted in this book. In the body of the text we have used "Oslo" rather than "Christiania" or "Kristiania" in the belief that this is likely to be least confusing to most readers. Whenever Grieg or one of his contemporaries is quoted directly, we have retained the name and spelling used by the writer but have added the modern name [Oslo] in brackets. When "Christiania" occurs in a proper name—as in "Christiania Theater"—we have retained the correct proper name.

The book contains a large and valuable collection of Primary Materials in translation—excerpts from Grieg's correspondence, critical reviews of public performances of his music, articles by and about Grieg, and so on. To make these materials accessible without interrupting the flow of the chronological text, they have been placed in marginal columns alongside the text throughout the book. A footnote indicates that a related item will be found among the Primary Materials.

A few terms occur in the text that are not meaningfully translatable into English. In these cases we have elected to retain the Norwegian terms in italics and provide brief explanations of them in a Glossary which will be found on p. 407. They are for the most part types of Norwegian dance tunes (*halling, kulokk, springar,* etc.). We could, of course, have used "cowcall" for *kulokk,* "roundel" for *springar,* and so on, but these terms—comfortingly familiar though they may be—tell one nothing about the unique characteristics that give each type of dance tune its special character. Casual readers will quickly understand from the context that a *springar,* for example, is a particular kind of dance tune; meanwhile, readers who wish to know something about the unique characteristics of a *springar* can consult the Glossary.

The translators have worked together on all phases of the translation and share equal responsibility for the final product.

We wish to thank the following groups and individuals for their invaluable contributions to the successful completion of this project: the staff of the music division of the Bergen Public Library for allowing us to study the valuable collection of Grieg letters and manuscripts housed there; the Norwegian Ministry of Foreign Affairs and the Norwegian Information Service in the United States for two travel grants; The Ohio State University for released time and travel support; Mr. Clair Strommen and Lutheran Brotherhood of Minneapolis for two travel grants; Dr. Patricia McFate, President of the American-Scandinavian Foundation, for her wise counsel regarding the publication of the book; and Marolyn Halverson for assistance in the preparation of the final manuscript. Special thanks are due to Professors Finn Benestad and Dag Schjelderup-Ebbe, both of whom read and evaluated the entire manuscript and spent many days in conference with us both in the United States and in Norway.

Finally, we acknowledge with gratitude a generous subvention from the American-Scandinavian Foundation, without which *Edvard Grieg: The Man and the Artist* could not have been published.

WILLIAM H. HALVERSON
LELAND B. SATEREN

Part One: The Foundation Is Laid

An Age of Conflict: Fertile Soil for Creativity

1. TRIBUTE TO BERGEN

You see, it is not just the art and the science of Bergen that have nourished me, it is not just Holberg and Welhaven and Ole Bull who have taught me . . . No, the whole Bergen milieu that surrounds me has been my very substance. Bergen scenery, Bergen deeds and initiatives of all kinds have inspired me . . . (Edvard Grieg in a speech to the people of Bergen on the occasion of his sixtieth birthday, 1903.)

The city of Bergen is and always has been a very special place, and Edvard Grieg bore the stamp of his native city in every facet of his being. As variable as the weather, his artistic temperament ran the gamut from mischievous joviality to deep melancholy. The "rowdy from Bergen" in him expressed itself especially when he was in the company of his closest friends, and on festive occasions he was truly in his element. Then he carried everybody else in the group along with him, and was sometimes so blunt as to be provocative. He was a brilliant writer; one marvels at his elegant and striking formulations, often laced with salty humor.

One might say that Grieg had a kind of love-hate relationship with Bergen. He loved the old houses, the narrow streets, the harbor, and the mountain surroundings. But the climate of western Norway always bothered him, especially the rawness and darkness of winter. What he truly despised about his native city, however, was its shallowness—the middle-class mentality that placed everyday business above the more spiritual and artistic values. Nonetheless, he never lost his love for Bergen.[1] He expressed this love in moving words on many occasions, but the most beautiful proof of his devotion to the city lies not in glowing words but in concrete action. Near the end of his life he willed his entire life's output as a composer to Bergen.

What kind of a city was this that Grieg both loved and hated, but that in his heart he was so proud of? It was the city that for centuries had been—in fact if not in name—Norway's true capital, with its face turned toward the sea and the outside world. Bergen, notwithstanding its provincialism, was the only city in Norway that bore the mark of international influences, and it has preserved its unique blend of distinctive and exciting traditions to the present day. A full 150 years before Grieg was born this milieu had served as an important backdrop for Ludvig Holberg's comedies. It is likely, for example, that Pernille's pithy retorts (in such Holberg plays as "The Weathercock" and "The Fussy Man") are derived from the glib shouts of the women who hawked their wares in Bergen's open-air fish market.

As early as 1765 Bergen had its own music society, "Harmonien" (the precursor of the Bergen Symphony Orchestra), in which Grieg's family played an essential role. From time to time the quality of the musical perfor-

Ludvig Mathias Lindeman—composer, organist, and the first person to engage in a systematic gathering of Norwegian folk tunes. He published more than five hundred folk tunes in simple piano arrangements. His collections proved to be of invaluable significance for later Norwegian composers, not least for Grieg. (Photograph by O. Vaering, Oslo)

mances undoubtedly left something to be desired, and perhaps the social dimension sometimes received too much emphasis, but in any case both professional and amateur musicians had a place where they could sharpen their skills playing the works of the great masters. Later, "Harmonien" became an institution in which the struggle for quality became a principal concern. During Grieg's active years, however, it was a question of preventing the music life of Bergen from sinking once again to the low level that it had reached during the early 1800s. Thanks to the efforts of Grieg and his successors, the Bergen Symphony Orchestra has in fact achieved international stature.

Viewed from a broader national perspective, the nineteenth century was a time of struggle for the Norwegian people—politically, socially, and to a large extent artistically as well. Under the influence of American and French ideas of liberty, the general unrest of the Napoleonic era combined with the struggle of the Norwegian people for independence from Denmark. The first triumphant result of this confluence was the Norwegian constitution signed at Eidsvoll in 1814. The Norwegian people were thus awakened from their "four-hundred-year night," and with proud enthusiasm set about the tremendous task of unleashing the forces that in the course of the next seventy-five years were to transform a very backward country into one of the most culturally advanced nations in the world.

Norway's emerging national consciousness during the years following 1814 laid the foundation for new economic development. At the same time it created the preconditions for the period of cultural growth that was about to begin—a period marked by a strong interest in that which was distinctively Norwegian. In the early stages of this "National Revival" movement the enthusiasm for that which was distinctively Norwegian was perhaps a bit naïve, but as time went on more and more people began to delve deeply into the cultural substance of their country. Ivar Aasen's dialect studies laid the foundation for the development of *nynorsk*—a new form of Norwegian based on a blending of many rural dialects—as a written language. At the same time there was a decisive awakening of interest in the ancient national traditions with their legends, folk tales, songs, and instrumental music. P. C. Asbjörnsen and Jörgen Moe explored the world of the folk tales, and M. B. Landstad did pioneering work in the area of the folk song. It was indeed time for such activity: Landstad once said that he felt as if he had helped rescue an old family jewel from a burning house.

As early as about 1840 L. M. Lindeman began systematically collecting folk tunes, and his first independent publication, *Norske Fjeldmelodier* [Norwegian Mountain Melodies], aroused considerable attention. During the years 1853–67 he published his monumental *Aeldre og nyere norske Fjeldmelodier* [Older and Newer Norwegian Mountain Melodies], a collection that has had an enormous influence on Norwegian music ever since. A number of Grieg's compositions owe a substantial debt to Lindeman's work. Lindeman continued his collecting over a period of many years, and he received a grant from the Norwegian parliament to support him in his travels throughout the country. He was the first musician in Norway to receive such a grant; the

Ole Bull. Portrait by E. J. Baumann.
Arthur M. Abell, in his book Talks with
Great Composers, *quotes Grieg in a 1907 in-*
terview as follows: "It was Ole Bull who first
convinced me that I should compose typically
Norwegian music . . . Ole Bull was my rescuer.
He opened my eyes to the beauty and original-
ity of Norwegian music." (Norsk Folkemuseum,
Bygdöy, Oslo, Norway)

members of Parliament probably had little sensitivity for art, but they demonstrated an appreciation of the national treasures that lay hidden in many a
remote area.

In the realm of classical music, in 1824 Waldemar Thrane made independent use of some distinctively Norwegian features in his musical play *Fjeld-*
eventyret [The Mountain Tale]. But the first composer who made a serious
attempt to incorporate a national style in songs, choral compositions, and
piano pieces was Halfdan Kjerulf.

It was not only in Oslo, however, that the quest for that which was
distinctively Norwegian found its expression in music. One of Bergen's own
native sons became the very personification of the truly Norwegian: that was
Ole Bull, "a Norse Norwegian from Norway" as he liked to call himself when
he was abroad. He was a character right out of a fairy tale, both in Norway
and on the international music scene, and the leading violinist of his day. As a
composer he was a captive of the virtuoso music of the time, but in a few

works he managed to reflect a genuine Norwegian atmosphere. This is especially true of the rhapsodic composition, *Et Saeterbesök* [A Visit to the Mountain Farm], which includes the piece "A Herd Girl's Sunday"—a composition that, with Jörgen Moe's beautiful text (added later), has become a folk treasure in Norway.

The quality in Ole Bull that was to have the greatest importance for those who came after him was his uncanny ability to inspire others with enthusiasm. One can hardly overrate the role he played for Björnson and Nordraak, and also for Grieg when he was searching for his Norwegian identity. Grieg spoke again and again of the unique importance this legendary violinist had for the future development of Norwegian music. At Ole Bull's funeral in 1880 he said: "Because you were an honor to our country like none other; because you raised our country up with you to art's glowing heights like none other; because you were a pathfinder for our young national music, a faithful and warm-hearted conqueror of the hearts of all like none other; because you have planted a seed that will one day sprout and for which future generations will bless you; with the deepest gratitude, *in the name of Norwegian music* I lay this wreath upon your coffin . . ."

As early as 1794 a theater company had been established in Bergen—a kind of sister institution to "Harmonien." This company provided a certain cultural element to the everyday life of the city. People learned to appreciate dramatic art, but there was no thought of establishing an independent Norwegian drama as such. Until 1850 Danish was the dominant language on the Norwegian stage.

But January 2, 1850 was a memorable day in the theatrical life of the city, for on that day "Det Norske Theater" [The Norwegian Theater] opened its doors. This is the institution that was later continued as "Den Nationale Scene" [The National Stage], the name under which it has continued in operation to the present day. The opening production was the first one in Bergen in which the cast consisted entirely of Norwegians. The founder of the venture was Ole Bull. The following year he engaged Henrik Ibsen as director and playwright-in-residence—a position that Ibsen was to keep for six years. Ibsen's successor was Björnstjerne Björnson. Both were then filled with enthusiasm for "Norwegianness," and exciting times arose for the people of Bergen.

Unfortunately, the theater had altogether too short a life span in this first attempt, despite the energetic contributions of Ole Bull. The support of the local population was not sufficient to keep a professional theater going. On May 17, 1863, the theater declared bankruptcy.

Bergen during these years would still have been considered a small town, for the population growth up to the year 1860 had been surprisingly slow. Around 1800 the city had 18,000 inhabitants. By 1863 the number was not greater than 25,000, but in the following decades the population grew much faster so that by the turn of the century it had reached 70,000.

These brief sketches can perhaps give some of the background for Edvard Grieg's creative activity, which essentially falls within the last forty years of the nineteenth century. At the time of Grieg's birth in 1843, Norway was regarded

Björnstjerne Björnson. Painting by Erik Werenskiold. On June 15, 1903—on the occasion of Björnson's sixtieth birthday—Grieg gave a talk in which he said, "The most beautiful and festive moments of my life I owe to Björnson. Where you were there was celebration. It was either your books, or your work for Norway, or your personal presence, that created the festive mood . . . You yourself were the fountain— Norway's mightiest torrent, that rumbled and roared and splashed and foamed until it was like a sea around you. It was precisely this splashing and this roaring that I and everyone else in my generation loved, and that led us to love you. And how the early spring sun shone upon this fountain! For what you said is true: it was spring then. You yourself were the bringer of spring . . . Yes, Björnson, as you sit here among us, you are the countryman whom we love most of all. And why? Because you are our ever wakeful conscience. Because it is through you that we feel the beat of Norway's pulse." (Nasjonalgalleriet, Oslo)

by other countries as a virtual nonentity. Politically, socially, and culturally it was viewed as a primitive country, relatively unknown by international standards, a province on the fringes of civilization. But during Grieg's lifetime there was an almost explosive development in a number of disciplines, so that by about 1900 Norway had to a certain extent become the cultural center of Scandinavia in the eyes of the rest of the world.

Tremendous conflicts marked these years in Norway's history. It was a time of such remarkable growth that we can scarcely fathom it today. The political tensions were at times unusually strong. A thoroughgoing process of radicalization accelerated the democratization of society even as the form of government was also becoming more democratic. The Norwegians displayed a steadily increasing dislike for Swedish political domination. The desire for independence was finally realized in 1905 with the termination of the Swedish-Norwegian union. Many had thought that war was inevitable, but reason prevailed on both sides of the border.

In the cultural realm the climax was reached earlier than 1905, led by the men associated with the "National Revival" movement and their successors. Several brilliant scientists and explorers earned world-wide fame for themselves and for Norway: the accomplishments of N. H. Abel, Armauer Hansen, and Fridtjof Nansen were shining examples of the Norwegian pioneering spirit.

Norway asserted itself relatively early in the area of pictorial art. The painters J. C. Dahl and Thomas Fearnley were soon followed by Adolph Tidemand and Hans Gude; these men and several of their gifted followers managed in their often sharply nationalistic paintings to distinguish themselves convincingly from the artists of other countries.

In the field of literature the radical writers Henrik Wergeland, Björnstjerne Björnson, and Henrik Ibsen stormed forward with irrepressible energy and a visionary outlook.

Grieg experienced quite early the tension that characterized these years of national conflict. One evidence of this is a newspaper article he wrote about Halfdan Kjerulf in 1879. A short excerpt from this article will be found in the text accompanying the picture of Kjerulf on p. 9.

Grieg himself became a radical, a tireless champion of the cause in which he believed so deeply. Zeal for the national cultural heritage was a powerful motive for him, but he never allowed himself to adopt conventional ways of thinking about anything. He had a natural desire and ability to reshape whatever he touched, and in one particular aspect of his music this quality expressed itself in a brilliant way—namely, in the realm of harmony. His starting point was German Romanticism, which was not particularly promising for a person of his bent. But quite early in his development the latent national consciousness came to the fore, strongly encouraged by Ole Bull's and Rikard Nordraak's zeal for that which was distinctively Norwegian. The emergence of this national consciousness led to profound conflicts in his attitude toward his mission as a composer, for he dreaded the danger of falling into a narrow-minded chauvinism. He would be Norwegian in his art, but at the same time he was determined to see his music against the background of a broader cosmopolitan setting. The artistic conflict between national and international influences marked his life's work in many ways.

However, Grieg's cultural work was not confined only to composing and performing. He became a leading figure in the cultural life of Norway, a personality whose opinions carried considerable weight. As an outspoken humanist, he stood in the front ranks in the struggle for social and national justice, politically conscious and progressive in his thinking as he always was. His basic attitude toward life and his view of art were permeated by the highest ethical ideals.

The conflicts in the spiritual life of Norway are reflected in a remarkable way in Grieg. Not least for that reason it is an absorbing and enriching experience to study his life and work. But it is first and foremost through his music that this brilliant man from Bergen continues to speak to the people of our time.

Halfdan Kjerulf. Upon Kjerulf's death in 1868, Grieg wrote of him as follows in Illustreret Tidende: *"He had no predecessors to show him the way. There was nothing but folk ballads, the outward expression of the most primitive cultural life. These he took as his starting point, and he chose the art song as the vehicle for his creative activity. For this we owe him thanks, for only in this area was it given to him to capture the national color by which our music can achieve its natural and healthy development." The following year he wrote in* Aftenbladet: *"Kjerulf had the good fortune to live at a time when the emerging national consciousness found its first powerful expression in virtually all of the arts and sciences of the Norwegian people, who in 1814 achieved their independence from Denmark. In painting there were Gude and Tidemand, in poetry Wergeland and Welhaven, in history the brilliant scholar P. A. Munch—all of whom expressed, each in his own way, distinct national tendencies." (Photograph by O. Vaering, Oslo, Norway)*

Coat of arms of the MacGregor clan. The Gaelic motto at the top means "My ancestry is royal." This claim is related to the fact that the MacGregors are believed to be the main branch of the Alpine clan, which descended from the eighth-century king, Alpine. The battle cry "Ard choille" presumably denotes a place with which the clan was once associated.

I. A SCOTSMAN WRITES ABOUT GRIEG'S ANCESTORS

It is generally known that the great Norwegian composer is of Scottish descent, but perhaps few are aware that his ancestors belonged to the unfortunate MacGregor clan. In 1611, in exasperation over the clan's riots and criminal acts, James VI ordered the Earl of Athole to expel the most troublesome among them from their highlands in Perthshire and force them to settle down in the cities and villages along the coast of Fife, Forfarshire, and Aberdeenshire. In the same year one of the clan's young families was forced, on threat of death, to relinquish the MacGregor name and to settle down in the village Kennoway in the county of Fife. They took the family name *Grig.*

The account of the descendants of these "aliens" appears in the church registry of the Kennoway parish where, for generation after generation, they were baptized, married, and buried. Most of them were farmers or small landowners. Some were, among other things, members of the governing council in the parish church.

After some time these "Grigs"—obviously displeased with the short surname they had been forced to use—added an "e" to the name. Thus the name was changed to both Grige and Greig. Charles, one of the Greigs from Kennoway, moved to Inverkeithing. He became the father of the famous Admiral Greig who stood so high in the favor of czarina Catherine of Russia. Another branch of the family settled in Peterhead. One of them—Alexander Greig, a fugitive from the gallows after the uprising of 1715—managed to escape with his wife, Ann Milne, on a ship bound for Bergen. The famous Edvard Grieg is descended from these two. (Quoted in *Zeitschrift der Internationalen Musikgesellschaft,* Vol. 7, No. 6, 1906, p. 244.)

Forebears: Some Scottish, Some Danish, but Mostly Norwegian

The family name "Grieg" is of Scottish origin. The spelling most commonly used in Scotland is "Greig" (pronounced "gregg"), but one also finds such other forms as "Grig," "Greg," and "Gregg." All of these are derivatives of "MacGregor," the name of a very famous Scottish clan. The Gaelic form is "MacGrioghair" (Mac = son of). Grioghair was one of the descendants of King Alpine, who reigned in the eighth century.

The MacGregor clan was continually involved in conflicts with other clans, and in certain periods it was declared outlawed. Under Charles II it received many privileges, but when William of Orange ascended to the throne in 1689 conditions again deteriorated for the MacGregor family. The difficulties continued until the battle of Culloden in 1746, when George II put an end to all opposition from the Stuarts. It is unlikely that the old censures against the clan were enforced after that time, but they were not formally eliminated until 1775 under George III.

On his father's side, we can follow Edvard Grieg's Scottish ancestors back to his great-great-grandfather, John Greig, who was married to Ann Milne. John was a tenant on the Mosstoun farm in the small coastal town of Cairnbulg, about fifty-five miles northeast of Aberdeen. In the cemetery in Cairnbulg one can still see today the gravestone which the children of John and Ann Greig erected after the deaths of their parents.

John's son Alexander moved from Cairnbulg to Bergen about 1770, and there has been a good deal of speculation about the reasons for this. A colorful but somewhat too imaginative Scottish account, written on the occasion of Edvard Grieg's visit to England in 1906, is given here.[1] One must read this account with some reservation because it contains a number of demonstrable errors. Ann Milne, for example, was not Alexander's wife but his mother. Nor could he have run away in 1715 since he was not born until July 19, 1739. It is possible that his father fought in the battle of Culloden, but his name does not appear among the many Greigs who participated on the side of the Stuarts. Since the family belonged to the MacGregor clan, however, one can assume that it had various problems in the 1760s, and that those problems had something to do with Alexander's decision to leave his homeland. The reason was probably no more dramatic than that.

Edvard Grieg's Family Tree

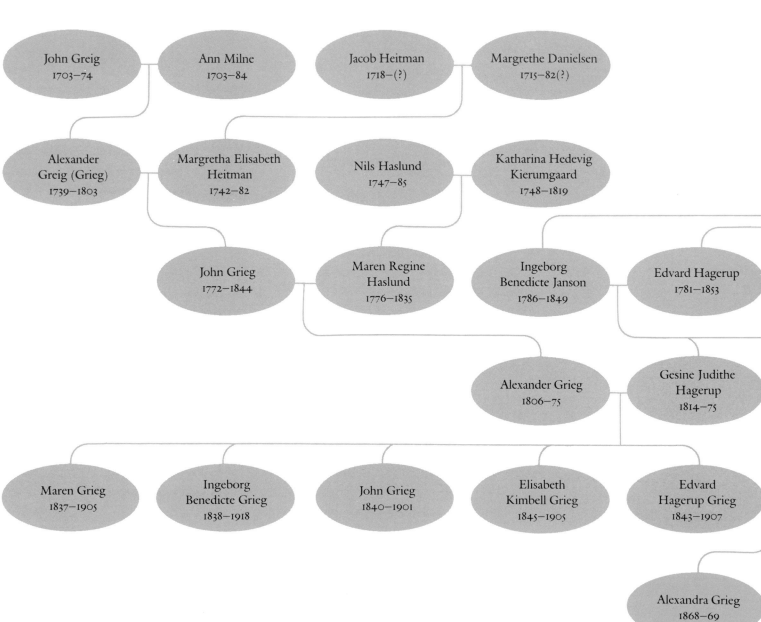

John Greig
1703–74

Ann Milne
1703–84

Jacob Heitman
1718–(?)

Margrethe Danielsen
1715–82(?)

Alexander
Greig (Grieg)
1739–1803

Margretha Elisabeth
Heitman
1742–82

Nils Haslund
1747–85

Katharina Hedevig
Kierumgaard
1748–1819

John Grieg
1772–1844

Maren Regine
Haslund
1776–1835

Ingeborg
Benedicte Janson
1786–1849

Edvard Hagerup
1781–1853

Alexander Grieg
1806–75

Gesine Judithe
Hagerup
1814–75

Maren Grieg
1837–1905

Ingeborg
Benedicte Grieg
1838–1918

John Grieg
1840–1901

Elisabeth
Kimbell Grieg
1845–1905

Edvard
Hagerup Grieg
1843–1907

Alexandra Grieg
1868–69

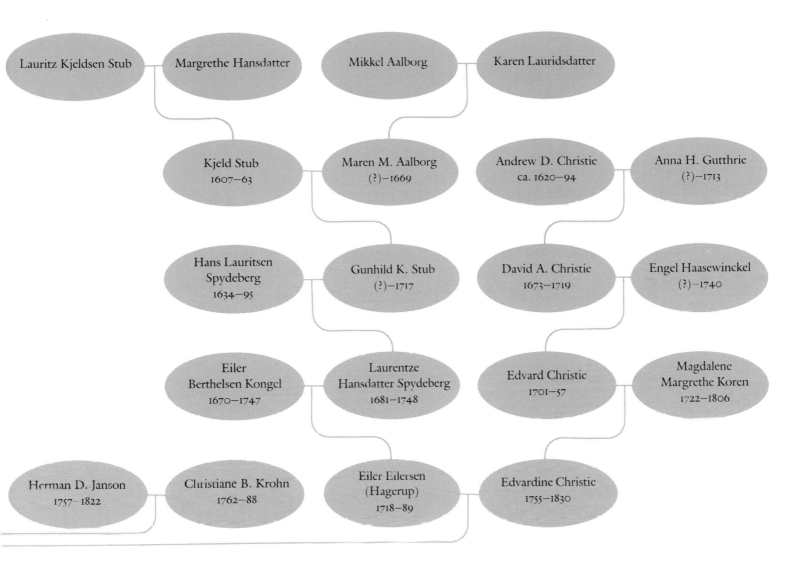

Lauritz Kjeldsen Stub — Margrethe Hansdatter

Mikkel Aalborg — Karen Lauridsdatter

Kjeld Stub
1607–63

Maren M. Aalborg
(?)–1669

Andrew D. Christie
ca. 1620–94

Anna H. Gutthrie
(?)–1713

Hans Lauritsen
Spydeberg
1634–95

Gunhild K. Stub
(?)–1717

David A. Christie
1673–1719

Engel Haasewinckel
(?)–1740

Eiler
Berthelsen Kongel
1670–1747

Laurentze
Hansdatter Spydeberg
1681–1748

Edvard Christie
1701–57

Magdalene
Margrethe Koren
1722–1806

Herman D. Janson
1757–1822

Christiane B. Krohn
1762–88

Eiler Eilersen
(Hagerup)
1718–89

Edvardine Christie
1755–1830

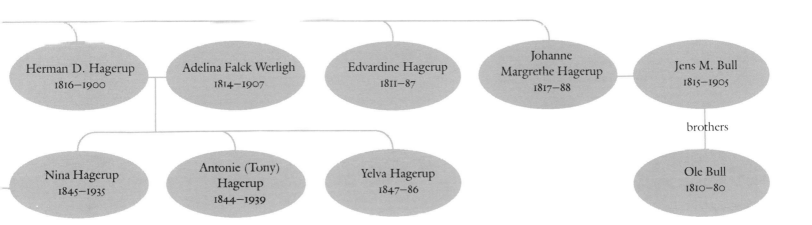

Herman D. Hagerup
1816–1900

Adelina Falck Werligh
1814–1907

Edvardine Hagerup
1811–87

Johanne
Margrethe Hagerup
1817–88

Jens M. Bull
1815–1905

brothers

Nina Hagerup
1845–1935

Antonie (Tony)
Hagerup
1844–1939

Yelva Hagerup
1847–86

Ole Bull
1810–80

On the trip to Norway, Alexander was accompanied by his brother James and two Norwegians of Scottish descent—Christie and Wallace—whose ancestors had settled in Bergen in the early 1600s. The two Norwegians were going home again after studies in Scotland.

The whims of destiny can be interesting now and then, for Alexander could not have imagined that the sister of one of his traveling companions would become the great-grandmother of his own great-grandchild, Edvard Grieg. Edvardine Christie was indeed the mother of Edvard's maternal grandfather, Edvard Hagerup. Thus there was a bit of Scottish blood in Edvard's veins on both his father's and his mother's side.

The other traveling companion, John Wallace, was the son of the British consul in Bergen at that time, and after his return he succeeded his father in that position. (John Wallace's son, Alexander, also became the brother-in-law of Edvard's paternal grandmother, Maren Regine Haslund.)

In his well-reasoned article, "Grieg and His Scottish Ancestry," J. Russell Greig suggests that the real reason for Alexander Greig's leaving Scotland was that the Wallace family had intimated that there might be a position for him in the consulate. A considerable emigration from Scotland was occurring at this time, and it would have been only natural for an ambitious young Scot to combine the desire for travel and adventure with the hope of achieving financial security in a foreign land.

Alexander found this security in Bergen. Here he quite rapidly built up a respected business exporting dried fish and lobster to Great Britain. The business yielded a good profit and was passed from father to son thereafter for many generations. On October 30, 1779, Alexander received his Norwegian citizenship, and at that time he changed the spelling of his name from "Greig" to "Grieg." The reason for this was that the people of Bergen had pronounced Greig the way it was spelled rather than the way it had been pronounced in Scotland. It is a little surprising that he didn't go all the way and take the name "Gregg," for that pronunciation is the closest of all to the Scottish.

Alexander Grieg was a deeply religious man, and twice each year he traveled to his home church in Cairnbulg to participate in communion services. He was married twice. With his first wife, Margretha Elisabeth Heitman, he had nine children. The entire Norwegian branch of the Grieg family is descended from Alexander and Margretha.

In 1797 Alexander became the British vice-consul in Bergen, but a year later he relinquished that post because of the huge problems created by the Napoleonic wars. He carried on an extensive correspondence with the government officials in London, but all his requests to be appointed the British consul after John Wallace were in vain. Following his death in November of 1803, however, his thirty-one-year-old son John got the consul position.

John Grieg was married to Maren Regine Haslund; through her, Danish blood came into the Grieg family. She was the daughter of Nils Haslund, a violinist who had come to Bergen from Aalborg. He had acquired Norwegian citizenship in 1776 as a purveyor of "Wine and General Merchandise," but what he is remembered for in his adopted fatherland is his contribution to the musical life of Bergen. As early as 1770 he became the conductor—or "leader" as it was called at that time—of the five-year-old "Harmonien." He held this position for fifteen years and earned much acclaim for his artistic achievements.

From the time of Maren Regine and on, music occupied a firm and permanent place in the Grieg family. Maren Regine's husband John soon became an active performer in the orchestra as well—the first of many Griegs who were to influence the musical life of Bergen. Maren Regine and John had a son, Alexander, who in his turn took over both the business and the title of consul. Alexander's wife, Gesine Judith, was the daughter of Edvard Hagerup, who was chief administrative officer in Bergen.

The Hagerup name is Danish, but Edvard Hagerup was thoroughly Norwegian. One must go back six generations to find a foreign element in the family: Lauritz Kjeldsen Stub, Edvard Hagerup's great-great-great-grandfather and father of the legendary Kjeld Stub, was an immigrant from Halland (in southern Sweden), which at that time belonged to Denmark. Moreover, Edvard Hagerup's family name was originally not Hagerup. His father, Eiler Eilersen, had a cousin on his mother's side, Eiler Hagerup, who was bishop of Trondheim. Eiler Eilersen lived for long periods with his cousin the bishop, and the end result was that he requested and received permission to change his family name to Hagerup. Like his namesake, he pursued a theological career and ended his days as bishop of Kristiansand.

Edvard Hagerup was married to Ingeborg Benedicte, the daughter of a respected citizen of Bergen—royal agent and consul Herman Janson. Both Herman Janson and Edvard Hagerup were very well-to-do and influential. Janson was head of one of Bergen's largest firms, and owned the country estate "Damsgaard" a short distance out of the city. He was widely known for his generosity. In 1811, when a campaign was launched to raise funds for the new university in Oslo, he immediately pledged the sum of four thousand riksdalers. This was an unusually high pledge for that time, and it made him the largest contributor from Bergen.

Edvard Hagerup was deeply involved in the issue of Norway's national independence. He was at Eidsvoll for the signing of the Norwegian constitution in 1814, and was one of the 112 representatives who participated in the first meeting of the "Storting" (Norwegian Parliament) on April 10 of the same year. He was elected representative from Bergen in the years 1814–24 and 1827–28. In 1827–28 he was president of "Lagtinget," the upper chamber of the Norwegian Parliament. In 1836 he was accorded the high honor of being offered a cabinet ministry, but he declined as it would have necessitated his leaving the Bergen that he loved so much.

Edvard Hagerup and Ingeborg Benedicte Janson had eight children. For our purposes it is two of these children—Gesine and Herman—who play the most important roles: Gesine became Edvard's mother and Herman became Nina's father. But the genealogy also reveals one other interesting detail. Gesine and Herman's sister, Johanne Margrethe, married Jens M. Bull, who was Ole Bull's brother. Through this marriage the Grieg and Bull families were connected, and Ole Bull—who thus was the brother of both Edvard and Nina's uncle by marriage—had continuous association with the Grieg family.

*Gesine Hagerup and Alexander Grieg,
Edvard's Parents ("Troldhaugen," Bergen,
Norway)*

His parents

Gesine Judith Hagerup and Alexander Grieg were married in 1836. They had five children: Maren, Ingeborg Benedicte, John, Edvard, and Elisabeth. Gesine is depicted—not least of all by Edvard—as a unique individual. It has been said that Alexander was not her first choice as a husband, but that her father—a minor government official—refused permission for her to marry the sailor with whom she was in love. That would not have been proper for a young lady of her social class. Gesine had to find someone, therefore, who was also acceptable to her father. The man she chose was Alexander Grieg, the prosperous son of the local consul. Once the decision was made Gesine went whole-heartedly into the marriage, and it was successful in every way.

Even as a child Gesine displayed unusual talent both as a singer and as a pianist, and her wealthy parents—who did their utmost to give their children a first-rate education—sent her to Hamburg to study music when she was still a young girl. That was a remarkable thing to do in those days. Gesine studied voice, piano, and music theory with Albert G. Methfessel, a German composer who in his day was held in high regard for his vocal compositions.

Upon her return to Bergen, Gesine began to play an important role in the musical life of the city. When she was just nineteen she performed with the Bergen Symphony Orchestra as a vocal soloist, singing Agatha's aria from Weber's *Der Freischütz*. Soon thereafter, however, she began to concentrate exclusively on the piano and became, among other things, an acclaimed accompanist. In 1863 she accompanied Ole Bull, and six years later—at the Bergen Symphony Orchestra's somewhat belated centennial celebration in 1869—she accompanied the violinist August Fries in the second movement of Grieg's F-major sonata. She also often appeared as a soloist and participated regularly in chamber music performances.

Gesine was considered the best piano teacher in Bergen. She was also the most expensive one, for she demanded what in those days was quite a substantial fee: half a riksdaler per lesson. Her favorite composers were Mozart and Weber. She often arranged musical evenings in her own home. Here her students and other amateur musicians in the area worked their way through a number of operas, portions of which they performed under Gesine's own direction.

She had many other interests as well. She wrote poetry and short plays, and was deeply involved in arrangements for the education of children and youth in the city. In the 1840s she was a member of the governing board of the "Sewing School for Girls." (Her husband was also on the board of the Bergen high school in 1834.)

Gesine had a distinguished but not particularly beautiful face. With her authoritative demeanor and pronounced sense of order it may well be that she sometimes appeared petulant, moody, and critical. But a strong will was a necessity for the matron of a large home where there were many guests. Moreover, in addition to attending to the needs of her husband and five children, she also had to serve as hostess at the many parties that were given in their distinguished consul's residence. For almost twenty-five years she was also the one principally responsible for seeing to it that "Landaas," her beautiful estate on the outskirts of the city, was properly maintained. She had received the title to this property when her mother died in 1849. "Haukeland," another estate that had been in the family for many years, was given at the same time to her brother Herman.

All of this activity contributed to a breakdown in Gesine's health, and in the last years of her life she was quite worn out. But her enthusiasm and concern knew no bounds. Not to be able to participate in the daily activities was the worst thing that could happen to her. In a letter of May 18, 1867, Edvard's father reported that she had stumbled over a cat and sprained her foot. Then he added, "I hope she doesn't have to sit around for too terribly long, for she who has always been like the north wind can't tolerate that kind of life, and her health will suffer if that happens . . ."

Edvard realized as early as the beginning of the 1870s that his mother's strength was beginning to fail. In 1873 he composed his musical tribute to her: "The Old Mother," a moving setting of a text by A. O. Vinje:

In a letter to the Bergen author John Paulsen of June 4, 1905, where among other things he discussed this song, Grieg wrote about his mother: "She was still living in Sandvigen at that time. I brought her the song, which had arisen from thoughts of her who with boundless energy and a sense of duty toiled and suffered until she dropped . . ."

Alexander Grieg was very different from his wife, outgoing and good-natured as he was. His children called him "daddy-man," and when he was in particularly good spirits he signed his letters "Paddy." He liked to have a lot of people around him, was always ready for a good joke, and preferred to immerse himself in the bright side of everyday life. The illustrious old firm of "Alexander Grieg & Son" had been as solid as a rock for many years, and Alexander had been a lucky fellow.

Toward the end of the 1860s, however, certain dark shadows were cast over this happy situation. The firm came upon hard times. Grieg's father mentioned one of the reasons for this in a letter to Edvard of July 9, 1866. Here he wrote that he had received "the most discouraging news from England. Yes, my friend, lobsters are now providing worse than a scanty living, for they are dying in such numbers that one can't get a thing for them. I dread every mail delivery, and I shudder each time I open a letter—I mean, of course, when it comes from that part of the world."

A new letter from England contained ominous news: of the entire cargo of 10,500 lobsters, 6000 had become spoiled enroute. The rest were "living or dead." It is no wonder that the usually optimistic consul was depressed. "Under these circumstances you can easily see for yourself that nothing can come of our trip to Copenhagen, which I have been looking forward to for such a long time . . ." The difficulties would only increase in the years to come. The time of greatness for the Grieg firm was over.

Other serious problems oppressed Alexander too. First, there was illness in the family. His daughter Benedicte suffered from chronic "anemia" and his wife was "constantly tired and exhausted." Also disturbing to Alexander was the cool relationship that had developed between him and his elder son John. This is clearly evident from a letter that Alexander wrote to Edvard on May 3, 1867, in connection with John's taking over the family business. In this letter Edvard's father first expressed his pleasure over the fact that all the money he

2. THE RELATIONSHIP BETWEEN JOHN AND EDVARD

Now I think I have told you a little about the whole family except for your brother and his wife, but I hardly dare to mention them—much less tell you anything about them—because then you come out with your unjustified remarks that not every father would tolerate. Notwithstanding a few very nasty remarks in your last letter, I have nonetheless understood, my dear Edvard, that you are still my loving son, and for that reason I forgive you all the more willingly for saying what you did . . . The year has brought us many things that have not been exactly pleasant—indeed, some things have been downright painful. Let us now promise each other that all of this will be forgotten as we begin a new year . . . (Alexander Grieg in a letter to Edvard, December 30, 1867.)

had used for Edvard's education had produced such good results. On the other hand, he deeply regretted that he had let John throw away two valuable years in cello studies in Leipzig (1860–62), for "what was spent there on your brother's music I regard as almost worse than wasted, for it has only served to make him unfit for the work that he is now to take up, and that hurts me so deeply. Our businesses are not such that they can support two families, and I have not accumulated enough so that I can leave the business, which is my highest wish. Thus I can look forward in my old age to nothing but financial worries, and I am quite prepared for the fact that this will be our last summer at 'Landaas.' That wouldn't be so bad if I could just have the pleasure of seeing my children happy around me, but unfortunately I can't hope for that either, and much less that the relationship between us parents and you children will ever become as I have always pictured it if I lived long enough to see you as grown men . . ."

One thing that appears to have affected the parents especially deeply during these years was the tension that had developed between the two brothers, Edvard and John. The basic reason for this bad feeling was in all likelihood the fact that John had been obliged to accept Edvard's going to the Leipzig conservatory when he was just fifteen years old, while he—the elder brother by three years—did not get his opportunity until two years later. Another reason was that, as the eldest son in the family, John had to totally abandon any thought of a musical career as a cellist because he—as is clear from Alexander's letter to Edvard—could not escape the business obligations.

Alexander spoke frequently in his letters about the relationship between the two brothers, and his own good-natured temperament is clearly evident.[2] He did not understand Edvard's almost aggressive attitude toward John, but he nonetheless excused his impertinent remarks. Rarely in these letters do we meet the stern father; it is rather the gentle mediator who was trying to smooth over the differences and find a common ground. Fortunately, Alexander and his wife saw the good relationship between the two brothers restored before their deaths in 1875.

There was an active correspondence between Edvard and his father. Many of the letters no longer exist; only two of Edvard's letters to his parents have been preserved. But in the Bergen Public Library there is a large collection of letters from Alexander written during the period 1866–75. All of them reflect his sincere love for his son, and his joy each time something went well for Edvard was deep and genuine.

The parents had a personal Christian faith that gave them strong support. In Gesine's few letters—and in many of Alexander's—we find expressions of the comfort and encouragement that they received from their religion. There are many admonitions, even in connection with the happiest events. In the autumn of 1869 Edvard and Nina had given a successful concert in Copenhagen, but after Alexander had expressed his pleasure over the success he went on to say: "I hope you won't let yourselves be ensnared by all of the praise that you have been receiving of late, but that you will both humbly give God the glory. For whatever we are able to accomplish comes from Him . . ." When things were at their worst for Alexander, it was his faith that sustained him. In a letter to Edvard of May 3, 1867, he wrote, after having discussed some apparently insuperable obstacles that had come in his way: "And yet there is a gracious and faithful Father over us all Who arranges all things for the best if we but yield ourselves to Him with complete trust and confidence."

Alexander, like his wife, was musically sophisticated, albeit not at the same level. He could at least play four-hand piano pieces with her, and on business trips to other countries he never failed to attend concerts. He must have been especially fond of operas and song recitals, for he reports in one place that he had heard more than 150 female vocalists in his lifetime. In one of his last letters to Edvard—dated May 26, 1875—he expressed his pleasure in music in these words: "Music has been my greatest joy throughout my life . . ."

Nina Grieg's parents

Herman Hagerup—Gesine's brother, who was one year older than she—was very different from his sister. He was handsome to look at, but it was rumored that his energy and willingness to work were not on a par with his appearance.

In 1841 Herman met his wife-to-be, Adelina Werligh, who had recently been widowed. She had been born in Denmark, and as an actress had traveled around Scandinavia with her husband, who was director of a traveling theater company. In 1841 they had gotten as far as Oslo, where her husband suddenly died. Thus chance brought Adelina, who on short notice had to take over the director's duties, to Bergen. Here she met Herman Hagerup, the handsome son of a local government official, and she quickly became enamored of him. Herman, naturally enough, fell for her unusual beauty and vibrant charm.

Herman's father was very unhappy when he heard of their plans to marry, and he did everything he could to prevent Herman's marriage to the Danish actress. But to no avail. He had to give in to Adelina's indomitable will.

As previously mentioned, after his wife's death Edvard Hagerup willed the "Haukeland" property to Herman. By that time Adelina and Herman had three daughters: Tony, Nina, and Yelva. They moved to "Haukeland" and made it their year-round home—in contrast to Gesine and Alexander Grieg, who lived at "Landaas" only during the warmer months.

Herman's income, however, was small, and it appears that the industrious Adelina once tried to run a kind of restaurant at "Haukeland," albeit with little success. Since she was also having problems learning to feel at home in Bergen, Herman agreed in 1853 to sell "Haukeland," and "gentleman farmer" Hagerup and his family moved to Denmark. Nina was then eight years old.

Growing Up in Bergen

During the 1800s Strandgaten (Strand Street) was in the middle of Bergen's foremost business district and was bustling with activity. It was the largest thoroughfare in that part of the city, and the noise of horses' hooves and cart wheels against the cobblestones could be heard from morning to evening.

Far out on this street, at No. 152 Strandgaten, lived consul Alexander Grieg and his family in a splendid white house. Here, on June 15, 1843, Edvard was born, and in this busy, lively street he grew up together with his brother and three sisters.

He was inquisitive and eager to learn, and he knew every street and alley in this part of the city. It was only a short distance to the Hanseatic buildings and the fish market, and when the great ships sailed off carrying his father's cargo of fresh lobster to foreign lands he could watch them until they were far out in the bay.

In the neighborhood surrounding his Strandgaten home he participated in the typical children's games—games with picturesque names like "not-full," "thirty-four," "cock-a-doodle," and—certainly the most popular of them all—"catch the last." But he was also fascinated by activities intended purely for adults. He often sneaked unobserved into the auction houses in order to feel the excitement of the witty verbal exchanges that occurred there. At the same time he had a strange awareness of—indeed, almost an inclination toward—sad occurrences. He could stand as though spellbound at the sight of a funeral procession, the somber impression of which was heightened by the weeping of the hired mourners and the black-garbed horse and carriage. Throughout his life he was fascinated by such things. During his first Italian journey in 1865 he wrote in his diary a detailed account of a funeral in Rome.

The impressions from his early childhood years etched themselves into the boy's mind. When Grieg spoke of this period in later years, it was always with heartfelt gratitude.

Unfortunately, we have very few sources for our account of these formative years of his life. The most important source is an autobiographical sketch, "My First Success," which he wrote in 1903. It is a stylistic masterpiece that conjures up the happiness of childhood, but it also discusses the disap-

1. CHILDHOOD THOUGHTS OF BECOMING A CLERGYMAN

If someone asked me what I wanted to be, I answered without hesitation: a clergyman. [The idea of] such a black-garbed shepherd of souls furnished my imagination with the most alluring characteristics I could imagine. To be permitted to preach or speak to a listening multitude seemed to me to be something great. Prophet, preacher—that was something for me. And how I recited in season and out of season for my poor parents, sisters, and brother! I knew all the poems in my reading book by heart. And every day after dinner, when father wanted to take a little nap in his easy chair, he couldn't get away from me; I, using a chair as a lectern, started reciting in total disregard of his wishes. I kept an eye on father, who appeared to be dozing. But once in a while, between his cat-naps, he smiled. Then I was happy. It was recognition. And how I could keep on pestering father. "O, just one more piece!" "No, now this must be enough." "O, just one more!" Yes, such is childish ambition! It knows exactly the exciting feeling of success. (From "My First Success.")

pointments and the joys of the conservatory period. Naturally enough, the account of some individual details is obviously influenced by the probably unconscious need of the sixty-year-old author to gild the memories. The accounts of the Leipzig period especially should be taken with more than one grain of salt. Grieg once said that "My First Success" was originally written for an American magazine, but for some reason it did not appear there. It was published in Norway in 1903, and in the foreign press soon thereafter. If it had been written for a European audience he would have developed the article in quite a different way. All objections notwithstanding, however, "My First Success" is an extremely interesting and important source document. Several excerpts will be found among the Primary Materials associated with this chapter.

As a child Edvard never thought of becoming an artist. He wanted to be a clergyman.[1] He imagined himself as a preacher in front of a listening congregation. He loved to recite texts that he had memorized; indeed, he claimed that as a school boy he knew all the poems in the reader by heart. The person who chiefly took the brunt of this proclivity was his father. Or shall we rather believe that the good-natured Alexander was gladdened by the first signs of artistic talent in his son? Edvard was not interested only in recitation and poetry, however. He expressed his lively imagination in enthusiastic reports of auctions and funeral processions. He even gave original funeral orations for "deceased" cats and birds.

School days

On April 1, 1853, when he was almost ten years old, Edvard became a student at the well-regarded Tank's School in Bergen. According to the school record, the basis for admission was his "general preparation." There was no compulsory grammar school at this time, but parents who could afford to do so commonly sent their children to private teachers who held classes in their own homes. Those who were wealthy engaged a private tutor to come to their home. The children who were lucky enough to have a good teacher could in this way get an education of relatively high quality. But this was possible, of course, for only a small minority.

So far as one can judge from "My First Success," the young Grieg got his "preparatory" instruction in a class consisting of thirty students.

Tank's School was a secondary school that demanded much of its students. Edvard seems to have had a strong antipathy toward the compulsion that was characteristic of the school, and his eagerness to get away from something that bored him on one occasion had an amusing result: he demonstrated his cleverness by coming to school soaking wet so that he could immediately be sent home again to fetch some dry clothes.[2]

He was not an especially good student, and his interests were at times quite different from the rote-learning on which the schools of that day placed such strong emphasis. It is clear from the school record that his effort during the five years that he attended Tank's School varied greatly. His grades at first

2. A TRICK TO GET OUT OF SCHOOL

From the time that I was ten years old my parents lived during the summers at the lovely country home "Landaas" just a short distance from Bergen. Every single morning my elder brother and I had to trudge off to school in the pouring rain for which Bergen is famous. But I used this pouring rain in what I thought was a very clever boyish prank.

The rule at school was that a student who came late would not be admitted to the class, but as a punishment had to stand outside until the end of the period . . . One rainy day when it happened—and it happened often—that I came to school entirely unprepared, I arranged so that I not only came a little late, but I stayed down on the street where I positioned myself under a downspout on a house until I became absolutely soaked to the skin. When I was finally admitted to the schoolroom such rivulets of water streamed from my clothes down to the floor that the teacher—for the sake of both my classmates and me—couldn't defend detaining me, but immediately sent me home to change my clothes. Because of the long distance to my home, this was the same as excusing me from forenoon instruction.

That I repeated this experiment rather often was already risky, but when I finally went so far as to come to school soaking wet one day when it was hardly raining, they became suspicious and sent someone out to spy on me. One fine day I got caught, and then I received a memorable introduction to the "percussion instruments." (From "My First Success.")

were good, but then they went rapidly downhill. By 1855 his grade average had fallen to 3.15. The result was that he had to take the third grade over again. Later he wrote, "Now fate decreed that because of an infected eye I had to miss school for a time. I who had never learned my lessons did not consider that a great loss. But my father thought otherwise . . ." According to the school record, this eye problem was no excuse for what happened in 1855, since absence due to illness is first noted in 1857.

But then he began to mature, and from the latter part of 1856 onward his grades became noticeably better. By 1857 his grade average had risen to a 2.36. He *could* learn when he wanted to. It is therefore not correct when he states in "My First Success" that for the most part he was lazy and a rebel against everything called school learning. His actual grades tell a totally different story.

We also know from Grieg's report card from Tank's School that the range of subjects was extensive: German, English, French, Norwegian, Religion, History, Geography, Arithmetic, Geometry, Natural History, Writing, Drawing, Singing, and Physical Education!

Edvard's report card, which is still in existence, shows an average performance in most subjects. He earned a final grade of 2.42 and ranked sixth among fourteen students. He was also then promoted to the fifth grade. He was lowest in written English and Norwegian, Arithmetic, and Physical Education, but his grades indicate that in all other areas his performance was equal to that of his classmates. Moreover, he was one of the few who received a 2 (a high grade) in effort, deportment, and manners.

In the autumn of 1858, two years before he would have taken the final graduation examination, Edvard suddenly left the Tank's School. In the school record one finds the following brief note: "Announced withdrawal August 31 to prepare himself to become a musician." On the same page of the record book the final grades for the various years are verified, and also the fact that Edvard went to the third grade for two consecutive years.

Musical development

Although young Edvard could not properly be regarded as a prodigy, no one in the music-loving Grieg home could fail to notice his definite musical talent. In his earlier years, however, he was somewhat overshadowed by two of the older children: John, who was an excellent cello player, and Maren, who later became a well-known piano teacher in both Bergen and Oslo.

It was Edvard's mother, especially, who realized that there was something unusual about Edvard's talent, for his musical imagination and joy in creating were evident in the fact that he liked nothing better than to sit and daydream at the piano. He hated lifeless scales and exercises.

He was no more than five years old when he first experienced the joy and the wonder of music's magical power of attraction. He wrote in "My First Success": "Why not begin by remembering the wonderful mystical satisfaction of stretching one's arms up toward the piano and bringing forth—not a

Strandgaten (Strand Street) in Bergen near the end of the 19th century. (Universitetsbiblioteket of Bergen, Norway)

melody. Far from it! No, it had to be a chord. First a third, then a fifth, then a seventh. And finally, both hands helping—O joy!—a ninth; I had found the dominant ninth chord. When I had discovered this, my rapture knew no bounds. That was a success! Nothing since has been able to intoxicate me like this. At that time I was about five years old."

It seems almost symptomatic of Grieg's later development that it was not a melody but a chord—and a quite dissonant one—that gave him such great pleasure at that early age.

At age six he began to get regular lessons on the piano from his mother. This did not always go smoothly. Gesine was wise enough to see that she had to be careful not to squelch the boy's joy in music and his need to experiment, but at the same time she was conscious of the need to maintain firm control of his musical training. Discipline was an important part of an artist's work. Edvard wrote of her in "My First Success": "Although it certainly must have gladdened her maternal heart that I sat there and tried to work out a little of this and that, she did not in any case allow herself to show it. On the contrary. She was not to be trifled with when I wasted my time dreaming away at the piano instead of busying myself with what I was supposed to be practicing. And when I had to get at my scales and exercises and all that other technical

3. MOSAK! MOSAK! MOSAK!

The word "Requiem" occurred in the text [that we were reading], and the teacher asked if any of us could name a famous composer who had written a religious work with that title. No one answered until I rather quietly ventured forward with: Mozart. The whole class stared at me as at an incomprehensible, strange creature.

That felt like a success, but I sensed immediately that it was a success that was likely to have some unpleasant consequences. And I quickly found that I was correct. For, as so often happens, the class didn't like having such a creature in its midst. From this time on my classmates pursued me in the streets whenever they had the chance and taunted me with the words, "Hey, look, there comes Mosak!" Off in the distance I could hear the words "Mosak! Mosak!" after I had escaped from my pursuers down a side street.

I felt this mistreatment to be an injustice and considered myself a martyr. I came very close to actually hating my classmates. It is certain that I withdrew from virtually all of them. (From "My First Success.")

deviltry—all of which gave my childish yearning stones in place of bread—it sometimes happened that she guided me even when she wasn't in the room. One day she shouted threateningly from the kitchen, where at that moment she was busy making dinner: 'But shame on you, Edvard, F-sharp, F-sharp, not F!' I was terribly impressed with her superiority."

Only later did Edvard realize that, had he followed his mother's "loving but firm guidance" more diligently, he would have had a still better foundation for a career as a concert pianist. "But my inexcusable tendency to be a dreamer began at this time to create for me the same difficulties that followed me far into the future. Had I not, in addition to the musical talent, inherited my mother's boundless energy as well, I certainly would never have been able to proceed from dreams to deeds."

He began quite early to jot down his musical impressions on note paper: he composed. The first pieces were written when he was nine years old. But everything he wrote at this time has been lost—"relegated to the wastebasket where it belonged," as he put it. No doubt it was not easy to be a musically gifted child in the midst of a gang of boys from Bergen.[3] The fact that Edvard was mocked by one of the teachers at Tank's School because of his composi-

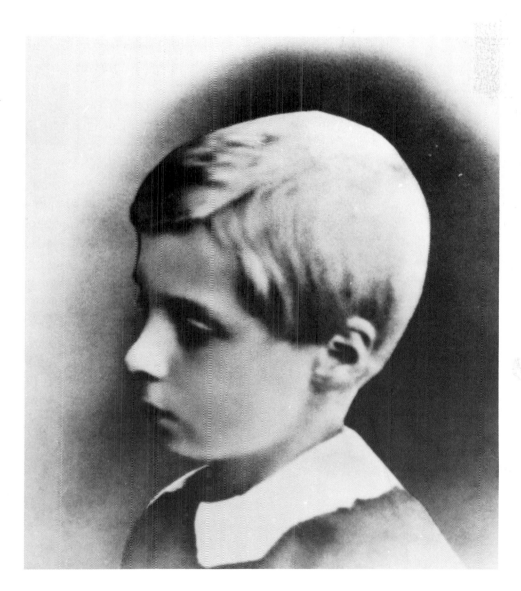

This is the earliest known photograph of Edvard Grieg. It is a detail from a daguerrotype made when Edvard was eleven years old. One rarely sees a more innocent-looking boy's face, almost dream-like in its appearance. One observes little here of the "rowdy from Bergen" which was also a part of Edvard's personality. (Bergen Offentlige Bibliotek, Bergen, Norway)

4. ASPIRING YOUNG COMPOSER MEETS ADVERSITY

So one day it finally happened—I was perhaps twelve or thirteen years old—that I brought to school a folder of my own music on the title page of which I had printed in bold letters, "Variations on a German Melody for Piano by Edvard Grieg, Opus 1." I had fun showing it to a classmate who seemed to be interested. But what happened? In the middle of the German class the same classmate was heard mumbling some unintelligible words that caused the teacher to shout almost involuntarily, "What are you saying over there?" Once again the indistinct mumbling, and once again a shout from the teacher, and then someone said quietly, "Grieg has something." "What do you mean 'Grieg has something?' "Grieg has composed something."

The teacher, with whom I . . . did not exactly enjoy any popularity, stood up, came over to me, inspected the booklet, and said in a clearly ironic tone of voice: "Well, well, the fellow is musical. The fellow composes. Look at that!" Thereupon he opened the door to the adjacent classroom, brought the teacher from that room into ours, and continued: "How about that! The little chap over there writes music."

Both teachers paged through the manuscript with apparent interest. There was general commotion in both classes. Already I felt confident of a great success. But one should not do this too early. The visitor was hardly out of the room before the teacher suddenly changed his tactics. He grabbed a mop of my hair so severely that I almost fainted and growled sternly, "Next time he will take the German dictionary along as he is supposed to, and leave such trash at home."

Alas! So near fortune's peak, and then in a moment cast down into the depths! How often in life something like this has happened to me. And always I have had to think back to that first time . . . (From "My First Success.")

tions naturally didn't contribute to nurturing his musical development either.[4] But great talent, as we know, does not allow itself to be stopped by lack of appreciation. Edvard continued to compose, and new works came forth one by one. On the manuscript of *Nine Children's Pieces* from the Leipzig period he wrote "Opus 17."

In the summer of 1858 he accompanied his father on a long trip to eastern Norway. He brought his sketch pad along and made a number of sketches from the trip. In Larvik he visited his mother's sister Edvardine, "aunt Kuehle." In the still extant drawing he made during the stay there, one can indeed discern a certain talent, but one can also see that the world did not lose a great pictorial artist when Edvard later laid aside his drawing equipment.

This summer became a turning point in Edvard's life. In the information that he gave to the biographer J. de Jong in 1881—information that was printed the same year in the Dutch periodical *De Tijdspiegel*—it is clearly evident that after the trip with his father he seriously began to regard himself as destined to become a musician.

He did not meet any great opposition from his parents on this point. The question was rather *when* he should go abroad to begin serious studies. Apparently his parents wanted him to finish his schooling at home before going away. To send a fifteen-year-old boy alone out into the world to study music seemed a bit hazardous. But later in the summer Ole Bull came to "Landaas" for a visit. Edvard now met his "uncle" for the first time, and this proved to be decisive. For—as stated in the above-mentioned Dutch periodical—"Ole Bull simply commanded that I be sent to Leipzig."

In "My First Success" Grieg gave a quite different account of the matter. Here he said nothing about the decision to become a musician having been made before Ole Bull entered the picture. On the contrary, he embellished the episode with the world-renowned violinist in such a way that one gets the definite impression it was Ole Bull who discovered his musical talent. That is not what happened, however. Ole Bull simply gave Edvard's parents a decisive push toward allowing Edvard to proceed immediately with his musical training, and in so doing expedited the young boy's departure to Germany.

It is also easy to believe that Ole Bull was keenly aware that Edvard's creative talents could be developed only through a systematic course of study at a conservatory. He had often realized how inadequate his own education in music theory and composition had been. For that reason he wanted now to try to prevent Edvard from suffering the same fate of remaining a self-taught composer. Grieg's vivid account of Ole Bull's visit to "Landaas" is included in the Primary Materials.[5]

It isn't clear which of his compositions Edvard played for Bull, but it seems most likely that they included, among others, *Three Piano Pieces* (CW 103). These pieces are preserved in manuscript form, but in the hand of his sister Benedicte. Edvard later included them, somewhat revised, in a collection that he put together in Leipzig in 1859, with the title *Short Pieces for Piano* (CW 105).

The beginning of the first of the three piano pieces, entitled "Longing," is reproduced below. This example gives some indication of Edvard's musical

5. OLE BULL SETS THINGS IN MOTION

The end of my time in school and with it my leaving home came more quickly than I had expected. I was almost fifteen years old but was still far from achieving senior class standing. Then one summer day at "Landaas" a rider came dashing down the road on a galloping horse. He drew near, reined in his magnificent Arabian mount, and leaped off. It was that storied adventurer I had dreamed of, but had never seen before: it was Ole Bull. There was something in me that didn't like the fact that this god, without further ado, dismounted and acted as if he were a mere man, came into the living room, and smilingly greeted us all. I remember distinctly that when his right hand touched mine something like an electric shock went through me. But at last the god began to tell jokes, and then I realized—with quiet sorrow, to tell the truth—that he was just a man.

Unfortunately, he didn't have his violin with him. But he could talk, and that he did in full measure. We listened speechlessly to his accounts of his travels in America. That was something for a child's imagination. Then when he found out that I was composing and improvising, there was no getting away from it: I had to go to the piano.

I don't understand what Ole Bull could have found at that time in my naïve, childish compositions, but he became very serious and talked quietly to my parents. What they discussed was not disadvantageous to me; for suddenly Ole Bull came over to me, shook me in his peculiar way and said: "You are going to Leipzig to become an artist!"

Everyone looked kindly at me, and I understood only this one thing, that a gentle fairy stroked me on the cheek and that I was happy. And my parents! Not a moment's objection or even hesitation. Everything was settled. And I thought that the whole episode was the most natural thing in the world . . . (From "My First Success.")

taste and skill before he went to Leipzig. We note the use of parallel fifths and octaves. It is possible that this was done consciously, but the most likely explanation is that he wasn't sufficiently grounded in traditional harmony. The compositions certainly bear the stamp of student works, but they are not badly written. One is especially struck by the harmonic boldness of the fifteen-year-old composer. All of the pieces are in quick tempo and require a considerable technical skill on the part of the performer.

"Longing," CW 103, No. 1 (CW 105, No. 2)

Photograph of Edvard as a young man, presumably taken while he was a student at the Leipzig Conservatory.

Professional Study at
the Leipzig Conservatory

Edvard was not the only member of the Grieg family who went to Leipzig to study music. One of his relatives in Bergen, Georg Grieg, studied piano at the conservatory in the mid-1850s, and it is likely that Edvard's father talked with him about the general situation in the renowned music capital. In 1860, when Edvard had been a student at the conservatory for two years, his brother John came there to study cello.

The conservatory records also reveal that there were several other Norwegians there. For the years 1854–58 one finds the names of such people as Otto Winter-Hjelm from Oslo, Claus Herman Brun from Norderhov, Martine Gudde from Trondheim, and Magdalene Mowinckel, Johan Beyer, and Georg Grieg from Bergen—most of them amateurs. Georg Grieg and Johan Beyer, who later became printers, played important roles in the musical life of Bergen, the former as a fine pianist and the latter as first violinist in the so-called Beyer quartet, which played together regularly for nineteen years. Johan Beyer was also the uncle of Frants Beyer, who was Edvard Grieg's close friend for more than thirty years. The only one of the group who made his living as a professional musician was Winter-Hjelm, who was to become a noted church musician and an influential music critic in the Oslo press.

The music conservatory in Leipzig was established in 1843, the same year that Edvard was born. Within a very short time it earned a reputation as perhaps the finest institution of its type in the world, with a faculty that was legendary. Many foreigners came to the conservatory: in Edvard's class of forty-five students there were Scandinavians, Englishmen, Russians, and Americans. Among the students from Scandinavia there was one with whom Edvard became an especially close friend—the Danish student C. F. Emil Horneman, whom Edvard later described as "a brilliant fellow student, a wild and irrepressible companion with a clear head and a warm heart."

But what could a fifteen-year-old from a provincial city in Norway present in comparison with mature young people who were among Europe and America's musical elite? Edvard was feeling unsure of himself when on October 6, 1858, he officially enrolled as a student at the conservatory. It must have been quite a shock to suddenly find himself independent and alone in the foreign metropolis. In "My First Success" he wrote: "It is no accident that the phrase 'was sent' comes naturally to mind in this connection. I felt like a package stuffed with dreams. I was sent under the care of one of my father's old friends. We traveled across the North Sea to Hamburg, and after a one-day stay there we continued by train to the medieval city of Leipzig whose tall, dark, and gloomy houses and narrow streets almost took my breath away.

"I was delivered to a boarding house, my father's old friend said good-bye—the last Norwegian words I was to hear for a long time—and there I stood as a fifteen-year-old boy alone in that foreign land among only foreign people. I was overcome by homesickness. I went into my room, and I sat and cried uncontrollably until I was called to dinner by my landlord and landlady. The man, a genuine Saxon post-office official, tried to console me. He said to me in German, 'See here, my dear Grieg, it is the same sun, the same moon, the same loving God you have at home!' Very well intended. But neither sun nor moon nor loving God could compensate for my father's vanished friend, the last thread that bound me to my home. Children's moods change quickly, however. I soon got over the homesickness, and although I didn't have the foggiest idea of what it really was like to study music, I was nonetheless cock-sure that the miracle would happen: in three years, after completing my studies here, I would go home again as a master of wizardry in the kingdom of sound. This is the clearest proof of my great naïveté and of the fact that it was purely and simply the child in me that was in control . . ."

The fifteen-year-old boy really was no more than a child then, either: he was short of stature, and he wore a fancy shirt with short sleeves as was the custom back in Bergen. At first some of his fellow students made fun of him, and one of them went so far as to take him up on his lap in jest—which, Grieg later reported, "brought me to despair."

But Edvard soon got hold of himself and proved to be an unusually talented student. Nor had he come to his studies unprepared. This is evident, for example, from the small piano pieces he had written before he left home—*Three Piano Pieces* from 1858 (CW 103).

Leipzig, with its old university and its newly established conservatory, was a well-known cultural center, and traditions dating from the time when J. S. Bach directed the Thomas School Boy Choir were carefully preserved by the townspeople. Especially important for Grieg's personal development was the music he heard at the so-called Gewandhaus concerts, where the conservatory students had free admission to the dress rehearsals. The finest musicians in the world came here to play with the world-famous Gewandhaus Orchestra or to give solo recitals. For the younger performers, a good review from Leipzig was the doorway to a career in the world of music.

A number of unforgettable musical experiences came Grieg's way in Leipzig. In "My First Success" he wrote: "It was fortunate for me that in Leipzig I was able to hear so much fine music, especially orchestral and chamber music. This compensated for the training in composition that I failed to get at the conservatory. It developed my spirit and my musical judgment consider-ably . . ." He had been in the city only a couple of months when Wagner's *Tannhäuser* was performed at the opera house. Grieg was enthralled by it and saw it fourteen times!

1. GRIEG ON HORNEMAN AND SCHUMANN

The very first day he [Horneman] came to Leipzig he got a ticket to the dress rehearsal for one of the Gewandhaus concerts. As he came into the concert hall somebody was singing an old concert aria to which he listened with the dispassionate respect for authority appropriate for a student. Then a lady sat down at the piano and began to play a piece with orchestral accompaniment.

After only a few measures Horneman became almost electrified. A new world opened up for him, a world full of that for which his whole being was longing, although he did not know it. He listened and listened, and it became more and more beautiful. Finally he could no longer stand not knowing what he was listening to. He turned to the fellow sitting next to him and whispered, "Who is this by?" "By Schumann!" "Schu—mann? Well, but then . . ." He looked up and realized that the fellow beside him was afraid he was sitting next to a madman. (It was Schumann's A-minor concerto he was hearing, and the lady at the piano was Clara Schumann.) But with this Horneman's fate was sealed. He swore that he would love this music no matter what a whole legion of teachers might say about it. (From an article written in 1881 for a Danish journal that ceased publication before the article was printed. Published in 1957 in Öystein Gaukstad, *Edvard Grieg: Artikler og taler* [Edvard Grieg: Articles and Speeches].)

Moreover, the spirit of Mendelssohn hovered over this city of music. He had been one of the founders of the conservatory, and in the years preceding its founding he had been principal conductor of the Gewandhaus orchestra. They wouldn't think of planning a concert season without including some of his works.

Schumann's star was also soaring high in the city, albeit somewhat higher in the Gewandhaus than in the conservatory at the time Grieg was there. When the conservatory first started, Schumann served for a year and a half as a teacher of composition, piano, and score reading, but he soon became too "modern" for the leaders of the conservatory. Furthermore, in 1834 he had founded the influential *Neue Zeitschrift für Musik* in Leipzig. Through this journal he became an enthusiastic spokesman for the newest trends in music, and he fought many a battle with the "philistines"—the narrow-minded, bourgeois crowd that in its reactionary zeal did its utmost to repress modern tendencies.

Grieg was much taken with Schumann's poetic music. He loved the songs and the piano pieces; once when he heard Clara Schumann play the piano concerto, which was to become a model for his own *A-minor Concerto* ten years later, it was a revelation for him. As late as 1907 he wrote in his diary: ". . . each tempo is indelibly imprinted in my soul. Youthful impressions such as these do not lie. The mind is as soft as wax, and impressionable, and the impression remains for life."

Schumann appealed to him much more than Mendelssohn. In Grieg's eyes, Mendelssohn was without doubt extremely competent, clear thinking, and elegant; but unlike Schumann, he did not succeed in expressing the secret longing that is at the heart of Romanticism. In Schumann's music Grieg saw the fulfillment of his own dreams. He got to play a number of the master's piano pieces during his time at the conservatory, especially after Ernst Ferdinand Wenzel—"Schumann's brilliant friend, who soon became my favorite"—became his piano teacher. Grieg later dedicated to Wenzel his first published work, *Four Piano Pieces,* Opus 1, which he composed toward the end of his stay at the conservatory.

Later, on a number of occasions, Grieg wrote enthusiastic articles about Schumann. In an article about his Danish friend Emil Horneman he also related an amusing story about how Horneman encountered Schumann's radical music for the first time—music that he had been sternly warned against back in Denmark.[1]

The thrilling musical experiences that Grieg had in Leipzig led him later to characterize this place as "the city of music." The cold reception that his own compositions received in the conservatively oriented music press there, however, hurt him deeply and resulted in a bitter attitude toward the city. In an undated but late letter to his biographer, Gerhard Schjelderup, he expressed this attitude in rather scornful words: "Leipzig, in spite of its conservatory and its university, never was and never will be a cultured city. The inhabitants of the city are by nature altogether too bourgeois and philistine for that."

This dislike for a city toward which he should have had every reason to feel grateful increased through the years. We find the same negative judgment of

In contrast to Svendsen, I must say that I left the Leipzig Conservatory just as dumb as I was when I was there. I had learned a bit, to be sure, but my own individuality was still a closed book for me. (Letter to Aimar Grönvold, April 25, 1881.)

* * *

How I envy you your technique, which each day I miss more and more. And it isn't just my own fault either; it is primarily the fault of that damned Leipzig conservatory, where I learned *absolutely nothing*. (Letter to Julius Röntgen, October 30, 1884.)

* * *

How I hate this conservatory in Leipzig! (Letter to Johan Halvorsen, December 6, 1901.)

* * *

I would have found it completely reasonable if neither the director nor the teachers at the conservatory had taken any interest in me. For I didn't accomplish anything during those three years that would create any expectation for the future. If, then, in these glimpses of the conservatory I have had to criticize various things about both the institution and the people within it, I must hasten to add that I take it for granted that it was due primarily to my own nature that I left the conservatory about as stupid as I was when I entered it. I was a dreamer with no desire for competition . . . (From "My First Success.")

the Leipzig milieu in Johan Svendsen who, like Grieg, was opposed by the local music critics. One finds this opposition not least of all in Edouard Bernsdorf, principal reviewer for the noted music journal, *Signale für die musikalische Welt,* who time and again almost automatically turned thumbs down on the Norwegian composers.

But Grieg and Svendsen were both to find that, in spite of everything, the musical and cultural level in Leipzig was higher than that which they would encounter at home in either Bergen or Oslo.

Grieg's teachers and their evaluations

It was not just the city of Leipzig that, as time went by, Grieg came to resent. The same thing happened—more or less unjustly—with respect to the music conservatory and its teachers. That there could be something to his criticism of the institution is obvious. This is altogether natural. A young, imaginative, creative spirit does not easily adjust to a system ruled by strict discipline, where rules are made in order to be enforced, where imagination is held in check and not released again until the fundamental technique has been thoroughly established.

In the Primary Materials will be found some of Grieg's most negative statements about the Leipzig conservatory.[2] It should be noted that they all date from a late period in his life, and that they are, therefore, probably colored by the aversion that he as a mature artist later developed toward the Leipzig milieu. The reality was undoubtedly somewhat different.

A fundamental question with respect to Grieg's judgment of his years at the conservatory is this: what expectations did the fifteen-year-old bring with him to Leipzig? He certainly had plenty of talent. But he was undeveloped, and as mentioned he himself soon came to realize this. In spite of his mother's skillful guidance, he had no training in how to work systematically toward a long-range goal. In "My First Success" it is evident that when he first came to the conservatory he did not understand the seriousness of the situation: "A few words of praise by a teacher during a lesson—that was a joy that lifted my youthful spirits quite differently than the applause of thousands later in life. At first, however, none of this kind of encouragement came my way. I was anything but an outstanding conservatory student. Quite the opposite. At the beginning I was lazy to the core."

This indolence went so far that Grieg's first piano teacher, Louis Plaidy, evidently lost his temper: "One fine day, as I sat and picked away at what I considered an abominable Clementi sonata that he had assigned, he suddenly grabbed the music off the piano and threw it in such a way that it flew through the air in a high arc and came to rest in the farthest corner of the large classroom. Since he couldn't very well do the same thing to me personally, he contented himself with shouting, 'Go home and practice!' I must confess that he had a right to be angry . . ."

In the article by J. de Jong in *De Tijdspiegel* (1881) from which we quoted earlier, Grieg wrote: "At the beginning it was all a dream to me. I looked and

3. POEM TO EDVARD
FROM HIS MOTHER

My son! Our loving God in His great
    mercy
Has shown you music's limitless domain,
Has offered you the pow'r to speak its lan-
    guage
And comprehend its innermost refrain;
Has giv'n your soul the wisdom to inter-
    pret
Its mysteries; to feel, to see and love
Its depth, its height, its fullness—yes, the
    essence
Of all that music's given from above;
Has in imagaination's dreams refreshed you
With joy that's greater and more pure by
    far
Than that which any earthly thing can
    offer—
A joy that nothing base can ever mar.

In ordinary life there's much that's trifling,
Much that seems silly, dry, or simply plain,
And in our youth we're tempted to regard it
As worthy only of our deep disdain.
Do not regard your music thus, but rather
With gentleness, love, and a cheerful mind
Direct its magic and its wondrous beauty
Upon the shadows that engulf mankind;
And when those shadows seem to be the
    darkest,
Let it shine forth with every rainbow's hue;
Thus will you reap with joy and under-
    standing
The fruit of that which God has given you.

(Written by Gesine Grieg during Edvard's
convalescence in Bergen in the summer of
1860.)

listened and didn't have the slightest idea that there was anything else I was supposed to do. In other words: I became lazy. Clementi's sonatas bored me. So did the rules about fifths and octaves. The things that excited me—the compositions of Chopin, Schumann, and Richard Wagner—were things that an ambitious student at the conservatory could not begin to study without committing a mortal sin . . ."

After the embarrassing experience during Plaidy's lesson, however, Grieg's Bergen temperament was aroused. He felt so offended by his teacher that he went directly to the Director of the conservatory, Conrad Schleinitz, and demanded to be excused from further instruction by that teacher. Surprisingly enough, he got his way. Wenzel became his new teacher, and somewhat later he also took piano from the most famous of the conservatory's pianists, Ignaz Moscheles.

From Grieg's report to J. de Jong we also learn how his ambition finally came to life, for he soon realized that his fellow students surpassed him in technical preparation. "The desire to compete spurred him on, for he realized that he, too, must work hard if he was going to make anything of himself. In order to get what he had missed he now began to work with such zeal that he damaged his health." In the spring of 1860, he came down with what was thought to be pneumonia, and according to an 1889 interview in the London *Pall Mall Gazette* his mother went to Leipzig to care for him. As soon as he was well enough to travel, she took him back to Bergen.[3]

This illness, which was actually the beginning of tuberculosis, was difficult to cure at that time, and his health was permanently weakened. One lung ceased to function altogether, with the result that for the rest of his life he had trouble breathing.

But his artistic ambitions had now come to life in earnest, and against the advice of the doctor his parents allowed him to go back to Leipzig in the autumn—accompanied this time by his brother John. At the conservatory they were called "Grieg the first" and "Grieg the second"—or, as the Scandinavian students put it, "Big Grieg" and "Little Grieg."

Edvard's instructors in harmony were Ernst Friedrich Richter, Robert Papperitz, and Moritz Hauptmann. He received the most thorough possible training in this discipline. Undoubtedly he was now an industrious student. This is clearly evident from workbooks that have been preserved from the classes of all three of these teachers. When he wrote that Richter, especially, was a pedantic old fogy he was guilty of a gross exaggeration. It is surprising to see the extent to which the teachers tolerated Grieg's inclination toward chromatic part writing. Here is a little example from Richter's class—Grieg's harmonization of the chorale, "Ich weiss mein Gott":

From Papperitz's class we have a similar exercise in harmony that shows Grieg's insistence on chromaticism:

Grieg took lessons in counterpoint from Richter and Hauptmann. His best student exercise in this area is Fugue in F Minor for string quartet, which dates from December, 1861 (CW 109). This fugue demonstrates a firm mastery of contrapuntal technique. In the example below it is interesting to note the conscious use of contrasting sounds. This characteristic points forward to the wealth of sound in the G-minor quartet (Opus 27) seventeen years later:

Fugue in F minor, CW 109

During his last year at the conservatory, Grieg had Carl Reinecke as his teacher in composition. He felt almost totally unprepared when he got his first assignment, which was to write a string quartet. Before he started, therefore, he made a careful study of Mozart's and Beethoven's quartets, and he finally threw together three movements. This "D-minor quartet" was played in class, and there was even talk of more public performances. This was prevented at the initiative of the violinist Ferdinand David, something for which Grieg was basically very thankful. Nonetheless, he put the quartet on the program in 1862 when he gave his first concert in Bergen. Since that performance nothing has been seen of it.

Grieg also started to write an orchestral overture, but the project came to naught. He never finished it, simply for lack of a rudimentary knowledge of composing for symphony orchestra: "I tackled the job with the unflinching courage of youth, but that time I nonetheless came up short. It is hard to believe, but there was not a single class in the conservatory where one could devote oneself to the elementary principles of writing for symphony orchestra."

He also tried to set a German text. On New Year's Eve, 1859, he composed a song to a text of E. Geibel, "Look to the Sea" ("Siehst du das Meer") (CW 106). It has been possible to reconstruct this song from fragments in one of his workbooks. The arrangement is far from dilettante, although musical interest lies more in the harmony than in the melody. The song also gives a foretaste of the style he was to use in the ten German songs he composed in the course of the following four years. We give here the four opening measures of this song, the first that Grieg ever wrote:

"Look to the Sea," CW 106

Grieg's first collection of German songs—*Four Songs*, Opus 2—also probably came into being while he was at the conservatory. In any case it was published by C. F. Peters in 1863–64 at the same time that the piano pieces of Opus 1 were published. The songs created a response in the German press. The renowned music theorist Hugo Riemann wrote that they revealed a power of musical expression that reminds one of Schubert at his best! Such an evaluation today seems greatly exaggerated. Undoubtedly, the songs are technically well written, and they have a certain mark of the "Sturm und Drang" that was so characteristic of Romanticism. Nonetheless, they strike one as rather insubstantial, and viewed in the larger context of Grieg's later compositions they are almost totally lacking in distinctive features. "I Stood Before Her Portrait" ("Ich stand in dunkeln Träumen")—a setting of a text by Heinrich Heine—is the best of the four, with a heartfelt expressiveness in the voice part and a rich, vivid accompaniment.

The piano was the center of Grieg's interest throughout his years at the conservatory. From 1853 to 1862 he wrote thirty piano pieces, including the small pieces he had written before he went to Leipzig (see p. 26). Later he felt rather embarrassed about these compositions, and on the title page of the collection *Short Pieces for Piano* (CW 105) he wrote clearly: "To be destroyed after my death. Must never be published." One can only regret this inscription, for the pieces contain so much of interest that they might well be published, for their value both as didactic music and as examples of the exceptional abilities of the sixteen-year-old who wrote them. The musical

Edvard and John Grieg ca. 1860, when John came to Leipzig to study cello. In a letter to Julius Röntgen May 3, 1904, Grieg related that during the time they were at the conservatory together John was often called "Grieg the first" and Edvard "Grieg the second." Among the Scandinavians, John was also called "Big Grieg" and Edvard "Little Grieg." That is not surprising when one sees the difference in their respective sizes. This difference is not due entirely to the fact that John was three years older than his brother. Edvard was always small: even as a grown man he weighed only about 110 pounds. (Troldhaugen, Bergen)

language here is very close to that of Schumann, and the melodies are merely a reflection of the Schumannesque model, but in his choice of harmony Grieg was somewhat more original:

"Prayer" CW 104, No. 4 (CW 105, No. 19)

It is interesting to note as a curiosity that the preceding example (CW 104, No. 4-CW 105, No. 19) is similar to the chromaticism in *Tristan and Isolde*, which Wagner was working on at this time.

But these small pieces were not the only things that Grieg later came to look upon with disfavor. He also regretted that he had allowed *Four Piano Pieces* to be published as Opus 1 in 1863–64. In a February 25, 1877, letter to Dr. Max Abraham, director of the C. F. Peters publishing firm, he wrote: "With respect to Opus 1, I would absolutely have been happiest if the work had not been published . . . but instead had been left in total oblivion. The pieces are such that not only do they lack independence and inspiration, but all things considered they are nothing more than student exercises."

Grieg's self-criticism with regard to Opus 1 strikes us as excessively negative. He played these pieces at his final examination in 1862, and according to his own report made a "formidable hit" with them at that time. Of course it is true that the pieces lack the striking melodies that distinguish most of his later works. They do, however, have a definite harmonic sophistication, and his mastery of piano technique and his confident ability to structure the music raise them above mediocrity.

One can generally say that Grieg's Opuses 1 and 2 were good "final exercises" in his composition class. They provide persuasive evidence that his years of study at Leipzig were not in fact the inhibiting ballast that he later thought they had been. Quite the contrary. The conservatory had given him a thorough technical training and laid a solid foundation for his future development as a creative musician.

Grieg said of himself that he was no "prize conservatory student," and it is evident from his statements that his effort at certain times—especially at the beginning of his study—was somewhat limited. But as his ambition grew his willingness to work grew stronger—with results to match. When one looks at his graduation diploma, which is still in existence, one can only marvel that an eighteen-year-old youth could obtain such laudatory reports from some of the world's leading music teachers.[4]

Moreover, he received an especially nice commendation from Moritz Hauptmann a few days before his final examination. Hauptmann's testimonial reads as follows: "Mr. Grieg from Bergen, a student at this conservatory who stands out as an excellent pianist, must also be counted among the best students in composition with respect to both theoretical mastery and practical application. An exemplary dilligence and love of study have always undergirded his natural talent. He has, therefore, acquired an exceptional level of training that promises great success in the future."

This commendation also had an endorsement by Carl Reinecke, who wrote as follows:

"I testify with pleasure that Mr. Grieg possesses a most considerable musical talent, especially for composition. It is much to be desired that he be given the opportunity to develop this talent to the fullest in every possible way."

Interlude in Karlshamn

In the Academy of Music in Stockholm there is a copy of *Three Piano Pieces* (CW 107). The original manuscript in the Bergen Public Library, which is dated April 1860, has at some later date been inscribed as follows: "Must not be published. To be destroyed after my death." The Stockholm version, possibly copied by Grieg's Swedish classmate Gustaf Smith of Karlshamn, has another inscription: "To Therese Berg from the Composer."

Who was this Therese Berg, and how did these piano pieces end up in Sweden? Is there perhaps a love story concealed in the dedication? The facts hardly provide a basis to suppose anything of the kind. Briefly, what happened was this: in the autumn of 1861, nearly a year and a half after these three piano pieces were composed, Grieg went to Leipzig by way of Sweden after having spent the summer vacation in Bergen. In Karlshamn, a city in southern Sweden, he interrupted his trip to visit Gustaf Smith and to give a public concert there. In the middle of August he had placed in the *Karlshamns Allehanda* an advertisement of the forthcoming concert, which was to be given in the "large lounge of the city courthouse." It does not appear from the program that Grieg performed any of his own works at this, the first of his public concerts. He did, however, play pieces by Mendelssohn, Schumann, and Moscheles. The concert was a success in every way. It was well attended, and Grieg received good reviews. His performance of Schumann's *Kreisleriana* was especially praised. It was probably on this occasion that Grieg met his young contemporary, Therese Berg, and gave her the manuscript copy of the three piano pieces.

Therese was an intelligent, well-educated, and very beautiful young lady who had mastered the finer points of piano playing exceptionally well. She was the daughter of C. G. Berg, a Karlshamn merchant and member of parliament who had taken a patent on the manufacture of Swedish punch, and with this industry had amassed a huge fortune. She accompanied her father when he resided in Stockholm, where she was called "The Rose of Parliament" because of her beauty and charming ways. She remained unmarried and died in 1932 at the age of 89.

It is possible that Grieg met Therese Berg on other occasions, but it is not likely. There is no evidence of any exchange of letters between the two, and not a single mention of her name is found in Grieg's letters. To weave a romantic story around the dedication on the manuscript copy and their brief meeting in Karlshamn—when both were eighteen-year-olds—has no basis in fact.

The three piano pieces, however, are interesting enough—especially the last two, which show the author's fresh imagination and developing talent. The first three lines of the second piece are given below:

CW 107, No. 2

"Arbeiderforeningen"—the Labor Union hall in Bergen where in 1862 Grieg gave his first public concert in Norway. The building is now called "Eldorado" and is used as a movie theater. (Photo collection of Universitetsbiblioteket in Bergen)

Grieg's first concert in Bergen

Grieg returned to Bergen in the spring of 1862 with his diploma from the distinguished Leipzig conservatory, and almost immediately he rented the Labor Union's large hall for a concert to be given on May 21—his first public concert in Norway. He received assistance from some of the city's leading musicians. The program included Beethoven's "Pathetique" sonata, some etudes of Moscheles, and three "Fantasy Pieces" by Grieg himself. The "Fantasy Pieces" are three of the pieces that were published as Opus 1. He also participated as the pianist in Schumann's piano quartet, Opus 47, and accompanied the singer Wibecke Meyer in his own *Four Songs*. Moreover, when these songs were published as Opus 2 they were dedicated to her. It was a comprehensive and demanding program, and in addition to all this the previously mentioned string quartet in D minor—the one that later vanished without a trace—was performed.

A brief report on the debut concert appeared in *Bergensposten* for May 23: "The praise that had preceded his arrival does not appear to have been

Portrait of Grieg taken in Leipzig, probably at the time he finished his conservatory studies. ("Troldhaugen," Bergen, Norway)

overstated. His compositions were particularly pleasing; as a composer Grieg seems to have a great future awaiting him. As a performer he also won general applause. This seemed especially to be the case in the Schumann quartet for piano and strings, which must be considered the high point of the concert."

Such a laudatory review provided fuel for Grieg's artistic ambitions. He wanted to get out and learn more. His father, who had paid for his studies in Leipzig, felt that he was not in a position to finance a new foreign visit. Grieg understood this and cheerfully sent a formal request to the Ministry of Education for a stipend to enable him to go abroad to further prepare himself as a composer.[5]

As was to be expected, the unknown Mr. Grieg from Bergen got no stipend from the Ministry of Education at this time. Thus he was not able to continue his studies abroad. He saw no alternative but to work on his own at home in Bergen. Profits from the concert were used to purchase, among other things, scores by the great masters.

He remained in Bergen an entire year, interrupted only by a long journey abroad with his father and brother John in the summer of 1862. Their journey took them to, among other places, London and Paris.

The Bergen milieu gave Grieg little or no support and could not stir his creative ability to any significant achievements. The only thing he composed was "Retrospect," a song for mixed choir and piano. It is amusing that a poem with such a title appealed to the nineteen-year-old would-be composer; that he ventured into a domain where life experience really is a presupposition gives undeniable evidence of a high level of self-confidence. Nor was there any future for "Retrospect," for after being performed in Bergen on April 27, 1863, this work of Grieg was "entrusted" to the aforementioned wastebasket.

But Grieg felt that he had to get away no matter what it might cost. In 1863 he got a loan from his father and headed for the alluring Denmark, which he had previously visited only briefly enroute to Leipzig. In a letter to Iver Holter on February 9, 1887, he wrote: "I was completely destroyed after my stay in Leipzig. I didn't know up from down when a vague longing drove me towards Copenhagen . . ."

5. GRIEG'S APPLICATION FOR A STIPEND

Bergen, July 12, 1862
To the King:

As may be graciously observed in the accompanying testimonials, I have lived in Leipzig for three and a half years and, as a student at the conservatory there, have sought to prepare myself to become a composer.

I trust that I will not be considered immodest if I humbly venture the hope that these testimonials will verify that I possess such an aptitude for composition and piano playing—and at the conservatory made such progress and received such training—that I should perhaps yield to hope that with further study I might achieve results that might be of some importance—not only for me but also for music in my native land, where it is my intention to remain.

It would be highly desirable for me, then, if while I am still young I could have an opportunity to visit the largest cities in other countries where the cultivation and practice of music are most advanced. But I do not have the means for this, and my father—Alexander Grieg, the British Vice-consul here in Bergen—also does not consider himself able to offer me the assistance necessary for this purpose.

Please note that I am nineteen years of age. I take the liberty, therefore, with reference to the foregoing matter, humbly to petition Your Majesty graciously to grant me a stipend out of public funds so that I may go abroad to further prepare myself in that art to which I have devoted myself, and to which my soul's entire interest is bound.

Humbly,
Edvard Hagerup Grieg

Grieg's drawing of Frederiksberg castle. This is undoubtedly Grieg's most successful effort as a sketcher. (Music division, Bergen Offentlige Bibliotek)

Formative Years in Copenhagen

I. IN SEARCH OF A NEW IDENTITY

I didn't want to be merely Norwegian, much less to be chauvinistically Norwegian; I just wanted to be myself. I wanted to find expression for the best that was within me, which was something a thousand miles away from Leipzig and its atmosphere. But that this "best" consisted in love for my homeland and an appreciation of the great, melancholy scenery of western Norway— that I did not realize, and perhaps I would never have realized it had I not, through Nordraak, been led to self-examination. (Letter to Iver Holter, February 9, 1897.)

In April of 1863 Grieg went to Copenhagen, and the months that followed became an especially important formative period in his life. We must now ask: Why did this young man from Bergen exchange Haakon's Hall for Frederiksberg castle, his hometown's familiar open-air fish market for the Höjbro market place, and the seven mountains surrounding Bergen for the idyllic, poetic charm of Copenhagen?

There were several reasons. As early as the 1860s Copenhagen, the principal metropolis in all of Scandinavia, was a city of considerable size with a population of some 170,000. When Grieg first visited the city enroute to Leipzig in 1861 it "made a powerful impression" on him, and he was captivated by its singular charm. The lively cultural life of the city was also very attractive to him. He had good contacts there in his close relatives—the family of his cousin Nina—and in Emil Horneman, his good friend from the conservatory.

Toward an artistic clarification

Grieg later made several interesting statements about his situation at the beginning of this Denmark period which was to prove so liberating for his creative abilities. As he tells J. de Jong, he was "more uncertain of himself than at any other time." He later wrote about this in some detail in a letter to Iver Holter.[1]

In an interview in *Dannebrog* on December 26, 1893, he was quoted as saying: "I was stuffed full of Chopin, Schumann, Mendelssohn, and Wagner, and it was as if I needed to find some elbow room and to breathe in a more personal and independent atmosphere."

We know that J. de Jong was building on Grieg's own statements when he went on to say, "This is when a light began to dawn for the twenty-year-old musician, as he was studying the Scandinavian legends and Scandinavian art. Distinctive ideals began to take shape in his imagination, and the compositions of Hartmann, Gade, and many younger composers who followed in their footsteps strongly attracted him. He, too, began to feel that he was a son of Scandinavia, but that he would nonetheless speak a language different from theirs when his creative juices began to flow." It is worth noting that Grieg here emphasized the *Scandinavian,* not the Norwegian, as the important thing—something he often did during this period.

It was clearly the new "beckoning sounds" from Scandinavia that fascinated him. Here were fresh and untapped sources in nature and in the soul of the Scandinavian people, sources from which one could simply take whatever one wanted. At first he approached them carefully, but as the 1860s progressed he delved deeper and deeper into them.

In all three of the Scandinavian countries the awareness of the unique values inherent in their folk music had been dramatically awakened. Major efforts had been launched to gather and publish these national treasures, and the folk tunes had become a rich source of inspiration for major composers as early as the first half of the nineteenth century. As mentioned earlier, the pioneers in this effort in Norway were L. M. Lindeman and Ole Bull.

Other Scandinavian countries had launched similar efforts even earlier than Norway. In Sweden, several large volumes of folk music were published by A. Afzelius and E. G. Geijer shortly before 1820, and in the 1840s by R. Dybeck and others. One also finds a national stamp in the original compositions of Geijer. It shows up again a bit later in the compositions of A. F. Lindblad, J. A. Josephson, and Franz Berwald, and even more strongly in those of August Söderman.

In Denmark the pioneers in this area were Werner H. Abrahamsen, Rasmus Nyerup, and Knud L. Rahbek, who jointly published a voluminous collection of Danish folk music in 1812–14. Their work was continued especially by A. P. Berggreen, who began publishing a series of volumes in the 1840s. The composers F. Kuhlau, C. F. E. Weyse, and J. F. Frölich (who also arranged folk melodies) were among the first to try to create a uniquely Danish sound in their compositions. But the central figures in these national endeavors were N. W. Gade and J. P. E. Hartmann.

Gade made use of Danish folk songs in his *Symphony No. 1 in C minor* (1841), and several of his compositions in the years that followed contain distinctively national elements. His principal work of this kind was the ballad "Elverskud" for solo voices, choir, and orchestra (1853)—a piece that is without doubt one of the most valuable contributions by a Danish composer to the corpus of Scandinavian national-Romantic music. But Gade failed to maintain this level of creativity, and his later works strike us today as significantly weaker and less original.

Hartmann, on the other hand—a far more original and gifted man than Gade (who, incidentally, was his son-in-law)—continued to grow artistically until he was very old (he reached the venerable age of 95). His work was somewhat uneven, but one often finds in his music interesting and bold ideas—for example, in the use of the church modes (i.e., diatonic scales other than major or minor). A distinctively Danish-Scandinavian musical language came to the fore in the opera *Liden Kirsten* [Little Kirsten] (1846). This language was developed further in his *Symphony No. 2 in E major* (1847–48)

2. GRIEG MEETS GADE
FOR THE FIRST TIME

"Herr professor, here is a Norwegian who is a musician." "Is it Nordraak?" Gade asked. "No, it is Grieg," Matthison-Hansen replied. "Well, so that's who it is," said Gade as he surveyed my diminutive body from top to toe with a scrutinizing glance. Meanwhile I, not without some awe, stood face to face with that man whose compositions I valued so highly. "Do you have anything to show me?" Gade inquired. "No," I replied. For I didn't consider any of the things I had finished good enough to show him. "Then go home and write a symphony," Gade suggested. (From an interview in *Dannebrog*. Copenhagen, December 26, 1893.)

and especially in a series of works associated with Scandinavian antiquity and mythology. Among the latter were the incidental music to *Haakon Jarl* (1857) and the ballets *Et Folkesagn* [A Folk Legend], Act 2 (1854) and *Valkyrien* [The Valkyrie], (1861).

Grieg's enthusiasm for the best in these two Danish composers is evident from his unpublished 1882 article about Horneman. Here he discussed the development of Danish music, how it "shone through the brilliant masters Hartmann and Gade." At Hartmann's death in 1900 he wrote to Frants Beyer: "Now Gade-Hartmann has become a saga! But a beautiful one. And how it is interwoven in the mystery of my own being."

It was primarily Gade's earliest works with their fresh naturalness that attracted Grieg. He made a point of this in a January 11, 1902 letter to E. MacDowell, in which he reported what Moritz Hauptmann, his teacher at Leipzig, had said about Gade's first orchestral works: " 'Sea gulls hover over his scores.' That is beautifully said."

With respect to Hartmann on the other hand, Grieg was highly enthusiastic about everything he wrote. He studied Hartmann's works to great advantage, and received important impulses from them. He heard the opera *Liden Kirsten* and the ballet *Valkyrien* in Copenhagen in 1863–64. Later he played a piano selection from this ballet at his own concerts, and in 1871 he performed parts of it with choir and orchestra in Oslo.

In honor of Hartmann's eightieth birthday on May 14, 1885, Grieg published a laudatory article in *Musikbladet* (Copenhagen) in which he wrote: "No one deserves more than he the honor of being crowned in the evening of his life as one of music's chosen high priests. For he never catered to the fashions of the day. He was guided only by the demands of his ideals. What musician in Scandinavia with a genuine feeling for the Scandinavian spirit is not reminded today of what he owes to *Hartmann!* The best and deepest thoughts that a whole generation of more or less influential minds have drawn upon were first expressed by *him*, and it was *he* who first made them echo within us."

While Grieg admired Hartmann only from a distance during his first stay in Denmark, he came in personal contact with Gade—"the sharp-clawed lion of Danish music," as he was called. But Grieg pointed out in the *Dannebrog* interview (1893) that he "never was his student, however, as is mistakenly asserted in several textbooks." He also stated in this interview that Gade's name had lured him back to Denmark: "I wanted to form a personal acquaintance with that significant artist who knew how to shape his thoughts so masterfully and clearly."

Grieg did not seek Gade out, however. He met him quite by accident some time after he had come to Copenhagen. He was taking a walk in Klampenborg one day with his friend Gottfred Matthison-Hansen, who happened to catch sight of Gade and introduced them to each other.[2] This meeting became the prelude to a closer relation between them shortly thereafter.

As mentioned earlier, Grieg underscored the fact that he was fortunate to have had Gade's clear, artistic judgment to lean on at that time. In an article in

3. NORDRAAK DESCRIBES HIS FIRST MEETING WITH GRIEG

Greetings to both Horneman and Grieg. I see that you still consider them good and talented companions, and I think you are right. Recently I ran into Kjerulf, who told me that Grieg's compositions had been sharply criticized in a Leipzig music journal. From the little that I was able to get out of him when I met him at Tivoli, I am inclined to share the opinion of the critics without having heard a single note that he has written. He appeared to be talented and deeply interested in his studies, and to be guided by noble ideas, but he also exhibited a pedantry that made no sense at all but by means of which he mistakenly thought he could reach his goal. He tries too hard to find the great within the small, and often elevates the latter at the expense of the former. Then there are his one-sided opinions, his exclusive preference for Schumann, etc., that will certainly hurt him in time if he really has the talent that I think he has; and when he stops this incessant searching for originality, then perhaps he will find it. The greatest original thoughts come of themselves; they come from the heart. In developing them it is all right to use one's measure of understanding, but one should not let it get in the way of one's feelings. (Nordraak in a letter to Louis Hornbeck, May 24, 1864.)

1900 he recounted how he had once shown Gade an immature work on which Gade then pronounced his opinion "in the following words, which were as telling as they were well chosen: 'Well, what good is it to have something to say when you can't say it?'"

But even at this early date Grieg wanted to stand on his own feet. He did not want to become, like some of the excessively dependent younger imitators, a kind of "Gade hireling."

There was another circle in Copenhagen—different from the one that revolved around Hartmann and Gade—of which Grieg became a part. It consisted of a group of younger musicians with progressive ideas. These colleagues became Grieg's firm supporters for many years to come. The center of the circle was Emil Horneman, a well-rounded, well-trained, and talented man with "brilliant foresight and inventive ability." The friendship between Grieg and Horneman was greatly strengthened at this time, though in spite of all they shared they were highly dissimilar in temperament. Indeed, they became such close friends that in a February 13, 1901 letter to Jonas Lie, Grieg could say of Horneman that he "knew the innermost wrinkles of my soul."

The circle around Horneman and Grieg included four talented artists who were to win renown as outstanding musicians: Louis Hornbeck, Gottfred Matthison-Hansen, Julius Steenberg, and August Winding. They became Grieg's closest friends in Denmark. Benjamin Feddersen, a writer and music teacher who was fourteen years older than Grieg, also became his mentor during his Denmark period, and Grieg dedicated to him the first piece that he now wrote: *Poetic Tone Pictures,* Opus 3.

Part of the voluminous correspondence that Grieg carried on throughout his life with these warm-hearted and vital individuals has been preserved and is of enormous value. It is characteristic of him that when he wrote of them he laid such great stress on their valuable human qualities.

In the summer of 1863 Grieg met Rikard Nordraak for the first time when the latter was on a short visit to Copenhagen enroute to Norway from Berlin. Grieg wrote about this meeting in an 1881 letter to Aimar Grönvold: "My first meeting with Nordraak as it really happened was so remarkable—for Nordraak—that I can recall it at this moment as if it were just yesterday. What happened was this. One evening at Tivoli in Copenhagen I was presented by Mrs. [Magdalene] Thoresen to a young man by the name of Nordraak who introduced himself thus: 'Well, shall we two great men really meet one another at last!' His bearing, his gestures, his voice—everything about him indicated that I was in the presence of a man who considered himself to be both the Björnson and the Ole Bull of the future. And yet there was such a touching naïveté and charm about him that he took me by storm. Until that moment I had never considered the possibility of being or even having the ability to become a great man. I was a student, no more. Moreover I was timid, shy, and sickly. But this cocksureness was just the medicine I needed. From that moment on it was as if we had always been friends."

The following year Nordraak wrote in a letter to Louis Hornbeck how *he* remembered that first meeting.[3] Shortly after this episode in Tivoli Nordraak went on to Norway, and the friendship between these two so diametrically

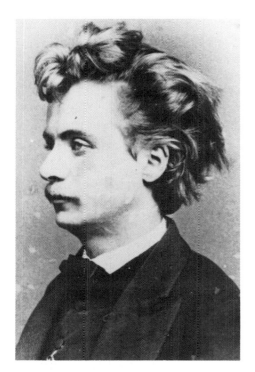

Grieg during his first stay in Copenhagen. (Photo collection of Universitetsbiblioteket in Oslo)

opposite young artists was not renewed until a year later, in the autumn of 1864 in Copenhagen.

Where Grieg lived during this first stay in Copenhagen is not known. He presumably took lodging with a "respectable" family and rented a piano so that he could work on his music in a private room—something that he always required. He practiced his already well-developed piano technique, but above all he wanted to compose.

During these first two years—up until the autumn of 1865, when he went to Berlin—Grieg wrote twenty-six songs, five choral pieces, thirteen piano pieces, one symphony, and two sonatas. The orchestral version of the symphony was not published until 1984 (see below, p. 53 ff.). During this period, Grieg also composed other pieces which are now lost, though we know some of their titles. In 1903 he wrote to Gerhard Schjelderup that he "remembered a big bonfire that [he] lit in a moment of despondency," and some of his early works undoubtedly went up in flames.

Grieg's production during his Copenhagen period, then, was impressive more for its breadth than for its quantity. The works that he later dared to acknowledge as his are very uneven in quality.

Enroute to self-discovery

Grieg now began to turn away from the musical language of German Romanticism, even though this remained the foundation from which he worked. A gradual liberation occurred in waves, depending in part on the kind of composition he was working on. He sought new directions, and this led to different forms of both melodic development and harmonic practice. The earlier "Sturm und Drang" type of expression was modified in the direction of a refinement of the musical content.

The principal result of this change was that simpler, naturally flowing melodies more often came to the fore. Meanwhile, he retained his interest in further exploring the world of harmony—not, however, the dark and obscure realm of German Romanticism, but the more accessible domain of the land and people and culture of Scandinavia.

The results of these efforts were not long in coming. Even in the first Copenhagen work of 1863—*Poetic Tone Pictures* for piano, Opus 3—there was an obvious simplification as well as an unmistakable connection to Norwegian folk music. The six pieces in Opus 3 are all significantly shorter and less demanding technically than those in *Four Piano Pieces,* Opus 1. The structure is relatively simple, though not uninteresting, and the various contrasting sections are usually repeated as variations rather than mere repetitions.

In Opus 3 Grieg also abandoned his earlier manner of expression in favor of a diatonic tonal language which he used in all of the pieces except No. 4. Meanwhile the chromatic parts that still remain in all six pieces are less radical than before and approach a kind of salon style. This is especially true of the second piece, which is the weakest of the six.

In Nos. 1, 3, 5, and 6, however, Grieg was well on the way toward something new, even though he was not able to maintain his inspiration at the same level throughout each of these pieces. The exciting thing here is that in certain very Norwegian-sounding sections of these pieces one finds—for the first time in Grieg's music—short, truly melodious motives with a national touch that is also carried over into the rhythm and the harmony. Especially interesting is the use of the church modes, which is typical of Scandinavian—not least of all Norwegian—folk music, both instrumental and vocal. They were carefully used on occasion by several of Grieg's predecessors and contemporaries in order to give their music a Scandinavian sound, and their use became one of the hallmarks of Grieg's music as he wove them into melody and harmony in a bold and personal way.

The most notable examples from Opus 3 reflecting characteristics of Norwegian folk music are given below. Norwegian folk-dance (*springar*) rhythms with accented second beats are combined with the Dorian mode on E in the first two measures. The pregnant rhythmic/melodic motive in these measures foreshadows the principal theme in the first movement of Grieg's second violin sonata (1867):

Poetic Tone Pictures, Opus 3, No. 1

In this case Grieg aimed at a certain "primitivism" by use of sustained notes and incomplete chords:

Poetic Tone Pictures, Opus 3, No. 3

The first four measures in this passage from No. 5 are marked by a D-Aeolian tonality in the right hand. Note the G-sharp appoggiatura alternating with G-natural in the left hand in measures 1–2:

Poetic Tone Pictures, Opus 3, No. 5

"Primitivism" caused by syncopations and incomplete chords is combined with a fluctuating use of the leading tone G-sharp and the modal G-natural. The dissonances are also quite evident, notably in measures 3–5:

Poetic Tone Pictures, Opus 3, No. 5

4. GRIEG ON THE
"GRIEG FORMULA"

There is one characteristic of our folk music that I have always liked: the treatment of the leading tone, especially when the note following the leading tone is the dominant. One also finds the same pattern in other composers, however. (Letter to H. T. Finck, July 17, 1900.)

In the first example (third measure) there is a melodic phrase that is especially associated with Grieg: a descending line in which a minor second is followed by a major third (c–b–g). This melodic pattern is found frequently in Norwegian folk music, as Grieg himself once observed.[4] David Monrad Johansen has called it "the Griegian *leitmotif*." It should be pointed out, however, that this phrase also occurs in another, less-noticed version with a descending major second followed by a minor third. It occurs in this form in the first two measures of the first example (e–d–b).

We will speak of these two melodic patterns as the major and minor forms of the "Grieg formula." We could also call the minor form the "modal" form of the Grieg formula, since the lowered leading tone that occurs in the descending minor scale is also characteristic of the Aeolian (natural minor), Dorian, and Mixolydian modes.

This formula occurs in both the major and minor form (in the bass and alto parts) in the second example (from No. 3) and in the minor form (in the alto line) in measures 6–7 in the fourth example (from No. 5).

We note with interest such precursors of Grieg's future style in several of these compositions. Grieg himself, however, didn't think much of them five years later, in light of what he had accomplished in the meantime. On November 2, 1868, he wrote to his Danish friend Niels Ravnkilde: "Excuse me, but when you praise *Poetic Tone Pictures* you are not being honest. That composition is nothing but immature nonsense that smells to high heaven . . . You will understand what I mean if you remember that, as Ibsen says [in *Peer Gynt*], the principle is not to be *sufficient* unto oneself but to *be* oneself."

In a much later letter (July 17, 1900) to his American biographer H. T. Finck, Grieg indicated, however, that he was aware of the national character of this opus. He wrote: "Norwegian everyday life, Norwegian sagas and history, and above all Norwegian scenery have exercised a strong influence on my creative work ever since my youth. But only later in life did I get an opportunity to immerse myself in Norwegian folk songs. When I wrote the piano pieces of Opus 3, and especially Opus 6—in both of which a national element appears in many passages—I knew next to nothing about our folk songs."

Although Grieg here spoke of "folk songs" rather than "folk music," one is inclined to be very skeptical about the statement, especially in connection with the work in which his national style first found full expression—*Humoresques*, Opus 6.

We have pointed out that *Poetic Tone Pictures* contains certain folk-like features. These have their roots in Norwegian folk music, not in the traditions that he encountered in Denmark. Grieg, in fact, emphasized that national characteristics are to be found in precisely this early composition. Thus it must have been clear to him that he was in the process of adopting a uniquely Norwegian stance, not one that was simply "Scandinavian." His strange, categorical statement about *Humoresques* cannot be accepted. There can be no doubt that Grieg already had a knowledge of the music of his homeland when he wrote his first composition in Denmark. He was occupied at this time not only with Danish (and to a lesser degree Swedish) classical music, and with collections of the folk tunes of these countries; but he was also especially occupied with Lindeman's and Berggreen's publications of Norwegian folk music. He certainly also studied and learned from Kjerulf's compositions, in which a national musical language is developed. All of these factors were present to light the spark of national consciousness. But the spark was fanned into flames in 1864–65, first during his association with Ole Bull in Bergen and then with Rikard Nordraak in Copenhagen.

After completing *Poetic Tone Pictures,* Grieg turned his attention to vocal music. He wrote eight songs and five choral pieces before starting work on his symphony.

Presumably the first song was "Sunset," which was published in 1867 as Opus 9, No. 3. It is his earliest non-German song, with a Norwegian text by the poet Andreas Munch.

> The style is greatly simplified. Several features contribute to a strong feeling of monotony—for example, the conscious avoidance of dynamic contrasts and the excessive repetition of certain rhythmic patterns and individual notes. Of the first fifty notes in the voice part the note "E" occurs no less than twenty-three times. Moreover, Grieg uses a very limited selection of chords, which is in general atypical of his music. For the first time since the compositions of his childhood the style is completely diatonic. Grieg tries to give the song a folk-like character, and for this purpose uses several of the same means he had used in Opus 3. Thus we find the Grieg formula in both forms, open fifths in the bass, and quite extensive use of modality. But the main impression one gets from this song is one of artificiality.

Grieg wrote another song having many of the same features in February of 1864, entitled "Devoutest of Maidens." The text was a Danish translation by Benjamin Feddersen of a German poem. One portion of the melody anticipates a phrase in "Solveig's Song" from *Peer Gynt:*

Allegretto   *"Devoutest of Maidens," CW 114*

Blik - ket   mod   Him' - len   gaa   Øn - sker - ne   vidt

In other respects the song is just as weak as "Sunset." In both of these songs the altered style that Grieg first employed in *Poetic Tone Pictures* is carried almost to an absurdity.

Among the first compositions that Grieg wrote in Denmark was *Four*

Songs for Male Voices, which he dedicated to the Students' Singing Society in Copenhagen. The texts of songs Nos. 2 and 3 were written by the poet Christian Richardt, who was also conductor of the Students' Singing Society. Only one of the songs—No. 3, "Student Life," which is certainly the least interesting of the lot—was performed by the choir, and that did not occur until December 20, 1866.

> Simplicity continued to be a basic principle in these choral pieces, but in all except No. 3 Grieg nonetheless created more variation and awakened stronger interest than in "Sunset." He did not, however, make use of the capacity for polyphonic singing. A diatonic style continues to predominate. A certain impression of boldness is caused by several markedly modal parts and some strong dissonances resulting from sustained notes in the middle voices. This is especially true of No. 1, "Norwegian War Song," to a poem by Henrik Wergeland—the only text by this poet that Grieg was ever to set.
>
> Here is a characteristic excerpt from the fourth song. "The Late Rose," text by Andreas Munch. The first three measures are in G Aeolian. Note that the harmonic progression is such that the roots of the successive chords move by seconds. Also interesting is the parallel motion of the two second-inversion seventh chords in measure 2—the earliest example we have of Grieg's use of this "impressionistic" harmonic device:

"The Late Rose," CW III, No. 4

After having expressed his Norwegian patriotism in the Wergeland song, Grieg again became Scandinavian, and on May 13, 1864, he wrote a new choral piece, "Denmark," to a poem by Hans Christian Andersen. This was his first setting of a text by this poet, who was later to inspire him so greatly. The composition is for mixed choir with an almost totally unimaginative piano accompaniment. It is undistinguished except for a short section in which Grieg suddenly demonstrates his harmonic boldness.

Six songs dedicated to Nina

Grieg wrote that what meant most to him at this time—and what also led to the writing of a series of songs—was his acquaintance with his cousin Nina Hagerup.

The first result of this acquaintance was six songs with German texts, Opus 4, which he dedicated to her when they were published in the early summer of 1864. None of them is a love song, however.

The style of the earlier German songs, Opus 2, is in many ways continued in Opus 4. But one change is that the voice part has been placed much more within the range of the performer. A general maturing is especially noticeable in the two more successful songs—No. 1, "The Orphan," and No. 5, "The Old Song." No. 5 is clearly the best of the lot. While Grieg in his Leipzig compositions paid attention primarily to the harmonic dimension and demonstrated no special talent for melody, he was now on the way to developing his melodic powers.

In both of these songs we find long sections that have a marked melodic and expressive character. In "The Orphan" these characteristics appear in a manner reminiscent of Schubert, and in "The Old Song" along the lines of Schumann. The latter has a folksong-like ballad stamp. In keeping with this, Grieg deliberately employed a somewhat archaic tonal language with a conscious use of modality. This is the earliest example we have of his use of this stylistic feature throughout an entire composition.

Moreover, the song is characterized by simplicity. In this case the simplification is not used to conceal lack of inspiration, but is a result of logical concentration. The same cannot be said, however, about the two least important songs in the set—the Heine song "Parting" (No. 3), with its extremely pessimistic autumnal atmosphere, and the strongly contrasting "Hunting Song" (No. 4), a setting of a text by Ludwig Uhland. Both are marked by monotony, the first especially with respect to rhythm, the latter as a result of an affected use of open fifths in the bass.

The two remaining songs—No. 2, "Morning Dew" (text by Chamisso), and No. 6, "Where Have They Gone?" (text by Heine)—are uneven. Both are relatively conventional, but they include isolated sections of harmonic daring, as in the excerpt from "Morning Dew" given below. This shows that Grieg was again on the verge of anticipating his later style. The passage has A as the tonal center. The first two measures are in A Aeolian. In the next measure we see a dominant seventh in G major (with the ninth, tenth, and eleventh in the voice part). But then comes a typical Griegian twist: the expected cadence in G major is omitted in favor of a triad in A minor. Thus the passage acquires a Dorian stamp:

"Morning Dew," Opus 4, No. 2

al - so muss wei - nen und schei - den, es ist ja die

Four Songs, Opus 10, to texts by Chr. Winther—perhaps the weakest of all Grieg's song sets—also dates from this period. The texts sound almost parodic at times. Consider, for example, these lines from "Thanks":

> *"Receive my thanks for every time*
> *Your lovely eyes and lips sublime*
> *Assuaged my spirit's sorrow,*
> *And like the sun in summertime*
> *Renewed me for the morrow."*

To be inspired as a composer of songs, Grieg was heavily dependent on textual quality. In these primitive and purely strophic songs he rarely rose above the level of the poems, even though he shines through in a few measures in each of them.

One section near the end of "Thanks" is noteworthy, however, in that the melody is identical to a few measures in the well-known lyric piece "Solitary Traveller," Opus 43, No. 2 (1886):

"Thanks," Opus 10, No. 1

"Solitary Traveller," Opus 43, No. 2

The "forbidden" symphony

Grieg was not exactly bursting with confidence when Nils Gade, at their first chance meeting in 1863, urged him to write a symphony—he who in Leipzig just a year earlier had not managed to put together an orchestral overture.

5. GRIEG ON GADE'S CHALLENGE

Gade's challenge to me, however, caused me to pull myself together and put all my energy into solving the task he had set for me. And within fourteen days I had actually composed and orchestrated the first movement of the symphony. (Interview in *Dannebrog*, December 26, 1893.)

"The sharp-clawed lion of Danish music" didn't frighten him, however. Grieg took him at his word and met the challenge with a completely different attitude than before. He wanted to see for himself what he was capable of, and with single-minded zeal he tackled that most demanding of all musical forms, the symphony.

In the beginning it went so quickly that the first movement was composed and orchestrated in the course of two weeks. At least this is what he himself reported.[5] He worked so hard that, when he was about to proceed to the remaining movements, both inspiration and the desire to work disappeared for a time. Thus the symphony was not completed until a year later: the score is dated May 2, 1864.

As soon as he was able to finish a fair copy, Grieg took the score to Gade. The Danish master was undoubtedly pleased, for he wrote an enthusiastic musical greeting in Grieg's autograph book.

In overall concept there is some similarity between Grieg's symphony and Beethoven's *Fifth Symphony*. The same motto could apply to both: "Through struggle to victory"—from the conflicts in the first movement to the triumph in the last. The primary tonalities in all movements are also identical in the two symphonies: C minor–A-flat major–C minor–C major. In the fourth movement Grieg used three trombones as Beethoven also had done.

But beyond this, Grieg's symphony has little in common with Beethoven's. It is the Schumannesque orchestral music that served as Grieg's point of departure. He was quite aware that Schumann was his model. Five years later he arranged the symphony's two inner movements for piano four hands, and in a letter to his Leipzig publisher he wrote: ". . . I have indeed orchestrated Opus 14; yes, I also heard them [the two inner movements of the symphony] played many years ago in Copenhagen. They sounded pretty good, but I would not for all the world publish the orchestral score now because this work belongs to a vanished Schumann-period in my life."

On Grieg's initiative the symphony was played five times in the middle of the 1860s. The premiere performance (just the last three movements) took place at Tivoli in Copenhagen on June 4, 1864, with H. C. Lumbye conducting. The complete symphony was on the Bergen Symphony Orchestra's concert programs in Bergen on January 19, 1865 and November 28, 1867. When Grieg made his debut as a conductor in Copenhagen on April 1, 1865, he had with him the two middle movements, and when he led "The Philharmonic Society" in Oslo on March 23, 1867, the last three movements were played. After the latter performance *Morgenbladet* reported that the symphony was received with applause, but the music gave the listeners a bit of trouble because "the main features were not always clearly evident." The reviewer thought that this was due to the fact that the work came into being during the flowering of Romanticism, when composers tended to stress "imaginative content" rather than formal beauty.

But after the performances in 1867 something quite dramatic must have taken place, for it was probably at this time that the score received the following inscription in Grieg's own hand: "Must never be performed."

What had happened? In October, 1867, Grieg attended a performance of the first symphony composed by his brilliant fellow countryman Johan S. Svendsen. It was a revelation to him, exhibiting as it did "scintillating genius, superb national feeling, and truly brilliant handling of an orchestra . . . Everything had my fullest sympathy and forced itself upon me with irresistible power."

Grieg had met his match and the effect was decisive: he withdrew his own symphony from the public after it had been played in Bergen in November.

Had Grieg any reason to be ashamed of his first attempt at composing a symphony? Most assuredly not. His symphony is an important work, full of life and enthusiasm. One is struck, not least, by the ease and fluency with which he wrote. The work flows so elegantly and smoothly that it is difficult to believe it was his first completed orchestral composition. It reveals no weaknesses in its orchestration; it is constructed with a sense of formal proportion.

On the other hand, it shows nothing typically Griegian. Moreover, the melodic invention is at times not particularly distinguished, and the harmony lacks originality. One feels that it is the product of a conservatory-taught youth under the influence of the Schumannesque world of sound. Certainly it is not the Grieg of the *A-minor Concerto* or of the *Peer Gynt* suites, lacking the markedly national modes of expression that characterize these works. In fact, it was not until 1865 that he found his national identity as a musician. But in the *Symphony in C Minor* we are, nonetheless, face to face with a bright young composer who displayed amazing skill in his first attempt at symphonic writing.

From the time of its withdrawal until 1980, the symphony lay dormant and unplayed in the Bergen Public Library, available only for study by students and researchers. When Bergen's new concert hall, the Grieg Hall, was to be dedicated in May 1978, it was proposed that the ban imposed by the composer be lifted, and that the symphony be performed on that auspicious occasion, but the trustees of the library's Grieg Collection voted against the proposal. Sverre Bergh, administrator of the Bergen International Festival and a composer in his own right, thereupon orchestrated the second and third movements of the work, using Grieg's piano four-hands arrangement of those movements (published in 1869 as *Two Symphonic Pieces,* Opus 14) as the basis for the orchestration. These were duly played at the dedication and it was presumed that the symphony in its original form would continue resting in the Bergen Public Library.

Such, however, was not to be the case. A photocopy of Grieg's handwritten score was surreptitiously spirited to the Soviet Union, the parts were copied, and the symphony was performed by the Moscow State Radio Orchestra under its regular conductor, Vitalij Katajev, in December of 1980.

The sensation—not least in Norway—caused by this modern "premiere" can easily be imagined, and the trustees of the Grieg Collection were again approached with the request that the symphony be made available for performance at the 1981 Bergen International Festival. This time permission was granted, and the symphony's second modern, *legal* "premiere" was given at a gala Grieg Hall Festival concert May 30, 1981—114 years after the work had been withdrawn. It was heard not only by those attending the concert that memorable evening, but by millions of Europeans via television and radio; and since then it has been performed all over the world. It has been published by C. F. Peters as Vol. II of *Edvard Grieg's Complete Works,* as well as in miniature score.

The main themes in each of the four movements are given below:

First Movement: Allegro molto

Principal theme

Secondary theme

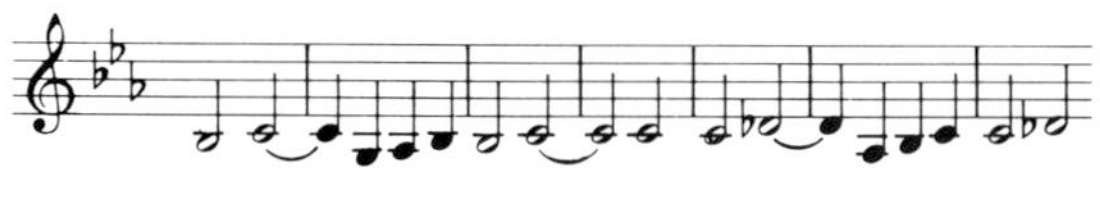

Closing theme

Second Movement: Adagio espressivo

Third Movement: Intermezzo–Allegro energico

A theme

B theme

Fourth Movement: Finale–Allegro molto vivace

Principal theme

Secondary theme

Closing theme

The first movement, *Allegro molto,* is constructed in accordance with the time-honored classical principles of the sonata form. A brief introduction in the shape of forceful chords builds up tension prior to the principal theme of the exposition. This contains a significant triplet motive which immediately captures our attention; it sets its seal on the whole movement and gives it buoyancy. The principal theme is presented, rather diffidently at first, by the violas and clarinet, to be taken up tutti somewhat later. A contrasting secondary theme is characterized by sequential passages. The ternary closing section embodies elements of the triplet motive presented earlier, but the most important thematic material in this section is in E-flat minor, as opposed to the E-flat major of the secondary theme. In the development the triplet motive of the principal theme is elaborated in a variety of keys. The recapitulation is wholly traditional, and a coda rounds off the movement with a flourish.

The second movement, *Adagio espressivo*, is in A-flat major. The mosaic-like form may be looked upon as a rondo in miniature—*ABA'CA''*, the *B* and *C* sections contrasting with the *A* section. A mood of serenity pervades the whole movement, and the melodic material is not without distinction.

The third movement, *Intermezzo–Allegro energico*, is a typical scherzo, *ABA,* in which the composer gives his talents full rein. The jaunty rhythms of the catchy *A* theme call to mind Norwegian folk music, and the ingratiating *B* theme bears a striking resemblance to the Norwegian folk tune "Astri my Astri." The movement ends with a spirited coda in the principal key, C minor.

The fourth movement, *Finale–Allegro molto vivace*, returns to the sonata form of the first movement, but this time it is in C major. The vigorous principal theme soon gives way to a secondary theme of elegiac character in A minor, a theme destined to be quickly superseded by a sprightly closing theme in D major. In the development section, which is largely composed of motivic material drawn from the principal theme, there is an extended passage in A-flat major. After a recapitulation on traditional lines, the coda opens exultantly with the secondary theme in E-flat major, this being repeated in C major towards the close. The symphony concludes on a triumphal note in true Beethovenian style. Grieg's choice of keys for the movements of his symphony, coupled with the clearly discernible "per ardua ad astra" philosophy that pervades the work, also strengthens the belief that Beethoven's *Fifth Symphony* may have served as a general model.

We can only regret that Grieg never wrote another symphony, for his later orchestral works fully demonstrate his mastery of orchestration. He evidently felt that a new symphony was beyond his powers.

Influence of Ole Bull

In the beginning of July, 1864, Grieg went to Bergen to stay for the summer. It was at this time that he first became well acquainted with Ole Bull, and he spent some exciting days in the violinist's home at Valestrand, near Bergen. Here Bull played and improvised for his young relative, for as his nephew (and Grieg's cousin) Schak Bull has reported: "Ole Bull often engaged in fanciful improvisation when he played for the family or among musical friends; it came naturally and easily for him."

In the absence of any special documentation, it has always been assumed that this association was important for Grieg. But only after the publication in 1961 of a conversation Grieg had in Berlin in 1907 with Arthur M. Abell did it become clear how epoch making it really was for Grieg's awakening national feeling. Grieg reported, among other things, that in Valestrand Ole Bull "used to take me with him down into a deep, almost inaccessible 'cave,' as he called it, and there he played for me the trollish Norwegian melodies that so strongly

6. OLE BULL:
"CREATE YOUR OWN STYLE!"

It was Ole Bull who first awakened in me the resolution to compose characteristically Norwegian music . . . He was my rescuer. He opened my eyes to the beauty and originality in Norwegian music. Through him I became acquainted with many forgotten folk songs, and above all with my own nature.

Had it not been for Ole Bull's fortunate influence I would have written colorless music à la Gade . . . He slavishly imitated Mendelssohn, of whom he was only an echo. After Ole Bull had heard a piano piece that I had composed under Gade's influence he said to me: "Edvard, this is not the way you are destined to go. Throw off Gade's yoke. Create your own style! You have it within you. Write music that will bring honor to your own land. You must develop a strong Norwegian tonal feeling. You can become famous if you do that, but if you follow in Gade's tracks you will only wallow in the mud."

Then the scales fell from my eyes. I followed Ole Bull's advice and developed the style that is regarded as characteristically mine. (From A. Abell's interview with Grieg, taken from *Talks with Great Composers*.)

fascinated me and awakened the desire to have them as the basis for my own melodies." Some of the most important passages in Grieg's statements to Abell are quoted in the Primary Materials.[6]

That summer Ole Bull introduced Grieg to several of the well-known fiddlers from western Norway, and he became very interested in the Hardanger-fiddle dances which he heard.

All these factors played a role, but it was especially Ole Bull himself—his violin playing, stimulating personality, and national enthusiasm—that had such a vivifying influence on Grieg's own development. This occurred, moreover, at the very time when Grieg was in the crucial period of his maturation as a composer. Bull's influence did not manifest itself directly in his compositions, however, until it was nurtured by his association with his fiery countryman, Rikard Nordraak. Then came the first genuine crystalization. But as Grieg put it many years later, "Nordraak's view of Norwegian folk music strengthened my own, but my national enthusiasm had already been awakened when I came to know him, though without its having yet borne any artistic fruit."

During that memorable summer in Bergen, Grieg and his brother John prepared a concert of chamber music together, and they did some of their rehearsing at Valestrand in order to take advantage of advice and suggestions from the experienced master. In 1907 Grieg told Percy Grainger with a chuckle about a delightful episode when the three of them were playing a Mozart piano trio. Ole Bull on one occasion was a little careless in his counting and failed to enter at the right moment. Too proud to admit that he had made a mistake, he interrupted the playing and cried out as though he was completely entranced by the music: "Oh, how wonderful, how wonderful!"

John and Edvard gave their chamber music evening in the Labor Union hall on September 19. They were disappointed that none of the Bergen newspapers published reviews of the concert. Nonetheless, they had reason to be pleased about a positive notice of the concert that appeared in *Bergensposten* the day before the concert was to be given.[7]

Shortly thereafter Grieg returned to Copenhagen, presumably in the beginning of October 1864. In the next months he wrote two piano pieces and a series of songs to texts by Hans Christian Andersen. He also wrote music for a stage play, *Courting on Helgoland,* which unfortunately has been lost except for one song.

The two piano pieces—"Album Leaf" (published in 1878 as Opus 28, No. 1) and "Agitato" (CW 116)—are in A-flat major. They have rapid tempos and are stylistically related to a somewhat chromatic melodic design. "Album Leaf" is a piece of no importance. In "Agitato," on the other hand, Grieg unites a hint of Chopin and Schumann with "Sturm und Drang"—a characteristic drawn from his late Leipzig period—in a fairly sophisticated and personal way.

The two first songs with Hans Christian Andersen texts—"Love" and "Folksong from Langeland"—were first published in Copenhagen in 1867 without an opus number, but were republished in 1870 as Opus 15, Nos. 2 and 3.

The texts are weak, and Grieg's music is of uneven quality. While the first song is quite unexceptional, the second shows that deliberate simplicity could

7. THE BERGEN PRESS URGES SUPPORT FOR THE GRIEG BROTHERS

We are pleased that gradually we can add more and more names to the still rather small number in our country who have reached or are attempting to reach a more elevated level than that which is acceptable to dilettantism.

Although we are not intimately familiar with the young men's artistic development, we do know that they have dedicated themselves to art with serious effort and unmistakable talent, and that their study both in Norway and abroad has been guided with unusual care and musical skill.

One of the brothers—Mr. Edvard Grieg—is already somewhat known as a composer. He performs as a pianist; his elder brother is a cellist.

We are confident, then, that the public will take advantage of this opportunity to hear the young artists. The program is attractive and substantial. (Notice in *Bergensposten*, September 18, 1864.)

8. *COURTING ON HELGOLAND* REVIEWED IN COPENHAGEN NEWSPAPERS

Berlingske Tidende stated on January 25, 1865: "The piece has a number of lively scenes, and the little love story in particular is drawn in brisk and attractive strokes." *Dagbladet* asserted (January 26) in part: "When one does not come to the performance with the boringly sensible demand that the action be probable, one can get a lot of enjoyment from the performance . . . Mrs. Hagen was such a lovely Helgolander that if there really are girls just like her on the island it would be a good investment to buy shares in Helgoland bathing resorts."

have a stimulating effect on Grieg's imagination with respect to both melody and harmony. But one will not connect this song with Danish folktunes. What Grieg employed here were rather elements of a more Norwegian style, toward which he had already shown certain tendencies somewhat earlier. In this thoroughly melodious song we find the Grieg formula in both forms, various scale forms, and fresh pedal-point effects.

Courting on Helgoland was a musical comedy freely adapted by Benjamin Feddersen from a German farce by L. Schneider, with "Music by Edvard Grieg." Between January 23, 1865 and March 17, 1867 the play was performed twenty times at the Casino, a Copenhagen theater devoted to the lighter genre (though it was also sometimes used for serious concerts).[8] The piece was revived in 1886 by the Dagmar Theater, but this time there was just one performance.

Of Grieg's incidental music for this play—his first attempt in this area—only one number remains, and it is preserved in the composer's own handwriting. It is entitled "Clara's Song from *Courting on Helgoland*," and is for voice and piano. It was to be included as No. 3 in a collection entitled *Fem Sange til min Ven Louis Hornbeck* [Five Songs to my Friend Louis Hornbeck], which Grieg prepared for publication in 1865. The collection was never published, but three of the songs—"Sunset" (Opus 9, No. 3), "Love" (Opus 15, No. 2), and "Folksong from Langeland" (Opus 15, No. 3)—were published two years later. "The Soldier" (CW 100, No. 5), the last piece in the planned collection, was published posthumously.

"Clara's Song" is in simple strophic form. It has a pleasant, sprightly melody written in a folk-like style. The accompaniment includes a number of daring passages in which chromatic lines are combined with dissonant inner pedal points.

In addition to songs and choruses, Grieg evidently wrote an orchestral overture for *Courting on Helgoland*. The evidence for this is a letter from Benjamin Feddersen to Grieg on April 3, 1869. Feddersen had attended the dress rehearsal for the premiere performance of Grieg's piano concerto in Copenhagen, and afterward he wrote: "Believe it or not, I think I recognized things from the overture to *Courting on Helgoland!*"

The play got a good reception in the press. Neither Feddersen's nor Grieg's name was mentioned, but it was said that the play was filled with "original music," something that had never occurred before at this theater.

Part Two: At the Artistic Heights

A Year of Significant Accomplishment

In October of 1865, Grieg left Copenhagen to go to Germany and later to Italy. Regarding the period from December, 1864, to October, 1865, Grieg told Aimar Grönvold in 1881: "Now came a happy time of triumph and accomplishment. This was in 1864–65. There in Copenhagen, during a period when I was spending some time each day with Nordraak and other young people who were enthusiastic about everything Scandinavian, I wrote a number of pieces: many songs, *Humoresques*, Opus 6, *Sonata*, Opus 7 [for piano], and *Sonata*, Opus 8 [for violin and piano]."

In his compositions prior to this winter Grieg had been continually searching for a personal mode of expression that would provide fertile soil for the cultivation of vigorous music. In *Melodies of the Heart*, Opus 5, and in the *Humoresques* for piano, Opus 6, which introduce his mature period, he succeeded in this for the first time. In the song "I Love But Thee" from Opus 5 he created one of the most cherished love songs of the Romantic period, and in the *Humoresques* the glowing embers of his "Norwegianness" burst into full flame.

Melodies of the Heart

In the statement to Aimar Grönvold cited earlier, Grieg could also have mentioned his cousin Nina as an important source of inspiration. The *Melodies of the Heart* of Opus 5—all to texts by Hans Christian Andersen—were finished in December, 1864, and a more beautiful engagement present can scarcely be imagined. At Christmas time, according to Nina, she and Edvard "(played) Schumann's B-major symphony [The 'Spring' Symphony] in a four-hand arrangement for piano—and became engaged!" For the time being, however, the engagement had to be a secret. Both sets of parents were opposed when they learned of it. Gerhard Schjelderup, in a book written in 1903, reports that Nina's mother "complained bitterly to a friend: 'He is nothing and he has nothing and he writes music that nobody wants to listen to.'"

Edvard's normally good-natured father expressed his concern in a letter to his son, calling it "this stupid engagement." On May 27, John consoled his brother with word that "under present circumstances" the parents certainly would soon "[give] their consent to a public announcement." John informed Edvard in July that he could finally announce the engagement.

In *Melodies of the Heart* (Opus 5) Grieg selected some of Hans Christian Andersen's best lyric poems to express his own love. The style of these songs is not especially Norwegian or Scandinavian. In two of them, however—the incomparable "I Love But Thee" and the beautiful tribute to youthful innocence, "Two Brown Eyes"—Grieg succeeded for the first time in maintaining the inspiration consistently throughout an entire song. Truly pregnant melodic phrases are linked together into a well-balanced whole, to which the accompaniments also contribute in a natural, unforced way.

In both of these songs simplicity has now become a strength. One's interest is held captive by small but subtle variations. The material is transformed both within the totality—in "I Love But Thee" according to the scheme *AA',* in "Two Brown Eyes" with the pattern *ABA'*—and in the details.

The harmony has its roots in the typical style of the Romantic period, but conventional clichés are for the most part happily avoided. In the accompaniment one can detect a certain Griegian stamp in the handling of chromatic passages and dissonances.

The remaining two songs, on the other hand—"The Poet's Heart" and "My Mind Is Like A Mountain Steep"—are of uneven quality. These fast and somewhat dramatically conceived songs contain short, fascinating parts which stand side by side with passages of lesser interest. Sometimes one encounters the artistic polish that one expects, at other times mere trivialities.

In "The Poet's Heart" we find a dissonant ending, a harmonic device that Grieg used later from time to time:

Opus 5, No. 2

In an article entitled "From Grieg's Youth," written in 1899, Grieg's friend Benjamin Feddersen stated that the composer could not find a publisher who dared to take a chance on publishing *Melodies of the Heart.* The set was therefore printed in Copenhagen in April, 1865, but at Grieg's own expense.

A review in *Illustreret Tidende,* published in Copenhagen on April 30 of the same year, stated that the songs were written by a young and talented composer and that they had "striking melodies and a sprightly accompaniment, though they are not altogether free of occasional abrupt transitions—a characteristic that seems to be due to a desire to imitate the great Schumann. But there is a liveliness in these songs that ensures that they will be heard with interest."

Rikard Nordraak at the beginning of the 1860s. In 1881 Grieg wrote to Grönvold: "I only know that he came as a good spirit upon my path, and that I am eternally indebted to him." (Det Kongelige Bibliotek, Copenhagen, Denmark)

Grieg wrote a counterpart to "I Love But Thee" at about the same time entitled "I Love You, Dear" (CW 100, No. 3). The text was by another Danish writer, Caspara Preetzmann, who published poems under the pseudonym "Caralis." Grieg's simple setting of this poem is quite sterile, and he wisely decided that it wasn't worth publishing.

The epoch-making Humoresques

His association with Nordraak in 1864–65 liberated Grieg's powers and led to the work that was to be the most important breakthrough for the development of his national style: the *Humoresques.* After his friend's death in March of 1866, he felt especially compelled to proceed along the road toward a characteristically Norwegian style of music—a road that Ole Bull had encouraged him to take and that Nordraak had further marked out for him.

Nordraak came to Copenhagen in the summer of 1864 and lived there for a year. Together with Louis Hornbeck he rented lodging from his widowed aunt, Birgitte Sanne, who lived at Vesterbro. Nordraak and Grieg had a common friend in Hornbeck; indeed, it was Hornbeck who brought the two young Norwegians together. The friendship that now sprang up between them was further strengthened in the spring of 1865.

Grieg wrote to Aimar Grönvold that "it was touching how fond we were of each other . . . I only know that he came as a good spirit upon my pathway, and that I am eternally indebted to him, and that without him I would perhaps have had to struggle for who knows how long without finding myself. We were so unlike each other, in spite of our intimate mutual understanding. Precisely for that reason his influence could be effective." In a letter to Iver Holter in 1897 he wrote: "Nordraak's importance for me is *not* exaggerated. It really is so: through him and only through him was I truly awakened."

Nordraak's purposeful and dynamic personality released latent powers in the heretofore shackled and insecure Grieg. In the letter to Grönvold, Grieg spoke about his friend's self-confidence and added: "But this confidence in ultimate triumph was just the right medicine for me."

Although Nordraak's musical training consisted of only sporadic, amateurish studies, Grieg discovered in him—undoubtedly to his surprise—a contemporary who had already found his own identity. Nordraak had created his unique national style in a series of mature songs and choral pieces, little pearls of melodic beauty marked by a deliberate simplicity of harmony. "How I . . . adored his songs," Grieg wrote; and another time: "I saw what Björnson in 'Arnljot' calls 'Norway in the rising sun'."

It was Nordraak's naturalness and spontaneity—both personally and musically—that had such a stimulating effect on Grieg's own development: "Suddenly it was as if the fog disappeared, and I knew what I wanted. It was not precisely what Nordraak wanted, but I think the road that led to me went first through him."

"We conspired," Grieg said later, "against the Mendelssohn-inspired, effeminate Scandinavianism of Gade, and we set out with enthusiasm on the new road on which the Scandinavian school now finds itself." (In 1889, however, Grieg retracted this statement which, he said, "belongs to my very green period . . . and to a greater degree than one might wish expresses mere youthful arrogance.")

The first concrete result of this "conspiracy" was the establishment of the "Euterpe" music society in the spring of 1865. In founding this society Grieg and Nordraak were joined by their friends Horneman, Hornbeck, and Matthison-Hansen. The name was borrowed from a similar society in Leipzig. This Copenhagen "New Music" society was dedicated to the propagation of contemporary Scandinavian music that would otherwise have had difficulty getting performed. Grieg said later that "Euterpe" was conceived as a society of militantly progressive young musicians, whose target was the established ruling cliques in the musical life of Denmark as represented by the conservative Music Association of Copenhagen.

The meetings of the leaders of "Euterpe" were a lively forum for the exchange of new ideas. Grieg wrote in *Politiken* on September 28, 1906: "Hornbeck had a hilariously dry sense of humor, with which, to our great delight, he spiced up our meetings in 'Euterpe,' and in our discussions essentially counterbalanced Horneman's brilliant but intense passion."

An advertisement in the Copenhagen newspaper *Dagbladet* on February 14, 1865, invited the public to three Saturday concerts, 5:00 to 6:30 p.m., for a subscription price of one riksdaler. During the next two years a series of concerts was given, but with decreasing frequency. The last concert was given on April 23, 1867.

At the opening concert in the Casino Theater on March 18, the actor Alfred Flinck recited a flowery prologue by Hans Christian Andersen. An audience of a thousand people—among them Hans Christian Andersen and the folk-music collector A. P. Berggreen, both of whom were specially invited—attended the event. Nordraak conducted an orchestra of thirty-nine musicians and a choir (which he reported was "scraped together with blinding speed") in several of his own works. "Kaare's Song" from *Sigurd Slembe* had to be sung twice, and the composer "became quite embarrassed about the noise from shouts of 'bravo!' and 'encore!' . . . and I was amazed at the outpouring of praise and attention."

The governing board of "Euterpe" sent Hans Christian Andersen a letter thanking him "who was always ready to lend credence to the hopes of the young."

At the next concert, given on April 1, Grieg was on the podium for the first time as an orchestral conductor in a performance of the two inner movements of his symphony. On April 4 it was stated in the *Berlingske Tidende* that these movements "reveal an extraordinary skill in composition, and although the originality is not particularly striking . . . they give evidence of independent study and imagination!"

Dagbladet's review of the same date was far more reserved. The reviewer reported that, after hearing Nordraak's and Grieg's works, he had "gotten a strong feeling that they need further study. The works of both composers give evidence of talent, which however is not easy to determine after such a simple test. Mr. Nordraak apparently strives more for naturalness than does Mr. Grieg."

It may have been this very review that prompted Grieg to subsequently write three larger works in the space of a short time. He later described his activity and general outlook during this period: ". . . we composed to beat the devil, so to speak," and again: "We hated the establishment with reckless abandon and dreamed about a new super-super-super-Norwegian future."

It was no small part of this dream of the future that Grieg realized when in April-May of 1865 he composed the four *Humoresques,* Opus 6, which are rightly regarded as some of the finest piano pieces he ever wrote. They mark the first major achievement in his career as a composer, filled as they are with sparkling ideas of singular freshness—ideas, moreover, that were deeply rooted in the music of the common people. Suddenly he emerged as a renewer within Scandinavian music.

Most striking is the marvelous confidence in the use of a national tonal language that one finds in these pieces, without parallel in Norwegian music prior to that time. The use of motives with small, concise "buds" that in subsequent variations are constantly sending out new "shoots" comes directly from the special variation technique of the Hardanger-fiddle music. Both melodically and rhythmically the pieces have a definite stamp of stylized folk dances. Everything happens naturally, so Grieg must have had a thorough knowledge of folk music. He demonstrates a convincing ability to enter into the essential spirit of this material. This is not to suggest that he had in any way merely copied from the dance tunes, however; the material is completely his own.

> The first and last pieces have the character of a *springar* (in $\frac{3}{4}$ time) while the third is reminiscent of a *halling* dance tune (in $\frac{2}{4}$ time). In the second piece—a minuet of the most singular character—the opening theme has a similarity to two little songs from L. M. Lindeman's collection: "Alle Mann Hadde Fota" [All Men Had Legs] (published in 1853) and, to an even greater extent, "Grisen" [The Pig] (published in 1863); Grieg arranged this latter song several years later as No. 8 in his folk-music arrangements, Opus 17.
>
> The melodies in the *Humoresques* are essentially diatonic with frequent use of elements from various modal scales. Lively, marked rhythms, often ostinato-like in character, are found throughout. Especially daring for his time is the harmony, with strong traits of such folk-music characteristics as modality, pedal point and other sustained-tone effects, and pungent dissonances. Here is a typical example taken from the first piece in the set:

Humoresques, Opus 6, No. 1

In some of their arrangements and in a number of original compositions with a Norwegian coloring, Lindeman and Kjerulf (especially the latter) had hinted at the possibility of combining stylistic elements from classical music and Norwegian folk music. However, it was Grieg who, with brilliant inventiveness, now made these possibilities a reality. The fusion of characteristics derived from these two sources is typical of his mature style.

The piano writing in these pieces is not intended to require a "bravura" performer, but substantial technical proficiency is needed to achieve a precise, clear articulation of the terse, concentrated texture. The *Humoresques* display here some tendencies toward the "de-Romanticized" piano writing of a later time.

> We give here the last three measures of the fourth piece, where Grieg characteristically concluded a piece that not only stands out markedly from the music of his contemporaries but also points far forward in the development of Norwegian music. Over a repeated G in the bass, Grieg wrote a rising melodic minor scale in the right hand while the left hand plays a descending form of the same scale, producing fairly sharp dissonances in measures 1–2. The progression from G major to G minor and back to G major is also typically Griegian:

Humoresques, Opus 6, No. 4

Grieg was making a conscious attempt to break new ground in this work. It is no wonder that this "music of the future" aroused opposition in conservative circles. He showed the pieces to Gade, whose reaction Grieg later reported to Iver Holter: "But he was one-sided; that is how we Norwegians felt. When I as a young man (1865) showed him my *Humoresques,* he sat and paged through the manuscript without saying a word. Then he began to grunt a little, then a little more, and finally he blurted out: 'Tell me, Grieg, is this supposed to be Norwegian?' And I, somewhat hurt, replied: 'Yes, herr professor, it is.'"

With these well-integrated piano pieces Grieg had realized the best that was within him. A path was open for him to go further, and this gave him courage to work even harder.

Grieg dedicated the *Humoresques* to Nordraak. He mentioned later to Aimar Grönvold that Rikard had shouted when he heard the Minuet: "Yes, it is as if I had written it myself!" Grieg undoubtedly smiled to himself when he heard this, for no matter how hard he tried Nordraak could not possibly have written such a piece. His style was too essentially different from Grieg's for this, and he didn't have the necessary technical training in composition to enable him to handle the harmony and the piano writing with anything approaching Grieg's competence and imagination.

Except for the concentrated simplicity that Grieg admired in Nordraak's

I. A BIRTHDAY GREETING
FROM NORDRAAK
ON GRIEG'S 22ND BIRTHDAY

It is with longing that I write to my won-derful colleague and Norwegian friend. Be assured that I remember your talent and your lovable character; I am glad that I got to know you so well and proud that you cared for me. I now send you my brotherly thanks for this and also my warm good wishes . . .

I must tell you this one more time: you really are a wonderful fellow. One shouldn't praise and coddle people like this, but now I've been gone so long that I have a right to miss you. And I have good reason to miss you and all my good friends in Denmark; I am so alone in the big, boring city . . .

How have you spent the summer? Each day happier than the previous one, I sup-pose. From forest to sweetheart and from sweetheart to forest: that's living! Be as-sured that I think well of your sweetheart—and of her sister, too. (Letter from Berlin, June 12, 1865.)

natural talent as a composer, his friend had not, *musically* speaking, supplied him with anything new. Grieg summed it up in the letter to Iver Holter: "I would willingly admit that the influence of Nordraak was *not* exclusively musical. But that is precisely the thing for which I am most grateful to him: that he opened my eyes to the importance of that in music which is *not* music." It was Nordraak's dynamic national consciousness that had a kind of spring-thaw effect on him. In his diary in 1907 he looked back on this period as "the Nordraak period, that wonderful time!"

At the end of May, 1865, Nordraak went to Berlin.[1] Grieg then moved to Rungsted, north of Copenhagen, where he secured lodging together with Benjamin Feddersen. He knew that he now had both the courage and the strength to tackle highly demanding tasks, and in the two sonatas from June-July he tried out his new national style for the first time in some larger works.

The Piano Sonata in E Minor

In an interview in *Dannebrog* of December 26, 1893, Grieg told with great delight of Gade's encouraging reaction to his two first chamber music works: "Whether it was the charming surroundings or the refreshing air that inspired me I shall not attempt to say. It is enough to say that my piano sonata was composed in the space of just eleven days, and soon thereafter I also finished my first violin sonata. I took them both to Gade at Klampenborg. He looked through them with pleasure, nodded, clapped me on the shoulder and said, 'That's pretty darn good. Now let's go and look at them more closely.' We then crept up a steep, narrow ladder to Gade's study, where he sat down at the piano and became completely enthralled. It has been said that when Gade was inspired he drank huge quantities of water. That day the professor emptied four large carafes."

The *Piano Sonata in E Minor*, Opus 7, is dedicated to Gade, and there are melodic and rhythmic affinities between it and Gade's sonata in the same key, Opus 28 (1840), especially in the respective first movements. Even more striking, however, is the influence of the brighter tonal language of Hart-mann's "Sonatine" (1863) and the piano piece "Vikinge fruens Dröm" [The Viking Woman's Dream] (1864). The latter piece anticipates to a considerable extent the third movement of Grieg's sonata, as is evident in the following examples:

A. Hartmann:

B. Grieg:

C. Hartmann:

Allegro moderato

D. Grieg:

Alla Menuetto

Grieg surpassed his Danish mentor, however, with his more substantial melodies and richer and more distinctive harmonies. There are places in the sonata, especially in the last movement, where the melodic interest is subordinated to the harmonic—something that was also the case in a number of compositions before 1865. But in the first three movements Grieg gave clear proof—as he had earlier done so convincingly in the *Humoresques*—that he had reached full maturity as a melodist. The stylistic elements derived from folk music are not nearly so obvious as in the *Humoresques,* though in certain sections of the sonata they are quite evident.

The harmonic boldness is kept under strict control, though there are some parts with truly daring chord progressions. The inspiration is not equally evident throughout, however.

In the overall concept as well as in the structural details, Grieg shows unquestionable talent. This is especially true of the first three movements. The first movement exhibits a mastery of classical sonata form united with youthful aggressiveness and the sheer joy of creating. Moreover, in accordance with prevailing ideas about how to create unity, there are certain similarities among the themes in each of the four movements.

The sonata generally distinguishes itself as a well-written piano piece with a Schumannesque flair. It is technically demanding, but without artificiality, and it clearly points toward the masterful piano style of the *A-minor Concerto* three years later.

The principal theme in the exposition of the first movement is introduced with a rhythmic and sharply accented four-measure motive:

Allegro moderato.

In the continuation the theme ascends in lively sixteenth-note figures, and the following section builds on the contrasts between these two characteristic melodic and rhythmic ideas.

The short secondary theme has *halling* rhythms. After four measures in G major it is transposed into B minor:

Some abrupt modulations lead to the closing theme, which also begins in G major but which, with its descending chromatic lines, has a completely different character:

The development is brief and concise. The principal theme is given first in E major, and we hear some colorful modulations to various keys, including A-flat minor, before the main key is reestablished near the end.

The recapitulation starts with material derived from the exposition but in a new rhythmic form, and the movement concludes with a rousing coda.

The second movement is constructed rather freely. It begins in C major with some charming melodic material that is presented in short, contrasting sections. The peaceful opening with its folk-song character and elements of modality (in C Mixolydian) is followed by some lively sixteenth-note figurations (sometimes in E Dorian). The subsequent crescendo is followed by a section in G major with lively *springar* rhythms. The rest of the movement

The Danish composer J. P. E. Hartmann, about whom Grieg wrote as follows in Musikbladet *in 1885: "No wonder that young people love him, for in all the changing moods of life he has had music for their longings and their hopes." (Photo collection of Det Kongelige Bibliotek, Copenhagen, Denmark)*

builds on the material from the first part. It contains some shallow chromatic passages, however, that are inferior to the overall style of the piece.

Here is the beginning of the second movement, Andante molto:

The sonata's most successful movement is the third, a minuet-like movement in *ABA* form. The *A* sections have a sharply drawn melodic line with a bouncy lilt to the rhythm; they surround an unusually expressive lyrical *B* section in E major.

Here are the first nineteen measures of the third movement, Alla Menuetto:

The last movement, which is also in sonata form, is far more uneven. The thematic material is interesting enough, but as the movement progresses it does not succeed in holding the listener's interest as did the first movement. This is especially noticeable in the development section, which sounds more like the cerebral exercise of a conservatory student than the living creation of a master composer. The tightly constructed coda, however, gives the movement and the sonata an effective, lively conclusion.

The first eleven mesures of this Finale are given below. The principal theme begins in the measure following the double bar:

As a whole, this piano sonata shows what Grieg had learned during his years of study in Leipzig, but it also illustrates the problems he had to contend with when he tried to work his own ideas into an old but still widely used musical form. The E-minor sonata is his "senior thesis" in this genre. Strangely enough, he never did write a "master's thesis" piano sonata. He turned his attention instead to other kinds of chamber music in which he created fully mature works.

The Violin Sonata No. 1 in F Major

The F-major sonata, Opus 8, can rightly be called Grieg's "Spring Sonata." The key is the same as that used by Beethoven in his "Frühlingssonate," Opus 24. It is also the key that traditionally has been regarded as the key of spring.

The work reveals a bubbling wealth of ideas, a wild adolescent love affair expressed in sound. Lively thematic ideas appear one after the other, shimmering with rhythmic suppleness and clothed in a harmonic garb that in its daring bears witness to a composer who has the courage to go his own way. The formal problems associated with sonata form are solved with deft elegance. And something new appears: Grieg here introduced for the first time a purely national element. It occurs in the Trio of the second movement, where the Hardanger fiddle is imitated in both the piano and violin parts in the form of a stylized *springar*.

In a letter to Björnson on January 16, 1900, Grieg referred to his three violin sonatas as some of his best works. Each represented an important period in his artistic development: "the first naïve, reflecting many antecedents; the second national; and the third with its wider horizons." This is a striking characterization, especially with respect to the last two works. As for the F-major sonata, one can think of two reasons why Grieg described it as "naïve." Compared with later works, it perhaps seemed to him rather superficial. He may also have looked back with a certain skepticism at the uninhibited boldness he had displayed in this sonata. Today, however, this lively recklessness strikes us as one of the most fascinating characteristics of the work.

2. GRIEG'S SUCCESS IN LEIPZIG

Mr. Edv. H. Grieg from Bergen, Norway, who was once a student at the Leipzig conservatory, and who is making a stop here on his way to Italy, in the last two weeks performed two of his own new compositions at evening concerts at the conservatory. One was a solo sonata for piano, the other a violin sonata that he performed together with a Swedish fellow artist, Mr. [Anders] Petterson from Stockholm. Both works were such as to awaken more than ordinary interest, thanks to their noble content and features of great distinction. They were warmly applauded. (From *Signale*. Leipzig, November 23, 1865.)

The antecedents to which Grieg referred are not easy to identify, however. Kjell Skyllstad has pointed out that the main thematic material in the second movement reminds one of a theme of J. P. E. Hartmann, but beyond this one can only say that it reflects stylistic characteristics that have their roots in Romantic violin sonatas generally. As a whole, however, the F-major sonata is a striking testimony to a young composer who had found his personal style and mode of expression.

The F-major sonata was written in the summer of 1865, just after completion of the piano sonata at the end of June. Dedicated to the violinist and orchestra conductor August Fries, who had championed Grieg's music in Bergen, it was published in 1866 by the Peters music publishing firm in Leipzig. The first printing, according to engraving records, was just 125 copies. One did not dare to risk much on a young, unknown composer in those days.

The first performance took place at a successful concert in the Gewandhaus in Leipzig in the middle of November, 1865, when Grieg was in Leipzig enroute to Italy. Grieg himself was at the piano, and the Swedish violinist Anders Petterson played the violin part. A review of the concert that appeared in *Signale* is quoted in the Primary Materials.[2]

The first movement, Allegro con brio, appears at first glance to be just a traditional movement in sonata form. When one examines it more carefully, however, one finds a number of subtleties which show that the composer was not merely following the beaten paths. The movement is introduced with a remarkably indefinite tonality: minor triads on E and A. After these vague and static opening measures, one is completely bewildered about how the piece is going to continue. Here, then, Grieg gives us his first surprise—a rousing, energetic principal theme with a marked rhythmic snap in a spicy harmonic setting. The theme is expanded into a section of fifteen measures, ending in the home key in measure 19, where the tonic (F major) is heard for the first time in root position.

The second surprise comes in measure 10. Here Grieg fires a daring harmonic arrow with a "brazen" introduction of the so-called Neapolitan sixth chord (a G-flat major triad) which, in an elegant way, is made autonomous and is carried on to a D-flat triad before the primary key is briefly hinted at in measures 12 and 14. The composer then steadily draws new arrows from his quiver. Notice, for example, the chromatically moving, consecutive six-four chords in measures 15–16 which are linked with the sustained note F in the piano part. The A-flat major chord becomes a dominant chord with the help of the added seventh and cadences to D-flat major in measure 17; the root of this chord is then reinterpreted as the diminished fifth in the following G chord—the so-called tritonal reinterpretation. The first twenty-three measures of the movement are given here:

The secondary theme has a certain rhythmic similarity to the principal theme, but it nonetheless provides a strongly contrasting effect with its resigned, slightly wistful mood. It begins in A minor (the upper mediant) without a modulatory bridge:

The closing theme is in C major (the dominant), as one would expect. It consists of two-measure motives and begins relatively softly:

Gradually, however, it acquires a sharp contour, marked by the energy of the principal theme, and it brings the exposition to an effective conclusion.

The development makes use of all three themes, each treated individually. The tempo change at the beginning—from Allegro con brio to Andante—is completely unorthodox, and here the principal theme is converted from major to minor. It is as if Grieg revealed a second aspect of the theme, perhaps reflecting the duality of his own temperament: youthful ardor gives way to tender melancholy. The threads are tied back to the subdued minor character of the four introductory measures. The pain of this first section is supplanted in an unusually beautiful manner a few measures later by a brighter section in F major before a more conventional continuation gets under way.

Thereafter a completely normal recapitulation ensues, with the traditional transposition of the secondary and closing themes down a fifth.

A five-measure coda, however, reverts to the mood of the beginning of the development, and the movement ends in a singular and very expressive closing cadence:

Grieg has been criticized because in the sonata movements he usually allowed the recapitulation to be virtually an exact repetition of the exposition, but with a transposition of the secondary theme section and no modulatory bridge between the thematic divisions. That is the case in this sonata as well. The transition from the principal theme to the secondary theme may be taken as an example. In the exposition he moved directly from F major to A minor, and in the recapitulation from F major to D minor. Criticism here is not altogether unwarranted, for even the slightest harmonic twist at just these points in the recapitulation would have added extra zest to the whole. On the other hand, it should be pointed out that Grieg wanted clear-cut and abrupt transitions like these. He stated this clearly in connection with the *String Quartet in G Minor* (see p. 227), and it is to his credit that he was able to create themes that fit so smoothly into such a framework.

The second movement, Allegretto quasi Andantino, which is a minuet-like piece in *ABA* form, has a captivating charm. The unusually melodious theme of the *A* section has, as was mentioned earlier, a certain resemblance to a theme by Hartmann. The Grieg formula appears in the very first measure: A–G#–E, which is in fact the core motive of the whole movement:

But how does Grieg manage to combine the dignity of the *A* section with the wildness of the *springar* imitations of the *B* section? The key is changed from A minor to A major, and the new tempo becomes Più vivo. For the listener the contrast between the two sections is enormous, but at the same time one feels a clear connection between them. The main reason for this is that the principal motive in both themes has the same starting point in the Grieg formula. We give here measures 51–58. In measures 53 and 55 the violin has the Grieg formula in its major form, while in the preceding measures the piano has it in both its major and minor forms:

The third movement, *Allegro molto vivace,* is cut from the same pattern as the first. The three-part exposition has exactly the same key progression and the same abrupt transitions between the themes. Nor does the recapitulation introduce anything that has not already appeared in the exposition. To be sure, the thematic material of this movement is richer than that of the first. The themes are as follows:

Principal theme:

Secondary theme:

Closing theme:

One gets the impression, however, that this material is merely broken up rather than being organically developed. The development begins with a cleverly constructed fugato, but otherwise cannot be said to be free of a certain rhythmic monotony that creates an impression of triviality. Nor is the harmony, except in a few places, generally as sparkling as in the first movement. The daring use of sequences in the last part of the closing theme, however, is especially captivating. Here a series of disjunct triads is progressively transposed upwards by thirds: C major, E minor, G major, B minor, D minor, and closing on a D-flat major sixth chord. In this way the feeling of tonality is thoroughly blurred.

Grieg himself did not play any string instrument. In view of this, it is noteworthy how accurately the sonata is adapted to the peculiarities of the violin. It is not really a virtuoso piece, but the fast concluding movement in particular demands a technical skill beyond the level of a competent amateur. The technical demands of the piano part are at a similar level.

The F-major violin sonata is the first Norwegian work in this genre of international stature. In its constant alternation between bold assertiveness and tender sensitivity it is typical Grieg.

Communion with nature in the North Zealand countryside

We have interesting diaries from two periods in Grieg's life—the first from 1865 to 1866 and the other from 1905 until his death in 1907.

The earlier diary covers two time periods: July 31 to August 9, 1865, and December 2, 1865 to August 28, 1866. In the intervening months when Grieg, among other things, visited the ailing Nordraak in Berlin, it appears that he did not keep a diary.

On the last day of July, 1865, Grieg left for a ten-day trip to North Zealand together with some Danish friends including Feddersen and Horneman. Partly by carriage and partly on foot, they visited various sights from Fredensborg and Helsingör to Tisvilde.

He described in great detail both important and unimportant experiences on the trip. Some of his accounts are very mundane, as when he referred to meals ("a contemptible dinner," "a fabulously cheap lunch"). Another such passage occurs in his description of the difficulties encountered on one of their hikes in the vicinity of Fredensborg: "Somebody got the unfortunate idea of designating Horneman as the leader—an assignment that he performed with great gusto, albeit anything but satisfactorily; for after having walked around endlessly in a forest jungle . . . we finally came out on a country road . . . But what did Horneman demand? That we should immediately leave the passable road and head out instead on one that led through a barley field to hell and back . . . We were all so tired that none of us was inclined to disagree . . . until

3. REFLECTIONS ON
THE DIVINE IN NATURE

Where does one sense God's greatness
more than in the roaring of the sea? In a
moment one becomes, as it were, an impo-
tent nothing who in gratitude dares only to
call upon the Father whose omnipotence
created his wonders! And how beautiful it
is that he has endowed his creatures with
powers by which they not only can understand and enjoy [the world], but can even
create works of art that are echoes of the
feelings about God's greatness which are
planted in the human breast . . . But—I
could not neglect also searching in my art
for a way to express the wild music in the
roar of the sea. Alas, my search was in vain.
I sensed the utter impossibility of expressing these mighty sounds in musical form.
There was in this rushing and roaring
something so boundless that it struck me as
presumptuous to consider even for a moment the idea of trying to reproduce it. But
here I also found consolation: the artist's
task is not to reproduce the physical event
itself, but rather to create a reflection of the
feelings awakened by that event; if this is
done with genius, the impression is equally
divine notwithstanding the absence of
those overpowering effects that belong to
nature alone. (From Grieg's diary, August 7, 1865.)

our feet literally got stuck in the muck; but then the anger broke loose, my
traveling companions sided with me, and soon there was a real commotion . . ."

Realistically colored entries like these alternate with passages more characteristic of the prose of the time—lyrical and florid descriptions of the twenty-
two-year-old's strong impressions of nature, sometimes combined with outbursts of religious emotion and declarations of love for Nina.[3,4]

His description of a sunset on August 7 is especially beautiful: ". . . and the
churning sea, over which the setting sun was spreading the most marvelous
illumination, lay outstretched before us. The endless surface of the water . . .
the desolate terrain bounded by pines and spruce forests, everything was
engulfed in the most dream-like mauve color, and over this fairy world there
stretched a vaulted heaven illuminated as from the mightiest conflagration. As
struck by a blow we sat speechless and gazed at all this magnificence . . . Little
by little the sun disappeared; it was as if it went to sleep in the sea's bosom.
Night lowered its veil over nature around us, and a marvelous soft, sad feeling
took hold of me. May it be granted me one day to linger in privacy with you—
my beloved!—in a time of communion with nature such as this. The awareness of God's great love must in such a moment rise to the highest level!"

It certainly was idealized memories of inspiring moments like these in
harmony with nature that he had in mind when, more than forty years later,
he recalled those youthful experiences in the Danish countryside and wrote of
them in a letter to Gottfred Matthison-Hansen. The date was December 19,
1906, and Horneman had just died. In his inimitably poetic style Grieg wrote:
"Now it is you and Steenberg who remain from that beautiful time of youth,
when the air and the beech forest on that beautiful Zealand were filled with
music and loveliness. How wonderful! It probably was not more beautiful
then than it is now. But we made it beautiful because we ourselves injected
our longing for beauty into the scenery and the life of the people, into the saga
and the history! The secret was that we ourselves were so filled with beauty!
And this has been enough to live on for a whole life. Shame on us if we have
not been overflowing with gratitude for it!"

Equally moving are some words in his diary written on June 3, 1907, just
three months before his death. After a "magnificent hike in the forest" in the
same region he had visited in 1865, he wrote: "The poetry of the Danish forest
is unique. And that first strong impression from my youth remains. As I felt it
then, so I felt it now. Equally strong—yes, perhaps even stronger."

The experiences during his trip to Zealand gave Grieg new energy, a fact
that he himself noted in the last diary entry from this period. It was written
after his return to Rungsted, "where beautiful letters awaited me, letters that
confirmed my resolution: to work with renewed strength toward my goal—
my great and beautiful goal!"

Grieg stayed in Rungsted until he went to Berlin about the first of October. That summer he met both Björnson and Kjerulf for the first time. When
Grieg told Kjerulf about his enthusiasm for Nordraak, Kjerulf clapped his
hands together and cried in dismay: "Now, I must say! Les extremes se
touchent!' (Opposites attract each other!)

4. FEELINGS ABOUT STORMY WEATHER ON NORTH ZEALAND— AND A DECLARATION OF LOVE TO NINA

The view from Frederikshöj is among the most spendid I have ever seen. Endless stretches of heath on high hills and in deep valleys—much like what one sees in the high mountains in Norway—surrounded by the rushing Kattegat, and a sky pregnant with the most terrible storms, and made even more interesting by the most piercing lightning flashes—all of these elements played a role in evoking this picturesque scene. Wild nature and wild weather belong together; [the combination] gives unity . . . Is it not as if from such a high vantage point—from which one seems almost to observe the whole world—one feels closer to one's God? In truth, in such a moment all that is earthly becomes distant to me and I feel my soul lifted up toward eternal reconciliation and love.

O, my Nina! If you knew with what tenderness my thoughts dwell on you here, with what endless longing I embrace you! Before I fathomed you and all your love it was as if I did not dare aspire toward the heights, as if all my longing was confined within a boundary beyond which I only peered into an impenetrable fog. It is with you, my beloved, that with confidence and clarity I dare cast a glance toward the infinite. It is as if you, my sweet angel, hovered beside me as my thoughts wander through the vastness of space—as if through your intercession I was given the power to break the links that bind me to this mortal body! May God shed His peace upon you during these days wherever you may be, you who are my treasure and the light of my life! (From Grieg's diary, August 1, 1865.)

His newly won desire to compose resulted in four songs which varied greatly in quality.

"Autumn Storms," a setting of an insignificant poem by Chr. Richardt, was published in 1869 as Opus 18, No. 4. Grieg here chose a through-composed form corresponding to the text's description of autumn, winter, and spring. The song smacks of exaggerated Romanticism. Bombastic sections alternate with others that seem insignificant and conventional, and there is little organic connection between the changing ideas. (The dramatic character of this song later led Grieg to use it as material for his orchestral overture "In Autumn," Opus 11, which was completed in Rome the following spring.)

The other three songs are settings of poems by Hans Christian Andersen. "Tears" (CW 100, No. 4) would in our day be regarded as a parody. Grieg chose a pale, diatonic melody which is at times harmonized chromatically with, among other things, consecutive augmented triads. The song remained unpublished during Grieg's lifetime.

"My Little Bird" (CW 100, No. 2) is dated August 12, 1865, but it was not published until 1896. Somewhat modal in character, it is much superior to the others and immediately captures one's interest. It also reveals a clear similarity to one of Kjerulf's loveliest songs, "Vidste du Vej, du lille Fugl" [If You Knew the Way, Little Bird], which was published in 1852.

"The Soldier" (CW 100, No. 5), the last of the four songs from 1865, is completely different from the others. Hans Christian Andersen, who is believed to have built his poem on a horrible memory from his childhood in Odense, wrote movingly of a soldier in an execution squad who was forced to shoot his best friend. (Schumann also set the poem in a German translation as his Opus 40, No. 3.) In the first part of his setting Grieg evokes the character of a funeral march:

"The Soldier," CW 100, No. 5

The conclusion—where the execution takes place—is in the style of a recitative. This is one of Grieg's most unusual songs. It exhibits a drastic, naked realism that is created in part by series of unresolved dissonances. In the development of the expressionistic style it stands midway between Schubert's "Letzte Hoffnung" (Opus 89, No. 16) and several of Mussorgsky's *Songs and*

Grieg in Copenhagen in the mid-1860's.
(Gamle Bergen museum, Bergen)

Dances of Death or Wolf's "Der Feuerreiter" (*Gedichte von Mörike*, No. 51).
Grieg employed a highly experimental tonal language unrelated to his Norwegian background, but his boldness remained under full control.

We do not know why Grieg never published this song. We can only speculate that the unpleasant subject and the radical mode of expression may have frightened the publishers.

Grieg and Nordraak

Toward the end of August, 1865, Grieg published in the Copenhagen newspaper *Flyveposten* a review of five Nordraak songs, Opus 2, which had been published in Denmark that spring. As far as we know, this is the first article Grieg wrote for publication. Although it can scarcely be characterized as a stylistic masterpiece, it nonetheless gives some hint of the engaged and lively mode of expression which was to become so characteristic of him as a writer.

What Grieg found attractive in Nordraak, and what he rightly emphasized, was his genuineness and originality. One might perhaps have expected a more lively enthusiasm on Grieg's part. His evaluations seem relatively restrained, and as a more experienced composer he permitted himself some cautious critical comments about form and prosody.

That Nordraak's style was described as Scandinavian rather than Norwegian is undoubtedly due to the fact that the article was written for Danish readers. Only in "En Underlig Vise" [A Strange Song] is Nordraak's connection to Norwegian folk tunes mentioned. But this text had already been set and published by Halfdan Kjerulf in 1859. Kjerulf had given it a far more national stamp than Nordraak, and in addition had created a stronger setting for what Grieg called "the half-crazy mood" of the text. Grieg's silence concerning Kjerulf's setting could indicate that he was not familiar with it, but it is much more likely that he simply did not wish to mention it in this connection.

One notes also that Grieg used equally strong words in his praise of "Solvejge"—a setting of an insignificant text by Jonas Lie—as in his comments on the song "Tonen" [The Tone] to a text by Björnson. In our day the latter little masterpiece is regarded as probably Nordraak's most exquisite song and the one that shows most clearly the influence of folk tunes on his music.

Liv Greni, in her biography of Nordraak, observes that when Grieg published "Solvejge" in his 1875 collection *Norway's Melodies,* he omitted Nordraak's postlude in its entirety. In the review he also criticized Nordraak for "the somewhat unrelated postlude," but indicated that he nonetheless "defers to the composer, who in just this interrupted thought process has found a true expression for his complaint." Grieg, however, did not defer to Nordraak at all in his arrangement in *Norway's Melodies,* substituting instead a postlude of his own invention.

Grieg immediately sent the review to Nordraak in Berlin, and his friend wrote back enthusiastically on September 2: "Thousands and again thousands of thanks for your good opinion of me! God grant that I may be worthy of it. And thanks because you have begun a revolution in the world of music criticism! It must continue, and we Norwegians—we who have felt the fresh, unpolluted mountain air—can discern more clearly than most the miserable, dishonest products of the spirit in the music of our time. You write it so well, one recognizes immediately the heart of the gifted artist who allows enthusiasm for a great idea to guide his pen; but, my friend, be calm, be calm, and again I say be calm in your treatment of those who until now have called themselves critics, no matter how much cause they give for raging in anger. Hold out, *don't allow yourself to be vexed;* I and others will take your side. Those stupid people with whom you have to deal in the newspapers—people who don't know any more about music than a cat about mustard—resort to their newspaper skills and try by one torrent of words or another to change the subject in order to be able to abuse and annoy someone who they feel might be a bit oversensitive. They hope thereby to get him to say things he later will regret."

It appears somewhat surprising that Nordraak here stressed the aggressiveness in Grieg's review. Grieg's manner of writing seems temperate enough. Nordraak was an agitator in no small degree himself, and when he asked his friend to take it easy it suggests that he had taken notice of Grieg's temperament. If this were displayed uncontrolled, it would undoubtedly create many enemies for Grieg and place unnecessary obstacles in the way of his artistic future.

The article was not the only one that Grieg was to write about Nordraak's music. Some years later he wrote a shorter but considerably more effusive essay about Nordraak's Opus 1 (six songs, of which four were to texts from Björnson's stories of peasant life). It must have been intended for a Danish publication, but it apparently was never published. It is undated, but was probably written about 1870.

One notices that in the unpublished article Grieg emphasized the genuinely Norwegian character of Nordraak's songs, and that he undertook a comparison of Kjerulf's and Nordraak's settings of "Synnöves Sang" [Synnöve's Song]. Oddly enough, he found Nordraak's setting "infinitely beautiful" and "more national" than Kjerulf's. The fact is that Nordraak's setting is primitive both melodically and harmonically, and to modern ears it sounds quite pale.

Grieg took the liberty of making alterations in this song, too, when he later arranged it for *Norway's Melodies*. In this case the alterations concerned a number of simplifications in the harmony. They included, for example, the elimination of a dissonance (a minor second) in measure 10. The alterations can only be characterized as a dubious favor notwithstanding his good intentions.

These two articles give an indication of an interesting fact. It was only after Nordraak's death that Grieg began to emphasize his friend's contribution as a Norwegian composer—as the prophet for the national ideas that he himself put into effect.

It is evident that as early as 1865 Grieg appreciated the greatness of Nordraak's unpretentious vocal compositions on their own merits, but he also realized clearly enough his friend's weaknesses and limitations. In 1881 he wrote to Grönvold: "With respect to me, it was just after his death that I came to an understanding of myself. His contempt for the technical side of art, which I did not share, became for me a stimulus for serious work." In a letter to Niels Ravnkilde on August 13, 1888, he wrote: "Nina is sitting downstairs and singing Nordraak's songs. It sounds so melancholy that it makes me feel completely strange. Yes, he also had something that all of us might desire. But it is good that he died because he was not a real musician, and when all is said and done a composer must be that to win complete victory."

In an article in *Verdens Gang* dated April 23, 1900, he summed up this realization even more sharply: "Nordraak unfortunately did not live to see that it ['Yes, We Love This Land'—the Norwegian national anthem] became the common possession of all Norwegians. Perhaps we ought not say 'unfortunately.' For more than one clear-sighted person is of the opinion that it was

5. GRIEG ON NORDRAAK'S ILLNESS

My dear friend Hornbeck!

So as not to be included among the un-
reliable people, I will try to get a letter
written to you today—though God knows
I am not in the mood for writing. To begin
with, I am physically ill after a grand night
at a tavern last evening—with gobs of oysters and Rhine wine. Secondly, I am currently depressed over all my bad luck. For
bad luck is what it must be called when I
arrive in Berlin to fetch Nordraak for the
trip to Italy and then the fellow goes to bed
and becomes deathly ill! He has now been
in bed for fourteen days with the most violent case of pneumonia, and he undoubtedly would have succumbed had not his
fabulous constitution sustained him.

Now the most dangerous part is past,
but Rikard is still suffering terribly. He
sweats so it pours off him, and he doesn't
dare—or, more correctly, isn't able—to
utter a word . . . How it will now go with
the trip I have no idea; I probably will go
to Leipzig on November 1 and await his arrival there—which will certainly not be before December 1. It is difficult because
traveling to Italy at Christmas time is never
a pleasant journey; it is even questionable
whether we could endure the hardships of a
winter journey.

Since I am not a fatalist, I dare to maintain firmly that everything would have
looked better for Rikard if he had followed
my advice. To begin with, last summer he
should have stayed in Copenhagen and
worked . . . Secondly, he should have left
immediately when I came here to get him
instead of telling me that he had reconsid-
ered and that he planned to stay here
through the winter, as he first said. However, the man is quite flexible, and it was
therefore not difficult to get him to give up
that crazy idea. The trip was thus set for
November 1, but oh my, then came the illness.

Berlin is a disgusting hole; would that I
were with you in Copenhagen—but that is
another matter. There everything is animated, there is poetry in the air, poetry in
the people—ah, that Denmark! The memory of the days spent there are my life's
brightest moments. (Letter to L. Hornbeck, October 22, 1865.)

good for him that he died so early. People who knew him intimately—among
them a psychologist with a world-wide reputation—have said that Rikard
Nordraak had to die because he was not made to live life as intensely as he did.
I also share this opinion. When, as a friend and artist, I consider him—almost
forty years after his death—I understand better than I did then his greatness
and his limitations. He could only express the feelings of the moment. He is
an outstanding example of the fact that a brilliantly endowed nature can fall
short for want of technical ability, the presence of which is an absolute
condition for further development. He did not have a sense for the larger
forms or for orchestration. The only technique he mastered was that required
to write art songs and compositions for male voices."

In the autumn of 1865 the two friends had planned to travel together to
Rome from Berlin, where Nordraak was living. Grieg's father wrote on
August 1: "You must not under any circumstances travel alone. I don't deny
that I wish you had a different traveling companion, for after what T. has told
me about Nordraak and what John says about his great self-conceit, it certainly seems to me that this is not the best daily company." He sent money for
the journey September 12: "You are a 'dear' fellow! That is both certain and
true in more ways than one."

A few days later Grieg received the following humorous little farewell
greeting from Hans Christian Andersen, who wrote in his autograph album:

Flee haunts of youth for eternal Rome,
Return with excitement abounding,
Create then a song for your Nordic home,
A song that for aye will be sounding.

Grieg went to Berlin at the beginning of October, but for the time being a
trip to Italy was out of the question because Nordraak had become very sick.
Grieg wrote about this in an indignant letter to Hornbeck, which happens to
be the earliest letter from him that has been preserved.[5] The injured and
remarkably unfeeling emotional tone adopted here with regard to his friend's
illness has a touch of the spoiled child, but can perhaps be explained as
youthful flippancy. It is unsympathetic in any case. If he had realized the
seriousness of the situation, he would undoubtedly have expressed himself
differently when writing to Nordraak's best Danish friend.

An entry in Nordraak's diary for October 12 states that the doctor's
diagnosis was that he was suffering from a severe liver attack (jaundice) as well
as pneumonia and inflammation of the chest with pleurisy. The doctor directed that the patient be watched over and that six leeches be attached to him
for three hours' bleeding!

Two weeks later, on October 27, Nordraak wrote: "For the first time since
my illness I slept [with the help of] sleeping powder; otherwise always awake,
so I was near to perishing."

The next day the pneumonia moderated and Grieg, who had contracted to
perform his sonatas at two concerts in Leipzig, decided to go without Nordraak. He left his ailing friend November 2 with a promise to return in a few

6. NORDRAAK REPROACHES GRIEG

My dear Grieg!

After being made a fool of for a whole month, I have now learned for certain from your latest and, indeed, welcome letter that you are not coming here. I couldn't dream of being angry about this; on the contrary, since you have found a good traveling companion I think the most reasonable thing you can do is to leave immediately for Italy and let Germany and its tight-fisted music publishers go to the devil. But what is and will always be a puzzle to me is the manner in which you have treated me since you left, and which, mildly speaking, I find contemptible toward someone that you call a friend, someone who was abandoned as you abandoned me; and I must say, of everyone I know you are the last person that I would have believed capable of such behavior . . . If the reason for your silence was that you didn't want to say to me what you had said to others—namely, that you weren't coming here—it was in the highest degree dishonest and cowardly; only at the beginning could I regard that as the thoughtfulness of a gentle spirit who didn't want to disappoint a sick man. But at the very least it was your duty, after you had given me your solemn promise, to apprise me as soon as possible, either directly or in-directly. When you left, you said you were going to be gone only a few days; the result, naturally, was that I lay and waited day after day for your arrival . . .

You must excuse me, Grieg; surely you know that I still think of you with deep affection. But my affection is burdened by a whole month's annoyances—the things that I have just told you, things that you, if you are thinking as you should, [will acknowledge] have their basis and justification . . .

And, dear Grieg, dearly beloved friend, I am afraid that . . . one fine day it will be all over . . . Never have I been in greater danger than now . . .

And now to close, dear friend, I wish you a happy and productive trip. Today you have gotten a letter filled with a mixture of good and bad, but from my heart I express the hope that only the good may follow you southward! And if there should be a moment when you hear the strains of Scandinavia, think of your sick friend whose heart is so full of those strains but whose voice is so weak; join him then in prayer to God that he soon can come and work with you toward our great common goal.

Your truly devoted friend, Rikard Nordraak. (From Nordraak's letter of November 30, 1865.)

Rikard Nordraak. Lithograph by J. Hassel. Grieg wrote to Iver Holter on February 9, 1897: "Nordraak's importance for me is not exaggerated. It really is so: through him and only through him was I truly awakened . . . The characteristics that we all are familiar with from Björnson were also present in considerable measure in Nordraak. He was a dreamer, a visionary, but he was not able to bring his own art up to a level corresponding to his vision . . . For me he became exactly what I needed . . . I willingly admit that the influence of Nordraak was not exclusively musical. But that is precisely the thing for which I am most grateful to him: that he opened my eyes to the importance of that in music which is not music." (Photo collection of Det Kongelige Bibliotek, Copenhagen, Denmark)

days. This, however, was to become an empty promise, and in a letter he sent to Nordraak from Leipzig on November 6 nothing is said about the return trip.

Grieg's concerts were highly successful and received positive press reviews. Another significant experience for him at this time was his first acquaintance with his unusually talented countryman, Johan Svendsen, who was now in the middle of his conservatory studies. Svendsen was greatly impressed with Berlioz, and on a later occasion (in a letter of May 9, 1872) he reminded Grieg that when they were together he persisted in trying to make Grieg into a Berlioz admirer, but in vain. Svendsen gave his new friend a warm farewell greeting in his autograph album: a transposed excerpt from the first movement of the splendid string octet he was writing at that time.

Meanwhile in Berlin, Nordraak was not at all improved. In his diary for November 11 he wrote: "They (the doctors) went out again, they couldn't bear to see it and they let me lie without a question or any examination. Later Mrs. Schmidt came in teary eyed. I knew this had to do with me, asked if I was given up. 'No, definitely not yet,' she said, 'but the doctors are afraid you don't have enough strength to hold out.'"

The next day he sent a penciled letter to Grieg: "For one small moment now I have strength . . . to send you a few words. Thanks for your precious letter; I cannot tell you how much good it did me." The preceding week had been the worst during his entire illness. He had had a terrible cough, and at the end of the letter he said: 'You must come now, Grieg. Do not delay longer, I must have you with me again. Write immediately to your devoted Rikard Nordraak."

This entry appears in Nordraak's diary the following week: "Letter from Grieg. He is coming soon." And the next day: "Grieg's letter yesterday tells of his two appearances in the Gewandhaus . . . tremendous success. Curtain calls. How I look forward to his coming."

Another letter from Leipzig dated November 30, however, came as a crushing blow: Grieg was not returning to Berlin but was going directly to Italy with a German friend!

Nordraak reacted angrily to Grieg's message in a letter of eight closely written pages. It was a letter trembling with rage, yet pervaded by devotion to his friend. Several characteristic excerpts are given in the Primary Materials.[6]

After Grieg had arrived in Rome he received a letter from Rikard's father, Georg Marcus Nordraak, who had come to his son's sickroom at the urgent request of the doctors. In this letter (December 15), the elder Nordraak discussed Rikard's complaints against Grieg. Here follow the most important sections of the letter:

". . . He is so weak that he can scarcely walk without help, and as it certainly will be a long time before he can write to you I will comment a little on the letter he has sent you and that undoubtedly was written in such a tone that you must certainly have understood the condition he was in when he wrote it. This was the last letter he wrote, and naturally it was without the knowledge and consent of the doctors that he concerned himself with such a task, one that must have had an extremely injurious effect on his weak nerves and enfeebled body."

"His despair over your leaving him—you who were his only solace and without whom he found himself forsaken and helpless—was so great that he had no choice but to use the last ounce of strength he could muster to bawl you out good and proper for the great treachery he thought you had committed by leaving him without informing him. Indeed, that must have been a difficult struggle for him to endure, to scold his best and dearest friend as sternly as he possibly could. God grant that I came to him in time so that I still can have some influence and calming effect on his condition. . . ."

"In conclusion, accept Rikard's and my friendly greetings. I hope that the trip that you have now begun will be enjoyable and satisfying for you and that it will bear rich fruit for your art . . ."

This letter, as well as Rikard's, must have affected Grieg deeply. From Rikard himself it contained only the most strictly necessary greeting in his father's formal conclusion.

It is difficult to find a convincing defense for Grieg's fickle behavior toward Nordraak, but there is reason to believe that he didn't dare to return to Berlin for fear that he himself might be stricken. He certainly realized that his friend had contracted tuberculosis, a great scourge at that time; and with his own lung impairment resulting from a tuberculosis attack during his conservatory period, he perhaps did not want to take any chances.

During his Italian sojourn in the winter and spring of 1865–66, Grieg undoubtedly reexamined his conduct toward his friend, and he developed a guilt complex that remained with him long after.

First Visit to Rome

In his diary for the period beginning December 2, 1865, when he journeyed southward from Leipzig, Grieg gave some fairly detailed reports of his trip to Italy—so detailed that one can follow him almost day by day for the next nine months. Compared to the flowery, Romantic language of the first part of the diary, the style here is much simpler. The entries typically consist of short, carefully worded observations, occasionally with a serious undertone. But he also broke out in effusive descriptions of Italy's scenery and art, and struck a more cheerful note when the opportunity presented itself.

The trip to Italy was by train via Dresden and Vienna. In Vienna he heard an opera by Lortzing and an operetta by Franz von Suppé, and he characterized the hotel bill as "a gigantic fraud." Of the journey from Vienna to Italy, he wrote that it was a "lovely trip" with a "memorable arrival in Venice." After a few days in Venice he went on to Padua, then continued "by omnibus" to Ferrara and by train to Bologna, where he stayed overnight. The next morning he continued southward to Pisa through the Apennine tunnels ("$3/_4$ of the trip under the earth"). His diary contains a poetic description of the Tuscany landscape that suddenly unfolded before him like a revelation of pure beauty.

In Livorno Grieg got "the first idea of what it is like to go to Rome. The closer one gets to the great world capital, the more impossible it seems that one will ever actually get there. Every possible difficulty is put in one's way. First, the passport inspections are almost ridiculously strict . . . and secondly, one cannot walk or drive ten steps without surrendering large sums of money for something or other that is never identified."

After traveling all night "by omnibus," he arrived in Civitavecchia "after being thoroughly smoked [for protection against cholera] and examined right down to the innermost parts." The same day—December 11—he arrived in Rome in the forenoon and with surprising energy immediately set about exploring the city: "Rented a room at Via Sistina 100, second floor. Then the Vatican. The first impression almost too overpowering to even think of enjoyment. The Laocoon group was lovely, as were also Raphael's frescoes . . . Café Roma. The Spanish Steps. Monte Pincio, evening tour."

The following day he rented a piano and initiated an acquaintance with

Franz Liszt at about the time Grieg first came in contact with him. (Photo collection of Det Kongelige Bibliotek, Copenhagen)

Niels Ravnkilde, a forty-two-year-old Danish composer who subsequently became his close friend. He met Ibsen for the first time, visited St. Peter's Cathedral, and stopped in at the Scandinavian Society.

During the following weeks he made short entries concerning visits to several of the city's most famous sights: the Colosseum, Forum Romanum, and Castel St. Angelo. He also went up to the St. Onofrio cloister "to watch the sun go down. Wonderful view."

During a concert he saw Franz Liszt for the first time and wrote laconically that he had observed Liszt "strutting about for some young ladies." Regarding a church concert he observed: "Terrible music . . . Bellini, Donizetti, Rossini. Two *castratos*, unnatural, repugnant." In the Lateran church he heard "a deadly boring concert of church music by some of the modern Italian masters (?). It was such a monotonous, uninteresting jumble of sounds, a single formless collection of tonic, dominant, and subdominant . . . Before the concert was half over I left the church, nervous and ravenously hungry. Outside the church I saw something interesting: a monk . . . dispensed for-

1. A NEW YEAR'S EVE VISIT
TO THE ROMAN FORUM

In the evening a wonderful moonlit tour to the Forum Romanum. This is the right environment in which to view the ruins. The impact of the Colosseum is indescribable. The French watchman who guards all the entrances used only a lantern to inspect all the gates and arches. The reddish light reflecting off the old arches and shining in among the ruins created an interesting contrast to the strange half-darkness produced by the blue-green light of the moon and made the whole scene even more ghostly . . . The moon shone so pale and cold, our imagination began to play tricks on us, and we hurried as fast as we could away from this admittedly romantic but nonetheless unpleasant world where assaults are anything but rare. Next we went to the Scandinavian Society to celebrate New Year's Eve, but it was so formal and uncomfortable in this "homey circle" that . . . after staying for only five minutes or so, and without telling anybody, I just left. We drank our chocolate in the Café Greco and talked about our beloved ones at home. By 11 o'clock I was sound asleep. (Excerpt from Grieg's diary, December 31, 1865.)

2. A HIKE IN THE CAMPAGNA

At 9:30 in the morning I and a group of other Norwegians gathered in Café Roma to take a hike in the Campagna. We went out through Porta St. Sebastiano on the old Roman highway in the most enormous heat—roughly like a July day at home . . . We had breakfast in a little restaurant out there; it consisted of dirty sausage and dirty spare ribs on even dirtier plates, and some almost undrinkable wine, but even so it was a singular delight. The mere thought that on the first of January—under beautiful green trees, and surrounded by the scent of roses—I was sitting out in the open air and eating my breakfast, made me almost intoxicated. From here we walked . . . under the dark blue sky and in the shimmering summer air toward the indescribably beautiful Alban Hills that lay in the distance. [Hans Christian] Andersen is right: Italy is the land of color. The light, clear air gives a wonderful harmony to the colors. The mountains look like dust, like ether, like things that are merely hovering in one's thoughts, and yet in such a way that one

sees and enjoys all of this with one's outer as well as one's inner eye. We chose another return route, went by the grotto of the nymph Egeria. Remarkably poetic . . . I couldn't resist going into the cool vault to taste the ancient spring water. (Excerpt from Grieg's diary, January 1, 1866.)

3. LISZT—BRILLIANT
AND AFFECTED

Heard a piece of a *musica sacra* for castrato singers, natural male voices, and harmonium by Franz Liszt. The performance was led by Liszt himself. That is to say: although someone else was conducting, Liszt led the entire piece with his black-gloved fingers that one moment were waving in the air, the next moment were busy at the keyboard.

The composition—*Stabat Mater Dolorosa*—is a sad proof of the decline of the newer German music. For it would be hard to find a more affected, pale, formless, shallow piece than this. It is unsound and un-

giveness to the sinners who knelt before him by giving them a fairly hefty blow on the head with a long stick . . . There were a great many sinners in the church, for the stick was going constantly."

Just before Christmas he witnessed a funeral: "powerful, gripping impression. The monks bellowed on two notes (interval of a sixth) with remarkable effect."

Grieg usually spent his evenings at the Scandinavian Society, where he became acquainted with the poet Andreas Munch and others. On Christmas Eve there was a big party at the Society; Grieg heard Ibsen talk, and the following day there was an informal "feast on the leftovers . . . Ibsen dead drunk." Grieg's colorful accounts of New Year's Eve[1] and of a six-hour hike on New Year's Day[2] are quoted in the Primary Materials, as is also his report on his strongly negative reactions to a piece of church music by Liszt which he heard several days later.[3]

He had mainly positive things to say, however, about a Liszt piano concerto, which was "the best thing by Liszt that I have ever heard. Brilliant from beginning to end. He throws out huge masses of sound with demonic power. The only defect is that the modulations are confused and altogether too frequent; if they were used a bit more sparingly they would be twice as effective. After hearing this I would call Sgambati one of the world's foremost piano *virtuosos*, not a pianist in the usual meaning of the word . . ."

Grieg was not unreceptive to the Mediterranean beauty of Italian women. "Wonderful Roman women" were admired from a distance, but also at closer range: "Flirted with a remarkable young Roman lady. The way she blushed ever so slightly as we were leaving the tavern was indescribable." The week-

true from beginning to end. The beginning did impress me, however; it was brilliant, mystical, and demonic—as Liszt can be in individual passages here and there. But the whole piece remained in this underworld. All too soon it became evident that he was not capable of mastering his thoughts—indeed, that he was rather the slave of those thoughts . . .

This much is clear, that if we do not fight with all our might against this genre the outlook for music in our time is very bad. It is almost as bad as the vulgar Italian school—yes, perhaps even more dangerous, because it ventures into an area that is of some interest to musicians, namely philosophy. But if the true art that consists in pure immediacy, in sparkling poetry—if that is to go forward, then philosophy must vanish, and the sooner the better, in my opinion . . .

Liszt looked splendid in his abbot's garb; one could see the visionary written all over him. (Excerpt from Grieg's diary, January 4, 1866.)

4. DIVINE WORSHIP AT THE SCANDINAVIAN SOCIETY IN ROME

. . . I for my part left with the same indignation that I always feel after a sermon in which the preacher appears with ecclesiastical decorations on his chest, trying through play-acting and an affected delivery to appropriate the dignity that he thinks he needs in order to impress his flock. And yet, I wouldn't have missed this forenoon for anything. It aroused me from my lethargy and provided food for thought. (Excerpt from Grieg's diary, February 17, 1866.)

5. THE SOCIAL CONSCIENCE IS AWAKENED

We walked out to St. Paul's Church, this elegant building that in some respects even surpasses St. Peter's. . . When one hears that this enormous church exists only for show, one cannot help asking the question: where in the world does all the money come from, for as everyone knows the country is anything but rich! Ah yes, the people are coerced into paying this enormous church tax because that is pleasing to God! The terrible illusion that the worship of God consists in building majestic temples that must, indeed, be admired—but for the sake of which the people sigh in bondage and misery. (Excerpt from Grieg's diary, February 17, 1866.)

6. ILLUMINATION IN ST. PETER'S CATHEDRAL

Such a thing I had never dreamt of. My imagination could never venture to create such a poetic, stupid, and colossal picture. The whole church was a sea of fire . . . even the cross above the dome, so it is no wonder that the man [a prisoner] who is assigned to place the lamps in this dizzying height always takes the sacrament of communion before he climbs up. But the thing about this that must not only astonish but outrage every thinking person is that people think they can please God by such nonsense. (Excerpt from Grieg's diary, April 1, 1866.)

long Carnival (pre-Lenten) celebrations that took place at the beginning of February, which interested him greatly, also provided an opportunity for closer contact with the life of the people: "To revive his spirits" he went to a tavern and "drank half a bottle of Foglietti, and this helped in a surprising degree and encouraged me to participate in the merriment."

He reported that one evening in Rome he saw beauty in all of the women in the balconies, "but the most enjoyable and stimulating were the processions . . . People were covered with big white cowls that came right up over the head, with the result that not only did one become unrecognizable but it even became absolutely impossible to distinguish the men from the women . . . and this circumstance undoubtedly helped to make the situation extremely provocative. That is how it came about that all of a sudden I found one of these apparitions under each arm (without any encouragement at all on my part), and only the soft outlines of the female body that pressed itself tightly against me enabled me to distinguish between the sexes. Moreover, I admit that I found myself in a somewhat desperate situation by getting into the middle of this comedy, because I couldn't answer a single word to all their Italian nonsense. I therefore made my escape by yelling at the top of my lungs . . . in shrill tones Holberg's inimitable 'Rinkolaveski spekave' and other nonsense words. Another time I got into trouble by patting a white figure very gently on the shoulder, whereupon another white figure—evidently a companion—who was behind us got so angry that all of a sudden I felt a clenched fist strike me from behind so hard that it rattled my backbone. When I turned around I saw the same fist raised toward me, accompanied by some words that sounded like a frightened howl . . . Hartman told me that the words meant: 'Don't touch the women!' I had no idea it was a woman that I had touched, and if only I had been able to speak Italian I would of course have said so; as it was I had to swallow my pride and bite the sour apple [let the misunderstanding remain]." (Grieg's companion was the Danish sculptor, Carl Christian Hartman, who also carved a bust of Grieg during his stay in Italy.)

The diary alternates between light-hearted reports like these and more serious observations in which he sometimes rather crassly stated his opinions about religion and about political and social conditions. Grieg already had radical ideas about these things at the age of twenty-two. Several characteristic statements from this period are quoted in the Primary Materials.[4,5,6,7]

Grieg participated in several evening chamber music programs at the Scandinavian Society. On March 24 he himself arranged a program for an audience of sixty that included the pianist Sgambati. At this program he performed his *Violin Sonata in F Major* with the famous Roman violinist Pinelli. He also accompanied the Danish sculptor C. F. Holbech in some arias of Bellini and Kuhlau: "It was an absolute comedy, for in spite of his good voice the man is so thoroughly unmusical that it was a hopeless task for me to keep him in time. One moment he was a half measure ahead, then a half measure behind with me trying to follow him, so the whole performance took on more the character of a farce than of art. We finally got through it, however, and the audience was delighted, and that's what counts . . . I was

7. MODERN ROMAN ART

Later I became convinced in a new and sad way that Rome is the ruins of a vanished greatness, and that is all . . . It is dangerous for a people—both with respect to politics and with respect to art—to have a great past. It leads either to what the Germans are sinking into, namely striving with all their might to hold themselves up, and with this striving to produce nothing but artificial, baroque, unnatural things; or else, as here among the Romans, quite phlegmatically to lull themselves to sleep and rest on their laurels. For one seeks in vain here for the slightest effort to do a good and serious piece of work . . . What is lacking here above all is just that same assiduousness that is also lacking among the present generation of Italians. And where art is handled with such a total lack of respect, it seems to me that the longing of the people for freedom must also be lacking. Where people do not respect the laws of art they also do not respect the laws of the state, and political freedom must then lead to complete degeneration and downfall. (Excerpt from Grieg's diary, March 16, 1866.)

asked to play my *Humoresques,* which I haven't looked at for a long time; I naturally winced at first, but that didn't help—I had to do it. I can't remember ever playing them so spontaneously and freshly. I loved them and felt happy with them . . . old memories were awakened, the whole situation gripped me. The thought that I was sitting here in Rome and making Scandinavian music for Scandinavians excited me, and that no doubt affected the performance . . . One after another they came to me to express thanks and appreciation. I held the daintiest, silky-soft hands of lovable, young girls in mine; I felt so thankful; in truth, this evening is one of the happiest of many happy evenings I have spent in Rome. Introduced to Sgambati; that, unfortunately, had to be the end of it, as we have no common language."

In addition to keeping a detailed diary, Grieg also wrote many letters. The diary tells about his active correspondence: with his family at home; with Nina, who was in Bergen; with Nina's parents and sister in Denmark; and with a long list of friends and acquaintances. This correspondence has not been preserved except for a letter from Benjamin Feddersen posted from Copenhagen December 25, 1865. In this letter Grieg got the good news that his *Humoresques* had "received an extraordinarily favorable review in [the Danish newspaper] *Dagbladet:* 'It is the first and the best thing that Norway has sent us in this genre.'" The letter reports further that Gade's concerts with Musikforeningen "have been quite brilliant . . . One might almost think that Gade wanted to crush 'Euterpe.' I will not deny that Euterpe's second concert [in the autumn] was less successful . . . It is doubtful that there will be a third one."

Feddersen proposed to Grieg in "the greatest confidence" that in the coming autumn he and Grieg should take over the Casino theater, with Grieg as the musical director: "I think I have a knack for such things, and sooner or later we would succeed in making the Casino into not only a decent theater but also a place where people would come to hear a good orchestra, and a place where we would have the joy of helping talented young musicians by giving their works the public attention they deserve." Grieg says nothing in his diary about his reaction to this idea, which was never implemented.

Grieg did in fact have plans at this time to become the conductor of a theater orchestra—not in Copenhagen, but in Oslo. The position of music director at the Christiania Theater had been vacant since 1865 and was now temporarily filled by Johan Hennum.

Grieg asked Ibsen for his advice on the matter, and he reported in his diary that Ibsen had "recommended writing to Björnson and Dunker [theater director and board chairman, respectively] about not filling the leadership post at the theater." It is not clear whether is was Grieg or Ibsen who was to write. In a letter to Ibsen from Copenhagen on June 10, 1866, Grieg stated that, in accordance with Ibsen's "friendly counsel" in Rome, he had written to Björnson six weeks earlier applying for the position. But since he had not heard a word from him, he now hoped that Ibsen might intervene.

In the back of the diary there is a draft of the specific conditions that he would set if he were to take the position. He wanted, among other things, a choir director in addition to himself, and wanted to have final authority regarding the musical repertoire. How bold a twenty-two-year-old can be! But what Grieg didn't know when he wrote to Björnson is that he was already too late, for Hennum had been given the position on March 1.

Thus Ibsen's support of Grieg's candidacy could not be of any help. His extremely friendly reply to Grieg's letter is cited on p. 99.

That Ibsen had a positive impression of Grieg's ability is evident from a calling card he gave Grieg as a note of introduction to a friend: "Warm greetings through a fine fellow, one who will give the future its direction." He beautifully expressed his belief in Grieg as an artist in the famous little poem that he wrote in Grieg's autograph album; he later published it in a slightly revised form in his Collected Works under the title "Fra en Komponists Stambog" [From a Composer's Autograph Album].[8] Grieg noted laconically in his diary on March 30: "Ibsen wrote in my album."

About this time Grieg also arranged a contact between his brother John and Ibsen regarding a German translation of *The Pretenders,* which John undertook with the help of his German-born wife.

From the overture In Autumn *to "Cradle Song"*

The hectic activities that occupied Grieg in Rome left little time for composing. The diary reports only four compositions that were written in the spring of 1866: the orchestral overture *In Autumn* (Opus 11), two songs to texts by Andreas Munch (Opus 9, Nos. 1 and 2), and *Funeral March for Rikard Nordraak* (CW 117).

In Autumn had evidently been started sometime in 1865. On January 31, 1866, he wrote in his diary: "Finished outline for the overture in D," and on March 14: "Completed the Autumn overture." The original manuscript no longer exists, so we know this overture only from a somewhat later arrangement for piano four hands and an 1887 orchestration of this arrangement (with minor rhythmic and dynamic changes). Grieg explained his reasons for arranging the two later versions in a letter to Iver Holter.[9]

> The overture opens with a thirty-measure slow introduction in D major, with short motives that become important later in the work. The fast main portion in sonata form follows in D minor, and the piece concludes with a brisk coda in D major.
>
> Some themes from "Autumn Storms," Opus 18, No. 4, are used as thematic material in the main section after having been subtly intimated in the introduction. The first section of the exposition is almost identical to the first part of the song. Later material from other parts of the song is also used, but with increasing dissimilarity. A contrasting part in F major is built on a variation in ⅜ time of the *springar* "Nordfjordingen" (in the tradition of Torgeir Audunsson [1801–1872]—better known in Norway as "Myllarguten"—who was renowned as a Hardanger fiddler). Grieg knew this tune from the collection *VIII Norske Slaatter for Hardangerfele* (VIII Norwegian Folk Dances for Hardanger Fiddle), published by Claus Schart in Bergen in 1865. Apparently he didn't have it clearly in mind as he worked out the details of the overture, for he asked his brother John to send him the melody. On March 12 he noted in his diary: "Received from John the haying song for the overture." He then

8. IBSEN'S POETIC GREETING TO GRIEG

To Edvard Grieg!
Orpheus with his golden lyre
Soothed the beasts, set stones on fire.
Stones our homeland has no lack of;
Beasts it also has a pack of.
Play so stones with sparks redound!
Play so meadows peal with sound!
(Verse written in Grieg's autograph album March 30, 1866.)

9. GADE REACTS NEGATIVELY TO *IN AUTUMN*

When I brought it to Copenhagen and showed it to Gade, he said, "It's nothing but a piece of trash, Grieg. Go home and write something better." I went home, too—and, I say with respect, I wept. The overture was not well orchestrated, that I remember. Then out of pure dejection I just let it lie. I arranged part of it for piano four hands and played this with Nina at home. Then [1867] I sent it to Stockholm for a contest being run by The Swedish Academy. The judges were Rietz in Dresden, Söderman in Stockholm—and Gade in Copenhagen. The overture . . . took first prize and was published for piano four hands in Stockholm. (Gade had evidently forgotten the whole affair.) Then in 1887 I reorchestrated the piece and had the score published by Peters. (Excerpt from Grieg's letter to Iver Holter, January 8, 1897.)

incorporated the tune in its original form in ¾ time in the coda, and two days later the overture was finished.

In referring to this melody as a "haying song," Grieg did not identify it as a *dance* tune. Strange though it may seem, he evidently had the idea that the word *slaatt,* which means "country dance," in this case had something to do with "slaattonn," which means "haying". Thirty years later he should have known better, but he perpetuated the error when he explained his concept of the overture in a letter to Louis Monastier-Schroeder April 1, 1895: "In the overture, both the poetical and musical contrasts derive from the fact that the piece is based on 'Autumn Storm,' Opus 18, which depicts the autumn storm, and on the farmers' merry haying song ('slaattesang'). There is no suggestion in the overture of a coming spring: it has to do only with a bringing together of the serious and the light-hearted elements that characterize autumn."

In the development, which is marked by surprising tonal leaps and strong elements of modality, the thematic material is reworked with a certain technical proficiency, and the recapitulation is interesting for the different form in which the original material is now repeated.

Harmonically, *In Autumn* is not a step forward for the composer. The harmonic devices are less refined, and the combination of musical styles is less successful than in the elegant and well-integrated works of the preceding year.

Neither the slightly idiomatic version for piano four hands—which appears to have been arranged in haste—nor the 1887 orchestral version is convincingly written. Although Grieg often included the orchestral version in his programs, and although it is also performed occasionally today, *In Autumn* does not show its creator in the most flattering light. The material from "Autumn Storms" is in itself of little consequence. Grieg certainly tried to give the piece coherence, but the musical material is heterogeneous and the loose and episodic form of the overture does not create the organic structure that must be present if a work is to live.

In Rome during the spring of 1866, Grieg became better acquainted with the fifty-five-year-old Norwegian poet Andreas Munch. As previously mentioned, Grieg had already written a song and a choral piece to texts by Munch in 1865. During a coach tour in which Munch was extraordinarily friendly to Grieg, the conversation eventually turned to Munch's poem cycle, *Kongedatterens Brudefart* [The Princess's Bridal Procession], which had been published in 1850. They agreed that this cycle was well suited for dramatic treatment as the basis for an opera text, and Munch was "not unwilling, if I was so disposed, that I should try my hand at it at some convenient time."

Nothing came of the plan for an opera. Grieg did find in a collection of Munch's poems entitled *Sorg og tröst* (Sorrow and Consolation) two texts, however—"The Harp" and "Cradle Song" (Opus 9, Nos. 1 and 2)—which he set to music at the beginning of April.

The two songs differ greatly in quality. With respect to the former, the less said the better. A hopelessly banal text is set in a way that seems almost to be a parody of Grieg's style.

"Cradle Song," on the other hand, is one of the very finest compositions of Grieg's youth. A father is singing to a new-born son whose mother has died in childbirth. The text movingly expresses Munch's own sorrow: his wife had died in 1850 while giving birth to twin sons, one of whom also died at birth.

Henrik Ibsen in 1866, near the time when he and Grieg first became acquainted. (Photo collection of Universitetsbiblioteket in Oslo)

10. GRIEG HEARS "CRADLE SONG"
SUNG AGAIN

J. Messchaert sang . . . my Cradle Song to [Andreas] Munch's "Sleep, my son" . . . thoroughly beautiful, with a shading and a tranquility that were just right. Only this choice of my song, this recklessness, characterizes the artist. Believe me, it was strange to sit here and listen to this thirty-five [thirty]-year-old product of my youth. I could hardly comprehend that I had written it. Really, it was almost like in Brahms's song "Mir ist, als wenn ich längst gestorben wäre!" But I felt a deep inward joy and gratitude toward the artist because he had not done violence to my most intimate intentions, but had actually understood them in such a way that he was able to interpret them to others. For I think I can say that I almost never experience this simply as a listener. (Excerpt from a letter from Grieg to F. Beyer, January 24, 1896.)

Grieg gave "Cradle Song" a strophic form, which seems appropriate for the mood of resignation that characterizes the text. After the four stanzas of the poem, however, he repeats the beginning unchanged, and then he repeats a line from the first stanza: "Sleep—though she who life you gave / Lies now in the cruel grave," in a new and exceptionally beautiful melodic setting.

It is remarkable how naturally Grieg made use of a modal style throughout this piece. The Aeolian mode dominates in the beginning, but later a harmonic background is used that cannot be clearly identified as any of the church modes. As we have seen, Grieg had tried using similar devices earlier, especially in brief sections of a piece. As he had done very carefully in "The Old Song" in 1864, so now he again allowed an entire composition to be permeated with modality. "Cradle Song" is an early example of the use of a modal style throughout a composition in the music of the nineteenth century.

Grieg once characterized this song as "one of my best," and when he heard it sung at a concert many years later he was deeply moved.[10]

The Funeral March for Rikard Nordraak

Grieg's diary reveals nothing about what he may have been thinking while Nordraak lay sick in Berlin. It is possible that he felt ashamed of his behavior toward his friend and for that reason did not wish to disclose his innermost feelings. In any case, he clearly was aware of the seriousness of Nordraak's illness. This is evident from a remark in a December 25 letter from Feddersen commenting on an earlier statement of Grieg with respect to the illness.

According to the diary, Grieg wrote to Nordraak on February 4 and March 8, but he heard nothing at all from his friend during his stay in Rome. He performed one of Nordraak's compositions, however: "Kaares Sang" [Kaare's Song] (with male chorus), from *Sigurd Slembe*. The chorus consisted of nine Scandinavian and German friends. The rehearsals were held in Grieg's own lodgings, and the work was performed at the Scandinavian Society on February 17: "The solo was first sung by Hartman, and the second time—when we were asked to sing the piece again—by Axel Prior." The shock came in an April 6 letter from Feddersen, reporting Nordraak's death on March 20. Grieg's feelings upon the death of his friend are most beautifully reflected in a composition that was written in the course of two days: *Funeral March for Rikard Nordraak* (CW 117).

The work was originally written for piano. The first fair-copy version differs, especially in the conclusion, from the edition that was published in Copenhagen the same year.

A year later Grieg arranged the piece, transposed up a half step to B-flat minor, for a large wind ensemble. He conducted it in his first subscription concert in Oslo on December 12, 1867, and wrote in a letter a week later that it "sounded wonderful."

When Grieg conducted this version of the funeral march in Copenhagen on October 9, 1869, it bore the title: "Upon Rikard Nordraak's Death. Tone Poem for Orchestra." He reorchestrated the work nine years later for a small military orchestra, and hoped some day to get it arranged and published for symphony orchestra. This, however, he never accomplished.

During the 1890s he expressed the wish to have this piece played at his own funeral. After Grieg's death, therefore, Johan Halvorsen—on the boat trip from Oslo to Bergen—hurriedly arranged the composition for symphony orchestra and performed it with the large orchestra that had been assembled for the funeral.

The funeral march is a valuable contribution in this genre. It clearly shows that Grieg had attained full maturity both as a melodist and as a harmonist. It also shows that within a short work he was able to create an organic whole. It is a compact piece without a single superfluous note.

The composition opens with three repeated A-minor triads. These are followed by a motive with sharply accented, compelling rhythms that becomes the core motive of the work:

This opening is further developed in a disciplined but creative way throughout the eighteen measures of the principal section.

The trio (also eighteen measures long) begins in A major. Here the core motive is transformed into a three-measure melody that resembles a folk dance. From the second measure and on the trio is marked by modality in both melody and harmony:

A subsequent series of powerful digressions into other keys provides the tension-filled high point of the work.

The funeral march both opens and closes with a modal section. The conclusion, with the chromatically altered sixth of the scale (in the bridge from A Dorian to A Aeolian) is quite unusual:

The style of this work was radical for its time. Grieg created sonorities of striking singularity—as he had also done in his "Cradle Song." These two works stand out in bold relief among his early productions. When he visited Liszt in Rome in 1870, he selected to take along as a gift—in addition to the

11. IBSEN COMMITS A FAUX PAS

And after all that, Ibsen—after a few glasses of Foglietti had gone to his head—got the idea that there should be a dance, and without further ado he had the table and chairs cleared away and urged Ravnkilde (!) to strike up a dance. When Ravnkilde naturally did not want to respond to the request, Ibsen got so angry that he took his hat and cane and left in a huff. When we are alone he is accustomed to having us obey his "Strike up the music, you fellows!" With this "strike up" the man means just music—any kind of music—and he still does not understand that it must seem very strange to an artist that so great a man can be so tactless and in this one area so obtuse. Just as if one were to ask Ibsen to recite Erik Bögh's ditties, we would then hear an indignant protest. No, an artist must first maintain his own integrity, for only then will the public learn to do so. (Extract from Grieg's diary, April 9, 1866.)

12. SLED TRIP OVER THE ALPS

When we had driven some miles into the Alps, we were so high up that we came into snow. We therefore had to let the omnibus stand and take a sled over the Alps. This was the apex of the trip. Ascending higher and higher, we came through almost impassable roads and dark tunnels; there was more and more snow, and at last we could see nothing but a gigantic carpet of snow. That was a marvelous sight. But a dangerous business . . . It was so cold up there that even with fur boots and blankets one became as stiff as a stone from the frost. Going down again, we warmed up in a rather peculiar way. The sleds whipped from side to side while moving with lightning speed . . . so one was constantly in danger of being dashed to pieces. One moment the sled was balancing on one side, the next moment on the other side, and it rumbled down over the chunks of snow and ice, so one had other things to do than freeze. On the contrary, one sat in such dread that the sweat flowed out from every pore. But even so, it was an interesting situation . . . and I would not have missed it for anything. (Excerpt from Grieg's diary, April 23, 1866.)

new G-major violin sonata—the *Funeral March* and the volume containing "Cradle Song." He played the march for Liszt and, according to Grieg himself, it was "also to his taste."

Grieg leaves Rome

On April 9, five Italian artists gave a big concert at the Scandinavian Society where, among other things, Sgambati "marvelously rendered" Chopin's *Fantasy in F Minor,* and he and Pinelli played a Tartini sonata in a distinguished manner. But Ibsen, according to Greig, committed a serious faux pas by proposing that they set up for a dance. Grieg's diary contains a cutting description of this episode.[11]

Two days later, Grieg and a Swedish friend by the name of Edman left for a week-long trip south to the region of Naples. Naples was "a magnificent city sparkling with life, greatest possible contrast to Rome." Together with Andreas Munch and Munch's new wife and others, he undertook an "exceptionally enjoyable and interesting trip by carriage in the most beautiful weather to Pompeii." Upon returning home he drank a toast to Nina of *Lacrima Cristi,* "a wine that I drink here each day until I am happy and relaxed."

He also took a trip by "a wildly rolling" steamship to Capri, where the passengers got into a small rowboat to visit the famous blue grotto. This caused great difficulties for "the poor ladies, among whom there was a wonderfully captivating little Russian. I wished I had been a sculptor, though the fact is that I drank in the beautiful female forms in all their voluptuousness as if I were a sculptor . . . When we were to go through the small opening leading into the grotto, the command *terra* [heads down!] was given. The sweet little Russian lady, so as not to be crushed, had to obey the order and cling tightly—half afraid, half bashful—to me."

On April 17 Grieg was back in Rome, where he got letters from his father and Nina and a check for 150 thalers from the Leipzig firm of Breitkopf & Härtel, which had just published his piano sonata.

Two days later, after farewell visits, he started north. He stayed briefly in Florence and Milan, and then went by carriage via Como over the Alps to Chur, Switzerland, "certainly the most remarkable trip I have ever taken." His diary contains a picturesque description of this mountain adventure.[12]

After staying overnight in Rorschach, he continued by steamship over "the lovely Bodensee" and by train via Augsburg and Nurnberg to Leipzig, arriving on April 29. There, he wrote, "I ran up to the Conservatory to see and talk with one of the old familiar people." The first person he met was his former piano teacher Wenzel, "who came running down from the top floor . . . I went with him for a walk down the street. He was the same splendid fellow as before."

Grieg visited Reinecke on May 1, and two days later he went to Berlin. Here he got a pleasant bit of encouragement. After he had purchased Berlioz's text on instrumentation in a bookstore, he asked for his own *Humoresques* and

I do not know how a father's love differs from that of a true friend; I only know that I loved Rikard with all my heart. I know what I have had to suffer in leaving him, my best friend, lying on a sick bed; in seeing my concern and love misunderstood; in having to live in uncertainty and concern for five long months in the south of Europe; and then at last, when hope once again began to stir in me, in receiving the harsh message that our young national art must fade in death because its champion is no more!

I know what I have lived through in those days down there in Italy, when I didn't dare to confide in anyone because no one understood my sorrow. Only music felt compassion; I turned to the mournful tones that never fail in time of sorrow, and from them I received consolation. They whispered to me that Rikard Nordraak's name will live in our Nordic art; his great, beautiful Ideal will carry it far beyond the grave and its oblivion—for that ideal has Truth's stamp upon it.

"He who has something to live for cannot die," he once said to me in an intimate, happy moment. This certainly did not prove to be the case in the ordinary meaning of those words, but only now do I clearly understand their deep significance; and perhaps he uttered them in the consciousness of the triumph of the ideal, even if the body should perish before the ideal has been realized. But it will be realized, for it shall be my life's mission to carry it forward in his spirit. I feel a double responsibility, but I feel that my strength and confidence have now also been doubled. Yes, it is as if he had given me this as a bequest—as if upon his death his fighting spirit flew to me and made its home in my soul.

We had both hoped that we could work together for the advancement of our national art. Since this was not granted us I simply have to hold loyally to the promise I gave him that his cause would be my cause, his goal mine. Do not suppose that what he aspired to will be forgotten. It will be my great mission to bring his few brilliant works to the people—our Norwegian people; to fight for their recognition; and to build further on their solid foundation.

What he wanted was still too new to take root among the people; but the time

will come when the national consciousness will be clearer, the need to assert it greater, and the name of each and every person who in his life work has struggled for it will be indelibly inscribed in our history. And among these, as surely as art has deep national meaning, will be listed as one of the first: Rikard Nordraak! . . .

May you not misunderstand these lines; they come from a heart that has felt thus for the friend, for the artist. Both the friend and the artist have been of equally great significance for me, and will be cherished in my memory with melancholy love . . . (Letter from Grieg to Georg M. Nordraak, May 7, 1866.)

"was told that all copies were sold out. The salesperson said the composer had so many friends in Berlin who were interested in him! A pleasant situation, for I didn't tell him who I was."

During the stay in Berlin he sought out the Jerusalem cemetery, where a month earlier Nordraak had been laid to rest. Only one person had been present for Nordraak's burial—a lovable old Jewish man by the name of Jacobi. Grieg took with him from the grave an oak leaf which has been preserved to the present day in the famous letter that he sent to Nordraak's father on May 7. The most important passages are quoted in the Primary Materials.[13] They give eloquent witness to his sorrow on this occasion and to the calling he felt to further his friend's ideas in spirit.

One other time, some months before he died, Grieg came to Nordraak's grave in Berlin. In his diary for April 13, 1907, he wrote: "This afternoon to Nordraak's grave. I laid a laurel wreath by his magnificent monument and in so doing was moved to reflection. Forty-one years have passed—that is to say, my whole life—since I stood at this grave. It was as if for a moment I stood face to face with what I have experienced—and above all, the wonderful Nordraak period!"

The trip to Italy brought to an end an important period in Grieg's life. In a letter to G. Matthison-Hansen on March 1, 1870, he summed up his impressions of the trip itself: "My first journey to the south [of Europe] was like a dream, and it was precisely as a dream that it had value for me at that time."

Back to everyday life

Grieg returned to Copenhagen from Berlin on May 10 "in the same miserable weather as when I left last autumn." The drab everyday life was about to resume. He remained in Denmark until early September; this became a difficult period for him, filled with uncertainty and anxiety for the future. The diary now suddenly becomes very terse; it contains nothing but purely factual information without a single personal comment.

On May 22 he wrote: "At Gade's with the Overture [*In Autumn*]. Gave him Opus 6, Opus 7, Opus 8." It was on this occasion that Gade expressed the harsh criticism of the overture that was so depressing to Grieg (see page 92). It seems surprising that he withheld this disappointment from his diary. Equally remarkable is the scant space given Nina in the diary: she is mentioned only a few times. She returned to Copenhagen on May 13 after a

Grieg "brought a developed keyboard technique together with excellent preparation in sight reading, and made such rapid progress that after just six weeks I could entrust to him the task of serving as my substitute at Frederikskirke during my summer holiday absence. If I were to characterize his merits more precisely I would emphasize his well-rounded, fine pedal playing, the well-developed sense of the tonal shading evident in his registrations, and surprisingly beautiful prelude playing . . ."

half year's stay in Bergen. Even then Grieg wrote only: "Nina's arrival from Bergen."

What the reason may have been for the infrequent mention of his fiancée we do not know, but their reunion does not appear to have been especially warm. Some candid opinions expressed in an August 10 letter from Benjamin Feddersen to Grieg show clearly that there were serious disagreements between Nina and Edvard at this time: "How I regard Miss Hagerup I would prefer to say to her directly. I am sorry that she has not understood her relationship with you; for no matter how much you may wish to excuse her I still maintain that she is not the woman who deserves to support and encourage you in the development of your talent . . . You call me your only friend. Then cast your sorrow on me as well; I will help you bear it . . . You have dreamt a mixture of the pretty and the ugly. Rejoice, you have awakened!"

Nor did Feddersen have a very high opinion of Grieg's prospective parents-in-law. "All they require for their daughter," he wrote, "is a man, preferably a rich one, whose life is assured for 100 years." But he emphasized that Grieg's art and life were one: "You sin against God if you fail to live in your art . . . The people who cannot understand this are not your friends. You cannot thrive among them: you will perish like a plant without air and sun."

For a young man who was engaged to be married, these were not exactly the most encouraging words from one of his closest friends who, moreover, knew the circumstances. Grieg was struggling within himself. Should he sacrifice his art or should he sacrifice himself for it? A possible compromise was to support a family by becoming an organist. In fact, he had already begun taking organ lessons from Gottfred Matthison-Hansen. His diary lists fifteen lessons during the course of the summer, and at the end his teacher gave him an excellent recommendation.[14] The acid test came when he went to Roskilde to play for Gottfred's father, cathedral organist Hans Matthison-Hansen, who was one of the country's leading church musicians. Grieg performed several works, including Bach's *Fugue in G Minor,* to the great satisfaction of the elder Matthison-Hansen.

Grieg also appeared as a pianist in a July 25 concert at Tivoli, given for the benefit of the victims of the great fire two weeks earlier in the city of Drammen, Norway. This appearance demonstrates his active social engagement already at this early date. It was the first of many benefit concerts that he was to give for a wide variety of causes in the course of his artistic career.

While he noted in his diary that the concert realized a profit of forty-two riksdaler, he wrote to Ravnkilde in Rome a month later that it "brought in about 250 riksdaler. I had the pleasure of being able to inspire the audience with my violin sonata. I don't understand how peasants suddenly acquire the ability to appreciate cucumber salad."

In the letter to Ravnkilde, dated August 28, he mentioned again the hope of becoming the conductor of the theater orchestra in Oslo. He also expressed anger that neither Björnson nor Ibsen had answered his letter. At the same time he gave his friend information regarding his future plans: "In eight days I will leave Copenhagen to visit my parents in Bergen. But this trip will be brief because by the end of September I must be in Oslo, my future home . . . The theater affair in Oslo went very badly. Björnson has not even deigned to answer a letter I sent him from Leipzig in August. I also wrote Ibsen several months ago asking him to persuade Björnson, who is after all his friend, to at least expend a few words in my behalf so that I would not have to go any longer than necessary with my future hanging by a hair. But he has not answered me either. Peculiar people, these Norwegian poets. I say Norwegian, because intellectuals in other countries have advanced so far that they use means other than arrogance and inconsiderateness to assert their intellectual superiority . . ."

Just before Grieg left Copenhagen, Ibsen finally sent him an amiable and encouraging reply: "Your letter was fairly old by the time it reached me down here, but I wrote immediately to Björnson . . . Whatever the outcome may be, however, you have no right to say that your whole future is at stake. No, dear Grieg, your future is surely something more and better than this conductor position. It would be ungrateful of you to estimate the talents you have been given by such a modest standard . . . Please be assured that I have stated your case briefly but well and have told Björnson what you are. Now I assume that the theater conflict will soon be resolved, and then I shall also hope to learn of your appointment. Don't be angry with Björnson . . . Write to him once more . . . Tell him that he *must* let you have the position. Tell him that you have a right to it . . . And f all this doesn't work, you will show in your musical work how poorly they have handled the matter . . ."

The letter is postmarked Frascati, August 24, 1866; but as mentioned earlier, the orchestra conductor position had already been filled without Ibsen's or Grieg's knowledge.

In the letter to Ravnkilde, Grieg also mentioned his plans to become an organist: "In the course of the summer I have become a grandiose organist. Well, don't laugh! You should hear the *Fugue in G Minor.* Yesterday I was in Roskilde and received a recommendation from Matthison-Hansen, which hopefully will have the result that they cannot refuse me an organist's position—even if Björnson rises up on his hind legs." Fortunately for both Grieg and the musical life of Norway, his future was neither as a theater orchestral conductor nor as an organist.

At the beginning of September, then, Grieg went to Bergen to visit his parents, whom he had not seen for two years. He remained for five weeks. During the stay—on October 5—he gave a concert in which he played, among other things, his piano sonata and three of his *Humoresques.*

For the next decade Oslo was to be his home. Before leaving for Oslo he announced his imminent arrival by placing an advertisement in the September 26 issue of *Morgenbladet,* offering his services as a piano teacher starting in mid-October.

The Young Composer Makes Himself Known

**1. GRIEG'S FIRST CONCERT
IN OSLO GETS GOOD REVIEWS**

There is something grand, daring, and powerful in his compositions, and one would have to be very accustomed to hearing his music in order to thoroughly understand it. But even the untrained ear is struck by it, and it is clear to everyone that here we are dealing with truly genuine music, not merely with an artificial cling-clang that tickles the ear and that is all.

In Grieg's own playing there is both power and a marvelous confidence, and above all there is a lucidity that allows none of the music's beauty to escape the notice of anyone who listens attentively to his performance. (From *Aftenbladet*, October 16, 1866.)

In early October 1866 Grieg went to Oslo. Except for a few visits of varying duration to Bergen (especially during the summers) and abroad, this was to be his home until 1877.

First efforts in Oslo

Immediately after Grieg's arrival in Oslo, where he took lodging at Kirkegaten 13, he made preparations for a big introductory concert consisting largely of his own compositions. The concert was given in the Hotel du Nord's banquet room on October 15. Grieg himself played three of the *Humoresques* and the last three movements of the piano sonata, and he also accompanied the Bohemian violinist Wilhelmine Norman Neruda in the violin sonata. Nina, who had come to Oslo for the occasion, sang *Melodies of the Heart*, Opus 5, as well as some songs of Kjerulf and Nordraak.

Grieg was not completely unknown in Oslo, for the very positive review in *Aftenbladet* the following day[1] spoke among other things of "the fame that had preceded" him. This refers to a long article of no less than 6500 words—entitled "Of Norwegian Music and Some Compositions by Edvard Grieg"—which had been published in *Morgenbladet* a month earlier. The author of the article was Grieg's fellow composer and elder by six years, Otto Winter-Hjelm.

In this article Winter-Hjelm had supported Grieg with a fairly enthusiastic discussion of several of his compositions. About the *Humoresques,* for example, he wrote that "there [Grieg] begins to rattle his chains, which doesn't happen except when there is a wild outcry of an exasperated soul that realizes that it has been imprisoned by alien hands." The piano sonata was commended for its freshness, but of the violin sonata it was stated that "some of the motives lack interest." The violin sonata, he added, also "suffers from the influence of Gade, who may indeed be very helpful with respect to form but is all the more hurtful when it comes to the content." About the *Funeral March for Rikard Nordraak,* Winter-Hjelm wrote that at first he was irritated by some "frills" in the piece, but he had learned to like it because it gave evidence of a truly outstanding talent.

2. THE OSLO CONCERT— A GOOD PRELUDE

It is my enthusiasm for the national idea that leads me to reconcile myself to the idea of living as an artist in my homeland. Nonetheless, in dark moments my future is clouded because of the total isolation and lack of outside influences [that one feels] up here. Still—if I have no individuality, then nothing has been lost; if I do, I will retain it no matter what; that is my consolation . . .

The relationship with Nina's parents, as you know, has been *rotten,* so stay away from them—though I think it is better of late because of a very successful concert I gave up here with the help of Mrs. Norman and my fiancée, both of whom were in Norway recently.

You should have heard Mrs. Norman play the violin sonata! I tell you, I hardly knew whether I should keep on playing or just stop and listen to her! The concert included nothing but Norwegian music (!) and earned me about 150 spesiedalers (!). This good beginning has given me courage and confidence in the future. (Letter to Matthison-Hansen, December 12, 1866.)

3. OLE BULL'S IDEA OF A MUSIC ACADEMY IN OSLO

I now propose to my colleagues the Norwegian musicians, that we join hands in a common effort . . . by establishing . . . an academy for instruction in music. Perhaps [in this way] we can finally plant the flag of Norwegian music where it belongs, and . . . from the heights can reach down to the other struggling artists and help them up as well. (*Illustreret Nyhedsblad,* Oslo, October 19, 1862.)

4. GRIEG AND WINTER-HJELM MAKE OLE BULL'S IDEA A REALITY

The evident and steadily increasing growth of our music life, and the highly appropriate effort to put a Norwegian stamp on this area of our life as well, make it ever more clear that we can no longer depend solely on foreign lands and their conservatories. The need for such an institution is evident if one but considers the development in the future of a larger audience for music— something that we think is more likely than people in general suppose if only we work devotedly toward that goal.

We entertain the hope that the amateur

After the successful concert Grieg immediately sent a telegram home to Bergen, and various members of the family wrote back expressing their delight. His sister Elisabeth wrote: "If my expectations were not so small as Father's, neither were they so great that they were not surpassed." His sister Maren reported: "Father ran throughout the house with the telegram in order to deliver the good news to all and sundry." Grieg's mother, in her typical manner, moralized a bit: "Yes, that kind of thing is uplifting; it inculcates the attitude that is a necessary condition for the completion of the vocation that you have chosen. It is . . . important for you and for your spiritual life to be understood and respected by the outside world . . ."

In a December 12 letter to Mathison-Hansen, Grieg described his feelings at this time. He also discussed the concert and touched on the delicate relationship with his fiancée's family.[2]

The beginning of his future work was therefore promising. Moreover, he had made good progress with his teaching and had secured a number of pupils. A greater goal beckoned, however: the realization of a plan to establish a music academy in Oslo. This was an exciting idea that Ole Bull had publicly espoused four years earlier, though nothing came of it at that time.[3] In the autumn of 1864 Winter-Hjelm had started an elementary-level music school with the hope of expanding it to a more advanced level at a later time.

Now Grieg—a young, professionally trained musician with pedagogical interests—came on the scene, and Winter-Hjelm contacted him. They decided to establish a music academy together, and they explained their plans in a long article in *Morgenbladet* on December 12.[4] The day the article appeared Grieg sent a copy of it to Matthison-Hansen, adding proudly: "You will be pleased to see such a weighty article here in our little part of the world."

The academy began operations on January 14, 1867, with the following instructors: the pianists Miss Kjölstad and Mrs. Lindholm; the violinist G. Böhn; the cellist H. Nielsen; the singer E. Meyer; and the organist Chr. Cappelen. Winter-Hjelm and Grieg taught theory, score reading, and composition. Grieg also taught piano. The students paid one spesiedaler a month for a weekly lesson.

musicians who will be sent out from such an academy will become a healthy and powerful nucleus among the people of our land. The unique growth that such students experience in an academy through association with teachers and fellow students will unquestionably have a refreshing effect on their musical sensibility; for here they will develop their ideas and become accustomed to seeing things elucidated from various angles—which is how one is freed from one-sided tendencies and narrow-mindedness in one's understanding . . .

Although we want the national element to be respected, we of course do not intend any kind of narrow isolation. Our desire is only that the music student shall also become acquainted with that which is our

own, that which is closest to him and is perhaps best suited to work fruitfully on his imagination; and when all that is great and mighty in the music of other lands is paraded before him it will not overwhelm him to such an extent that his impression of our own music is erased—which, unfortunately, is often the case at present.

The academy will include a *music school,* . . . a higher *academy,* and a *college* for the training of teachers. . . Instruction will be offered in piano, ensemble playing, violin, cello, voice, choir, harmony, and composition as well as score reading, elementary music theory, and methodology. Lectures will also be given from time to time on the history of music. (*Morgenbladet,* December 12, 1866.)

There does not appear to have been much need for advanced musical training of this kind, however. The academy limped along for a while, but when Grieg went abroad in the autumn of 1869 it just disappeared from view and died a quiet death. The conservatory idea was not revived until 1883, when L. M. Lindeman started his school for organists. This school was the forerunner of the modern Oslo Music Conservatory.

Grieg found little time for composing during the years that he was attempting to get the music academy under way; a few songs and piano pieces were all that he was able to produce. In the letter to Matthison-Hansen he wrote: "I finished two pieces for piano and cello in Bergen, and now I am stuck in the middle of the first movement of a symphony."

This symphony is totally unknown, but the cello pieces have been found in a manuscript that has come down to us. Here they are presented as two movements in a suite. One of these pieces—"Intermezzo" (CW 118)—has been preserved in its entirety and published in volume 8 of *Edvard Grieg's Complete Works*. It is a fine little composition—not exactly typically "Griegian" in character, but not totally lacking in individuality either. Of the other piece—"Humoresque"—only one manuscript page has been preserved. This contains an E-major version of the beginning of the last movement of Grieg's second violin sonata (in G major), Opus 13.

On November 5 Grieg wrote to his Danish publisher, Emil Erslev, that he had composed a long ballad-like song—"Outward Bound"—that he thought was pretty good. One can well understand Grieg's opinion of this song, which was published by Erslev in 1867 as Opus 9, No. 4. The text, by Andreas Munch, portrays a young married couple who go to Italy, where the wife dies. Grieg applied this to his own sorrow over Nordraak's death, and he succeeded in creating a deeply poignant work. Except for a short and rather uninspired section in the middle, the song is representative of the best works that Grieg produced during his early years as a composer.

On December 12 he composed a song, "Little Lad" (CW 119), to a text by Kristofer Janson. This was his first setting of a text in *nynorsk*. This melodious little song, which Grieg never released, has a marked similarity to genuine Norwegian folk music.

Another manuscript—*Musical Bonbons for the Christmas Tree*—is dated December 24, 1866. It includes his two best-known waltzes for piano. The first of these was published one year later with a few insignificant changes in *Lyric Pieces I*, Opus 12, No. 2. The other came out as No. 7 in *Lyric Pieces II*, Opus 38, with a number of important improvements.

One activity that occupied Grieg greatly during the winter and spring of 1867 was conducting the Oslo orchestra, The Philharmonic Society. For two years the orchestra had been conducted by Winter-Hjelm, who now turned the baton over to Grieg for three concerts on February 2, March 23, and April 13. As the principal work at the opening concert Grieg selected Beethoven's Fifth Symphony. A review of this concert stated: "The conductor appeared to display considerable calmness and energy and on the whole acquitted himself with great distinction. We would only note that the tempos in the overture to *The Magic Flute* and in the first movement of the symphony certainly were slow."

At the second concert he gave, among other things, a successful performance of the three last movements of his own C-minor symphony. At the last concert the program included Winter-Hjelm's B-minor symphony and several works by Nordraak. In a letter to Emil Horneman he wrote: "*Sigurd Slembe* [by Rikard Nordraak] has caused a tremendous sensation up here. I have re-orchestrated it to make it sound more powerful. You should have heard our choir of students . . . I myself was so deeply moved as I was conducting that I trembled . . . You have no doubt been working like a dog with 'Euterpe' this winter. But no more than I have here with the Philharmonic. And in addition to that I have the Music Academy and private lessons. What has become of the composer under these circumstances is easy to say. But just wait, it will come."

Wedding and family complications

On December 12, 1866, Grieg described his future plans to Matthison-Hansen in beautiful and lyrical terms: "After a *fortunately concluded* winter I will come down to the green forests happier than I have ever been. Yes, down there under the summer sky I will meet my little sweetheart, will go with her into the church, and from there will head homeward with her toward Norway, the place where I will live and work. Oh, it is a wonderful thought, a strange mixture of joy and sadness . . ."

Grieg's financial situation had become sufficiently secure so that it was now reasonable for him to marry. The circumstances in connection with the wedding proved, however, to be tinged more with sadness than with joy. This was due primarily to the relationship of the young couple to their parents and their prospective parents-in-law. As mentioned earlier, the Hagerups didn't think much of Edvard. The engaged couple had never been able to be together in Nina's home, nor was Nina well regarded in the Grieg home in Bergen. Soon after the engagement, Edvard's sister Benedicte wrote to her brother telling him that he had acted foolishly and that he had better get ready for a fight: "You must also greet Nina from me; I will be fond of her, even though I do not expect to regard her in the bright light in which you portray her." Even after Nina's half-year stay with the family in Bergen in 1865–66 there was no visible improvement in the relationship, and the chilly tone continued.

The wedding was set, however, for the spring of 1867. Definite information about this was sent to Bergen, but strangely enough Edvard's parents were not invited. Edvard asked only that a few furnishings be sent to his new apartment at Övre Voldgate 2 in Oslo, where he and Nina were going to live. An undated letter from Edvard's mother contains a list of these furnishings: bed linens, mattresses, slippers, a silver-coated horn, a silver fork, an inkwell, a matchbox, a mahogany table, Hans Christian Andersen's works in twelve volumes, and many other things. An excerpt from this touching letter will be found in the Primary Materials.[5]

Such a letter should melt the coldest of hearts, but it didn't melt Edvard's at that time. As late as May 18 his father wrote: "Believe me, it pains me that I am not able to be present for your wedding . . . You certainly will not be

5. "SOCKS FOR THE BRIDEGROOM" FROM HIS MOTHER— WITH "PRAYERS AND WISHES KNITTED INTO THEM"

The gray socks are the sixth pair, the ones I didn't have time to finish knitting before you left last autumn. The striped ones, however, I have thought of as something for the bridegroom to wear unless you have something better. They are not fancy, but I don't know what your needs are in that respect. My prayers and wishes are knitted into them. The round table, too, is always covered with [my prayer and wishes]—if you have a healthy, uncorrupted eye with which to see them. I ask you to treat it with respect. The plate belonged originally to my dear parents. What better use could I make of it than to give it to my dear son as a small token of my constant love—however intermingled with pain that love may be. My beloved and honored son will surely, with God's help, reclaim and feel the joy of the need for that childlike reliance and secure love that have made me strong and happy so many a time. Nicolai Knudsen has repaired the foot of the table, which I had thought of sending you for your birthday to supplement your other furniture. But since the piano is being sent today, I am also sending the table together with my blessing on the important step that you are about to take. God bless us all. Your loving mother. You must get Hals's people to take care of the piano for you. (From Edvard's mother's letter to him before his wedding.)

6. WEDDING CELEBRATION WITH FRIENDS

And now thanks so much for the last time we were together, for that pleasant wedding day when I got married twice and ate the chocolate at the altar in all solemnity. We were actually together much too little, but I was so thoroughly tied up that it was impossible to break loose. (Letter to Matthison-Hansen, July 30, 1867.)

7. QUARRELING BETWEEN FATHER AND SON

It is now a long time since you have heard from me, and that should not surprise you as long as you continue to write letters like your last one. It appears that you don't know how to handle your good fortune, for you are becoming arrogant, and that—as you know good and well—is what I am least willing to tolerate. I have been wondering for a long time if I shouldn't rather write to Nina in the hope that she might understand me better; but it seems to me unnatural that she, who scarcely knows me, should be needed to establish the right relationship between a father and son who have always treated each other with love. When I think back, [what I remember is that] since you were grown you have always been to me a loving son, and inasmuch as I am absolutely sure that my attitude toward you has not changed in the slightest—except insofar as I perhaps understand your faults better than I once did—your behavior, as I have said, remains a mystery to me, unless it is to be ascribed to the aforementioned cause . . . When I encounter meanness, and that where I have the least reason to expect it, it upsets me so much that it absolutely destroys my health and renders me unfit for everything . . . And now good-bye for this time, my dear Edvard! Let me see a change of heart; show yourself to be a true Christian, conciliatory and loving.

Loving greetings from your parents and sisters to you and Nina. With all our hearts we wish happiness and every good thing to both of you. (Letter from Alexander Grieg to Edvard, July 24, 1867.)

surprised that I am staying away, since I have not heard either from you or from anyone a word to the effect that I or any of the family would be welcome at your and Nina's marriage. Still I would like to know on what day you are planning to get married, for I would like to follow you in my thoughts as you take this important step and send up my fervent prayers for your future happiness."

Nina's parents were not invited to the wedding either. The marriage ceremony took place on June 11 in Johanneskirken (St. John's Church) in Copenhagen, followed by a party with some friends.[6] It must certainly have been a strange experience for the bridal couple that none of their parents was present—not a very promising beginning for a marriage. A few days after the wedding the newlyweds went to Oslo.

The belated wedding greetings from Edvard's sisters in Bergen, which were mailed on June 15, were—to put it mildly—of mixed character. Elisabeth wrote to her brother that she would try to stop remembering Nina as a drill sergeant. Benedicte sent this greeting to the bride: "Let all of the old and unpleasant things be forgotten, and think only about the fact that we really are fond of you."

The wedding greetings did not lead Edvard to a reconciliation with his family, and some even angrier letters were sent to his childhood home. It was difficult to break out of the vicious circle. Edvard's arrogance was hard for his generally good-natured father to take; on one occasion he sent his son a conciliatory letter which clearly shows the tension that existed between them at this time.[7]

Several months went by before the breach was healed. In February, 1868, Alexander learned that he was going to become a grandfather, and from then on the tone between father and son became more cordial. When Nina and Edvard's daughter, Alexandra, was born on April 10, 1868, Edvard learned anew of the love that surrounded him in his childhood home.

One cannot avoid asking about the reason for the strained relations between Edvard and his parents in the middle of the 1860s. The real reason evidently was that Alexander and Gesine Grieg disapproved of Edvard's engagement to his first cousin, especially to a daughter of the fickle Herman and his extremely outspoken wife Adelina. This attitude caused Edvard to react very angrily, and one harsh word led to another. We must not conceal the fact, however, that it was Edvard who—in his letters to his parents—persisted in making the problem worse rather than better; but it is also clear from the correspondence that it was he who in the beginning of 1868 reflected upon the situation and contributed much to the restoration of the strong family ties that had existed previously.

The Lyric Pieces *take shape*

One project that Grieg was working on at this time was an album containing eight small piano pieces. It was published in Copenhagen in December, 1867, with the title *Small Lyric Pieces (Lyriske smaastykker)*, Opus 12—the first in a series of ten such albums that he was to produce during his lifetime. In these

8. BJÖRNSON WRITES WORDS FOR GRIEG'S "NATIONAL SONG"

But the very next day I met him, to my surprise, brimming with enthusiasm for his writing: "It's going great! It will be a song for all the young people of Norway. But there is something at the beginning that I still haven't been able to get right. A specific battle cry. I feel that the melody requires it, and I can't put my finger on it. But I'll get it." Then we parted. The next forenoon, as I sat up in my attic studio on Övre Voldgate [a street in Oslo] giving a piano lesson to a young lady, I heard the doorbell ringing as if it were going to ring right off the door. Then there was a racket as if a herd of wild animals had broken in and a roar, "Forward, forward! Hurrah! Now I've got it! Forward!" My pupil trembled like an aspen leaf. My wife, who was in the next room, was scared out of her wits. But then when the door flew open and Björnson stood there, happy and glowing like the sun, everybody joined in the excitement. Then we heard the beautiful poem, which was nearly completed. (Grieg in *Björnstjerne Björnson. Festskrift,* Copenhagen, 1902.)

9. GRIEG ON THE G-MAJOR SONATA

Today marks three weeks that I have been on vacation, and in these three weeks I have written a new violin sonata that I am looking forward to hearing when my countryman [Johan] Svendsen comes in the near future. He is the only one, in fact, to whom I dare to give it. The other violinists all hate me, apparently out of envy. They prefer, as [Hans Christian] Andersen says someplace, to expose one's weaknesses, and don't see the good qualities—or don't want to see them. It might appear as if I were fortunate in the new circumstances that surround me, but in reality that is not the case. Most people hate my compositions, even the musicians. For a few they are undoubtedly a closed book, and in such cases the reaction is of course pardonable; but there are others who understand them and to my face express only admiration, but have nothing good to say about them when they talk about them with others . . . (Letter to Matthison-Hansen, July 30, 1867.)

volumes Grieg enriched the piano literature of the Romantic period with well-written and easily understood music intended primarily for piano students and amateurs.

These "lyric pieces" — sixty-six in all — were primarily responsible for bringing Grieg into thousands of homes not only in Norway but around the world, and many of them have maintained their popularity to the present day. This is due to the melodic charm, the rhythmic and harmonic freshness, and the national flavor that absolutely abound in the best of these pieces.

In Opus 12, which also contains some pieces from the preceding years, Grieg set a very high standard for this type of music—i.e., music written primarily for didactic purposes. All of the compositions exhibit his fresh melodic vein, and the uncomplicated harmony is highly appropriate to the melodic material. Some of the melodies are quite folk-like in character. In two of them—"Folksong" (No. 5) and "Norwegian" (No. 6)—the national features are artfully stylized; the *springar* character of the latter sounds completely genuine. In the rest of the set, too—pieces exhibiting a natural, unforced musical language—Grieg rose far above the typical maudlin "salon" style that was so characteristic of current instructional music.

In his last lyric piece—"Remembrances," Opus 71, No. 7, written in 1901—Grieg harked back to the sentimental little "Arietta" that stood as the first piece in the Opus 12 collection of 1867. "Waltz"—the second piece in Opus 12—is definitely one of Grieg's most successful pieces in this genre. It is followed by the beautiful and chorale-like "Watchman's Song" with its mysterious middle part. The graceful "Fairy Dance" (No. 4) and "Album Leaf" (No. 7) reflect typically Romantic moods and are both of high quality. "National Song" (No. 8) brings the volume to a rousing conclusion.

The melody of "National Song" appealed strongly to Björnstjerne Björnson. Indeed, at Christmas, 1868, according to Grieg, Björnson stated that he "liked it so well that he wanted to write a text for it." Grieg added, "That made me happy. Then I said to myself: he'll never get around to it." Grieg's vivid account of what actually happened is quoted in the Primary Materials.[8] Grieg used Björnson's text when, some time later, he transcribed the piano piece as a song for male chorus (CW 133, No. 17).

The Violin Sonata No. 2 in G Major

The exciting feelings associated with his engagement had left their mark on Grieg's first violin sonata. Now, in the space of just three summer weeks in Oslo, he created his second violin sonata "in the euphoria of my honeymoon." In a letter to Matthison-Hansen he described the rather unpleasant outward circumstances at this time, with obstinate musicians, animosity, and outright lies.[9] But in the midst of this situation—not to mention the problems in the relationship with his parents in Bergen—he nonetheless wrote one of the cheeriest pieces of his entire career: the *Violin Sonata No. 2 in G Major*, Opus 13. It sparkles with talent and is Grieg's first fully mature work in one of the larger musical forms.

The sonata, which is dedicated to Johan Svendsen, was performed for the

10. GRIEG ON THE
NATIONAL ELEMENT

The music of every country starts with folk songs which in time make their way into the smaller forms and thereby into the larger, fuller, more combined [forms] . . . (From an article about Halfdan Kjerulf in *Illustreret Tidende,* Copenhagen, 1867–68.)

first time at an "Edvard Grieg Music Evening" on November 16, 1867. Grieg himself was at the piano; the violin part was played by Gudbrand Böhn, a colleague at the Music Academy. The piece was immediately received with great enthusiasm, and it has had a secure place in the standard repertoire of Norwegian violinists ever since.

The G-major sonata can certainly be called Grieg's "national" sonata. In no other piece of chamber music did he make use of elements drawn from Norwegian folk music to the extent that he did in this work. That is not to say that he borrowed directly; but the rhythmic and melodic features of Norwegian folk music inspired his creative consciousness and thus permeate the entire composition. This is especially true of the outer movements with their *springar* character. In the middle movement the folk element is much less prominent, but toward the end of the movement there is a short section that faintly suggests the sound of a Hardanger fiddle.

There is reason to believe that in this sonata, more than in any other cyclic work, Grieg wanted to demonstrate that elements drawn from folk music could be used to good advantage within the confines of classical sonata form.[10] He made his point convincingly. The music flows naturally and freely and does not sound at all episodic.

The sonata marks an important step forward in Grieg's artistic development. It shows the same great spontaneity in its wealth of musical ideas as the first violin sonata, but its structural development is firmer and more assured; there is not a superfluous measure.

The development section in the first movement is free of the rhythmic "tramping" that to some extent characterizes the first sonata. The compositional technique throughout is the same, however, with extensive use of sequences.

The handling of the violin part is brilliant; one might almost think that Grieg himself was a violinist. There are, as a matter of fact, more difficult passages for the pianist than for the violinist, but the sonata is by no means a virtuoso piece.

The first movement, Lento doloroso–Allegro vivace, is a model of motivic-thematic composition. The composer demonstrates a remarkable ability to extract the melodic material from a seminal motive, namely the Grieg formula in both its major and its minor forms. This formula occurs frequently and is integrated into a variety of melodic contexts, but Grieg used it so flexibly that one scarcely takes notice of it.

This is also the only sonata movement that Grieg ever wrote which starts with a long introduction. It begins in G minor, the parallel minor key, and its somber character seems to foreshadow a gloomy, almost tragic atmosphere. But what comes instead—quite unexpectedly—is a flamboyantly vigorous and lively allegro in G major whose principal theme incorporates characteristic *springar* rhythms. This is followed in typical Griegian fashion by a secondary theme in the mediant key (B minor). This section contrasts sharply with the preceding one, but is nonetheless completely built on the original motivic material. The closing theme is in the dominant key (D major), and here the Grieg formula is dramatized by means of steadily increasing dynamic effects. The key changes among these three sections correspond exactly with those in the first movement of the F-major sonata. The key changes in the recapitulations in the two sonatas are also parallel.

A careful study of the exposition of this movement shows how completely Grieg had mastered the problems inherent in sonata form. It is also noteworthy that the principal theme section (measures 26–86) in and of itself exhibits sonata form in miniature: the exposition occurs in measures 26–45, the development in 46–67, the recapitulation in 68–80, and the coda in 81–86.

The exposition is quite extensive, and it is balanced by a short development in four sections in which motives from the principal theme and the secondary theme are interwoven. This music contains a number of interesting features, harmonically and otherwise. We shall concentrate, however, on the most characteristic feature of this movement, namely the unifying effect that results from the use of the Grieg formula in its two forms (marked G1 and G2 in the examples that follow). It is difficult to determine with certainty whether and to what extent Grieg consciously used this technique. There surely is reason to believe that for the most part he used it intuitively, as is often the case with the great masters; but it was an intuitive application that could only have been achieved on the basis of a solid technical mastery of the musical elements. When one gathers up the motivic threads in this movement, one gets a better understanding of the composer's creative process because the musical ideas behind the work stand out more clearly. In other words, we catch a glimpse of the composer at work.

We give here the first eleven measures of the introduction to the first movement, the whole of which is permeated by the Grieg formula in various forms. The several versions of this formula are identified as follows: G1 = the major form, G2 = the minor form, G1v = a variation of the major form, G2v = a variation of the minor form, and G2o = inverted minor form. The chord in measure 2 is a combination of the subdominant with an added sixth and the dominant:

The next example consists of the first seventeen measures of the exposition of the first movement. Note the continued prominence of the Grieg formula. The pedal-point effect on the tonic in the first system is characteristic. In the second system the pedal point is replaced by sustained notes alternating between D and A. One is struck by the similarity of the violin part to Hardanger-fiddle music:

The opening measures of the elegiac secondary theme of the first movement are based on a variation of the Grieg formula in its major form:

The second part of the secondary theme is based on a variation of the minor form of the formula:

The beginning of the closing theme once again employs the modified major form of the formula:

In the second part of the closing section Grieg returns to the secondary theme, but now in a strident major form that has little in common with the original elegiac character:

The tender second movement, *Allegretto tranquillo,* is for the most part lyrical in character. It forms a striking contrast to the first movement which, though highly varied, is basically dramatic. Its form is three-part: *ABA,* with the key signature changing from E minor to E major and then back to E minor.

The *A* theme is fascinating in its utter simplicity. Especially striking is a constant shifting between E minor and G major that gives a certain ambiguity to one's sense of the key that one is hearing. The theme is built entirely on the motive announced in the first measure, a motive that is a transformed version of the Grieg formula. In the course of the movement this theme appears in eight different forms.

The beginning of the *A* Theme in the second movement

A has two sub-sections based on the same motivic material. The two sections employ this material in essentially different ways, however. In the

second section the composer develops the principal theme melodically, rhythmically, and dynamically in a series of figurations fraught with tension. Thus it
is this part that stands out as the real contrast to *B*:

B is a lyric pearl of exquisite quality:

The opening measures are similar in some ways to the corresponding measures
in the second movement of the third violin sonata, which was written some
twenty years later.

B is followed by an almost exact repetition of *A*. In the subsequent coda
there are a few measures containing an imitation of the Hardanger fiddle. (We
note, however, that the performer is here required to play at times in the
second position, which is quite out of character with the Hardanger-fiddle
tradition.)

The third movement, Allegro animato, takes us back to the home key of G
major. The themes are as follows:

Principal theme:

Secondary theme:

The form of this movement is somewhat puzzling. At first glance the
movement appears to have an expanded two-part form: *AA'*. In reality it is a
sonata rondo, i.e., a piece in which elements of both sonata form and rondo are
combined in a mixed form. The pattern in this movement is: exposition —
contrasting section — recapitulation — coda. (If one analyzes the movement
in terms of the *AA'* pattern, *A* consists of the exposition and the contrasting
section, *A'* of the recapitulation and the coda.)

The exciting thing about the exposition is that it constitutes a complete
miniature sonata-form movement in itself with a principal theme, development, and recapitulation. It replicates in many ways the pattern that we found
in the presentation of the principal theme of the first movement, but this time
the various sections are much longer. (The introduction comprises measures
1–4, the exposition measures 5–59, the development measures 60–89, and the
recapitulation measures 90–108.)

Instead of the usual development after the exposition, there is a contrasting
section in E-flat major. The theme in this section seems quite different from
the rest of the melodic material, and it has an ethereal beauty that stands in
sharp contrast to the wonderful blending of *springar-*, waltz-, and mazurka-
like themes in the exposition. The bright sound of E-flat major is soon
obscured as the music turns toward the darker minor regions (B-flat minor,
E-flat minor, and A-flat minor), but toward the end a bridge is built to the

recapitulation by a series of passages in major keys. We give here the beginning of the contrasting section at the point where the violin enters:

The recapitulation is a somewhat modified version of the exposition. Contrary to the usual practice, Grieg here allowed the secondary theme to keep the same key as in the exposition, starting once again in B minor.

The coda brings the movement—and therewith the entire sonata—to a brilliant conclusion. Here the theme of the contrasting section appears—most surprisingly—in fortissimo in G major and with a codetta in the form of a small presto section. This coda crowns the piece magnificently. It is as if Grieg gathered up everything that preceded it in a concluding apotheosis. In later works as well—such as the *A-minor Concerto,* the *String Quartet in G Minor,* and the *Violin Sonata in C Minor*—Grieg brought the concluding movement to a similarly grand culmination.

The Grieg formula, which permeates the first movement, is also represented in the last movement, albeit more indirectly. Indeed, it is an interesting feature of this sonata that there is a certain similarity in the melodic contour of the various themes in all three movements. Remarkably enough, even the secondary theme in the finale shares this similarity:

Principal theme, first movement:

B theme, second movement:

Principal theme, third movement:

Secondary theme, third movement*:

(*This theme is in E-flat major in the original. For the sake of comparison it is here transposed to B-flat major.) Thus does Grieg demonstrate his considerable ability to create unity and wholeness with the help of thematic ideas that do not appear to belong together, but which in reality have sprung from the same root.

We have scarcely touched on the harmony in this analysis, though in this respect the sonata bears further witness to Grieg's artistic growth. If one compares it with the F-major sonata, for example, it is clear that Grieg here made more economical use of his harmonic resources and depended more heavily on smooth transitions. The characteristic Griegian boldness is still indisputably present, but now it is fully integrated into the whole.

It has been claimed that Grieg never mastered the large classical forms. We

11. DIFFICULT WORKING CONDITIONS

I am so busy with all kinds of nonsense that I wish the day had forty-eight hours, or at least that the twenty-four it has could all be used for work . . .

Lately I have, as the tailors say, prepared myself in my profession to such an extent that I now perform as a conductor par excellence. . . It doesn't earn me a penny—don't think for a minute that it does—but I must have something like that to keep my sanity; otherwise I spend the day giving lessons so that my wife and I won't croak up here. For it is as Ibsen says in *Peer Gynt:* each of us here "is sufficient unto himself." Ergo, each must provide for himself. I'm not composing at all—I have neither time nor inclination. I have become totally unmusical. (Letter to G. Matthison-Hansen, December 23, 1867.)

12. OSLO'S PROVINCIALISM

The public's attitude at that time was so primitive, and their understanding of artistic interpretation was far too barbarous for them to be able to appreciate performances that gave major emphasis to the life of the spirit. It got to the point where we only made music at home or in our own circle of friends. But in Copenhagen, where I gave concerts almost every year, my wife became a favorite among both musicians and music lovers. (Letter to Finck, July 17, 1900.)

totally disagree with such a view. Not least, the G-major sonata is resounding proof of Grieg's sense for consistent structure, balance, contrast, and unity—essential conditions for viable music within the confines of any musical form.

Opposition in the capital city

Grieg had many problems to contend with in Oslo after his marriage. For one thing, he was compelled to work very hard just to make ends meet.[11] He had to give countless lessons for a small fee, and orchestra rehearsals with contentious and amateurish musicians were like a yoke around his neck. He also found little sympathy for his ideas in what he considered an obdurate press and an underdeveloped public.[12] The curiosity he had awakened in the beginning had been replaced by mistrustful ill will. People were slow to accept this young outsider from Bergen who, temperamental and conceited as he was, thought to reform the music life of Oslo.

It is no wonder that Grieg felt frustrated in such a restricted milieu. In the years to come it was not Oslo but Copenhagen that was to become his artistic and spiritual home.

The heaviest burden resulted from his inner struggle. The circumstances in which he was working gave him little opportunity to concentrate on what he desired most of all: to compose. This led to an almost total loss of the inspiration to create music of high quality. Nothing could be more depressing and tragic for a sensitive artistic spirit.

This enervating struggle robbed him of his creative power. The compositions from the following three years in Oslo bear the mark of stagnant routine, with the happy exception of a few short songs and the folk-music arrangements of Opus 17. Characteristically enough, however, it was when he fled the confinement of Oslo and again encountered Danish friendship and warmth in the summer of 1868 that he recovered his creative powers. For in that summer he opened up, as it were, and in a few hectic weeks expressed his genius in one of the most marvelous inspirations in Norwegian music: the *Piano Concerto in A Minor,* Opus 16.

In the autumn of 1867, however, he threw himself into his duties with fresh determination, writing optimistically to Matthison-Hansen on October 8: "Things are getting better for us up here now. Next month I have a concert, nothing but my own compositions, Svendsen on Saturday also doing just his own compositions; already in my mind's eye I see my honorable countrymen gaping like cattle at painted red doors. But let them do what they will for now; with several of us working together the recognition will eventually come."

His own concert was given on November 16. He played the G-major violin sonata with the violinist Gudbrand Böhn. Three new compositions were also presented: a rousing and melodious "Gavotte" for violin and piano, and two short and unimportant pieces for male chorus—"Evening Mood" (CW 121) and "The Bear-Hunter" (CW 120). He made use of the gavotte five years later in the incidental music to *Sigurd Jorsalfar,* Opus 22 (No. 3); here, however, it

13. LONGING TO GET AWAY

I am sitting up here in a remote corner of the world and I feel a need to live and make my contribution to art. If you have an organist position for me I will come immediately to Denmark and will gladly write you a song every week. When I am willing to leave Norway on such conditions you can judge for yourself what circumstances are like up here. I will soon say as Björnson says in *De Nygifte* [The Newlyweds]: "Something within me is dying"—if I don't get away. Well, this summer I shall hope to greet you in beautiful Denmark. Then I am going to compose and forget all this lethargy and pettiness. That Norway has no musicians in the true sense of the word is not due to the fact that none is born here; it is because they are stifled in their home country before they have had a chance to develop, and because as a rule material want prevents them from freeing themselves. A sad truth. But just as I clearly understand this state of affairs, so also I am determined not to take it lying down. If I can get a stipend I am going to go to Leipzig with the hope of being able to live there. (Letter to Emil Erslev, December 29, 1867.)

was transformed into the march "At the Matching Game," which has understandably become very popular.

It was at this time that Grieg wrote his first song to a text by Björnstjerne Björnson: "The Fair-haired Maid" (CW 100, No. 1). Both the poem and the setting are love lyrics and are somewhat grandiloquent in character. The song was not published until after Grieg's death.

The Philharmonic Society had again engaged Grieg as conductor for the winter; soon thereafter, however, the Society disbanded. Grieg, therefore, took the opportunity to establish an orchestra himself, and on October 31 he invited the public to four of his own subscription concerts. The announcement indicated that the concerts would include symphonies by Mendelssohn and Schubert, Beethoven's *"Emperor" Concerto,* and Gade's oratorio *Korsfarerne* [The Crusaders].

At the first concert on December 12 the program included Mozart's *Symphony No. 40* and a new arrangement for large wind ensemble of Grieg's *Funeral March for Rikard Nordraak.* At the end of this month, however, in two letters to Denmark he expressed his dejection and his longing to get away.[13]

A few days later he got an encouraging letter from Johan Svendsen, who was in Leipzig. In this letter dated January 1, 1868, Svendsen wrote in part: "First, thanks for all the demonstrations of true and sincere friendship that you showed me during my stay at home . . . It would be splendid—I dare to think, for both of us—if we could soon arrange to work together. We are basically striving for the same goal, and if our inclinations and views on some things are not the same, I nonetheless know that our personal friendship—united with the artistic universal humanity that more or less distinguishes all true artists—is more than adequate to hold us together."

Svendsen's gratitude probably had to do especially with Grieg's effusive review of his concert in Oslo on October 12, at which time his *Symphony in D Major* had its premiere performance. As far as we know, this was the first critical review of a concert that Grieg ever wrote; it is given in part in the Primary Materials.[14]

Grieg's only activity as a composer in the spring of 1868 was to put together a cantata for male chorus and wind instruments (CW 123) for the unveiling of a statue of W. F. K. Christie in Bergen on May 17, Norway's Independence Day. Christie was one of the signers of the Norwegian Declaration of Independence and also a cousin of Nina and Edvard's grandfather, Edvard Hagerup. Grieg regarded the cantata as nothing more than occasional music, and it has never aroused much interest.

At the same time he was struggling once again with orchestra problems. On March 18 he wrote to Matthison-Hansen regarding the rehearsals of two of the latter's works: ". . . on this matter I need only to note that the orchestra is awful. They all boom and crash as if their lives depended on it . . . I warned the orchestra that we were going to keep on practicing until they got it right. That caused a bit of an uproar. The result was that yesterday it went exceptionally well."

Grieg's activity as a conductor now earned him a bit of appreciation. After the fourth subscription concert *Aftenbladet* wrote in its issue of April 8 that, in

14. GRIEG REVIEWS
SVENDSEN'S CONCERT

Today Norwegian art has celebrated one of its triumphs. For triumph it must be called when a musically unenlightened audience—an audience of only a few hundred people—is so carried away by that which is absolutely new and great that it forgets its arch-enemy, the symphony—"that artificial music," as it is called—and breaks out in enthusiastic applause.

The concert opened with [Johan] Svendsen's *Symphony in D major,* a work that provides insight into an individuality that is so great that it would be easier to write books about it rather than pages. What first and foremost is so refreshing in this symphony . . . is the perfect balance between the [musical] ideas and the technical [competence with which they are developed] . . .

That an artist such as Svendsen, after such meager financial rewards, will pack his bags and leave as quickly as possible is only to be expected . . . We have only a few national talents—enough, however, that through their mutual effort a true artistic life might be established.(*Aftenbladet,* October 15, 1867.)

15. GRIEG NEEDS PEACE
AND QUIET FOR COMPOSING

I pounded on the piano like a madman in order to forget everything around me, for only then can I get in the right mood. But then fate willed that I should hear the next-door neighbors come home—and all I need say about them is that they are Scandinavians. The mere thought of being criticized while I am working completely destroys my ideas, and I can just as well quit immediately . . . (Grieg in a letter to his parents from Rome, February 17, 1870.)

* * *

To have the ability to withdraw into oneself and forget *everything* around one when one is creating—that, I think, is the only requirement for being able to bring forth something beautiful. The whole thing is—a mystery. (Grieg in a letter to Agathe Backer Gröndahl, November 17, 1905.)

spite of the meager monetary reward, Grieg could be assured that "the interest of our musical public in these concerts is not diminished but rather has been steadily growing."

Two days later Nina and Edvard had another reason to rejoice: they became parents of a daughter. Alexandra, as she was named, was to be their only child.

The happy father now found inspiration to write a song that is one of his true pearls: the simple and tender "Margaret's Cradle Song" from *The Pretenders,* his first attempt to set a text by his great contemporary, Henrik Ibsen. It was published in Copenhagen in December as Opus 15, No. 1. The fourth song in the same opus—"A Mother's Grief," to a text by Christian Richardt—was also written in 1868. It is a beautiful contrast to the cradle song, deeply tragic in character.

The Piano Concerto in A Minor

During the years in Oslo the best—and not infrequently the only—time available to Grieg for composing was during his holidays. In June of 1868 he went to Denmark with Nina and Alexandra in order to begin the largest task he had undertaken to date: a work for piano and orchestra. Nina and the child stayed with Nina's parents in Copenhagen while Edvard himself settled down at Sölleröd, a picturesque spot in the heart of Zealand. Two of his friends, Emil Horneman and Edmund Neupert, were with him there. Neupert was at that time Norway's—indeed, Scandinavia's—leading pianist. Benjamin Feddersen had rented a small summer house with a piano for Grieg in Sölleröd. Here he was able to work entirely undisturbed by the crying baby and everyday chores. Grieg himself reported how dependent he was on complete quiet whenever he was composing. A few trenchant statements to this effect are quoted in the Primary Materials.[15]

In periods of profound concentration the work progressed on a wave of inspired enthusiasm. Not least stimulating was Neupert's constructive criticism, by precept and example, as the work gradually took shape. Thus it was only natural that the concerto should be dedicated to him.

In a little-noticed letter to Ravnkilde, Grieg wrote from Oslo on November 2: "The heat was unbearable, but even so I look back with pleasure on this period. I undoubtedly felt rather lethargic owing to the temperature, but I also felt that now was the time to get on with it. The result is that I have written a concerto for piano and orchestra which I believe contains a number of good things. If only I could find time now during the autumn evenings to orchestrate the first movement. But . . . the time! I am even being robbed of my evenings. Neupert, in fact, will be playing it in Copenhagen at Musikerforeningen [The Musicians' Society] just before Christmas." It is clear from this statement that—contrary to what has often been maintained in the past—the work was not completed at Sölleröd. What Grieg composed there was the piano part and an outline of the orchestral score. The work was given its final form in fits and starts during the following winter in Oslo.

16. FEDDERSEN WRITES ABOUT THE CONCERTO

The Casino's large auditorium was about as full as at the Musikforeningen's concerts. Gade, Hartmann, Rubinstein, Winding, Neruda, and the chamber musician Hansen (the composer) had seats together in a reserved section. The queen was also there together with a large company of ladies and gentlemen, as well as the crown prince and his younger brothers and sisters . . .

Your composition was listened to with considerable interest. While my ears attended to your sounds I kept my eyes steadily on the loge where the notables were sitting; I observed and understood each expression, each motion, and I can assure you that Gade, Hartmann, Rubinstein, and Winding were filled with joy and admiration for your work. At the very beginning Gade said something to Rubinstein, who was listening with such rapt attention that he only acknowledged Gade's remark by nodding his head without looking at him. When Neupert came for the first time to the rest in the first section—the place where the bassoons come in—Rubinstein spontaneously clasped his hands together; and throughout, wherever it was appropriate to clap, he and Gade, Hartmann, and Winding joined in the general thunderous chorus of applause. How I regretted that you yourself did not have the joy and pleasure of hearing this unusual work. Believe me, it will contribute greatly to your being recognized as one of the most brilliant composers of our time. You can believe me when I tell you that the applause was thunderous! But Neupert also did his job exceptionally well, and you owe him sincere thanks for the interest and the love with which he approached the playing of the piano part. Paulli also conducted the rehearsals with great care, and Rubinstein's piano contributed a bit as well with its incomparably rich and sonorous tone. (Feddersen's letter to Grieg, April 4, 1869.)

Grieg failed to complete the score in time for Neupert to premiere the work shortly after Christmas, as had been planned. Thus the *A-minor Concerto* was not launched until April 3, 1869, with Neupert as soloist and Holger Simon Paulli, chief conductor at The Royal Theater, wielding the baton.

The performance, which took place in the large Casino concert hall, proved to be a notable event in the Copenhagen concert season. No less a person than Queen Louise, who had a great interest in music, added luster to the occasion. Denmark's leading musical personalities were there as well, notably Hartmann and Gade. Also in the audience was the world-famous Russian virtuoso pianist, Anton Rubinstein, who was on a concert tour in Denmark. He had generously placed his own grand piano, which he brought with him, at Neupert's disposal for the occasion.

The scene was set for a sensational event. Rumors from the rehearsals had created an air of tremendous expectation, and this proved fully justified. Contrary to usual practice, the soloist had participated in no fewer than four rehearsals with the orchestra, and together they gave a sparkling performance. The audience was wildly enthusiastic, and a storm of applause interrupted the performance on several occasions. This occurred not only between movements but also after the superb cadenza in the first movement.

Sad to say, Neupert was not able to share his triumph with the composer. Grieg, who was in Oslo at the time, felt that he could not take time off from his duties with the orchestra there.

He was also unable to attend the second performance (the first in Norway) a few months later. On August 7 Neupert performed the *A-minor Concerto* in Oslo, with Johan Hennum conducting the Oslo Theater Orchestra. Unfortunately, Grieg had long since left for Bergen to spend the summer months with his family at "Landaas." On that occasion Neupert shared the platform with one of their mutual friends, Julius Steenberg, whose repertoire included Grieg's song "Thanks," Opus 10, No. 1. Neupert also played Rubinstein's Piano Concerto in G Major.

This summer concert was poorly attended, but according to the August 9 issue of *Aftenbladet* the audience was in high spirits, particularly after hearing "Grieg's new, original, and inspired composition." Strangely enough, this was the only account of the *A-minor Concerto* appearing in the Oslo press after its first performance there. Clearly, music did not enjoy a very big following in those days.

After the world premiere in Copenhagen, however, Grieg received a number of overwhelmingly enthusiastic letters. Matthison-Hansen called the work "the most splendid piece" he had ever heard, while Horneman spoke of his friend's "magnificent and inspired concerto." Feddersen wrote two lengthy letters, one immediately after the dress rehearsal and another after the actual concert.[16] For Grieg, however, it must have been most interesting to hear Neupert's delightful first-hand account.[17]

Earlier Grieg himself, in a letter to Ravnkilde, had spoken very cautiously about the qualities of the work. This might suggest that at the time he did not fully realize how great a work of genius he was creating. But the supremely favorable reaction to the first performance was of tremendous importance to

17. NEUPERT ON THE PREMIERE PERFORMANCE

On Saturday your divine concerto re-
sounded through the Casino's large auditorium. The triumph that I achieved was
really tremendous. Already at the conclusion of the cadenza in the first part the audience broke out in a true storm [of
applause]. The three dangerous critics—
Gade, Rubinstein, and Hartmann—sat up
in the loge and applauded with all their
might.

I am supposed to greet you from
Rubinstein and tell you that he is really surprised to have heard such a brilliant composition; he looks forward to making your
acquaintance. He spoke very warmly about
my piano playing. I had at least two curtain
calls and at the end I got a big fanfare from
the orchestra.

You should have seen Emil [Horneman]
and [Matthison-]Hansen after the concert;
they were almost ready to eat me up for joy
because everything had gone so splendidly.
Gade thought very well of the first and second movements, less about the third. He
spoke with genuine warmth, however. Old
Hartmann was ecstatic. Feddersen, who sat
in the balcony, cried the whole evening . . .
(Neupert's letter to Grieg, April 6, 1869.)

him: the *A-minor Concerto,* Opus 16, was to become his gateway to international fame. From this time on he was to be considered among the foremost
composers of his age.

Grieg's concerto has achieved enormous popularity. Most pianists include
it in their standard repertoire. making it one of the most frequently-per-
formed works in its genre. It has stood up extremely well to the passing of
time, and it exercises just as strong a hold on audiences today as it did when it
was first played more than a century ago. It is not easy to explain why this is
so, but it certainly is not due to any attempt to create superficial effects. Grieg,
in fact, never played to the gallery. The music that fades and dies is precisely
the kind that caters to people's taste for the superficial, the mediocre stereo-
type. Hundreds of competent composers—including some of Grieg's contemporaries—have been consigned to oblivion precisely because they sought
success by currying favor with the popular taste of their age.

Not so Grieg. Through the years the *A-minor Concerto* has lived a life of its
own by virtue of its enduring fine qualities. It possesses an unusually many-
faceted charm, fascinating melodies, varied rhythms, finely polished harmony,
instrumentation that is at times brilliant, and an effective solo part that
combines elegant virtuosity with lyric beauty. When people speak of "the
A-minor Concerto" it is always Grieg's concerto they have in mind, just as
"the B-flat-minor Concerto" is forever associated with the name of
Tchaikovsky.

Grieg undoubtedly took as his model Schumann's piano concerto, which
had made an "indelible impression" when he heard Clara Schumann play it
in Leipzig in 1858. One must not overemphasize Grieg's dependence on
Schumann, however, for this concerto stands as an entirely independent
work, imbued with unique vitality, not least in its melodic lines. These two

*Edmund Neupert, renowned Norwegian pia-
nist who played the A-minor Concerto at its
world premiere performance in Copenhagen in
1869. (Photo collection of Universitetsbiblioteket
in Oslo)*

concertos can in a way be regarded as a pair of musical siblings: the family likeness is obvious though they are very different. Schumann's concerto may perhaps be said to possess a larger measure of gracious charm, whereas Grieg's is in part marked by boyish exuberance. Yet they both possess power and ardent lyricism in full measure. And while each in its own way had broken away from its precursors, the Schumann concerto remained firmly anchored in the German romantic tradition. Grieg's concerto also reveals the strong influence of this heritage, but in addition it possesses something quite new: a touch of the Norwegian national temperament combined with a special folkloristic character.

The *A-minor Concerto* is happy music, permeated by sheer delight. Strangely enough, Grieg expresses his joy in a minor key. In the opening bars he literally hurls his "musical signature" at the listener as the Grieg formula— from the octave to the seventh and the fifth—is announced in the piano in cascades of sound. (See the facsimile of p. 1 of the original score on p. 120.)

The principal theme, introduced by the clarinet, is not exactly gay, but with its springy, pointed rhythms it contains an undercurrent of good-natured and infectious humor. After four measures a typical Grieg feature emerges: bold use of augmented fourths. Here is the principal theme in the piano version:

After the conclusion of this section comes a transitional passage containing lively *halling* rhythms. It contrasts markedly with what had preceded it, and the tempo is somewhat accelerated:

The magnificent secondary theme (in C major) shows Grieg's superb melodic skill. This theme is today always presented by the cellos; but both the original manuscript and the first printed editions assigned it to the trumpet, in typically Lisztian fashion. Not until an 1882 edition do we find it assigned to the cellos.

After four measures the secondary theme is taken over by the piano soloist, who introduces a number of embellishments:

Like Schumann, Grieg dealt more freely with the concerto form than did the Viennese classical masters. Neither of them, for example, included any separate orchestral exposition. Both the principal and secondary subjects are divided between orchestra and soloist.

In the development Grieg starts boldly enough with motives from the piano's opening fanfare, but now in C major and with full orchestra. In its continuation, for the first and only time, he strikes more plaintive notes as he develops motives from the principal theme in various keys. This touch of melancholy is only for the moment, however. Immediately before the recapitulation, fragments of the opening fanfare occur in the piano part in an interplay with the orchestra playing the beginning of the principal theme as they unite in a thunderous fortissimo in the dominant key.

The development is concise and concentrated. The most typical thing about it is that, through all the compositional subtleties, there is a melodic stream of the same high quality as in the exposition.

In the recapitulation both the opening cascade in the piano part and the orchestral statement of the principal theme are omitted. Otherwise this section proceeds as in the exposition, apart from certain variations in key and a few minor changes in the orchestration. At the end of the recapitulation—before the start of the solo cadenza—Grieg inserts an extra touch. According to tradition one would expect at this point a tonic six-four chord as a means of heightening the anticipation. This is not what happens. What comes instead is a subdominant sixth chord (D minor with F in the bass), and—quite unexpectedly—the soloist starts the cadenza on this chord. The masterfully written cadenza unites technical brilliance at the highest level with rich musical content, in the form of a compressed adaptation of the essence of the principal theme. It concludes in a most unusual way: in pianissimo it slips almost imperceptibly into the further continuation of the principal theme in the orchestra.

A tremendous tension is created in the coda, which culminates in a rhythmically varied version of the opening fanfare in the piano undergirded by pithy tutti chords. Thus the movement ends with the same musical exclamation with which it began.

The second movement, Adagio, contains some of the loveliest music Grieg ever wrote. It is as if he, in an unbroken burst of inspiration, captured something of eternity in temporal vessels. The mood is that of a nocturne—not a Mediterranean nocturne, but the gentle shimmering light of a Scandinavian midsummer night.

To give a technical musical analysis of a poetic revelation such as this may seem something of a sacrilege. Its individuality lies to some extent in the

Grieg at the time he composed the Piano Concerto in A minor. (Photo collection of Det Kongelige Bibliotek, Copenhagen)

melodic waves that flow into and out of one another, surrounded as they are by a rich harmonic fantasy in which Grieg waves his magic wand in such a way that functionality, chromaticism with enharmonic changes, and hints of modality all unite in a characteristically Griegian synthesis.

The movement starts in the remote key of D-flat major, but moves freely through several keys where the distinction between major and minor seems almost to be a matter of no importance.

The framework is an utterly simple three-part form (*ABA'*). Notwithstanding its brevity it contains a wealth of subtle details. The entire first part is purely orchestral. Here the melodic material is assigned to muted strings, with brief contributions by the woodwinds and horns. Here is the *A* subject:

Not until *B,* which begins in the tonic, does the piano come in with some finely woven filigree. It reminds one in some ways of Chopin's nocturnes, but it is nonetheless unmistakably Grieg. Here the orchestra plays only a supporting role, partly with motivic material from *A,* after which occur the most suspenseful modulations in the movement. The beginning of the *B* section is given below:

In the recapitulation (*A'*) the piano takes over the thematic material, but now in fortissimo in contrast to the orchestra's pianissimo in the first part. The piano part consists of a series of full chords. From time to time the melody is reinforced by the woodwinds and a few strings.

The soft nocturnal mood returns toward the end of the movement. Over the fading sounds of the strings in D-flat major we now hear a mysterious dialogue between the piano and solo horn, a passage of almost magical power in which D-flat major gradually slips away and is resolved in a concluding turn toward D-flat Phrygian.

This *adagio* is also the only slow movement in Grieg's cyclical works in which the same basic tempo is maintained throughout. The result is a high degree of internal unity.

The last movement, *Allegro moderato molto e marcato,* begins with four measures in a pronounced rhythm played pianissimo by the woodwinds. This is followed by some brilliant passages in the piano part before the soloist introduces the intense and driving principal theme:

This theme has always—and rightly—been considered the most typically Norwegian theme in the entire concerto. Its character is that of a lively *halling*: one hears the sound of the Hardanger fiddle, greatly refined, in the piano part:

The first page of Grieg's manuscript of the A-minor Concerto. This manuscript, owned by the University of Oslo Library, is the only one known to survive. Presumably there was an earlier manuscript in Grieg's hand, but this is not completely certain. The University of Oslo manuscript was a printer's copy for the first printed edition in 1872. In later editions Grieg constantly made changes in various details. It was not until the 1894 edition that the first measure received its final form. It acquired at that time, for example, a much more powerful effect than that shown by the facsimile on this page. The whole orchestra joins in the first chord in measure 2. (All the changes made by Grieg are discussed in the Editorial Commentary in Volume 10 of Edvard Grieg's Complete Works *[Peters, 1983].)*

there are pedal-point effects, open fifths, and sharp dissonances. The theme receives broad and varied elucidation throughout the exposition.

The secondary theme section is introduced with three powerful chords in C major on the piano. Then follows a completely new motive with sprightly dance rhythms. The new motive stands more or less by itself, however, for at this point Grieg surprises us: the secondary theme quickly gives way to motives that clearly have a strong relationship to the principal theme. The extended secondary theme section almost has the character of a development of the principal theme; in the last part we are again back in the tonic (A minor). In the following example we see the introduction of the secondary theme and its continuation by the violins together with the sparkling broken chords in the piano:

Grieg seldom used principal and secondary themes that are so similar. One is almost tempted to say that the exposition in this case consists of a principal theme and variations. This is a unique idea on Grieg's part, but it is in line with the desire for unity that is characteristic of Romanticism.

The first truly contrasting theme in this movement is in F major. Its lyrical "nature" mood gives it a moving effect, and it contains a number of such typically Griegian elements as the Grieg formula, double appoggiaturas, and triplets. There is also a hint of the Mixolydian mode when E-flat is occasionally used instead of E. The theme is introduced by the flute, and the tonal picture with the harmonic foundation being played tremolo in the upper strings has something characteristically Griegian about it. Here is this theme as it is presented for the first time in the piano:

This lovely theme is worked out in a long section that takes the place of the traditional development. There is, then, no attempt whatsoever to elaborate any of the material that had been presented earlier. This contrasting section stands as a complete and well-rounded whole; toward the end the ethereal sounds of the melody simply disappear into infinity.

The third movement is constructed in such a way that we cannot speak here of sonata form in the usual sense; it is, rather, a "sonata rondo." Grieg must clearly have liked this form, for as previously mentioned, he also made deliberate use of it—and very successfully—in the last movement of the *Violin Sonata in G Major*. Later he would also use it in the finale of his String Quartet in G minor.

As was usually the case with Grieg, the recapitulation proceeds essentially unchanged up to the concluding part of the exposition. Here, however, a broadening occurs and new keys are introduced. The recapitulation concludes with a rousing piano cadenza.

The coda begins quite differently than one would expect: the *halling* theme is now transformed into a sprightly *springar* in ¾ time. Thereafter the piano part becomes more and more intricate until we get a new and final surprise in the gigantic climax with which the movement concludes. Here, in a bright A major, the contrasting theme is heard once again in a brilliant tutti. Intermingled with this mass of sound we hear the sparkling sounds of the piano playing a series of powerful passages. Grieg had used the idea of a concluding apotheosis of the contrasting theme once before, in the last movement of his second violin sonata. The effect is even more impressive in the piano concerto, however.

Grieg plays his last trump card at the very end. It gives the piece a singular and most original ending: the two impressive Mixolydian concluding cadences, in which the lowered leading tone (G instead of G-sharp) in the dominant chord "dots the final i." It was at this point that Liszt, the first time he played through the concerto, exclaimed with delight: "g, g, nicht giss! Famos! Das ist so echt schwedisches Banko!" [G, G, not G-sharp! Fantastic! That's the real Swedish article!] This conclusion is reproduced in its entirety on p. 123. (Grieg's own account of the Liszt episode is given on p. 137.)

There is no reason to conceal the fact that this fine piano concerto has also been the object of some criticism. However, its inherent musical qualities have always survived even the most outspoken and sometimes pedantic academic criticisms.

One of the main criticisms of the work has been that Grieg made too little use of the possibilities for variation in his recapitulations. This objection has some plausibility, but only from a purely theoretical point of view. Grieg's point of departure was indeed the classical sonata form, but he never allowed himself to be slavishly bound by traditional ways of thinking. New material requires new handling; so also in this case. For the material in the expositions is so copious and varied that in Grieg's view a further emphasis on the variation possibilities—with new modulations, for example, and radical changes in the orchestration—would only have detracted from the purity of the form.

Another objection concerns the episodic character that some critics think they find in Grieg's sonata-form compositions. Grieg himself emphasized, however, that it was his express wish to set dissimilar musical elements up against each other in sharp relief so the contrasts could stand out as clearly as possible. A certain episodic character is part of the price that Grieg was willing to pay for this. The idea has its roots in the esthetics of Romanticism, which Grieg—notwithstanding his thorough classical training—also made his own. It is obviously inappropriate to judge his music on other premises.

If one looks at the *A-minor Concerto* in relation to Grieg's earlier works, it is clear that he here turned toward a much broader public. It can be said without

condescension that the piano sonata and the two violin sonatas were intended primarily for a Scandinavian audience. In the concerto, Grieg instinctively managed to give the local color an appearance that elevated it to the international level. He created a work that has proven its viability—not because the national and Griegian elements make it "interesting," but because those elements have been naturally integrated in a genuine musical whole that has a message for everyone.

Grieg and Neupert in the early 1870s. Neupert spent most of his professional life abroad. He made a significant contribution as a piano teacher in the conservatories of Berlin, Copenhagen, Moscow and New York. Grieg was much indebted to Neupert for his pioneering efforts in behalf of the A-minor Concerto all over the world, and regarded him as the ideal interpreter of the work. (Bergen Offentlige Bibliotek, musikkavdelingen, Norway)

Grieg and Liszt

The period from the winter of 1868 to the summer of 1870 brought both good and ill for the Grieg family. The joy of anticipation was followed by the sadness of their daughter's sudden death. But Grieg overcame sorrow through his work on an important composition: the twenty-five arrangements of Norwegian folk tunes for piano, Opus 17. He also received a new zest for life when his career led him to Italy and an encouraging meeting with Franz Liszt.

The Liszt letter and hope for the future

In the autumn of 1868 Grieg fervently desired to get away from Oslo for a while, and he launched a bold campaign to get a stipend from the Ministry of Education for a trip abroad during the coming year. In the hope of strengthening his application for the stipend, he wrote to several famous musicians including Moscheles, Hartmann, and Gade asking for recommendations. All of them obliged his request.

His greatest aid, however, was to be Franz Liszt. With a view to securing Liszt's help, he wrote on November 2 to Ravnkilde in Rome: ". . . things look pretty bleak for me: students seven hours a day, choir rehearsals and orchestra rehearsals and concerts and—botheration . . . Your letter awakens a longing for the south of Europe, a longing that becomes stronger day by day—and with God's help I will overcome all of the obstacles. Remember that I am now married and must make all kinds of arrangements [in order to take a trip like this]—but *I will:* that is my watchword. As you can see by the enclosed letter, I am already trying to secure the means to make my plans a reality. I am seeking a stipend for next spring and am now asking Liszt for a recommendation. Do you think he will give me one? Encouraged by your recent report that he has played my violin sonata, I have confidently ventured this step and hope that you will use whatever method you think best to make sure that my letter reaches him."

Ravnkilde transmitted Grieg's request to Liszt, who on December 29 sent Grieg a most gracious recommendation. It reads as follows:

Monsieur,

It is with the greatest pleasure that I express to you the sincere joy that I felt upon reading through your sonata, Opus 8.

The sonata bears witness to a great talent for composition and shows a well-conceived, inventive, and excellent treatment of the material; it demonstrates a talent that needs only to follow its natural bent in order to attain to a high level. I hope and trust that in your homeland you will receive the success and the encouragement that you deserve, for anything else would be grossly unfair. If you should come to Germany this winter, I cordially invite you to make a visit to Weimar so that we could meet.

Receive, monsieur, the assurance of my deepest regard.

Franz Liszt

Liszt did not mention in his letter that it was Grieg who had asked for such a statement. Perhaps it is this omission that made Grieg "forget" the exact circumstances when, in 1881, he wrote to Grönvold: "It was recognition of the greatest significance for me when in December, 1868—precisely when the gloom in Oslo seemed the darkest—I received one day a letter from Liszt, who brought some sunshine into my life. There was at that time no one in my homeland who paid any attention to me as a creative artist. I expressed my feelings of discouragement in a letter to a friend in Rome. My friend passed it on to Liszt, who he knew was warmly interested in me. It shows a noble trait in Liszt that he immediately sat down at his desk [and wrote to me] in the awareness of the good that he might thereby bring about. I was thinking just then about applying for a stipend, but I didn't have much hope of getting it since I was not well regarded by our conservative old musicians and other

Edvard and Nina at a family gathering at Landaas in the summer of 1869. L. to r. are Edvard and Nina, Edvard's parents, his sisters Benedicte and Maren, his brother John, John's wife Marie, Edvard's cousin Marianne Riis, and Edvard's sister Elisabeth.

1. BJÖRNSON DELIGHTS GRIEG BY SUPPORTING HIS CAUSE

Grieg has not received any obvious encouragement as a composer here in Norway, but has in fact encountered many, many kinds of obstacles. Elsewhere, however, he has received wide acclaim. In Germany, and especially in Denmark, he is regarded as the man of the hour. Moreover, when he recently solicited recommendations from Europe's most famous composers in support of his application for a fellowship, he received the most excellent encomiums. Moscheles, Rubinstein, Hartmann, Gade, Liszt, etc. have given him much encouragement in his work . . . (Björnson in *Norsk Folkeblad*, April 10, 1869.)

* * *

Björnson wrote a nice piece about me in today's issue of *Norsk Folkeblad* that you ought to read. He says there that I am a painter of landscapes—how appropriate, for my life dream is to express the Scandinavian scenery in music. (Letter to Matthison-Hansen, April 10, 1869.)

2. PLANS FOR THE SUMMER AND AUTUMN OF 1869

You are expecting me in Denmark this summer. Unfortunately, I'm not going to make it. I'm getting the stipend, all right, but I'm going to have my wife with me so I don't want to use up any of it before the trip. I'm going to stay with my parents at their country home near Bergen this summer; that won't cost me a penny, you see. If I can also earn a little there by giving concerts, then I will come to Copenhagen for a month this autumn enroute to Italy . . . But what you said about Gade—that he takes back what he said and sends his greetings—I don't understand. Did he really say that? . . .

This summer I want to write something for chorus and orchestra. I have the feeling that I could do something of that sort, but I can't find a text. Since we were last together I haven't composed a note. Just given lessons and concerts. I have become so unmusical that it now seems to me an impossibility to be creative. But it has happened before; that is my consolation.

Would you believe that I recently got a letter from Liszt—really! It almost made me dizzy . . . Just think, he invites me to visit him at Weimar. But I'm stuck up here with a wife and perhaps children! (Letter to E. Horneman, April 24, 1869.)

musical dilettantes who would be making the decision. But Liszt's letter worked wonders."

On January 10, 1869, after receiving the recommendation from Liszt, Grieg sent to the Ministry of Education his application for a stipend of 500 spesiedalers. The stated purpose of the stipend was "by a visit abroad to secure time and leisure for creative work as well as an opportunity—through association with art and artists—to rejuvenate my mind and broaden my view of the ideal, which, under the circumstances in which I am living, can only become narrower."

That which Grieg considered unlikely happened, thanks not least of all to Liszt. He got the stipend, but only after a delay of half a year.

He wrote to his Danish friends about his working conditions and feelings at this time. In a January 31 letter to Winding he said: "Believe me, it's a real joy to be a Norwegian artist in Norway! If I didn't work like a slave the whole blasted winter I wouldn't be able to take my trip to Denmark—and my life depends on it."

Then from Denmark came the truly great encouragement: the report of the successful April 3 performance of the piano concerto. On April 10 Grieg wrote exuberantly to Matthison-Hansen: ". . . I then received five different letters from dear Denmark, all of which told of art and friendship down there. Among these was also yours. A report of recognition like that comes like a ray of sunshine into my lonely home. For I lack anything like that here, and you know full well that the life of the spirit depends on it. For that reason I thank God for my kinship with the Danes, as a result of which my music is understood in Denmark. Here there is coldness and severity, both in nature and in the temperament of our people. No doubt there are many here too who at bottom are kind hearted, but an artist needs to see evidence of it; he cannot use his gifts if he must engage in an endless quest in the most out-of-the-way places just to find a crumb of understanding . . .

I want very much to get away from here. Just think: all winter long I have not heard any music except that which I have produced myself. For I got into a conflict with the orchestra, because some first violinists demanded five spesiedalers each for a concert with three rehearsals. The result was that I didn't get an orchestra established, since I wasn't willing to go bankrupt over the matter . . . But I wanted to . . . put on my concerts, and they went all right . . . But to tell the truth, I am thinking a lot these days about what is to become of me . . . I feel that I am standing at one of life's turning points, and it should not be passed by blindly."

The same day Grieg received some gratifying and unexpected recognition from a Norwegian source: Björnstjerne Björnson strongly supported his young artist friend in an article in *Norsk Folkeblad*.[1]

Two weeks later Grieg described his plans for the future in a letter to Horneman.[2] In the same letter he also touched on his relation to Gade, which for some unknown reason had deteriorated.

When Grieg, in the letter to Horneman, used the expression "perhaps children" in speaking of his own family, it could indicate that another child was on the way. In the Grieg family's correspondence from later years it is intimated that Nina had a miscarriage. It is possible that the reference in this

But one knows nothing in this world. I learned this the hard way recently: barely arrived here for a visit with my parents when my little girl—our only child—came down with brain fever [meningitis] and died. My joy in being a father is now but a dream.

You can understand that this has been a difficult time for me. It is hard to watch the hope of one's life lowered into the earth, and it took time and quiet to recover from the pain. But thank God, if one has something to live for one does not easily fall apart; and art surely has—more than many other things—this soothing power that allays all sorrow!

Your last letter included, as I recall, enthusiastic words in praise of marriage, and certainly it can contain a peace and a truth that one seeks in vain elsewhere; but perhaps the other side of the scale—the side that contains sorrow—is as full as the side that contains all of life's joys. In this matter you are the one who is deserving of envy. But the secret is really to find the right glasses—the optimistic and bold ones—with which to look at life. He who does this is equally happy whether he be a married man or a bachelor. (Letter to N. Ravnkilde, June 29, 1869.)

later correspondence is to this very point in time. If so, the miscarriage could have been caused by the shock of Alexandra's sudden illness and death.

Just a month earlier Grieg had written to Matthison-Hansen about his happiness as a father: "I am writing to you on what for me is a day of celebration. It is my little daughter's first birthday. It is so nice to see this joy around me."

In the middle of May the Griegs left for their long-awaited summer visit to Bergen, but were struck by a terrible tragedy: on May 21, Alexandra died. This was a blow that they would not get over for a long time. It appears, however, that with the help of his art Grieg managed to work through the sorrow. He wrote very directly about this in a moving letter to Ravnkilde.[3]

During the visit to Rome the following winter Grieg wrote to his parents on February 17, 1870: "Our home has become empty—yes, I think much about the time when we shall return to Oslo: perhaps then the loss will really sink in. I ask only for strength to work and accomplish something; then everything else will follow."

Grieg cherished the memories of Alexandra throughout his life. A Belgian friend, Frank van der Stucken, told about the time in 1883 when they were together in Rudolstadt: "How tenderly he thought of her, and he liked to report his memories of her short life." When Julius Röntgen—a Dutchman who was one of Grieg's best friends—lost his little daughter in 1904, Grieg wrote consolingly on March 22: "For me the memories [of my child] are a beautiful dream. It will be so for you too. But what if the dream had never really existed? Would that not have been preferable? I am reminded of a poem by Andreas Munch [the poem is actually by Tennyson] in which he says: 'Tis better to have loved and lost than never to have loved at all.' Maybe he is right. I don't know."

Intimations of "hidden harmonies" in Norway's folk melodies

After Alexandra's death Grieg found a certain consolation in composing, and he set to work on a task that was new for him: arranging folk music. *Twenty-five Norwegian Folk Songs and Dances,* Opus 17, for piano, was his first contribution in an area that was to become quite central in his art. It was also an area in which he was to do some of his best work.

In a letter to H. T. Finck on July 17, 1900, Grieg looked back upon the "mystery" of his unique relationship to Norwegian folk music: "The realm of harmony has always been my dream world, and the relation between my sense of harmony and Norwegian folk music has always been a mystery for me. I have found that the obscure depth in our folk music has its foundation in its unrealized harmonic possibilities. In my arrangements in Opus 66 and elsewhere I have tried to give expression to my feelings of the hidden harmonies in our folk melodies. In so doing I have been rather especially fascinated by the chromatic progressions in the underlying harmonic structure."

Two important predecessors—Ludvig M. Lindeman and Halfdan Kjerulf—had already made pioneering efforts in this area. What they had done was to clothe the folk music material in the garb of serious music and make it available to a broad audience in relatively simple piano arrangements. Grieg now carried this task further, but on the basis of his own background and experience.

Lindeman's harmonizations are of uneven quality. Now and then he sparkles with striking turns of imagination, but the arrangements often sound primitive and at times quite experimental. Grieg put it accurately in 1905 when he characterized Lindeman's arrangements as "awkward and impractical." It should be remembered, however, that in 1875 Grieg had thought so well of these arrangements that he included eight of them unaltered in the collection *Norway's Melodies.*

We shall now see how Lindeman, Kjerulf, and Grieg each handled the same folk melody, "Jölstring" [Dance from Jölster]. Our first excerpt shows the opening part of Lindeman's version. Note the pedal point on the dominant in measures 1–4, the secondary dominant (with B instead of B-flat) in measures 9–11, and the perhaps ill-considered change to F major near the end:

Lindeman: *Ældre og nyere norske Fjeldmelodier*, No. 402

Kjerulf published two collections containing piano arrangements of folk music. In comparison with Lindeman's arrangements of such melodies, Kjerulf's are more carefully crafted and harmonically varied, and Grieg undoubtedly got some ideas from them. Kjerulf often managed to unite elements from the Romantic harmony of his day with typical Norwegian features in a more natural and spontaneous way than did Lindeman. His arrangement of "Jölstring" sounds harmonically bland in the first four measures, but it gradually becomes more interesting, especially through the judicious use of chromaticism. The change to F major, which occurs in measures 8-9, is accomplished more colorfully by Kjerulf than by Lindeman, but it also gives the impression of being somewhat experimental. (There appears to be a printer's error in measure 10. Presumably Kjerulf wanted F-double-sharp, not F-sharp, as in the preceding measure.)

Kjerulf: *25 Udvalgte norske Folkedandse nr. 2* [Twenty-five Selected Norwegian Folk Dances, No. 2] (1861)

The source for all of the pieces in Grieg's Opus 17 was Lindeman's transcriptions in volume two of his collection, *Aeldre og nyere norske Fjeldmelodier* [Older and Newer Norwegian Mountain Melodies]. In three of the pieces (Nos. 2, 13, and 19) Grieg used the folk melodies just as Lindeman had recorded them. In the rest he, with great reverence, made various small melodic and rhythmic changes. Beyond that he provided the arrangements with repetitions—sometimes with altered harmony—and occasionally added preludes, interludes, and postludes. Naturally he did not consider himself bound in any way by Lindeman's chord progressions.

Most of the arrangements in Opus 17 make no great demands on the technical skills of the performer. As in all of Grieg's mature piano music, the style is decidedly idiomatic. That is also true of the few somewhat more demanding pieces in the collection. There is not a hint of virtuoso pianism in these pieces; but although the work is intended for amateurs, the pieces are so varied and full of contrast that if they were to be played seriatim they could without doubt be used as concert music.

Most of the pieces are arrangements of folk songs, but there are also some lively folk dances for violin or *langleik*. Grieg generally chose melodies of high quality. Each of the arrangements has the character required by the melody. There is a balance between simplicity and cautious sophistication in every respect: in the piano writing, in the harmony, and in the formal development of each piece. The choice of chords is often quite imaginative, and there are several passages that nicely illustrate the composer's hallmark: an organic fusion of functional and often chromatic chord combinations that more often than not are liberally spiced with dissonances and modal elements.

The artistic high point in Opus 17 is achieved in two totally different kinds of pieces, namely "Solfager and the Snake King" (No. 12) and "Dance from Jölster" (No. 5). The former is based on a wonderful folk song from Telemark that undoubtedly has its roots in the Middle Ages. The melody, the key of which is somewhat indefinite, is enhanced by an expressive and varied harmony. "Dance from Jölster," on the other hand, is based on a dance tune for violin (not Hardanger fiddle). It is interesting both rhythmically and harmonically. This *halling*-like piece, in Grieg's lively and imaginatively harmonized version, is one of the finest achievements of his early work in this genre. He played it often at his own concerts.

Here is the first part of "Dance from Jölster" as arranged by Grieg. Its superiority to the previously cited arrangements of Lindeman and Kjerulf is immediately evident. It is harmonically much richer, and the harmony is well suited to the melody. Note the simple but nonetheless very effective prelude and the typically Griegian use of chromaticism in the accompaniment:

Grieg: Opus 17, No. 5

In inspired arrangements such as "Solfager and the Snake King" and "Dance from Jölster," Grieg succeeded for the first time in implementing the idea of giving expression to "the hidden harmonies" in Norwegian folk music. Later he would probe even more deeply into the depths of these folk melodies.

Grieg was to use many of the melodies collected by Lindeman in his own future compositions. He did this in Opuses 24, 29, 30, 35, 51, 63, 64, and 74, as well as throughout *Norway's Melodies*.

Grieg and Lindeman never became personal friends, partly because of their age difference of thirty-one years and partly because of their dissimilar temperaments. That Grieg and Winter-Hjelm did not make use of an expert such as Lindeman at the Music Academy is due to the "chorale controversy" which was going on at just this time. Winter-Hjelm and Lindeman were on opposite sides in this controversy, which concerned the rhythmic form of the old chorale melodies to be used in a forthcoming Norwegian hymnal. It is quite possible that Grieg also got involved in the matter in support of Winter-

Hjelm, who advocated a return to the original rhythmic form of the chorale melodies.

But it must have made Lindeman happy when, in September of 1873, Grieg honored him and his wife by composing a little song for their silver wedding anniversary (CW 129, No. 2). Although a typical occasional piece, it is nonetheless of great interest because the middle section has a clear similarity to that exquisite part of "Solveig's Song" where there are no words. It was not until a year later, however—when he wrote the *Peer Gynt* music—that Grieg succeeded in giving this material an adequate artistic form. The difference is readily apparent when one compares the two versions:

Passage from song "For L. M. Lindeman's Silver Wedding Anniversary":

Corresponding passage from "Solveig's Song":

Nor was Grieg ever very close to Kjerulf. In a bitter letter to Matthison-Hansen on July 30, 1867, he wrote: "It might appear that I am a lucky man because of the new circumstances that surround me, but I am not. Most people—even musicians—hate my compositions. For some, to be sure, they are a closed book, and in their case it is forgivable; but there are others who understand them and express nothing but admiration to my face, but who don't have a good word to say for them when they speak of them to others. That is less honorable—and Kjerulf is one of them." These words were undoubtedly written in a moment of dejection, for they stand in sharp contrast to Grieg's later adulatory statements about his older colleague.

That same year Kjerulf wrote a little greeting in Grieg's autograph album in the form of the prelude and postlude of one of his loveliest songs, "Hvile i Skoven" [Rest in the Woods], a setting of a text by J. S. Welhaven.

Immediately after Kjerulf's death on August 11, 1868, Grieg wrote an obituary for *Illustreret Tidende* in Copenhagen. Here he mentioned among other things Kjerulf's illness (tuberculosis) "that allowed him for so long a time not only to live, but even to retain the most undiminished creative power and youthful warmth and enthusiasm." He said further that Kjerulf "with determination and true love of his art stuck to his principles among people who still have not sensed his significance."

Grieg expressed himself in a particularly beautiful way in the Oslo newspaper *Aftenbladet* on February 1, 1879, when he allowed publication of a long and detailed article about Kjerulf as a composer of songs. He wrote: "The time cannot be far off, then, when the Kjerulf songs . . . will be hailed as the creations of a truly beautiful soul."

In the spring of 1869 Grieg gave several concerts in order to raise money for a memorial for Kjerulf. One such concert, according to a letter to Matthison-Hansen, brought in no less than 220 spesiedalers. For the unveiling of the statue at Kjerulf Square in Oslo on September 23, 1874, he wrote a cantata in the form of two songs for male chorus using a text by Andreas Munch. This, too, is a typical occasional piece, but as a whole the cantata is better than the song for the Lindemans' silver wedding anniversary.

Of Kjerulf's compositions it was above all his songs that Grieg regarded most highly. He often included them on his concert programs along with his own. In the Kjerulf obituary he wrote that "nearly all of the songs have a surprising freshness and originality," and he studied them thoroughly when he published the article in *Aftenbladet* in connection with a new edition of the songs. In the *Aftenbladet* article he wrote: "What melodies he coaxes out of his lyre, what nobleness hovers over their sound! . . . The collection as a whole can be warmly recommended to all friends of genuine and noble song. There are pearls of great price among them." Grieg pointed to "Hvile i Skoven" as "one of the most wonderful inspirations of his genius" and to "Skovbakken" [The Forest Hill] as "wonderful, light, and airy, but difficult to perform." In "Nökken" [The Water Sprite], he wrote, "despite its great simplicity [there dwells] a true enchantment."

Against the background of such expressions it seems strange to read Grieg's matter-of-fact statement about the relation between Kjerulf's art and his own in the biographical information he gave to Aimar Grönvold in a letter of April 24, 1881: "I am not aware of any significant influence by Kjerulf [on me] notwithstanding my admiration for many of his songs." Kjerulf had an unusual ability to integrate the national tonal feeling with the musical tools of his day, a fact that Grieg emphasized in his obituary. One can assume, therefore, that Kjerulf had been the model for Grieg's own efforts since early in his career. But to admit this to his biographer was certainly not easy. That is all the greater reason to base one's judgment on his clear-sighted summation of Kjerulf's contribution as stated in the quotations from the obituary and the 1879 *Aftenbladet* article cited earlier. In *Aftenbladet* he allowed his insightful evaluation to come forth clearly in the statement that Kjerulf "was above all the first person to have emphasized the great significance of the Norwegian folk melodies for our national music. He accomplished this in a noble and pleasing way: it must, therefore, be acknowledged that in the history of Scandinavian music he fulfilled a mission the magnitude of which should not be underestimated."

Opus 17 was dedicated to that other great inspiration for Norwegian nationalism, Ole Bull, with whom Grieg spent a good deal of time during the summer of 1869. Just before he left Bergen to start the trip to Italy made possible by his stipend, he gave a farewell concert. *Bergensposten* reported that "among the many listeners was Ole Bull, who often showed his approval."

Some weeks later Grieg's father reported (in a September 29 letter to Edvard in Copenhagen) that Ole Bull was very interested both in the *A-minor Concerto* and in Opus 17. He wanted to help get these works published in America and suggested that Edvard might earn a lot of money if this were to occur. Grieg, however, preferred to have the concerto published in Germany and Opus 17 in Bergen. When Bull got word of this his interest cooled.

That autumn (1869) Grieg put the final touches on a new volume of songs, Opus 18, which was published in Copenhagen in December. This collection, which was dedicated to Nina, contains nine songs, most of them to texts by Hans Christian Andersen. One of them—"Autumn Storms"—was written four years earlier, but the rest apparently are from 1869.

The songs in Opus 18 vary in quality. Most are kept in a simple style, with a light melody undergirded by conventional Romantic harmony. "Moonlit Forest," "The Poet's Farewell," and "Poesy" are in this vein. One finds a somewhat more intense side of Grieg's personality in "My Darling is as White as Snow," "The Cottage," and especially in "The Young Birch Tree"—a sensitive, folk-like setting of a beautiful text by Jörgen Moe.

The least inspired songs in the collection are "The Rosebud" and "Serenade for Welhaven." Both are colorless songs in the "drawing-room" style of the day; the latter is nothing more than an occasional piece originally written for male chorus to be sung in an 1868 students' parade in honor of Welhaven.

"Among Roses" apparently also dates from this period, but it was not published until 1884 when it appeared as Opus 39, No. 4. In its terse and clean-cut style it is similar in many ways to both "The Young Birch Tree" and "The Old Mother" (1873). It portrays eloquently a mother's sorrow at the death of her child; one senses that Alexandra's death was the underlying inspiration for the song.

Liszt's advice

In mid-September, 1869, Nina and Edvard made their way via Oslo to Copenhagen, where they stayed for eight weeks and gave two successful concerts. In 1893 Grieg recalled that it was on this occasion, his first independent concert in Denmark, "that I really made my breakthrough down here. I conducted my piano concerto, which Neupert played superbly. My father-in-law said, 'I like the tuttis best.'"

On November 14 Grieg wrote to Ravnkilde in Rome: "I have now spent two months in Copenhagen in a constant whirl. I had hoped to find leisure for work, but I shall probably have to wait until I get to Rome." He asked his friend to help him find lodgings in Rome, "preferably on Monte Pincio."

Fourteen days later the Griegs traveled southward. They stopped briefly in Berlin and Leipzig and spent ten days in Vienna, where their friend August Winding and his wife joined them for the journey to Italy. They traveled via Venice and Florence, reaching Rome just before Christmas.

The visit to Italy lasted four months, and according to Grieg entailed a few disappointments but many more occasions for encouragement. In March of 1870 he wrote somewhat disconsolately to Matthison-Hansen that it had been a miserable winter, cold and rainy. "From the Eternal City my thoughts turn in a mood of dissatisfaction back to the land where it is my vocation to work."

What Grieg is referring to here appears to be a certain feeling of frustration that the compositional work on which he had pinned his hopes had not produced anything significant. For, as he wrote to the Ministry of Education in September in his report on the Italian tour: "On the journey itself and during my stay in Italy the impressions I received were so numerous and overwhelming that one immediately eclipsed the other, so to speak. The result is that while I have made a number of preliminary sketches, and have written various lyrical trifles, I have not had the peace and quiet necessary to concentrate on the larger forms. But I have retained in my memory a wealth of ideas, which is really the main thing. If in addition I succeed when I get home in infusing some of the exuberance and belief in the future of our art that the journey has reawakened in me, then I am convinced that the Ministry will recognize in my journey, as I do, its importance to me and thus to the art of my native land."

But the most important result, he wrote, is to be found in the fact that "life here has filled me with an infinite number of impressions . . . In Rome I discovered what I needed . . . leisure to concentrate on myself and the great world around me, the daily influence of a world of beauty. It is of the greatest importance for a Scandinavian musician who has received his elementary training in Germany to later spend some time in Italy, for in so doing he can clarify his ideas and purge them of that one-sidedness that only results in further concentration on German things. The national character of a Northerner contains so much that is heavy and introspective, which in all truth cannot be counterbalanced by an *exclusive* study of German art. In order to serve national interests we need mental balance, an intellectual soundness that can only be acquired by discovering what can be learned in Southern Europe."

The Italian interlude was marked by two great and entirely different highlights: a ten-day excursion to the Naples area with seven Scandinavian friends at the beginning of April, and two days in the company of Liszt.

Grieg gave an exuberant account of the journey southward from Rome in an April 9 letter to his parents. He wrote: "All the impressions throng together in my mind, creating a vast chaos . . . Last evening we came back here full of impressions, in fact satiated with pleasure . . . A drive to Amalfi . . . well, what am I to say since I have called Castel [Gandolfo?] a paradise, and this place is still more beautiful . . . and then to cap it all the warm sun, the fresh wind, the blue sky, and the horizon clear to its very extremities—what more could one ask? The memory of *one* day of this kind enriches one's whole life. The next day we left the ladies behind in Salerno and drove out to see the temple ruins at Paestum. The reason was that the road is not very safe, and none of us felt particularly keen to see robbers making off with our wives. For this reason we proceeded like cautious generals. The Temple of Neptune at Paestum is, next to a temple on the Acropolis in Athens, the most beautiful artifact that has come down to us from Greek art. You will get some idea of the truth of this when I tell you that everything in Rome is a mere bauble compared to this temple."

The meetings with Liszt were undoubtedly the most rewarding result of the Italian tour. Grieg emphasized this in his report to the Ministry of Education: "But what for me personally has been of the greatest importance is my acquaintance and contact with Franz Liszt. In him I have gotten to know

My dear parents!

Liszt came up to me with a smile, and said in the most amiable fashion: "We've exchanged a few letters, haven't we?" I told him that it was thanks to his letter that I was now here, a remark that elicited a truly Ole Bullian laugh from him. All the while he eyed with a sort of voracious expression the parcel I was carrying under my arm . . . And his spidery fingers hovered so menacingly that I decided the wisest course would be to use my own fingers to open the parcel without delay. He then started to leaf through it—that is to say, he read the first part of the sonata [Opus 13] through rapidly, and that this was no mere bluff was immediately obvious when he indicated the best passages with a significant nod of his head, a *bravo*, or a *sehr schön*. My spirits rose, but when he asked me to play the sonata, my mood dropped below zero. It had never occurred to me to play the violin sonata on the piano, and on the other hand I was anxious to avoid having to sit there and turn over the pages for him. All to no avail, however.

So I started off on his lovely American grand piano. At the very start, where the violin breaks in with a somewhat Baroque but Norwegian-sounding passage, he exclaimed: "My, how dashing! I like that! Play it once more." And when the violin comes in again in the *Adagio*, he played the violin part an octave higher on the piano with expression that was so beautiful, so absolutely correct and *cantabile* that I smiled to myself.

Those were the first notes I heard Liszt play. Off we went, at a great rate, into the Allegro; he took the violin part, I the piano. My courage steadily increased, because I was so pleased with his approval, which in truth flowed so abundantly that I felt the most wonderful gratitude. When we had finished the first movement, I asked if I might play something for piano alone, choosing the minuet from the *Humoresques*, which you of course remember. When I had played the first eight measures, and repeated them, he sang the melody with a certain heroic expression of power in his gesture, which I very readily understood. I did note that it was the national peculiarities that appealed to him. I had already suspected this, and for that reason had

not only the most brilliant of all piano players, but, what is more, a phenomenon—intellectually and in stature—unmatched in the sphere of art. I took him several of my compositions, which he played; and it was of supreme interest for me to observe how the national element in my work at first made him hesitant, but then enthusiastic. A triumph of this kind for my efforts and my views on the national is itself worth the journey."

In a March 1 letter to Matthison-Hansen, too, he gave rein to his enthusiasm over his visits to Liszt and the master's piano playing: "As an unheard-of favor I was asked to visit him, and he proceeded to play—I tell you, I don't care if I ever hear anyone else play the piano. The point is that this is not piano playing. One forgets the pianist, the instrument, and all that nonsense; one is alone with a giant who marshals a legion of spirits in headlong flight with all of his unbridled fancy. In a moment of cool reflection this is a reproach I could make, that he has no 'bridle.' I wish you had heard him play my latest violin sonata, sight-reading it from beginning to end. Yes, you should have heard it—and the brilliance of his conception! I left convinced that he can do the impossible."

Grieg elaborated on his impressions of his meetings with Liszt in two letters to his parents—the first dated February 17, the second April 9, 1870.[4] Here he enthusiastically provided a number of candid humorous descriptions. In the April 9 letter he wrote: "Since my first account amused you, I've added this one, but I do hope that this will be reserved for a smaller public. Anything that is to be read by a larger audience would have to be weighed more carefully."

This "weighing" was to be carried out with meticulous care more than twenty years later, in 1892, when he allowed some passages from the two

brought along a number of pieces in which I had tried to touch some national strings. (Letter from Grieg to his parents, Rome, February 17, 1870.)

* * *

My dear parents!

Winding and I were very eager to see whether he [Liszt] would really sight-read my concerto. I personally considered it impossible. Liszt, on the other hand, was of an entirely different opinion. He said to me: "Would you like to play it?" I hastened to say that I couldn't! Liszt then took the manuscript, went to the piano and, with a smile peculiar to himself, said to all those who were present: "Well, now I'll show you that I can't, either." Then he began. And in view of what he now achieved, I must say that it would be impossible to imagine anything of the kind that would be more sublime. He played the first part rather rapidly, and the result was that the opening passage sounded rather slapdash; but later on, when I had an opportunity to indicate the tempo, he played as he alone and no one else can.

It is significant that he played the cadenza, which is among the technically most difficult parts of the concerto, perfectly. His gestures are priceless. You see, he doesn't merely play; no, he converses and criticizes at the same time. He carries on a brilliant conversation, not with one person, but with the entire audience, distributing significant nods to right and left, mainly when he is particularly pleased with something. In the *Adagio,* and to an even greater extent in the *Finale,* he reached a peak both in execution and in the praise he gave.

Finally, as he handed me the score, he said: "Hold to your course. Let me tell you, you have the talent for it, and—don't get scared off!" This last is of infinite importance to me. It is almost like what I will call a sacred mandate. Time and again when disappointments and bitterness come I shall think of his words, and the memory of this hour will have a wonderful power to sustain me in days of adversity; that is my confident hope. (Letter from Grieg to his parents, April 9, 1870.)

letters to his parents to be printed in the Oslo periodical *Samtiden* (pp. 219–24). A comparison of the original letters with the printed version, however, reveals that Grieg changed the wording in a number of places. On the whole these alterations are of minor importance, apart from one noteworthy addition: in the second letter in *Samtiden* Grieg inserted an entirely new paragraph. This is the oft-quoted "divine episode" when Liszt "roared the theme" in the concluding measures of the *A-minor Concerto*. In its entirety the paragraph reads as follows:

"There is one perfectly divine episode I cannot forget. Towards the end of the finale, as you will remember, the second theme is repeated in a great fortissimo. In the very last measures, where the first note of the first triplet of the theme—G sharp—is changed to G in the orchestra, while the piano in a tremendous scale passage traverses the entire keyboard, he suddenly stopped, rose to his full height, left the piano, and with mighty theatrical steps and raised arms strode through the great monastery hall, literally roaring out the theme. When he got to the above-mentioned G, he gestured imperiously with his arm and cried: 'g, g, nicht giss! Famos! Das ist so echt schwedisches Banko!' He then went back to the piano, repeated the whole phrase, and concluded it."

Liszt in a typical pose in front of his admirers. In 1870 Grieg described Liszt's playing thus: ". . . a giant who with all of his unbridled imagination sets a host of spirits in wild flight." (public domain)

The originals of both letters and of the manuscript of the article in *Samtiden* are preserved in the Bergen Public Library. The manuscript bears the following inscription, formulated by Grieg: "Extracts from two letters written in his younger days from Rome, with Edvard Grieg's kind permission placed at our disposal by the composer's brother, Consul John Grieg." (In *Samtiden* the inscription was reproduced in a footnote.)

There can only be one reason for this inscription. Grieg had been asked to publish extracts of the two letters, because they were naturally of general interest. He thereupon composed the new version—with the famous additional paragraph—and by allowing the periodical to acquire the material through his brother John he managed in a natural way to include the above-quoted inscription as a neutral footnote.

There is, of course, no reason to suppose that the "divine episode" is pure invention on Grieg's part. It undoubtedly took place, but when Grieg wrote his letters to his parents he for some reason failed to include it.

It is equally certain that the encouragement he received from Liszt in 1870, which he brought to life so vividly, gave him a great deal of much-needed confidence. It was to prove a valuable resource in the demanding years ahead.

Years of Productive Collaboration

The years 1870–75 were by far the most important ones in Grieg's "Oslo period." Norway's capital during those years was his principal place of work as a conductor and teacher. It was also important to him to be able to spend the summer months in Bergen, however, for only then did he find the time and the tranquility to devote himself wholly to composition. Both quantitatively and qualitatively, this period in Grieg's life is extraordinarily significant.

The paramount feature of this period was the collaboration he initiated with three leading figures in Norwegian cultural life: Björnstjerne Björnson, Johan Svendsen, and Henrik Ibsen. With Björnson and Svendsen Grieg also established a close personal friendship.

As early as 1868 he had been attracted by Björnson's strong personality. On November 2, 1868, he wrote to Ravnkilde: "Björnson is here, and where he is there are also vitality and imagination."

The poet's comprehensive and self-confident ideas stimulated Grieg in more ways than one—musically and otherwise—as Björnson's cousin Nordraak had also done when the young Grieg needed it most during his Denmark period. Among other things, Björnson fully awakened his political consciousness; but Grieg also received musical inspiration from the great poet. This inspiration expressed itself in a number of ways, including a series of songs. Its most important fruits, however, were several large dramatic works.

Svendsen's rich personality and artistic versatility also came to mean much for him. Grieg and Svendsen were very different both in temperament and in musical expression, but each had a liberating effect on the other. They became aware of this fact rather early, and the collaboration they initiated became unusually successful. Indeed, an almost brotherly relationship grew between them, and it lasted throughout their lives.

The artistic culmination for Grieg in this period was his collaboration with Ibsen on *Peer Gynt*. But since Ibsen stayed abroad during most of these years, they were able to have contact with each other only by letter. Later, however, the acquaintance of 1866 was renewed to some extent, though as a human being Ibsen always remained inscrutable for Grieg.

1. TWO GRIEG LETTERS ABOUT THE POSSIBILITY OF PUBLISHING THE *A-MINOR CONCERTO*

Will you take a risk and publish my piano concerto? Because I don't want to come out with a mere trifle for Christmas, and the concerto shall and must come out now . . . Please, if you will, be so kind as to determine the honorarium yourself. It is of course difficult for me to say anything about this undertaking, but judging from the numerous inquiries to me and to people in Norway, and from the manner in which audiences in Denmark took to the concerto, I can't help but think that it wouldn't take long for it to pay for itself. (Letter to Sophus Hagen, July 6, 1870.)

* * *

Regarding the publisher stories, be assured that I, too, can serve up wastepaper. But it is really not worth losing one's integrity for the sake of some paltry music dealers. When something like this happens to me, I am happy when I recall Schumann's words: "Always strive only to be a greater artist, then everything else comes of itself." A statement like that from a man like Schumann is capable of sustaining one's good humor. Don't you agree? (Letter to N. Ravnkilde. December 6, 1869.)

2. JOHAN SVENDSEN RECOMMENDS THE *A-MINOR CONCERTO*

I have spoken at length with Fritzsch concerning your piano concerto—without being familiar with it—and made his mouth water. I am completely confident that he will publish it . . . He is an honest man of the rarest kind, and he bets everything on something that he believes has a future. (Letter from Svendsen to Grieg, July 14, 1871.)

Two frustrating years

After the long and satisfying tour to the south, the Griegs returned to Copenhagen on April 20 and remained there for two months. Then they went on to Bergen to spend the summer with Edvard's family at "Landaas." In the hope of getting the piano concerto published, Grieg wrote to the publisher Sophus Hagen in Copenhagen.[1] But the Danish publisher—like the Leipzig publishers whom Grieg had contacted during the preceding winter—did not dare to take on such a risky venture. The publisher E. W. Fritzsch had returned the concerto with a note stating that it did not interest him enough to print it. Grieg commented about this with deliberate irony in a March 5, 1870 letter to an unnamed German friend: "Really, he is able to pronounce judgment on a large score after giving it only a hurried reading!" Later, however—after Svendsen had given his support to the concerto—Fritzsch changed his mind and decided to publish it.[2]

It is surprising that Grieg allowed this summer at "Landaas" to slip by without doing any composing worthy of mention. He wrote only four songs in 1870, three to texts by Björnson. His first setting of a text by Björnson had occurred some years earlier when he wrote the insignificant song "The Fair-haired Maid" (CW 100, No. 1), published posthumously in 1908. Far more vigorous is a piece for male chorus, "Norwegian Sailors' Song" (CW 124), completed in 1869. It has an unusually attractive melody that quickly won the hearts of the Norwegian people.

The three Björnson songs of 1870 are of uneven quality. "Good Morning!" (Opus 21, No. 2) is rather impersonal in character, but it is nonetheless well written and quite effective. "The First Meeting" (Opus 21, No. 1) and "From Monte Pincio" (Opus 39, No. 1), however, are among the finest songs Grieg had written up to this time. In "The First Meeting" he created—as he had done in "I Love But Thee"—one of the most beautiful love songs of his day. Within the confines of a very simple three-part form (*ABA'*), the material is varied in the last part in an exquisite manner, like three melodic waves of sound in a steadily rising curve. The singular intimacy and warmth of "The First Meeting" have earned it deserved fame as one of the pearls among Grieg's songs.

"From Monte Pincio" reflects a profound mutual understanding between composer and poet. With intense inspiration, and in an almost impressionistic way, both managed to capture some rapidly shifting mood pictures from this best known of Rome's six hills. With its flaming, southern coloring, the piece has become one of Grieg's most cherished concert songs.

The fourth song from 1870—"The Odalisque" (CW 125)—is much less successful. This coarse Danish poem, with its exotic theme of a harem slave girl's passionate longing, was little suited to call forth the best in Grieg. He nonetheless allowed it to be printed in the July, 1872 issue of *Nordiske Musikblade*, an inter-Scandinavian publication that he edited in collaboration with Horneman and the Swedish composer August Söderman until 1875. It was, however, the only composition Grieg published in the periodical.

In September Grieg resumed his work in Oslo. Winter-Hjelm had con-

3. THE *A-MINOR CONCERTO* GETS A
NICE REVIEW IN THE OSLO PRESS

Grieg's *A-minor Concerto* was also presented, with the piano part being brilliantly
performed by Miss E. Lie. It is a fresh and
rich composition, though its themes are
perhaps not always developed with sufficient clarity to enable one to comprehend
them on a first hearing. Nonetheless, the
concerto provides strong evidence of the
composer's genius. (*Dagbladet*, April 28,
1871.)

ducted the subscription concerts while he was abroad, but now he took over
this work again. The season was to consist of four concerts, all of which would
require the assistance of large choirs. The plans included performances of
excerpts from Wagner's "Lohengrin" at the first and last concerts. One of the
highlights of the season was a memorial concert celebrating the centenary of
Beethoven's birth on December 17. This concert began with a spoken prologue written by Jonas Lie, and included Beethoven's *Symphony No. 7* as well as
his *Fantasy,* Opus 80, for piano, solo voices, chorus, and orchestra. At the
concluding concert on April 27, 1871, Grieg conducted his *A-minor Concerto*
for the first time in Oslo. Erika Lie was praised for her performance as
soloist.[3]

Grieg was concerned that this period in which he had composed very little
had lasted for nearly two years. On May 25 he wrote dejectedly to Ravnkilde:
"I have done nothing; either I am an unmusical beast or else all my creative
power is going into conducting concerts." Shortly thereafter, however, he
went to Bergen and his desire to compose was reawakened.

Pictures from Folk Life

In Bergen during the summer of 1871 Grieg worked on several compositions.
The most important of these was *Pictures from Folk Life,* Opus 19—three
technically demanding works which he often performed at his concerts.

He probably had made a rough draft of these pieces as early as the time of
the trip to Italy, since he mentioned some sketches and "lyric trifles" in his
report to the Ministry of Education. In a concert in Larvik on September 6, he
played a composition which in the program is called "Humoresque in A
Minor (New)," and which in all probability was the first version of "In the
Mountains," Opus 19, No. 1.

He completed his new opus at "Landaas," and that is why a fair copy of the
manuscript of "Bridal Procession" has the inscription "Landaas July 24, 1871."
Moreover, he played both "Bridal Procession" and "In the Mountains" at
concerts in Bergen on September 12 and 19. On the program the latter was
called "Ballad of Revolt," which is the exact title of the best-known composition of the twentieth-century Norwegian composer Harald Saeverud.

As a subtitle for this opus Grieg wrote "Humoresques for Piano," and it is
in fact the style of the epochal Opus 6 *Humoresques* that he took up once more.
Elements drawn from folk music were again employed in a natural and
organic way, with a thoroughgoing originality in the tonal language.

"In the Mountains" is characterized by rhythms drawn from the *springar.*
The melodic material is Grieg's own, but the opening section is somewhat
similar to the folktune "Brita Valaas" (No. 408 in Lindeman's collection). On
two occasions Grieg explicitly stated that the material was not borrowed from
folk music. On July 17, 1900, he wrote to Finck: "When the late talented
French composer Edouard Lalo, in his *Norwegian Rhapsody for Orchestra,*
simply made use of the first piece in my Opus 19 in the belief that it was a folk
tune, I take the liberty of regarding this thievery as a compliment." Three

4. FOREWORD TO THE FIRST
EDITION OF *PICTURES FROM
FOLK LIFE*

It should be noted that familiarity with the
first two pieces is necessary to an understanding of the last. For in the carnival, in
the midst of the milling crowd, one
glimpses in the distance a Norwegian wedding procession. The wedding procession is
then replaced by giant figures that in a series of big *halling* leaps (to motives from
"In the Mountains") clear the stage, as it
were. Lastly comes the flying ride, which is
indicated by the open fifth in A major that
occurs after the "Stretto." At this point the
carnival turns into a scene of complete
wildness. The whistling and yelling of the
crowd, plus the snorting horses that in one
unified motion pierce the air—everything
blends together to create a picture of the
most abandoned wildness. In part the ideas
derive from the Carnival season in Rome,
but with no effort to depict it in detail. In
part it is also the memory of folk life in
general that has later given the composer
some vague ideas. In order to facilitate understanding of the composition, I thought
it best to explain these things.

years later—on April 21, 1903—he wrote to Frants Beyer from Paris that Lalo
"has stolen a whole section of my 'In the Mountains'." These irascible words
are probably due to the fact that Lalo's son had just given Grieg's Paris concert
a poor review, whereas "a few years ago he praised the same things he now
derogates."

"Bridal Procession" (No. 2) has rightly become one of Grieg's most
celebrated piano pieces. It is one in which his distinctive quality is expressed in
a particularly effective way. With a sure sense for the national element,
Grieg—in a moment of fortunate inspiration—fused melody and harmony
into a magnificent whole.

In the first edition of Opus 19 Grieg included a foreword on the inside of
the dust cover. It is given in its entirety in the Primary Materials.[4] Today, of
course, the programmatic allusions in Grieg's account strike us as rather odd.

According to this foreword, "From the Carnival" illustrates the moods of
the Carnival season in Rome. Grieg observed these festivities for the first time
in 1866, when he described them vividly in his diary, and he saw them again in
1870. Now the time had come to let the figures from the Carnival swarm
forward in musical garb. The composer recreated rhapsodic snapshots with
charming melodies in which the Italian and Norwegian temperaments are
united. Toward the end some short phrases from "Bridal Procession" are
quoted, and in the coda elements of the *springer* from "In the Mountains" are
converted from a minor key and $\frac{3}{4}$ time to a *halling* in A Lydian in $\frac{2}{4}$ time.
Finally, after some repeated open fifths, comes the part that Grieg characterized in the foreword as a "flying ride" in the course of which the Carnival
"turns into a scene of complete wildness."

Pictures from Folk Life was published in Copenhagen in January, 1872. But it
seemed clear to Grieg that the publisher, Sophus Hagen, did not think
especially well of the work; he noted dryly in a letter to Hagen that he got only
forty-five riksdalers "for dealing with the life of the people." In an April 18
letter to Frants Beyer, he expressed regret at not being able to send him a copy
of the piece: "My publisher is a stingy pig, as a result of which I am as short of
copies as a church rat."

In the same letter Grieg gave a vivid description of his performance of the
work in the Student Association in Oslo: "It is true, since I am speaking of the
langleik: Pictures from Folk Life was published several weeks ago. Some time
back I played 'Bridal Procession' for the Student Association, and believe it or
not it brought tears to their eyes. I first explained to them what I had in mind,
and then I played, and understanding struck them like a bolt of lightning.
There was a shout: Encore! Encore! And was I happy! For it was the language
of the heart on both sides."

On the continent the pieces were soon judged on their merits. Grieg took
note of this in a letter to Beyer from Leipzig on March 30, 1875. The Norwegian pianist Johanne Rytterager had appeared in a concert in which she
played both the *A-minor Concerto* and Opus 19. After this concert Grieg
wrote: "I have had a very good time during my stay here, and have gotten no
less than three works performed without doing a thing . . . And what is even
more remarkable is that all of them have been successful—even the *Pictures*

5. A GERMAN REVIEW OF
PICTURES FROM FOLK LIFE

Grieg's pieces are highly characteristic, with an originality that should not be underestimated. They are not easy to perform but are all the more rewarding when done by a gifted performer. They depict three completely different scenes with equally great lucidity. The first piece refers to "the mountains"—not, of course, the gentle, forested German mountains, where vines or beech trees or oak trees grow. But neither is it "in the highland," to which Gade pays homage. It seems to begin in the dark crevices of the jagged, rocky wastes of which there are so many in the composer's native land. A serious, almost sinister tone characterizes this first piece . . .

In No. 2 the composer feels at home, as well he should since it depicts a "Norwegian wedding procession."

In No. 3 Grieg has made a daring move into the folk life. He parades before us various groups "from the carnival" . . . but the raw material is refined at the hands of the composer. (From a review in the *Leipziger Tageblatt*, March 15, 1875.)

from Folk Life, which the Germans find good . . ." He then quoted a laudatory review in *Leipziger Tageblatt.*[5] Especially encouraging for him was the statement that "the raw material is refined at the hands of the composer." As we know, the German press was not always so positively disposed toward him at this time.

Initial cooperative efforts with Björnstjerne Björnson

In 1881 Grieg told Aimar Grönvold of the significance that Björnson had for him: "I must not forget to mention a man who, during the musically empty years 1868–72 when I was in Oslo, filled me with his powerful personality. That was Björnson. He was a true friend to me in those years, and it was essentially he who kept me going. Although he did not understand music, he believed in what I was trying to do—and that gave me courage."

The first time we hear of a possible musical-dramatic collaboration between the two is in a November 8, 1870, letter from Björnson to Margrethe Rode: "I am now in the process of writing a new musical drama (*Klokker-Familien*) [The Sexton Family] with music by Grieg." Björnson never completed this piece, nor do we know if Grieg wrote any music for it.

Björnson was Grieg's principal stimulus during the period 1871–74. That spring he started writing music for a short excerpt from the dramatic poem *Arnljot Gelline.* The section he chose was a piece called "Before a Southern Convent," which he set for soprano and alto soli, female chorus, and orchestra. During the summer he completed the composition in rough draft.

Arnljot Gelline takes place during the time of Saint Olaf. In the excerpt Grieg chose for his composition we find ourselves before a convent in Italy. The young Jemtland chieftain's daughter Ingigerd has seen her father murdered by the plundering heathen Arnljot. He was also on the verge of raping her, but in pity he let her go. However, Ingigerd—despite the ghastliness of what had occurred—felt an attraction for the assailant. This naturally leads to a strong guilt complex on her part, and for this reason she seeks expiation by asking to be accepted as a nun in a foreign country.

Ingigerd knocks on the gate of the cloister. In the ensuing dialogue she is asked about the background for her decision, and she speaks openly about what has happened. The piece then ends with a nuns' choir bidding her welcome: "From guilt and sin, to God come in . . ."

In *Before a Southern Convent* (Opus 20) Grieg created a consistent and well-written little piece. Although it does not exhibit great originality, it contains several expressive sections. The work opens with a long and somewhat chromatic prelude. Its musical value, however, lies especially in the handling of the dialogue between the young girl Ingigerd and the nuns. This section contains some unpretentious and sensitive music. It culminates with the choir solemnly intoning a series of simple but highly effective chord progressions.

After the work was completed, Grieg wrote modestly to the publisher Sophus Hagen on July 14: ". . . I don't know if this is suitable for publication." But when Hagen decided to publish it, Grieg sang a different tune: ". . . it

Bjørnstjerne Björnson. In a letter to Iver Holte dated February 9, 1897, Grieg wrote: "It is a solemn duty to call attention to the great influence that my association with Björnson from the autumn of 1866 to the spring of 1873 had on my art. He shaped my personality in many ways—that is, he contributed greatly to its development. He made me a democrat, artistically and politically. He gave me the courage to follow my own instincts. This period (the 1870s) was a marvelous time with its surplus of courage and faith!" (H. Aschehoug & Co., Oslo, Norway)

6. GRIEG ON DEDICATION PLANS FOR *BEFORE A SOUTHERN CONVENT*

I want to ask you to be content instead with something in which you personally can't have the interest, but which I nonetheless don't want overlooked because of the *common* nationalistic tendency that characterizes it, namely: a collection of piano pieces that is coming out for Christmas called *Pictures from Folk Life*.

It was, by the way, a strange coincidence that ruined plans for the first dedication . . . I told Björnson yesterday about what had happened, and he was quite amused by it. (Letter to Hartmann, October 12, 1871.)

would please me even more if, like me, you found that *Before a Southern Convent* is the best thing I ever wrote. That would show that you understood me." He was offered fifteen riksdalers as an honorarium, which led him to write sourly: "Fifteen riksdalers for six pages! I don't want to be arrogant, but that it wasn't worth more is hard to take. How will the title page be? Beautiful, I hope!" The honorarium was then increased, and—to use Grieg's ironic words to the publisher—he got "twenty-five riksdalers for mourning at the Southern convent."

The work was published in a piano edition in December, 1871, with a dedication to Liszt. Originally Grieg had planned to dedicate it to Hartmann, but when he learned that Hartmann himself had recently written music for the same text he naturally abandoned that idea. Hartmann's name was placed instead on the title page of *Pictures from Folk Life*, Opus 19.[6]

In a letter from Bayreuth on July 5, 1872, Johan Svendsen was happy to report that Liszt appreciated the dedication: "Liszt spoke with great interest about the piece dedicated to him and promised to write to you."

7. GRIEG REPORTS ON A PERFORMANCE OF *BEFORE A SOUTHERN CONVENT* IN GERMANY

Why do I write today? Because I am so overjoyed, and because you are the first one who must know about it. Last evening *Before a Southern Convent* was performed in "Euterpe" and was a great success. I myself conducted. Nina sang. Many curtain calls. Emma Dahl's translation had to be abandoned when competent people found it to be—awful. The well-known librettist-composer Franz von Holstein has now translated the poem to everyone's satisfaction—also to mine and, I hope, to yours. Emma Dahl: what shall I do with her? I may face the consequences and send her a letter telling her exactly what happened; in that way I suppose the offense would have some limits—though I am afraid that after this Oslo will be even more sour toward me than before. (Letter to Björnson, March 18, 1875.)

8. GRIEG FINDS FAULT WITH THE PERFORMANCE IN PARIS

Then came *Before a Southern Convent*. Except for the orchestra, everything was mediocre: Ellen [Gulbranson] gives nothing of the spiritual quality that is needed, the alto was disgusting, the chorus tiny (twenty) and poor. Colonne dares to offer this to me because he himself isn't responsible! Even the organ was much too weak. In short, a performance that I would have been ashamed of *at home*. The little piece, which I dearly love, then also got a meager "success d'estime." (Letter to Beyer, April 21, 1903.)

9. BJÖRNSON ON THE *BERGLIOT* MUSIC

[My son] Björn said that you had heard I didn't like *Bergliot*. Nonsense. I didn't find the beginning on a level with the subject; but some things there were magnificent, and the conclusion is [so exciting] that one could not listen to it and remain seated. (Letter to Grieg, October 13, 1889.)

The piano edition was later reissued in a somewhat revised form, and the orchestral score was published in 1890.

In the spring of 1875 the work scored a big success when Grieg conducted it at "Euterpe" in Leipzig.[7] Two years later it was performed in New York; on December 21, 1877, Grieg wrote to Beyer: "Believe me, I was happy [to hear of the performance in New York], for this has a certain significance for me." Grieg later heard that the piece enjoyed an "enormous success" in Amsterdam in 1894. In Paris, however, it failed—primarily because of poor singing, according to Grieg.[8]

It must be said that *Before a Southern Convent* has, generally speaking, been neglected—notwithstanding Grieg's earnest faith in the composition and the fact that he performed it a number of times, both at home and abroad. Nonetheless, with this work he began his journey with Björnson toward the saga period's heights.

In an interview in *Dannebrog* in 1893 Grieg said: "After I had written *Before a Southern Convent*, Björnson, who easily became enthused, was beside himself with excitement." Encouraged by the poet's enthusiasm over the fortunate result of this collaboration, he quickly started working on a new and larger task—the melodrama *Bergliot*, which was completely drafted the same summer.

Grieg's idea was to create a colorful orchestral work with declamation, but there was no possibility of getting such a composition published at this time. Even the piano concerto originally generated no interest in publishing circles. For this reason *Bergliot* was put aside for fourteen years, until the autumn of 1885, when he finally completed it. Grieg commented on this in a letter to Ravnkilde, and also looked at the piece with self-critical eyes.

At the premiere, which he conducted at the Christiania Theater on November 3, 1885, the composition received an enthusiastic reception from the audience and the press. According to *Nordisk Musik-Tidende,* the actress Laura Gundersen, with her "brilliant, artistic rendering, contributed immeasurably to the glowing success." Grieg acknowledged this by dedicating the work to her when it was printed in 1887 as Opus 42.

Some years later, in a letter to the composer, Björnson offered an interesting critical assessment of Grieg's music.[9]

Björnson's work, which is regarded as one of his major writings, is a sharply chiseled portrait of Bergliot, the wife of Einar Tambarskjelve and one of the principal female characters from the period of the sagas. Depicted first is her despair over the fact that King Harald Hardraade, protected by an armistice, had lured her husband and their son, Eindride, to a meeting where he treacherously had them murdered. In mighty strokes Björnson paints Bergliot's flaming anger and her goading of her cowardly kinsmen to wreak vengeance for the atrocity.

The closing stanzas are absolutely thrilling; with their heavy rhythms they are like a muffled funeral march in poetic form. Thoughts of retribution have had to yield. Vengeance will not be hers: "The new god in Gimle, the dreadful one who took everything, let him also take vengeance, for he understands it!"

This epic poem evoked Grieg's power of imagination and liberated his

10. GRIEG'S THOUGHTS ABOUT
BERGLIOT AS A MELODRAMATIC
ART FORM

In September I completed a melodrama with orchestra, a work for which I had had some sketches lying around for a long time. I then went to Oslo where I . . . conducted, among other pieces, the aforementioned melodrama, which was excellently declaimed by our brilliant actress, Mrs. Gundersen. The piece is called *Bergliot,* a beautiful poem by Björnson with which you are undoubtedly familiar.

It has always annoyed me that Heise could dream of setting this piece for solo voice, for in this way the whole thing becomes, in my opinion, ridiculously weak and unnatural. Certainly [in this way] he has the advantage of being able to keep the whole thing musically nice whereas I, in order to achieve a realistic effect, often was obliged to forsake the musical domain and write things that get their value only in the dramatic situation. Now, be that as it may, I would be the last one to defend the melodrama as an art form; but when I was finally going to set this poem "Bergliot," it just *had* to be melodramatic. There was no other choice.

My piece has many weak points, that is only too clear; but on one point I will insist as long as I live: the basic idea was right. (Letter to Ravnkilde, February 14, 1886.)

* * *

Even in a melodrama I have taken every possible precaution, and still—after the first orchestra rehearsal I had to make changes. *First and foremost,* it is a matter of making sure that the listeners are able to understand the text—every word of it—without difficulty. The competition between *voice* and *music* is a terribly sensitive problem. And how *amazingly little* it takes before the voice is drowned out! (Letter to Frederick Delius, December 9, 1888.)

11. INVITATION TO THE
ESTABLISHMENT OF THE
"MUSIC ASSOCIATION"

Whereas we assume the desirability of an association in this city in which, at all times, the art of music can be advanced, we take the liberty of inviting our fellow citizens to join a "Music Association." This may be regarded as a continuation of the

artistic gifts far more strongly than "Before a Southern Convent" had done. The poet's *alfresco* technique was transferred to his own palette, and in powerful musical strokes he painted an intense picture of the gloomy and severe world of the saga.[10]

The music sounds de-Romanticized; it leans in the direction of a harsh realism, with sharp dissonances and a weakening of the conventional major/minor tonality. It makes extensive use of chromaticism and modality. This is especially striking in the two great funeral marches. The first of these (Andante molto, for full orchestra) occurs after Bergliot realizes that her loved ones have been murdered. The other (Tempo di marcia funébre) takes place in the closing scene where, in bitter resignation, she rides away in the carriage bearing the two corpses: "Drive slowly, for we shall get home soon enough." The musical character here is highly reminiscent of the *Funeral March for Rikard Nordraak,* but the expressive power is more concentrated and gripping.

Another fine song to a Björnson text—"The Princess" (CW 126)—was also written in 1871. It had been set earlier by Kjerulf. Grieg, in his comments on Kjerulf's songs in *Aftenbladet* in 1879, rightly identified it as one of the composer's "most beautiful" songs. Grieg's setting can be placed alongside Kjerulf's, for it complements his predecessor's simple, folk-song-like interpretation of the poem with more refined means.

Grieg founds the "Music Association" and Svendsen joins in

In the autumn of 1871 Grieg decided that the time had come to create a permanent orchestra in Oslo, and he succeeded in making the project a reality. On October 14, in cooperation with several leading figures in Oslo's cultural life—among them L. M. Lindeman, piano manufacturer Karl Hals, and Consul T. J. Heftye—he published an invitation to establish a "Music Association."[11] Winter-Hjelm was not among the signers of the invitation; it is evident that some problems had developed between him and Grieg.

Morgenbladet, which immediately gave its full support to the undertaking, observed that interest in orchestral music had been steadily growing, thanks not least of all to Grieg's efforts as a conductor. The governing board of the

"Philharmonic Society" and virtually a continuation of the subscription concerts that have been given in recent years.

We will take over the leadership of the "Music Association" for the time being. The undersigned Edvard Grieg will be musical director.

We propose to present four concerts in the large Freemason Auditorium during the winter season. The cost for all four concerts will be one and a half spesiedalers. (Oslo newspapers, October 14, 1871.)

12. THE FIRST CONCERT OF THE "MUSIC ASSOCIATION"

The "Music Association"'s first concert took place Saturday in the large Freemason auditorium, as a full house was expected. The Association's orchestra is composed of the Christiania [Oslo] Theater Orchestra's personnel, augmented by our ablest amateurs and other musicians to a number of almost sixty. The chorus of women's and men's voices included almost 150 voices.

Mr. Grieg is to be commended both for his choice of selections and for their performance, which bore witness to the energy and ability with which he was able to combine and enliven the many and varied resources that are available to him. The concert as a whole, as in its individual parts, won the most decided applause. (*Morgenbladet,* December 4, 1871.)

13. GRIEG'S FRUSTRATION WITH THE PRESS

I still have not, so far as I know, been given a mention [of "Before a Southern Convent" in the Danish newspapers] except for two lines in *Faedrelandet,* which I don't consider anything at all. And I must say, if anyone has any concern for my individuality, it should show itself there. I am disappointed. Remember, I need these rays of sun from persons of feeling down there. As Björnson said upon concluding his work with *Folkebladet* last year, "Up here, one thing is missing: *spirit.*" And he is right. Surely it will come, but it is hard for representatives of the spirit to function in this barren place where questions of food and railways are of prime importance to most people . . . If you see a review that is truly a review of my things, then, by all means, send it to me. People here need to know that spirit is appreciated amongst you. You understand that I myself, through my friends, must coerce local newspapers to reprint foreign reviews. You wouldn't believe how insignificant I am considered here in my own country . . . The fact is that the philistines who control the press here have agreed to kill me with silence. But it won't do any good. As surely as I write from the bottom of my heart, so surely shall what I write prevail. And I see the best sign in this, that my supporters are as enthusiastic as my enemies are bitter. That is always a secure beginning. For without enemies on the one side and friends on the other one never succeeds. (Letter to S. Hagen, January 13, 1872.)

society could now relieve him of administrative duties so that he could devote himself to purely artistic concerns.

The first concert of the Music Association was on December 2. The program included Beethoven's *Symphony No. 2* and Gade's "Elverskud." Nina sang one of the solo parts in the latter. The reviews were very positive.[12]

Grieg had some great triumphs as an orchestra conductor. In a letter to Winding on January 3, 1872, he wrote enthusiastically: "Yes, believe me, it is quite a load that I am carrying on my weak shoulders—to awaken a taste for the ideal in music. But it is good to have a mission in life, and that I have. It demands a willingness to sacrifice, that's certain, but I also have moments of truly glowing joy. You understand me: it is when chorus and orchestra swell around me and I feel that I and everything about me are being elevated."

Even if his contribution as a conductor was appreciated in Oslo, he thought he was being overlooked as a composer. In a letter to Sophus Hagen, his Danish publisher, on December 6, 1871, he expressed his disappointment: "This town's music dealers (I won't mention them by name!) take private pleasure in hiding my things away in the most obscure places, so no one knows they exist until after Christmas when nobody buys anything." He also touched more directly on his economic situation, and he wasn't especially gentle with Hagen himself either: "You once turned down my piano concerto. I am nonetheless willing to offer you my smaller things and have them published by you provided that you don't pay less than other publishers. It is embarrassing to speak of such things, but if you only knew how poorly I am situated and how I long for artistic freedom. I often feel such a marvelous yearning for creative work, but I am stuck up here in daily tasks and must resign myself to it!"

A month later he again addressed himself to Hagen with bitter statements about the tepid reception he encountered as a composer—not only at home, but also in Denmark.[13] In Sweden it was a different story: the Royal Swedish Academy of Music, under the patronage of Crown Prince Oscar, had appointed him a foreign member. Oscar, who had a personal interest in music, became king that same year. From Germany, too, came good news. On February 27 he wrote to Hagen: "Today I had the pleasure of hearing from Leipzig that Erika Lie played my concerto in the Gewandhaus last Thursday [February 22]." Grieg, however, expected heavy criticism from the music periodical *Signale,* which had frequently been negatively disposed toward him. But he would survive it—a fact that he expressed with sardonic humor: "So now they will speak badly of me in *Signale.* 'It's just a passing phase' said the fox as he was being skinned."

The Music Association's third concert on February 24, 1872, was devoted primarily to chamber music. In addition, Grieg presented choral works by the Swedish composers Lindblad and Söderman, as well as some by the young Norwegian composer Johan Selmer.

Among the singers in the chorus was a young man from Bergen, twenty-one-year-old Frants Beyer, who was studying law in Oslo. He became Grieg's student in piano and music theory at this time, and though he only cultivated music as a hobby, a number of songs he later wrote bear witness to an unmistakable talent. Beyer's warm personality enriched Grieg immeasurably throughout the lifelong friendship that now was established. Through the years Grieg wrote hundreds of letters—some very candid—to his friend; they are among the most important Grieg documents we possess.

Both Grieg and Beyer were nature lovers, and they went on a number of trips together to the mountains. Already in Grieg's first letter to Beyer—dated April 18, 1872—plans for a mountain trip are mentioned: "My dear Beyer! . . . If I don't go to Denmark this summer, we must take a trip to the mountains together. We must write to each other about this. Then we would really have fun with the *langleik* and fiddle." Grieg went to Copenhagen, however, so plans for the trip had to be postponed.

In the same letter he insisted that Beyer must soon come back to Oslo: "It would be so wonderful. I have only enemies here, and in you I know I have a friend! Is that not so? That I have! I rarely offer my friendship, but you have it completely, and that is my final word! Write soon, and let's be rid of all this unnecessary formality [i.e., the formal and polite form of address]. From now on I will just be your devoted friend, Edvard Grieg."

Two weeks later, on May 4, the Music Association gave its final and grandest concert of the season. Grieg presented Mozart's *Requiem,* and for the first time he conducted a work by Svendsen: *Symphonic Introduction to "Sigurd Slembe,"* Opus 8 (1871). *Aftenbladet*'s critic asserted that Svendsen's composition "was for many a closed book—that kind of music can hardly be wholly and correctly understood on first hearing." Grieg, on the other hand, in a letter to Matthison-Hansen on April 29, 1881, characterized the work as "a brilliant, powerful piece," although he missed the Scandinavian element.

Svendsen expressed his pleasure over the performance in a May 25, 1872 letter to Grieg from Leipzig, where he was employed as concertmaster in the music association "Euterpe." He wrote, ". . . thank you for your encouraging words, thank you for the speed with which you got *Sigurd Slembe* performed, above all thank you for your faith in me. If there is anyone whose friendship makes me proud and happy, it is you." He also took up a thread from a letter he had sent Grieg the year before: "You wouldn't believe how happy and proud I am over every proof of friendship I receive from you, you noble, unbiased, and brilliant friend. Your words of praise for my violin concerto are for me all the more valuable because I am convinced of your unshakable integrity and sincerity. It is regrettable for me—perhaps for both of us—that we are so distant from each other; how stimulating and, therefore, profitable it would be if we could work together."

In the summer of 1872 Grieg realized his plans for another visit to Denmark. On June 28 he wrote from Copenhagen to Ravnkilde in Rome: "I am a lazy beast who does nothing—who can do nothing, I should say, because I don't know exactly what I want . . . I'll be here this summer . . . What do you say to a trip to Bayreuth next summer? I'm strongly considering it."

In September he was back in Oslo, with teaching and concerts. That autumn Svendsen returned from Germany and took up residence in the city, and a productive collaboration between the two began. In this dynamic fellow artist Grieg got the most active supporter he could have desired in the struggle to raise the musical level of the city and to win sympathy for authentically Norwegian music. He summed up his situation prior to Svendsen's

14. GRIEG EXPRESSES HIS OPINIONS REGARDING THE WORKS OF TWO NORWEGIAN COLLEAGUES

I wish you were here this evening and could go along to Svendsen's concert, which includes [some] truly brilliant things. I am sending you the program, which shows that we have some talent up here. The carnival ["Carnival in Paris"] is the best. Here rhythm and harmony vie with an instrumentation that is not only masterful, but often entirely new. For this occasion he has managed to put together an enormous orchestra (and for once the musicians are donating their services; the "Music Association," which has to pay its musicians, simply can't compete). He conducts well, so for once we can indulge completely in pure enjoyment of the music.

You should hear his orchestration of Liszt's *Rhapsody* [No. 6]! In his arrangement, the piano passages turn into the most original and imaginative orchestral play . . . and I won't now talk about the dynamic level. Here it is as it should be, but sometimes in the other pieces it assumes such dimensions that I—once the initial surprise is over—become almost numb and then weak, unreceptive to everything, no matter how wonderful it may be.

Johan Selmer, another Norwegian musician whose name you see on the program, is also talented, albeit in his style less clear than Svendsen. Like Svendsen, he has a strong revolutionary tendency . . . and all this demonic stuff is, of course, a result of the French influence. Now the demonic element certainly has its place in life and in art, just as surely as [the Norse god] Loke rides alongside [the Norse god] Thor, but, but—but he [Loke] should also be away once in awhile.

But as I said, we have talent up here—and better to have something demonic that is kept under control than that German morbidity which isn't capable of vigorous development. (Letter to Winding, October 26, 1872.)

entrance into the arena in a letter to Aimar Grönvold in 1881: "I would rather skip over my long stay in Oslo. To write my biography of these years would be to write primarily about the artistic life in Oslo, and that, God knows, was thin. I stood alone. Kjerulf, who warmly supported me in the beginning, fell away in 1868. Of the following years I can only say that, until Svendsen won the hearts with his homecoming, it is only with bitterness that I can think back on the indifference—yes, the contempt and disdain that were shown for Norwegian music. I could tell things about this period that sound unbelievable. But there was actually at that time a total lack of what is called artistic morale."

On October 26 Svendsen gave a big concert with the Christiania Theater Orchestra. The program included, among other things, two premieres: his own *Karneval i Paris* [Carnival in Paris], Opus 9, written during the summer, and Johan Selmer's *Nordens aand* [The Nordic Spirit], Opus 5, for chorus and orchestra. Grieg's comments on the concert give a valuable insight into his artistic point of view at this time.[14]

Grieg and Svendsen shared the podium at the Music Association's first subscription concert on November 30. Svendsen premiered his violin concerto with Gudbrand Böhn as the soloist; Grieg conducted Beethoven's Fifth Symphony and *Before a Southern Convent,* with Nina as soloist. *Aftenbladet*'s review on December 2 stated: "Grieg's music for *Before a Southern Convent* completely fulfilled the expectations we had formed beforehand for this work . . . The composition is gripping with its grand simplicity and striking veracity; it is faithful to the text in the most beautiful way, and the handling of the orchestra—especially in the colorful introduction—was highly effective."

The work was repeated at the next concert on December 21. This concert also included two Danish works: Winding's *Nordisk ouverture* [Scandinavian Overture] and Gade's Fourth Symphony, as well as Beethoven's *"Emperor" Concerto* with Neupert as soloist. *Aftenbladet* reported two days later: "Everything performed by the orchestra and choir gave evidence of the most skillful and careful rehearsal." On December 26 Grieg wrote to Winding that he had had three "detailed rehearsals," and that the string group consisted of twenty violins, seven violas, four cellos, and four double basses "plus a new and quite competent timpanist who gave life and rhythm to the whole, so it won't surprise you [to hear] that something came of your beautiful piece . . . Neupert played splendidly and enjoyed a triumph such as he has never dreamed of up here . . . Gade's symphony also went very well." He added a somewhat ironic note, however: "When *Aftenbladet* states that [Gade's symphony] has a *powerful* sound, I think that is going too far."

In early January, 1873, Grieg went to Stockholm, where he gave two very successful concerts. At the first, which was given on January 12 in the large stock exchange hall, he conducted the *A-minor Concerto* with Neupert as soloist. Two days later he had an evening of his own in the Royal Theater. The prime mover for this visit was August Söderman, to whom Grieg sent his thanks in a letter of January 25: "You were incomparably generous and gracious towards me; I shall not forget it."

As in the preceding year, the Music Association concluded the concert season with a large choral work: Mendelssohn's oratorio *Elijah* (Part 1). On May 2 the Griegs then left on a four-week concert tour enroute to a long-awaited summer stay in Bergen. They first visited Drammen, then Arendal, Kristiansand, and Stavanger. Arriving in Bergen, Edvard gave concerts on June 11 and 15. On August 11, for the first and only time, he appeared in concert with Ole Bull, whom he accompanied in two of his own violin pieces: "Minuet" (the second movement of the violin sonata in F major) and "Gavotte" (which Grieg included in *Sigurd Jorsalfar* under the title "At the Matching Game").[15]

That autumn, just before Grieg left for Oslo, something nice happened: at the instigation of Björnson—without Grieg knowing that *he* was back of it—some citizens of Bergen presented him with three hundred spesiedalers (the profits of a song festival) as a travel grant.

Meanwhile, in Oslo plans were being made to collect funds to expand the activity of the Music Association. The result of an ingathering was that on November 26 the Board was able to issue a press announcement that two thousand spesiedalers had been received, and that it probably would be possible for sixteen concerts to be given under the direction of "Messrs. Grieg and Svendsen."

From this point on Svendsen took over the purely orchestral evenings, while Grieg had responsibility for the concerts where a choir was involved.

The 1873–74 season actually comprised eleven concerts. Of these, three consisted of chamber music, with Svendsen playing viola in a string quartet in which Gudbrand Böhn played first violin. Grieg conducted three concerts that included large choral works, among them Schumann's *Paradise and the Peri*. On May 3 Nina wrote to Fredrika Stenhammar: "Grieg is well, thank God. He rests, in a way, after his concert exertions. I say 'in a way' because he gives a great many lessons, and that really isn't the sort of work that refreshes one's spirits."

O. M. Sandvik has given a rich characterization of Svendsen's and Grieg's conducting activities at this time.[16] The two of them collaborated very well,

15. GRIEG REPORTS ON A CONCERT WITH OLE BULL

I remember a similar celebration here in Bergen . . . It was in 1873. Ole Bull gave a concert—[to raise money] for Leif Erikson's monument—in that beautiful hall called "Ekserserhuset." He had invited Björnson. And Björnson came. Bull played, Björnson gave a lecture on Leif Erikson, and I conducted. Yes, Bull and I also played together, and the interesting thing for me was that this was the only time in my life that he and I performed together in public. After the concert we got together for a private party. And then you spoke, Björnson . . . among other things, in support of [the restoration of] Haakon's Hall [a medieval banquet hall in Bergen]. You wanted to have it made into a mausoleum honoring Norway's cultural leaders, with Ole Bull standing in the place of honor with a lowered bow. But that was when Ole Bull jumped up from his chair: "Why with a lowered bow? No! I don't want to die. I want to live!" (From Grieg's response to Björnson at Grieg's sixtieth birthday celebration on June 15, 1903.)

16 GRIEG AND SVENDSEN AS CONDUCTORS

The two leaders appear to have shared the work and the laurels equally. Svendsen's excellent abilities as an orchestra man, though, put him a bit ahead of Grieg. The critics constantly underscored his eminent leadership. On the other hand, Grieg's programs of choral works were always well received by the audiences. As instructors they were not equally successful, at least with the orchestra. Svendsen was of course the decidedly superior absolute ruler against whom no one dared to protest, and moreover he was so good-natured and likable that all conflicts were avoided. Grieg, on the other hand, was more irascible, and his joint rehearsals with chorus and orchestra could sometimes make the somewhat undisciplined musicians impatient—all the more because Grieg sometimes had the bad habit of making them repeat a whole section without explaining in what way it was unsatisfactory the previous time. This happened one time too many at one of the rehearsals of *Paradise and the Peri*. When Grieg—after endless repetitions—finally said, "All right, now we will take the whole thing over once again," the concertmaster, Fredrik Ursin, replied, "Yes, let's do that!" and struck up a rapid folk-dance tune for solo violin. Everybody laughed, and Grieg bowed and said: "Yes—well, thanks for today!" (O.M. Sandvik in *Norges Musikhistorie*, Vol. II, p. 165.)

17. BJÖRNSON ON *ARNLJOT GELLINE*
AS AN OPERA SUBJECT

I shall rewrite *Arnljot* as an opera for him
up there, and it will be done soon. The
whole design, scene by scene, is complete.
(Letter from Björnson to Gotfred Rode,
January 23, 1872.)

* * *

Hurry up now! You can do it, I'm sure:
broad, plain music that costs you nothing.
Read the saga and get yourself into the
mood. (Letter from Björnson to Grieg,
September 24, 1872.)

and that was good both for the musical life of the city and for their personal
friendship. There was never a hint of any rivalry between them. Grieg touched
on this in his 1881 letter to Aimar Grönvold: "More and more I have been
attracted by Svendsen's art, although nothing could be more different than
our artistic natures. He has taught me to believe in myself and in the power
and legitimacy of individuality. As you know, there was a time in Oslo when
to be an individual was the same as to be a criminal. But then Svendsen came,
and he was also an individual, and then the miracle happened: from that time
on I too was tolerated. There are, therefore, few artists to whom I feel
gratitude such as I feel toward Svendsen. When he returned home in 1872
there were a number of people who wanted us to become enemies. But—
thanks to our mutual appreciation of the art of the other—the plan completely misfired."

Further work with Björnson

Grieg's work as a composer during the years 1872–74 continued to reflect the
influence of Björnson, with musical dramas occupying the center of his
interest. Once it occurred to him that he might make more out of *Before a
Southern Convent.* On January 3, 1872, he sent the work to Winding in the hope
that he would like it: "I have thought of this as a scene in an opera. You
undoubtedly understand the connection with Liszt. Do you remember when
we stood before that southern convent beside the Titus arch, and what
unforgettable hours we spent out there?"

Björnson immediately jumped at the idea of writing a libretto based on
Arnljot Gelline, and considered going with Grieg to Valdres that summer so
they could work together on the opera. Instead, Grieg went to Copenhagen.
But Björnson proceeded with the project, and in September he sent the
manuscript to Grieg with words of encouragement.[17] Nothing ever came of it
on Grieg's part, however, except for some rough drafts, including a sketch of a
section from "Bjarkemaal" (in *Heimskringla*). Again in 1875 Grieg mentioned
to Björnson that his interest in the project had reawakened, but without
result.

As the new year 1872 began, Grieg was busy with another task: writing
music for Björnson's new play, *Sigurd Jorsalfar.* On January 14 the poet
reported to his Danish friend Gotfred Rode that Grieg was at work on the
project. On February 2 he mentioned to Mrs. Rode that the play, with music
by Grieg, was "being copied at top speed" for delivery to the theaters in the
Scandinavian capitals and in Gothenburg. At the same time he wrote to
Grieg: "The music, therefore, must be ready within a month. Naturally, you
will be paid for it. You'll get the complete text in a couple of days—as soon as
Karoline [Björnson's wife] has finished copying it."

With the exception of Oslo, however, all the theaters mentioned in Björnson's letter of February 2 rejected the play. Christian Molbech, the consultant
in Copenhagen, went so far as to characterize it as a play written by a "careless
and affected playwright." This made Björnson furious, and in a letter to

18. GRIEG'S ACCOUNT OF THE PERFORMANCE OF *SIGURD JORSALFAR* ON MAY 17, 1872

It was packed from floor to ceiling. The curtain went up. I almost regretted that I had taken Björnson there. To begin with, it was obvious that he was not enjoying himself. And I understood why. On the stage there was absolutely no trace of direction. One played hither and one thither . . . Although Björnson came with the best intention of being charitable and of looking open-mindedly at the whole production, he was perceptibly nervous. There were moments when quiet, ominous grunts suggested that the interior of the crater was not to be played with . . .

[During the first intermission the poet went over to an acquaintance and said:] "This is really rough!" . . . Björnson returned to his seat. When the curtain went up again it was Mrs. Gundersen who had [the first] lines. Her monologue was thrilling. On the whole, from this point on the acting exhibited more momentum . . . No further expressions of displeasure were heard from Björnson. He sat there like a school boy, calm and nice . . .

But now came my turn to be nervous—yes, almost to forget where I was. It isn't always desirable for the composer to listen to the musical rendition from up in the rafters. Hammer [Hjalmar Hammer, the twenty-five-year-old actor who played the title role] certainly was a gifted actor. Here in the role of a court poet, however, he was also supposed to be a singer. He did his best. But when he got into "The King's Song," I had a strong feeling of displeasure that developed into such a confused torment that I wanted to go away and hide. Instinctively I leaned forward more and more. Finally I was so far down in the seat that, bracing myself on my elbows, I could hold my hand in front of my face. I relate this to illustrate the degree to which Björnson now realized what the situation required of us. Because suddenly he gave me a fairly hard jab and whispered, "Sit up!" I straightened up as though I had been stung by a wasp and sat thereafter in irreproachable immobility in my seat until the very end. But then Independence Day jubilation broke out in earnest. The applause, which previously had been warm, now became tempestuous. (Grieg in *Björnstjerne Björnson. Festskrift*, Copenhagen 1902.)

Frederik Hegel he called Molbech "that cream-barrel fly who drags his legs behind him."

Although it is true that Grieg had only a short time to write the incidental music, he certainly exaggerated quite a bit in the *festschrift* honoring Björnson on his 70th birthday when he stated: "The play was to be staged . . . on such short notice that I had no more than eight days to write and orchestrate the music. But I had the flexibility of youth, and the job got done."

The music shows no sign of having been a rush job. Grieg did, however, take advantage of the opportunity to use an earlier violin piece—"Gavotte"—which was included unaltered as a march under the title "At the Matching Game."

The premiere took place on April 10. Laura Gundersen played the role of the heroine, Borghild, and Johan Hennum conducted the orchestra. *Morgenbladet*'s long but somewhat reserved review appeared two days later. It stated in part: "The incidental music composed by Edvard Grieg to unite the two halves of Act I and that written for the first entr'acte . . . was highly praiseworthy, while [that written for] the two laudatory poems struck us as less successful . . . There were shouts for Mrs. Gundersen to come out and take a bow, but she did not respond. Mr. Grieg was also applauded for a curtain call, which created some dissent among those present."

The author of the play was not present for the premiere because, according to Grieg, there were "such misunderstandings that for a long time Björnson would not set foot in the theater." But he let Grieg talk him into going along to the performance on May 17, and the composer gave a delightful account of this visit to the theater.[13]

A humorous high point of the evening was an episode that occurred after the play was over—an episode the comical effect of which Grieg said he "would never forget." A certain professor X strode onto the stage and criticized Björnson for having one of the characters in the play quote Gunnar Lidarende's famous words in Njaal's saga: "How beautiful is the mountainside; never has it seemed to me more lovely!" "But," said the learned gentleman, "Njaal's saga had not yet been written at that time." Then, according to Grieg, Björnson—striking a magisterial pose—stretched out his arm imperiously toward the director of the play, a fellow by the name of Bucher, and thundered, "Out, Bucher!" And the best part was that Bucher took this command so literally that he "bowed deeply to Björnson, turned around, and . . . in a double-time march disappeared between the wings."

The performance was duly celebrated afterwards at the Björnson home in Piperviken with "marvelous Norwegian cheese." The joint creators of the musical drama "enjoyed [their triumph] like happy children." The culmination occurred when Björnson's children came running in shouting, "Just think, we were up in the balcony and saw father and Grieg come onto the stage!"

Sigurd Jorsalfar was a genuine public success, and not only on Independence Day (May 17). It was performed nine times during the spring season of 1872, and it remained in the theater's repertory continuously in the years that followed.

19. BJÖRNSON'S STAGE DIRECTIONS FOR "BORGHILD'S DREAM"

. . . Borghild lies partially clothed upon the coverlet. Her hair is disheveled, her sleep restless . . . Soft music begins before the curtain goes up, and as it rises it reveals her restless sleep little by little until it comes together in a great terror; she screams, awakens, and sits up. The music reflects the awakening, confused thoughts that swarm to the fore; it stops and she whispers: "Still burns my anger like glowing iron!" The music follows her as she slowly comes forward, stops, and leans against the back of a chair.

The music for the play consisted of eight numbers—six purely orchestral and two songs. They were published in a piano version in Copenhagen in December, 1874, as Opus 22. In 1892 Grieg revised portions of the work, and the following year three of the orchestral pieces were published separately as Opus 56. This orchestral version, which the composer often conducted abroad, was generally well received by Grieg's contemporaries. The British dramatist George Bernard Shaw, who at one time was a music critic in the London press, was an exception, however. After a Grieg concert in May, 1894, he characterized Opus 56 as "pure foolishness, apart from an imaginative and sensitive movement for muted strings in pianissimo, with an abrupt shudder in the timpani. This movement depicts somebody or other's restless dreams."

The movement to which Shaw was attracted was "Borghild's Dream," the middle movement in Opus 56. To modern ears, on the other hand, this movement sounds like the absolutely weakest part of the entire piece. Musically it is thin and cliché-ridden compared to the rest of the *Sigurd Jorsalfar* music, where the composer's profile is far more prominent. "Borghild's Dream" functions well, however, in its original setting as purely illustrative music in connection with Björnson's stage directions.[19]

Grieg built the music around a subdued, flowing opening motive. In the agitated midsection this motive is reshaped to depict the heroine's nightmare and awakening, and in the concluding part it expresses pain and sorrow.

"Borghild's Dream" appears in the middle of Act I of the play. As a prelude to Act II we find the march "At the Matching Game" (fomerly "Gavotte"). This piece begins with a heroic theme in A major. This theme, which is quite striking melodically, will characterize the departing Sigurd, one of two competing royal brothers in the play:

The quiet middle section in A minor depicts the more cautious Eystein, the brother who stayed at home. We cite here a modally colored section, where the concluding phrase in the first line differs markedly from the tonal cadence in the second line:

In both of these pieces from Opus 22 the harmonization was changed in several places for Opus 56. Among other things, major sevenths were added to a series of triads in the first section of the march.

The song "Northland Folk" concludes the second Act. Björnson's powerful poem is set in four identical stanzas, the first two being sung by Haldor, the third by a nobleman, and the last by King Sigurd. A refrain for male chorus follows. With simple means, Grieg here created one of his most popular compositions. He wrote to Max Abraham on August 5, 1892, that "here in Bergen 'Northland Folk' is so ridiculously popular that after being performed at concerts in the park it is even being sung by the street urchins . . . More than once I have had to go another route to avoid hearing these stanzas, which are yelled with terrible coarseness."

It does not appear that Grieg himself thought especially highly of the piece. In connection with the program for a concert in Oslo in 1896 he wrote to Iver Holter: "You will undoubtedly understand that on this occasion I don't want to be represented with 'Northland Folk' but with works in which the best of my personality is clearly expressed."

"Homage March" marks the reconciliation between the two kings midway through the third (last) Act. The theme, one of Grieg's most rousing melodies, is introduced pianissimo by the cellos in a four-voiced setting. It is carried forward with steadily increasing excitement to a grandiose climax with augmented note values for full orchestra. In the revised version of 1892 (Opus 56) the march is greatly expanded: in addition to an introductory pompous fanfare, Grieg inserted a long Trio midsection. Both melody and harmony—sometimes by virtue of the deft use of chromaticism—here bear the distinctive stamp of Grieg's compositional style during the 1890s.

This march in its final form is an especially effective concert piece. Its orchestral splendor is fully equal to that of Svendsen's "Festpolonese" [Festival Polonaise], and its expressive power even surpasses it. It is festive music at its brilliant best.

In the three stanzas of "The King's Song" that bring the play to an end, court poet Ivar Ingemundson pays homage to the two brother kings. In the first two stanzas Grieg has the soloist declaim in a recitative-like style. In the last stanza, however, he changes to a broad melody of folk-like character which is then taken up by the male chorus.

In 1903 Grieg prepared a complete score of *Sigurd Jorsalfar* for a staging at the Stuttgarter Hofbühne, including three additional orchestral pieces: a prelude to Act I (forty-one bars taken from "The King's Song") and two interludes (mostly music from "The Homage March").

May 17, 1872 was also memorable for Björnson and Grieg in another way: that forenoon a bazaar was held at the Akershus fortress to raise money for the restoration of the Nidaros [Trondheim] cathedral, and here *Land Sighting* was premiered. Björnson's poem by this name was based on the writings of Snorri Sturluson—"Snorre," as he is usually called in Norway—the twelfth-century Icelandic poet and historian who wrote a history of the Norwegian kings. According to Snorre, Olav Trygvason—on his return to Norway in 995—had plans to build a church in Nidaros. Taking this report as a starting point, Björnson wrote his enthralling poem, which was planned explicitly for the big event at Akershus. On May 12 he wrote to Grieg: "I love this song! I expect a *big* sound!" A "big" sound he got in Grieg's music, and Grieg used

20. GRIEG COMMENTS ON A
PERFORMANCE OF *LAND SIGHTING*

The day before yesterday I gave a concert to raise money for the Haakon's Hall project, and was well received. Your *Land Sighting* made a great impression and had to be repeated. I have now changed the declamation and am pleased with the piece. But those Bergensers can really sing. N.B.: when I am the conductor! Through the entire piece you could sense a unified, noble sound which can only be attained when *everybody* is thoroughly caught up in the piece. I'm sending you the program so you can see how it reeks of *Bear [Björn]* steak! (Letter from Grieg to Björnson, June 17, 1873.)

this same expression when he told Björnson about a performance in Bergen the following year.[20]

At the Akershus premiere *Land Sighting* was performed by two male choruses, baritone solo, wind ensemble, and organ. Grieg revised it two or three times before it was published in 1881 as Opus 31, dedicated to Karl Hals. The wind ensemble was then replaced by a symphony orchestra and some new interludes were added. The piece, which has become very popular in Norway, has also enjoyed some success abroad.

Land Sighting depicts Olav Trygvason's experience of nature's might and culminates on a solemn note with a religious undertone. In the first section (Allegro moderato) the male chorus sings the three introductory stanzas using the same terse melody throughout, but there are harmonic and dynamic changes from stanza to stanza. In the 1881 version the orchestra plays a more important role than in the original version. The new interludes especially illustrate the text's changing pictures in a striking manner.

The chorus also sings the fourth stanza, but when we come to the words "sounds as of church bells chiming" the melody is changed and Grieg employs modal harmonies to create an archaic, church-like stamp in accordance with the text:

The rest of this stanza proceeds by way of E minor to B major. Grieg then moves directly to G major, the key in which the last part of the composition (Andante molto e religioso) begins. This very expressive section consists of three stanzas with virtually identical settings, each containing two contrasting subsections that alternate between G major and E major. The first two stanzas are sung by the soloist. The choir takes over in the last stanza, which leads to a powerful climax in the concluding line, "Spirit nature's height attaining, Fill'd by Him all things sustaining." The piece ends as a veritable apotheosis with a brief coda-like cadence on the words, "filled by Him!"

Land Sighting is undoubtedly one of Grieg's most successful choral works. He himself regarded it as merely an occasional piece, but it pleased him greatly to see the effect it had on people. After a performance in Oslo on December 7,

1905, he wrote in his diary: "*Land Sighting* went so well that even I was completely thrilled."

Before the summer of 1873, when Grieg started on his next big project—the unfinished opera *Olav Trygvason*—he wrote five songs to texts by Björnson. In 1872 he completed *Four Songs,* Opus 21, which had been begun two years earlier. The work was dedicated to August and Clara Winding. Both "To Springtime my Song I'm Singing" and "Say What You Will" are short and compact and have an attractive Griegian freshness about them. The former is a lyric tribute to springtime, the latter a striking picture of longing for the sea—indeed, it is as if one perceives a salty wash of waves in the captivating melody and pounding accompaniment.

One of the most important songs from the 1870s is "Hidden Love," Opus 39, No. 2, which was written in Bergen in 1873. It interprets Björnson's gripping poem with small but nicely varied musical material. Two other Björnson songs written during the summer of 1873, on the other hand, show little evidence of inspiration. They are "The White and Red, Red Roses" (CW 128) and "Sighs" (CW 101, No. 4), neither of which was published during Grieg's lifetime.

Olav Trygvason

The great enthusiasm awakened by *Sigurd Jorsalfar* and *Land Sighting* in the spring of 1872 whetted Björnson's appetite. He started working on a long-planned play about Olaf Trygvason, a project in which he also wanted to get Grieg involved. On May 30 he wrote to Dikka Möller: "Well, now I am sitting here in possession of everything that is mine . . . my precious things . . . the opera text that I am working on and my reading material, which at the moment is Scandinavian mythology." Impulsive and erratic as Björnson was, however, the *Olav Trygvason* project never got much beyond the idea stage at this time.

During the following summer he wrote a poem commemorating the battle of Hafrsfjord in 872—a "cantata for the millennial celebration of the Kingdom of Norway." The intention was that Grieg should write music for this cantata, but to the composer's disappointment he received the text so late that he couldn't find time to do it. Some misleading statements that appeared in the press made Grieg feel that he had to say something publicly to set the record straight. On July 27 he wrote in *Aftenbladet:* "I therefore want to report that *I could have been finished* if I had been given an opportunity *to start at a reasonable time;* but I was only given eight days to write the whole cantata (consisting of eight sections)—which, I need not add, is an absolute impossibility."

After Björnson finished the text for the cantata, he revived the idea of *Olav Trygvason* and gave Grieg to understand that he was now going to get seriously under way on the project. The work proceeded in fits and starts, however. On November 29 he wrote to E. Stjernström: "I am exuberant! I am working on *Olav Trygvason,* a large dramatic work." But then he evidently

21. BJÖRNSON'S AND GRIEG'S FIRST LETTERS REGARDING *OLAV TRYGVASON*

Dear Grieg:

This is a finished section so I will send it to you. The [remainder of the] act will follow shortly. The piece must be ready by autumn and could earn you a lot of money. The music must go like the wind! That's no joke. It must rush all over the place. It must get steadily wilder and wilder. Then comes a hell of a hullabaloo over the miracle—and then more miracle, frenzied possession, dance, delirium—wow! (Letter from Björnson to Grieg, July 10, 1873.)

* * *

Dear Björnson!

Thanks for the piece you sent me recently. It is pervaded by an incredible sense of mystery, and I look forward to working on it. I have borrowed a cottage from Rolfsen in Sandviken, and that's where I'm going to get started on the project. But I should have liked to know a bit more. Is this the last nocturnal sacrifice prior to Olav's coming? In reading it through it struck me that it needs to be handled melodramatically, and in that case you must give me a completely free hand. I have learned a lot that will be of great help here. But above all: send the next section as soon as possible. (Letter from Grieg to Björnson, July 17, 1873.)

stopped working on the project. Not until the middle of the summer of 1873 did Grieg receive the first three scenes. He was ebullient in his enthusiasm and wrote expectantly to Björnson asking for more text.[21] Within a few months he had drafted the music for the three scenes, and on September 19 he could write to Winding: "This summer I sketched out a bit of dramatic music, but don't mention it to anyone because I don't yet know if anything will come of it." Grieg lived at this time with his parents at Sandviken in Bergen; this was now their home, since they no longer owned "Landaas." Poor health and financial difficulties had forced them to dispose of the beautiful estate. Grieg, however, secured a tranquil place to work in an idyllic cottage at "Elsero," the country estate of a local shipowner and brewer, Rasmus Rolfsen. This cottage served as his "composer's hut" for two or three years.

Björnson visited him in the middle of August on the occasion of the Leif Erikson concert, but he did not bring with him the promised continuation of *Olav Trygvason*. He was about to leave for Austria and then Italy, where the family was to live for several years. With respect to the continuation of *Olav Trygvason*, Björnson emphasized to Grieg that it was essential they be together while they were working on the project, and he urged that he and Nina join him in Italy later in the autumn. In order to make this possible he made arrangements in Bergen for Grieg to receive a travel grant of three hundred spesiedalers. Grieg, of course, understood that he needed far securer financial support for such a trip; further, his obligations to the orchestra in Oslo stood in the way.

Björnson and Grieg parted in Bergen. They could not have imagined that it was to be seven years before they would see each other again—this was at Ole Bull's funeral—and that they would not meet again as friends until 1889.

In Italy Björnson turned his attention to writing contemporary plays, and the dream that he and Grieg once shared of creating an opera based on the sagas was never fulfilled. Instead of scenes for *Olav Trygvason*, Grieg received a mundane cantata text in honor of Karl Hals's silver anniversary as a manufacturer of pianos. This he dutifully set to music (CW 130), but it—like the text—was a trifling occasional piece that, however well intended it may have been, sounds today almost like a parody. Grieg had slightly better luck with another occasional piece that also dates from this time: a lively and folk-like song to a text by Johan Bögh honoring Christian Tönsberg on his sixtieth birthday (CW 129, No. 1).

The work with the orchestra in Oslo greatly taxed Grieg's strength. He felt a steadily increasing need to tear himself away from everything that tied him to Oslo so that he could dedicate himself completely to creative work. In February of 1874, therefore, he and Johan Svendsen joined in sending to the Storting (the Norwegian Parliament) a long and carefully argued petition for an annual composers' stipend.[22] Neither of them was especially optimistic, for five years earlier, when a similar private recommendation had been made for public support for Svendsen, the stipend and pension committee had voted against it on the ground that the two thousand spesiedalers already provided annually by the Storting for scientists and artists to travel abroad was certainly all that could reasonably be expected of them.

22. SVENDSEN AND GRIEG APPLY FOR COMPOSERS' STIPENDS

To the Storting:

The undersigned hereby request an annual public stipend of 400 spesiedalers each in order that they may be enabled thereby to dedicate themselves entirely to their work as composers.

Oslo, February, 1874.

> *Johan S. Svendsen   Edvard Grieg*

Since our economic circumstances compel us to spend nearly all our time in routine teaching, which totally destroys the creative power that we feel is necessary to proceed successfully on the path that we have chosen, we venture to send forward the present request.

We want to call your attention to the way in which provision is made for musicians in other countries. In the larger countries artistic activities abound: there are sinecures, positions for artistic consultants under a wide variety of forms and titles, all of which exist exclusively to give creative talents an opportunity to develop and thereby enrich their country. But in the smaller countries, with which the comparison in our case perhaps is most appropriate—and restricting ourselves to Scandinavia, and especially Denmark—all the outstanding creative musicians have public stipends. And we would especially stress that such an arrangement must appear even more necessary here in our developing artistic environment, where we still have none of the things that in other countries have a stimulating effect on the artist's imagination; for we lack the foundation that is to be found in a national opera with an orchestra and a chorus corresponding to the requirements of art and of our time. Finally, we venture to call attention to the fact that, in accordance with our talents, we have worked for the advancement of our art here in Norway, and with respect to the essential facts about our circumstances we refer to the enclosed biographical summaries.

In 1873, however, the "Venstre" (Left) Party had won the parliamentary election, and Grieg had an inkling that there might be a more liberal attitude toward the arts in the new Storting. Björnson had whole-heartedly supported the petition with a warm recommendation to his good friend Johan Sverdrup, who was president of the Storting. Grieg wrote about this to O. A. Thommessen on September 30, 1898: "I remember what old Björnson wrote one time in a letter that he gave me for Sverdrup when Svendsen and I in 1873 [1874] sought and with his help received a federal grant. He wrote, 'Let us heed the time of our visitation!' Vintage Björnson!"

There was undoubtedly a lot of "corridor politics" in the Storting concerning this matter. The ten-member budget committee split down the middle, five for and five against. Fortunately, however, the chairman of the committee, B. I. Essendrop, voted for the proposal; and since the chairman's vote counted double, the committee supported the petition in its report of May 20, 1874. This report states in part: "Five members of the committee, including the chairman, now wish to support the petition. They assume that the great importance of music for our cultural development is generally recognized and that art no less than science warrants public assistance . . . These members assume, however, that the petitioners will dedicate their abilities to the furtherance of music in their fatherland."

During the decisive consideration of the issue in the Storting on June 1 the outcome was uncertain, but Sverdrup had played his cards well: the recommendation was adopted by a vote of 61 to 44. In the debate, considerable weight was given to a statement that had been obtained from the Music Association. It was read in its entirety. Sverdrup gave a long speech from which some excerpts are given in the Primary Materials.[23] Grieg and Svendsen were each awarded an annual stipend of four hundred spesiedalers "until the Storting decides otherwise."

A few days later Grieg had occasion to discuss the grant in a letter to Beyer: "One thing that dampers my joy [in receiving the grant] is the fact that everybody around me gives me the impression that I am very lucky rather than deserving of the four hundred spesiedalers. As a matter of fact, I hear from

23. FROM THE DEBATE IN THE STORTING

The Storting [the Norwegian Parliament] had appropriated funds for the gathering of a rare treasure of national melodies; they lay there like dead things, and it couldn't have been the intention that the job should remain unfinished. If they were to be further developed in various ways it was necessary that the important musicians that we possessed be given an opportunity to work with this material. The experience of nations everywhere showed that music deserved to take its rightful place beside the other arts, and that it must do so if the cultural life was to be full and complete . . .

The speaker now wished to add that the gentlemen who had influenced him toward supporting the proposal were men of recognized artistic talent who by their diligence had shown themselves in all respects to be worthy of the nation's support. Testimonials had been received from the most knowledgeable authorities stating that these men, according to all the evidence, had before them an even greater future as artists, and that they must be regarded as possessing such ability and training that one could confidently expect that a grant to them would fall on fertile ground and that it would be an important step toward the development of the art form in question . . . (Abstract of Johan Sverdrup's speech.)

some quarters that it is an injustice . . . against the civil servants who received either too little or no increase. Now there's an uplifting attitude for you! It's like I always say: one does not find one's best friends in one's own family . . . I sent a thank-you telegram to Sverdrup. I feel moved in a wonderful and quiet way by what has happened—and I feel a great responsibility, for now I am starting a new life; the time has come."

On June 26 Björnson wrote to Grieg: "I send you my hearty congratulations on the composers' stipend that you and Svendsen received! I think I played a part in this, which makes me all the happier. For the same reason I rather expected to hear a word from one of you now that it has happened. But you artists are the most egotistical people on earth. You expect the whole world to wait on you hand and foot; if it doesn't, then to hell with it, and if it does—well, then it is only doing its duty."

Grieg was not able to muster much of a defense against Björnson's complaints when he replied on July 5: "Thank you for your letter. It made me very happy. But I don't grant a bit of what you say about egotism. No, you see, in recent years I have been living suppressed, without being able to express myself, and under those circumstances much can appear to be egotism that really isn't that at all . . . Sincere thanks for your letter to Sverdrup. It was not made public, for we preferred to do everything possible to prevent a public discussion of our petition ahead of time. The reason that I did not answer you at that time was, of course, that I was angry with you. And surely you know why? Because now I am sitting here composing music to *Peer Gynt* instead of to *Olav Trygvason*. That's the nub of the matter. But how can I carry a grudge against anybody now when I feel so happy—and least of all against you, whom I hold in such high regard because of both what you are in yourself and what you awaken in me! We will not see each other soon, for now I am spending the summer here in order to work undisturbed in the beautiful cottage in Sandviken . . ."

Björnson had sent a poem along with his letter and in connection therewith had written: "As thanks for the grant, in gratitude toward farmers, Sverdrup, me, and other notorious fighters for freedom, you are to write a first-rate melody for the enclosed Battle Hymn for the Freedom Lovers of Scandinavia. To tell the truth, I don't think there is a composer in Scandinavia other than yourself who dares to do it under present circumstances. But for that reason it will also be noted and remembered that you dared."

Grieg replied enthusiastically: "Your battle hymn, which I received this morning, is completed, and if it is not democratic then nothing is. Moreover, it is a solid piece; it comes marching up like a whole battalion—the kind that takes its objective by storm."

This little composition (CW 131), which is not really distinguished in any way, was sent to Denmark where it was published in *Dansk Folketidende* three weeks later.

Greatly irritated because Grieg was in the process of writing music for Ibsen's play, Björnson wrote on July 14: "For one who is busy with other literary projects, it is a great loss of both time and money to write opera texts. Nonetheless, I offered to get at it as soon as you appeared. But without your

Björnson in a typical pose as depicted by a contemporary caricaturist. (Olaf Gulbransson, c. 1900; public domain)

presence my text was written haphazardly, not the way you would want it—*at once,* thus requiring revision after revision—as a result of which I had no time whatsoever. Already in Bergen we had an agreement that you would follow me to Italy. *That is why* I scraped up the money for you there . . . *That is why* I supported your petition for a grant. Who has broken his word in this matter? You or I? My offer was repeated at the beginning of the summer, at the very time when your new freedom to work was about to begin. Once again in vain. Now you're working on *Peer Gynt!* It has *some* parts that lend themselves to poetic music, but the totality is a flight away from such music—a flight that often leads through comical and dry places that you will not conquer. Once again you are wasting your time and talents. This my solemn warning I will not neglect to send to you, even if it rubs you the wrong way. Possibly some day as an *older man* you will be able to master such material in its entirety, but you can't do it now."

It was two months before Grieg answered. In September he went to Denmark, where he was to remain until January of 1875. On September 12, enroute to Denmark, he wrote from Kristiansand: "Your last letter was indeed highly original! Do you think that I willingly neglected to go to Italy last winter? Since you had a part in [securing] the three hundred spesiedalers that I received in Bergen, I do thank you most sincerely; but with just those funds could I take my wife and go out into the world and devote myself exclusively to composing? And yet, I would have done it if I had gotten rid of my lodgings. No! It was certainly *good* that I stayed home, for otherwise the four hundred [the composer's stipend] would hardly have been forthcoming. It really is a fact that if I had gotten your text I would have said no to Ibsen and thus would have avoided *Peer Gynt* with its many perils. I hope to be finished with it this autumn (it is only a matter of a few fragments here and there), and then I am enthusiastically ready for *Olav Trygvason.* But—I must be in a place where I can hear good dramatic music, stay in touch with the times, and have frequent contact with art and artists in general. As much as I would have liked to first take a side trip to Italy to meet you and discuss everything that we need to discuss, I just can't afford it, since I seriously hope for the time being to be able to work undisturbed abroad. I feel that the moment that has come for me will not come again, and it must not be wasted in traveling and pleasure: it must be used. So even if you were to send me the most tempting letter from Italy, I would have to be like stone and push all the feelings away . . . Just write away at *Olav!* Do it! If you have grand scenes they will be suitable for opera, that I know. You have now lived for so long with contemporary images that it will be a joy and an urge for you to get to work on the saga again."

Björnson thought Grieg was writing an opera to the text of *Peer Gynt,* and wrote ironically to S. A. Hedlund on September 10: "Now Grieg is writing one opera after another. Ça ira! [So goes it!]" But Grieg's letter succeeded in satisfying the offended author on this point. In his answer dated September 17, Björnson acknowledged that he had been mistaken: "I am very glad that it is not an *opera Peer Gynt* that you are working on. Very!" But even so he could not resist giving Grieg a little jab in the ribs: "You have traded Olav Trygvason—for Peer Gynt; you certainly are a modern philistine!!?? Boo!"

24. BJÖRNSON'S IDEA FOR
THE CONCLUDING TABLEAU
IN *OLAV TRYGVASON*

Olav before the burnt-out temple, with the bishop and people standing further down the steps singing God's praise; and from above, from the surrounding forest, the throng of white-robed people desiring to be baptized . . . white-robed men and women who come singing from every direction, white [sic] music, a white sun shining on the land and in their faces . . . (Letter to Grieg, September 17, 1874.)

25. BJÖRNSON AND GRIEG ENJOY
THEMSELVES AT WAGNER'S EXPENSE

Wagner is sick; there are entire keyboards in his soul that are completely locked up. This autumn I saw *Tristan and Isolde*. It is the most enormous depravity I have ever seen or heard, but in its own crazy way it is so overwhelming that one is deadened by it as by a drug. Even more immoral . . . than the plot is this seasick music that destroys all sense of structure in its quest for tonal color. In the end one becomes just a glob of slime on an ocean shore, something ejaculated by that masturbating pig [Wagner] in an opiate frenzy! (Letter to Grieg, September, 1874.)

* * *

I have almost laughed myself to death over your statement about Wagner, and because of those two lines I hesitate to send your letter to Holmboe. If I don't get it back again I will hate him for the rest of my life. (Letter to Björnson, October 1, 1874.)

Meanwhile, he intimated to Grieg that the *Olav Trygvason* project could be taken up again: "As soon as you come I will lay everything else aside and we will begin at once. But *before* you come—no, I'm not going to work in a fog or by guess. Tell me when you are coming and the draft will be ready when you arrive . . . How many opera plots do I not have [in my head], and how willingly would I not write them!" Thereupon he sketched in poetic terms how he had conceived the conclusion of the opera.[24]

In the same letter Björnson reported his impressions of some Wagner operas he had attended recently, and we are given an astonishing insight into his opinion of this composer. It is clear that Wagner was not the model for his own operatic ideas. Grieg in no way disagreed with Björnson's grotesque statements about *Tristan and Isolde,* including an expression that today sounds totally shocking. To the contrary, in his October 1 reply he absolutely gloated over Björnson's coarseness.[25]

In this letter Grieg also wrote: "Your letter was marvelous! It contained so many things for which I thank you again and again. It opens possibilities for me of the very kind that I love!" But for the time being, he said, he had to continue working on the *Peer Gynt* score, which he had promised to have ready by Christmas, in order to earn money for the trip to Italy. It would be, he wrote, "foolish of me to waste time and money on a *short* visit to Rome. That is how I see it, and *I* cannot act otherwise. There are times when I want to abandon the whole thing and flee southward, but no—that must not happen. If you will still be there for a full year starting next spring, I will move heaven and earth to spend that year with you in Italy, because that is how much time will be needed. For to write an opera will take *ten* times as long as it takes to write a play—N.B., a contemporary opera."

He asked further whether Björnson could really think that the decision to write music for *Peer Gynt* was a "voluntary choice on my part! I was exhorted by Ibsen in the spring and naturally I bridled at the idea of writing music for that most unmusical of subjects. But I thought about the 200 [spesiedalers, i.e., the honorarium for writing the music], and about the trip—and I made the sacrifice. The whole thing hangs over me like a nightmare; if I could be done with it I would leave in a moment. If I had not had to write music for the unveiling of the monument to Kjerulf I would be done with it now. It is awful to be in a certain way the only one [who can do these things], as I have sometimes been; one is used as the organ grinder of the day, and one has no time to write what is in one's heart—one is always doing something else. For that reason it is high time that I get away. I've had enough realism for now."

In connection with *Peer Gynt* Grieg made an illuminating remark about his understanding of the play, and solicited Björnson's opinion as well: "I can only marvel at how it is filled with a mixture of witticism and bile from beginning to end, but it will never engage my sympathy. Nonetheless, it strikes me as the best thing Ibsen has written. Don't you agree?"

In his sarcastic reply on December 8, Björnson made a crass statement which certainly indicates that it was not only Wagner who he feared might contaminate Grieg, but his Norwegian fellow poet as well: "You say that Ibsen must take precedence. Well, may God grant it! That is how I have seen it

26. GRIEG IS IMPATIENT
WITH BJÖRNSON

He [Björnson]—as he may have told you—
has promised me a text for a Norwegian
musical play, which I have already done a
little work on. But unfortunately I have
other obligations that I must take care of
first before I can do any more with this
project; and besides, Björnson refuses to
give me any more text unless I am near
him—a harsh demand, but one I wish I
could accede to, because I really am very
fond of him. Greet him and tell him that I
wait longingly for a letter from him, and
that I will wait as long as I must, albeit not
as long as Solveig in *Peer Gynt:* for a lifetime. (Letter to Ravnkilde, January 9, 1875.)

27. GRIEG HAS PLANS TO FINISH
ARNLJOT GELLINE

Would you believe that during the past few
days I have read through both of the first
two acts (*Olav* [*Trygvason*] and *Arnljot*) and
have come to the conclusion that my musical-dramatic interest leans towards *the latter?* . . . It's good that I neglected *Arnljot*
for a while; I have become more able, have
developed a better eye for the dramatic, and
I now have a definite feeling that it will develop into something. But please don't
think that I have gone absolutely mad.
Though I note that in life it is dangerous to
have two subjects at one time. (Letter to
Björnson, May 14, 1875.)

for a long time. But he is so damned vicious and filthy that he only provides
more food for scorn, more fuel for his critics; it is above all the pedants who
use him for their own purposes."

In early January, 1875, Grieg went to Leipzig, and from there wrote to
Ravnkilde in Rome about his collaboration with Björnson and his growing
frustration.[26] On February 21 he thanked Björnson "sincerely" for a letter and
mentioned that in order to finish *Peer Gynt* by April 1—which he had set as a
goal—he now had to "work like a horse." To come to Rome was utterly
impossible, but by the middle of May he hoped to be able to join Björnson in
the Tyrol "at least for a few months, for I need that much time to get anything
accomplished . . . If your wife is going home, I intend also to let Nina go
home so that our time in the Tyrol can be given exclusively to *Olav Trygvason.*"

Björnson had also suggested that Grieg write music for one of his new
contemporary plays. This did not appeal to him, however. "To paint Norwegian scenery, Norwegian country life, Norwegian history and folk poetry,"
on the other hand, "seems to me to be the sort of thing wherein I think I could
accomplish something. What you are talking about certainly has my complete
sympathy as well, but I am not the one to do it—not in this period of my life
in any case. For at this stage Romanticism in all its glory still beckons me!"

The meeting in the Tyrol never came about, however. Grieg tried instead
to persuade his friend to visit him in Leipzig before he left for Denmark at the
end of March: "I am in great need of a sketch of the whole story, but more
about that when we meet . . . You must tell me *definitely* when you are
coming." Björnson accepted the invitation but on the condition "that there
would be no carousing" until they had finished discussing his rough draft. On
May 14 Grieg wrote: "I am terribly anxious to see you and talk with you, but
you must not scold me for not going to the Tyrol . . . Nina sends her greetings. She is fine and thinks you are a funny guy." Grieg also mentioned that
now it really was the *Arnljot Gelline* project that interested him most.[27] And
he wrote in perfect honesty: "The entire blood-sacrifice scene in *Olav* is fine,
but there are many places where I can tell that you have been thinking in terms
of melodrama, not opera. Especially the beautiful monologue: it is too long,
as is the chorus that follows. That is also the exact place where I am hung up."

It is quite possible that Björnson could not tolerate this cautious criticism
and that this was the real reason that he did not go to Leipzig—and that now
he completely severed his relationship with Grieg.

Thus the collaboration on *Olav Trygvason* came to an end. From Björnson's side the premise for completing the project was always this: Grieg had to
be with him over an extended period of time. Until this requirement was met
he would not deliver a single new line of text. Thus the project was at an
impasse. Eventually the patience of both men was exhausted.

On May 20 the Griegs went to Denmark, where they were able to borrow
Winding's country home at Fredensborg. They remained there until the
middle of August, then went to Bergen because of the serious illness of
Edvard's parents. Not until the following spring did Björnson hear from
Grieg; in his letter of May 2, 1876, the composer asked warm-heartedly for

28. GRIEG AGAIN REACHES OUT THE HAND OF FRIENDSHIP TO BJÖRNSON

Now I am really living, although it is only in these lovely spring days that I have awakened from a long, long period of lethargy. Heavy waves have swept over me since you last heard from me. Perhaps you have heard that last autumn both of my parents suddenly passed away, and I ended up spending the winter here. It has been dark and miserable, and I have been living as if entrapped by reflections of the most various kinds. What I have written during this time also bears the stamp of the condition I was in. But, although I have grown ten years older, it is nonetheless as if the reflections of these days have led back in time; the child in me came forward once again, and with it the love of everything in life that is beautiful. You had to hear this, because the first thing that comes to mind when I once again see my goal in life is *you!* You, who like none other have shown me that art and life must permeate each other. I am coming to you and I now demand of you that you understand me, and I long to hear from your own lips that you do.

If that is true, then also do not refuse what I now request: Give me a draft of the plot of *Olav Trygvason*—and do it *immediately.* My God, as I write this the desire to get started once again is becoming a veritable suffering! And it is good that this time has passed, for I have become a different person and I look at things differently and more broadly. Dear friend, do it . . .

And then I have one more request: I am very excited about the idea of restoring Haakon's Hall and am thinking about calling all of the singers from western Norway to a meeting here next summer . . . If you will write a kind of cantata or whatever we might call it—something beautiful, something over which hovers the spirit of the saga—I will with great enthusiasm write the music for it.

And now—write, so I can see that you are still the old Björnson. If you have lost interest in me, I just want to tell you that I do not deserve it. But I know there are funny monster-like things in me—unfortunately! But never has the urge to drive those things out been stronger than now. (Letter to Björnson, May 2, 1876.)

understanding and expressed the hope that they could resume their friendship.[28] So far as we know, Björnson never answered this letter.

It was twelve years—near the end of the 1880s—before Grieg again turned his attention to *Olav Trygvason.* As he wrote to Iver Holter in 1897, he discovered one day "that my drafts for the first act could be orchestrated and turned into a concert piece. I got to work on it at once . . ." He rewrote the sketches, which were published by Peters in Leipzig in a piano version. He later prepared an orchestral score, which is dated November 30, 1888, but was published in 1890. It was given opus number 50.

In autumn, 1889, Grieg prepared the premiere performance of *Olav Trygvason* for an October 19 concert by the Music Association orchestra in Oslo— a concert that he himself was to conduct. In connection with this concert he sent some interesting comments about the piece to the resident conductor of the orchestra, Iver Holter.[29]

The time had now come for a reconciliation between the two cultural leaders. Grieg took the initiative. He suggested to Björnson in an October 6 letter that he come to Oslo from Aulestad, his country estate near Lillehammer, to attend the concert, and he went on to say: "I ask for your permission to dedicate to *you* the music for those scenes from *Olav Trygvason* that were completed, and in so doing I offer you proof that ever since we parted I have continued to love you and what you are fighting for—and I express a fervent hope that this work, which was the cause of our losing each other, might also be the thing that later brought us together! So blot out all the little things, and let these dramatic sketches, which are the products of a full heart, also find their way to your great heart—that heart that I loved in days gone by, and that I continue to love in the confidence that it has not changed in the intervening years!"

On October 31 Grieg wrote to Beyer: "I waited anxiously for several days. Finally I got a letter! . . . Just this one passage I must give you right away, for it is so characteristically Björnsonian: '*When you write: Blot out all the little things, I answer: they are blotted out! But I do it only out of obedience, for nothing of the sort was necessary!*'" In his letter of October 13 Björnson wrote further: "You have the greatest lyric power of any musician living today, and it is beyond my ability to remember what else might be in the way . . . I am not going to come down to hear *Olav Trygvason;* I am apprehensive about the old text—I don't remember it any more."

29. GRIEG WRITES ABOUT *OLAV TRYGVASON* IN 1889

As an introduction to the piece itself, I will just tell you that the first drafts date back to 1873! I have undergone enormous development since then, so I cannot honestly say that it is flesh of my flesh and bone of my bone as I am today. But on the other hand I felt that there are things in there that deserved to be rescued from oblivion in the wastebasket. On stage I am sure that it would go well; with respect to the concert hall I confess to some doubt, although I have hope [that it will sound all right there too]. That the piece was not finished years ago is due to the fact that Björnson chose not to send me any more text. That was characteristic of him and his stage of development at that time. Obviously there will never be any more—nor should there be. To continue it now would destroy the unity of style both in his part and in mine. I say this to you quite privately as a friend and an artist. (Letter to Iver Holter, September 24, 1889.)

30. GRIEG'S MUSIC GETS AN ENTHUSIASTIC REVIEW IN THE OSLO NEWSPAPERS

The text of the poem is alliterative and heavy . . . it would have been difficult to maintain this monotony through several acts. Grieg's music for these scenes, as one would expect, is beautiful and interesting . . . It must also be said that the whole score is inspired, noble, captivating, so to that extent it is a pity that the play remains "unfinished." (Otto Winter-Hjelm in *Aftenposten,* October 21, 1889.)

* * *

We venture to say that neither in our music literature nor in that of all Scandinavia can one find another work as magnificent and powerful in its construction as this one; there are some passages where the concert hall is too small to accommodate the dimensions of the music. The entire piece is a brilliant musical poem that has an overwhelming effect. Despite the fact that the text is so nationalistic that it often speaks in riddles, and that it is more reflective of the time in which it was written than of the current cultural period, Grieg's music is completely free of any kind of exaggerated "Norwegianness." Except for the fact that it of course is Grieg's offspring, as a musical composition it could just as well have been composed by a powerful creative spirit in Germany as by a Norwegian . . .

Everything joins together in a picture of extraordinary dramatic effect that includes orchestral passages of great originality. (*Morgenbladet,* October 20, 1889.)

Grieg wrote back two days later: "Thank you again and again for your reply! You don't know how happy you have made me!" He then reported that he had just had the first rehearsal: "I am dead tired, soaked through and through—but it was wonderful! My God, how it is going to sound! With regard to your not coming to Oslo, I had already resigned myself to that . . . Still, it is hard to accept. For there is a prophetess [the prophetess is one of the main characters in *Olav Trygvason*] here who is marvelous! The young woman from Sweden, Miss Ellen Nordgren! That you are apprehensive about the text is touching. That you don't remember it any more is equally touching! It is *brilliant.* That is a fact. But that neither you nor I could work on it again *now* I understand full well. Perhaps it is best as it is. Little but good, as the farm girl said. And now *you* have given me courage and enthusiasm [in a degree] that cannot be overestimated. What you say about my lyric ability is not true, however. On the other hand, I do have some dramatic ability. *Olav T.* is proof of that."

Although Björnson was not present for the premiere performance, he decided nonetheless to show up when the piece was performed again one week later (October 26). Once again he and Grieg could celebrate a great triumph together.[30] *Morgenbladet* reported the next day that Grieg, after five

The collaboration between Grieg and Björnson as seen by a caricaturist in the satiric journal "Korsaren." (c. 1905; public domain)

31. GRIEG REJOICES OVER HIS RECONCILIATION WITH BJÖRNSON

Believe me, I am jubilant about the reconciliation with Björnson after a lapse of sixteen years. He was completely taken with *Olav Trygvason,* and now he is thinking about resuming work on the play. During these days I have experienced moments that I never dreamt could be possible here in Norway. The whole experience was like a spring thaw. (Letter to H. L. Braekstad, October 31, 1889.)

* * *

And then the meeting with Björnson! . . . You should see how wonderfully nice and gracious he has become. For me it is as if I had suddenly become sixteen years younger! For it is that long since we talked to each other. How much I have allowed to get away from me! But I suppose it had to be that way! (Letter to Beyer, October 31, 1889.)

or six curtain calls, shouted from the podium: "To this I have just one thing to say: Long live Björnstjerne Björnson!" Whereupon Björnson "[shouted] through the auditorium that he was proud and glad to be a Norwegian this evening, when we have a man who can write music like that. Long live Edvard Grieg!" Björnson then led a nine-fold "hurrah" for the composer.

Grieg was almost ecstatic when he wrote to Max Abraham: "Last evening I . . . experienced something that I did not consider possible. Even [my success in] London must pale . . . First the audience gave me a cheer, then the chorus, and finally Björnson . . . Also floral gifts, a wonderful lyre, and a huge laurel wreath (which I had not purchased myself!). In short, I hardly knew where I was. But this much I know, that it was much more than I deserved . . ." And in a letter to Beyer on October 31 he wrote: "The artistic satisfaction over *Olav Trygvason* has been extremely great. It sounded, if possible, even more beautiful and impressive than I had dared to anticipate."

The resumption of a warm friendship with Björnson was like a veritable spring thaw in Grieg's soul; he wrote enthusiastically about it in several letters.[31]

Olav Trygvason was also to be performed in Denmark the same autumn, and on October 23—three and a half weeks before the November 16 concert—the music critic Harald Hansen wrote a sarcastic article about the piece in the Copenhagen newspaper *Morgenbladet.* Björnson reacted with strong indignation, and in a letter to Otto Borchsenius, editor of the offending newspaper, he wrote that the critic "is a slanderous, vicious . . . rascal . . . He has written me a letter in which he says straight out that he had it in for me personally, but now regrets it . . . [The article] shows that he has led you astray. For one thing there is *nothing* unclear in my text, and for another there is nothing disjointed in Grieg's music; it is *unified* and powerful."

Grieg himself conducted the concert, and he wrote to Holter on November 21: "Believe me, the performance here was like a cold shower after Oslo. Please greet the chorus from me and say that I now really appreciate for the first time what they did. Here there were 130 singers, but they didn't come close to equaling the result that was achieved at home. But I tell you, this Danish language is the confoundest thing; it makes one more seasick with each passing year."

The reviews were mixed. The most positive one came from Angul Hammerich in *Nationaltidende;* he called Grieg "a man of genius." The composer thanked him for his review on November 21: "It did me much good, because it was the only review of my composition that seemed to me to be dictated by understanding and sympathy . . ."

Grieg now had a newly awakened hope that the piece could be finished. Writing from Paris on December 26, he proposed to Beyer: "If you should some day have an idle moment, write to Björnson as only you can do. He has a great heart, and he will understand you and agree with both you and me if you ask him to continue with *Olav Trygvason.* He really wants me to write music for *Kongen kommer* [The Arrival of the King] (a play that he is working on), but I told him it was not for me and I will not do it for any amount of money. I only want to do *Olav Trygvason* or a Norwegian fairy tale. Well, whatever will be will be. I will write only what I want to write and am able to write."

It does not appear, however, that Björnson had any interest in the idea, for some days later he wrote to his daughter Bergliot: "Yesterday I got a letter from Frants Beyer . . . containing the most earnest appeals for me to finish writing *Olav Trygvason* for Grieg. Well, that's the way it is: everybody wants to use me. Everybody!"

On March 10, 1890, Grieg wrote to Beyer thanking him for having approached Björnson, but said resignedly: "I don't think he feels up to the task or wants to spend time on it. He has gone on to totally different things. I shall not complain, however, for there are so many other things I want to do."

On August 20, however, he wrote to Björnson: "Isn't *Olav Trygvason* coming? Just think, it will soon be a year since we discussed it together—and still no sign of progress. I don't want to talk you into it, for that sort of thing must come from within. Meanwhile, your fragment is still in manuscript while my score has now been published. So you will certainly understand that I do not want to be the only one to gain material advantage from our mutual efforts. Permit me, therefore, to send you the enclosed 1000 kroner from the honorarium that I received. Whether you continue or not—well, the future will tell. If there is to be no more, let me just tell you how happy you made me when, many years ago, you sent me the fragment."

Björnson replied on September 3: "I hear that Björn [Björnson's son] has told you that for the time being I am not working on *Olav Trygvason*. No, I was waiting for you to come . . . Without consultation I'm just not going to proceed . . . [The] first scene is *too long*, and the overall structure obviously has to be changed . . . The treatment must be much more compact."

Grieg wrote back a week later: "Do you really think that a conversation could resolve the matter? I rather doubt it. For I am a big dunce when it comes to conversation. I am happiest when I get the roasted doves ready to eat—as you have let me get them in the past. Then they are delicious!"

Even though the dove of peace hovered over the waters that lay between them, Björnson's pegasus never managed to rise to any further flight with Grieg. Grieg commented resignedly on this in a letter to Iver Holter on February 9, 1897: "There was a lot of talk in those days about Björnson wanting to continue with *Olav T*. But—it was a passing fancy. He was busy with more important tasks and could no longer get excited about things that he had long since left behind—which was certainly understandable. So *Olav Trygvason* will always be a torso."

Thus *Olav Trygvason* remained a fragment with respect to both the text and the music. It bears the stamp of being a broadly developed introduction to a long musical drama, a prelude with nothing that follows. The Björnsonian ideas about opera were totally out of step with the esthetic standards of the 1870s, grounded as they were, more or less, in the spectacularly staged opera (*grande opéra*) with magnificent dance and ballet scenes—a genre that was almost totally out of date.

The three scenes have a tableau-like construction that points more in the direction of a cantata than of an opera. This impression is strengthened by the absence of movement in the somber treatment and the schematic figures in typical dark tones.

The first scene is set in a pagan temple near Nidaros [Trondheim]. The heathen throng is anxiously awaiting the arrival of "the evil Olav," herald of the new faith. After an orchestral introduction, two soloists—a priest-chieftain (baritone) and a woman (mezzo soprano)—alternate with a male chorus and a female chorus in progressively louder shouts to the Norse gods for help in their struggle: "Only gods can contend with gods!" The scene culminates in an extended section for mixed chorus.

In the second scene the third soloist, a priestess (contralto), appears. She utters sinister incantations, chanting magic formulas and writing runic characters that are cast into the holy fire as a "terrible crashing sound shakes the temple." After further supplications to the gods to demonstrate their power, one sees—as in a mirage—the temple disappear and then reappear once again. This miracle shows, sings the chorus, that Olav's gods will lose in the contest with their gods. If, on the other hand, he himself were to step out of the temple unharmed, "then we will believe him!" But "the flame will light him to his grave!" The scene ends with the priest-chieftain lifting "our father Odin's [Wotan's]" horn and the chorus announcing that sacred dances are to be held in honor of Odin.

In the third scene the orchestra and chorus take turns accompanying dances around the sacrificial fire—first a circle dance, then an intense sword dance with constantly changing dance formations. The music is wild and provocative, but lyrical passages for the choir are interjected at two points before the scene is brought to a culmination in great waves of powerful sound.

Grieg was at first enamored of Björnson's concept, but with his sure artistic instinct he undoubtedly soon developed an intuitive premonition that it could go very badly. Today it is also easy to see that it would have been almost impossible to blow life into this torso of rough-hewn granite. He touched on this point in a June 1, 1889 letter to Frederick Delius. In this letter he wrote that *Olav Trygvason* had become "a strange, crude thing—Wagnerian, actually—and it has to do in reality with the Scandinavian gods. This is undoubtedly a mortal sin, but then we are but sinful beings. A dozen sins more or less don't make any difference . . . When I'm done with all this Nordic crudity I will try to wash myself clean again with some genuine songs."

What Grieg identified as Wagnerian—in addition to the historical-mythological subject matter—must have been primarily the treatment of the arias in the soloists' parts. Here we find not melodic arias, but a declamatory song style that might indeed remind one of the Wagnerian *Sprechgesang,* though in its essence it is Grieg's own. The Wagnerian influence in *Olav Trygvason* is in reality scarcely discernible. The connecting lines lead back rather to J. P. E. Hartmann, who in the ballets *Valkyrien* and *Thrymskviden*—both of which were inspired by Norse mythology—and especially in the cantata *Völvens*

Spaadom, had tried to create an "old Norse" style, not least in the handling of the music. Grieg had high regard for these pieces; indeed, in his opinion *Völvens Spaadom* bore "the stamp of genius" like no other work of Hartmann.

If one wishes to look for traces of earlier works, they can be found first and foremost in Grieg's own "historic" compositions *Bergliot, Sigurd Jorsalfar,* and *Land Sighting.* There are many lines of connection between these and *Olav Trygvason.* But *Olav Trygvason* is most clearly stamped with the flavor of the sagas.

Grieg's dramatic talent strikes sparks several times in the course of this thirty-minute piece. He demonstrated a marked ability to build suspense, and made every effort to develop the music in a manner consistent with his understanding of the Vikings' heathen rituals. One notes this already in the first somber tones of the orchestral introduction.

The three main characters—the priest-chieftain, the prophetess, and the woman—are characterized with the help of melodic lines that make one think of the past. In the priest-chieftain's first recitative the Lydian influence is striking:

The augmented fourth—"diabolus in musica"—also appears frequently in the part sung by the priestess and in the chorus. Similar striking devices are used as important elements in recreating the mood of ancient times.

The priestess has the most demanding solo part. Grieg himself was well aware that the effectiveness of *Olav Trygvason* depended entirely on the performance of that part by someone with exceptional talent. Before the piece was performed in Copenhagen in 1889, therefore, he wrote to Otto Malling: "With respect to the solo parts, it is the dramatic contralto who is of first importance . . . It must be a deep and powerful voice, one that can declaim stirringly."

In the dramatic development there are also obvious weaknesses, however. This is less true of the largely effective choral sections than of the principal arias of the solo parts. The latter are not altogether free of a certain monotony, both rhythmically and melodically. Grieg's predilection for merely transposing his themes often becomes rather trite. An example of this occurs in the first scene, where a long section is simply repeated in steadily higher keys (E minor, G minor, and B-flat minor) instead of being further developed. It strikes one as a somewhat too superficial way of increasing the dramatic tension. On the other hand one is often captivated, both in the choral pieces and in the solo parts, by the robust realism of the music. There is not a trace of the mawkishness that was so characteristic of the time. There are a number of abbreviated motives that from time to time are virtually chiselled into the listener's consciousness. The principal weakness, however, lies in the fact that the melodic material in itself is not sufficiently pregnant to hold one's interest.

That which most of all gives *Olav Trygvason* a certain nobility is the composer's imaginative use of the orchestral palette. With his indisputable talent for tonal shading, Grieg frolics with the instruments to produce passages that are sometimes coarse and full of contrast—tonal colors that cause the dark contours of the work to stand out sharply. A good example of this is the opening measures of the orchestral part, where the deep bass instruments announce the principal theme over a pedal point in the horns and tremolo strings:

Also effective are the sharp, piercing sound of the piccolo flute during the ominous incantations of the priestess and the frenzied instrumental wildness in the concluding temple dance. The orchestral writing is generally on a level with Svendsen's. What a pity that Grieg did not orchestrate in this way more often!

A unique example of thematic kinship with other works occurs in the introduction to the third scene. Here one is reminded of both the *A-minor Concerto* and the characteristic thematic motto of the string quartet, Opus 27:

This motive is used very sparingly, however. Only toward the end does it appear again—in the choral part, and then slightly altered.

32. GRIEG ON A TEXT FOR A MUSICAL PLAY

Perhaps now you can understand why I often go and stare up at the clouds as if I could find there the Norwegian drama in Norwegian music that I dreamt of—indeed, that I have always thought I should be able to write some time, but that I am now beginning to think has been decreed by fate to come from someone else. But—it will come. And if it comes profound and great like the Wagnerian operas, perhaps after our time, then—though there must also be people like you to receive it—then I will go as happily to my grave as if I myself had written it. For man's yearning undeniably has an insatiable need to encompass everything, and I must remember—alas! I say it with sadness—that the circumstances of my life have been such that I have expressed myself in the lyrical. But—apart from that, and however that may be, I still have never seen a text that had the power to ignite my soul. And if I don't get one like that, I know somebody who would leave the musical play unwritten rather than write a piece of rubbish. (Letter to Beyer, August 27, 1886.)

33. ADVERTISEMENT FOR *NORWAY'S MELODIES*

This work will be a collection of everything in Norwegian music that is beautiful, distinctively Norwegian, familiar, and attractive. The songs will be arranged for piano in *easily playable* arrangements, yet with constant attention to the artistic requirements . . . Everyone will find here something of interest, because the popular treatment makes it unnecessary to deal with the great difficulties that one would otherwise have to overcome in order to get acquainted with the music of one's own country. (From an advertising circular for *Norway's Melodies* that appeared as an enclosure with the first volume. E. Wagners Forlag. Copenhagen, 1875.)

It was not to be Grieg's lot to compose a complete Norwegian national opera. He wanted to, and he certainly had the ability to do it, but he never managed to get a text that appealed to him strongly enough to make him undertake and complete such a task. That we can only regret.[32]

Norway's Melodies

Grieg financed his trip abroad in the autumn and winter of 1874–75 in part with a publication designed to popularize Norwegian music. This was *Norway's Melodies,* a collection of simple piano arrangements of the music of his homeland, by various composers. The collection was published in Denmark.[33]

It was not generally known that it was Grieg who compiled and edited this work, for when the collection was published in 1875 he insisted that his name not be mentioned. Not until after Grieg's death, when a new edition was published (1910), was it stated on the back of the dust jacket that Grieg was primarily responsible for the collection.

Two years after the appearance of the first edition of this collection, Grieg looked back on it with regret as he revealed the story of its origin in a letter to Matthison-Hansen on March 7, 1878: "In 1874 I was urged by the music publisher E. Wagner of Copenhagen to collect and arrange some pieces for *Norway's Melodies,* which was to be published by his firm. The project had absolutely nothing to do with art; the publisher regarded it as a very simple money-making project, and since he insisted that everything be arranged to suit the 'vox populi' it obviously became for me something that held no artistic interest whatsoever. I would, therefore, have said 'no thanks' and had nothing to do with the whole mess except for the fact that I needed the money for a trip abroad that I was about to take. Thus I went along with his suggestion on the explicit condition that my name was not to be mentioned either publicly or privately in connection with the work in question. Wagner was reluctant to accept this, but when I stood firm in saying that either my name would not be mentioned or else I would have nothing to do with the whole thing he chose to accede to my demand . . . I am no better and no worse because I, like many people more important than I, have worked for money's sake."

After the bankruptcy of the Wagner firm in 1878, Grieg went on to say, the estate in bankruptcy wanted to put out a new edition of the volume "complete with my name," and he was asked "for a relatively large fee to write a foreword—just eight or ten lines—to the new edition . . . Isn't that the limit, to want to buy me in this way." His reaction was violent; he wrote saying "if my name is published I will be compelled, first, to publish a protest in the Danish press and, second, to get a Danish lawyer." Fortunately, no such actions became necessary.

Grieg's agitation is a little difficult to understand. His arrangements in *Norway's Melodies* strike us as an honest piece of work, something he had no need to be ashamed of. Even though the publisher's advertising indicated

34. GRIEG'S OPINION REGARDING THE POPULARIZING OF FOLK MUSIC

If, on the other hand, you want to harmonize or arrange folk songs with the goal of getting them widely disseminated among the people, then you must put away your "oysters and caviar" and get out the "rye bread and butter." One must forget about heaven and remain on earth. Moreover, such publications are entirely justified if they are intelligently and carefully organized—not unwieldy and impractical like Lindeman's collection. *Norway's Melodies,* which you judged so harshly, is just that kind of unassuming publication; and that it has served its purpose is evident from the fact that many thousands of copies have been sold in just one generation. I got a good laugh over your statement [that *Norway's Melodies* was] "scandalously bad." For just between you and me I will tell you that it was I who as a young man—N.B.: in response to a request—harmonized the whole thing from one end to the other! The requirements were that the harmony be simple and that the pieces be as easy to play as possible. I needed the money and demanded complete anonymity. Voila tout! I remained anonymous, too, except—as I recall—for five or six folk songs in which the harmonies were such that it might have been suspected that it was I who had written them. To these I attached my name as the arranger. Wasn't that clever? If you will take the trouble to look once again at *Norway's Melodies* and judge the treatment according to the standards appropriate to it, I am confident that you will take back the expression "scandalously bad." It makes no sense to try to shoot sparrows with cannons, just as it makes no sense to create idylls and pastorales out of pathos à la *Tristan and Isolde.* (Letter from Grieg to G. Schjelderup, November 24, 1905.)

certain artistic pretensions, this clearly was not the primary goal. The main objective was to meet a need for easy arrangements of Norwegian music, in Denmark no less than in Norway.

Grieg appears to have made a judicious choice of material, and the 152 pieces included in the collection are ably arranged for amateurs. Popular songs by composers of various periods and folk tunes alternate with less well known but generally worthwhile pieces from other sources. Ole Bull, Kjerulf, and Nordraak are represented by some of their finest songs. In several of Nordraak's songs Grieg, surprisingly enough, took the liberty of changing some of the chords. Among other things, he introduced dissonances in some places and removed them in others. The collection includes ten of Grieg's own songs written during the period 1865–71.

Norway's Melodies also contains fifty arrangements of Norwegian folk tunes, forty-four of which were derived from the first two volumes of Lindeman's collection, *Ældre og nyere norske Fjeldmelodier* [Older and Newer Norwegian Mountain Melodies]. Eight are taken note for note from this source, which Grieg acknowledged with the notation "arr. by Lindeman." Six of the folk tunes are designated "arr. by Edv. Grieg."

In four of the folk-tune arrangements, Grieg used melodies that he had already employed in Opus 17 (Nos. 10, 15, 16, and 25); but surprisingly enough, the same chord selection is not used in *Norway's Melodies,* where the harmonization is decidedly less advanced. This could indicate that these arrangements were done before Opus 17 (1869), but Grieg's own statement about the time of origin of *Norway's Melodies* makes such a supposition most unlikely.

Three of the folk melodies in the collection were also used by Grieg later in a new harmonic dress in Opus 29, No. 2, Opus 30, No. 1, and Opus 51.

Grieg's own early harsh judgment of *Norway's Melodies* as a work that had "nothing to do with art" is noteworthy in light of something he wrote thirty years later. By that time he was able to view the work from a greater distance and clearly recognized its positive qualities. He was almost offended when Gerhard Schjelderup, in a letter, inadvertently made a condescending criticism of the quality of the collection. Grieg rejected the criticism in a somewhat humorous reply in which he referred to the six "folk songs" that he, in *Norway's Melodies,* had "subtly" identified as his own arrangements and consequently had wanted to acknowledge himself. This part of the letter to Schjelderup is quoted in the Primary Materials as an example of Grieg's attitude toward popularization for pedagogical purposes.[34]

Grieg also published these six arrangements as an independent work in 1886 with a few minor changes. The title was *Six Norwegian Mountain Melodies* (CW 134), and Lindeman's collection was the source for all of them. The arrangements are quite simple, and Lindeman's own arrangements here appear more clearly to have been Grieg's model than was the case in *Twenty-five Norwegian Folk Songs and Dances,* Opus 17. But they also bear a Griegian stamp in their chromatic coloring and modal elements.

Here follows one of the loveliest passages in *Norway's Melodies:* the last eleven measures of "Lullaby" (Children's Song from Valdres), No. 59. (This piece also appears unaltered in *Six Norwegian Mountain Melodies,* No. 2.) Note the Mixolydian strain in the harmony:

ja - ga øl - lø vil-lø Dyr. Æ han kvit, so kjøjr' en hit,

æ han graa so lat en gaa, æ 'n brun i

Bo - ge so lat en gaa i Sko - ge.

Grieg and Ibsen

I have now also read your magnificent Brand. There is something remarkable about the truth. People can tolerate it when it is expressed in poetry; it doesn't touch one's life so closely but that one can enjoy it. When it is expressed in pure prose, however, it is—as Kierkegaard has said—too sharp, too impudent. In no other way can I make any sense out of the enormous furor that Brand has created in the huge circle of readers that daily devours it. (Letter to Ibsen, June 10, 1866.)

To create incidental music for Ibsen's powerful drama, one of the masterpieces of world literature, was a task that called for the very best of which Grieg was capable. A less gifted man might well have come to naught in the face of such an apparently insurmountable challenge. For although, as he wrote to Björnson in October of 1874, he complained about having to write music for "this most unmusical of all subjects," he nonetheless did not avoid the challenge. He wrestled with this "nightmare" that haunted him, and he won.

As is often the case when great works of art come into being, the creation can be credited to a happy coincidence. Grieg was the right man who appeared at the right time to give Ibsen's play its appropriate musical garb. The same thing happened later when he wrote his Vinje and Garborg songs.

It is not generally known that Grieg was not the first person to write music for *Peer Gynt*. The Swedish composer August Söderman did it in the late 1860s, when he wrote a set of pieces for voice and piano based on the Ibsen play. These songs were to have been used at a performance at the Stockholm Opera House on June 16, 1871, in connection with the opening of the railroad between Stockholm and Oslo, but this performance never occurred. The first performance of the Söderman songs—at the Konsertföreningen in Stockholm—did not take place until 1892, sixteen years after the composer's death. Three years later, nine of these pieces were printed for the first time. It is highly unlikely that Ibsen was aware in 1874 that Söderman had written music for his play.

Grieg and Ibsen decide to collaborate

As early as 1866, when Grieg and Ibsen were together in Rome, Ibsen had realized how gifted this man from Bergen was, intellectually as well as musically. His positive opinion of Grieg's maturity and deep understanding of his plays was strengthened by a letter that he received from Grieg dated June 10, 1866. The insightful comments that Grieg here made about *Brand* gave Ibsen further evidence of his ability to internalize purely poetic values.[1]

2. IBSEN INVITES GRIEG'S COLLABORATION

Dear Mr. Grieg:

I am writing to you in connection with a plan that I propose to implement, and in which I wish to invite your participation.

The plan is this. I propose to adapt *Peer Gynt*, which will soon go into its third printing, for the stage. Will you compose the music that will be required? I will indicate briefly how I am thinking of arranging the play.

The first act is to be retained in its entirety, with only a few cuts in the dialogue. I would like to have Peer Gynt's monologue treated either as melodrama or perhaps in part as a recitative. With the help of ballet, much more must be made of the wedding scene than is done in the current version of the play. For this a special dance melody must be composed, which can then continue to be played softly until the end of the act.

In the second act the scene with the herd girls may be handled musically in whatever way the composer thinks best, but there must be deviltry in it! The monologue I have thought of as being handled melodramatically, with chords played in the background. The same goes for the scene with Peer and The Woman in Green. Some kind of musical accompaniment must also be created for the scene in the hall of the Mountain King, although the speeches in this section are to be considerably shortened. The scene with the Great Böyg, which is to be given in full, must also have a musical accompaniment; bird calls must be sung, and church bells and hymns must be heard in the distance.

In the third act I need a few chords for the scene with Peer, the Woman [in Green], and the Troll Child. I have also thought that there should be a soft accompaniment for [the scene depicting the death of Aase].

Nearly the whole of the fourth act is to be omitted. In its place I have imagined a large-scale tone picture suggesting Peer Gynt's wandering throughout the world; American, English, and French melodies might be interwoven, growing and fading one by one.

The chorus consisting of Anitra and the other girls is to be heard singing behind the curtain at the same time that the orchestra is playing. While this is occurring the curtain will go up and the audience will see, as in a distant dream picture, the tableau de-

Against this background it was obvious to the playwright that Grieg was the man he had to bet on when, in 1874, he began making plans to have *Peer Gynt* staged with music interwoven throughout. In a letter to Grieg from Dresden dated January 23, 1874, he asked the composer if he would accept the task of writing the music, and in the same letter described in considerable detail his own interesting ideas about how the music might be developed.[2] That Ibsen wanted to completely omit the fourth act indicates that he was concerned that this least poetic part of the play might lack public appeal. The entire letter bears eloquent witness to the fact that it was written by an experienced man of the theater. It also gives clear expression to Ibsen's explicit appreciation of the role of the music as an integrated part of the dramatic whole—a concept that was sure to prove tempting to the composer. In addition, Ibsen offered one further piece of bait: the honorarium that was to be received from the Christiania Theater for performance rights—400 spesiedalers—would be divided equally between them. He also suggested the possibility of productions in Stockholm and Copenhagen, but asked Grieg to "keep the matter secret until later."

Grieg immediately sent a positive reply, which is now lost, and Ibsen wrote back on February 8: "From your friendly letter I note with pleasure that you agree with my proposal. How much music and for which scenes you will compose it I naturally leave entirely to you; in this a composer obviously must have a completely free hand. I regard this matter with great interest, and it is my hope that you will do the same. I will probably visit Norway this summer, and then I could perhaps have the pleasure of discussing this project with you—and also of reviving our common memories of Rome."

Two days earlier Ibsen had written to the director of the Christiania Theater, Ludvig Josephson, about the project. In this letter he said, among other things, that the new version of *Peer Gynt* was an "*adaptation*, such that in an *abbreviated* form it will be suitable for public performance. The piece is being arranged as a musical drama . . . The music will be composed this summer. I am confident that under your skillful direction it will be very effective on the stage, especially when it is accompanied by good music." The outstanding Swedish director had won great renown for his romantic-realistic

scribed where Solveig, now a middle-aged woman, sits singing in the sunshine outside her house. After her song the curtain will be slowly lowered. The orchestra will continue to play, but the music will move toward a description of the storm at sea with which the fifth act begins.

The fifth act, which in performance will be called either the fourth act or an epilogue, must be shortened considerably. A musical accompaniment is needed [for the scene with the Stranger]. The scenes on the overturned boat and in the graveyard are to be omitted. Solveig will sing [Scene 5]; thereafter the music will accompany Peer Gynt's lines, and will then become an intro-

duction for the choirs [Scene 6]. The scenes with the Button-moulder and with the Mountain King will be shortened. The churchgoers sing on the forest path [Scene 10]; the ringing of bells and the distant singing of hymns are suggested in the music that follows, and this continues until Solveig's song brings the play to an end. As the curtain falls, the hymns sound nearer and louder.

That is more or less how I have conceived the whole project. Please let me know if you are willing to undertake this task. (Letter from Ibsen to Grieg, January 23, 1874.)

Henrik Ibsen in a caricature by Olaf Gulbransson. (public domain)

productions of large dramatic works. His staging of Meyerbeer's opera *L'Africaine* at the Stockholm Opera House in 1867, especially, had aroused international attention.

As one might expect, Josephson was enthusiastic about the plans. But with respect to the staging of the last part of *Peer Gynt* he had his own ideas, and Ibsen went along with them. The playwright commented on this to the theater's consultant, Hartvig Lassen, in a letter of August 16, 1875: "That *Peer Gynt* can be staged only in an abbreviated form is self-evident. When I first wrote to Grieg about the music, I explained to him how I had thought that the fourth act should be replaced by a tone poem that would suggest the content and that would be accompanied by a few vivid pictures or tableaux depicting the most appropriate events from the omitted act . . . I reported this plan to Mr. Josephson, but he did not agree with me. He proposed instead some cuts in the dialogue—cuts that struck me as being undertaken with great understanding, and to which I gave my consent. He has assured me that if his intentions are followed the play will be both a popular and a box-office success."

It was clear to both Ibsen and Grieg that the latter had to take whatever time might be required to complete so demanding a task. During the summer of 1874, in the peace and quiet of Rolfsen's little hut in Sandviken (near Bergen), he got seriously under way, starting with the parts that especially appealed to him. From Sandviken he wrote to Beyer on August 27: "The work on *Peer Gynt* is proceeding very slowly, and there is no possibility that I can finish it by autumn. It is a terribly difficult play for which to write music, with the exception of a few places—as, for example, the scene where Solveig sings; that part I have finished. I have also written something for the scene in the hall of the Mountain King—something that I literally can't stand to listen to because it absolutely reeks of cow pies, exaggerated Norwegian nationalism, and trollish self-sufficiency! But I also have a hunch that the irony will be discernible, especially when Peer Gynt later is obliged to say, 'Both dancing and playing—may the cat claw my tongue—were pure delight.'"

On August 23 Josephson had written to Grieg asking when he expected to finish the job. He told Grieg that there was no thought of trying to produce the play until January at the earliest. He reported further that Ibsen was in Oslo and was working with him on the necessary changes. "If you need to know about these," he wrote, "I will send you a revised copy of the script." Josephson recommended that Grieg come to Oslo before going to Denmark because "there are a lot of things we might want to talk about." Grieg replied on August 28, however, that he was traveling by way of Kristiansand. He was pleased to hear that the play could not be produced until the following year, because "the job is proving to be much larger than I had thought, and in some places I am encountering difficulties that have me absolutely stymied."

Josephson sent the revised text to Grieg in Copenhagen on October 18. He reported that Ibsen had been very receptive to his suggestions for changes— changes that he hoped Grieg would understand and for the most part come to like. Naturally, he said, the composer has a completely free hand in deciding which parts of the play are most suitable for musical treatment. He also asked

3. MUSICAL EXPERIENCES
IN LEIPZIG

You would be astonished if you knew what
a tremendous amount of music I have listened to during these three weeks that I
have been here. Almost every day a concert
and frequently rehearsals in the forenoon.
How it has gone with my own work under
such circumstances you can well understand, but I really look upon it as a kind
of duty to gather as much honey as I possibly can while I am here. To be sure, one
often gets poor honey. But recently in St.
Thomas Church I heard [in rehearsal] three
Bach cantatas that still have not been performed publicly. I have never heard anything so beautiful by Bach; they are marvelous, great, profound, childlike, and sincere.
(Letter to Winding, February 4, 1875.)

Grieg to complete *Olav Trygvason,* which, he said, could launch "a new and
perhaps great epoch" in theater history: "Whatever you send I will receive
with the greatest joy!" He concluded by saying, "I have neither rest nor peace.
I live in a constant fever, now more than ever."

Grieg replied a week later in a thank-you letter that the revised text
requires that "I have to revise a few things, but there must also be much more
music than I had ever dreamed of."

The completion of the project was to take another full year. Grieg discussed the problems in several letters to Björnson. On January 2, 1875, he
wrote from Denmark: "With *Peer Gynt* it has gone as you predicted: it hangs
over me like a nightmare, and I can't possibly be done with it until spring. It
was the need for money—or, more precisely, it was the offer of money—that
drove me. Perhaps that should not have happened, but the prospect of travel
and visions of great beauty loomed before me . . . Besides, the performance of
Peer Gynt just now can do some good in Oslo, where materialism is trying to
rise up and choke everything that we regard as high and holy. There is a need
for one more mirror, I think, in which all the egotism can be seen, and such a
mirror is *Peer Gynt;* then you will come home and rebuild. For it cannot be
denied: the people must see their own ugliness before you can do any good,
but once their eyes are opened you are just the man to lead the parade."

It was with no great enthusiasm that Grieg continued working on *Peer
Gynt* after coming to Leipzig in the spring of 1875. It was much more tempting
to participate in the rich concert life of the city.[3] While continuing work on
Peer Gynt he became concerned about the quality of the orchestra at the
Christiania Theater; in a letter to Björnson dated February 21 he wrote:
"Yesterday I heard how things stand with respect to music in the Christiania
Theater, as a consequence of which I am today writing to both Ibsen and
Josephson that I consider it a duty not to deliver anything . . . so long as the
orchestra is not adequately staffed. It is absolutely scandalous, the worst that it
has ever been, and Svendsen says that if the situation continues we will in the
course of a few years have no orchestra at all in Norway's capital city—a city
of nearly 100,000 people. Old Mozart operas won't be destroyed, that we
know, but to deliver a score with modern orchestration to the Christiania
Theater *now* would be to contribute to a grand fiasco."

In his reply of March 5 Ibsen expressed his complete agreement with Grieg
and stated emphatically: "I earnestly beg you not to make any concessions to
poor orchestral resources. Arrange your music according to an ideal standard
and let them worry about how to perform it. Anything less than that would be
unworthy of a man such as you and moreover would harm us both."

On April 5 Grieg wrote dejectedly to Winding: "With respect to what I am
working on there is, unfortunately, little to say. I am still plugging away at the
music to *Peer Gynt,* and it doesn't interest me."

It was at Winding's summer home in Fredensborg that he finally finished
the project, and on July 27 he was able to tell Ibsen that the music was
completed. On August 20 Ibsen wrote expressing his pleasure over this and
asking him to send the score to Josephson and to "share with him any
comments you wish to make . . . Play rehearsals should be hurried up as much

Johan Hennum, orchestra leader at Christiania Theater 1866–94. He conducted the premiere of "Peer Gynt" in 1876 and "Sigurd Jorsalfar" in 1892. Grieg had great respect for his musical insight. (Photo collection of Universitetsbiblioteket in Oslo)

as possible. That you yourself will be present for the music rehearsals is, naturally, a foregone conclusion; but these will probably not begin until sometime in October."

Grieg was not able to be present for the rehearsals in Oslo, however, as he had to go directly from Copenhagen to Bergen, where both of his parents lay on their deathbeds. On September 2 he sent the score to Josephson, and in the cover letter he made several interesting comments: "That there are so innumerably many details about which, for the sake of the dramatic effect, I wish that we could talk together, you will readily understand. In many places the text is such that one must simply abandon any thought of real music for the sake of the outward effect. So that you will not search in vain, I must not forget to tell you that I have not written a hymn for the graveyard scene— partly because I think this scene will be omitted, and partly because Hennum [the theater's orchestra conductor] can simply make use of one of the traditional hymns."

In early September Josephson did Grieg the honor of giving three performances of *Sigurd Jorsalfar* at the Christiania Theater. The last of these occurred on September 12. Grieg's father died in Bergen the following day.

On September 28 Grieg wrote to the theater director: "You can well understand that I cannot leave Bergen until Mother has passed away, but on the other hand you can also understand that I am extremely reluctant to let the so-called music to *Peer Gynt* be performed without being present, at least at a few rehearsals, in order to make sure that my intentions are followed."

Grieg's mother died on October 23, and for the funeral John Grieg wrote a poem that Edvard set to music. This piece no longer exists, however, and nothing is known about it.

Thirteen years later, when his friend Julius Röntgen had lost his mother, Grieg sent a consoling letter in which he gave extraordinarily beautiful expression to his thoughts about chastening through sorrow.[4]

After the hard blows that he had endured in the course of a short time, Grieg could not bring himself to go to Oslo for the rehearsals of *Peer Gynt*. A whole year was to pass before he would return to the capital city.

On December 14 he instead sent Hennum a letter of no less than twenty-

---

4. REFLECTIONS ON SORROW

I have just received the sad news of the passing of your dear mother. It is strange what can befall one in this life. That nature not only permits such agonies, but even demands them! Now you also know what it means to lose one's dearest possession. How different the world suddenly becomes, and how gloomy everything around one! But there is a consolation. It is one that heretofore you have known only in theory, but that you can joyfully depend on: that the selfsame nature that gives such deep wounds also contains a healing power, and that this wonderful healing is denied to no one. You can scarcely grasp this just now. But, praise God, it is true. I know it from my own experience. Time covers the pain of loss like beautiful, soft clouds, and you will come to acknowledge with gratitude how you are matured by the law of necessity. When my mother died, my love of art died with her. But not permanently! To the contrary: when joy reawakened, it was greater than before.

You will find, dear Röntgen, that art still carries within itself undreamed-of happiness. How certainly and beneficently is nature arranged in such a way, then, that we first reach the highest satisfaction in art through life's most traumatic shocks! (Letter to Röntgen, August 4, 1888.)

During the winter we had heard much about the extraordinary effort of many kinds that the theater staff was having to put forth in order to complete the task—by our standards a nearly colossal one—of producing this splendid, remarkable work. We were expectant, and it should be said that our expectations were more than fulfilled. The performance lasted more than five hours without any indication of waning interest on the part of the audience. One thing that contributed greatly to this result was the music that Edvard Grieg has composed for the play. The music is certainly in its totality a most exceptional piece of work—insofar as one dares to judge after this single performance, when many in the audience displayed such a lack of appropriate interest and regard for the composer that they carried on noisy conversations during many of the numbers. One of the pieces—Anitra's song—was omitted because of Mrs. Asmundsen's illness. Such pieces as the music to the wedding scene, to the parades in the hall of the Mountain King, to the scene with the three herd girls, etc., give evidence of a special gift as a dramatic composer, and there is a bold originality in the whole musical treatment. (*Morgenbladet,* February 25, 1876.)

eight pages in which by way of introduction he wrote: "The fact is that there are many things in the score that are not stated as clearly as one might wish, and I have recently observed a few places in which the orchestration could be improved . . . Only in a few places is the music just music; it moves out on the thin ice of caricature, and it often does this so crudely that it is important to bring it off in such a way that the audience will understand the intention. There is so much that I wish we could talk about that does not lend itself to a simple summary. I will therefore set the score in front of me and go through it, and I ask you to now do the same."

The letter contains a wealth of information about Grieg's intentions with respect to the music. Some relevant passages are quoted in the Primary Materials in connection with the detailed analysis of the music for the various parts of *Peer Gynt*.

The earliest performances of Peer Gynt

The first performance took place on February 24, 1876, and according to Josephson's memoirs of 1898 it was "an unqualified success." The critics whose comments appeared in the newspapers the following day were on the whole extraordinarily enthusiastic. In *Aftenposten* it was stated, among other things, that "Grieg's music was especially effective and adapted itself nicely to the various situations in the play." *Aftenbladet* said that "of the great contributions he has made to the performance we would especially call attention to the lively . . . and highly characteristic overture, Solveig's Song, the ballet in the desert, and an Adagio for string orchestra preceding Act 3 that was a little symphonic masterpiece; but we confess that last evening, as the impressions flooded in upon us from all sides, we did not immediately grasp all of the music which, however, was in all essentials characteristic of the composer and will certainly reward a closer acquaintance." *Morgenbladet*'s review will be found in the Primary Materials.[5]

The success of *Peer Gynt* was due in large part to the outstanding performance of the thirty-two-year-old actor Henrik Klausen in the title role. In his memoirs, Josephson characterized Klausen thus: "One could scarcely hope to achieve a finer portrayal of the demanding role of Peer Gynt than through the excellent and manifold talents of Mr. Klausen. No one can have had a better opportunity than I to observe his flexibility and receptivity to new ideas and possibilities." *Dagbladet* singled out Klausen's performance as "in its entirety some of the most polished that has ever been presented on a Norwegian stage."

The public's reaction to the event was effusive. *Peer Gynt* was the great sensation of the season, and it was performed thirty-six times during the spring of 1876.

Josephson sent Ibsen a telegram telling him of the success, and the playwright replied elatedly on March 5: "Thank you for *Peer Gynt!* Your friendly telegram was the preface to a series of happy messages that I have received from home during the past week. This outcome of the theater's daring

Scene from the premiere performance of "Peer Gynt": Henrik Klausen as the aging Peer. (Photo collection of Universitetsbiblioteket in Oslo)

venture has exceeded all my expectations, although I have really not had any fear on that score. I knew that the matter was in your hands and that nobody else in our country could carry it off as well as you."

On March 15 Grieg wrote to Ibsen: "It is, therefore, a double joy for me to be able to congratulate you on the marvelous result produced by the stage version of *Peer Gynt*. If I have contributed even a little to that result, I have repaid only a portion of the debt that I feel I owe you. I was unfortunately unable to be there myself (terrible events in my home have for the moment made all public activity loathsome to me, so this winter I have just withdrawn into my hut and into my thoughts) . . . What I regret the most is that the ending—where I think I have written some of my best music—has, because of a thoroughly mangled musical performance, made a weak impression." Ibsen replied on March 30: "Allow me, however, to offer you my warmest and friendliest thanks for the large share that you have had in the success of my play on the stage back home!"

6. GRIEG COMMENTS ON THE INSTRUMENTATION OF THE ORIGINAL VERSION

I have recently received requests from several foreign musical organizations for the score and orchestral parts for the *Peer Gynt* music, but I have always declined because I don't want it spread around like that in its present form. The instrumentation was, as you remember, adapted solely to the limited orchestral resources of the Christiana Theater. The instrumentation didn't please me then, and it does so even less now. On the title page of the score I have also protected myself against the possibility of a concert performance by explicitly noting that the music is intended for a "theatrical production" of the play. (Letter to Hennum, November 12, 1882.)

7. GRIEG TELLS ABOUT THE STAGING OF *PEER GYNT* IN COPENHAGEN

This afternoon I had the first rehearsal with the singers for *Peer Gynt*. As I came up the stairs . . . I heard the herd girls yelling at the top of their lungs—naturally in a wrong tempo, exactly at half speed, so I am certainly glad that I am here. But the voices are good, and the girls appear lively, so I'm not worried about that scene, the new instrumentation for which is much improved. Then I tried Solveig's Song with Mrs. Oda P., but since Solveig [Oda P.] is in an advanced stage of pregnancy the illusion is not very convincing. Otherwise she handles the part well and exhibits a musical temperament. Then came the thief and the receiver [of stolen goods], who performed their parts so stupidly that I asked them to be quiet and listen to me. Whereupon I rendered the piece and—incomprehensibly—so masterfully that the listeners broke out in wild applause. (Letter to Beyer, December 22, 1885.)

* * *

But now I am at work on the last part—fortunately, for it is about time. In the cafe I am bombarded by copyists and music directors who grab the pages from me one at a time as soon as I am finished with them. Thus we rehearse a little at a time. Two pieces gave me much satisfaction at the first rehearsal. They were the introduction to the second act and the scene with the herd girls. The latter you wouldn't even recognize. When I first conceived it I felt something, but now I *know* something: that is

Another and more interesting explanation of why he was not in Oslo, however, is given by Grieg in a letter to Johan Selmer dated April 12: "Yes, one can take satisfaction in acclaim when one has a good conscience in relation to one's own artistic ideals; but that does not apply to me and that wretched *Peer Gynt* music, for every moment I had to banish my ideals in order to cover up for a poor orchestra and enhance the popular stage effects. If I had had the strength to be my better self, it goes without saying that I would have been there to see to it that my intentions were realized; but you can surely understand that under these circumstances I preferred to be elsewhere."

Grieg did not see *Peer Gynt* until November of the same year, and both after "Solveig's Song" and at the conclusion the audience gave him a thundering ovation. A short time later—on January 15, 1877—there was a big fire in the theater. The scenery for *Peer Gynt*—part of which had been painted by Frits Thaulow—and all the costumes were totally destroyed, and it was fifteen years before the play was staged again in Oslo.

As early as March, 1876, some excerpts from the music ("Anitra's Dance," "Solveig's Song," and "Peer Gynt's Serenade") were printed in a piano arrangement in Copenhagen as Opus 23, and several additional excerpts came out during the summer and fall.

There was much in the orchestration of the Peer Gynt music that Grieg himself was dissatisfied with.[6] When the play was to be performed in an abbreviated form at the Dagmar Theater in Copenhagen ten years later, Grieg decided to undertake a thorough revision of the music "so that it could present itself decently clothed." This was in the autumn of 1885. On February 3, 1886, he wrote to Julius Röntgen that he had "almost totally reconceptualized and reorchestrated the music. What a job that was!" In connection with the performance he wrote three letters to Frants Beyer in which he made a number of informative and humorous remarks.[7]

Grieg also included four new pieces: "Bridal Procession" (Opus 19, No. 2) preceding the wedding scene in Act 1, and three of his *Norwegian Dances*, Opus 35, "as an extended interlude" in the hall of the Mountain King. These pieces were orchestrated by two Danish composers, Georg Bohlmann and

the difference. It has acquired life, color, and deviltry—which really were not there before because the instrumentation was so defective . . . Enormous preparations are being made for the performance, which will certainly be something totally different from the one in Kristiania [Oslo] so far as the scenery and the music are concerned. (Letter to Beyer, January 5, 1886.)

* * *

You would have had fun watching me at the rehearsals. I was so anxious to make sure that my intentions were realized that I personally took command here and there. One moment I conducted the orchestra, another I instructed the singers, yet another I was on stage and played director. It was es-

pecially in the scene with the herd girls that I was determined not to give up. But it turned out to be quite a performance. I . . . stopped them every moment with shouts like, for example: "It says you are supposed to kiss him—please, help yourself!" And when they finally crossed the Rubicon they became absolutely wild and crazy and everything was the way it was supposed to be. At the dress rehearsal there was great applause after this scene, but at the first performance there wasn't a single clap. The scene obviously merely astonished the audience. But as a whole the music was a great success, that I can certainly say, and the execution was quite good. (Letter to Beyer, January 21, 1886.)

8. GRIEG PRAISES ODA NIELSEN AS
SOLVEIG IN *PEER GYNT*

Your Solveig was free and graceful, just as
you are. I don't know if it was Ibsen's Solveig, but this I know, that both the character and the music were suffused with
fragrance and music and purity and delicacy. Thank you for that and for so many
other unforgettable memories of your brilliant artistry. (Letter to Oda Nielsen,
May 7, 1902.)

9. THE *PEER GYNT* MUSIC FOR
FLUTE AND BASSOON?

Many thanks for the new editions. It is becoming downright unpleasant that my
compositions are being disseminated in all
kinds of arrangements. All that is lacking is
a *Peer Gynt* suite for flute and bassoon, [or
perhaps] . . . the hurdy-gurdy. The arrangements of *Album Leaves* actually look pretty
good. The *Peer Gynt* suite, however, is arranged in a completely unmusical way.
Thank God I am totally innocent in all this.
(Letter to Max Abraham, September 22,
1896.)

Robert Henriques, because he himself was, as he said, "up to my ears with the orchestration of the rest of the music, otherwise I would of course have done it myself."

Henrik Klausen again performed in the title role, and Grieg reported to Beyer that he "was the same as in Oslo ten years ago—a little less spry, perhaps, but it appeared to me that he handled the concluding acts better than before." Of Oda Nielsen as Solveig, Grieg said that she was "a comely and poetic figure, though not the Solveig we usually think of. But she sang beautifully and naturally."[8]

The production was grandly conceived. The press reported that "at least 100 people are on the stage," among them "fifty troll children in brown monkey suits, . . . half a score of elf maidens" and "a swarm of animal figures." The artistic triumph at the premiere was complete. Georg Brandes wrote in *Politiken* that here "notwithstanding the lavish but totally sensible merriment, splendor, music, and dance of the production, Ibsen's satire shows through so sharply that one is forced to ask oneself how a whole generation has managed to avoid understanding. The satire hits the audience in the face, as if it had been written about Denmark, and written quite recently."

The audience was no less enthusiastic, and Grieg was able to report with pride that the production played to a full house for a long time.

It was with the two suites from *Peer Gynt* that Grieg had the satisfaction of seeing the music he had written for this play become a truly great success. This occurred during the last twenty years of his life. The suites were played throughout the musical world—in the orchestral version, in the composer's own arrangements for piano, and in countless other arrangements. The first of the suites, Opus 46, he delivered to C. F. Peters (Grieg's German publisher) on January 18, 1888, at which time he received 3000 marks in payment. Immediately after it was printed it began its triumphal tour through the concert halls. After its performance in London on March 14, 1889, Grieg was able to report to Beyer: "At the conclusion there broke out a jubilant demonstration that was like a pack of animals! You understand what I mean: this hullabaloo that finds expression only in moments of great enthusiasm." In 1891 the publisher told Grieg that the suite was being performed in Asia, Africa, and Australia.

Nonetheless, he had to put up with certain surprises. After a performance by the Monte Carlo orchestra in March of 1893 he mentioned to Beyer in a letter dated April 2 that he was indeed greeted with ovations, but "that wasn't enough to keep me from all harm. For 'The Death of Aase' as a polka and 'Anitra's Dance' as a fast waltz—that's the limit! The most remarkable part about it, though, is that people can stomach that sort of thing and even like it."[9]

In 1890–92 he revised the orchestration for the four pieces that were printed in 1893 as *Suite No. 2*, Opus 55. Originally this suite did not include the "Arabian Dance," but included instead "Dance of the Mountain King's Daughter" as the final movement. Before the work was printed, however, the latter piece was removed—"quite unkindly, with all due respect and love for all trolls," as Grieg expressed it in a letter to Julius Röntgen on February 19,

10. "FOLKEBLADET" REVIEWS BJÖRN BJÖRNSON'S PORTRAYAL OF PEER GYNT IN OSLO IN 1892

One must remember the circumstances under which Björnson has created his *Peer Gynt.* At the same time that he was overburdened with his duties as both set designer and director of this colossal work, for which the stage settings alone are more than enough work for one man, he has had to work through the role. When this is taken into consideration, . . . then it must be allowed that Björnson, in his triple role, has accomplished a monumental feat that few if any will ever duplicate. And, all things considered, it must be acknowledged that his *Peer Gynt,* in its overall construction and intent, holds promise of mastering the enormous task of creating a realistic *Peer Gynt* according to the demands of the times. I have no doubt that this promise will sooner or later be fully realized.

11. GRIEG ON THE REHEARSAL IN 1892

It is a pure stroke of luck that I have driven you mad, because madness is an absolute necessity for a good *Peer Gynt!* . . . With that Böyg *you* have driven me mad! But as I said: I am trying to write this music. It is a pity that I will not be there before the performance. There is so much concerning which my presence would be of the greatest importance!!! (Letter to Björn Björnson, February 7, 1892.)

12. GRIEG ON THE NEW MUSIC FOR THE SCENE WITH THE GREAT BÖYG

Considered simply as music it is very easy, but the trick is to relate it properly to the theatrical. The horn players must blow as if they had twenty lungs! (Letter to Hennum, February 16, 1892.)

1893. What had happened was that Grieg himself had conducted the piece in Leipzig twelve days earlier and had come to the conclusion "that it belongs *only* in the theater and not in the concert hall." The composer also considered at one time incorporating "Peer Gynt's Serenade" and "Solveig's Cradle Song" in the suite, but eventually abandoned the idea.

In 1892 Björnson's son Björn, who was then director of the Christiania Theater, produced *Peer Gynt* once again in the capital city,[10] but as he reported, "Just the first three acts; I couldn't manage any more." Björn himself played the title role, and twenty-five-year-old Johanne Dybwad got her big break as an actress by playing Solveig.

The scenery for this production was created by Jens Wang. Grieg was also asked to prepare some new music, but in a February 7 letter to Björnson[11] he stated that he had no desire to create any more music for *Peer Gynt* "because I am *done with* that period!!" On February 12 he wrote indignantly to Max Abraham of C. F. Peters: "This fellow Peer Gynt gives me sorrow as well as joy . . . They're requiring me to write *more music* for a few scenes. At first I refused. Then they wrote back and said that in that case the additional music would be written by somebody else. In other words, they are forcing me. So now I'm in the middle of it, and I had to give up another project that I had barely begun. It's shameful, that's what it is."

The newly composed piece was an expansion of the music for the scene with the "Great Böyg" which, according to Grieg, was what Björn Björnson had asked for.[12] In the letter to Björnson cited earlier, Grieg expressed regret that he was not able to be present for the rehearsal. One week later he sent the new version to maestro Hennum.

Immediately after the turn of the century, Ibsen's play with Grieg's music began its triumphal tour outside of Scandinavia. Eduard Hanslick, the famous Vienna critic, had written in 1891 after a performance of *Peer Gynt Suite No. 1:* "Before long it may well be that Ibsen's *Peer Gynt* will continue to live only through Grieg's music, for so far as I am concerned this music contains in each of its movements more poetry and artistic insight than all five acts of Ibsen's play put together."

Although this prediction has not been fulfilled, it is nonetheless Grieg's music that in great measure has ensured the popularity of the play. In Berlin alone the work was performed more than a thousand times prior to the Second World War.

Grieg never felt that he was completely finished with the *Peer Gynt* music. As late as 1901, therefore, he reworked the instrumentation of the prelude to the first act and also started working on a revision of the scene with Peer and the herd girls. On August 15 of the following year he wrote to Julius Röntgen that he had "recaulked the scene with the Great Boyg." This apparently was done in connection with a new performance of the play at the National Theater (in Oslo) in February of the same year. The performance was conducted by his close friend, Johan Halvorsen, orchestra conductor at the theater since its opening in 1899. Grieg was not present for this performance, which he characterized in a letter to Beyer of February 14, 1902, as very important, since it would "more or less fix the style for the future: it has to do

13. GRIEG'S DISAPPOINTMENT OVER THE 1902 PRODUCTION AT THE NATIONAL THEATER

I realized immediately that the play had not been a great success, for then there would have been a telegram already yesterday. And if *Peer* isn't up to par—well, so what? That's not my concern. So far as the music goes, I relied confidently on Halvorsen, although despite his great ability he does not have what I would call flexibility—which is precisely what is needed for the *Peer Gynt* music. I deeply regret that I was not there to clarify my intentions so far as possible. There are places where the music needs to be coordinated almost to the second with what is transpiring on stage. And then of course there are other things that could have been improved with just a few strokes of the pen. But never mind. If I am granted a few more years of life I will arrange *all* of this music as I have conceived it, and as I am capable of making it sound. (Letter to Beyer, March 1, 1902.)

14. PROBLEMS GETTING THE *PEER GYNT* MUSIC PUBLISHED IN ITS ENTIRETY

It isn't so easy for me to get the scores that I want printed either. If it were, the entire score of the *Peer Gynt* music, for example, would have been printed long ago. (Letter to Gerhard Schjelderup, May 11, 1904.)

15. GRIEG'S COMMENTS ON INDIVIDUAL PIECES OF THE *PEER GYNT* MUSIC:

Act I (no. 1): Prelude. At the Wedding
The two fragments of "Halling" and "Springar" I have thought of as being played by a *solo viola*. They must sound as if from afar, but sharply accented and authentic. (H) [Here and in what follows "(H)" indicates that the quotation is from Grieg's letter to Hennum of December 14, 1875.]

Act I (nos. 2 and 3):
"Halling" and "Springar"
The beginning of the "Halling" must be heard as coming from very far away . . . It is my intention that the fiddler be seen in the distance on the meadow . . . There is one thing I would insist on: the fiddler must know both dances, not as an orchestral part, but almost by heart, and both dances must be played in perfect accord with folk-dance traditions, with sharp ac-

precisely with my intentions, many a time even with respect to minute details."

The new production evidently was not the unqualified success that Grieg had hoped for, and in a letter to Beyer written shortly thereafter he expressed his regret about not being present to assist in the final polishing.[13]

As early as the 1890s Grieg was busy with plans to someday have all the *Peer Gynt* music printed, and in 1902 the prelude to the first act and "Peer Gynt and the Herd Girls" were published by C. F. Peters as "rental material." It appears that the project went no further, however, and in the final years of his life Grieg was greatly vexed over the publisher's failure to print all of the *Peer Gynt* music.[14] It was Halvorsen who, in 1908—the year after Grieg's death—got the job of preparing the score for printing. Based on manuscripts and earlier editions of individual pieces, including both orchestral suites, the Peters score contained twenty-three numbers.

How close Halvorsen came to the ideal score Grieg had desired is difficult to say, but he certainly did not prepare a *complete* score. The following items are lacking: "Peer Gynt and the Woman in Green" (No. 6), "Peer Gynt and Anitra" (No. 18), and "The Shipwreck" (No. 22). On the other hand, Halvorsen's score contains pieces that Grieg definitely would not have included, i.e., "Bridal Procession" (in Halvorsen's orchestration) and the purely instrumental version of "Solveig's Song" prepared by Grieg for *Peer Gynt Suite No. 2*. Halvorsen also made use of an abbreviated version of "Solveig's Cradle Song" that Grieg prepared for the edition of *Six Songs with Orchestra* (1896), but that was not intended for the stage. In addition, Halvorsen placed "Peer Gynt at the Statue of Memnon" (No. 20) at the wrong place in the score.

In our detailed analysis of the *Peer Gynt* music, therefore, we will use the first complete score, published by C. F. Peters as Vol. 18 of *Edvard Grieg's Complete Works* (1987), and we will relate the music to the production of 1876. In the Primary Materials will be found for each number a quotation from Grieg himself—mainly from his letter of December 14, 1875 to Hennum, but occasionally we also cite a letter that Grieg wrote to Louis Monastier-Schroeder on April 1, 1895.[15] The opening measures of each number are given in the entry for Opus 23 in the Catalog of Works with Thematic Incipits.

cents against the beats and powerful strokes, so as to make the picture credible and authentic. (H)

Act II (no. 4): Prelude. The Abduction of the Bride. Ingrid's Lament
Above all, much weight must be given here to the contrasts that portray different characters—the "Andante" Ingrid who toward the end complains beseechingly, even threateningly, and the "Allegro furioso" Peer Gynt, who tells her to go to the devil! (H)

Act II (no. 5): Peer Gynt and the Herd Girls
This is a difficult piece that will either make a very bad impression or an altogether

splendid, wild, devilish, and sensuous one—all depending on how the performers *sing* and *play*. This is just one of the places where I think the music ceases to be merely music. The herd girls must first scream the words: "Trond of the Valfjeld!" etc., as if they were shouting just to one another. They must not pay any attention to the audience, but only to the mountain scenery around them. Later they must . . . not stand still for a second, but must circle around Peer Gynt in wild desire . . . Then comes the resulting laughter, that must sound altogether witchlike and be accompanied by mime and gesture . . . In the concluding *Quasi presto* the orchestra has a demanding task, and if they get it right I think it should sound absolutely devilish. (H)

Act II (no. 6):
Peer Gynt and the Woman in Green
The oboe solo portrays the Woman in Green; the basses, however, depict Peer Gynt. The "amorous gestures" mentioned by Ibsen must, therefore, be adapted to the music. (H)

Act II (no. 7): Peer Gynt: "You can tell great men by the style of their mounts!"
In this piece there is nothing to do but to go strongly ahead and then make a clear *diminuendo* to indicate that the actors are leaving the stage. (H)

Act II (no. 8):
In the Hall of The Mountain King
I have also written something for the scene in the hall of the mountain king—something that I literally can't stand to listen to because it absolutely reeks of cow pies, exaggerated Norwegian provincialism, and trollish self-sufficiency! (Letter to Beyer, August 27, 1874.)

* * *

When the choir comes in there must already be a crowd on stage. The troll children's lines—"May we slash his fingers?" etc.—must be spoken right in time with the others, and as I have conceived it the troll children, one by one, come running toward the troll king at the front of the stage, and do not speak their lines until they reach him. This will enhance the effect. Thus the speakers gather expectantly in front of the troll king until he shouts with a thundering voice: "Ice water in your blood!" . . . The bass drum and cymbals must thunder and crash for all they're worth. (H)

Act II (no. 9): Dance of the Mountain King's Daughter
Here the music must be an absolute parody, and in such a way that the audience understands that it is a parody. Only then will the effect be comical. (H)

Act II (no. 10):
Peer Gynt Hunted by the Trolls
Yet another piece where it is essential that everything happens without pause and that what occurs on stage be exactly what is prescribed . . . The *low-pitched bell* in the distance I would like to have tuned to D in order to form a diminished fifth with the basses' tremolo on G-sharp: that should give quite a frightening effect. (H)

Act II (no. 11): Peer Gynt and the Böyg
Naturally, this is not a matter of making music but simply of trying to make the chord sound as hollow and muffled as possible. (H)

* * *

The difficult thing here is that this is absolutely not supposed to be music, and photographic expertise in orchestration has never been my strength. (Letter to Röntgen, August 15, 1902.)

Act III (no. 12): The Death of Aase
This piece is played twice, first from the orchestra pit as a prelude to Act 3, and again as Aase dies—this time off stage, and infinitely softly. (H)

* * *

Off stage *pp* Aase's death, and so incredibly softly that one notices the music only as an indistinct sound that does not disturb the dialogue. (Letter from Grieg to Louis Monastier-Schroeder, April 1, 1895.)

Act IV (no. 13): Prelude. Morning Mood
This piece has merely to be treated as music, so everything depends on the musical execution. It is a morning scene where I think of the sun breaking through the clouds at the point in the score where the force first appears. (H)

Act IV (no. 14): The Thief and the Receiver
A very fast tempo, and the whole thing must sound conspiratorial . . . It is important that the text be clearly heard. That is why I have kept their [the thief's and the receiver's] music so simple, so that anybody can sing it . . . (H)

Act IV (no. 15): Arabian Dance
A piece which I think will be effective . . . I hope that each of the dancing girls will have a tambourine, for that is the only way to get the sound I have in mind. I heard something similar this winter, and it sounded wonderful . . . The contrabassoons and bass drum *pp* must sound genuinely Turkish. (H)

Act IV (no. 16): Anitra's Dance
A delicate little dance that I hope will sound lovely and beautiful. It is essential that there be only a few dancers. For in order that Peer Gynt's lines during the dance shall be comprehensible to the audience it is orchestrated in such a way that if necessary the whole thing can be played *ppp*. I would be grateful if you would treat this piece with special affection. (H)

Act IV (no. 17): Peer Gynt's Serenade
It must sound half amorous, half ironic. During the intermezzo and the instrumental conclusion Peer Gynt must handle his instrument with a certain affected passion. (H)

Act IV (no. 18): Peer Gynt and Anitra
Here the strings must play with sharp accents. (H)

Act IV (no. 19): Solveig's Song
The actress who sings this song must make the most of it, for it reveals Solveig's character. Once in a weak moment I noted in the score that if the actress couldn't manage the humming part it could be played instead by a solo clarinet, and Solveig could sit spinning until it was finished. But I have totally abandoned this idea—first and foremost because it doesn't make sense to have her spinning in $\frac{3}{4}$ time, secondly because it is inconsistent with the character of the song, and finally because then the unique character of the piece is ruined. So you absolutely must rehearse the humming with the actress . . . A folk-song style must be preserved throughout. (H)

Act IV (no. 20):
Peer Gynt at the Statue of Memnon
The four horns must be played very softly, and the whole piece must have a foreign flavor. (H)

Act V (no. 21): Prelude. Peer Gynt's Homecoming. Stormy Evening on the Sea
The task of this piece is to characterize a stormy evening on the sea. Every crescendo and diminuendo must therefore be strongly emphasized and the tempo must be very agitated. (H)

Act V (no. 22): The Shipwreck
The foundering of the ship is depicted. The actual grounding is indicated by the bass drum, timpani, and the tremolo in the basses, which should accordingly make a murderous noise . . . The presto and the outcry must sound absolutely frightening, and the following timpani solo depicts the expectant calm. (H)

Act V (no. 23): Solveig Sings in the Hut
Off stage. Subdued and solemn. (H)

Act V (no. 24): Night Scene
This piece . . . depends heavily on [a proper] understanding. Where the woodwinds begin off stage, they must make the strongest possible crescendo. Likewise the strings, which shortly thereafter come in

playing tremolo, begin *pp* and each time make a big crescendo and diminuendo . . . Thus the overall effect must be this: first soft, distant, and then as time goes on increasing greatly. The unison chorus must sound more and more ominous, and there must be a bit of stretto character as the piece progresses. (H)

Act V (no. 25):
Whitsun Hymn: "Oh Blessed Morning"
The hymn that Ibsen has written in the play . . . must only be hummed softly off stage, not sung loudly. (H)

Act V (no. 26): Solveig's Cradle Song
Here I am hoping for a poetic effect using simple means. My concept is that, during the prelude, Peer Gynt lies as though hidden in Solveig's arms while the horizon heralds the imminent sunrise . . . I hope that the actress will sing quietly and sincerely, then louder and fuller toward the end . . . Therefore the strings must always stress the beginning of the measure and then immediately change to *pp,* so that the whole song becomes almost dream-like when the off-stage organ and voices join in, *distantly and softly* . . . Likewise Solveig's last stanza [must be] very broad and fervent. The curtain must fall *very* slowly, as Solveig remains sitting bowed over Peer Gynt. (H)

The Peer Gynt *music: a major accomplishment*

Before the curtain goes up the orchestra has a prelude—a kind of potpourri-overture—with some characteristic themes. Bright *halling* rhythms depict the blustering, bragging Peer. Later we hear the first part of "Solveig's Song." There are also some short excerpts from "Halling" and "Springar" (Nos. 2 and 3), here for viola solo.

"Halling" and "Springar" are original compositions by Grieg, who here displays an exceptionally accurate and sensitive understanding of the tradition associated with the uniquely Norwegian country dance tunes known as *slaatter.* In lieu of a Hardanger-fiddle player on stage the music may be performed by an orchestral violinist concealed in the wings while an actor dressed in a colorful national costume acts the part of the fiddler for the dancers. He sits toward the back of the stage, where the dance is going on, so as not to interrupt the dialogue. Grieg was so pleased with the "Halling" that he arranged it for piano as one of the *Lyric Pieces IV,* Opus 47, No. 4.

The prelude to Act II elicits the strong contrasts between Peer the bully and the broken-hearted Ingrid, the bride whom he had carried off and whom he was about to abandon to her sad fate. Little fragments of Peer's gay *halling* motive from the prelude to Act I are now transformed into an almost grotesque caricature in a minor key, representing the evil facets of his nature. The main theme, however, is Ingrid's intense and deeply moving lament. This piece is incorporated in *Peer Gynt Suite No. 2,* Opus 55, No. 1.

The music for the mountain scene (No. 5) between the three lustful herd girls and Peer, who never said 'no' to an adventure, is unfortunately little known. It was not included in either of the suites for the simple reason that it requires solo voices. Grieg was especially pleased with this piece. In an interview in *Dannebrog* on December 26, 1893, he was quoted as saying: "Concerning the scene with the herd girls—which, remarkably enough, I have never published although I consider it to be the best of all of my *Peer Gynt* music—Ibsen wrote to me: 'You must handle that however you will, but there must be deviltry in it.'"

It is easy to understand Grieg's enthusiasm, for this music may be regarded as some of the most spirited in the entire work. One is totally caught up in the jubilant *joie de vivre* of the young women. They are hunting for trolls, and Peer truly can manage all three of them: "I'm a three-headed troll and a three-woman man!"

This scene contains some of the most folk-like music that Grieg ever wrote. The herd girls' song with its lively dance rhythms has an extraordinarily simple, almost stylized melody with a deliberate monotony relieved only by a series of augmented fourths. Just at the time he was working on *Peer Gynt* Grieg was searching for a uniquely Norwegian style. In a letter to Beyer on March 20, 1875, he wrote: "So you're going to Lindaas, Haus, and Hosanger! Well, at least you get to touch and smell a few things that way. But perhaps you will also get to hear something? Some augmented fourths or some other hocus pocus. If you should run into something that is characteristic of the

Peer and the herd girls. From Ny illustreret Tidende *following the premiere in February, 1876.*

peasants of that area, write it down for me. You know I'm crazy about that kind of stuff."

The entire piece is brilliantly well written. One cannot but be impressed with how realistically Grieg elicits the feeling of the great outdoors high in the mountains, both through the song and perhaps most of all through the transparent orchestration.

Now Peer meets The Woman in Green (No. 6). This piece is a pure idyll: a solo oboe depicts The Woman in Green (the daughter of the Mountain King) with a theme that—somewhat modified rhythmically, and with a low leading tone—anticipates "Morning Mood" (No. 13). There is also a strain of Peer's motive from No. 1, but this time in slow tempo. The next number follows the text, "You can tell great men by the style of their mounts." This is where Peer and The Woman in Green ride off into the mountains on a pig. Her theme is now converted into a wild presto, while Peer's motive is left out altogether.

With "In the Hall of the Mountain King," Peer—and Grieg with him—takes his first step into the realm of the trolls, a new and unexplored world. This was a challenge that appealed to the boldest elements in the composer's imagination. The result was a pure stroke of genius that is linked with Grieg's name in a very special way. The piece is developed in a remarkably unique manner, as one continuous intensification of both dynamics and tempo. This idea was later picked up by Ravel (*Bolero*), Honegger (*Pacific 231*), and Harald Saeverud (*Ballad of Revolt*), to name but a few. A four-measure ostinato melody with a kind of spastic motion begins deep down in the basses. It works its way relentlessly through the various instrumental groups with growing frenzy and steadily louder dynamics.

At the middle of the piece the choir enters with refrains in which the trolls rage over Peer's seduction of The Woman in Green: "Slay him, Christian man's son . . ." "In the Hall of the Mountain King" concludes *Peer Gynt Suite No. 1*—without the choir voices, of course.

Scene from the premiere performance of "Peer Gynt": Johannes Brun as the Mountain King. (Photo collection of Universitetsbiblioteket in Oslo)

The trolls and Peer are entertained by The Woman in Green, who performs a grotesque dance that, according to Grieg, was supposed to be as "ludicrous and ugly" as possible. In its own way this troll music is just as bold as the previous piece. It is the only completely modal piece that Grieg ever wrote. The key is D Lydian, and the augmented fourth (G-sharp) figures prominently in the piece. It is as if the trolls are here caricaturing folk music, an effect that is further underscored by recurring open fifths in the basses. This piece (No. 9) was originally included in *Peer Gynt Suite No. 2* as the fifth and last movement, and was also performed as a part of this suite in Leipzig in February of 1893, but was removed just before the work was printed.

The visit to the home of the trolls culminates with the Mountain King giving the troll children permission to play with Peer, but the game degenerates to such an extent that it appears they are about to kill him. He is saved at the last minute by the sound of church bells and hymns which break the power of the underworld. The music builds on motives from "In the Hall of the Mountain King," now converted from $\frac{4}{4}$ to $\frac{3}{8}$ meter. It has a certain dramatic energy, but the overall effect is somewhat superficial with stereotyped ascending and descending chromatic progressions.

This scene leads without interruption into the meeting with the Great Boyg, a mysterious character whose voice personifies Peer's conscience, and whom he cannot overcome by his own power. But Peer's mother, Aase, gets the people in the village to ring the church bells, and with that he is saved.

In the original score Grieg experimented with some sound effects using horns off stage. A choir was to "imitate the horns and have these to go by." Grieg had visualized a "frightening blast of sound toward the end." In 1892 he wrote some new music for this scene, and revised it again ten years later. The printed score now calls for an organ (off stage) instead of a chorus. The organ is supposed to "suggest hymns being sung in the distance." Based on purely outward effects without musical substance, the music for this scene is some of the weakest in the entire work. The movement really consists of nothing more than a series of augmented fourths that are shifted chromatically, with tremolo strings and muted horns giving distinctive shadings of sound.

"The Death of Aase" is played twice: first as a prelude to Act III and again as an accompaniment to the action in the fourth scene. For this scene, where Peer comes to visit his dying mother, Grieg has chosen an altogether different approach than that suggested by Ibsen. Instead of mirroring Peer's merry fabrications about the sleigh ride with the horse Grane, Grieg takes a quite different tack: the music describes the solemnity of death. Thus Grieg deliberately sets Peer's all-too-typical flight from reality, which Ibsen stresses, in sharp relief.

Rarely has a deathbed scene been painted so movingly in sound. In "The Death of Aase" Grieg picks up the threads from the *Funeral March for Rikard Nordraak* and the two funeral marches in *Bergliot*. But in "The Death of Aase" the style has become even simpler and more concentrated. Grieg's careful attention to the subtlest tonal nuances finds here its most sublime expression. This piece appears as No. 2 in the first *Peer Gynt Suite*.

Ever since the first production, "Morning Mood" has been used as a prelude to Act IV, although the piece was originally intended for use in connection with Scene 5, "Early Morning."

"Morning Mood" is a nature sketch, the gripping effect of which is due to its shimmering brightness and its gentle successions of third-related chords. It transcends any particular time or place. In the play it is supposed to depict a sunrise on the coast of Africa, but with its pentatonic character it could just as well depict a Norwegian dawn. Remarkably enough, Grieg has also used here—with a few changes—the same melodic material that he had used as the principal theme of "The Woman in Green." "Morning Mood" is the first movement in *Peer Gynt Suite No. 1*.

The short scene with "The Thief and the Receiver" [of stolen goods], for two bass voices, takes place in the desert. The music, too, has a somewhat arid character. The terse lines of the dialogue are chanted by the two voices on the note of G while the orchestra softly suggests oriental tone colors. Only the delicate orchestration, which is worked out most artistically, lifts the piece a shade above pure banality.

In the scene where the "Arabian Dance" occurs, Peer plays the role of a prophet while the Bedouin girl Anitra and a group of slave girls entertain him with songs and dances. The exotic, which to some extent was intimated in the preceding piece, now comes through in full force. Grieg shows here a remarkable capacity to enter into an entirely new musical sphere. This pastiche was written at the same time as *Carmen* and about fifteen years before the *Nutcracker* ballet, in which Bizet and Tchaikovsky, respectively, also make use of oriental musical sounds and devices. Grieg's contribution in this area is not inferior to theirs.

Grieg achieved an oriental coloring with some daring orchestration, including the subtle use of various percussion instruments. But he also elicited an exotic feeling by the use of unfamiliar scales. The piece is set in C major with a middle part in A minor, but there are abrupt shifts in tonality to, for example, B-flat Lydian and then A-flat Lydian. "Arabian Dance" is the second movement in *Peer Gynt Suite No. 2,* again without the vocal parts.

"Anitra's Dance" is one of Grieg's most charming orchestral pieces. Oddly enough, at this point in the play he has smuggled an amorous little waltz right into the middle of a desert oasis. In addition to its graceful elegance, it also contains an unmistakable hint of seductive sensuality. Anitra possesses—in

Scene from the premiere performance of "Peer Gynt": Peer (Henrik Klausen) seated beside a beduin tent in the desert. (Photo collection of Universitetsbiblioteket in Oslo)

Scene from the premiere performance of "Peer Gynt": Thora Neelsen as Solveig. (Photo collection of Universitetsbiblioteket in Oslo)

mind if not in body—much of the wildness of The Woman in Green. The ambiguity of her character is expressed clearly through the graceful innocence of the opening motive, which immediately afterward is spiced up with a dash of distorted trollish chromaticism. The unusually thin orchestration—strings plus a solitary triangle—clothes this scene in an alluring way. "Anitra's Dance" is the third piece in *Peer Gynt Suite No. 1*.

In "Peer Gynt's Serenade," Peer extols Anitra's supposed virtues in a quasi-exotic aria sung in mock operatic style. He sits in front of the tent and pretends to be playing an Arabian lute. Grieg wants to show that Peer is now totally captive to this foreign milieu, and he does this with suggestions of modal shifts and a static rhythm.

After the serenade, a short melodramatic episode occurs in the scene where Peer rides through the desert on horseback with Anitra in the saddle in front of him. This music is supposed to depict the trotting of horses.

"Solveig's Song" is the composition that is most often popularly linked with the name of Edvard Grieg. This wonderful melody possesses the finest characteristics of the folk tune, suffused as it is with the ultimate in naturalness and simplicity. Grieg himself was well aware of the song's close relationship to the style of the folk tune. In a letter to Finck on July 17, 1900, he wrote: "So far as my songs are concerned, I don't think that in general they have been influenced by the folk song to any great extent. Such influence did occur, however, where local color *had* to play a dominant role—as, for example, in 'Solveig's Song.' But this may be the only one of my songs where an imitation of the folk song can be demonstrated."

Grieg never indicated which folk song he had in mind. It could have been either the Norwegian song "I laid me down so late" or the Swedish "O Värmeland the beautiful." With respect to the wordless passage in the second part of the song, there is an obvious similarity in concept to Kjerulf's "Synnöve's Song." One also finds a forerunner of the "Solveig" melody in the song that Grieg wrote the preceding year for L. M. Lindeman's silver wedding anniversary (see p. 132).

Grieg also prepared music for the scene at the statue of Memnon.

The prelude to Act V, where Peer returns to his homeland as an old man, is a striking tone painting with the title "Peer Gynt's Homecoming" or "Stormy Evening on the Sea." The howling wind and churning sea are vividly portrayed through bold use of the resources of the orchestra. Powerful contrasts, marked rhythms, and extensive use of chromaticism are characteristic of this type of music. It is the Wagnerian style as displayed especially in *The Flying Dutchman* that Grieg here had not managed to avoid. This piece appears as the third movement in *Peer Gynt Suite No. 2*.

There is also music for the scene where Peer is clinging to an overturned lifeboat. Grieg depicted the shipwreck with banging and crashing.

Meanwhile, Peer makes it safely to land, for as it says in the play: "One does not die in the middle of the fifth act."

Finally Peer comes home again, and in a forest scene where he is picking wild onions he approaches the cottage that he had once built for himself and Solveig. He recognizes it, and suddenly he hears Solveig singing in the cottage: "All is made ready for Whitsuntide."

The original version of this song has a simple string accompaniment that was supposed to be played off stage. The melody is the same as in "Solveig's Song."

In "Night Scene" Peer's bad conscience makes itself heard: thoughts he should have thought, tears he should have shed, and so on. Unfortunately, Grieg's melodramatic handling of this section fails to plumb the depths of the poetry. The composer moved strictly on the surface, with tedious, uninterrupted repetitions—no less than six times—of the same musical material, each repetition being a half step higher than the previous one. That Grieg's own artistic conscience was sorely tried in this connection is evident from his very thorough comments to Hennum; he attempted to conceal lack of inspiration by a demand for outward effects at the performance.

As Peer approaches the end of the road, in deep despair over his wasted life, he hears the churchgoers singing on the forest path (No. 25).

In the concluding scene with "Solveig's Cradle Song," it is the innocent Solveig who brings Peer the peace for which he is yearning. The fundamental idea is the religious concept of redemption, here expressed in exceptionally beautiful poetic form. Grieg, with his genius, was able to give the poetry new dimensions. He almost outdid himself. The song is developed with infinite care, with a sublime melody surrounded by ethereal sounds in the orchestra. Its character is similar to that of his famous song, "Last Spring," Opus 33, No. 2.

This scene was an especially demanding task, and in the original version Grieg did not follow Ibsen's instructions. Toward the end of the scene he interrupted the lullaby with a repetition of the preceding hymn tune (accompanied by full orchestra) at the point where the Button-molder speaks his concluding line: "We'll meet at the final crossroad, Peer; and *then* we'll see— I'll say no more."

The *Peer Gynt* music became Grieg's greatest triumph. While he was working on it, however, his attitude toward it was ambivalent. Sometimes, when Ibsen "fired his imagination," he was confident of complete success. At other times he was thoroughly fed up with the entire project. The music also certainly contains some weak sections that could not have pleased his artistic conscience. This is probably one of the reasons why he was glad not to be present for the first production. He simply was not sure that the music would catch on, or that the notes he had written on paper would sound the way he

Detail from a poster by Edvard Munch for an 1896 performance of Peer Gynt *in Paris. (Edvard Munch Museum, Oslo, Norway)*

Caricature of Ibsen by Ragnvald Blix.

had imagined them. He had, as we know, no great confidence in the quality of the orchestra. Strangely enough, he also did not attend the premieres of either the 1892 or the 1902 productions of the play in Oslo. The overwhelming successes that he later had with this music, however—both on the stage and in the concert hall—must have convinced him that in all essentials he had created a work of global stature.

It is unfortunate that in some music circles it has become customary to turn up one's nose at the *Peer Gynt* music, with condescending remarks to the effect that it is nothing more than light popular-romantic music. Such an evaluation is in our opinion completely unfounded. Good music is not cheapened merely because the public at large takes it to its heart. All of the pieces that make up the two much-loved orchestral suites and most of the other numbers are free of banal sentimentality. They are equally fresh and living for each new generation. This is especially true when one hears the music in its proper setting, as an integral part of a stage production. It is, to be sure, a product of its time, but in addition to its purely lyrical qualities it often has a realistic and dramatic intensity that is completely in keeping with Ibsen's intentions.

The dramatic qualities of the music, of course, are realized first and foremost in the theater. Grieg understood this, and even after the worldwide sensation that he created with the two orchestral suites, he emphasized the importance of experiencing this music in its proper setting. On July 30, 1905, he wrote to Finck: "If it were possible for you to [attend the play], you would see that the musical intentions can be clearly understood only in the context of a dramatic performance."

After dinner we had some music. One of our host's beautiful daughters performed "Solveig's Song" using Grieg's melody . . . The song was new at that time, and it had been prepared especially for the enjoyment of the playwright, who was present for the evening. But dear old Ibsen just sat quietly and serenely, without any outward sign of either approval or disapproval. He had obviously paid as little attention to the text as to the music. And when someone in the group finally called his attention to the fact that it was his own poem that had been sung, it elicited a courteous reply that scarcely concealed his indifference.

His feelings toward composers bordered on contempt. I have every reason to believe that he regarded their calling as essentially useless.

One time, talking about a well-known author who, though intellectually shallow, was emotionally rich, he said to me: "He's no poet, for poets have not only emotions, but also thoughts. He's a mere lyricist, a *composer.*"

I had to smile at this definition, and I thought: Now Grieg, who regards his art as the highest in the world, should have heard you. It could have been the beginning of a delightful argument. (John Paulsen in *Mine Erindringer* [My Recollections], pp. 186–87.)

Grieg's assessment of Ibsen

The meeting between Peer Gynt and Edvard Grieg laid the foundation for one of the most fortunate collaborations in the realm of theater music that the world has ever seen. Grieg found in Ibsen's imaginary character a rich originality that stood in remarkable contrast to the Ibsen that he knew. For Grieg never made genuine contact with Ibsen. Unfortunately, they never managed to open up to one another. The closest they came was in August and September of 1876, when they were together every day for several weeks in the German village of Gossensass near the Brenner Pass.

In April of that year Grieg had received a letter from Ibsen, who was in Munich. In this letter of March 4 the playwright wrote among other things that "it would be especially nice if we could get together." When Grieg and John Paulsen, the young poet from Bergen, visited the music festival in Bayreuth, Grieg received—in a letter dated August 4—the following gracious invitation from Ibsen to visit him in Tyrol: "You will be heartily welcome here, and I hope you don't make your visit too short. After the strenuous pleasures of Bayreuth you will certainly need some fresh mountain air, and that you will find up here."

In his autobiography, *Mine Erindringer* [My Recollections], Paulsen gave some interesting descriptions of their time together with Ibsen in Gossensass. He wrote of their first meeting (pp. 10–11): "Grieg introduced me. The usual greetings were exchanged. Ibsen's face revealed neither pleasure nor displeasure at seeing us. It was totally expressionless . . . It was as if I stood in front of a solid rock wall—an impenetrable mystery." The two young artists had little success in penetrating this rock wall during their stay in Gossensass.

Paulsen wrote further (pp. 17–18): "Ibsen was taciturn and unapproachable throughout the day. He often invited me to go on walks, but didn't speak a word . . . Nonetheless, when we parted he never failed to thank me for my 'pleasant company,' which amused me. In the evening, however, he usually loosened up and became talkative and jovial. Grieg had a special ability to get him going . . . I cannot recall Ibsen ever using an enthusiastic expression, a spontaneous word—anything that revealed a deeper inner life. He was the soul of negation."

In the summer of 1880 Paulsen was present at a dinner given in Berchtesgaden in honor of Ibsen, and in connection with this he had occasion once again to discuss the playwright's relation to Grieg and his music.[16]

The following year Grieg wrote to Paulsen from Karlsbad (letter of June 3, 1881): "But the association with Ibsen does not yield what you thought it would. I can understand that. A person who is as caught up in distrust as he is cannot appear warm and pleasant when he is with others, even if he really is."

At a party in Rome in 1884, Nina sang most of the songs that Grieg had written to texts by Ibsen. The composer wrote in a letter to Beyer on March 19 that he was surprised at Ibsen's reaction: ". . . and just think, after 'Little Haakon' and especially after 'Album Lines' [Op. 25, No. 3] and 'A Swan' [Op. 25, No. 2] (!) the icy exterior melted, and with *tears* in his eyes he came over to the piano where we were, and pressed our hands almost without being *able* to

*Henrik Ibsen, for whose play Grieg wrote the
famous "Peer Gynt" music. (Aschehoug, Oslo,
Norway)*

say anything. He mumbled something to the effect that this was true understanding . . ."

Grieg toyed with two ideas for operas based on plays written in Ibsen's youth. Paulsen reported in his book *Samvaer med Ibsen* [In Ibsen's Company] that Grieg "in his dream of writing a lyric opera" was always on the lookout for a good libretto. Ibsen had said to Paulsen concerning *Olav Liljekrans* that "if it wasn't good for anything else, at least it was good enough for an opera text." Paulsen then arranged the contact. In the *Dannebrog* interview of 1893 Grieg reported: "In 1876 I met Ibsen in Tyrol. He was very cordial toward me. 'I owe you sincere thanks for the music for *Peer Gynt*,' he said. 'Furthermore, I have an opera text that I started working on many years ago: *Olav Liljekrans*. It was really intended for another composer, but now I wouldn't want anyone but *you* to compose the opera. It will be ready for you within a year.'"

On June 20, 1877, Ibsen wrote to B. E. Bendixen, manager of the National Stage in Bergen, asking to borrow their library copy of the play: "I am planning to rework my old play *Olav Liljekrans* into an opera text for Grieg . . . But please keep this matter quiet so that it doesn't get into the newspapers."

Ibsen wrote a draft of the beginning of the opera. He never sent it to Grieg, however, for in the interview of 1893 the composer said: "I neither saw nor heard anything about *Olav Liljekrans* thereafter. Later I abandoned any thought of writing operas. However, if I could get hold of a suitable Norwegian story—one handled in the manner of *I Pagliacci*—I would more than likely throw myself into such a task with energy and determination."

Nothing ever came of the *Olav Liljekrans* project. Paulsen reported that Grieg nonetheless retained a secret hope that Ibsen would write something especially for him. In June of 1893 Grieg mentioned in a letter that Ibsen had visited him at the Grefsen Spa and was absolutely determined to write an opera text based on *The Vikings at Helgeland,* which in his opinion was remarkably well suited for a musical treatment. Grieg wished that he were healthy enough to tackle such a project, but said that for the time being he would just think about the idea and wait and see how Ibsen, who was nearly finished with one act, had developed the material. Paulsen wrote in his memoirs (1913) that Grieg had confided to him "that he finally had gotten his fondest wish fulfilled. Ibsen was going to write an opera text for him based on *The Vikings at Helgeland.* Grieg was ecstatic."

Ibsen sent Grieg a draft of the first act, but according to Paulsen the composer "had misgivings when he began to read through Ibsen's manuscript. He quickly realized that the playwright had not condensed the material and emphasized the main features, but had kept the original play largely intact and had limited himself to rhyming the lines." This was not the new and spontaneous material that Grieg was looking for, and the project was immediately abandoned.

Although Grieg was not attracted to Ibsen's early national romanticism, he was at times enthralled by his modern plays. Needless to say, he did not look upon them as suitable material for operas.

Grieg made a number of incisive statements about Ibsen's later plays that reflect his attitude toward the playwright's fundamental ideas. These comments, quoted in the Primary Materials, demonstrate the human and artistic distance that existed between these two giants of the spirit—a distance that was too great to be bridged.

That the chasm between them need not have been so impassable is evident from a diary entry made in London on June 23, 1906. In this brief note Grieg, with generosity and sympathetic understanding, summed up his judgment of Ibsen the man after learning of his death: "Although I was prepared for it, the news came as a shock. How much I owe him! Poor, great Ibsen! He was not a happy man, for it is as if he carried within him a chunk of ice that would not melt. But under this chunk of ice lay a fervent love of humanity."

A Year of Reflection

Last week I saw my father to his grave, and my mother will not live through the winter, so you see this is a lot at one time. Life for me, not to mention art, has for the moment lost its fragrance. Of the sorrow of others one can well speak in musical tones, but if it comes too close to one personally, then— . . . Moreover, I think that such periods in life yield material which later—in beauty's moment—can be made use of. And so in the last analysis one reaps something good when one sees the eternal law fulfilled in those one loves most. It is unspeakably hard, but it is good.

What is hardest, however, is the doubt and struggle to which one is exposed. The other evening I was with one of my closest friends who said that to him it was a beautiful thought that the dead now had "eternal" peace and had entered the eternal rest. In other words, that it was over. The terrible thing about it was that for a while this thought wholly possessed me, but then afterwards I became utterly empty. No, you can have all the dogmas, but the thought of immortality I must have! Without that everything is nothing. (Letter to Winding, September 28, 1875.)

The year 1876 proved to be a demanding one for Grieg. During the preceding autumn his life was saddened by the loss of both of his parents. He expressed his feelings at this time in an unusually beautiful way in two letters to Winding—the first at the end of September, 1875,[1] and the second on December 17 following. In the latter he wrote: "Now I sit here unspeakably lonely and forsaken. I have not been able to pull myself together for anything whatsoever. Life and death and eternity, religion and art—everything creates hazy pictures before my inner eye, pictures that I still have not been able to comprehend. I thought that I would compose a great deal, but although my feelings are so strong that they overwhelm me at this time, the urge to reflection is even stronger. I live in a continual struggle among these elements and find no resolution. May this transitional life soon find an ending, for there is something agonizing about it—even if it actually bears fruits. I will remain here this winter and live with my brother. I give a few lessons; other than that I live in complete seclusion and am glad to be free of the public . . . Any thought of concerts is now loathsome to me."

The Ballade *in G minor*

When Grieg in the following months repeatedly emphasized that he was in a period of depression, it is unlikely that this was solely because of the death of his parents.[2] Presumably it was caused as much by an increasingly problematic relationship with his wife. There is no tangible evidence concerning this matter, but in various circles in Bergen there has long been a widespread belief that at just this time Nina was having an affair with Edvard's brother John. This, according to the rumor, hurt Edvard deeply and weighed heavily upon

2. MARIE BEYER REGARDING
GRIEG'S PROBLEMS

In addition to this sorrow, which deeply affected the good and loving son, Grieg also had some other traumatic experiences—a crisis that left deep scars and later gave rise

to several of his most significant compositions, including the string quartet and "The Mountain Thrall." (Unpublished manuscript from 1924 in the National Archive in Oslo.)

him for several years to come, and may account for the hiatus in his compositional activity at this time. But the problem must nonetheless have been resolved, for in 1883 Edvard dedicated the cello sonata, Opus 36, to his brother. Later—in the 1880s and again in the 1890s—when new marital problems arose, they had different causes.

In 1875 Grieg tried to get through this crisis by throwing himself into his work. The first composition reflecting the struggle that he was experiencing is the *Ballade in the Form of Variations on a Norwegian Melody,* Opus 24, which was completed in the spring of 1876. This piece—his largest composition for piano—he rightly considered some of the finest music he had ever created. It was, as he said, written "with my life's blood in days of sorrow and despair."

Throughout his life he felt a very special relationship to the *Ballade.* It appears that the feelings he had here reduced to music affected him so strongly that he was never able to perform the piece in public. Iver Holter's account of the "unforgettable impression" he received when he first heard the *Ballade* also reveals something of Grieg's attitude toward the piece. In late July, 1876, when passing through Leipzig on his way to the Bayreuth Festival, Grieg played it for Dr. Max Abraham, director of the Peters publishing firm. According to Holter, he put his entire soul into the interpretation; and when he was finished, not only was he so physically exhausted that he was bathed in sweat: he was also so agitated and shaken that he could not say a word for a long time. We also have Grieg's own account of this performance.[3] Dr. Abraham found the work so engaging that he proceeded to publish it without delay.

Internationally, the composition did not receive an immediate response, and this disappointed Grieg. He placed some hope in Liszt, however, who had earlier shown himself sympathetic toward Grieg's music. In a letter to Matthison-Hansen on February 10, 1878, he wrote that he had sent Liszt "several things that should not be killed by neglect—for example, the *Ballade* which you know and about which I have literally not seen a *single* public statement. This business of not writing for the masses has, in addition to its joy, some moments of discouragement and despair."

The *Ballade,* with its extremely demanding technical problems, is a challenge to concert pianists quite apart from matters of interpretation. It has a playing time of about twenty minutes. With its deep emotional content and its sterling quality, it deserves to be regarded as one of the most interesting and profound set of variations for piano from the nineteenth century.

Grieg took the melody that he used as the theme for these variations from

3. GRIEG LOOKS BACK AT THE *BALLADE*

I still remember that many years ago I was extremely unhappy over having to play my *Ballade,* Opus 24, for Dr. Abraham because I was convinced that it would not be to his taste. When I was finished, however, to my surprise he said: "A great, serious work which it will give me pleasure to publish and which will add even greater luster to your name." Those were approximately his words. And time has shown him to be right. But there is something strange about this so-called success, especially when it is "artistic." Sometimes a work like that falls flat to begin with, and yet the success is there—N.B.: for one who has a wide horizon. (Letter to Henri Hinrichsen, July 21, 1904.)

4. THE NORTHLAND PEASANTRY

I know so many a lovely song
Of beautiful lands elsewhere,
But ne'er have I heard a single song
Of my home in the north so fair.
So now I'm going to try my skill
To write a song so that people will
See that life up north can be happy
    and gay—
No matter what folks down south
    might say.

L. M. Lindeman's collection *Ældre og nyere norske Fjeldmelodier* [Older and Newer Norwegian Mountain Melodies]. This melody appears as No. 14 in the second volume (1858) under the title "Den nordlanske bondestand" [The Northland Peasantry]. Lindeman, while on his trip collecting melodies in Valdres in 1848, had written it down as it was sung to him by fifty-one-year-old Anders Nilsen Perlesteinsbakker from Modalen in South Aurdal. Given below is a facsimile of Lindeman's original notation of the melody. The text as recorded by Lindeman is not easy to read (even for a Norwegian!); it is given in translation in the Primary Materials.[4]

According to the research of Öystein Gaukstad, the text was written by Kirstine Aas (nee Colban). It was printed without the author's name in *Finmarkens Amtstidende* of March 17, 1832. Jörgen Moe published the poem in a song collection in 1840 with the instruction that it should be sung to the melody of "Å kjöre vatten, å kjöre ved" [Hauling water, hauling wood], which has exactly the same metrical structure. Both melodies are cut on the same last; the lines of the verses have the same structure: *AB AB CC AB*. It is hard to find any other connection between them, however. The Valdres melody is in minor as well.

The greatest oddity, however, as Gaukstad points out, is that the first ten measures of the *Ballade* are virtually identical to a drinking song from Lista, "Saa tæge mi naa glaset fatt." It was written down by Hartvig Lassen and printed as No. 90 in A. P. Berggreen's *Norske Folke-Sange og Melodier* [Norwegian Folk Songs and Melodies], Copenhagen, 1861.

Perlesteinsbakken's beautiful melody is simple and cleanly cut. It moves only within the first five notes of the G-minor scale aside from a lower and an upper auxiliary tone (F-sharp and E-flat).

The melody's mournful, almost tragic character was consistent with Grieg's state of mind at this time. He also empathized with the text of the song. Intuitively he must have experienced it almost as a motto for his own creative task: to show the outside world that composers of the far north, too, could honorably make their musical contribution to the great world chorus.

In his adaptation Grieg took occasional small liberties with Lindeman's version—some in the melody, more in the rhythm.

The theme of the *Ballade* is introduced with an unusually varied and expressive chord underlay:

The basic somber mood is established through the use of chromaticism in the first four measures. Without the usual closing cadence, the piece moves directly to a repetition of the melody in a slightly altered harmonization. The single tone of the upbeat is followed by successively fuller chord support, culminating in complete four-part harmony in measures 7–8. In the contrasting section (measures 9–12) a momentary brightening occurs as Grieg brings in the relative major—B-flat—before a chromatic cadence in measure 12 leads back to the main tonality. Then the opening phrase of the melody is repeated with a chordal accompaniment that is a synthesis of the progressions in the first eight measures. In contrast to what occurs in the folk melody, the last half is repeated.

This beginning establishes the pattern for the work's formal and tonal construction. Except for a few minor departures, the pattern is maintained in the first eight of the fourteen variations. This results in a certain deliberate staticity which Grieg counteracts with some quite stirring alterations of tempo, rhythm, texture, and dynamics from one variation to another and, at times, within a single variation. The melody is transformed in highly imaginative ways and appears now and then in the inner voices. Its changing character is illuminated by similarly changing chordal accompaniments within a framework of unassailable logic.

Melancholy and somber variations (Nos. 1, 3, 5, and 8) alternate with others that are sometimes intense (Nos. 2, 6, and 7), sometimes folk- and dance-like (Nos. 4 and 10). In No. 7 the right and left hands engage in a bit of imitation. A temporary but altogether unique climax is reached in No. 8—surprisingly, in pianissimo. Here the melody rises like a mighty cathedral from a tonal foundation that has an impressionistic tinge.

The slow, lingering ninth variation, with its 9 + 17 + 17 measures, breaks the symmetrical pattern of the preceding variations and forms a bridge to the

5. TEMPO ALTERATION
IN THE *BALLADE*

We talk a lot about it, but he wants the
ending to be very fast. The tempo marking,
however, is *un poco allegro*—which, therefore, is not correct. (J. Röntgen in a letter
to his wife, November 28, 1899.)

much freer and more radical variations in the last part. These latter carry the *Ballade* forward to the grand display of power with which the piece concludes.

The tenth variation has bouncing dance rhythms which are also retained in the variations that follow. According to Julius Röntgen, who had rehearsed the work with the composer for a concert in Copenhagen in November, 1899, Grieg wanted a very fast tempo at this point.[5]

The tenth variation also starts the process of building greater suspense. In the closing measures Grieg used no less than twelve dominant seventh chords in the second inversion. They move up chromatically until they reach the secondary dominant of the main key, which is reinterpreted to become a secondary dominant of D-flat major.

The eleventh variation, which starts in D-flat major, is the first to begin in a key other than G minor. After five measures comes a transition to E major, and four measures later another to G major. The tension is not released by the cadences, however, because the dominants of these three keys (with a lower auxiliary tone to the augmented fourth) are being played the entire time as pedal points in the left hand. A temporary release occurs in the twelfth variation (G major), where sonorous chords present a version of the theme with tripled note values.

The two last variations—Allegro furioso and Prestissimo—are once again in G minor. With their *springar* rhythms and violent accents, they both have an absolutely frenetic character. They lead toward a climax of such bold intensity that one is put in mind of the "barbaric" style of the twentieth century. The culminating point comes in a left-hand E-flat octave (the chromatically lowered fifth of the secondary dominant chord) which, after a long fermata, moves down to the dominant D. Then comes the ending: just the first eight measures of the folk melody (with harmonization altered so slightly that the changes are scarcely noticeable) without the brighter contrasting section. After a fruitless, unresolved struggle, Grieg thus allowed the *Ballade* to end in much the same mood with which it began—dying away in resignation.

We have Grieg's own comments on this ending in a letter to Beyer from Leipzig dated March 27, 1898. Eugène d'Albert had played the *Ballade* in the Gewandhaus "so brilliantly that it took the audience by storm. Think what that means! He had virtually *all* the requirements: with both refinement and grand style he played that mighty passage that increases in intensity until it breaks out in sheer fury. And then after that you should have heard the daringly long fermata on that low E-flat. I think he held it for half a minute. But the effect was colossal. And then he completed that old, sad song so slowly, quietly, and simply that I myself was deeply moved . . ."

The Ibsen and Paulsen songs

The inner turmoil that Grieg experienced when he wrote the *Ballade* was such that once again—and now for the last time—Ibsen's poetry kindled his creative spark. This occurred in the late winter and spring of 1876. It was not the riotous tales in *Peer Gynt* that interested him now. He felt instead an attraction toward the spiritual poems where Ibsen, in an almost aphoristic style, gave short mood pictures with a universal message. The result was *Six Songs,* Opus 25. The most important of these songs have to do with the autumn of life. In a few pieces, however, Grieg focused upon the somewhat lighter sides of Ibsen's poems, and this led quite naturally to the intimations of spring in the less problematic lyrics of the young Bergen poet, John Paulsen. The Paulsen poems that Grieg selected resulted in the song collection *Five Songs,* Opus 26.

Among the Ibsen songs, "A Swan" is a jewel of the most excellent quality; it is among the finest songs Grieg ever created. The rare poem about the mute swan that only in death receives the ability to make a sound became for Grieg a symbol of his own situation: only through art are life's greatest troubles overcome.

In Grieg's setting the poem acquires undreamed-of dimensions, not by outward bravura but by revealing the inner radiance of the ruby's deep color. Already in the melancholy opening measures, elegantly simple as they are, the concentrated world of emotion is captured masterfully. Note the tonic followed by the subdominant with a major seventh in the first measure. This sequence is repeated in measure 3, but this time with a minor third in the subdominant. The effect is sublimely beautiful:

It is remarkable how Grieg, in the midsection of the song—purely intuitively, and here for the first time—anticipated the delicate nuances of impressionism. In the passage below, Grieg created a static sound effect with the help of pillar-like chords. The entire passage is constructed over a pedal point on the dominant C. In measure 2 of this example Grieg has moved the melody up a third (relative to the passage immediately preceding), but on the same tonal foundation. Meanwhile, in the right hand of the piano part the former B-flat

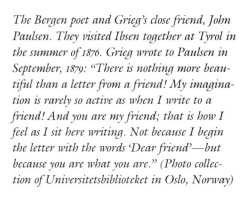

The Bergen poet and Grieg's close friend, John Paulsen. They visited Ibsen together at Tyrol in the summer of 1876. Grieg wrote to Paulsen in September, 1879: "There is nothing more beautiful than a letter from a friend! My imagination is rarely so active as when I write to a friend! And you are my friend; that is how I feel as I sit here writing. Not because I begin the letter with the words 'Dear friend'—but because you are what you are." (Photo collection of Universitetsbiblioteket in Oslo, Norway)

has been raised to B-natural. The result is that almost imperceptibly the harmony has changed: the chord has become an "incomplete" secondary dominant (VII[11] cf V) in F major: B–D–F–A–C–E (with C in the bass).

The eleventh (C) has functioned as a pedal point throughout, but in measure five it is transferred from the bass to an inner voice. It is subsequently resolved to B, as this note becomes the third of the incomplete dominant of the dominant with the minor ninth (A flat) in the bass. The ensuing chromatic progression in the bass strengthens the movement toward the tonic chord in measure seven. The varied recapitulation then follows.

The release comes toward the end of the song, where the listener is elevated to a supernatural world:

Among the remaining five Ibsen songs, "Fiddlers" is the most significant. Grieg undoubtedly identified himself with the main character of the poem, i.e., the artist who came under the spell of the water sprite and who, when he had finally "mastered" it, realized to his dismay that he had wasted his own happiness.

Grieg gives his first hint that he, too, had personal problems like those told about in the text of the song, with regard to his work on the string quartet, Opus 27. The thematic basis in Opus 27 is, in fact, the melodic material from "Fiddlers." The intimate connection between these two works will be discussed more thoroughly in connection with our analysis of the quartet (p. 222 ff.).

"Fiddlers" has been sung surprisingly seldom both in Norway and abroad. This is probably due largely to its wide range (an octave and a fifth) and the

In you I see much of myself of earlier days. Therefore I can tell you: get steel, steel, steel! And when you ask: where do I get it? There is only this one, terrible answer: it is bought with one's heart's blood. God knows that I speak from experience. Believe me, my friend, I hardly know if I should wish steel for you, because it is so costly!! May God strengthen you! (Letter to J. Paulsen, June 27, 1876.)

high tessitura in the dramatic midsection, but the interpretive problems in the somewhat obscure text undoubtedly play a role as well.

The song's weakest section is the middle part, where a single phrase is transposed up a minor third three consecutive times. The triviality of this procedure is relieved, however, by the exciting and daring world of sound in the varied repeats. The harmonic crassness here results from series of dissonant chord columns erected on thirds—this in a context that is neither major nor minor, but one that cannot be classified as belonging to a specific modal scale either. It is precisely in this way that Grieg underscored the absence of release, which is entirely in keeping with the basic mood of the poem.

"Album Lines" and "Departed!" are closely related. It is not always easy to grasp the meaning in these very terse poems. Grieg's concentrated settings, too, have something cryptic about them. Both exhibit an arid sparseness and are written in a recitative style. Their most characteristic features are the frequent use of diminished fourths and tritone effects. While in the two preceding songs—and especially in "A Swan"—Grieg anticipated *impressionism,* it is obvious that he was here approaching an *expressionistic* musical language. He had come close to doing this once before in "The Soldier," that remarkable song from 1865. In "Album Lines" and "Departed!" Grieg set before himself—to use Ibsen's words—"the demand of the Ideal": *truth* before *beauty.*

In the two remaining songs Grieg once again became a full-blooded Romantic—indeed, almost too much so. "With a Water Lily," which is unmistakably Schumannesque in character, fell right in with the popular taste of the time and came to be regarded as almost a "hit tune." It is a captivating and somewhat ambiguous song with a distinctive accompaniment. For the first and only time in his career, Grieg allowed the voice part to be accompanied almost slavishly by piano octaves distributed between the right and left hands, and with the chords as off-beat figures.

In "A Bird-Song," on the other hand, Grieg never seems to get into motion. The tune itself has something of the innocence of a good children's song about it, but it gradually gets lost in stereotyped sequencing: long sections lack the variation and development that could have raised the song to greater poetic heights.

The optimistic tone that emerges in "With a Water Lily" and "A Bird Song" is heightened in the Paulsen songs. In a letter to Björnson of May 2, 1876, Grieg wrote that the winter had been dark and oppressive and that he had been surrounded by reflections of the most diverse kinds. This had been mirrored in his compositions. He had "only now in these lovely spring days awakened from a long, long period of lethargy."

Paulsen's rather weak, sentimental poetry certainly lacks the stamp of genuineness that comes from personal experience. Grieg went—almost cruelly—right to the point about this with his friend in a letter sent to him after Opus 26 had been completed.[6]

It is entirely characteristic of Grieg that he was heavily dependent on textual quality. He was rarely able to turn a mediocre text into a good song. This is clearly evident in "Hope," and even more so in "You Whispered That You Loved Me" and "Autumn Thoughts." The songs have a certain ambitious

A typical caricature of Richard Wagner

appearance, but they are so artificial as to be quite unconvincing. In "I Walked One Balmy Summer Eve" and "The First Primrose," however, he succeeded in a surprising manner in ennobling the texts to produce mature songs of high quality. Both songs are excellent and overflowing with lyric feelings. They complement each other despite the dissimilarity of styles. "I Walked One Balmy Summer Eve" has an attractive, natural simplicity and a slightly modal diatonic style; the music clothes the words attractively. Grieg was not especially adept at expressing himself by means of chromatic melodies, but "The First Primrose" is an exception. Here he managed to add to his stature as a melodist. From the ingenious chromaticism of the voice part emerges a supple, graceful melody that immediately kindles one's interest and takes root in one's mind.

Enthusiasm in Bayreuth—frustration in Scandinavia

The great experience for Grieg in the summer of 1876 was his encounter with Wagner's art during the opening of the first festival in Bayreuth with *The Ring of the Nibelung*.

Grieg wrote Johan Selmer on April 12 that Dr. Abraham had sent him tickets for the performances, and he asked his colleague to obtain piano scores for him so that he could study the operas thoroughly. In a May 2 letter to Björnson he referred to *The Ring* as "the strangest work our culture has brought forth, and doubly remarkable because it is miles ahead of our time."

Grieg had obtained an assignment from *Bergensposten* to cover this event for the newspaper, and the six long articles he wrote in the course of ten days bear witness to his extraordinary ability to write meaningfully about music. In a captivating and very personal manner, he described his impressions with delightful turns of speech. His evaluations also provide interesting proof of his ability to enter into the Wagnerian world, a world toward which he felt both fascination and repugnance.

Grieg was accompanied to Bayreuth by his friend John Paulsen. Immediately after they arrived in the festival city, Grieg wanted to attend the dress rehearsals which began on August 6. But King Ludwig II wanted the exclusive right to attend these rehearsals, so there were problems getting into the building. The prankster in him awakened, however, and he found a solution that he later described to his American biographer, H. T. Finck. Conductor Hans Richter had been obliged to deny him entry, but he had done so in such a kindly way that Grieg asked: "But what if I came in without permission?" To that Richter replied: "Well now, something like that I obviously cannot prevent." It was no sooner said than done. So even though Wagner's "most intimate friends . . . did not get in, I watched for my chance and slipped into the auditorium . . ." When the king arrived in the hall, however, Grieg and the other "sneak previewers" stood up noisily, and Wagner angrily reprimanded them from his box!

The next day, however, Grieg was able to tell *Bergensposten*'s readers that the king had changed his mind: "Today we hear that Wagner has helped the

I have received a firm promise of admission to them [the dress rehearsals], but the matter has nonetheless become . . . very dubious because the king of Bavaria arrived during the night (he always travels at night merely because he finds it romantic) and wants to have the dress rehearsal all to himself (that is because he is shy). From what I hear, he will not attend the public performances. It is unfortunately all too likely that Wagner will be obliged to obey his royal friend and patron, who has contributed so much to the great results which are now at hand. Well, we shall see. I am determined to attend the dress rehearsals, one way or another. One does not come all the way from Norway just to stand outside. (Article to *Bergensposten* dated August 6, 1876.)

* * *

One does not really sympathize with these mermaids, giants, gods, and goddesses. One looks at them, one admires them on the stage, but where—as here—they do not appear in contrast to human beings, who can speak to our human emotions, one becomes tired of them. (Dated August 6.)

* * *

I go home and tell myself that despite everything one might find fault with—despite the restlessness with which the gods are depicted, despite the many chromatic passages, the constant change of harmony as a result of which one little by little is overcome by a nervous irritability and finally complete exhaustion, despite the considerable filigree and the total absence of moments of relief [from the dramatic tension], despite the extremity of complete exhaustion, despite the outer limits of beauty's border on which the whole work stands—despite everything, this musical drama is the work of a giant the equal of whom has perhaps been seen in the history of art only in Michelangelo. (Dated August 7.)

* * *

Here we also occasionally find traces of something definitely old Norse, something which naturally cannot be attributed to Wagner. But that these are present shows how strong his inspiration has been. What one cannot finally hold against him, but

king understand how important it is for him to hear how everything sounds in a full house, and that the king therefore has permitted the distribution of free tickets."

On August 12 Grieg described the unique atmosphere in Bayreuth, which now had become the center for the Wagner cult: "As I sit here now I can hear Wagnerian motives being hummed, sung, yodelled, and bellowed from below. I go to the window and see both valkyries and Rhinemaidens, both giants and dwarfs, both gods and human beings walking around and enjoying life on the tree-lined streets. I slam the window down so as to have rest . . . but Erda's mighty alto voice penetrates the thick walls. It's no wonder that I sit here bewildered."

It appears that the labor of writing had completely drained Grieg's energy, and to Paulsen's great disappointment he declined the honor of attending a reception at Wagner's home. In his memoirs Paulsen wrote: "Grieg and I were invited to a soirée at Wagner's villa Wahnfried, an invitation that must be regarded as a great honor . . . Thus we had to count ourselves among the chosen few. But Grieg was not in the mood to go out that evening, and accordingly I had to forgo a pleasure that in a childish way I had anticipated."

Some excerpts from Grieg's *Bergensposten* articles are given in the Primary Materials.[7] From these articles one can see that he did not swallow Wagner's ideas indiscriminately, but weighed them with great care. Especially important, not least of all in relation to his own vocal music, are his thoughts about Wagner's handling of the human voice; he had strong reservations about the fact that the soloists often "do no more than provide a background of inner voices."

From Bayreuth, Grieg and Paulsen left on the previously mentioned pleasure trip to the Tyrol in response to Ibsen's invitation to visit him in Gossensass.

After meeting several of the giants of cultural life, Grieg had to return to the trivialities of everyday life in Oslo. He wrote dejectedly to Paulsen on November 15: "Yes, believe me, everything here is just dandy; you can greet Ibsen and say that. It was a transition to come from the South up here again this time, more so than I have ever felt before. I was met by icy coldness from every quarter, and it wouldn't have taken much to get me to take to the road again." There were problems on every hand, not least with the orchestra. On December 29 he wrote to Winding, "Up here I live icebound in more ways than one. It goes badly with the music in all quarters. We can't use music for a

must nonetheless regret, is that the Nordic folk music is foreign to him. I mean, of course, merely that one might wish that he had used it here where he depicts the Nordic lands of long ago—a unique product of which is our heroic ballads. (Dated August 13.)

* * *

Much of that which is most profound in the material that previously has been a closed book for me will become clear and

be popularized by the dramatic presentation. It is as when one gives pictures to children: the eye aids the thought. For a time such as ours, with its marked tendency to create halves and parts instead of [whole] personalities, it can also certainly be a good medicine to take to heart these broad, heroic figures with their strong passions, their big self-sacrificing deeds, and their full, warm personalities. (Dated August 18.)

8. GRIEG DEFENDS HIS ARRANGEMENTS OF MOZART'S SONATAS

Much of it really sounds very good—indeed, so good that I have reason to hope that Mozart "won't turn over [in his grave]." (Letter to Winding, April 23, 1877.)

* * *

The writer of this article has himself tried, by the addition of a second piano, to give some of Mozart's piano sonatas a sound that commends itself to modern ears; and in his own defense he wants to add that he did not change a single note that Mozart had written, thus showing the master the homage that is his due. I do not think that this was something that had to be done—far from it. If one does not do like Gounod, who transformed a Bach prelude into a sentimental and trivial (albeit modern) crowd pleaser—an act of which I emphatically disapprove—and further, if one seeks to preserve the unity of style, then there is no reason to get upset just because someone attempts a modernization in order to show his admiration for an old master. (From an article about Mozart originally published in *The Century*. New York, November, 1897. Republished in a slightly different form in *Samtiden*, 1898.)

full orchestra in our [Music] Association because two bassoonists act as if they are crazy and won't play for all the gold in the world—and they are the only two to be found in the whole city! I have little to do—altogether too little—and still I am composing nothing."

To earn money, he and Nina gave concerts in Stockholm and Uppsala—but they "didn't get much," he wrote to Winding. As a further frustration, they got such a silly review that Grieg felt compelled to write an angry article in the Swedish press (see p. 302).

A sad chapter in Grieg's work as a composer occurred at this time. He did a very curious thing: he provided a freely composed second piano part for four of Mozart's lovely, innocent piano sonatas. This version (CW 135), which was written for pedagogical use, "sounded surprisingly good in the concert hall," he wrote to Dr. Abraham on May 27, 1877. But Dr. Abraham's firm was not interested in publishing it. (In 1879, however, the work was published by E. W. Fritzsch.) It is hard to understand why Grieg would embark on such a task, and in time he himself was embarrassed by the whole affair.[8] The leading Swedish music critic, Adolf Lindgren, articulated clearly in *Svensk Musiktidning* (April 1886) the opinion that we share today: "Grieg's transcription of Mozart's fantasy for two pianos [sic] is only a bungling and in part a Norwegianizing of Mozart, for whom a true musician ought to have more respect."

A bright spot in Grieg's otherwise gloomy life was a concert on June 2 when he performed his first violin sonata together with the world-renowned violinist Henri Wieniawski. Grieg wrote to Winding on August 13 that while the audience "usually sits and yawns over my music, now they were about to tear the house down . . ."

A short time later Nina and Edvard shook the dust of the "tiger city" (so called because of its reputed lack of cordiality toward strangers) off their feet and headed westward. The Oslo period was over once and for all.

The First Visit to Hardanger

1. GRIEG'S HATRED FOR OSLO

The conditions in Oslo are wonderful: the vilest cliques poison the air there . . . Lies and slander are now being flung at me, but—they can't touch me. If you come to Oslo you will first encounter a courtesy and friendliness that will surprise you so much that you will say: Here there can surely never be any treachery! But—that's when you have to watch out for the sly old fox. Yet, what am I really talking about? It can only be intimated. If you work for your own ideals, sooner or later you will run into this monster of prejudice, of half-this-half-that, of flabbiness, of egotism, of hate, of envy—yes, of bestiality, of low slavery. Only your own good genius can advise you how to escape it, but a warning from some-one who wishes you well can also be a good thing. (Letter to John Paulsen, August 19, 1877.)

In 1877 Grieg's long-suppressed irritation over the constricting circumstances in Oslo reached a critical point. He felt that now he had to burn all of the bridges with city life and renew his strength in a different and healthier milieu—one that would allow him to give himself wholly to his creative work. He wrote to Dr. Abraham on January 31: "You talk about composition. But here I sit and give lessons and conduct rehearsals, choir practices, and that sort of thing. I will be glad when summer comes so I can go out in the country and work."

He was not greatly tempted by an invitation from Winding to come to Copenhagen once again, or by an offer from Dr. Abraham to use his home in Leipzig for an extended period of time. To the contrary. He wanted to steal away to the solitude of western Norway in the hope that he might recover his creative energy. On April 23 he wrote to Winding: "I will probably stay at a Norwegian farm someplace. I'm thinking about Hardanger."

This is the first time Hardanger is mentioned in Grieg's letters as a possible place to live and work. What gave him the idea of heading for that part of the country we do not know; perhaps it was only an impulse of the moment. Be that as it may, it was lucky for him—and for Norwegian music—that he went to Hardanger that summer.

Toward the end of June, Nina and Edvard settled down on a farm called "Övre Börve" in Ullensvang, near the village of Lofthus. It was a uniquely beautiful place, with the fjord (Sörfjorden) immediately below and the spar-kling glaciers of Folgefonnen high up on the other side of the fjord—pastoral charm and majestic grandeur in perfect harmony.

They stayed at "Börve" all summer. Grieg loved the place. On August 13 he wrote enthusiastically to Winding: "You couldn't help but get well if you were here! The air is so light that one feels like a feather—or, that one could feel that way if one did not have to bear the burden that is an integral part of the happiest and the unhappiest lot on this earth: to be an artist."

One week later, ecstatic about having left Oslo once and for all, he ex-pressed in the harshest possible terms his hatred for that city and everything it represented. The statement occurs in a candid letter to his friend John Paulsen, the poet, who at just that time had plans to move to Oslo.[1]

Grieg had rented a little schoolhouse in the village in order to have peace and quiet for his creative work. At first he didn't compose much, however. In the letter to Winding he wrote: "Here I am spending a lot of time cod fishing, and much too often the musical ideas I catch are, unfortunately, not unlike these noble creatures . . ."

But although Grieg loved "Börve," he soon discovered that he could not stay there through the winter. The farm lacked "the minimal comforts required even by a native," as he put it. But he wanted to stay in Hardanger, so he decided to move to Lofthus—a small village on the fjord, about five miles north of Börve. Here the Griegs took lodging at the local inn, where Brita and Hans Utne were the innkeepers. A warm friendship developed between the two families, and in later years Nina and Edvard went back to Lofthus summer after summer. The first year they did not live in the inn itself, but in an old building that originally had been a general store. They took all of their meals with the Utne family. A few years later Grieg also became godfather to Sverre, one of twelve sons in the Utne family.

Grieg became close friends with the local clergyman, Johann A. Budtz Christie, a distant relative who was about the same age as Edvard. They carried on probing discussions about religious questions, a topic that was further developed in their later correspondence. *Four Psalms,* Opus 74— Grieg's last composition—was dedicated to Christie.

Lofthus and the story of the "composer's hut"

In a letter to Matthison-Hansen on February 10, 1878, Grieg wrote about the "beautiful, noble, and enlightened farm folk." The people he primarily had in mind were undoubtedly his innkeeper friends, the Utnes. The truth is that seldom or never did he manage to win the confidence of the farmers to any great extent. The local residents had a long-standing mistrust of visiting tourists from the city. They just turned away with a sly smile when the diminutive Griegs, all bundled up in warm clothing, took their walks in the area—she with short-clipped hair, he with an artist's mane; she with tiny little steps, he with longer strides—with rubbers over his boots.

On one particular occasion, however, the farmers came to Grieg's rescue. It is well known that Grieg could not tolerate having anyone nearby when he was composing, and for that reason he arranged to have a little work hut built for him at some distance from the inn. This was done in September and October while he was in Bergen, where he gave two concerts in order to secure funds for his winter stay in Lofthus. The hut was jokingly called "Komposten," a play on words suggesting both "compost heap" and "the composer's hut." Grieg gave a highly amusing account of his hut in an 1886 issue of *Norden, Illustreret Skandinavisk Revue.* The article, which had the title "Komposten," was illustrated by Wilhelm Peters, an artist friend of Grieg from Oslo. The Griegs, as a matter of fact, had lived with Peters just before their trip to Hardanger. An excerpt from Grieg's jovial reports is given below.

Concerning "Komposten" Grieg wrote: "Truly a bad-sounding name for

Brita Utne, Grieg's beautiful hostess in Hardanger for many years. She was 25 years old when Edvard and Nina came to Lofthus in 1877, and she did everything she could to make it pleasant for them. It is rumored that she and Grieg were more than friends, and it is known that he wrote several letters to her which have never been made public. (Troldhaugen, Bergen)

an artist's abode! But that is how the country folks in Hardanger humorously christened the little room I arranged to have built during my hibernation there; . . . and unfamiliar with the area as I was at that time I chose a remote hill, to which no visible path led, in the hope of getting away from people. But as luck would have it, a time-honored old footpath—about whose existence I was ignorant—led right to the place. And the farmers—let me tell you, they surely found that path! They wanted to 'listen in.' So all winter, except when the weather was bad, I had the pleasure of hearing stealthy footsteps outside the house while I sat and worked. And many a time when I got up from my writing table to try out a new musical idea on the piano, the idea got nipped in the bud by the farmer-critic who stood behind the house listening in the hope of becoming the godfather of the new musical child . . .

"Eventually the situation became intolerable. I decided, like a new Aladdin, to move my whole castle, and I was lucky enough to find a sheltered and quiet place—one with a view toward Folgefonnen's glaciers—far down by the fjord between the cliffs and the woods.

"It was already nearing Easter when I proceeded to carry out my plan. I got about fifty farmers—it couldn't be fewer than that—who with great willingness promised to help. N.B.: they promised to help not as workers—I couldn't get them to do that—but as friends and acquaintances. For our farm folk have the custom, as old as it is nice, of helping each other with jobs requiring a lot of manpower and expecting no remuneration other than food and drink. Their word for this sort of thing is 'dugnad.'

Nina and Edvard in characteristic attire. Caricature by O. Hartmann. (public domain)

Lofthus in Grieg's day. In an April 8, 1878 letter to Frants Beyer he wrote: "I cannot begin to tell you how beautiful it is out here now. Weather as never before, a cloudless sky, and awakening nature all around! Not to mention the starlings. There is a veritable concert here, no matter where one goes." And in a February 10, 1878 letter to Matthison-Hansen: "Yes, 'this Lofthus' as you so scornfully say. But you should see 'this Lofthus'—see the towering mountains, snow-covered right down to the water, see these millions of picturesque things, see and talk with the handsome, noble and enlightened inhabitants here; then I think that if you could you would move 'this Lofthus' lock, stock and barrel over to Danish soil." (Photo by K. Knudsen. Universitetsbiblioteket of Bergen, Norway)

"One lovely morning at the stroke of nine, the whole crowd of able-bodied men gathered together in an obviously festive mood, which was in no way diminished by the sight of abundant preparations for the serving of food and drink—for which I had wisely made provision. A barrel of Hardanger beer, famous for its strength, stood ready for serving beside adequate stocks of genuine Norwegian aquavit and appropriate delicacies such as flat bread, lefse [a thin Norwegian potato bread that resembles a soft tortilla], cakes, and the like . . .

"The tasks were now assigned, everyone was ordered to his place, and I will not soon forget that glorious moment in 'Komposten's' history when, with a mighty heave, it was torn from its foundation to the thunderous applause of the assembled peasants. Meanwhile the pupils from a nearby girls' school, who had gathered en masse to watch, waved their handkerchiefs and filled the air with an enthusiastic 'hurrah' that was full of youth and springtime. It was as if all of us were electrified by these light and cheerful female voices, and with much shouting the house was moved—sometimes dragged, sometimes rolled on large logs—to its new home. A delightful situation developed during a rest break when Messrs. Grieg and Peters went from man to man serving aquavit left and right, and all the while wise cracks were being made around us bearing witness to the general sense of well being that obviously was present. Then we continued forward, and with renewed cries of 'hurrah' we reached the chosen spot. When the house was finally lifted up on its new foundation it looked quite splendid, nestled between the birch and the mountain ash beside the crystal clear fjord. Then the ale bowls were passed around, and they were needed too; for many a husky fellow was seen wiping the sweat from his brow after the exertion . . .

"But the work was still not completely finished, for now the piano had to be moved to its place. A detachment of troops was sent off, and a few minutes later in a mood of excessive gaiety they came galloping with the heavy box as if it were a ball of feathers. Meanwhile, the guests who had stayed behind had been guzzling the beer to such an extent that the atmosphere was becoming more animated than one might have wished. A couple of drunken fellows could already be seen lying like dead bodies on the grass. The rest of the crowd now insisted that I play—which I obviously neither could nor would refuse to do—and the little hut was so jammed full of listeners that I could scarcely move my arms. Those who couldn't find standing room inside stood in the open door or sat in the window, while the rest of the listening crowd stood outside and craned their necks to see the 'performance.'

"To the accompaniment of a listener to my left, who constantly staggered against me so that I almost fell off the piano stool—and another to my right, who recited with such fervor that the saliva sprayed out onto the piano keys— I struck up the Norwegian folk dance called 'Stabbelaaten.' I must admit that now there was a moment in which it was perfectly quiet—but it was only for a brief moment. Suddenly a husky voice in the corner of the room pronounced, 'Thanks. Now, may the devil take me, that's enough for today!' A most encouraging review! I didn't let that scare me away, although the laughter made it hard to keep on playing; but I kept on until the dance was finished, fired up by the fact that the fellow who so rudely interrupted got what he deserved by being—to speak literally—kicked out of the 'concert hall.' When the last note had faded away, one of the group who was still sober congratulated me on my new house, to which I replied by expressing thanks to everyone who participated in the 'dugnad' and offering a toast to all the local inhabitants.

"Meanwhile, outside the house things began to get even wilder. People began throwing stones and clumps of turf. First they tried to hit each other, but they soon got tired of this sort of thing. Then the ale bowls, which were being passed from one man to another, became the chosen targets. Their aim was remarkably accurate. Beer and pieces of dirt showered down upon the bystanders in such quantity that the air itself seemed to be darkened; and when one person or another got himself a regular 'beer bath' there was a deafening shout of laughter. It was a grotesque sight! While this was going on up by the house, some tipsy fellows for whom the beer keg had a magical power of attraction were down by the sea. . . [One of them] had selected a place directly under the spout so the beer could run right down into his open mouth. At last the wantonness took over completely. One poor fellow, who had collapsed dead drunk on the grass, was actually buried alive under clumps of sod while the onlookers laughed demoniacally. At this point in the festivities I found it wisest to slip away unnoticed . . ."

Wedding procession on the Hardanger fjord in the latter part of the nineteenth century. Grieg witnessed something similar. He wrote to John Paulsen from Börve on August 19, 1877: "It is a beautiful Sunday morning. I am sitting in the schoolhouse, where I have taken over a little studio, and see the church-goers as they pass by out on Sörfjorden. They are going to Ullensvang. Meanwhile, I am going into another church—the great one that exists in memory—there to let my thoughts rise like pillars high up towards beauty and light. (Photo by K. Knudsen. Universitetsbiblioteket of Bergen, Norway)

There is no doubt that Grieg let his imagination run wild in this description, and the people whose behavior he was allegedly describing reacted angrily to the sometimes insensitive exaggerations which they felt assailed their honor. Brita Utne, who was there herself, also protested Grieg's account.

In 1880 Grieg sold his work hut to the Ullensvang rectory, where for a time it was used as a playhouse. Later it was moved to Bokn, where it served as a wash house for the employees of a steamship company. But in 1949, on the initiative of the Ullensvang Youth Society, it was purchased and brought back to Lofthus. Here it was placed in a beautiful setting close by the fjord, and the Ullensvang Hotel has outfitted it as a miniature Grieg museum.

It is clear that Grieg was much occupied with nationalism during his first year at Lofthus. On October 17, after he had moved from Börve to Lofthus, he wrote to Matthison-Hansen: "For you must not say that since the old masters did not often use national themes, therefore we should not use them either—in other words, that we should not relate differently and more closely to the national folk tunes than they did, for *that's what we are doing.* I do not think, as Gade said, that one gets tired of nationalism, for if that were possible it would not be an idea worth fighting for. But regarding myself, I think that I have been stagnating because of a total lack of technical compositional skill—and

2. REFLECTIONS ON THE PAST AND THE FUTURE

You ask why I am leaving Oslo and what it is that is drawing me to spend the winter at Ullensvang. Well, the point is just this: it had to be done if I was not to cease to be an artist. Perhaps it surprises you, but if you only knew what an inner struggle I have waged these last years you would understand me. Every possible outer circumstance has prevented me from following my calling, and no one has been more dissatisfied with what I have achieved than I myself. There have been bits and pieces, to be sure, in which aspiration has now and then been present, but the integrated whole that I began to grasp when I was twenty-five—and for a few years thereafter—has since, year by year, slipped away from me. I have lost the ability to manage the larger musical forms—and if one loses that, after once having had it, which I really did at one time—then it is farewell to the future! In a word, I felt that things were beginning to go askew, the ideal picture was becoming stunted—and for that reason something had to be done. And I have not been as happy as I am now for a long time—yes, as thankful, as innocently happy. I am again busy immersing myself in my art, and with God's help something will come of it. (Letter to Winding, October 28, 1877.)

lack of experience with the larger musical forms. But I can take a hint, and in one thing you are right: I won't go hunting for national themes. I intend to discard all reflection and write from the heart, whether it turns out to be Norwegian or Chinese. It is for this reason—in order to have peace and quiet to do this—that I have chosen a place like Ullensvang. In Leipzig or anyplace else down there I wouldn't get this peace and quiet. I know how, the last time I was down there, I was made unsure of myself by what I heard around me. The thing is, I dare not and will not go to Germany without having something 'in the portfolio.' I think that in a way one must regard musical impressions just as one regards impressions of nature. One lives on them, but one must not go searching for them in order to use them *simultaneously* in one's creative endeavors. For my experience has been that that doesn't work. It isn't for the sake of the impressions of nature that I have chosen Hardanger either. All I need is peace and quiet—but *concentrated* peace and quiet . . . but you must remember: it is not my intention always to isolate myself, but only at a moment that is as critical as the present moment is for me."

Four months later, however, it appears that he had had all the "Norwegianness" he could stomach. On February 10, 1878, he wrote to his friend: "Not writing for the crowd has its joys, but it also has its discouraging moments—especially for us Scandinavians who, to put it bluntly, live among a people 'possessed' by populism. I love the *idea* of the folk high school, but now when I see how it is run (by one of our most important citizens) I often need an honest-to-goodness aquavit from time to time to keep from getting nauseous. There is a self-righteousness and a mutual setting-up-on-a-pedestal that really is morally enervating." But Grieg needed "this bath in solitude and in nature." He needed leisure to work, and—he wrote—"that I have found, perhaps more than is good for me."

Hints of serious personal and artistic problems

Grieg remembered the Hardanger period as a time of struggle, but it was a struggle on two different levels: the artistic and the personal. At the conclusion of the "Komposten" article he wrote: "For nowhere has my heart's blood flowed as in the music that I wrote here . . ." Then he was able to see it all in a larger perspective. But as early as August 13, 1877, he bared his soul to Matthison-Hansen: "There is something that I must do for the sake of my art. Day by day I am becoming more dissatisfied with myself. Nothing that I do satisfies me, and although I think I still have some ideas, I can neither escape nor give form to my ideas when I proceed to the development of some larger project. It's enough to make one lose one's mind—but I know well enough what the problem is. It's lack of practice, thus lack of technique, because I have never gotten beyond composing by fits and starts. But that is going to end. I am going to fight my way through the large musical forms, cost what it may. If I go mad in the process, now you know why. I tell you this because I know and feel that you have been more supportive of my art than most people."

Similar thoughts were expressed to Paulsen on August 19: "I would not say that you should call me our first 'skald of music,' that's for sure! I don't ever want to hear it again because it is a lie. I could have become that . . . but I didn't. However, it is my intention to challenge fate to a struggle; I still have enough strength to chance it, and we will see if I can win." He summed up the situation very thoroughly in a letter to Winding at the end of October.[2]

Grieg was in a situation that was fraught with tension. He had finally gotten the leisure that he had been seeking, but he was not sure that he was going to succeed in renewing himself artistically in areas that he had paid little attention to in the past. This uncertainty undoubtedly provides *some* of the background for his behavior when the newly married Marie and Frants Beyer came to visit him at "Börve." He apologized to Beyer in a letter on September 2: "I know very well that I was not in very good humor, but please don't be angry with me for that. A lot of things were irritating me at that time, but I shouldn't have let it show—least of all during the visit of such dear friends."

Moreover, the artistic problems were interwoven with a profound frustration that he was feeling during this period of his life. The irritations he alludes to in the letter to Beyer were in reality only the outward symptoms of an agonizing inner turmoil. Art and its uncompromising demands became a kind of scapegoat, a camouflage for something quite different. The real cause of his simultaneously defeatist and aggressive attitude appears to have been his relationship with Nina.

When David Monrad Johansen published his biography of Grieg in 1934, Mrs. Grieg was still alive, and in deference to her he left the issue "in abeyance." However, he mentioned that "when all the material concerning this part of Grieg's life becomes available perhaps it will show that also at this time there was the closest relationship between his life and his art." He also stated unabashedly that "hand in hand with the artistic crises he was experiencing at this time went also some personal experiences that appear to have deeply affected the course of his life."

It does not appear that the materials to which Monrad Johansen alluded can ever be made publicly available, but the vaguely concealed hints can be interpreted with the help of other materials that we do know about.

As early as September 18, 1876, Grieg's sister Elisabeth wrote an admonishing letter to her brother expressing her sadness about the fact that Nina and "Vardo" had grown so far apart. There was no way out of this impasse, she told him, unless they talked the matter out together.

Shortly after the tension-filled year in Hardanger, Grieg expressed his pent-up feelings in a long and revealing letter to John Paulsen. In this letter, dated September 8, 1879, he wrote: "Lost illusions! It would not be good if one did not lose them. Remember that for each one you lose you take one step toward the truth—and surely we can agree that however beautiful the illusions may be, truth is still more beautiful—although, to be sure, it is often unpleasant. As for myself, I cannot speak of one lost illusion at a time; no, with me they have showered down in hundreds like rotten fruit in the gusty wind. Yes. I have been out in the gusty wind. Perhaps a little of the good fruit has been blown away too—unfortunately; but I still have some left, and that of the best—of the kind that does not fall to the ground in stormy weather . . . You must not get too close to the world! Especially to women! I think I can read a 'love story' between the lines of your letter. Remember: women want to play and that is all! That sounds hard and materialistic, but there is some truth in it all the same. Women have never comprehended and never will comprehend that which is great, that which is wild, that which is boundless in a man's—an artist's—love. And if I am right in this, it follows that an artist should not marry . . ."

The bitterness that permeates these lines is expressed even more clearly—albeit as an understatement—in a letter to Iver Holter nearly twenty years later: "I don't know if you have taken notice of a song by Ibsen:

> *My dreams were of my beloved*
> *Through the warm summer night,*
> *But by the river I wander'd*
> *In an eerie and pale moonlight.*
>
> *Heigh, do you know song and terror?*
> *Can you dazzle the heart of the fair,*
> *That in mighty halls and cathedrals*
> *She'll covet to follow you there?*

It was the theme from this song (from 1876) that I used in '77 in the string quartet. And in this, as *you* will understand, there lies a piece of personal history. I know that I had a big spiritual battle to fight, and I used a great deal of energy creating the first movement of the quartet there among the dark mountains of the Sörfjord in that sad summer and autumn."

That Grieg underlined the word *you* in this letter is no doubt related to the fact that in 1876 he not only had been with Holter in Leipzig, but also had confided in him about his personal problems. May it not be that the key to the understanding of this "piece of personal history" is to be found in the rest of Ibsen's poem? Perhaps the poem became for Grieg an unveiling of an extremely delicate point in his relationship with Nina. For the last part of the poem ("Fiddlers") is revealing: art has indeed been mastered, but in the struggle for the mastery of art the artist, against his own will, lost the dearest thing he had!

> *I conjured the sprite of the waters,*
> *He lured me to regions wide,*
> *But when that dread sprite I had mastered—*
> *She was my brother's bride!*
>
> *In mighty halls and cathedrals*
> *I fiddled tunes refined,*
> *But evil songs and horror*
> *Were ever in my mind.*

Those who had the most to do with Nina and Edvard's problems—not only at this time, but also in the years to come—were Marie and Frants Beyer. See Marie Beyer's comments that are quoted in the Primary Materials on p. 199.

3. THE STRING QUARTET IS TRIED
OUT IN BERGEN

I am in town these days to hear my string
quartet. I have had a caterwauling rehearsal, but I hope it will be better tomorrow.
(Letter to Matthison-Hansen, March 7,
1878.)

Fortunately, the "evil songs and horror" eventually faded from Grieg's memory, but many tense years were to pass before mutual confidence was restored between Edvard and Nina. When art was at stake he was capable of being something of a despot who insisted on having his way unmindful of Nina's objections. He did not hesitate, for example, to compel her—this fragile city woman with ambitions as a concert singer—to settle down in the lonesome, isolated world of Hardanger. Indeed, he actually considered the possibility of making that their permanent home. This frightened Nina. Loneliness and the overpowering mountain scenery had a depressing effect on her. It is no wonder that this also led to constant quarrels between two such strong and independent natures.

From Grieg's point of view, the decision to spend the winter of 1877–78 in Ullensvang was final and irreversible. In the middle of all these difficulties, however, there now occurred a series of short, hectic work periods that produced some of the finest works in all of Norwegian music. It is because of them that Börve and Lofthus are memorable in Norwegian music history. Isolated and in inner turmoil, struggling for high artistic ideals, harboring a kind of love-hate attitude toward the national elements—in such a period, when life and art were interwoven in a remarkable way, Grieg created what is perhaps his finest chamber music composition: the String Quartet in G Minor.

The String Quartet No. 1 in G Minor, *Opus 27*

From Börve Grieg wrote Winding on August 13 that he was working on something that interested him. He reported that what he was finding in that musical vein was not all gold, but "one must be content with a nugget now and then." He also mentioned his new project in a letter to Matthison-Hansen written the same day: "The next thing you see from me will be something for string instruments; I'm in the middle of it, but God knows when it will be finished. Just now I am in a situation that is not conducive to work—a situation that must change . . ."

This is the first hint we have of the string quartet—the composition that, together with the *Ballade,* constitutes the strongest expression of Grieg's inner tension. It is almost autobiographical in character, as Grieg himself was well aware. On March 18, 1883, he wrote to Aimar Grönvold: "For I feel that in this work are hidden traces of that life's blood of which the future will hopefully see more than mere drops . . ."

About eight months passed before he could place the final double bar on the quartet. It was completed in February, 1878,[3] and a month later he sent it to the Cologne violinist Robert Heckmann, first violinist in one of Germany's foremost string quartets. Heckmann had also appeared in concert in Oslo on October 10, 1875, at which time he performed, among other things, the second and third movements of Grieg's first violin sonata.

Grieg felt a strong need to obtain an expert critique of his new work, especially with respect to the technical dimensions when writing for string instruments. An extremely fruitful cooperation arose between Grieg and

The first page of the manuscript of the string quartet. The notations in the left and right margins were made by the publisher. "Pariser" indicates the format in which the quartet was to be printed.

Heckmann with the exchange of many letters. Seven of the seventeen Heckmann letters which the Bergen Public Library has in its possession contain detailed suggestions for changes. Grieg accepted most of them when they had to do with the actual performance of the work, but now and then he wrote a clear *no* in the margin when Heckmann moved into the purely compositional area. He showed his gratitude to Heckmann by dedicating the quartet to him.

Unfortunately, the Bergen Public Library has only one Grieg letter from this correspondence, but in the Pierpont Morgan Library in New York there is an unusually important letter (dated July 22, 1878) to Heckmann in which it is stated that the composer was in the process of fair-copying a completely new score. This score is among the manuscripts that Grieg willed to the Bergen Public Library, but it is not identical to the manuscript in response to which Heckmann wrote his comments. Because of this, it is sometimes difficult to relate Heckmann's comments to the score. The original manuscript has evidently been lost.

Grieg also made radical changes in the publishing proofs which were not subsequently entered in the manuscript. The third movement, for example,

4. BERNSDORF'S VILIFICATION OF GRIEG'S STRING QUARTET

The Heckman Quartet from Cologne gave a concert in the Gewandhaus on November 30 . . . to step into the breach for a composer of our own time, Mr. Edvard Grieg from Kristiania [Oslo]. Thus it was a purely propagandistic concert . . . and Mr. Grieg has every reason to be grateful to Mr. Heckmann and his colleagues . . . Would that we could have been as grateful to the gentlemen from Cologne as Mr. Grieg! That, unfortunately, we could not be . . . For the Griegian products have given us no joy or pleasure at all—not the G-minor sonata [sic] for violin and piano (Opus 13), not the still-unpublished string quartet (also in G minor), and not the many songs or the little piano pieces from Opuses 6, 19, and 28. Quite the opposite. We have felt only displeasure and repugnance toward all the boorish and absurd stuff that is gathered together under the guise of a Norwegian national stamp, toward the mediocrity of the compositional inventiveness that lurks behind the rough-hewn and exaggerated Norwegian exterior (something non-Norwegians must accept in good faith), and toward the lack of any talent for structure and development—indeed, the lack of any ability whatsoever to create—adequately, without patchwork—a continuous whole in a movement (as here in the sonata and the quartet) . . .

Finally, we must acknowledge that—no matter how curious it may appear from our standpoint—performers and compositions at the concert were almost without exception received with great enthusiasm. Indeed, Mr. Grieg even had to repeat "Bridal Procession" . . . (Excerpts from the review in *Signale,* 1878, p. 1046.)

5. PROBLEMS OF FORM IN THE QUARTET

You have no idea what difficulty I have with the forms, but that, too, is a result of the fact that I was stagnating—and this, in turn, resulted in part from [devoting myself to] numerous commissioned works (*Peer Gynt, Sigurd Jorsalfar,* "and other unpleasantries"), in part from catering too much to popular tastes. (Letter to Matthison-Hansen, February 10, 1878.)

was given a completely different ending than that which appears in the Bergen handwritten copy.

The work was premiered by the Heckmann quartet in the Cologne Conservatory concert hall October 29, 1878. Grieg, who was present for the occasion, also played the G-major sonata with Heckmann as well as several solo pieces for piano. The concert was a great public success. Grieg was much in demand: he gave four performances in the space of five days.

But in the venerable Gewandhaus in Leipzig, on November 30, 1878, the quartet was dealt a major blow. Six years earlier the *A-minor Concerto* had been scathingly criticized by Edouard Bernsdorf in *Signale.* Grieg, naturally enough, was concerned about the dreaded critic's reaction to his new work, and his worst fears were realized. Bernsdorf's pen spewed venom and gall; he virtually denied that Grieg had any talent whatsoever as a composer.[4]

Grieg was not sufficiently thickskinned to let such an unsympathetic criticism go unnoticed. He never forgot it. As late as March 26, 1901, he wrote to his Danish friend Robert Henriques: "In Leipzig, after the first performance of my quartet, the reviewers all scorned it. I had given my best, my very heart, and I met only contempt. I was so depressed that I wanted to burn my piece. But time has made amends."

It was especially painful to Grieg that Dr. Abraham of the Peters publishing firm rejected the quartet—as he also had done with the *A-minor Concerto.* To his credit it must be said, however, that he did this before the unfavorable reviews had reached him. Grieg had written him the day before the premiere: "I was eager to hear my string quartet . . . and I can only say that the work sounds the way I had imagined it would. It is a fact that it is not fashioned according to Leipzig Conservatory requirements. But that it is not violinistic—or, indeed, that it is pianistic—is a false conclusion. I have great respect for your judgment, but you must grant me as an independent artist an independent judgment as well. I can only take it as a mark of friendship that you so openly stated your opinion . . ." So it was the Fritzsch publishing firm, not Peters, that printed the quartet in 1879.

One of those who realized the significance of the work quite early was Franz Liszt. In a letter to Grönvold on March 18, 1883, Grieg reported what Heckmann had heard from Liszt after the quartet had been performed in Wiesbaden in 1879. Liszt, according to Grieg, spoke in considerable detail about its significance: "It is a long time since I have encountered a new work, especially a string quartet, which has interested me so strongly as this singular and excellent work by Grieg."

Because of the nature of the overall plan for the quartet, it was inevitable that Grieg would have to come to grips with serious problems of form in working it out.[5] He also had a difficult time getting started on the first movement. The problem here was to find a captivating theme for the opening section. With the help of recently found sketches in the Bergen Public Library, one can now trace the evolution this material underwent as the quartet took shape. Originally Grieg worked with two completely different themes, both of which, however, were eventually discarded. The first is sluggish and lackluster:

The second takes up a melodic thread from the introduction to the "Temple Dance" in *Olav Trygvason* (see the excerpt on p. 170):

Grieg evidently felt that there was more to this theme. He did not use it as a principal theme, but in a slightly altered form he used it no less than three times in the exposition of the first movement (see first movement, example 3 on p. 223).

The first draft of the principal theme is both featureless and uninteresting, not least because of the monotonous motivic repetitions in the two middle measures:

Only after having discarded this material did Grieg hit on the idea of using the "Fiddlers" motive as a kind of motto for the quartet. This idea took root, and it is clear that it was the basic spirit of this song which attracted him anew:

One should note, however, that in the introduction Grieg dramatized the "Fiddlers" motive very effectively by changing it from major to minor (see first movement, example 1 on p. 223). Not until the appearance of the secondary theme do we encounter it in its major form (see first movement, example 4).

This melodic idea satisfied Grieg on two related but nonetheless dissimilar levels: the motivic and the thematic. The motivic core in both its major and minor forms pervades the entire quartet and gives cohesion and unity to the whole. This is clearly evident when one places the motives of all four movements side by side:

FIRST MOVEMENT:

Introduction, m. 1:

Beginning of allegro, m. 20:

Just before secondary theme, m. 89:

Secondary theme, m. 95:

Dev. of secondary theme, m. 127:

Dev. of secondary theme, m. 135

Augmentation, m. 275:

Coda, m. 564:

Coda, m. 600:

Coda, m. 608:

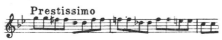

SECOND MOVEMENT:

Measure 1:

Measure 8:

B section, m. 20:

THIRD MOVEMENT:

Measure 1:

Measure 55:

Measure 85:

Coda, m. 250:

FOURTH MOVEMENT:

Introduction, m. 1:

Beg. of Presto section, m. 20:

Contrast section, m. 269:

Contrast section, m. 277:

Coda, m. 631:

Coda, m. 651:

Coda, m. 679

Sometimes the motive is conspicuous, at other times it is more hidden; but as the overview shows, it is always there in one way or another. Here we can speak of the core motive's structural power on a *micro* level.

But there is also a *macro* level in which the core motive is built into a larger melodic phrase or into a theme of major significance. The version in minor appears in the introductions to both the first and last movements. The version in major, in addition to constituting the secondary theme of the first movement, is also brought in as a constituent element in the codas of both the first and last movements. In the latter it appears as a mighty apotheosis—in augmented note values, and right in the middle of a witch's cauldron of chords.

Grieg did not originate the idea of unifying an entire composition in this manner. Liszt, among others, made prominent use of the same technique. But in this string quartet Grieg used the principle in a more thoroughgoing way than had ever been done previously in a chamber music work. Fifteen years would pass before Debussy did something comparable in his G-minor quartet—a composition that has many other similarities to Grieg's quartet, not least motivically.

In many places Grieg calls for an almost orchestral sound that is quite unorthodox in a string quartet. He uses, for example, fortissimo double stops in several instruments simultaneously. This sort of thing was unacceptable to

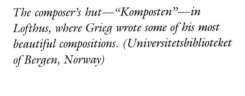

The composer's hut—"Komposten"—in Lofthus, where Grieg wrote some of his most beautiful compositions. (Universitetsbiblioteket of Bergen, Norway)

many, and he received some criticism on this point—a not uncommon phenomenon for a composer with progressive ideas. The tremendous expansion of sound was, of course, completely intentional on his part. He wrote Matthison-Hansen September 10, 1878, that the quartet was "not intended to deal in trivialities for petty minds. It aims at breadth, flight of imagination, and above all sonority for the instruments for which it is written."

Another feature of the quartet about which objections were raised is its marked homophonic style. Criticism on this point is easier to understand, though it is inherently unreasonable; one obviously cannot tie a genre to an unchanging model. Time has vindicated Grieg here as well, not least in the fact that many quartets written since that of Debussy have in this respect followed the direction first taken by Grieg. It should also be mentioned that there are a number of places in the G-minor quartet where one finds subtle polyphonic passages which demonstrate that Grieg had mastered this technique. He did not use a predominantly polyphonic texture more extensively because it was not consistent with his overall plan.

The introduction to the first movement immediately establishes the basic tragic mood. After sixteen measures follows the *allegro* (in sonata form). The principal theme is marked by an uneasy, almost nervous, conversation in a texture of imitation between the first violin and viola over a tonic pedal point in the second violin and cello:

The impression of an irrepressible will to fight given by this movement comes to the fore not least through what might be called a process of motivic contraction. It is a compositional technique that arose during the Viennese Classical period and one that Beethoven, especially, exploited with great mastery. It appears chiefly in connection with sequences, and consists in the progressive shortening of the elements of the sequence—partly through the diminution of note values, partly through the successive deletion of whole groups of notes in each repetition. The latter occurs to a most unusual degree in the first part of the allegro (measures 17–45), in connection with the typical Griegian pattern of ascending by thirds. In measures 45–60 the tightening is achieved by a progressive diminution of the note values.

The increasing tension culminates at *A*. The first part of the principal theme is then reiterated, but this time fortissimo in a powerful outpouring of sound. The technique of "motivic contraction" is used once again: the basic tempo is the same throughout but the note values are diminished little by little in such a way that there seems to be a constant acceleration.

The excerpt is also interesting harmonically. Look, for example, at the fourth system. The harmonic foundation is the dominant, but sharp dissonances (e.g., the diminished octave F-sharp–F-natural) also set their un-

6. GRIEG EMPHASIZES THE SIGNIFICANCE OF THE CONTRASTS IN HIS MUSIC

The four Italians played excellently, and as early as the middle of the first movement applause broke out, so it was no longer possible to hear what was being played. I must explain myself a little better. You know that in my larger works I have the habit—the weakness, or whatever I should call it—of ending in the primary key before the second subject enters, instead of bringing in a transitional passage that leads imperceptibly into the second subject, as most composers do. I do this for the sake of the architectonic effect and the contrast of the themes. The same thing occurs again after the return of the first subject following the development. But this is what caused the difficulty: the general public, which does not really understand the overall design, thought the movement was over! For a moment it was no laughing matter for the players who, naturally, couldn't hear each other . . . (Letter to Beyer, February 15, 1884.)

mistakable stamp on the music. The bold chord progression starting in measure 3 of the fifth system is also worthy of note. Here Grieg employs a series of parallel seventh and ninth chords, sometimes with added sixths, and with appoggiaturas and suspensions in the first violin. From the point of view of functional analysis, what we have here is a series of dissonant chords based on a fifth relationship between the roots of the respective chords—i.e., roots that are either sounded or implied: B-flat (= E via tritonal reinterpretation) A D G C F B-flat E-flat (= A) and so on. As one proceeds through the series one must make enharmonic changes from time to time to make it come out right. It is, however, an instructive example of how Grieg mastered the difficult art of uniting an advanced chromaticism with an approach which is basic to the later system of functional analysis. How conscious he was of this technique is impossible to say, but it is such a typical feature of his style that it cannot be accidental.

The secondary theme creates a powerful contrast to the driving strength of the principal theme. It enters abruptly after a G-minor cadence. The key is now B-flat major. But suddenly—after only twelve measures—Grieg breaks off completely and inserts a four-measure motive fortissimo. Moreover, it is the very same motive as that with which he concluded the principal theme section. One is wrested totally away from the lyric mood that had been struck by the secondary theme. The secondary theme is immediately moved to F minor, but once again we are jarred abruptly out of the lyric mood by the dramatic four-measure phrase. With this second interruption the lyric aspect of the exposition becomes a mere memory, and we get instead an extended section of an almost developmental character. In the middle of the secondary theme section there appears, moreover, a completely new motive that serves no real thematic function. There is a strong relationship between this motive and the closing theme in the last movement of the F-major violin sonata.

In the development there is continuous alternation between material from the principal and secondary themes. The section begins with the principal theme's basic motive in B-flat minor. A series of short passages where this motive dominates is pushed chromatically upwards: from B-flat minor to B minor, C minor, C-sharp minor, and D minor before B-flat minor again wins the upper hand. A rather sophisticated passage where the principal theme's basic motive is augmented rhythmically, first with quadrupled and then with doubled note values, appears just before the recapitulation. This is exactly opposite from the diminution technique which marked the principal theme section of the exposition.

The recapitulation proceeds quite traditionally. As usual, Grieg concludes the principal theme section with a solid chord in the tonic (G minor). Thereafter, without modulation, the secondary theme is introduced in E-flat major. Such a compositional technique—we encountered it earlier in the F-major and G-major violin sonatas—created a good deal of surprise among both critics and audiences at that time. In a letter to Beyer, Grieg gave an enlightening comment on this following a concert where an Italian quartet had performed his composition. It was clearly necessary for him to explain the effect that he was seeking by the use of such abrupt transitions between the themes.[6]

Motives from the secondary theme completely dominate in the coda, and the movement ends in a wild prestissimo with an enormous discharge of tension.

The second movement, "Romanze," has a distinctive structure. Two quite different thematic ideas are brought into collision: a lyric *A* section and a dramatic *B* section. The theme of the *A* section is introduced by the cello:

In the *B* section the mood is radically altered; something breathless and violent displaces the dignified calm of the *A* section. Now the voices seethe and bubble, the tempo is increased to *allegro agitato,* and the key is a gloomy B-flat minor. The first violin has the theme, but one should also notice the viola's ostinato figure in which the principal notes are clearly related to the *A* section's main motive and to the principal theme of the first movement:

The *B* section sounds fragmented as the theme passes through a number of keys. One of the things that ties it together is the Grieg formula, which follows immediately after the ascending scale movement.

The movement is structurally ambiguous. In its overall outline it reminds one of a complex three-part *ABA* form, but it has some features of the rondo and sonata-rondo by virtue of the fact that fragments of both *A* and *B* are inserted in the last part of the movement. The modified *A* section at the end rounds off the whole in a gripping way: a kind of resigned calm that in spite of everything is given the final word in the stormy conversation.

The third movement, "Intermezzo," has the same monumental grandeur and seriousness as the first. The Grieg formula now appears in a completely new rhythmic setting, with syncopated motions in which a two-pulse feeling absolutely wrestles with the three-beat meter. We know of no other composition by Grieg that contains such a clear and consistent example of rhythmic conflict: it is as if the composer stubbornly and aggressively wished to emphasize that a battle will be fought here and now:

The dramatic character is altogether different from that in the material he originally had intended to work with, and which is found among his sketches in the Bergen Public Library:

The form of this movement is very simple: *ABA* + coda. But on closer examination of the *A* section one discovers that the composer here—in a manner similar to that employed in the G-major violin sonata—structured it as a sonata movement in miniature. The design of the form is as follows: exposition = measures 1–48 (principal theme in G minor, 1–16; transition modulating to D minor, 17–32; secondary theme in D minor, 33–48); development = measures 49–112 (largely based on the principal theme, but with a contrasting section in measures 85–106); recapitulation = measures 113–166 (principal theme in G minor, 113–128; transition modulating but returning to G minor, 129–150; secondary theme in G minor, 151–166).

The *A* section has a decidedly homophonic stamp, but two ingenious canonic sections are inserted as well. In the first of these the second violin pursues the first violin; in the second, the viola is the pursuer. In both cases the imitation occurs at the distance of a quarter note. The *A* section also contains a contrasting lyric passage (see third movement, example 3 on p. 223), but the real contrast first appears in the *B* section with a *halling*-like theme that sounds as if it were taken directly out of Norwegian folk music. It starts in the cello, but gradually passes through all the instruments:

After the *A* section is repeated there is a brief coda that gave Grieg quite a bit of trouble before he achieved what he wanted. The final form was reached only during the correction of the print proofs and, therefore, does not appear in the manuscript in the Bergen Public Library. After the grave G minor of the *A* section, the G major of the coda comes as a veritable ray of light. The beginning of the coda is quoted in the third movement, example 4 on p. 223.

The fourth movement, "Finale," has a slow introduction in which the motto theme from the first movement is taken up again, but this time with imitation in all four voices. A sparkling *Presto al Saltarello* is then introduced, and one is swept along in whirling dance rhythms. Once again the Grieg formula is integrated into the thematic material.

The form of the movement is that of a sonata-rondo. The principal theme in G minor and ⅜ meter is developed briefly before the secondary theme, scherzando e vivace, enters in B-flat major and ¾ meter. Finally, we get an extended closing section that starts out in D minor and contains some violent dynamic outbursts as it runs its course. The following example is representative:

The exposition is rounded off with an abbreviated version of the principal theme in G minor. Then follows a longer contrasting section that begins in G major—one in which the Grieg formula manifests itself once again (see fourth movement, example 3 on p. 223).

In the recapitulation both the secondary theme and the closing theme are transposed down a fifth. Towards the close Grieg adds a powerful coda with continuous rhythmic changes and sheer cascades of sound. Here it is as if the whole quartet is being summarized with thematic elements from both the first and third movements. The motto theme is played twice in G major. There is, nonetheless, an undercurrent of unresolved defiance; this is underscored by, among other things, strong dissonances that constantly tear to shreds any tendencies toward a "harmonic" conclusion. Only at the very end, after a crescendo from *pp* to *fff*, do we get the actual resolution in G major with two triads—like hammerstrokes—followed by a final unison G. Even after this dynamic culmination, however, one sits back with a feeling that the drama has not been brought to a wholly liberating resolution. The conflicts have been too strong, and the intense struggle continues to live within us.

Into new musical fields

Grieg had ideas for several other compositions, some very significant, at the time he was working so energetically on the string quartet: a movement for a piano trio, Andante con moto (CW 137); the last of the *Album Leaves*, Opus 28; *Improvisations on Two Norwegian Folk Songs*, Opus 29; *Album for Male Voices*, Opus 30; and *The Mountain Thrall*, Opus 32.

When he had first provisionally completed the quartet (i.e., before undertaking extensive revisions in collaboration with Heckmann), he wrote Matthison-Hansen February 10, 1878: "Now I'll get to work on another piece of chamber music. I think that is the way I will find myself again." The work he referred to here can only be the piano trio, the completion of the slow movement of which is dated June 17 of the same year. But he never got further with this work, and the trio, therefore, is merely a torso.

The carefully constructed trio movement shows solid craftsmanship, but musically it does not really call for superlatives. It was never performed during Grieg's lifetime. After his death, Nina sent it to Julius Röntgen in Amsterdam to get his evaluation. Röntgen performed it at a Grieg memorial concert in Copenhagen on January 22, 1908, but thereafter it remained unplayed for many decades. In recent years, however, it has been performed a number of times both in Norway and abroad. It has now been published in *Edvard Grieg's Complete Works,* Vol. 9.

> The Andante con moto is solemn music, well adapted for the instruments (violin, cello, and piano). The principal key is C minor, but the piece moves through many keys. The form is quite unusual in that the movement is basically in sonata form, but with a touch of the rondo: exposition (with the secondary theme in G minor); development (that starts out in E-flat major); recapitulation (with the secondary theme still in G minor); a second development section (now in C major); coda (in C minor).
>
> The movement's funeral-march character is announced in the opening measures. The following excerpt shows the thematic core material:

> The secondary theme (beginning with measure 17) brings little variation, and it can be said that the movement as a whole exhibits a certain monotony. One looks almost in vain for typically Griegian subtleties in melody and harmony.

Grieg can hardly have been satisfied with this trio fragment. He never said anything about it, which probably indicates that it was quickly laid on the shelf and never taken down again.

Three piano pieces with national associations date from the Lofthus period. The most noteworthy is *Album Leaves,* Opus 28, No. 4. An elegiac folk-like section in C-sharp minor (Andantino serioso) frames an Allegro giocoso in D-flat major in which syncopated dance motives seem to sound in the distance. Grieg himself recounted to Röntgen how he got the inspiration for this midsection when he heard Hardanger-fiddle playing out on the Hardanger fjord.[7]

The piece must be considered one of his most successful piano compositions incorporating a stylized Norwegian flavor. It was published by Warmuth in Oslo in December, 1878, together with three others in the same genre written in 1864, 1874, and 1876. These latter, however, are not of the same quality. Apart from a fresh, folk-like midsection in the third piece, they all sound like ordinary salon music.

At the same time, Warmuth separately issued a fifth Album Leaf (CW 136B) and *Improvisations on Two Norwegian Folk Songs,* Opus 29. Grieg contributed the 100-kroner honorarium for the latter work to a fund for the Holberg monument in Bergen. He took some of the melodic material of Opus 29 from Lindeman's collection, but he then altered it rather freely.

> After a short introduction, No. 1 opens with the first part of the folk tune "The Lad and the Lass in the Cow-Shed Loft" as a cantus firmus in one of the inner voices. The second part of the tune then follows in an Allegro in which the meter of the folk melody is changed from ¾ to ⅜, thereby completely shifting the accents. The initial melody is finally repeated in the upper voice with a new harmonization. (Grieg had previously harmonized this folk tune in *Norway's Melodies,* No. 126, and it also appeared with this harmonization as No. 6 in *Six Norwegian Mountain Melodies.*)
>
> No. 2 builds on the very lovely Valdres melody "There Once Was a King," a tune that Lindeman got from S. J. Agervolden in 1848. The midsection of the piece—*Presto leggiero,* which has the character of a *springar*—is, however, Grieg's original composition.

Opus 29 provided a well-written contribution to Romantic nationalism, but the pieces signal no truly new aspects in Grieg's development.

A major work written in Hardanger is the *Album for Male Voices,* Opus 30. It includes twelve arrangements for male chorus, most with baritone solo— "freely arranged Norwegian folk tunes" taken from Lindeman's *Ældre og nyere norske Fjeldmelodier.* Grieg was at work on this project as early as August of 1877.[8] On May 3 of the following year he told Warmuth in Oslo that the volume was completed, but in December—before Warmuth had printed the collection—he had written yet another arrangement ("Rötnams Knut") that was also included in the collection. The origin of this piece is rather humorous. Bastian Reimers, a friend of Grieg who was the proprietor of a popular bakery in Bergen, had that summer presented Grieg with a half barrel of rye rusks. Since Reimers was an enthusiastic member of the "Concordia" male quartet, on September 9 Grieg sent him "Rötnams Knut" with the inscription "A musician's whim, with hearty thanks for a baker's ditto." The old barter economy was still going strong: rusks were exchanged for art.

In Opus 30[9] Grieg picked up the thread of his earlier folk-music arrangements, but now in a new genre. Melodic material of high quality became the starting point for a strikingly confident treatment. In these small choral jewels he mastered the demanding medium with consummate skill, constantly creating new and diverse choral effects. Although the chord progressions are sometimes chromatic, the voice parts move in a natural and singable way.

---

7. HARDANGER FIDDLES ON THE HARDANGER FJORD

While composing I suddenly heard soft music in the distance—it came from fiddlers who were rowing on the fjord. The sounds marvelously matched my piece and inspired its midsection. (J. Rontgen: *Edvard Grieg,* p. 19.)

8. GRIEG REGARDING THE *ALBUM FOR MALE VOICES*

Since you left me I have been working on something that has interested me, namely, a free treatment of folk songs for five solo voices. What beauty is hidden in these things! But one can't accuse Lindeman [in his piano arrangements] of having exposed much of that beauty to the light of day. I've now arranged one song that is tragic in character, two that are humorous, and two hymns, and I wish I could hear them in Bergen. (Letter to Beyer, September 2, 1877.)

* * *

For contrast and relaxation after finishing the quartet I have just now freely arranged a few folk songs and folk dances for men's voices, soloists, and choir—an interesting task. I need some of that kind of thing for concerts. (Letter to Matthison-Hansen, February 10, 1878.)

9. DEBUSSY GIVES OPUS 30 A FAVORABLE REVIEW

In the Norwegian folk songs one notes some of the striking melancholy in Edvard Grieg . . . In "Voyez, Jean" [presumably "Rötnams Knut"] the style is perhaps more instrumental than vocal, but we were won over nonetheless by his use of the male chorus. This music has the icy coldness of the Norwegian lakes, the fleeting warmth of the nippy, short-lived Norwegian spring. (Debussy in *Société Internationale de Musique Bulletin,* March 1, 1914.)

Between the Sörfjord mountains in winter garb, at the time I wrote this [*The Mountain Thrall*] and much else of the best I've done (the string quartet, for example), I also got hold of Landstad's collection of folk poetry. I was looking for some more text of the same quality and flavor as that which I used in *The Mountain Thrall*. I would then have included parts for chorus and a large orchestra. But I didn't find the text I was looking for, so all that came of it was this fragment. This was during the years 77–78. It was an important period in my life, filled with significant events and emotional upheavals. (Letter to G. Schjelderup, September 18, 1903.)

* * *

I could think of no one better to dedicate it to. I know that you are one of these dreadful people who insist on seeing blood, and it won't take someone like you long to find here and there drops and traces of pure life-blood. But who has a sense for such things? I wrote to [Wilhelm] Hansen that he would lose money, for life-blood doesn't sell well. So now I've done my duty; the rest is up to Hansen. (Letter to G. Matthison-Hansen, September 18, 1881.)

* * *

I have also sought to emulate in the music the compact brevity of style that is expressed so movingly in the old Norse poetry. (Letter to H. T. Finck, July 17, 1900.)

Opus 30 shows a high degree of variety. It includes two religious folk tunes—the Brorson hymns "Fairest among Women" and the exquisitely beautiful "The Great White Host"—but it also contains lyric love songs, lullabies, and humorous, ribald dance and drinking songs. Grieg achieved especially attractive effects in "Kvaalin's Halling" by adding a contrasting midsection, where the *halling* melody is sung in minor by a baritone soloist while four other solo voices create accompanying chords on the syllable "du." Even more amusing is the realistic cat-meowing in the *springar* entitled "Children's Song."

As a group these arrangements are artistically related by the simplicity and refinement that distinguish Grieg's most successful efforts.

Grieg had plans to write a large work for baritone solo, choir, and orchestra based on folk-song material, but he had to abandon the idea because he could not find a suitable text.[10] Instead, he took a short epic poem from M. B. Landstad's 1853 edition of *Norske Folkeviser* (Norwegian Folk Poetry). It is the tale of "The Mountain Thrall," a young man who is lost in the forest and who, after being bewitched by the daughter of a mountain troll, is thereafter unable to resume a normal love life.

It seems hardly a coincidence that Grieg chose such a text at just this time, for it gave him an opportunity to express some of his innermost feelings. This fact is strongly emphasized in a letter to Matthison-Hansen some years later, when the work was to be published by Wilhelm Hansen in Copenhagen as Opus 32.[10]

The Mountain Thrall is written for baritone solo, two horns, and string orchestra. Its intensely concentrated musical form is wholly in keeping with the expressive terseness of the text, a fact that Grieg himself pointed out in a letter to his American biographer, H. T. Finck.[10]

The poem's seven stanzas, each of four lines, are chiseled in simple rondo form. A moving orchestral introduction of fourteen measures establishes the basic grave mood. Following are the first six measures:

The musical form of the poem's first and seventh stanzas is almost identical to this introduction. Most of it is also used as an interlude following stanzas two and four.

After the slow first stanzas there is a contrasting section in G minor. Its mood is also one of pathos, but the tempo is allegro agitato. This is where the youth tells of his meeting with the troll.

In stanzas five and six, where the poem describes the harmony in the world of nature, a lighter sound suddenly intrudes marked by some unusually simple chords in C major. Gravity returns toward the end of this section, emphasized by the use of an expressive chromaticism. Nature is out of balance: "All of them—all have their own true love, But I—all alone am I." Here and in the

11. GRIEG TELLS ABOUT A PARTY GIVEN IN HIS HONOR

After a decent supper I was escorted into the auditorium to deafening applause, and what do you suppose greeted me there: the walls were covered with huge illustrations relating to *The Mountain Thrall*. You would have laughed yourself sick if you had seen it. The painters Munthe and Bloch had done it. Above the pictures they had written the voice part in huge notes. Then came the pictures and under them a collection of all the animals with their mates. These animal couples were so funny that one could die laughing just looking at them. And then yours truly on his knees in front of the daughter of the mountain troll while the troll himself—the sculptor Bergslien—was running after me! (Letter to Beyer, October 25, 1885.)

12. OLA MOSAFINN WITH GRIEG AND OLE BULL

Grieg also asked if he wouldn't play something, but the fiddle was absolutely "obstinate" and "she wouldn't respond" in the way he wanted . . . But when he had played a few dance tunes the fiddle started to improve. Everybody sat and listened to the fiddler. Bull and Grieg had by then become especially interested. They listened carefully and talked about the special characteristics of the dance tunes . . . Bull and Grieg escorted him out and talked about "his unique music" . . .

Bull played some Norwegian folk tunes and then a *springar*—probably "Store-Mylnaren" . . . And when Bull had played for awhile, Member of Parliament Aga said: "No sir, I don't understand this kind of playing. I'd much rather hear Syrefloten [the well-known fiddler Sjur Pedersen Aga]." (Arne Björndal: *Ole Bull og norsk folkemusikk* [Ole Bull and Norwegian Folk Music], pp. 37–39.)

closing stanza the essential tragedy of the situation is stressed: the despair that cannot be conquered. The music of the first stanza is repeated almost verbatim, but with a dynamic tension that leads forward to the climax: "Could not find the pathway home."

The Mountain Thrall was first performed in Copenhagen on April 5, 1879. The soloist was Thorvald Lammers, a superb vocalist who came to be regarded as the ideal interpreter of this profound work.

Grieg was deeply involved emotionally in the composition. After a concert in Oslo in 1885 he wrote to Beyer: "Then came *The Mountain Thrall*, which sounded much better than I have ever heard it before . . . The tale had such a strikingly demonic effect that I was completely enraptured. Curtain calls and shouts, albeit with moderation, for this is fortunately not accessible to everyone. It is a glorious thought to be able to say here with Björnson: 'God knows that it was written with devotion!' It is as if with this piece I have done one of the few good deeds of my life."

After the concert Grieg was invited to a lively party arranged in his honor by the Artists' Society. In a letter to Beyer he gave an amusing account of the evening's surprises.[11]

In April, 1877, Grieg had applied for a travel grant from the Ministry of Education, but in spite of a unanimous committee vote in his favor the application was not approved. The following year, however, he got the grant, and he now began a "suitcase" existence that was to last for almost two years. In the autumn of 1878 he went abroad. On October 29 his string quartet got its baptism of fire in Cologne (see p. 221). There were several concerts in Bonn and Leipzig. He spent the winter in Leipzig, where he presumably met Brahms for the first time. After the premiere of Brahm's violin concerto he received a valuable souvenir from the composer: an autograph consisting of the first measures of the second movement of the concerto.

In the spring of 1879 Grieg spent a few months in Copenhagen. The king and queen were present at one of the two concerts he gave there.

At the end of May we find him again in Hardanger. On May 24 he wrote to Beyer: "For the first time here I feel the oppression of loneliness. The quietude of nature is too cold for me after all the human feelings I have shared recently. The company of many people has both good and bad points. But I believe I will be more content when I get to work." The desire to create did not return, however. The loneliness became too depressing.

But there was gaiety on Grieg's birthday, June 15, when Ole Bull came to visit and the well-known fiddler Ola Mosafinn played *slaatter* to the great delight of the two world-traveled artists.[12]

Grieg gave two concerts in Bergen in October. Toward the end of the same month he performed the *A-minor Concerto* with success in Leipzig's Gewandhaus. Then it was on to Copenhagen, where he had appearances before standing-room-only audiences in February, 1880. Toward spring he had four sold-out Sunday chamber music matinees in Oslo, the last on April 18.

Shortly thereafter he was in Bergen. By April 28, in an attic room on Strand Street, he had set "The Berry"—the first of the glorious Vinje poems which now ignited the creative spark in him once again.

The Vinje Songs

For Grieg as a creative artist, the "winter" that began when he left Hardanger in 1878 lasted almost two full years. Not a single new work from his hands saw the light of day during this period. Only when he was back in Bergen in April, 1880, did there occur—almost magically—a thawing. It melted the ice in his soul and drove him into a hectic creative period. In the course of a few weeks he wrote some of the finest art songs in all of Scandinavia—*Twelve Songs to Poems by A. O. Vinje,* Opus 33 The inspiration from Hardanger was upon him once again.

Grieg himself related how during the spring of 1880 he was deeply captivated by the practical wisdom enshrined in Vinje's poetry. Anxious as he was lest the artistic vein in him was perhaps drained dry forever, this world of thought must have been what he subconsciously had been searching for. In Vinje he met an artistic temperament similar to his own. He had not been able to find any solution to the crisis in which he found himself. Vinje, however, had managed to stake out a path that he thought might lead him out of the thicket. The path was not an easy one, for according to Vinje the ripening of the soul is accomplished only through trials and suffering:

Now stand upon the ruins you've made of your own life's hope,
Then first to view, with eyes grown wise, the wider scope.

In Vinje, this positive attitude toward life was clothed in the most beautiful *nynorsk* poetry. Vinje's poems were exceedingly rich in pictures drawn from Norway's majestic scenery. Grieg was enthralled.

The songs were published in 1880 by Wilhelm Hansen of Copenhagen. Originally there were fifteen songs, but before the collection was sent for publication Grieg specified that three of them—"The Young Woman" (CW 138, No. 2), "The Forgotten Maid" (CW 138, No. 1), and "On the Ruins of Hamar Cathedral" (CW 101, No. 1)—should be omitted. "On the Ruins of Hamar Cathedral," which is by far the weakest of the entire set, was printed posthumously in 1908. The other two omitted songs, which were thoroughly deserving of publication, have now been printed in *Edvard Grieg's Complete Works,* Vol. 15.

In stating that all the Vinje songs were composed in the spring of 1880,

I. THE BACKGROUND OF THE VINJE SONGS

They all came into being one after another in my boyhood home on Strandgaten in the spring of 1880. It is fairly certain, as you say, that in addition to the purely spiritual element, the Hardanger scenery also lies hidden in these songs. For a few years it really took hold of me and set its stamp on everything I wrote at that time. Moreover, its influence has continued right up to the present day. (Letter to J. Paulsen, June 4, 1905.)

Grieg toward the end of the 1870's. (Photo collection of Det Kongelige Bibliotek, Copenhagen)

Grieg was exaggerating.[1] The gripping song "The Old Mother" was in fact written several years earlier. The text and melody of this song are given on p. 18. It captures, in a completely unaffected way, the purity and simplicity of the folk-tune style. It has somewhat the same character as the Norwegian religious folk song, "I Know a Fortress in Heaven." At the same time it testifies to Grieg's affection for his own mother, who "with boundless energy and a sense of duty toiled and suffered until she dropped."

Another Vinje song, "Beside the Stream," is also of earlier origin: the manuscript is marked July 8, 1877. It is undoubtedly one of the "golden nuggets" Grieg alluded to during his first stay at "Börve." It is interesting that as early as 1877 he was already receptive to Vinje's idealistic message, and was able to enter deeply into this beautiful poem and give it such a suitable tonal garb.

In "Beside the Stream" Vinje, with an insight born of personal experience, depicts life's struggle using the analogy of the flowing brook that unceasingly digs downward beneath the bending trees. The main idea appears in the second stanza: "Like you, how many a time I see how false love's wakening can be, when youth, though one most gallant, he will kiss the hand, then soon run free."

Grieg varied the two stanzas with subtle nuances in such a way that the song seems almost through-composed—a form seldom found in his songs. The accompaniment, like the river, flows steadily onward. It seems to be completely independent of the voice part, and creates a pronounced syncopated effect. In the first stanza the bass has nothing but open tonic fifths, while the musical development is discreetly reflected in the right hand on the piano and in the voice part.

The rhythmic pattern in the piano part is maintained in the second stanza, but the melody becomes progressively more active. The chords are continually altered, with chromatic downward shifts in one voice after another.

The conclusion, with its remarkable coda, is of incomparable beauty. In the passage just preceding that given below there is a short section in F Aeolian (F natural minor). In measure 1 of the excerpt Grieg returns to a kind of A-minor tonality. Then comes a highly expressive cadence (measure 2) in which the dominant seventh chord starts out with a suspended fourth and a diminished fifth (beat 1), and then has its third lowered from G-sharp to G-natural (beat 3). The melody strengthens the Phrygian color. What we have here is a characteristically Griegian combination of the functional-harmonic and the modal.

The coda, which begins in measure 3 of the excerpt, is based on a tonic pedal point. Above this the middle voices descend chromatically, sometimes with dissonances, while the melody in the right hand in the piano part echoes the core motive from the first stanza.

In the last six measures Grieg repeats the words "Du Skog" ["Still Woods"] three times, but with enormous dynamic contrasts. The song reaches an appropriate culmination in a beautiful Mixolydian cadence:

Aasmund Olavson Vinje (Universitetsbiblioteket of Bergen, Norway)

"Beside the Stream" was the only song to come from Hardanger, and three years were to pass before Grieg returned once again to the poetry of Vinje. However, "The Old Mother" and "Beside the Stream" had—each in its own way—set a standard that was difficult to surpass.

The first three songs in the published collection are completely strophic and are very similar to each other both textually and musically. All exhibit the unaffectedness of melody and rhythm that is characteristic of folk tunes, but Grieg's distinctive accompaniment gives the emotional content of the poems a greater depth.

"The Youth" is an especially compact piece. In the space of just eleven measures the voice part—"freely recited," according to Grieg—rises in a great melodic and dynamic arch from *b* (sung piano) to *f-sharp″* (sung fortissimo) before returning to *b'* in the last measures. Grieg had great respect for the artistic judgment of his colleague, Johan Svendsen, and he must have been delighted to hear his friend's positive evaluation of this song. On June 22, 1882, Svendsen wrote: "Here music and poetry have been sensitively united to create passion of such magnitude, that I know of no equal in the whole of song literature."

Grieg's melodic gift never manifested itself more beautifully or more loftily than in "Last Spring." What Grieg expressed here is not merely the coming of spring as a natural phenomenon. Far from it. It is the individual's joyful gratitude for the opportunity to experience *one more time*—before the flame of life is extinguished—this eternally youthful wonder of nature. The music reflects perfectly the inner spirit of the poem. It stands forth, clean cut in every detail, free of turgid sentimentality—deeply serious, albeit in major.

"The Wounded Heart" exhibits the greatest pathos of any of the songs in the cycle. It is much bolder harmonically than either "The Youth" or "Last Spring," but it lacks the latter's openness. A mood of anguish is established at the very beginning, where on the first downbeat we get a searing chord—a C-sharp minor triad with the tritone F-double-sharp that clashes with the fifth (G-sharp). This dissonance recurs throughout the piece. Only toward the end does the song begin to brighten, and it ends in a liberating D-flat major.

"The Berry" deals with the theme of self-sacrifice: as the ripened berry yearns to be plucked, so also do mature human beings attain their greatest joy by giving themselves for others. This through-composed song also has elements of a modified strophic form. The melody has an unmistakable folk-tune flavor, with an obvious strain of the Gypsy scale when the raised leading tone to the fifth colors the text in a distinctive manner. The song's most expressive phrase occurs in the last line. Note the insistent, tension-filled intervals:

In the sequence established by Grieg, "Beside the Stream" follows as the fifth song in the cycle. Then, in marked contrast to the first five songs, comes the first of the two fast pieces in the collection: "A Vision." This is a love poem about a woman whom the poet saw only fleetingly, but could never win. Grieg has made the song into a kind of *springar* (in minor!) with characteristic folk-music features, though with a touch of the routine. Stanzas 1, 2, and 4 are identical. Stanza 3, on the other hand, interrupts the dance-like character with a series of sustained chords in the piano. This stanza also receives the most interesting harmonic treatment. The sense of key is vacillating because of the use of independent seventh chords with lowered leading tones, in both major and minor.

After "A Vision" comes "The Old Mother" (from 1873), discussed earlier, and then "The First Thing." Here Vinje emphasizes that a life without the ability to love signifies the end of any existence worthy of a human being:

> *"The first thing, man, you're called upon to do is simply die,*
> *When you wish no more the maid to woo that's caught your eye."*

It was altogether natural for Grieg to use a purely strophic form for this song in which the two short stanzas express the very same thought. It is one of the best songs in the cycle. Here simplicity truly yields strength. The introductory phrase, which contains two characteristic motives, forms the basis for everything that follows. The most remarkable thing about the song is the way in which Grieg breaks out of the major-minor system. The folk-like melody is completely blended with a deliberately archaic use of chords.

The song's first motive is harmonized in C major, but the second motive, which ends on *e*, achieves an almost magical effect through the cadential chords: A minor, G major. E minor (to the words "is simply die").

The next phrase is a melodic rhyme, transposed to natural minor (A Aeolian), this time with a cadence in C major.

In the third phrase both motives are altered. The first now appears in C Aeolian, while the cadence in the second is in F Mixolydian.

The first part of the fourth phrase is a melodic rhyme of the corresponding part of the preceding phrase, now in F Aeolian. In the cadence motive, however, there is a new twist, with chords in C Aeolian: A-flat major, B-flat major (as a six-four chord), C minor.

Right at the end, three chords appear under the C in the melody. These are in C Dorian, but with a divergent chromatic coloring of the third last chord with the help of a G-flat: E-flat minor (with C), F major, C minor. (This remarkable but typically Griegian cadence has a striking parallel seven years later in the conclusion of the first movement of the *Violin Sonata in C Minor*, Opus 45. See the music excerpt on p. 280.)

"At Rondane" is one of the most exquisite songs in the entire literature of Norwegian lyric poetry dealing with the beauty of nature. The poet, in viewing the mountain range Rondane at sunset, is reminded of the mountains of his childhood. He expresses much of the same humble sense of gratitude as in "Last Spring" and he marvels at the fact that *once again* he will experience the beauty of nature and "feel sunset's magic fire dispel my fear."

Grieg caught the nostalgic mood of the poem in a gripping way, and

Agathe Backer Gröndahl, to whom Grieg dedicated the Vinje songs. After her death he wrote in his diary (June 4, 1907), "No artist has ever walked purer paths than she. I loved her solemn idealism. It had its unique charm. If a mimosa could sing, its sound would be like her loveliest and tenderest music." (Photo collection of Universitetsbiblioteket in Oslo)

created a setting that is the epitome of profound lyricism. It has the character of a folk song, and partly for this reason is especially cherished by his countrymen.

Everything in the cycle is not equally good, however. The next two songs—"A Piece on Friendship" and "Faith"—show Vinje's misanthropic side. Warm lyricism gives way to bitterness and biting irony. Nor are Grieg's settings of these texts especially successful. The bitterness in "Friendship" has its musical counterpart in a cold, uninteresting melody with cutting dissonances in the piano accompaniment.

In "Faith" it might appear that Grieg misunderstood the poet's sarcasm regarding the hypocrisy of many Christians, for he chose to create a simple hymn-like setting for this text. It is more likely, however, that he allowed the irony in the poem to be expressed in his own way—emphasizing it, in fact, through the glaring disparity between the derisive words and the pious melody.

The twelfth and last song, "The Goal," was intended by Vinje as a proclamation in support of the proponents of *nynorsk*—"New Norwegian"—an alternative form of the language combining elements of many Norwegian dialects. It was an exhortation to hold the banner high until the final victory was won. The poem was published in his paper *Dölen* as an appeal to its subscribers. According to a letter to Finck of July 17, 1900, Grieg was not clear about this rather prosaic relationship: "I thought that the spirited poem was addressed to a friend, or perhaps even to the poet's wife!" Thus it seems clear that the appearance of this "New Norwegian" battle song at the end of the cycle is the result of a misunderstanding on the part of the composer. Grieg viewed the text from a broad, universal perspective. This robust and rousing song in a way departs from the sphere of what we think of as "songs" from the Romantic period; it is more akin to a heroic aria in a dramatic opera. In contrast to the other songs, it requires a special kind of ostentation in order to come off well. Its distinctive character consists in its combination of the heroic and the almost exaggerated national elements: *halling* rhythms, open tonic fifths in the bass against dominant chords in the upper voices, the "Grieg formula" in both forms, and the strongly contrasting lyric midsection that contains a hint of a "*kulokk*."

As previously mentioned, Grieg set three additional Vinje poems: "On the Ruins of Hamar Cathedral," "The Young Woman," and "The Forgotten Maid." We do not know why these three songs were not included in Opus 33. One can well understand that Grieg himself rejected the rather undistinguished piece, "On the Ruins of Hamar Cathedral." It is harder to understand why he allowed the other two to be omitted, for they are of much better quality than either "A Piece on Friendship" or "Faith."

There is some reason to believe that the Danish publisher did not want to have fifteen pieces in the collection, and that Grieg was forced to limit the number to twelve. It is equally possible, however, that the composer deliberately omitted "The Young Woman" and "The Forgotten Maid," since it is clear that in terms of their content they do not fit naturally in the cycle. The songs that were included are in every case concerned either with *man* (the

2. *TWO ELEGIAC MELODIES* ARE PLAYED IN WEIMAR

Ah, last evening you should have heard "The Wounded Heart" and "Last Spring." It was simply marvelous to hear how they played them. Beautiful crescendos and pianissimos beyond one's wildest dreams, and a fortissimo that was like a world of sound. And believe it or not, the Germans liked it! In addition to the applause of the audience, from the orchestra I heard "Bravo, bravo!" after some of the best passages; and from the box to my left (I was on the stage conducting the piece) I heard Liszt's grunt, that well-known sound that he makes only when he hears something he likes. (Letter to Beyer, October 17, 1883.)

* * *

The first time I performed them for a German audience was in Weimar. I can't recall many times in my life when I have been so moved. I hardly knew where I was, whether in the court theater in Weimar or in the melancholy, dark mountains of Norway. The truth is that I wasn't in either of these places; I was floating about the room on the ethereal wings of lovely harmonies. (Letter to J. A. B. Christie, December 28, 1883.)

male of the species) or with that which pertains to *humanity in general*. In "The Young Woman" and "The Forgotten Maid," on the other hand, the focus is exclusively on *woman*.

In "The Young Woman" the message is that the most important thing is not to find a mate but to find oneself.

"The Forgotten Maid" has a touch of sardonic humor: the "overlooked" spinster regrets that in her youth she did not swallow the bait of the miser who had wanted to marry her.

> Both songs are strophic. Rhythmically they are similar to a *springar*, and both contain a number of typically Griegian characteristics.
>
> "The Young Woman" is melodically and harmonically more advanced than "The Forgotten Maid." It starts in C major and sounds at first a bit like a folk song (*stev*), but as early as the fifth measure it departs from the folk-tune style with a sudden tonal shift to the dominant seventh chord in B minor. The return to the original key is also accomplished in a quite unorthodox manner.
>
> "The Forgotten Maid" has an equally clear-cut melody. It is more uniform tonally, although it contains a strong element of the Gypsy scale and concludes with an ascending melodic phrase in natural minor with an Aeolian cadence in the accompaniment. A postlude sounds the Gypsy scale again, but with a standard authentic cadence at the end.

When Grieg became conductor of the Bergen Symphony Orchestra ("Harmonien") in the fall of 1880, he found himself in need of orchestral music which he himself had composed. With this in mind he arranged "The Wounded Heart" and "Last Spring" for string orchestra. In so doing he joined such composers as Dvořák (*Serenade*, 1875) and Tchaikovsky (*Serenade*, 1880), initiating a renaissance of the string orchestra in the Romantic period.

These two pieces, published by Peters in 1881 as *Two Elegiac Melodies*, Opus 34, were also given slightly different titles. Grieg gave an explanation for this in a letter to Finck of July 17, 1900: "The profound sadness in these poems is the background for the solemn sound of the music, and this led me . . . to clarify their content by giving them more expressive titles. Therefore [I have decided to call them] 'Last Spring' and 'The Wounded Heart.'" ("Last Spring" was originally called simply "Spring.")

The pieces are brilliantly orchestrated, and Grieg used them frequently in the ensuing years on his concert tours. They made the same strong impression wherever they were played.[2] Grieg himself realized their high artistic merit, and in keeping with the intensity of the tonal language he always performed them with great emotion.

Façade mod S.C.

Façade med S.V.

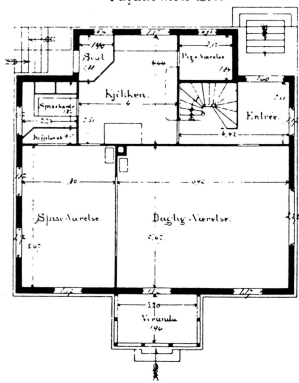

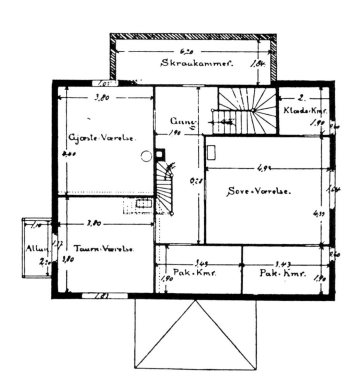

Architect's drawings of exterior elevations and
proposed floor plan for "Troldhaugen."

Part Three: The Wanderer

Struggles in Art and in Life

1. DEPARTURE FROM HARDANGER

I sought peace, insight, and self-understanding, and all of this I found in the magnificent Hardanger district. The place became so dear to me that for 4–5 years I continued to go back every summer. But finally it was as if the mountains had nothing more to say. I became stupid looking at them and decided that it was high time to get out of there. (Letter to G. Schjelderup, September 18, 1903.)

2. WORK IN "HARMONIEN"

As you know, from the fall of '80 and until the spring of '82 I conducted the Bergen Symphony Orchestra ["Harmonien"]. That was quite a contrast to life in Lofthus! How imperfect in comparison! But how important in my development! But the musicians—especially the winds—were terrible, and after two years I couldn't stand it any longer. Still, I wish you had heard what we achieved in Schubert's C-major symphony and in Handel's anthems. Because I really brought the chorus up to something. But naturally I got on the outs with the governing board, which neither could nor wished to understand me, and I found myself wallowing in rubbish, anonymous criticism, and all that kind of stuff. (Letter to G. Schjelderup, September 18, 1903.)

The years 1880–84 were a difficult period in Grieg's life, a period marked by exhausting work with the orchestra and stagnation in his artistic growth. Indeed, at times the desire to create was totally absent. There are many indications that this state of affairs was largely a result of a shattered emotional life, and the situation eventually became so exacerbated that in July of 1883 he left Nina for half a year. A number of letters he sent to his friend Frants Beyer during this time show, as Marie Beyer has expressed it, "the overwhelming ferment in which he was living: as he says in these letters, he required solitude in order to understand himself more clearly."

Grieg becomes conductor of "Harmonien"

In the summer of 1880 Grieg came to the conclusion that as a permanent home Hardanger was too confining for him.[1] In July, when he applied for the position of conductor of "Harmonien"—the Bergen Symphony Orchestra—he undoubtedly understood clearly what he was letting himself in for. The status of music in Bergen was no better than that in Oslo. It is readily understandable that he had a desire to devote a year or two of his life to art in his native city, but it seems strange that he chose to do this at a time when he had just demonstrated his artistic vitality in the Vinje songs. In our opinion, the reason was that he sought refuge in routine orchestra work in order to suppress the inner discord that he felt was destroying his creative gifts. It gave him an excuse for neglecting the creative side of his nature.

Grieg began his new duties in September, and through two demanding seasons they totally absorbed his time and energy.[2] With respect to his goal as conductor of "Harmonien" he wrote to Matthison-Hansen on April 29, 1881: "I have told myself that once I got the opportunity to give a few months to my native city I would work with all my might to push its awareness of art forward a step or two."

The season got off to a promising start on October 22. The local newspaper stated that a new spirit had come into the orchestra, as a result of which it played with a precision and delicacy that it had never achieved before. The

3. CHORUS MEMBERS GO TO THE DANCE

. . . I have tried to maintain the artistic standards of the music society, of which I am the director this winter. Well, there was a whole group of chorus members who, after we had rehearsed a large, difficult work, decided to miss the dress rehearsal and concert because a *dance* was being held at the same time. The people involved had signed pledges committing themselves to participation in the chorus. I therefore used my authority and informed the deserters that I regretfully found it necessary to prohibit their future participation . . . Yesterday I even received a statement signed by the women's chorus (about sixty members) in which they frankly sided with me. That was a nice gesture—in contrast to the city gossips and the press, all of whom have branded my course of action as *crude*. (Letter to Winding, December 27, 1880.)

4. THE ARTIST'S LOT IN NORWAY

You are currently in a productive period—which is something that every true artist has. That is a lovely time. *My* productive period was so short. I have waited and am still waiting for it to return. But the delicate web of circumstances must be in order before this can happen. During these days I have just finished a long and exhausting work [as a conductor] . . . But the result has been too costly. However that may be, I am through with it . . . It goes as Björnson once said: among us no sensitive man can hold out for more than a moment at a time. So there is a spurt [of artistic creativity] now and then. But the unfortunate thing is that a Norwegian artist's activity also becomes intermittent and discordant because of the muddled circumstances [in which he must work]. I can therefore in a way understand those who have enough insight to turn their backs on Norway and become European. But I could not do that. No, never! Unfortunately, I have a heart! (Letter to J. Paulsen, April 28, 1881.)

program consisted primarily of Viennese classics, but it also included two pieces by Norwegian composers: Johan Svendsen's *Norwegian Rhapsody No. 3,* and Ole Bull's "The Shepherd Girl's Sunday." The Ole Bull piece, with which the concert began, was played with the audience standing in tribute to the recently deceased violinist. At his funeral on August 23 Grieg had expressed his gratitude in words of exceptional beauty (see excerpt on p. 6).

Grieg's troubles in his new position began in December when several members of the chorus, contrary to their written commitment, failed to attend the dress rehearsal for Handel's *Coronation Anthem* because it conflicted with a large public dance. Grieg decided to make an example of them. He gave the miscreants their walking papers, an act that aroused great indignation. Someone went so far as to publish a letter in *Bergens Tidende* of December 11 defending the singers: "That those young ladies were looking forward with keen anticipation to a dance—who will blame them for that? And that for this reason they could not take part in the dress rehearsal is obvious."

Grieg, however, was unyielding. He knew that he was right, and that one could not compromise on artistic demands. Some weeks later he received welcome vindication in the form of a scroll signed by about sixty members of the women's chorus.[3]

In the spring of 1881 the church authorities—to Grieg's indignation—refused his request to use Nykirken ("New Church") for the last three concerts of the season. The concerts were scheduled for March and April; the program was to consist of Mozart's Requiem, in which Nina was to be one of the soloists. The stated reason for the refusal was that the church was dedicated to worship service use and, in addition, the work was a Catholic mass for the dead. Instead, the concerts had to be held at the Labor Union Hall which, as *Bergens Aftenblad* wrote, was "much too small and confining a place for such an undertaking."

In the above-mentioned letter to Matthison-Hansen, Grieg wrote: "Now I have another 3–4 months of drudgery behind me. Since New Year's Day ten concerts—three "Harmonien" concerts, two repeat concerts, three chamber music evenings, and the others done gratis for various worthy causes. For up here artists are used to raise the money that every damned merchant ought to shell out." He wrote further that "the season's conclusion was a complete triumph. I was greeted with an orchestral flourish, got a laurel wreath and flowers and, when I came home, a pretty silver mug from the women's chorus. As a result of this I have now become so cocky that no one can stand me." He did not think that the work had been in vain. "But *I* cannot stand this any longer," he wrote. "Now somebody else will have to carry on the work . . . Yes, time marches on, and it yields meager results. Would to God that this line of reasoning were merely the result of an upset stomach, but I see what is going to happen . . . I have not given a single lesson this winter, have not composed a note, so you can deduce the rest."

In a letter to John Paulsen, Grieg discussed in exceptionally strong terms the nagging concern that this stagnation might be permanent. Indeed, he even suggested that his creative activity was a thing of the past.[4]

5. REGARDING THE "CURE" AT
KARLSBAD

Only the gods know what good this is
doing. I am weak and incapacitated in both
body and soul. Just imagine getting up at
5:00 every morning, drinking four big
glasses of warm water with walks in between, getting no breakfast until late forenoon, and maintaining the strictest diet
consisting mainly of eggs and milk and
bread! Yes sir, it will make a better man of
me! (Letter to J. Paulsen, June 3, 1881.)

* * *

I have chronic inflammation of the stomach, enlarged intestines, and a swollen
liver . . . I have always admired augmentation—N.B.: when it has to do with intervals. But now I think I will settle for
diminution, at least for a little while. And
then I will end up with the pure triad . . . I
will have to contend with my illness for a
long time, though the doctor has assured
me that I can and will be well again. (Letter
to G. Matthison-Hansen, June 17, 1881.)

Grieg took advantage of his newly won freedom in April not to resume composing, but rather to write a eulogistic article about his friend Emil Horneman in response to a request from a Danish periodical. Meanwhile he felt that he was badly out of shape, and he wanted to spend the summer quietly at home. After a severe gastric attack at the end of May, however, he had to go to Karlsbad for treatment at the insistence of his physician. "In this matter," he said, "it is not I who am the conductor."

He arrived at the health spa on June 1, but without Nina. Two days later he wrote to Paulsen, "I had to obey, disappointing though it was to have my only working time ruined—this time that I had awaited with such longing." After four rather unpleasant weeks[5] he returned home by way of Hamburg, where he boarded a boat to Bergen.

Norwegian Dances

Soon after his return to Bergen, he and Nina left for another summer stay in Lofthus. His will to work awakened once again, and the result was *Norwegian Dances*, Opus 35, for piano four hands.

Throughout his life Grieg enjoyed playing piano four hands, and his pleasant experience with this form of music-making is amply reflected in Opus 35. It is brilliantly arranged for the performers. Grieg had two things in mind in composing this opus. First, he wanted to write good music for instructional purposes: "You can use it for your better students," he said to Matthison-Hansen after it was printed in November. Second, he wanted to present Norwegian folk music somewhat differently than he had previously.

These *Norwegian Dances* have a character that seems to call for the sound of an orchestra, and it is strange that Grieg himself didn't make some attempt to orchestrate them at the same time that he wrote the four-hands version. The reason probably was that he was intimidated by Johan Svendsen's achievements in this area. He greatly admired Svendsen's *Norwegian Rhapsodies,* in which the composer had made liberal use of folk tunes. With skill and elegance, Svendsen had succeeded in giving these folk tunes a dazzling orchestral dress. For the time being Grieg did not dare to invite comparison with Svendsen since—as he put it to Robert Henriques on April 24, 1887—he "did not possess Svendsen's brilliant technique."

Grieg took the melodic material for the four *Norwegian Dances* from Lindeman's large collection (Nos. 302, 102, 8, and 50). The first piece is the "Sinclair" march from Vaagaa; the other three are *hallings*. Grieg took some liberties with Lindeman's notation; in his hands the short dances became the basis for an independent adaptation in which he developed and varied the material to create larger forms. All the dances have contrasting midsections.

> In No. 1 (D minor) Grieg reshaped the last part of the march into a lengthy contrasting midsection in doubled note values and in D major, whereas in Lindeman it is harmonized in A major.
>
> No. 2 (A major) is built on a folk tune that Lindeman got from Arne Thingstad of Aamot in Österdalen. It is an easygoing and very charming and

I note to my surprise that I compose very well when I am, so to speak, forced to do it. I think if somebody or other paid me 1000 German thalers a year in advance royalties my conscience would not rest until I had finished composing the required quantity of music. (Letter to Dr. Abraham, August 22, 1881.)

* * *

In accordance with your proposal, I have the pleasure of sending you herewith 3000 German marks with the request that, for this amount, you produce by next September a piano concerto, some piano pieces, and a concert overture or a piano trio or a violin sonata or some pieces for violin and piano. (Letter from Dr. Abraham, September 7, 1881.)

* * *

What I dashed off in jest you have taken seriously! Nonetheless, since you're willing to give it a try I will too. But every project has its "but," and this one is no exception. If I were free this winter I would immediately have complied with your friendly directive . . . But if you can give me another half year—i.e., one and a half years altogether—it will be a matter of honor for me to do what I have agreed to do. By the way: must it absolutely be a piano concerto? If by chance it should take the form of a violin concerto, would it be all the same to you? (Letter to Dr. Abraham, September 16, 1881.)

graceful dance. Melodically it is the strongest piece in the set, as a result of which Grieg was also inspired to display his mastery of harmony. The short contrasting section consists of the last four measures of the original—transposed, however, to F-sharp minor and extended to twenty-four measures in a frenetic allegro that virtually makes the sparks fly.

In No. 3 (G major) the dance theme in Grieg's version is twice as fast as in the original. In the midsection the same thematic material is transposed to G minor and given doubled note values.

No. 4 (D major) is the most fully developed of the dances. It has an introduction of Grieg's "own invention" in D minor, and this material is exploited dexterously in the contrasting section with an almost symphonic effect.

Kjerulf had arranged two of the *hallings* (Nos. 3 and 4) for piano in 1861, and No. 4 occurs also in the first of Svendsen's four *Norwegian Rhapsodies* of 1876.

The work with the *Norwegian Dances* went surprisingly fast. They were completed in August, and after Grieg got back to Bergen he sent them to Peters in Leipzig. In a letter to Dr. Abraham on August 22 he suggested, with tongue in cheek, that a yearly advance could do wonders for his future compositional output. The publisher promptly took him at his word and sent him 3000 marks.[6] The agreement they reached gave Grieg a measure of financial security and became the basis for his later advantageous contracts with the firm.

In 1882 Robert Henriques made an orchestral arrangement of the *Norwegian Dances*. Grieg was so pleased with this arrangement that in 1886, when *Peer Gynt* was to be produced in Copenhagen, he asked if he might use the first three dances in the ballet that was to be inserted in the scene in the Hall of the Mountain King (see pp. 181–82).

Hans Sitt, the violist in the renowned Brodsky quartet, somewhat later undertook a new arrangement. Grieg wrote to Delius in April of 1888 that Sitt certainly "revealed colossal erudition" but that "his manner of orchestration at times seems coarse." When Peters two years later wished to publish this version, Grieg suggested that the orchestration should be done by a Frenchman—Lalo, for example. But the firm did not comply with Grieg's wishes and in 1891 printed Sitt's arrangement, which is in fact quite effective. In this form the work has achieved great popularity in the concert hall.

Despite his earlier reluctance, Grieg nonetheless said that he was willing to continue for one more year as conductor of "Harmonien," but only on the condition that the salary be doubled to 2000 kroner. The board of directors did not look favorably on such a demand and inquired of both Svendsen and Ole Olsen if they would take over, but without success. The upshot was that the society had no choice but to accept Grieg's offer. Thus he became "an expensive dog," as his father had once called him. The following autumn when Iver Holter took over as conductor, the "Harmonien" account showed a balance of only 8.92 kroner! The high salary paid to Grieg as conductor was cited as one of the reasons.

The 1881–82 season was no less stressful than the preceding one, and although Grieg swung the baton brilliantly he didn't compose a single note. A

7. DESPONDENCY IN BERGEN

I am bound hand and foot here again this winter . . . I am in poor health and will probably have to go to Karlsbad again in the spring. But if I survive that, then there will follow a new era where I . . . will find myself—in something else. (Letter to J. Paulsen, September 16, 1881.)

* * *

For my part, I give each day its due and feel embarrassed about it . . . Indeed, I am so changed you will hardly recognize me. I live on a strict diet and am abstemious in every respect. That is not so bad, but I do miss being in good spirits. But—I have as much hope now as at any time. (Letter to G. Matthison-Hansen, November 18, 1881.)

* * *

When Mrs. Thoresen says that a human being's most beautiful feeling is longing, then I say no, no, no. *Hope* is the most beautiful feeling we have! Long live hope! (Letter to J. A. B. Christie, December 14, 1881.)

* * *

My health has improved so much that at least I have had strength enough to conduct the orchestra ("Harmonien"). But I would not do it for another season for all the gold in the world. One is infected by all the pettiness and indifference that surrounds one. By next summer I will be a philistine and a provincial, but then if I am still living I will shake the dust off my wings. (Letter to J. A. B. Christie, December 19, 1881.)

8. WANING INSPIRATION AND PROBLEMS WITH HEALTH

It appears as if I have lived a more peaceful life than ever before, but in reality it has been a life filled with inner strife. I have no outside work at present; I give a few lessons and that is all. But I am ill both mentally and physically. Every other day I decide not to compose another note because I am less and less satisfied with myself. When one has to struggle for technique as I do—and, strange to say, with greater and greater intensity—the delivery finally becomes so difficult that it drains all of one's strength. Just recently I have come to see more clearly than ever before what I lack. But still I have the feeling that I can overcome it if that confounded stomach . . . (Letter to Matthison-Hansen, December 20, 1882.)

number of letters express his frustration over the conditions, but also suggest the hope of better days ahead.[7]

According to Marie Beyer, Grieg played chamber music for recreation during both this winter and the following one. The other members of the group were August Fries and Carl Rabe, violinists, and Grieg's brother John, cellist. Grieg played the piano parts in trios and quartets, and the musicians met alternately in Edvard's and John's homes and at the Beyers.

In April, 1882, Grieg retired as conductor with a performance of Mendelssohn's *Elijah*. The audience gave him a standing ovation and "Harmonien" arranged a big farewell celebration in his honor.

Several honors were accorded him at this time. In June he was named a Knight of the Royal Norwegian Order of St. Olav, and he received an inquiry from Helsinki inviting him to become director of the newly established conservatory that was to begin its activities in the fall. He declined this offer, however.

The first part of the summer he was again in Karlsbad for treatment, this time with Nina. He found a companion in suffering in this "lonely, monotonous, and melancholy world" in the person of his cousin Schak Bull, who was an architect. Grieg considered asking him to make some sketches for a house he was planning to build near Bergen, but nothing came of the idea at this time. Not until two years later did the plan to build a house become a reality.

With his "increasing crankiness and Karlsbad-bellied dissatisfaction," he longed more and more for home—"for you and the mountains, for you and the sea—in short, for you and the poetry of home," as he wrote to Beyer on June 5.

After a short stay in Denmark, he was back in Lofthus in July. He stayed there through the summer and began working on the first sketches of a larger work, a cello sonata for his brother John. Now he was free as a bird and could wholeheartedly commit himself to holding up his end of the agreement with Dr. Abraham. He had already received the first royalty check.

The Cello Sonata in A Minor, *Opus 36*

When Grieg returned to Bergen in the autumn of 1882—free at last of burdensome orchestral duties—everything should have been conducive to creative work. Something, however, was troubling him; despite his outwardly calm life, progress on the new sonata was very slow. Poor health became the scapegoat;[8] in later years as well he frequently pointed to illness as the principal reason for his long unproductive periods.

It took more than six months for him to finish the sonata. The last movement is dated April 7, 1883. It was published by Peters in late autumn of the same year.

The first two performances took place in Germany in the autumn of 1883. The premiere was at the Tonkünstlerverein [Musical Art Society] in Dresden on October 22, with Grieg and Ludwig Grützmacher. Five days later Grieg

Detail from a 1901 painting of Grieg by Leis Schjelderup. (Rasmus Meyers Samlingen, Bergen)

played it with Julius Klengel in the Gewandhaus in Leipzig. It goes without saying that the *Signale*'s reviewer pronounced a crushing verdict on the piece, but he had to admit that the composer had a remarkably good hold on the audience.

Grieg was not at all satisfied with this work, and as early as May 23 he wrote to the publisher that he had lacked inspiration: "And now to talk about Pegasus: no doubt he has been here, but I would not exactly call him 'Presto,' nor can he be called 'Allegro.' If I were going to christen him, his name would have to be 'Andante, quasi lento.'" As late as December 27, 1903, he wrote to G. Schjelderup: "Of my large works I think you are altogether too kind to my cello sonata. I myself do not rank it so high, because it does not mark a forward step in my development."

What is hidden behind these self-critical remarks? Grieg evidently felt that in the cello sonata he had begun to repeat himself, for to a considerable extent it consists of melodic materials that we have encountered earlier. Without trying to track down each and every example, one is nonetheless struck by a number of things. The lyric secondary theme of the first movement, for example, presents the much-used Grieg formula in both forms, but without bringing in anything new. It appears also as a secondary theme in the last movement. The principal theme in the second movement is virtually a copy of the "Homage March" from *Sigurd Jorsalfar*. The piano part in the closing section of the first movement has an unmistakable similarity to the conclusion of the first movement of the *A-minor Concerto*. The principal theme of the sonata's last movement, with its exaggerated folkloristic coloring, strikes one almost as a caricature; and the augmented major form of the theme in the closing section sounds quite stereotyped.

The harmonic development of the material is not nearly as imaginative and sparkling as in Grieg's other chamber music works, and does not help at all to retain one's interest. It is as if the composer is steering around all the reefs in order to be perfectly safe. Mechanical skill tends to take command.

With respect to form, it is evident that Grieg adhered rather slavishly and unimaginatively to traditional concepts. All of the movements are cast in sonata form, but with a considerable amount of segmentation. This is especially true of the last movement. Here the composer could have used a red pencil to good advantage and, with an iron hand, stricken long, tedious sections with enervating sequences that seem to go on forever (the movement is 828 measures long).

Notwithstanding all of these objections, however, there is something about the sonata that makes one listen to it willingly, especially the first two movements. The first has a melodic and rhythmic fervor that is quite captivating, and one certainly has to marvel at Grieg's ability to adapt the music so sensitively to the instruments. The cello is brilliantly exploited, gliding smoothly in and out in a playful dialogue with an unusually sonorous piano part. The composer gambols about with considerable technical skill and insight. It is presumably this aspect more than anything else that has brought the sonata into the standard repertoire of cellists.

The first movement has a dramatic character that is immediately made evident by the intensity of the principal theme:

A gentler, more lyric mood prevails in the second movement, where the principal theme instantly sets the tone:

The third movement, as we mentioned, is unusually long. It begins with a recitative-like cello solo of twenty measures. This material returns in a new form at the end of the development, but serves no other function in the movement. Despite its minor key, the principal theme with its stimulating *hailing* rhythms is quite lively—but it cannot support the heavy load that Grieg demands of it as the movement progresses. The metronomic marking must be taken with some reservation:

In the letter to Dr. Abraham cited earlier, Grieg mentioned that he had also made a stab at a new piano concerto, but inspiration failed him. Thus the *A-minor Concerto* never had a sequel. The concerto was to have been in B minor, but only a few measures from the first and third movements are known to exist (see CW 142). The existing opening measures of the third movement are reproduced below. Their Griegian character is readily apparent:

Grieg also composed the exposition of a first movement of a piano quintet in B-flat major (CW 162). He never mentioned this work in any of his correspondence, and it is not known when he wrote it, but it is quite possible that it was in 1883. Parts of this exposition are included in *Edvard Grieg's*

Complete Works, Vol. 9 (1978). It consists of a principal-theme fragment of sixteen measures plus a somewhat longer secondary theme in F minor. The former is rather anemic; the latter, on the other hand, has a melodic and harmonic charm that immediately identifies it as Griegian.

Around the same time that he wrote the cello sonata Grieg also finished two other works: *Waltz Caprices,* Opus 37, for piano four hands, and *Lyric Pieces II* for solo piano, Opus 38. On June 25, 1883, he sent all of the recently composed pieces (Opuses 36, 37, and 38) to Dr. Abraham with the following note: "Will you be sufficiently pleased with these three works so that I can finally feel that I have paid my debt to you?" Dr. Abraham was in fact very pleased with them, and published them immediately. There was a demand for this kind of music.

The two waltzes are not at all in accord with the tastes of the twentieth century. They are pure salon music. They do not come from the fresh mountain streams of Norway as did the *Norwegian Dances* of Opus 35. They reflect, rather, the wide rivers of the continent with an unmistakable scent of Chopin. Grieg's hand is discernible only in the skill with which the pieces are constructed.

The eight piano pieces in Opus 38 are much worthier of their creator, even if all are not of the same quality. Most of them were written in 1883, but earlier versions exist of No. 7, "Waltz" (1866) and No. 8, "Canon" (1877–78). With this volume Grieg established a link with his first collection of lyric pieces (Opus 12), thus continuing the series of similar compositions that were to make him famous all over the world. Compared with Opus 12, the pieces in Opus 38 are much more grandly conceived, and technically they are considerably more demanding. Yet stylistically the collection is less uniform. It ranges from the inspired "Cradle Song" and the captivating "Waltz" to the melodically bland "Melody" and "Elegy." Between these two extremes are the fairly successful folk-music pastiches—"Folk Song," "Halling," and "Springar"—plus an ingenious little polyphonic exercise entitled "Canon."

On December 20, 1882—as the fateful year of 1883 was about to begin—Grieg summed up his situation for Matthison-Hansen in these words: ". . . I have no desire to stay home any longer. I become altogether too depressed and philosophical here at home!" About his future plans he wrote: "Just think, I am studying French for an hour every day—because next winter I intend to be in Paris if nothing unforeseen prevents it." But what was it that suddenly gave rise to this talk about Paris?

Breach and reconciliation

There is no avoiding the fact that the relationship between Nina and Edvard was not the idyll that many people like to think it was. The friction that arose at a fairly early stage increased during the 1870s and 1880s. Temperamental and obstinate, they were pronounced individualists who had difficulty adjusting to each other.

Very little written material exists regarding their relationship, for Nina saw

John Grieg (Gyldendal, Oslo)

9. DESTRUCTION OF GRIEG'S LETTERS

On all my letters from Grieg I have written: To be burnt unread after my death. Do you agree with this? (Letter from Nina Grieg to Percy Grainger, September 25, 1923.)

* * *

I have also received many requests to allow Frants Beyer's letters [to Grieg] to be published. These letters do not exist. Grieg burned them, together with all of his other correspondence, a few years before his death. He had neither the time nor the energy to sort and organize the great mass of letters, and he did not want them to fall into the wrong hands after his death. He said this to my husband, who agreed that the letters should be destroyed and later told me of their conversation.

Frants Beyer proceeded in the same spirit [with respect to the Grieg correspondence in his possession]. During the many years when he was preparing EG's letters for publication he destroyed a large number of them. They contained vigorous and direct expressions of EG's mental suffering and inner struggles with regard to intimate and personal problems—matters concerning which Beyer was his only confidante. But he preserved and . . . released for publication almost everything written by EG which, without injury to those still living, might serve to fulfill his burning desire to give the Norwegian people a complete and true picture of their great composer. (Marie Beyer in an unpublished manuscript from 1924 in the National Archive, Oslo.)

10. EDVARD AND THE FAIR SEX

Great artists are always subjected to flattery and devoted admiration from women. Grieg was no exception; but despite his weakness for "the fair sex," this [flattery etc.] occasionally disgusted him and led him to misjudge them. (Letter from Nina Grieg to L. Monastier-Schroeder, February 1, 1917.)

to it that all letters exchanged between them were destroyed.[9] Fortunately, however, Edvard also carried on an extensive correspondence with his closest friend, Frants Beyer, for some thirty-five years, and in these letters he revealed his inner feelings to a far greater extent than in any other surviving source. A selection of these letters was published in book form by Mrs. Marie Beyer in 1923 [*Breve fra Edvard Grieg til Frants Beyer 1872–1907*, Oslo, not available in English]. The remaining extant letters, deposited in the National Archives, Oslo, were also included in Bjarne Kortsen's book *Grieg the Writer*, Vol. 2, published in Bergen in 1973. Before Edvard's death, however, Frants had destroyed the letters in which his friend touched on the most intimate personal matters.[9] Even Mrs. Beyer's reverent edition of the letters evoked hurtful memories for Nina as she wrote to Percy Grainger on May 5, 1924: "Now that I have read the Grieg letters published by Mrs. Beyer—for she wouldn't let me read them beforehand—all I can say is that I find them infinitely moving and profound, and I well understand that both you and everyone else regard them only thus. But for me, since I *know*, their publication also has another quite different and painful effect."

Nina is seldom mentioned in Grieg's letters, and when she is it is usually in surprisingly matter-of-fact terms. There is little tenderness and loving consideration in his words except during the last few years, when a hint of gratitude towards her begins to creep in.

Earlier—especially in connection with the Lofthus period—we discussed the aggravated marital situation. On several occasions Edvard stated more or less directly that all was not well in their married life. In his own way, he felt frustrated. Nina and her life style seemed to constitute a barrier between him and art ("women want to play"), and in the mid-1870s he also felt personally neglected. His dissatisfaction was such that he allowed himself to be enticed into some questionable relationships. The temptations were naturally very considerable, as is often the case with lionized artists. Nina herself wrote of this in no uncertain terms.[10]

In the early 1880s another woman entered the picture. That is why Grieg left home in the summer of 1883, and we do not know whether he ever intended to return. In April he unburdened himself to John Paulsen, referring to himself as a fleeing bird: "But now spring is coming, and the annual scrubbing of ceilings and walls. I can assure you that I am going around here like a person in need of a thorough cleaning. Would that I could, mentally speaking, take a steam bath and emerge from it twenty pounds lighter! One's soul becomes as heavy as lead here. For that reason I shall, must, and will go abroad again, however I can manage it . . . But home, of course, is where one's sense of beauty lies, so away, away! Yes, a Norwegian artist is really a strange bird, with his monotonous song: away, away! and home, home! With this song life passes by!"

On June 25 he wrote to Dr. Abraham: "I can't stand it in this cozy little place any longer. I must see and hear and talk about art." These words undoubtedly conceal a double meaning: he laid the blame on his longing for art, but the real problem was something quite different.

He especially wanted to go to Paris. The reason was that Leis (Elise)

Self-portrait of Leis Schjelderup, painted on wood, now belonging to her nephew, Alv G. Schjelderup, Oslo. In the 1880's she lived in Paris with her brother, Gerhard Schjelderup, a composer who also became Grieg's first Norwegian biographer. Grieg was very attracted to Miss Schjelderup during this critical period of his life. A number of letters that he wrote to her during this period are extant but have not been made public.

11. UNWILLINGNESS TO RETURN HOME

How am I!! I wish I could tell you! If I were to try I would start twenty letters to you and then tear them up again. I am too confused to give my thoughts expression through my pen . . . Let me *live*—really live life—during the time that still remains to me! I don't mean *enjoy;* I mean live so that I feel that it is I who am living, not a potential for something or ruin of something . . . I repeat: to come home now would be my undoing. It would be like putting me back in school, aborting my development—the process of fermentation that I can only undergo where I am. (Letter to Beyer, July 29, 1883.)

Schjelderup, a twenty-six-year-old painter whom he had met in Bergen, was now living there. Miss Schjelderup was a native of Bergen and the daughter of the local senior magistrate. The adversity he was encountering in his own life made him very susceptible to her extraordinary charm.

Grieg did not make the trip to Paris that summer, however. He went first to Rudolstadt in Thüringen, where he visited the young "Belgian friend and musician," Frank van der Stucken, a composer. Together they traveled to Bayreuth for the world premiere of *Parsifal* in July. After this he stayed in Rudolstadt for several weeks, spending his time "mainly practicing the piano" and taking daily French lessons from his friend. A stream of letters from Beyer encouraged him to return home, but to no avail.[11]

Grieg had applied for a grant to enable him to "travel to Paris," as he subsequently told Matthison-Hansen (March 27, 1885). "I didn't get it, I was furious, and I swore that I would raise the money in some other way . . ." This he did by means of an exhausting three-month concert tour in Germany and

12. BEYER TRIES TO BUILD A BRIDGE

All in all, you write in such a way that it's literally seething inside me. Dear Frants, I wish I could communicate to you the gratitude, the joy of having a true friend that permeates me whenever I read your letters. I am thinking and thinking, almost going mad, but I don't even want to try to dig around in that anthill of feelings, moods, and impressions which make me feel all the same that I should stay where I am. For I really couldn't give you a clear picture of my condition. Life must be allowed to develop in its own way, and in the fullness of time everything comes if one can wait for it and believe in it. It's just that it's often so hard . . . If only I could know that I will some day find Norway again, and at the same time find joy in the thought of going home, then all this would be something in which to rejoice. But *happiness* for me is to be found nowhere, if I cannot find it—in myself. (Letter to Beyer, November 15, 1883.)

13. GRIEG'S FEELINGS FOR BEYER

Dear, dear Friend! Well, I must speak a few words with you before the old year comes to an end. I cannot thank you for it, I can only tell you that without you I would probably not have survived it, that you are my best friend, and that as long as this heart of mine continues to beat I shall cherish you more than anyone else. As unhappy as I was when I left, and also later during the first part of the summer, and how much less unhappy now—no, I wouldn't have thought it possible! Happy! That's something else. Why should I be happy, too? I am entirely happy only with your friendship, for you are the only person in the world who has never let me down. With my art I *should* be entirely happy—but I am not, because I have not always forged straight ahead, and for this reason I have not achieved what I was called to achieve . . . I open my arms to you, to the new year, to spring, to the new spring of the spirit and of Nature, to joy and peace—I could embrace the whole of mankind in gratitude for the bright star which, despite everything and through the mist, shines on my existence. (Letter to Beyer, December 29, 1883.)

the Netherlands: "It was strenuous. Every day travel, rehearsal, and concert." The tour started in October in Weimar, where he played his piano concerto and was delighted at the performance of *Two Elegiac Melodies,* Opus 34 (see p. 241). "It was a brilliant start, and for that I can surely first and foremost thank Liszt. My, how wonderful he was to me. Then once again to Leipzig— the central point from which, like a spider, I could survey my entire web." He performed the cello sonata in Dresden and again in Leipzig. Then came concerts in Meiningen, Breslau ("[Max] Bruch was there, a boring pedant"), Cologne, Frankfurt (where, among other things, he visited Clara Schumann), Karlsruhe, and a number of cities in the Netherlands.

During these months he was carrying on a thoughtful correspondence with Beyer, a series of letters in which his inner turmoil is reflected. Unfortunately there are gaps in this correspondence, and we must assume that nobody other than Beyer ever read the frankest letters. From the ones that have been preserved it is clear that Frants did his utmost to mediate between Edvard and Nina, and he did so in such an earnest manner that Edvard constantly felt compelled to ponder deeply the consequences of what he was about to do.[12]

During this critical autumn Nina stayed with the Beyers. It is symptomatic of Edvard's attitude toward her that in November, when he was going to send her a birthday greeting, he merely asked Frants to greet her from him.

Finally he had to make a decision. Should he go to Paris and resume his relationship with Miss Schjelderup, thus precipitating a final break with Nina? With the help of Beyer's conciliatory efforts he made his choice: he would stay with Nina. When all was said and done, the bonds between them were too strong to sever. They would both have to make a fresh start— together.

A heavy burden was lifted from Grieg's shoulders when that decision was finally made. The letter of thanks that he sent to Beyer from Amsterdam at the end of the month glows with a sense of liberation and inner joy.[13]

The plans for a trip to Paris were abandoned, and he also turned down an invitation from the Royal Philharmonic Society in London. Instead, he remained in Amsterdam for three weeks as a guest of the young Dutch composer Julius Röntgen, who in the years ahead was to become his closest foreign friend.

The final reconciliation with Nina occurred in mid-January when she and the Beyers met Edvard in Leipzig, and they all traveled together to Rome. To Nina and Edvard's great disappointment, their friends were able to stay in Italy for only a couple of weeks. The reason was that they were in the process of building their new home, "Naesset" [The Promontory], at Hop on Lake Nordaasvann, some six miles south of Bergen. The Griegs, however, stayed in Italy for four months, and among other things gave the concert at which Ibsen was so charmed by Nina's singing (see p. 195).

One product of this trip was the beautiful portrait of Nina executed by the famous German painter, Franz von Lenbach (see p. 256).

Just before the Griegs left for home, Nina wrote to her good Danish friend, Clara Winding, telling her something of what she had been through. Her letter, dated May 5, also expressed the hope that everything had now

Rom 7. Mai 1882

14. THE PERILS OF
"DOLCE FAR NIENTE"

I am becoming an absolute cripple in my art as a result of this indolent life. I am beginning to feel that gold, too, can be bought too dearly. Still, as we make our bed, so must we lie. (Letter to Beyer, April 8, 1884.)

15. WORK MAKES ONE YOUNG

I am sure that the first thing I will say to myself when I see my home again is: How old you have become! For me there are only two ways to cure this morbidity. The first is "go to the mountains"; the second, "liberation through work." Each piece I write from now on will make me a couple of years younger in spirit, and just you wait and see how wonderful it will be when we are together again. (Letter to Beyer, April 16, 1884.)

A famous portrait of Nina by the German painter Franz von Lenbach. The picture, which now hangs at Troldhaugen, was painted in Rome in the spring of 1884 shortly after the reconciliation between Nina and Edvard. Grieg wrote to Beyer on April 30, 1884, "It is most generous of him that he will allow us to have the picture that he is painting; it will surely be a fine ornament for that home that I am always dreaming of."

finally changed for the better: "It's so long since I wrote to you, my dear Clara, and I have been through so immensely much recently, both loneliness and a lot of other evil things; but thank God I believe all the same that there is still much that is beautiful to live for, even if there is no one to carry on after one is gone."

Early in the spring, Edvard began to feel a certain distaste for the life of idleness he was leading.[14] He longed for firm Norwegian rock beneath his feet, and wrote on March 1 to Beyer: ". . . there is something within me that cries out for this: a home, a home! Only with a home can I achieve anything, and it's high time. But I am having the same problem that one has so often in art: I am groping for the right form. I am tired of the sort of home that is intended to last just a year or two and then be broken up. Admittedly, traveling still has its attractions, but not a vagrant existence as such. And as for setting up a permanent home outside of Norway, I don't think I could stand that for long. I would be consumed with longing . . ."

The Holberg Suite

The troubled autumn of 1883 was the beginning of a long unproductive period for Grieg. Until the summer of 1886, when he finally got to work in earnest once again, he managed to produce only one large composition of lasting value: the *Holberg Suite,* Opus 40 (1884). On February 10, 1885, he wrote to Winding: "This year I have taken no permanent position because I wanted to compose. But the Muse does not approve of a total lack of spiritual vitality, and she manifests herself altogether too often by her absence." His entire output in 1885 consisted of finishing the orchestration of *Bergliot,* Opus 42, and a few compositions of minor importance.

The period 1884–88 was Grieg's weakest as a song writer, which is evident from the three songs that he wrote during these years. "Upon a Grassy Hillside" (Opus 39, No. 3), to a text by Jonas Lie, is just another song with no distinguishing features, and "Hearing a Song or Carol" (Opus 39, No. 6, to a Nordahl Rolfsen translation of a poem by Heinrich Heine) sounds dry and uninspired. "Beneath the Christmas Tree" (CW 129, No. 4, text by Nordahl Rolfsen), printed in 1885, is also musically thin.

That same year Grieg published a volume of piano arrangements of some of his songs, Opus 41. Several of them, including "The Princess" and "I Love But Thee," were given a vastly different character. "The Princess," as a matter of fact, was actually made into a virtuoso piano piece, totally different from the song.

Upon his return from Italy, Grieg viewed creative work as a "fountain of youth" for which he felt a distinct need.[15] It is a youthful composer that we meet in the *Holberg Suite,* which was written in Lofthus in the summer of 1884. This suite is one of the most curious compositions in all of Norwegian music. The immediate occasion for its creation was the festivities marking the bicentennial of the birth of the Norwegian-Danish playwright, Ludvig Holberg. Grieg had always felt a kinship with Holberg with respect to the

16. GRIEG DISCUSSES THE *HOLBERG SUITE*

. . . my suite in the old style, "From Holberg's Time" [*Holberg Suite*], which I have completed. Once in a great while it really is a good exercise to conceal one's own individuality. (Letter to Röntgen, August 26, 1884.)

* * *

Just think, a Danish critic says that I have struck out in a new direction. That's nothing but *sheer nonsense*. (Letter to Röntgen, December 15, 1884.)

* * *

. . . for that reason I have arranged that poor *Holberg Suite* for string orchestra. It may sound pretty good. (Letter to Röntgen, February 1, 1885.)

* * *

. . . my own *Holberg Suite,* which compared to Sinding's piece [*Suite in A minor for Violin and Orchestra,* Opus 10] sounds so very French, as well it should. But Sinding's work lays claim to a much greater profundity—and it really is profound, too. (Letter to Beyer, December 25, 1887.)

17. GRIEG COMMENTS ON THE *HOLBERG CANTATA*

I am bored by having to write a piece for male chorus for the Holberg celebration. Well, I may be writing poor music, but on the other hand I'm doing all right as a fisherman. Yesterday I pulled in seventy of them. (Letter to Beyer, October 9, 1884.)

* * *

Moreover, so far as music is concerned I've been bored silly because I've had to spend my time writing a cantata for male chorus a cappella. I have to conduct the thing on December 3 on the main square in Bergen, where the monument is to be unveiled. I can see it now: snow, hail, storm, and thunder, a large male chorus with open mouths into which the rain pours, and me conducting with a rain coat, winter coat, galoshes, and umbrella! Then, of course, a cold or God knows what other kind of illness! Ah well, that is one way to die for one's country! (Letter to Röntgen, October 30, 1884.)

* * *

There were umbrellas, naturally—it wouldn't have been Bergen without them—but otherwise everything went very well . . . the cantata . . . *sounded* good any-

way, albeit a bit crude in a rustic sort of way. (Letter to Röntgen, December 15, 1884.)

* * *

Father Holberg has cost me two months of hard labor—but he deserves it too, that

splendid fellow . . . The truth is that I really haven't known him until now . . . But now I have come to realize that his vision was as broad as that of anyone in history that I have heard of. (Letter to Ravnkilde, December 17, 1884.)

universality of his personality and humor, his breadth and satire, and he was delighted at the opportunity to clothe Holberg's old figures in modern dress and give them a personal touch as well. His point of departure was the stylized French dance-suite form (as used by Couperin, Rameau, and Bach in the eighteenth century), and he recreated some of the most characteristic musical forms of Holberg's day. The basic spirit is the precision of French classicism, the musical language is Romantic, the synthesis is Griegian.

The first movement, "Preludium," resembles a *perpetuum mobile* and fairly bubbles with genuine musical delight. The same ebullient joy in music-making also permeates the strikingly graceful "Gavotte/Musette" (third movement) and the concluding "Rigaudon," which, despite its inherently eruptive character, is nonetheless held in check. The other inner movements—"Sarabande" and "Air"—play on deeper strings; indeed, the expressive "Air" is one of Grieg's loveliest creations:

The suite, which was first written for piano, was finished in August, and Grieg immediately arranged it for string orchestra.[16] He wrote to Beyer on September 11 that he had scored the work and was looking forward to hearing the orchestration as soon as the opportunity presented itself. He got the opportunity on March 15 of the following year, when he conducted the premiere of the suite in Bergen.

Once again Grieg revealed his unusual ability to write sonorously for strings. After the orchestral version was published in 1885 it began its conquest of music lovers all over the world, and it has retained its original freshness to the present day.

In connection with the actual memorial festivities for Holberg, Grieg was asked in September to write a cantata (to a text by Nordahl Rolfsen) for a cappella male chorus. It was to be sung on December 3—Holberg's birthday—for the dedication of a statue of the great playwright by the Swedish sculptor Johan Börjeson. Grieg dutifully accepted the assignment, and the music (CW 143) unfortunately sounds like something he wrote from a sense of obligation.[17] It is uninteresting and not at all characteristic of him.

In Grieg's own opinion, his most important opus during this period was neither the *Holberg Suite* nor the *Holberg Cantata,* but the work he was doing on his new home, "Troldhaugen."

The Building of "Troldhaugen"

I. PLANS FOR TWO HOUSES ON BEYER'S BUILDING SITE

Our building site consisted of two promontories, and the original plan was that [we would build on one and] the Griegs on the other. But when our house was built we found that the lot was not big enough to provide the space and privacy that one would want for two homes. (Marie Beyer in an unpublished manuscript from 1924, State Archive, Oslo.)

2. RUMORS ABOUT GRIEG'S MEGALOMANIA

Mrs. Grieg wrote a friendly letter to Miss [Christiane] Schreiber that gave Miss S. occasion to spread among strangers a rumor to the effect that the Griegs were suffering from megalomania, in proof of which she reported that Mrs. G. wrote that "for fourteen days her husband has been driving around on the estate with *three horses*." I said immediately to Ravnkilde that this was utter nonsense; and sure enough, I read in *Aftenposten* that Grieg had spent fourteen days at the farm "*Hestetred*" [a proper name that in Norwegian is somewhat similar to the words for "three horses"], where he plans to build a house! (Henrik Ibsen in a letter to his son Sigurd, Rome, September 24, 1884.)

During the stay in Italy Grieg eagerly followed Frants Beyer's developing plans for "Naesset," a peaceful and incredibly beautiful building site about six miles south of Bergen. He was delighted that the work was proceeding so quickly; on March 16, 1884, he wrote excitedly to his friend, "What a lucky fellow you are—to be able to hang a wreath on your very own house! For a wreath like that I would gladly exchange ten thousand wreaths of the kind that are used to honor musicians at the end of a performance!"

"Naesset" reinforced for both Nina and Edvard the idea that they now *must* get themselves a home that would be truly theirs. This idea got a further boost when Beyer wrote suggesting that it might be possible to build two houses on the site. Marie Beyer has written about how this was the original plan.[1]

The Griegs came home from Italy in the late spring of 1884 and immediately moved into "Naesset" as guests of the Beyers. When it became evident that the site was too small to accommodate a second house, they were deeply disappointed. It then occurred to them that it might be possible to build on an adjacent site—"Hestetred," a part of the farm of Salomon Monsen Hop. This odd name, which means "an enclosure for horses," occasioned a misunderstanding that gave Ibsen a good laugh.[2] Grieg was able to buy the outermost part of the property for 500 kroner. Beyer, who was an attorney, drew up a contract specifying, among other things, that sheep and goats would not be allowed to graze on the property. Ever wary of strangers, Grieg also got written assurances that the adjacent land could not be sold without his knowledge.

The site was a wilderness of trees and undergrowth, with a surrounding deep hollow called "Trolddalen"—The Valley of the Trolls. Grieg was captivated by the beauty of this unspoiled place; it appealed to the artist in him to be able to participate in the creation of a home in this little piece of western Norway.

After the purchase of the site was completed, he wanted very much to take a summer trip to his beloved Hardanger. Nina, who had never really felt at home in Lofthus, had been uneasy about Edvard's earlier vague notions about settling down there permanently. Happy over the purchase of the property,

3. GRIEG'S BIG, NEW "OPUS"

I spent fourteen beautiful days with Frants Beyer at his new little country home near Bergen, and then I came here where it is more beautiful than the most beautiful place imaginable. But before I left I made preparations for a new opus—the best I have ever produced—by buying a piece of land about six miles from Bergen. This autumn I intend to realize here an old dream of building my own home. It might seem crazy from an artistic standpoint, but at the moment I am as happy as a child with this project.

No opus has filled me with greater excitement than this one. I spend half the day measuring and drawing: rooms, basements, attic rooms—including one in which you can rest on soft cushions when you come. (Letter to Ravnkilde, July 21, 1884.)

4. THE PLANNING OF "TROLDHAUGEN"

I think I wish that we could get a house the interior of which would be almost exactly like yours—but then we would have to have it a bit different on the outside so it wouldn't just be a copy. Edvard draws and studies hour after hour until he gets crazy in the head, but we still haven't arrived at any final plans. Now and then in all modesty I venture to come forward with a proposal, but of course as a rule it is silly. Ah well, I only wish we might end up with something as nice as you have. (Letter from Nina to Marie Beyer, June 24, 1884.)

she wrote to Marie Beyer on June 17 while enroute to Hardanger, "But you know, Maisie, I am so glad that it was not *there* that Edvard decided to build—not only because you don't live there, but Hardanger has always struck me as a somewhat melancholy place to live. Perhaps I am silly—as I am so often; I have so frightfully many different kinds of feelings and sensations, as you well know . . ." That Grieg was having similar thoughts is evident from what he wrote to Frants Beyer the very same day: ". . . for even if I can talk with farmers, I am no longer so crazy about them that I want to live only among farmers." Complete isolation from the pulsating life of the city could be too much to take.

In a letter to Ravnkilde sent from the Utne Hotel in Lofthus, Grieg wrote excitedly about his building plans: this was going to be the "best opus" he had ever produced.[3] He threw himself intensely into the planning. At the hotel he met a distant relative—a Bergen architect by the name of E. C. Christie—who encouraged him to consider building a house modelled after those typical of the Gudbrandsdal Valley in eastern Norway. In a letter to Beyer, Grieg included sketches of the floor plan of such a house, but at the same time he asked his friend to make some pencil drawings of "Naesset." It is clear that both he and Nina wanted above all to get a house that resembled "Naesset" in every respect. Nina wrote about this in another letter to Marie.[4]

The two families were already at work trying to find a suitable name for the place, and this led to some minor controversies. Grieg himself had settled on "Knausen," which means "the knoll." Beyer proposed "Klubben," which is another word for "knoll". That made Grieg angry, and in a fit of temper he wrote: "If the place is called 'Klubben' I'll never go there again, I don't care what the name means. And if you call it by that name, I'll never want to see you again, either. Damn! The whole knoll becomes a dung heap when I hear the word 'Klubben.' No, if 'Knausen' isn't good enough, then I stick with Nina's idea, namely, 'Troldhaugen' [The Hill of the Trolls—derived, obviously, from 'Trolddalen']." Thus Nina won the argument over the name.

That fall Grieg's cousin, the outstanding architect Schak Bull, was engaged to draw the plans for the house and supervise its construction. Nothing now remained of the idea of a house in the Gudbrandsdal Valley style. What was built was a Victorian country house in the style typical of the time, with a large porch and—in accordance with Grieg's special wish—a tower on top with a room.

In late fall Grieg left Hardanger and spent the winter in Bergen. He threw himself heart and soul into the building project. He wrote jokingly to Dr. Abraham on March 14, 1885: "I really don't know these days whether I am a musician or a builder. Every single day I take the train back and forth to the house. All my ideas are used up there, and masses of unborn compositions are smothered by the newly excavated dirt. When you come for a visit some time, all you have to do is dig around and Norwegian chorus, orchestra, and piano pieces will gush up from the bowels of the earth! We must not be confused by the fact that these works will look like peas and potatoes and radishes—for there really is music in them."

Nina and Edvard in Rome in the spring of 1884. (Photo collection of Universitetsbiblioteket in Oslo)

A few weeks later the house was finished, and Nina and Edvard could finally move in. They had a home of their own.

The financing of "Troldhaugen" was not without its problems, for the Griegs' economic situation was far from secure. Building costs totaled 12,500 kroner, a very substantial amount in those days; and conscientious as he was in financial matters, Grieg was concerned about how he would meet the obligations he had now assumed. As early as August 26, 1884, he wrote to Julius Röntgen in a humorous vein—but with a hint of seriousness too—about what he had gotten himself into: "I have completed a volume of songs [Opus 39], and hope with these to be able to scrape up at least enough money for the basement windows."

Once the building was completed it was necessary to start making payments on both the principal and the interest. These weighed heavily on him for some years to come—until one day he happened to mention the problem to Dr. Abraham. Quite unexpectedly, the yoke was then completely lifted from his shoulders: the publishing company gave him a large sum of money that enabled him to pay off the loans he had taken in Bergen. The money was represented as a loan from the firm; in reality, however, it was a most generous gift, for he was never asked to repay it.

Grieg's house stands today pretty much as it was when it was built over a century ago. Some people, to be sure, have reacted negatively to a building of this character on this site; most, however, are immediately captivated by its charm. It has a light and breezy elegance, free of the often bombastic exaggerations that were characteristic of the period. The architect and contractor succeeded in giving it a friendly and distinctive stamp. Understandably, Nina and Edvard put their personal stamp on the interior. One is perhaps a bit surprised at the rather unusual juxtaposition of rustic wood walls—the only feature that was retained of the country style they had originally planned to use—and late Romantic plush-covered furniture. But the whole has a highly personal touch created by two artistic natures who in this case worked together in complete accord. One feels "at home" in these rooms with their very special atmosphere.

The good and evil trolls

The year during which "Troldhaugen" was being built had been uncommonly strenuous for Grieg, both physically and psychologically. One would think that with the completion of the new home his innermost wishes would have been satisfied, but such was not the case. Artistically, he felt undernourished. From a purely musical point of view Bergen, for him, was a provincial, out-of-the-way place marked by "extreme lethargy and materialism." "Troldhaugen," in a way, isolated him even more.[5]

Against this background, one can well understand—even though it seems strange to us—that after living in his new home for only a few weeks he could write these words to John Paulsen in Rome (April 30): ". . . I am filled with

"Troldhaugen" (Photo by L. K. Örnelund, Oslo, Norway)

envy when I think of you, you lucky fellow—sitting down there in a country where you can bathe yourself in impressions of beauty of every sort . . . In the fall I must make up some kind of devilish excuse to get out of here again . . ."

The "ten thousand wreaths" seem already to have been forgotten. Once again his two natures were in conflict: one sought contemplation for creative work, the other drove him steadily away from peace and quiet in response to a restless, almost insatiable need for stimulation in the form of new, colorful experiences. Grieg himself was painfully aware of this and often cited, with reference to himself, the striking aphorism of the German poet Schmidt von Lübeck: "Happiness is where you are *not*."

This lack of contentment was not of recent date. Even during his Oslo period it had manifested itself time and again, and throughout his life he felt, as he once said, a certain kinship with "the migratory birds and their monotonous song: away, away, home, home!"

Both sunshine and clouds were to hover over "Troldhaugen" for Grieg. In a letter to Beyer on October 24, 1892, he put it like this: "That Troldhaug, that Troldhaug: it harbors both good and evil trolls." How are we to understand this? The answer appears to be that he transferred the division in his own mind to his home and its surroundings.

It is certain nonetheless that some of his best times were spent at this marvelous place that was his home. Most of his later significant works came

6. IDLENESS

. . . while up here on my "troll hill" [Troldhaug] I can't think of anything that I like better than loafing. To write [music] without wanting to is something I never do now as long as I am not starving—and fortunately I'm not doing that. (Letter to Horneman, July 23, 1894.)

The formal living room at "Troldhaugen" (Photo by L. K. Örnelund, Oslo, Norway)

into being in waves of inspiration that occurred at "Troldhaugen." But there he also endured the most discouraging thing that can happen to a creative artist: periods when nothing succeeded for him.[6]

The total solitude that he always needed for composing he found in his composer's hut down beside the lake—"the office," as he called it. It had been planned in 1886, but was not built until five years later.

Sigmund Torsteinson, in his charming book about "Troldhaugen" (1959), reports that when Grieg was finished with his day's work in the composer's hut he always placed the following little message on top of his papers: "If anyone breaks in he is asked to please spare the music, for it has no value for anyone other than Edvard Grieg."

Unfortunately, the hut was both drafty and damp; the very first winter that he used it—1891–92—he contracted a severe attack of rheumatism.

When the weather was in its best mood and "Troldhaugen" displayed its loveliest garb, it had an immediate effect on Grieg. In a letter to his Danish friend August Winding of June 3, 1895, he exulted: "It's a pity you are not here now. A bird song with enough motives for twenty-seven symphonies and

7. SUMMER TRIPS ON THE FJORD

During the middle of summer, when the weather was dependable and the air warm, we took advantage of Sundays for all-day boat trips. The boat was loaded with things to drink from "Troldhaugen" and food from "Naesset." Happy as children, we set out with Frants at the oars. He guided us with a sure hand through the various channels, past the verdant banks, and out toward the open fjord. Here we always stopped at the same place in a cozy little inlet, spread a cloth on the green grass, and enjoyed to the utmost summer's beauty and the great outdoors. Toward evening we went in the boat again and threw out our fish lines. Grieg was an enthusiastic fisherman, albeit not exactly a particularly lucky one. If he actually hooked a sea trout or pollack he got terribly excited. We usually had our evening meal as we neared our homes—on one of the small islands that lay beckoning in the evening sun. (From Marie Beyer's unpublished manuscript in the State Archive, Oslo.)

8. A FISHING STORY

One day . . . Grieg went out fishing in a small boat with his friend Frants Beyer. After a while a musical theme suddenly came into his head. He took a piece of paper from his pocket, quietly jotted it down, and put the paper on the bench at his side. A moment later a gust of wind blew it overboard. Grieg did not see it, but Beyer saw it and picked it up. Being himself something of a composer, he read the melody and, after putting the paper in his pocket, whistled it. Grieg turned like a flash and asked: "What was that?" Beyer answered nonchalantly: "Only an idea I just got," whereupon Grieg retorted: "The devil you say! I just got that same idea myself!" (H. T. Finck, *Grieg and his Music*, p. 72.)

twenty-four operas." But instead of symphonies and operas, that summer he created eight of his most beautiful songs: *The Mountain Maid,* Opus 67 (the *Haugtussa* cycle).

One of the things Grieg enjoyed most during the summer was the family excursions on the fjord, when he and Nina and the Beyers rowed out to nearby islets in a small fishing boat. The arrangements for food were always substantial: a lunch basket from "Naesset" and wine from "Troldhaugen." In the Primary Materials will be found a description of these excursions by Marie Beyer[7] as well as an account of a delightful episode from one such fishing trip.[8]

But often, even in the summer, western Norway's weather showed its trollish side and ruined any opportunity for summer pleasures. And when fall and winter storms came along and made the large house—exposed to the weather as it was—feel like a summer cabin, Edvard and Nina shivered through the days. Then dejection and irritation came to the fore. Grieg wrote to John Paulsen, for example, on January 21, 1887: "Outside it is dripping and pouring, the wind is howling and screaming. The road is impassable. Ice patches and mud holes that will break your arms and legs. Thus we sit imprisoned in our loneliness, and not a living soul dares to come this way . . ."

Because of experiences like these, the Griegs managed in all to struggle through only four winters at "Troldhaugen." By and large, it served as their home only during the warmer months of the year.

Notwithstanding the inclement weather, the relationship between the Griegs and the Beyers grew steadily closer as they lived side by side in their newly built homes. The two families even developed their own private communication system, necessitated by the fact that Grieg absolutely refused to install a telephone at "Troldhaugen."[9]

The friendship with Frants Beyer came to be one of the most important things in Edvard's life—a fact that is often movingly expressed in the many hundreds of letters that Grieg wrote to his friend. Best of all, of course, were the times when they could be together. Edvard especially enjoyed their long Sunday hikes together in the mountains. Weather permitting, they would hike all the way to Mount Lövstakken, leaving early in the morning. When the weather was uncertain they sometimes took a shorter hike through the lovely Tveteraas woods to the completely unspoiled scenery on top of the Nattland hills. Then Grieg shared his innermost thoughts, as if to a confessor. For Frants had a unique ability to draw him out of his self-centeredness—the endless circling of the lonely artist within the confines of his own world. Many a heavy burden was lifted from Grieg's shoulders as a result of their stimulat-

9. SIGNALING BETWEEN "TROLDHAUGEN" AND "NAESSET"

During the first twelve years there was no telephone at "Naesset," nor was there any at "Troldhaugen" as long as Grieg was living. To facilitate communications between us, we gradually developed a rather complicated signal system that conveyed messages and decisions: the flag was raised or lowered, a light was turned on in the tower window at "Troldhaugen," and so on. A bed sheet or towel hanging out on the balcony also had a special meaning. But we sometimes also just shouted to each other. (From Marie Beyer's unpublished manuscript in the State Archives, Oslo.)

10. MARIE BEYER ON FRANTS'S CHARACTER

His heart was filled with moving compassion and love, and the quest for the truly human—the attempt to understand the individual human being—was like a scarlet thread that ran through his entire life. His own life was marked by the simplicity and moderation that were his innermost nature . . . A harsh and unkind word or an unfeeling judgment were unthinkable for him; thus he also became for all who were close to him the dearest, surest friend in sorrow as well as joy . . . As different as they [Edvard and Frants] were, they still had many points of contact. Perhaps it was precisely the difference in their makeup that was the connecting link in their strong friendship. (From Marie Beyer's unpublished manuscript in the State Archive, Oslo.)

Frants Beyer, Grieg's close friend and confidante during most of his adult life. (Music division, Bergen Offentlige Bibliotek)

ing conversations. Marie Beyer has beautifully described her husband's noble character, especially the deeply human qualities that bound him so strongly to Edvard.[10]

Often in his letters Grieg expressed himself warmly and with singular feeling about Frants and what his friendship meant to him. On October 27, 1895, for example, he wrote: "Yes, dear Frants, life is mysterious and complex—most of all, perhaps, for him who lives in my skin. That is also why I must get home again and be with you, for with you I can always learn anew the simple, *un*complex joy in being alive! That is not the smallest part of the great beauty that your friendship has been for me and will be until my last hour."

On March 2, 1901, he wrote: "Until my last hour you will stand for me as an example of the noblest and best that I have met on life's pathway. But it is true: *strictly speaking,* it is not you who deserve the thanks, but the powers that allowed us to meet! Just imagine if that had not occurred! For it is conceivable. But—I am incapable of imagining that. I would then have become a completely different person. That is how influential you have been in making me what I am."

In view of their likes and dislikes, it is in some ways almost surprising that Nina and Edvard managed to maintain a very hospitable home. They had little inclination toward practical affairs, and Nina's interests did not exactly lean toward responsibility for housekeeping. Indeed, it is said that what she preferred most of all was life in a fashionable hotel. Marie Beyer reports that Edvard, on the other hand, "was a homebody and an excellent host. In the little circle where he felt secure, composed basically of his and Nina's closest relatives and the Beyers, he freely displayed his amiability. His luminous intelligence, good spirits, interesting stories, and warm disposition made those gatherings unforgettable and cherished by all who were so fortunate as to participate in them."

Grieg impulsively threw out invitations for a "troll visit" to his large circle of acquaintances without fully realizing how much he was letting himself in for. As early as March 26, 1886, he intimated something of this in a letter to Beyer: "I'm not sure to what extent I'll be able this summer to get away from the many foreign friends who will disturb the peace and quiet that I need for my work. For that reason I have thought seriously about building a little 'composer's hut' down in Trolddalen—similar to the one I had in Hardanger, but about twice as big."

Down through the years there were many who accepted Grieg's invitation to visit "Troldhaugen," and they stayed for varying lengths of time. For Nina and Edvard, these visits served as stimulants in their otherwise quiet life—but it could also be tiring to try constantly to live up to their reputation as the perfect host and hostess, especially when it became evident that some of their guests were taking advantage of their hospitality. After the visit of some foreign guests in 1888, Grieg wrote to Frederick Delius on November 6 with a bit of trollish tongue-in-cheekness: "A fresh breeze like that from the outside world does one good, but I must admit—the rural peace and solitude after they leave is much better!"

The interior of the composer's hut with its idyllic view of Nordaasvannet. (Photo by L. K. Örnelund, Oslo, Norway)

Grieg's greatest worry in this connection was the uninvited guests—friends of friends who arrived suddenly, but often departed much more slowly. These sometimes became a burden for both Nina and him. He once found it necessary to write reproachfully to Julius Röntgen, one of his closest foreign friends, in connection with an unexpected visit by a Dutch composer: "And even if Mr. [Johan] Wagenaar is a god, I will nevertheless say: I hate you when you burden me with him and thus deprive me of my rustic peace and quiet. Such visits are the bane of my life . . . Needless to say, [when he arrives] the day after tomorrow I shall be thoroughly amiable." (Letter of August 15, 1906.)

Perfect host that he was, Grieg managed to conceal his annoyance toward Mr. Wagenaar, for the following summer he actually turned up for another visit at "Troldhaugen." This time Grieg's irritation was obvious.

The good and evil trolls took turns dominating Grieg's life throughout his years at "Troldhaugen." Sometimes even during the summer, the loveliest time to be there, he felt an urge to go away. At such times he sometimes fled, like Peer Gynt, to the mountains—without Nina. When Nina was along they went instead to Hardanger or some other place in western Norway.

In the unbearable wintertime they fled to more distant places, preferably abroad; in later years they sometimes went to Oslo. Indeed, the struggle with the strange forces at "Troldhaugen" often became so difficult that Grieg seriously considered selling the property. At the turn of the century he very nearly decided to take up permanent residence in Oslo. The ties to "Troldhaugen" were too strong to be severed, however. In spite of everything, it was there that he and Nina belonged.

Concert Successes and Creative Brilliance

Summer at home, autumn and winter abroad

I. SUCCESS IN OSLO

Sold out. Grand, overwhelming ovation. The whole audience stood up. Shouts of "Long live Grieg!" A torrent of flowers. Endless curtain calls. Inform Frants. Affectionate greetings, Edvard. (Telegram to Herman Hagerup, October 18. 1885.)

Grieg spent the early part of the summer of 1885 at "Troldhaugen," and he invited Julius Röntgen and his wife from Amsterdam to become the first foreign guests in his new home. Röntgen, together with the singer Johannes Messchaert, had also visited the Griegs the previous year at Lofthus, where they "made music for 3–4 hours almost every forenoon" while "the Hardanger beer was passed around to the great delight of our guests."

The Röntgens, unfortunately, had to decline the invitation when Mrs. Röntgen became ill. Grieg wrote to them on July 20: "My flag hangs at half mast, and the studio couch that just arrived I shall drape in black!" He consoled them, however, by saying that the weather had been miserable, so they hadn't missed out on very much. He also mentioned that he was in the process of studying Brahms's Piano Quintet, Opus 25, "a work of genius! In my opinion far more beautiful than the *Third Symphony*, which I now know thoroughly."

At the beginning of August, Grieg and Beyer took the first of many expeditions that they were to take to the Jotunheimen mountains. In the years that followed, these trips became Grieg's principal opportunity for close contact with nature and were, he said, a continual source of "vitality for both body and soul."

Nina and Edvard planned to spend the winter of 1885–86 in Denmark, but first they went to Oslo where he participated in four concerts. On October 17 and 21 he played some of his own piano works. He also accompanied Nina and Thorvald Lammers in a number of songs and performed the cello sonata with his brother John. These concerts were enormously successful, as is evident from the enthusiastic telegram he sent to his father-in-law, who had now returned to Bergen.[1]

At the Music Association on October 24 Grieg conducted selections from the *Peer Gynt* music and the *Holberg Suite*, and Lammers sang *The Mountain Thrall*. It was after this concert that the Artists' Society held the celebrated banquet reported in the Primary Materials on p. 234. On November 3 he experienced a new artistic triumph when Laura Gundersen premiered *Bergliot*.

Then the Griegs left for Copenhagen, where Edvard participated in five

2. LETTERS TO BEYER FROM COPENHAGEN

After the concerts we have it cozy, believe me. Then we gather . . . with musicians, painters, poets, and other friends and often talk and celebrate far into the night. Then comes the sour, painful morning after . . . [The Stavanger author, Alexander] Kielland is a splendid fellow, I would definitely like him. Svendsen is amiability itself toward us, but he is so complex that in fact he will always be an enigma to me. He is on the outs with virtually all the musicians here, so we don't see anything of him at our post-concert gatherings . . . He comes to our house a lot and tells Nina about his marital problems . . . Christmas Eve we'll be at Winding's together with Professor Hartmann . . . (Letter to Beyer, December 11, 1885.)

* * *

A toast for the New Year and for our friendship, for your understanding, forbearance, kindheartedness, and all the other good things . . . I sent you a postcard with a request for my practice keyboard. For I am to play my concerto in Svendsen's Philharmonic concerts the latter part of January, and I want to practice on technical exercises at top speed, something that under these circumstances I really don't want to do at the piano—not to mention the fact that it makes me nervous . . .

For my part, I say what you once wrote to me: you are not a friend, you are *the* friend; therefore I say: receive a friend's handshake and gratitude for everything good. (Letter to Beyer, December 22, 1885.)

3. FAILING HEALTH

Perpetually cold hands and feet, and a leaden feeling—a kind of paralysis—in my arms and legs threatens to render my musical life impossible. All physical and mental energy vanishes. Today I finally went to the doctor. He concurred with the earlier doctor's opinion that the problem is anemia, but also nerve impairment . . . Would to God it were spring, for then I'd certainly head for home. (Letter to Beyer, January 21, 1886.)

concerts in the space of just one month. Two of these—on November 23 and 27—were evening programs consisting entirely of his own compositions. A "glorious concert" took place December 10 at the Concert Society. Both Gade and Horneman took part as conductors; Grieg himself wielded the baton in *The Mountain Thrall,* in which the opera singer Niels J. Simonsen "[sang with] personal involvement and dramatic power! This was genuine!" Indeed, the work was so well received that it had to be repeated. Beyer, in Bergen, was kept continually informed about these successes.[2]

Grieg, meanwhile, was also busy reorchestrating the *Peer Gynt* music for the triumphant performance at the Dagmar Theater in Copenhagen in January, 1886 (discussed on p. 181): "In the cafe," he wrote to Beyer on January 5, "I am bombarded by copyists and music directors who grab the pages from me one by one as soon as I've completed them. And so we rehearse a little at a time." But the press of work and a too active social life began to take their toll on his health.[3] Nonetheless, he was still able to give his best when he played his piano concerto on January 30, with Johan Svendsen conducting and the entire Danish royal family in attendance. "Everything went well and made a tremendous hit," he wrote to Beyer the following week. He continued: "I have a feeling that Svendsen [who since 1883 had been the music director of the Royal Theater in Copenhagen] will end up in Oslo again; he is homesick for Oslo, and he'd like to have me there as well. We are together daily, and although I never really feel that I know him completely, I must say he is more amiable toward me than ever. He often nearly reveals his inner self, but then one suddenly bumps into a brick wall. Just between you and me, there is one thing that worries me—and I have said this in all candor to Svendsen himself: I am worried about *his art,* for his future as an artist. He has peculiarities of character which hinder the unfolding of his rich creative gifts. This hurts me so much that I could weep, for there is no one from whom I have expected greater things. I will not give up hope yet . . ."

Unfortunately, Grieg's fears were to come to pass, for Svendsen in fact did not compose anything of importance in the years to come.

Grieg's health problems at this time were caused in part by financial worries related to the financing of "Troldhaugen." On February 14 he mentioned to Ravnkilde that he had a desire to go to Rome: ". . . hardly a day goes by that we don't talk about it. But there are so many reasons not to do it. The travel money must be used for 'Troldhaugen' . . ." At the end of March Nina and he were to leave on a concert trip to Jutland: "The whole thing stinks for me—but, but, that damned Mammon!"

On February 12 he wrote to Dr. Abraham: "Believe me, to be obliged to give concerts in order to exist when one isn't well—that's not an especially pleasant life. You will no doubt reply that I don't really have to give concerts unless I want to, because I can take care of myself best by writing music. But a person can't compose all the time—I can't, in any case!"

A performing artist deserves his wage, however, and when someone in Berlin wanted to book him free of charge it made him furious: "If it were important to me that I perform in Berlin it would be a different matter—but it emphatically is not, and I wouldn't perform without an honorarium even if I

4. NINA'S SISTER IS BURIED

We went to Copenhagen because we didn't know that she was so near to death; but just as we arrived we learned that she had died. So we went back to attend the funeral, a strangely melancholy ceremony— with some of the realism that is characteristic of our rural funerals . . . And the little motherless children, lively and boisterous, dashing around and noisily slamming doors after themselves—in truth, it was startling and hardly appropriate to the mood we have been brought up to associate with such circumstances. But there is something natural and wholesome about it, which I can easily accept. (Letter to Beyer, April 9, 1886.)

5. GRIEG COMMITS A FAUX PAS

Norwegians find it difficult to understand a joke, and later in the evening he gave expression to his bad humor in a most unfortunate speech. At the dinner table old Hartmann proposed a toast to Grieg and his wife, and as always he gave a fine and elegant speech. Then it was Grieg's turn to respond. After a remark about the many fermatas [i.e., facsimiles thereof used as table decorations] that swarmed about like "bedbugs," he alluded to the Danes' propensity for fermatas, and thereupon took the occasion to say that he and many of his countrymen recalled the 400-year fermata which, politically, Norway had been obliged to endure under Denmark. General consternation! (L. B. Fabricius: *Traek af dansk musiklivs historie,* pp. 65–66.)

was invited to give a concert before God in heaven. Those fellows probably perceive me as a conservatory student who is hungry for recommendations— but I am not what they think, nor have I ever received such a demoralizing offer . . ." (Letter to Robert Henriques January 27, 1886.)

The Jutland tour in the middle of March brought in some money—2000 Danish kroner—and it did not prove to be the journey to a musical hinterland that Grieg had feared. In Aarhus he performed, among other things, selections for string orchestra from the *Peer Gynt* music and—as he wrote to Beyer—"got twenty-five men together who played so impeccably that we had to repeat the entire piece." No less than seven concerts were given in the space of two weeks—in Aalborg, Randers, Aarhus, Horsens, Vejle, and Ribe. Nina sang, Edvard played some of his own piano pieces, and they performed together as a piano duo. He summed up his impressions for Ravnkilde in a letter on April 20: "Despite being snowbound for six days in Aarhus, on the whole we had a good time on our Jutland tour. There were always many people, and they obviously were delighted over the music we gave them."

The tour kept them busy for the most part with "a load of comical details." It was a sad contrast, therefore, when upon their return to Copenhagen they learned that Nina's thirty-eight-year-old sister, Yelva Nommels, had died of tuberculosis at her home in Fyn.[4]

Grieg's poor health in the spring of 1886 tended to make him irritable, and his irascibility led on several occasions to behavior that the Danes must have found painful. In his book *Traek af dansk musiklivs historie* (From the History of Danish Music Life), L. B. Fabricius reports that Grieg's untoward conduct began with a concert in the Copenhagen Chamber Music Society, when according to the official records of the society he aroused a bit of ill will by some talks he gave. The climax came, unfortunately, at a large banquet given for Edvard and Nina by the Copenhagen music society "Fermaten" [The Fermata] in the Concert Palace on April 14. Thirty-four ladies and gentlemen were gathered to witness the distinguished composer being honored with a performance of a strange work for piano and orchestra which a large number of Danish composers had created together. It was entitled "From Norway to Norway," or "Around the World in Eighty Melodies"—an allusion to Jules Verne's famous novel, *Around the World in Eighty Days.*

The music of various lands was artfully interwoven with Grieg's. The journey went through Sweden, Denmark, Germany, France, Spain, and Italy; it continued, Fabricius reports, "through the Dark Continent [Africa], to the Canary Islands, up the Himalayas—from the summit of which sounded Grieg's *Oppe, oppe!*—across the Pacific ocean, which steadily became more and more pacific as in *Meeresstille* [in Danish this is a play on words meaning "more peaceful"], then the Pacific railroad through America and over Greenland back to Norway, where the orchestra played the Norwegian national anthem while Bendix struck up Grieg's piano concerto on the grand piano."

Irritated by this unceremonious use of his music, the honored guest committed a monumental faux pas: in his thank-you speech, he shocked his hosts by talking about "the 400-year Danish fermata" in Norwegian history when Norway was politically subject to the Danish crown.[5]

6. HOMESICKNESS CREATES MUSIC

Spring is spring, and birdsong is birdsong. Down here I have both in rich measure, and yet it is as though I had neither. And friends are friends, and I also have many of them here; but none of them understands, as you do, what it is that draws me toward the scenery of home. Because of that I also have the feeling that as far as I am concerned all those other people more or less fade into oblivion at this time. What do you say to a quiet morning in the boat, or out between the rocks and small islands! The other day I was so filled with this longing that it took the form of a quiet song of thanksgiving. There's nothing new in it, but it is genuine; and since it is basically nothing more than a letter to you, I'll include it here: [Then follows the score for "In My Native Country."]

If the setting for "Naesset" and "Troldhaugen" had been more expansive, the music would have been different. But I'm glad that setting is as it is, and this quiet joy about the fact that everything up there is just as it is—that is what is being expressed in this music. The colors are the soft colors of western Norway, but the heart of the piece was beating for you, old friend, as I was writing these notes. (Letter to Beyer, April 26, 1886.)

Jacob Fabricius was then to raise a toast to the great Danish musicians Hartmann, Gade, and Paulli, and Chr. Barnekow angrily urged him to repudiate Grieg's "at the very least—*tasteless* speech." The situation was hardly pleasant, but Fabricius handled it nicely. He sketched the history of Danish music and showed the significance it had had for the Norwegians. They, in turn, had delighted the Danes by using their music "as a stepping stone into the wider world." As the chairman of the Concert Society, he said, he had had abundant opportunity to experience this. He expressed the hope that Grieg, "as in the past, will continue to use us to try his wings before flying over the admiring world, and that he, as in the past, will settle down among us for the winter months and enjoy it in spite of our shortcomings, and that he will join all of us in a resounding 'hurrah' for our great triumvirate: Hartmann, Gade, and Paulli."

Spring-like piano pieces and summer-like songs

There was little opportunity for composing during this stay in Denmark. On March 6, 1886, Grieg noted in a letter to Beyer that he was never able to work without interruption in his apartment. For that reason he had borrowed a back room from Robert Henriques's father "where, accordingly, I sit and work. Unfortunately, however, there's no possibility of working in the true sense of the word; my health just isn't up to it." He managed, nonetheless, to produce two little gems for the piano. One of them exists in two versions. The earlier version is dated April 16 and is called "Butterfly," a title that probably was given to it the following summer when the piece was included as No. 1 in Grieg's third collection of *Lyric Pieces*, Opus 43. On May 10 he presented Clara Winding with a new version which he then called "Windingiana (Album Leaf)".

The other piece, "In My Native Country" (Opus 43, No. 3), he enclosed with a letter to Beyer dated April 26. In this letter Grieg described in lyric terms how the thought of "Troldhaugen" and of Beyer himself had been the inspiration for the piece.[6]

On May 19 Grieg went back to his home in Norway where, in June-July, he completed the volume of new piano compositions that he had begun in Denmark. The melodic quality of Opus 43 is uniformly excellent, and the harmonic palette is sparkling and imaginative. Because of these qualities, Opus 43 ranks with Opus 54 as the finest and most successful of his *Lyric Pieces*.

In a July 23 letter to Dr. Abraham, Grieg characterized Opus 43 as a collection of "spring songs." It is just this feeling of spring in connection with nature and emotion that marks this music, particularly in the last piece, "To Spring." This tone painting is the very essence of a lyricist's tribute to the coming spring. Several of the other pieces can also be perceived as spring-like declarations of love—for Nature's harbingers ("Butterfly" and "Little Bird"), for his friendship with Beyer ("In my Native Country"), and for Nina ("Erotikon").

The two pieces written in Copenhagen are marked by longing; it is possible that the moody "Solitary Traveller," which is a kind of musical self-portrait, was written there as well. Such a supposition is supported by the fact that the melody in the opening section is borrowed from an earlier song—also written in Copenhagen—entitled "Thanks," Opus 10, No. 1 (see the musical excerpt on p. 53).

Opus 43 shows Grieg's mastery of concentration, his ability to create sophistication within simplicity, and his gift for uniting details into a fully developed whole. To illustrate these characteristics we have chosen to look more closely at one of the pieces, "Little Bird." Its original inspiration probably is indicated in the following extract from his April 26 letter to Beyer: "It is sad to have property and not be able to be home early in the spring, for that is when one gets fresh new ideas. Oh, the birds' nests that I have forgotten! It is exasperating because now it is too late. If only some of those little creatures would come and stay with us! For I tell you truly, I need surroundings that can bring a little cheer into the everyday cares! I can't write music about this need, for no matter what I write I can't seem to give wings to longing."

Nina and Edvard in the latter part of the 1880's. (Photo collection of Det Kongelige Bibliotek, Copenhagen)

With consummate skill Grieg, in the opening measures, paints a musical picture of these hopping and singing "little creatures" whose "chirp-chirp-chirp" is clearly the source of the first motive:

The first four measures are then developed, with an increase of tension and a modulation to the dominant (A minor). After a repetition of this *A* section follows the contrasting section (*B*) in A Phrygian with an inserted non-functional passage that descends chromatically. The *B* section is succeeded by a varied repeat of *A,* with a cadence in the home key (D minor). An eight-measure coda begins in D Phrygian with an allusion to the opening of the *B* section.

The melodic, rhythmic, and harmonic core motives introduced in the first eight measures constitute the material for the entire piece. As it progresses, this motivic material is developed and constantly modified in a way that is both logical and natural. The result is a piece of just thirty-six measures that stands out as a masterpiece of musical cogency. This is greatness in smallness!

This piece can be viewed as an approximation of a sonata movement, with *B* serving as the development. Some of Grieg's other compositions (e.g., *Humoresques,* Opus 6, No. 4; "To Spring," Opus 43, No. 6; and "Puck," Opus 71, No. 3) are similar in their construction. Brahms also used this model from time to time—for example, in the two rhapsodies of Opus 79.

*View from Eidfjord, where Grieg and Drach-
mann visited the painter Nils Bergslien at his
farm in July of 1886. Drachmann wrote poems
in honor of both Bergslien's wife Johanne and
his daughter Ragna. Grieg set these poems in
Opus 44. (The picture postcard dates from the
late nineteenth century.)*

7. AN UNFINISHED REQUIEM

In 1886 Holger Drachmann was a guest at "Troldhaugen" for a couple of weeks. Then the days and the light summer nights merged into one another, filled with high spirits and, of course, with a good deal of partying. Plans were made for a joint project, a Requiem. In order that they not disturb each other, Drachmann spent the forenoons at "Naesset" while Grieg worked at home. A blotter on which the introduction to the Requiem had been written down was preserved at "Naesset" for a long time:

I see it rising slowly, slowly
Through the still air, like wisps of smoke;
Thus toward perfection's glorious day
Mankind doth strain beneath his yoke.
Sometimes, sometimes there is no movement,
Mankind bows down, surrenders, dies.
O man, O man, look all around you,
Like shipwrecked men, lift now your eyes.

Whether Drachmann ever got further than this first verse, I don't know. (From Marie Beyer's unpublished manuscript in the State Archive, Oslo.)

8. GRIEG ON THE "PROLOGUE" AND "EPILOGUE" OF THE DRACHMANN SONGS

I regard the "Prologue" as one of my best songs. But the daring poem must, if possible, be declaimed in its original language if it is to be fully realized. The "Epilogue" fails because of the banal phrase "Auf der Alm, da gibt's 'ka' Sünd." Drachmann sang this phrase for me as he had heard it sung in the Tyrol, and in a way he obligated me to use it. Perhaps I will *eliminate* it in any future edition. (Letter to Finck, July 17, 1900.)

Opus 43 was among the piano works that Grieg himself liked to perform in public. As a matter of fact, a 1906 recording of him playing "Butterfly" and "Little Bird" is still in existence. It provides a charming glimpse into the Romantic style of playing—a style in which one is not afraid of spontaneity and personal expression, as evidenced by the marked use of rubato.

At the beginning of July the Danish poet Holger Drachmann paid Grieg a visit. Marie Beyer has written about their jovial time together and also about a Requiem that they began but never completed.[7]

From "Troldhaugen" Grieg and Drachmann went first to Hardanger (Eidfjord and Lofthus), where they stayed for a short time, then up to a cottage called "Tvindehaugen" in the Jotunheimen mountains. On July 30 Grieg sent a postcard to Beyer in which he reported that they had just climbed Mt. Skinneggen, "but unfortunately, it was overcast and many of the peaks were lost in the clouds. But I was enchanted and so was Drachmann . . . Have had an unbelievably glorious trip with Dr[achmann]. Have become positively young again! And a new zest for work!!"

In an August 18 letter to Röntgen, Grieg wrote that on the trip "the brilliant lyricist wrote poems like a man possessed, which I set to music." On September 3 he told a bit more about this in a letter to Winding: "For once life was the way it ought to be. He is quite a character, this Drachmann of yours. There is something of the troubadour or minnesinger—or whatever one should call it—about him, and he seems like such a queer duck against the background of our age that is so preoccupied with 'reality.' In the poems he wrote for me I got him to be brief—which, as you know, he often is not."

The first fruit of the collaboration between the two artists was the song cycle *Reminiscences from Mountain and Fjord*, Opus 44. Here Drachmann portrayed four young girls and women to whom he had been attracted on the trip, and he surrounded these portraits with poems that have something to do with the Jotunheimen mountains: "Prologue" ("On Mt. Skinneggen") and "Epilogue" ("Farewell to Tvindehaugen").[8] Unfortunately, what he achieved is nothing more than a few disappointing pieces of "occasional" poetry. His powers of self-criticism must have been on a holiday when, for example, he allowed the following lines to stand:

Your breasts are glorious, Ingeborg,
Like glaciers white and bold—
But no poor mountain climber may
Those wondrous breasts behold . . .

As might be expected, Grieg's inspiration completely failed as a result. He sounds like a foreign tourist in his own country. The "Norwegian" traits, such as the *springar* color in "Ingeborg," this time sound strangely artificial. There is no fresh mountain water in his melodic veins in these songs. He does, however, have some harmonic surprises in store that perk things up a little. This is especially the case in "Prologue" and "Epilogue," which he tied together by giving them the same recitative-like style and by using the same strongly modal concluding cadence in both.

On August 19, after he had returned to Denmark, Drachmann sent Grieg a

9. DRACHMANN PROPOSES
A MOTTO FOR HIS NEW OPUS

"From Troldhaugen to Tvindehaugen," lyrical, musically collegial Gypsy band in three parts: 1. End, 2. Beginning, 3. Continuation, thereby signifying the work's undying, i.e., unending, character. (Letter to Grieg, August 19, 1886.)

10. GRIEG SEEKS BEYER'S
ADVICE REGARDING THE
DRACHMANN SONGS

There are several songs that I can't send off [to the publisher] because, in fact, I myself can't decide between two versions of the same song. Do you remember "Ragnhild"? I have completely redone it. Also "Christmas Snow" [Opus 49, No. 5]. There are also some things where my self-criticism says stop. And there is not a *single* person here except you—professional musician or amateur—whose judgment has any importance for me. (I hope this tiny bit of honey doesn't injure your stomach!) (Letter to Beyer, September 6, 1886.)

letter of thanks. The trip, he wrote, "has given me air in my lungs and under my wings . . . I've temporarily forgotten myself (the highest point one can reach in these flat parts)—I have felt nature's firm foundation under my feet . . . When I close my eyes, I dream of Ragna . . ." He also suggested to Grieg, half jokingly, a motto for the song cycle.[9]

Grieg himself was not satisfied with the work. On August 28 he wrote to Beyer, who was in Karlsbad, that the collection was finished; a week later, however, it appears that he had written a new version of "Ragnhild" and wanted to hear Beyer's opinion of it.[10] The cycle was published in Denmark in December, 1886.

The third violin sonata

Only two years separated Grieg's first two violin sonatas, but between the second and the third nearly twenty years elapsed. These two decades provided ample evidence of the unevenness of his creative work. We have watched him ascend to the highest peaks of artistic self-realization, but we have also seen him in periods of dark depression and gnawing doubt, the telltale signs of which were a decrease in productivity and the creation of uninspired compositions that lacked the creative spark to cause lifeless notes to blaze up into living works of art.

Grieg commonly used minor keys with flats when he wanted to express the grand, the dramatic, and the tragic. There is a line here that runs from his Beethoven-inspired C-minor symphony, through the conclusion of *Bergliot* in C minor, the *Ballade* in G minor, and the String Quartet in G minor, to the third—and last—violin sonata in C minor, Opus 45. All of these works, dissimilar as they are, have something in common: a profound, expressive intensity that positively tears at one's innermost being. That Grieg was aware of this with respect to the C-minor sonata is evident from an article in the Czechoslovakian periodical *Dalibor* of March 14, 1903. The article was written by the violinist Karel Hoffmann, who had met Grieg in Vienna in 1896 when they performed the work there together. Hoffmann wrote: "Grieg was very sick and wanted to be careful. I had two rehearsals with him at the hotel. We practiced his violin sonata, which I was to perform publicly for the first time in my life. He was an excellent pianist who, in spite of his nervousness and ill health, played with unusual passion, and he asked me to put all the intensity I could muster into the performance. He had only a few dynamic markings. He played the first movement in a wild allegro, and he wanted the lyrical sections to be done as expressively as possible . . ."

The C-minor sonata moves on a different plane than the earlier works. In the *Ballade* and the string quartet, Grieg was in the middle of a difficult struggle; he was a participant wrestling with the material and with himself. In the sonata there is a greater distance between him and his material. Thus he was able to give it a stronger stamp of classically balanced control than he was able to give the other works. The eagerness of youth, with its innate tendency to exaggerate, is gone. The deliberate emphasis on national elements has had

Grieg at Troldhaugen in 1887, shortly after he had written the C-minor sonata. This charcoal drawing by August Johannessen now hangs in the lobby of Grieghallen in Bergen.

to yield to an orientation toward "the wider horizon," as Grieg himself expressed it in a letter to Björnson. The sonata is dramatic, but it has a clarified and elevated tonal language that makes it one of the gems of violin literature.

Grieg wrote his sonata at about the same time that César Franck composed his A-major sonata, but three years before Brahms's D-minor sonata saw the light of day. Different as they are in many respects, all three have the same intensity of expression. The inspiration for the second movement was undoubtedly Johan Svendsen's *Romance,* Opus 26 (1881), which quickly became world famous. The two pieces have the same lyric quality and are constructed according to the same formal pattern.

Grieg's earlier chamber-music works had aroused interest not least because of their "Norwegianness"—the folk-like element that tickled the ears of people out in the wider world. That is not the case in the C-minor sonata. It has won international acclaim solely on the strength of its inner musical qualities. The purely folkloristic element is gone. What remains is typically Griegian.

The C-minor sonata was the last chamber-music composition that Grieg completed. It was written at "Troldhaugen" in the latter half of 1886. In a July 25 letter to Dr. Abraham, Grieg wrote: "I'm now under way with a chamber music work. Only the gods know when it will be finished, for I suffer the most unbelievable interruptions from foreign summer guests. Believe me, I am almost desperate. As you know, I have fled to Lofthus, but to no avail. July and August appear to be impossible months . . ."

The project went better after the trip to the mountains with Drachmann. Grieg wrote to John Paulsen from "Troldhaugen" on January 21, 1887, that for the moment he was on a "composition vacation." "I have just written a violin sonata," he continued, "which I shall now have the satisfaction of having lying in my desk until autumn before I shall hear it. For in the autumn I want to get away."

He played the sonata for Frants Beyer in the summer of 1887, but he wasn't completely satisfied with it. Some small corrections were undertaken in Leipzig later in the autumn, and it appears that it was Johan Halvorsen who came to his assistance. Halvorsen was a pupil of Adolph Brodsky at this time. In an unpublished collection of materials preserved in the University of Oslo library, Halvorsen reports that Brodsky "created" the C-minor sonata, "but I was nonetheless the first one who played it. One day Grieg came to my room with the manuscript, and he wanted to hear how the violin part sounded. I think I was of some help to him at that time. We played the sonata through a couple of times, and I was completely enthralled by that beautiful work."

On November 22 Grieg wrote jubilantly to Beyer from Leipzig: "I've just returned from the home of Professor Brodsky, Halvorsen's teacher. We played the new violin sonata together—the one that you got such a poor impression of last summer. I was as disappointed then as you were, but tonight (albeit after changing the shortcomings) I experienced a joy that is seldom granted to an artist. He played *absolutely incomparably,* and was himself completely enthusiastic about my work. I assure you, I didn't recognize it. It was indeed what I had intended, but I just didn't think my intentions could be made real."

This frog was Grieg's mascot for many years. After Nina's death it was given to one of Grieg's Danish friends, Haagen Falkenfleth, editor of "Nationaltidende." It was later given to Dag Schjelderup-Ebbe who in turn presented it to Troldhaugen. It is said that Grieg always carried the frog with him when he gave public concerts, and that it was his custom to stroke it as he was mounting the podium.

On December 11, 1887—the day after the premiere in the Neues Gewandhaus in Leipzig—he was able to report to Beyer: "During the forenoon I had a fight with Brodsky, who wanted the top of the grand piano down. But I didn't give in; I kept it up and promised to play more softly. When he still wasn't satisfied I said, 'das ist ein norwegisches Versprechen!' [That is a Norwegian promise!] And then he believed me! And how he played! After each movement there was prolonged applause, and two curtain calls after the finale . . ."

It was a great success, even if *Signale*'s notorious critic Bernsdorf once again did his utmost to downgrade the composer. To be sure, he praised both Brodsky and Grieg for a performance marked by warmth and fervor. But the sonata itself, in his opinion, was seriously flawed: it lacked organic development, the harmony sounded contrived, and the composer's lack of talent was plain to see in the tastelessness and musical trickery with which the piece abounds! A review like that says more about the critic than about the composer. In any case, the C-minor sonata immediately became very popular. On March 21, 1887, Grieg wrote to Beyer: "Just think: the new violin sonata, which has been in print for only a few months, has already sold about 1500 copies. Dr. Abraham says that is unique, including even Brahms. He gave me 3000 marks for it, and 300 more for the *Peer Gynt Suite* [Opus 46]; and for a collection of *Lyric Pieces* [Opus 47] which is now ready, and for *In Autumn* [Op. 11]. I can undoubtedly expect enough to bring the total to a goodly sum . . ."

The first movement, Allegro molto ed appassionato, is without doubt Grieg's most successful use of sonata form. There are several reasons for this. The themes have an unusually strong appeal to both performer and listener, and they are easy to remember. In comparison with his earlier sonata movements, this one shows a much freer use of resources within a simple formal pattern. The coordination of the two instruments in both solo and ensemble passages is brilliant. The movement has a powerful expressive intensity. The smooth bridge passages between the various thematic groups, the concentrated development, and the daring but consummately controlled harmony are also striking.

Grieg begins with a principal theme in the violin that immediately establishes the dramatic intensity and soars upward on the G string in a series of typically Griegian sequences:

In his sonata movements Grieg often employed two secondary themes or a secondary theme and a closing theme. This is not the case here. Instead, the thematic material of the principal theme is expanded in such a way as to create two independent subjects. The second has a milder character than the first, but the suspense is constantly present. It starts on the open G string and, like the opening subject, rises steadily upward in flowing legato passages undergirded by tremolo chords in the piano:

The two principal subjects sound very different, but when one examines them carefully one discovers that they in fact spring from the same root. The second subject might be considered a simplified and rhythmically extended (augmented) version of the first one. This is clearly evident when they are placed one under the other:

When one says that these subjects "spring from the same root," it means that they have a common core, a common melodic "skeleton" that can be discerned in both. But this does not mean that they are immediately perceived as being related. In order to see the structural similarity one must be prepared for a certain amount of manipulation, especially rhythmical manipulation. In the example given above, the "common notes" of the two themes are placed one under the other. In that way the impression of an underlying unity is plain, even though the sound that one hears when the two subjects are played is somewhat different. Musicologists call this phenomenon a "metamorphosis." It is usually impossible to determine in a given case whether the composer was aware that what he had written was a transformation of musical material used earlier.

After an uncomplicated modulatory bridge, the melodious secondary theme enters in E-flat major. It is a theme of surpassing beauty. Especially effective is the so-called mediant shift from E-flat major to G-flat major in measure 12 of the following example, where the theme, with no bridge of any kind, is simply transposed up a minor third. One often finds this sequence—melodic rhyme—in Grieg's music:

The lyric stamp is indisputable, but the piano's syncopated after-beats nonetheless give the theme a certain restless character. It is also interesting to note that the first motive of the theme has a strong similarity to the beginning of the trio of the "Homage March" from *Sigurd Jorsalfar* (which was inserted in the revision of 1892). In this case the similarity is readily apparent: the two themes have similar tempos and note values, and they also appear for the most part without melodic "camouflage":

The development is something virtually unique in Grieg's music. It begins quite unexpectedly—in broad augmentation—in pianissimo with a completely altered version of the first motive in the principal theme. The key is changed from C minor to B-flat major, and the register is raised by more than two octaves. The original dramatic two-measure motive has been transformed and expanded to a full twelve measures. The heavy piano chords have been replaced with harp-like arpeggios that give to the whole an almost luminous radiance. The expressive effect is also strengthened by the typically Griegian chromatic bass line:

After an intense four-measure outburst, Grieg now repeats the preceding section a semitone lower, in A major. Then the drama recommences with a sophisticated use of motives from the principal theme section as well as small rhythmic elements from the secondary theme. Toward the close of the development there is a series of powerful outbursts, but the decisive climax—the real release of tension—is reserved for the re-entry of the principal theme in the recapitulation.

The beginning of the coda is of singular effect. Here we get the feeling that there is going to be a new development section, for suddenly the augmented motive from the principal theme returns—this time in A-flat major, which is to say a semitone lower than before. For eighteen measures it proceeds just as in the two earlier occurrences, but then it breaks off abruptly; it is not the ethereal world of sound that is going to triumph but, rather, the more somber world. The movement ends in a strange but infinitely beautiful C-minor cadence in the lower range. There are some harsh dissonances, and we sense a certain ambiguity about the tonality; but the note C is repeated throughout and gives unity to the whole—with some help from the bass line, which struggles toward the tonic. A drama in sound is brought to its conclusion:

The second movement, Allegretto espressivo alla Romanza, is one of Grieg's loveliest tone paintings, equal to both the adagio movement of the *A-minor Concerto* and the second movement of the string quartet (with which it shares the same title, "Romanze"). Both listener and performer experience a kind of elevation of the soul upon being ushered into this world of beauty. A verbal description scarcely touches the fringes of the musical experience itself.

The structure of the movement is *ABA'*. Grieg had a special liking for this uncomplicated formal pattern, and in his most inspired moments—as in this case—he used it to unite the various elements into a harmonious whole. The outer sections with their fully developed and large melodic span are in a radiant E major, while the succinct midsection is in E minor. The contrast between the solemn C minor of the first movement and the luminous E major of the second movement is tremendous, for the keys have very few notes in common. Such a tonal contrast does not appear elsewhere in Grieg's chamber music. A similar relationship exists between the first two movements of the piano concerto, however: A minor and D-flat major.

The theme of the *A* section is introduced by the piano, which was also the case in the slow movement of the G-major sonata. This time, however, the theme is spun out in a broad melodic arch of forty-four measures. Once again, as in the first movement, we find an extended use of the melodic rhyme wherein a number of four-measure phrases are shifted about in a highly artistic way.

The first seventeen measures of the movement are reproduced below. They reveal Grieg's melodic gift in one of its richest moments, and at the same time they show how naturally he creates, out of relatively simple elements, an infinitely beautiful framework of sound surrounding the expressive melody. This is Grieg's distinctive, wonderful world of harmony:

The melodic material is repeated by the violin while the piano has a purely accompanying role. The *B* section then follows with a radical change of mood: it becomes insistent, almost aggressive, not least because of the syncopation in the piano part:

The bridge from *B* to *A'* is one of the summits in Grieg's harmony, a marvelous realm of distinctive sonorities:

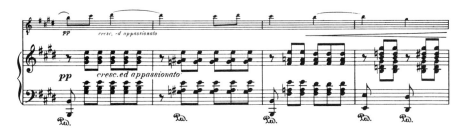

Even within the context of Grieg's richly faceted harmony, this bridge section is unusually luxuriant and imaginative. The chord progressions are logical according to the principles of functional analysis, but unfortunately a rather complicated analytical terminology is needed to explain this passage.

At the beginning of the excerpt we move from E minor to C minor, but without a single C-minor triad appearing. There is a continual intervallic tension in the passage, with descending chromaticism in the bass, rising chromaticism in the inner voices, an inner pedal point (D–F) in the piano right hand, and ascending chromaticism in the violin (with enharmonic changes in relation to the notation in the piano part). The dominant seventh chord in C minor is reached in measure 6 of the example.

This chord (G–B–D–F), with the help of a so-called tritone substitution, is reinterpreted as a secondary dominant ninth chord in B major, with the implied root (C-sharp) omitted and with a lowered fifth (G) in the bass and a minor ninth (D). Thus the chord has the notes E-sharp (= F)–G–B–D (with G in the bass). It is followed (in measure 7) by a suspension chord on B with the fifth (F-sharp) in the bass; this chord, according to standard practice, should lead to an F-sharp major chord in root position. Here Grieg gives us his first surprise: the suspension chord has an added minor seventh (A), with the result that the chord is construed as the second inversion of the dominant seventh chord in E major. Thus Grieg deftly skips over the expected F-sharp major chord to an ordinary dominant seventh chord in E major in measures 9–10.

But then comes a new and surprising twist. Instead of E major, which our ears are now expecting, we get something completely different: the dominant seventh chord in E major is reinterpreted as a secondary dominant ninth chord in E-flat major—parallel with what we previously observed in measure 6. (B = C-flat, the lowered fifth of the chord, in the bass; D-sharp = E-flat, the seventh; F-sharp = G-flat, the minor ninth; the root of the chord [F] is omitted.) The chord that follows is not, therefore, the E-major tonic that we expect but rather something quite unexpected: a six-four chord in E-flat major, with the fifth (B-flat) in the bass, and with a violin melody in E-flat major in a high register. This is a most colorful turn, and it is one which our ear quickly approves despite the fact that it seems to occur "without warning." That this sequence sounds right notwithstanding its somewhat unorthodox character is due to the inherent functional logic of the harmonic progression as explained above.

In the last measure of the third system there occurs another tritone substitution, but this time Grieg goes in the opposite direction: the dominant seventh chord on C is reinterpreted as the secondary dominant in E major, an incomplete ninth chord on F-sharp, with a minor ninth (G), and with a lowered fifth in the bass. This is then followed by an ordinary resolution to a six-four chord in E major.

The appearance of contrast between *A* and *B* is so marked that these sections seem almost to represent two completely different musical spheres. Nevertheless, there is a thematic connection between them that perhaps is not easily perceived on first acquaintance. As a matter of fact, there is an even clearer relationship between the *A* theme in this movement and the *B* theme in the second movement of the G-major violin sonata. When all three themes are set side by side, their mutual affinity becomes quite evident:

Opus 13, second movement, beginning of *B* section:

Opus 45, second movement, beginning of *A* section:

Opus 45, second movement, beginning of *B* section (transposed):

We don't know whether or not these thematic relationships were intentional on Grieg's part, but the similarity is definitely there. Consciously or subconsciously, the basic pattern must have been in Grieg's mind. And a remarkable thing happens: a common basis in no way prevents the composer from working out his melodic ideas in such a way that the contrast between the *A* and *B* subjects becomes considerable. This obviously is also due in part to their great difference in tempo. What keeps the movement from becoming utterly disjointed, however, is just this common point of departure. Diversity is created out of unity; it is thus that the mark of wholeness is preserved. This appears to be a musical law with wide validity.

In the third movement, Allegro animato, we are abruptly brought back to the basic mood of the first movement. The ethereal world of sound that prevailed at the end of the second movement is swept away by a rhythmically pregnant subject in C minor that is introduced by the violin in its low register accompanied by broken chords (open fifths) in the piano:

A kind of echo effect occurs in measure 6 in the piano's left hand, and thereafter the motives are thrown from one instrument to the other, like a mischievous question-and-answer game. A surprising harmonic twist occurs in measure 93: a dominant seventh chord in the home key, which one expects to be followed by a tonic triad, is succeeded instead by an E-minor chord, and the subject itself appears in E Dorian. This little aberration continues for eight measures before C minor again reasserts itself and brings the principal theme section to a close. Impudent little harmonic twists such as this do much to add color to the music.

After a pause in measure 112 comes a strong secondary theme that completely alters the character of the music:

This firmly chiseled material, which starts out in A-flat major, takes the form of a broadly spun-out melody in which the motives move higher and higher and the dynamic tension steadily increases from the first note to the last.

After the secondary theme has been stated one would expect a development as in normal sonata form. Grieg surprises us, however: he skips the development and returns immediately to the principal theme in C minor as in a conventional recapitulation. Then follows the secondary theme, now transposed to a triumphant C major, accompanied by rippling harp-like chords in the piano.

The triumphant mood is strengthened in the coda, for here the original, dark C-minor subject is transformed into a jubilant, prestissimo C-major passage. The violin and piano seem almost to be chasing each other toward the goal.

The structure of this movement is the simplest Grieg ever employed in the finale of a larger work. It is *AB-AB'* plus a coda; but as we have already intimated one could, paradoxically enough, equally well describe it as a sonata movement without a development. That Grieg chose to omit the development undoubtedly is related to the fact that both thematic sections are in themselves so rich in variation and motivic exploitation that further development would only have made the movement unbalanced.

Grieg's last sonata is a stirring work, his personal *per aspera ad astra*.

After finishing the C-minor sonata in the summer of 1887, Grieg turned his attention to the scaling of peaks of a different kind—those provided by Norway's rugged mountains. In an October 17 letter to Ravnkilde he recalled some memorable experiences hiking in the Sogn mountains: ". . . my beloved Jotunheimen, where for two weeks every summer, together with my noble friend Frants Beyer, I bathe myself in that which is timeless. Yes, here one stands face to face with greatness: it is Shakespeare, Beethoven, and every genius you could want all rolled up in one! I would not trade this for a dozen Gewandhaus concerts. I must tell you about something that happened one marvelous, sunny August day right between the Skagastöl peaks. We wanted to cross a ridge called Mt. Friken, but we couldn't get a mountain guide . . . Then two very pretty milkmaids appeared from the summer farm in the mountain—one an older girl and the other a young blond girl named Susanne. They offered to show us the way. Laughing and singing we headed up

The Skagastöl Peaks as seen from Turtagrö. The tourist lodge in the foreground was often the starting point for Grieg's walks in the Jotunheimen mountains. In an August 11, 1890 letter to Frederick Delius he called this place "the threshold to the holy of holies." (Universitetsbiblioteket of Bergen, Norway)

the mountain, and when we got to the top we sat down and enjoyed whatever our knapsacks had to offer us. Cognac and ice-cold glacier water raised the mood of the party to absolutely ethereal heights. But the most beautiful part was still to come, for Susanne had with her a small, national instrument—a goat horn that sounds only *three* notes; and when the girls had bid us farewell up there at the top of the mountain (because now they had to go down again to milk the cows), and as Frants and I just stood there absorbed by the beautiful sight as we watched them hiking along the mountain's edge, blond, slender, and erect, with the blue horizon as background—suddenly they stopped, Susanne put the goat horn to her mouth—I will never forget the picture, their silhouette against the luminous summer sky: then we heard a gentle, melancholy sound, as if from the mountains surrounding us:

When that final G died away in the distance, we looked at each other—and we were both in tears! For we had felt the same!"

Experiences like these were overwhelming; they further deepened the friendship between Grieg and Beyer and made the pulsating artistic life of Europe seem infinitely distant and unimportant. Nevertheless, it was toward the European milieu with its "satin gloves" that Grieg would soon set his course.

Toward a Cosmopolitan Outlook

I. A NEW ZEST FOR LIFE

It is a long time since life has been so bright and good for me as at this time. I am well again, better than I have been at any time here in Karlsbad . . . And what is obviously of greatest importance: Nina is healthier and more lighthearted than at home . . .

I am negotiating about three concerts in Vienna . . . My fingers itch to get hold of a conductor's baton. I am also in discussion with Amsterdam and Berlin, but everything is uncertain at the moment . . . I long for Leipzig—its art and its artists—more than I can say. (Letter to Beyer, October 8, 1887.)

By autumn of 1887, two and a half years had elapsed since Grieg had been outside Scandinavia, and he again felt drawn toward the great metropolitan centers of music. In the next two years he was to expend a considerable amount of effort in behalf of his own music in such places as Leipzig, London, Birmingham, Berlin, and Paris. During this period and until the spring of 1890, he stayed abroad for twenty-one months and was at home for only nine.

Great successes on the continent

At the beginning of September Grieg left "Troldhaugen" for Germany. After a brief stay in Leipzig he arrived at the Karlsbad Spa in Bohemia, which he had visited on two previous occasions. Here he revised and reorchestrated his early concert overture, *In Autumn*, Opus 11, which was published by Peters a year later. The pause for "the Karlsbad cure" gave both him and Nina new strength, and he looked more cheerfully on life than he had for a long time.[1]

From the middle of October he spent a half year in Leipzig, where he became the dynamic center of a circle of Norwegian and foreign colleagues. He was also stimulated by his many successes as a composer.

Things were not especially promising at the beginning, however. On October 31 he wrote Beyer that he had just "sneaked away" after the first half of a concert in which his F-major violin sonata had been "very musically played by a sweet little twelve- or thirteen-year-old English girl accompanied by a teacher from the conservatory, Herr Rehberg, who played in such a way as to remind one of a train. Yes, it is surprising, but soon we will not look for music among musicians! It is becoming something else, a kind of sport for which I know no name!"

Grieg himself took up a more exhilarating sport. On November 22 he wrote Beyer: "I have thrown myself into gymnastics in earnest, and after 14 days I am no longer the same man. Zest for life, power, energy—everything is coming back. Why? Because the body gains resiliency and buoyancy . . . My outings are gymnastics in my bedroom! The other day I weighed myself: forty-seven and a half kilos [104 pounds]! Lighter than ever before!"

2. THE BRODSKY QUARTET PLAYS GRIEG

Since you are touching the very cockles of my heart, let me continue in the same vein and tell you about the quartet—this strange piece of music which I almost call a composition by both of us! . . . It was played extremely well, passionately, and in heroic style, albeit in my opinion sometimes at the expense of beauty of sound. After each movement there was loud applause . . . Then when the performers and I came forward, a couple of loud hisses mingled with the applause, almost like whistles. It almost took my breath away. It was Bernsdorf and a couple of his cronies. But it didn't do any harm. On the contrary, it increased the applause of their opponents—which fortunately included almost the entire audience. (Letter to Beyer, February 20, 1888.)

3. TCHAIKOVSKY MEETS GRIEG

As they were playing through Brahms's new trio, a man walked into the room—very small of stature, middle aged, extremely sickly in appearance, shoulders of uneven height, head covered with large, blond, tousled locks. His beard and moustache were most unusual . . . indeed, almost youthful. The facial features of this man, whose appearance for some reason immediately appealed to me, are not especially noteworthy; one cannot call them either handsome or unusual. But on the other hand, he has unusually attractive, medium-sized, sky-blue eyes of irresistibly charming character, eyes that remind one of an innocent, adorable child. I was glad in the very depths of my soul when, upon being introduced to each other, it was revealed that the bearer of this inexplicably attractive exterior was a musician whose deeply felt music had long since secured for him a place in my heart. It was Edvard Grieg.

4. TCHAIKOVSKY ON GRIEG'S MUSIC

Perhaps Grieg's mastery is a good deal less than that of Brahms, the development in his music less elevated, the aspiration and goal less broadly conceived. A subconscious striving toward the unfathomable depths seems to be entirely lacking. But on the other hand, he is closer to us, he is more understandable and kindred precisely be-

The first of Grieg's concert successes during this period occurred in Leipzig on December 10, 1887, when he joined Adolph Brodsky in the premiere of his *Sonata in C Minor* for violin and piano (see p. 277). He celebrated new triumphs on February 18 and 19 of the following year when the Brodsky quartet played his *String Quartet in G Minor.*[2]

There were two Norwegian musicians in Leipzig with whom Grieg associated at this time: Christian Sinding and Johan Halvorsen. The British composer, Frederick Delius, also became a close friend. He was called "The Hardanger Plateau Man" in this circle of friends: "Delius is 'Norway crazy' and has been to Norway four times, staying out on the Hardanger Plateau for fifteen days at a time and things like that," Grieg wrote Beyer following a lively Christmas Eve party in 1887. "What a Christmas Eve!" he continued. "If you had been with us you would have said you had never experienced one more beautiful and interesting."

A New Year's party at Brodsky's became an event in music history—a meeting of three princes of the Kingdom of Art: Brahms, Tchaikovsky, and Grieg. Tchaikovsky's impressions of Grieg and his music are cited in the Primary Materials.[3,4] There is also another and quite delightful account of this party. In *Recollections of a Russian Home* Anna Brodsky wrote: "We went to the table. Nina Grieg was seated between Brahms and Tchaikovsky, but we had scarcely sat down when she jumped up and cried: 'I can't sit between these two. I get so nervous.' Grieg stood up and said: 'But I can.' So the two exchanged places, and the three composers sat together in the best of spirits. I can see Brahms picking up a bowl of strawberry jam, saying that he wanted it for himself, and that no one else would get any. It resembled a children's party more than a gathering of great composers."

Four weeks later Grieg was again a guest at the Brodsky's, this time with Tchaikovsky, Sinding, Halvorsen, and others. On January 29 he wrote home excitedly to Beyer: "We made music the entire time. First, at Tchaikovsky's request I played my new sonata with Brodsky. Then Sinding's piano quintet was rehearsed with Sapelnikov, and lastly my string quartet. Those fellows can play! My God, how it sounded! Sinding's quintet is a large-scale work, at

cause he is so deeply human. When we hear Grieg we realize instinctively that this music was written by a man driven by an irresistible longing to give expression by means of sound to the stream of feelings and sentiments of a deeply poetical nature—without being a slave to a theory, to a principle, or to a banner hoisted aloft as a consequence of this or that accidental circumstance of life—but rather yielding to the prompting of a living, sincere artistic feeling. Perfect form, cogency, and faultless logic of thematic development we shall not find in the music of the renowned Norwegian (although the themes are always fresh and new, colored by the characteristic features of indigenous Teutonic-Scandinavian na-

tionalism). On the other hand, what enchantment, what spontaneity and richness in the musical inventiveness! What warmth and passion in his singing phrases, what a fountain of pulsating life in his harmonies, what originality and entrancing distinctiveness in his clever and piquant modulations, and in the rhythm as in everything else— how endlessly interesting, new, original! (From Tchaikovsky's "Autobiographical Account of a Foreign Journey in 1888," quoted in translation from Jon-Roar Bjørkvold's "Peter Tchaikovsky og Edvard Grieg—En kontakt mellom to aardsfrender" [Peter Tchaikovsky and Edvard Grieg—A Meeting of Two Kindred Spirits].)

*Photograph that Grieg dedicated to Tchaikov-
sky February 1, 1888, with the words, "From
your ardent admirer."*

times too garish, even brutal (which Sinding considers a merit!), but of great,
rare power. In Tchaikovsky I have gained a warm friend for my music. He has
as much affection for me as I have for him, both as an artist and as a human
being. You will learn to know him because he undoubtedly will come to
'Troldhaugen.' Just think that d'Albert has promised to play my concerto at
the [Scandinavian] Music Festival [in Copenhagen] this summer! . . . He is a
wonderfully gifted artist."

It was undoubtedly in this connection that Tchaikovsky ventured the often
quoted opinion of Sinding's quintet: "I have allowed myself much in my
time, but never anything like this!"

Earlier in January Grieg had been on a four-day trip to Berlin, and in
February he returned for another short visit. The Belgian singer Désirée Artôt
had sent him a telegram inviting him to a supper to which Tchaikovsky had
also been invited. He went immediately. "That was a very strange evening. A
big party, including many of the musical elite," he wrote to Beyer on February 13. "Later there was dancing, and from the fact that Mademoiselle Artôt

5. ANXIETY ABOUT THE LONDON CONCERTS

Since the first of February I have been practicing the piano for several hours a day so that I won't disgrace myself in London. I regret terribly that I have promised to play my piano concerto, but I have given my word and I can't go back on it. (Letter to Beyer, February 13, 1888.)

* * *

If only I had this confounded England tour behind me. There is nothing to gain, and I will lose a good part of my health. I feel more and more that I can't give my best by running around and playing for people, and it isn't going to happen again either. Chamber music and small pieces don't bother me, but when I have to use a sledge hammer on the piano I can't achieve the intended effect, and I only destroy myself. (Letter to Beyer, March 21, 1888.)

* * *

I'm not looking forward to the trip, that's for sure, and I have a sort of dark premonition that something will happen that is not good. Everything within me draws me homeward, and absolutely nothing draws me to England—for that damned "pound sterling consciousness" is no feeling at all. I have considered committing some stupidity or other to be rid of the whole thing—but once before I said that I was sick, so that won't work again, and I don't know any other way out. The "Hardanger Plateau Man" [Delius] suggested that I say an old aunt of mine has died! That's like him! (Letter to Beyer, April 12, 1888.)

suddenly grabbed me and pulled me out towards the dance floor you can readily understand that there was a carnival atmosphere! . . . She wanted to dance the polka and I the galop, so the net result was some truly ludicrous movements . . . Her figure defies description. She sang some inferior music—but she sang it all ravishingly. The next evening we attended Tchaikovsky's concert, and then we were at a big dinner with him at a restaurant. The next morning we came here again and had the feeling of having read a fairy tale."

On March 21 Halvorsen went to Aberdeen, where he had become concertmaster, and Grieg wrote jokingly to Beyer that he had instructed the young musician to find a sweet little Grieg girl over there to be his wife: "Those relatives of mine who stayed in Scotland naturally have reproduced to their heart's content, so it isn't impossible that I will see Halvorsen and a Scottish Miss Grieg paying a visit to 'Troldhaugen' one beautiful summer day." Grieg's light-hearted comment was to come true, but in a slightly different way: in 1894 Halvorsen actually married a Miss Grieg, Edvard's niece Annie, the daughter of his brother John.

Some plans for concerts in Vienna unfortunately did not work out. Instead, he began making plans for a trip to London. As the time of his departure approached, however, Grieg became more and more concerned about how things would go.[5] On March 2 Tchaikovsky wrote from Paris that he had telegraphed to London proposing that he "should appear together with *my friend Grieg*" at his big concert March 22. But Grieg felt that the proposal for such an appearance came on too short a notice, so he declined the flattering offer.

During this time Grieg completed the four-part *Peer Gynt Suite No. 1*, Opus 46. With this work, which Peters printed immediately, the publisher certainly acquired a small gold mine. The honorarium was three thousand marks, and on March 21 Grieg wrote Beyer that he could also count on "a good return for a volume of lyric pieces now ready." The reference here is to Opus 47, published in autumn of the same year. "Springar," No. 6 in the set, had appeared in January, 1885, in the Oslo *Nordisk Musik-Tidende;* sketches for

Christian Sinding in the latter part of the 1880's. (Photo collection of Universitetsbiblioteket in Oslo)

"Album Leaf" (No. 2) and "Waltz-Impromptu" (No. 1) are respectively dated June 29 and September 1, 1887.

Opus 47 marks a decidedly backward step when compared with Opus 43. Melodic and harmonic vitality have become more lackluster, especially in the two weakest pieces, "Album Leaf" and "Melancholy." In "Melody" and "Elegy," however, and especially in "Waltz-Impromptu," one encounters a handling of sound which is more worthy of the composer. Grieg's individuality comes to the fore best in the two stylized dances, "Halling" and "Springar."

Grieg seems to have had no problems at all with finances at this time. Quite the opposite. On April 20 he sent Beyer 9000 marks in Prussian bonds for deposit.

Frederick Delius, whom Grieg described as "a talented and up-to-date musician." While in London in the spring of 1888, Grieg persuaded Delius's father to allow Frederick to devote himself completely to composing.

Three days later he arrived in London with Nina and Dr. Abraham. Here they were lodged as guests of Peters's British agent, the well-known music publisher George Augener.

Stage fright increased as the time for the concert series approached. According to Nina, Grieg was completely out of sorts, was annoyed by everybody and everything, and vowed that "he would never come to London again." But seldom was he so wrong.

The opening concert on May 3 with the orchestra of the Royal Philharmonic Society was one of his greatest triumphs. Beaming with joy, he was able to telegraph home to Beyer, "Yesterday magnificent. Joyful, boundless acceptance. Colossal success. Conducted 'Last Spring' da capo." He was completely overwhelmed by the public's enthusiasm. When he stepped onto the podium in St. James's Hall he was met by an ovation that lasted more than three minutes!

Grieg was soloist in the *A-minor Concerto,* and to Beyer he wrote that it "went well enough so far as I was concerned. To be sure, my own performance does not come close to satisfying me; but it was all right nonetheless. It was best after I got warmed up." The orchestra under the direction of Frederick Cowan "left much to be desired. But believe me, I evened things up when I conducted the string orchestra [in "Last Spring" and "The Wounded Heart"]. What an orchestra: almost sixty string players, all of absolutely first-rank quality! . . . There were places where one could weep for joy, it sounded so wonderful. I had rehearsed the minutest details, and all the players vied to give their best, so the effect was altogether captivating . . . it was like a song of harmonies from ethereal heights."

The lengthy reviews of the concert in the London press the next day were exuberant. The *Times* called Grieg's interpretation of the *A-minor Concerto* a revelation: the composer had played it in his own way with excellent execution, both technically and intellectually. Regarding the *Two Elegiac Melodies* for string orchestra, the *Daily Telegraph* stated that one rarely heard more beautiful ensemble playing than that produced by the magic baton of Edvard Grieg.

The concert on May 16 was an evening of chamber music. Nina sang some songs, Grieg played a number of piano pieces, and he also accompanied violinist Wilhelmine Neruda in the F-major sonata and the last two move-

They have invited me to conduct in the
Philharmonic Society, and to contribute to
the "Monday Popular Concert" series with
my chamber music. I shall try this for one
time and, let us hope, never again. I would
rather be home, but "Troldhaugen"
urgently begs me for some pounds sterling!
(Letter to Delius, September 23, 1888.)

* * *

I *must* exert myself precisely because of
these pounds sterling. I certainly don't do it
for pleasure. It is completely stupid that I
have to do this, for I haven't the talent to
play in public. But conducting doesn't
bring me pounds sterling. (Letter to Delius, November 6, 1888.)

ments of the C-minor sonata. The concert exceeded all expectations. The
Times reviewer wrote that the poetry and indescribable charm of his playing of
such pieces as "In the Mountains" and "Bridal Procession" again impressed
the listeners in such a way that even those who knew them best felt as though
they had never heard them before, so full of individuality were the interpretations.

After a brief vacation on the Isle of Wight the Griegs returned to Copenhagen, where Edvard immediately began preparing for the first Scandinavian
Music Festival, a grand display of the best of Nordic music which was to be
held from June 3 to June 10. That became a huge gathering. The orchestra
numbered 106 musicians, and there was also an inter-Scandinavian choir of
554 voices, of which seventy were from Oslo (forty from the Music Association and thirty from the Student Male Chorus). The newly built concert hall
accommodated an audience of 2100, and during the intermissions people
fortified themselves with such things as "22 whole roasts of beef, 900 pounds
of fish, 8000 open-face sandwiches, and 7000 bottles of beer," according to
the restaurant ledger.

At the opening concert Grieg conducted his piano concerto, with Erika
Lie Nissen as soloist—not Eugene d'Albert, as had originally been planned.
Charles Kjerulf wrote in the Copenhagen daily *Politiken* that the *A-minor
Concerto* was unquestionably the high point of the evening.

At a Norwegian-only chamber music evening, Grieg accompanied Thorvald Lammers in some of his Vinje songs and played the C-minor sonata with
violinist Fr. Hilmer.

After the music festival Grieg left for "Troldhaugen," where he remained
until the middle of August. Then he set out once again, this time across the
North Sea enroute to Aberdeen and onward to a music festival in Birmingham. Here he observed once again how popular he and his music were in
England. On August 29 he conducted the *In Autumn* overture, and a day later
the *Holberg Suite*. The applause was tremendous.

The stay in Birmingham also came to mean something for him in another
way. It was here that he first came in contact with Unitarianism, whose
dogma-free religious outlook was very attractive to him. (See p. 380.)

Beyer had been with him on this tour, and after brief stops in London and
Copenhagen they were back in Bergen by the end of September. But new
tours were already being planned. Especially enticing was the thought of
earning some pounds sterling.[6] From Paris and Prague invitations had also
come which Grieg felt he could not refuse, and on Tchaikovsky's initiative he
was invited to Moscow and St. Petersburg as well. But it was not until 1903,
and again in 1906, that he visited Prague; and notwithstanding repeated
invitations, a Russian tour never materialized.

In the autumn of 1888 Grieg orchestrated the incidental music for *Olav
Trygvason*, which was published as Opus 50 in 1890. In a letter to Delius on
November 30, 1888, he was able to report some very pleasant news: "A few
days ago I was sent a gift—a wonderful piano from the Pleyel firm in Paris
which I don't know at all. The man must be out of his mind."

Nina and Edvard stayed at "Troldhaugen" until January 2, 1889, when they

7. ENTHUSIASTIC BERLIN REVIEWS

But of even greater account than this overture [*In Autumn*] was the orchestral suite, the incidental music for Ibsen's *Peer Gynt*. In these pieces poetry and form stand on the same level . . . The second piece, "The Death of Aase," is an important composition in every respect. The theme is extremely attractive and moving, the harmony remarkably original and pleasant to listen to. The effect was gripping and overwhelming. . . (*Berliner Tageblatt,* January 22, 1889.)

* * *

One's ear listens attentively to the harmonic subtleties which give the simplest melodies an original stamp. Everything seems to develop in an unforced and spontaneous way—an effect which in reality is a result of extensive study and a manifestation of one of the most sensitive talents of our time. (*Nationalzeitung,* January 22, 1889.)

"went by sleigh over the mountains in a terrible but magnificent snowstorm, arriving in Oslo six days later," as he reported to Delius in a letter on February 4. Here Grieg also told about his concerts with the Berlin Philharmonic on January 21 and 29: "The critics scolded, but on the whole the concerts were a great success. And I have become so blasé that the approval of an unbiased audience means more to me than all the critics put together, whether they commend or condemn!"

At the first concert he conducted, among other things, the *In Autumn* overture and the *Peer Gynt Suite No. 1.* At the second concert—"when the crowd was so great that *hundreds* had to go home"—the program included the *A-minor Concerto,* with Erika Lie Nissen as soloist again.

Grieg's statement that the critics "scolded" does not square with the facts, for the city's leading newspapers had many positive things to say about the concerts.[7]

Berlin was followed by a trip to Leipzig, but without concerts. From here on March 15 he sent Beyer 9000 German marks for deposit, a "small gold mine . . . naturally from the bosom of [Dr.] Abraham." The amount should be seen in relation to the contract he had signed with Peters in which he had assigned rights to all his works to the firm. Its highly favorable terms assured his financial security for the rest of his life.

On February 16 he set out once again for London, his third visit there in ten months. As in the previous year, he was invited to stay at Augener's. Concerts were scheduled one right after another: eight in five weeks. Nina, although somewhat indisposed following a serious illness, participated in the first of them on February 23. Grieg played his cello sonata with "the cellist who (just between us) is as boring as he is famous: [Alfredo] Piatti. That was torture for me," Grieg wrote Delius the day after the concert. But the enthusiasm of the audience was great and genuine.

On February 25 he performed the F-major violin sonata with Wilhelmine Neruda, who in the previous year had married the seventy-year-old German-English conductor Charles Hallé. "Thank God, she has fire and vitality," Grieg wrote. In Manchester on February 28 Grieg conducted the celebrated Hallé Orchestra. Hallé, who had been a student of Kalkbrenner, was soloist in the piano concerto. The program also included the *Two Elegiac Melodies,* and Grieg accompanied Nina in several of his songs.

There was a series of three chamber music concerts in London on March 9, 20, and 31. At the March 9 concert Grieg performed his second violin sonata with Joseph Joachim, and at the other two he performed in the third violin sonata. The soloist at the March 20 concert was the Belgian violinist Johannes Wolff, and on March 31 it was Wilhelmine Neruda. On these occasions he also played some of his piano compositions, and Nina appeared both as a singer in some of Edvard's songs and as a pianist together with her husband in the *Norwegian Dances* for piano four hands, Opus 35. G. B. Shaw was present at the last concert, and in a review in *The Star* written over his pseudonym "Corno di Bassetto" remarked wryly that the music reminded him of the style of Grieg's late great countryman, Ole Bull.

On March 14 Grieg conducted the Philharmonic Society in the *Peer Gynt Suite No.* and Nina sang five of his songs. Two weeks later, with Agathe Backer Gröndahl as soloist, he conducted the piano concerto with the same orchestra. For the first of these concerts Grieg had stipulated a fee of fifty pounds, but for the second he wrote the orchestra's secretary, F. Berger: "I would like to relinquish my honorarium as I desire to do everything in my power for my outstanding woman compatriot."

From the newspapers it seems that a veritable "Grieg fever" raged in London at this time. Grieg, much encouraged, went to Paris at the beginning of April. There he reached an agreement with Édouard Colonne, conductor and founder of the famous "Concerts du Chatelet," regarding some concerts to be given at the turn of the year. The trip home included a two-week stopover in Leipzig; then it was on to Bergen by way of Berlin and Copenhagen. By the middle of May (1889) he and Nina were back at "Troldhaugen."

At the end of July he went on a mountain tour over Laerdal to Lake Gjende in the Jotenheimen district with Sinding, Delius, and Augener.

Drawing from 1887. (Photo collection of Det Kongelige Bibliotek, Copenhagen)

Two new song collections

In October, 1889, Grieg declared in unusually strong terms that he had turned away from the purely national in order to achieve something broader (see further p. 332 ff.). In the two song sets that comprise Opuses 48 and 49—settings of German and Danish texts, respectively—we see the first evidences of the change. Grieg here made no attempt to give the music a Norwegian flavor; nonetheless these twelve songs, though of uneven quality, bear the stamp of his authorship.

The *Six Songs* of Opus 48, dedicated to Ellen Nordgren (Gulbranson), are clearly superior. Here Grieg chose fine poetic texts, and Nordahl Rolfsen's translations into Norwegian are excellent. Dates in the manuscripts show that the first two songs were written five years before the others (at Lofthus on September 16–17, 1884), while the last four were written on August 15–20, 1889.

For the first time since 1864 Grieg, in these songs, turned to German lyric poetry, but it was now the mature artist who entered the domain of the art song. He thought, and rightly so, that he had reaped enough experience to set his own stamp on this genre, which he did with respect to both melody and harmony.

Of exceptional charm, with the flavor of a German folk song and a simplicity becoming to fine art, is the melodic richness of "The Way of the World" and "The Nightingale's Secret." Small but exquisite strokes also mark "One Day, O Heart of Mine." The voice part is much more recitative-like than is usual with Grieg, while he attempts to enhance the text primarily by harmonic means. Elements of the church modes especially characterize the style, as Grieg here transfers them to a lyrical German Lied. This introspective song forms an interesting contrast to Hugo Wolf's much more radical interpretation of the same poem six years later in his *Spanisches Liederbuch* (No. 22). While Grieg limits himself to interpreting the passion and release in the text within the confines of a strophic form, Wolf has through-composed the song. Unlike Grieg, he assigns an active role to the accompaniment.

The other three songs in Opus 48 are almost Schumannesque in their chromaticism, but have a Griegian sound in the unexpected harmonic relations that are so characteristic of him. The most conventional is "Greeting," while "The Time of Roses" and especially "A Dream" show more distinctive contours. "A Dream" has rightly taken its place among Grieg's most popular love songs.

At the beginning of May, 1889, Grieg had also set "Easter Song" (CW 144), a minor German poem by A. Böttger, but he judged it unworthy of publication. Nonetheless, it was published by Peters fifteen years later. The text describes the Easter bells heralding the coming of spring, and Grieg tried consciously to imitate the sounds of bells in the accompaniment by means of clever chord progressions based on pedal-point effects and a series of open fifths. "Easter Song" is a preliminary exercise for the later impressionistic harmonic experiments in "Bell Ringing" (Opus 54, No. 6) and "In Ola Valley, in Ola Lake" (Opus 66, No. 14).

In the summer of 1889 Grieg was again attracted by the florid lyrics of Holger Drachmann. The result was *Six Songs,* Opus 49, dedicated to Thorvald Lammers. "Christmas Snow"—that beautiful poem, as Grieg called it—had been composed toward the end of August, 1886, and "Spring Showers" at the beginning of September, 1887. The remaining four were written July 2–5, 1889. Two other Drachmann songs also date from this time: "You Often Fix Your Gaze" (CW 145, dated July 4) and "A Simple Song" (CW 101, No. 3, undated). He did not allow either of them to be published during his lifetime, but the latter was published posthumously by Röntgen in 1908. These closely related songs are cast in a drawing-room style, and the musical substance is thin—melodically and rhythmically monotonous, and with trite chord progressions.

Opus 49 is exceptionally uneven in quality. "Christmas Snow," "Rocking, Rocking on Gentle Waves," and "Now Is Evening Light and Long" show a striking lack of stylistic unity. The melodic lines are dry and the composer's harmonic imagination clearly failed him as well.

Grieg sharpened his pen, however, for "Tell Me Now, Did You See the Lad" and "Kind Greetings, Fair Ladies"—two bravura songs of liveliest character, with attractive melodies and fresh rhythms and sounds. The first is perhaps a bit stereotyped and mannered, but the latter ranks among the most brilliant and resplendent in Norwegian art-song literature.

"Spring Showers" is in a class by itself. Here the poet has drawn a delicate little mood picture: "The branches, quivering, release a shower of silvery tones cascading on the pebbles." With a gentle touch Grieg has captured impressions of nature with successions of blurred dissonances. In this song the composer has moved to the borders of Impressionism and created a counterpart to the French musical "raindrop poetry." Here he has become truly cosmopolitan in the best sense of the word:

8. GRIEG CONDUCTS WITH A BROKEN BATON IN BRUSSELS

Everything was sold out, and as we had not been able to hold a rehearsal in the concert hall itself I was quite nervous when I made my entry. I was very warmly received, but when I was ready to start conducting there was no baton. Orchestra stage managers everywhere are idiots, so after a moment's waiting I had to leave the podium. Finally the brute came with a baton that was about as long as I am tall, but fortunately as thin as a reed. I did what you also would have done: under the furious glance and energetic protest of the stage manager, I broke a piece off and threw the rest in a corner, whereupon I went back to the podium and struck up the sound of the *In Autumn* overture. You won't find this in the reviews, so I give you this private account of the little episode. (Letter to Beyer, December 14, 1889.)

Fresh triumphs in the concert hall

In October Grieg was again in Oslo. He premiered the two new song collections in cooperation with Ellen Nordgren (Gulbranson) and Thorvald Lammers, and on the 19th the public had an opportunity to hear for the first time the incidental music for *Olav Trygvason,* with the composer conducting. But the greatest pleasure he had on this occasion was not the overwhelming public success (see further pp. 165–66); his greatest pleasure was that his friendship with Björnson was renewed after a lapse of twenty years. Three parties were given in Oslo in honor of Grieg. The first occurred at the Student Association on October 23. Here Grieg lifted a toast to Björnson, "Norway's beating heart," whereupon Björnson improvised a speech of thanks with characterizations of Kjerulf, Nordraak, and Grieg: Kjerulf as the deep and calm one, Nordraak as the impulsive one, and Grieg as the man with the "face like an open book."

The next day Grieg's friends held a large party for him in the Grand Hotel with Björnson as the principal speaker. Grieg's response was rather strange. At a time when the people of Oslo were almost wild in their excitement over him ("even London pales in comparison"), he could not resist alluding to the city's unfriendly attitude toward art and artists. According to the *Nordisk Musik-Tidende* he said, among other things: "All the people in the country with talent and ability sought refuge here, gave their best, then drifted away. It was as if this city wouldn't let them go until their backs were bent." In conclusion he toasted an Oslo that in the future would be "a happy city."

After the Artists' Society's party on October 28, the Griegs went to Copenhagen, where the music for *Olav Trygvason* was performed at the Concert Society on November 16. It went well, but nothing could overshadow the Norwegian premiere. They then continued on to Brussels, where Edvard gave three concerts. At one of these the Belgian pianist Arthur de Greef was soloist in the *A-minor Concerto.* Grieg wrote about an amusing incident at the December 8 concert in the opera house.[8]

The following day Nina and Edvard traveled to Paris, where they remained for six weeks. They visited the poet Jonas Lie and formed ties with a number of well-known French artists, including Vincent d'Indy. Grieg's three concerts of his own works were exceptionally well received by both the public and the critics. On December 22 and 29 he conducted the Colonne orchestra in a concert that included the *Two Elegiac Melodies, Bergliot,* the *Peer Gynt Suite No. 1,* and the *A-Minor Concerto* with de Greef as soloist. On December 26 Grieg wrote Beyer about the first concert: "Believe me, last Sunday was

9. GRIEG AND BRAHMS MEET AGAIN

But the two masters didn't come near each other. The mood just wasn't right! Grieg played "Bridal Procession" from Opus 19, and Brahms his G-minor *Rhapsody.* I had the impression that neither liked the other's piece. On the other hand, Brahms spoke very warmly to me about Grieg's *Ballade,* Opus 24. Only much later in Vienna [in 1896] was a very cordial relationship established between them. (J. Röntgen: *Edvard Grieg,* p. 25.)

wonderful. I was received with continuous applause as a dear friend. You should have heard the *Peer Gynt Suite.* It surpassed my fondest dreams."

On January 4 there was to be a chamber music evening for specially invited guests: "Everybody who is anybody in Paris is invited." It was a marvelous success. Of the opening number—the *Violin Sonata in C Minor,* which Grieg played together with Johannes Wolff—he wrote Dr. Abraham on January 5 that it "created a tremendous sensation." He also reported that Nina had sung his songs "*so expressively* and so beautifully." Influenza unfortunately prevented Grieg from being present at performances of his string quartet on December 28 and January 11.

The Griegs planned to go to Prague, but had to forgo the trip for political reasons. "There was a plan that I would be used as a symbol by the Czech nationalists against the Germans, but Dr. Abraham got wind of this in time," he wrote to Beyer on January 11. They went to Germany instead—first to Stuttgart, where he conducted the court orchestra February 1, and then to Leipzig for two concerts at the Gewandhaus. *Olav Trygvason* was a great success on February 27, even though the critic Edouard Bernsdorf once again used the occasion to attack Grieg who, in his opinion, was a prodigal son of the Leipzig conservatory. Bernsdorf wrote that the work was totally lacking in what a musician understands as careful construction—which is absolutely essential in so large a composition—and that it consists merely of a pointless search for novelties and a host of harmonic "atrocities."

During the Leipzig stay Grieg again met Brahms, who was passing through. Röntgen, who was also there, wrote about this third meeting in his book on Grieg, and remarked about how distant the two composers were from each other on this occasion.[9]

On March 21 Grieg performed the G-major violin sonata with Brodsky, and in a letter to Beyer four days later reported that the piece awakened lively applause. "I was recalled three times, and the critics also were in good spirits. But my spirits will not be positive until I am on the way home."

In April he was finally home again at "Troldhaugen," and he remained in western Norway until October. He was working on a large set of variations about which he wrote Delius on August 11: "I have completed a piece for two pianos, and now I am enormously happy to be free of everything called music!" He was thinking about taking a two-week trip with Beyer to the Jotunheimen mountains.

The work referred to in the letter to Delius is *Old Norwegian Melody with Variations,* Opus 51, which is dedicated to the French composer Benjamin Godard. It is a broadly conceived work with obvious elements of the grandiose virtuoso style; it reflects the influence of Schumann, Liszt, Brahms, and Saint-Saëns. The theme of the variations is the lovely melody of the heroic ballad "Sjugurd and the Troll Bride" from Hallingdal (No. 22 in Lindeman's collection), which Grieg had harmonized for *Norway's Melodies* and also published as the fourth of *Six Norwegian Mountain Melodies.* Johan Svendsen also used this folk tune in the second of his four *Norwegian Rhapsodies.*

In the opening phrase, the alternation between the major and minor third in the key of F undoubtedly appealed to Grieg's harmonic imagination:

Edvard and Nina near the turn of the century.

The work consists of a short introduction, the theme with fourteen variations, and a very long finale. The design is quite effective, but the piece never has caught on because of a certain monotony and drawing-room conventionality that stamp both the harmony and the music as a whole. The same turns of phrase are repeated a bit too often, and as a consequence the piece is not sufficiently interesting.

During the years 1900–03 Grieg orchestrated the work, and this version was performed on February 21, 1904 by the National Theater Orchestra under Johan Halvorsen. When publication was discussed "various friends, including Nina and especially Halvorsen, urged me to delete two variations and some of the finale. They think the piece currently is too long and, for that reason, tiresome," Grieg told Röntgen in a letter of November 24, 1904. At the same time he asked for Röntgen's advice because he felt it would be an "act of violence" to make alterations in the finale. Only when Svendsen had given his opinion—after having performed the work in Copenhagen on November 18, 1905—did Grieg delete the tenth variation and substitute eight new measures for the last thirty-six in the finale. In spite of these changes, however, the composition still seems too drawn out.

In the summer of 1890 Grieg also wrote a new collection of piano pieces, Opus 52, based on his own songs. Here, as in the comparable collection of 1884, Opus 41, he demonstrates a sense for effective pianism. Some artificiality creeps in, however, when simple songs—for example, "The Old Mother"—are converted into ornamented piano music for recital use.

The third work from this period—Opus 53—consists of two arrangements for string orchestra of his own songs: "Norwegian," based on the Vinje song "The Goal" (Opus 33, No. 12), and "The First Meeting," based on the Björnson song of the same name (Opus 21, No. 1). These arrangements are overshadowed, however, by the *Two Elegiac Melodies,* Opus 34.

Edvard and Nina as performing artists

Grieg gave his first public concert when he was just eighteen years old, and through the years activities as a performer continued to make great demands on his time and energy. Even after "Troldhaugen" had become their home, he and Nina continued to lead the lives of traveling musicians—with the result that for long periods of time their real "home" was a series of hotel rooms.

Why did they arrange things in this way, and why did Edvard not devote himself exclusively to composing? Many circumstances must be considered

10. THE PERILS OF FAME

You think that staying abroad can undermine one's morals. Dear friend, do you think I am so low? Since my early youth I have traveled abroad and learned what is important to acquire. It is true that in the beginning I met rust and rubbish, but now as I travel I meet only the best and the noblest . . . I have, however, been well aware of the danger of a certain kind of moral deterioration, and that is the danger that results from too much recognition and admiration. I have certainly met that in richer measure than ever before, and to the degree that it does one good—thrown into one's life like sunbeams at the very moment when one needs light and warmth—to that same degree it becomes dangerous when it continues without interruption. (Letter to J. A. B. Christie, December 28, 1883.)

* * *

Yes, dear Jonas Lie! We have become famous men. But for my part I find that a dubious fortune, for fame exacts a price. Good Lord, how dearly bought it is! If fame would ever consider the debt fully paid, one could be done with it. But it wears and tears at the very fabric of one's life, and it doesn't rest until it has unraveled so much that one swings and sways in every wind. (Letter to Jonas Lie, August 28, 1887.)

* * *

I only wish him [Fridtjof Backer-Gröndahl] and myself the same: that the concert demon doesn't spoil us! That fellow should be in *our* pockets—and not we in his! One would think that it would be easy to say "no thanks" to all invitations, but it isn't! There is something devilishly alluring about the concert hall for one who receives enthusiastic understanding and sympathy there. (Letter to Agathe Backer Gröndahl, May 15, 1907.)

when we attempt to answer these questions. We have mentioned some of the reasons in the chapter on "Troldhaugen." Some of them were utterly trivial, such as irritation over the unpleasant climate of western Norway. Grieg also realized that Nina was not a homebody and that she needed to get away from the daily treadmill. She blossomed in other surroundings.

There was another and deeper reason for the Griegs' flight from their homeland, however. Isolation from the pulsating life of the rest of the world preyed on their minds. Both of them longed for the great metropolitan centers of music where they could meet the world's leading artists—places where they could receive life-giving impulses from others, and make stimulating contributions of their own.

In time, Grieg developed a reputation as a fine pianist and conductor. The public understood and appreciated this special "son of the North" and flocked to his concerts. This led to impresarios virtually standing in line to engage his services, because large sums of money could be made in his company. For Grieg personally, there was much honor and fame as a result of his concert activities. Like every artist, he had his share of vanity. But it was not just the honor of performing—even when the presence of royal personages added luster to the concerts—that first and foremost appealed to him. It was, rather, the opportunity to do his best for the great crowds of music lovers who came to his concerts. That gave him a feeling of genuine success and made the concert triumphs the high points in his life as an artist. But Grieg understood quite early the perils of fame. In 1883 he expressed this in a letter to the clergyman J. A. B. Christie, who had become his trusted friend at Lofthus; later he expressed similar thoughts to Jonas Lie and Agathe Backer Gröndahl.[10]

In addition to the honor that came to him in this way, one should not forget the attraction of the financial gains connected with the concerts. He very much needed the income he got in this way, for at this time there existed no international law guaranteeing royalties each time his music was performed. He was entirely dependent on his own efforts. The Peters publishing firm was more and more whole-heartedly advancing his cause, because it recognized that in him it had a veritable gold mine. Thus it encouraged him to give concerts, for that was very important for the dissemination of his printed works at a time when there were no radios or record players. Grieg was his own best advertisement.

One other factor must be mentioned. In difficult times Grieg threw himself with a vengeance into hectic concert work. It happened especially when his creative inspiration was blocked. Then he virtually ran away from the problems and toward something he felt satisfied with, but something that nonetheless robbed him of his strength. Composing was then entirely set aside, and he went around with a chronically bad conscience because he knew very well that composing was his true vocation. As time went by and illness entered the picture, the concerts absorbed more and more energy—but then it was too late to stop; he simply couldn't do it. Even in the last year of his life he planned long concert tours, some of which he completed. On February 12, 1906, he wrote to Oscar Meyer of his love-hate sentiments about giving public

The statue in the park at the University of Washington in Seattle. Arthur M. Abell, in his book Talks with Great Composers, *reports that when financier John Wanamaker built his supermarket in Philadelphia in 1903, he wished to get a world-renowned musician to inaugurate the concert hall which was part of the building. Grieg was offered $25,000 and expenses, but he declined with the words: "I would not cross the Atlantic for a million dollars; indeed, I doubt that I would get to New York alive. I suffer terribly from seasickness. The short journey across the English Channel is always a nightmare for me." Wanamaker's next choice was Joseph Joachim, and then Lilli Lehmann, but it ended with Richard Strauss accepting an offer of $6000. (Photo by Darlene Crawford)*

concerts: "You may well wonder why I continue to give concerts. The fact is, however, that people lure me into it, and I unfortunately don't have enough character to quit. The worst thing I know is to perform publicly. And yet: to hear my works in a wonderful performance in accordance with my intentions—that I can't resist."

Grieg was completely aware of the enormous demands of public performance. Dilettantism was an absolute abomination to him, but equally bad in his eyes was the soulless technical virtuosity that characterized some performing artists. Technique was essential, but only as a servant of expression.

In piano music he was meticulous about including clear instructions so that the richness of the expression could be brought out. He considered it important, for example, to indicate the correct fingering, which was always prescribed either by himself or by someone in whom he had confidence. He wanted personally to approve the fingering in each individual case. He was angry, therefore, when the Peters publishing firm, in an 1897 new edition of a collection of his *Lyric Pieces,* inserted fingering instructions which he himself had not authorized. He wrote to Dr. Abraham on December 28 of that year: "No matter how good the fingering is it is not mine, and when all is said and done it isn't what I want either. A big disappointment, however trivial the whole matter may appear."

After Grieg had become a well-established artist he took very few students. Occasionally he assumed the task of rehearsing certain compositions with younger pianists such as Fridtjof Backer-Gröndahl, in whom he saw an unusually gifted interpreter of his works. But others he had to struggle with. Of the pianist Martin Knutzen, who was to play three dances from Opus 72, he wrote Beyer on February 12, 1904: "The Lord deliver us, how I work with him. He is so willing, but spirit! soul!"

To the Norwegian-born singer Dagmar Möller, to whom *The Mountain Maid,* Opus 67, was dedicated, Grieg wrote on November 4, 1896: "You must strive to interpret the *totality* of what the soul of the artist has breathed into the music, for there is no art except that which comes from the heart's blood." In her memoirs of Grieg (1940), Dagmar Möller commented about how exacting he was at rehearsals: "He was insistent that even the smallest dynamic signs should be carefully observed. 'That they are there means that that is how I want it,' was his standard retort."

He nurtured his own technique with great diligence, and to maintain it he often brought with him on his travels a silent keyboard. He demanded as much of others as of himself in both technique and execution. That is undoubtedly also one of the reasons that he accepted so few students. Once when a young pianist wished to play for him in order to secure a recommendation, he wrote to Julius Steenberg: "I cannot give her individuality if she doesn't have it in her nature. And I lack the stamina to inject my own. For it is more than merely listening to a single play-through and then saying a few words. When it is a matter of seriously trying to realize my intentions, I can sit for hours with sixteen measures . . ."

It was precisely the lack of respect on the part of some for the composer's intentions that so endlessly irritated him and precipitated many strong protests against performers, not least of all against female singers. In his diary for January 7, 1907, he wrote: "What is a female singer? She is the epitome of vanity, stupidity, ignorance, and dilettantism. I hate the whole lot of them! 'Also your wife?' someone asks. But I reply, 'Excuse me, she fortunately is not—a female singer.'" To Beyer he wrote petulantly on February 12, 1904: "We have solo concerts almost every evening. Mostly female singers, God pity us! And when occasionally I am so unlucky as to wander into such a concert in order to be with Nina, who wants to hear what the young people are achieving, I always know that my songs will be wretchedly sung." In annoyance he took a shot at pianists as well: "That is now the third time that sexless artist has sat there and played absolutely wrong, with incorrect harmonies, etc., etc., in my poor songs. And yet, so far as I know I've never done him any wrong in my life!"

As a pianist Grieg earned much recognition. He was by no means a great piano virtuoso, but his technique was sufficient to allow him to tackle even his own extremely demanding piano concerto. At the end of the 1880s he first noticed that his strength was not always equal to the task. He wrote to Beyer on March 31, 1888: "Chamber music and small pieces don't bother me, but when I try to use a sledge hammer on the piano I don't achieve the intended effect but only destroy myself." On September 14 a year later, it appeared that he had wholly given up playing the piano concerto, for he wrote to Julius Klengel: "My piano concerto, however, I no longer play. It unsettles me too much. And it also requires great strength to play the work effectively." It is heartbreaking to read his letter to Röntgen of September 1, 1905: "In recent days I have been very sad about the fact that it is becoming steadily clearer that I can no longer endure playing the piano. It isn't only that I lack breath, but I just don't have enough sheer physical strength when I come to a loud, fast-moving passage."

Nonetheless, a year later in Leipzig he recorded a number of pieces on the so-called Welte-Mignon rolls (for player piano), the best method then available for recording sound. These reproductions show his playing in his old age—charming and impulsive, and characteristically Romantic in expression. The recordings are still in existence and have recently been reissued using modern enhancement techniques.

How did his contemporaries judge him as a performer? He had unusual public appeal, which generally expressed itself in ovations whenever he gave concerts. But Grieg the pianist also heard words of highest praise from the critics. He was known for his fresh and brisk manner of playing, and the rhythmic verve he brought to the music was legendary. If one is to judge by the metronomic markings on his works he must have had a tendency to play very fast; indeed, one can't help wondering if his metronome wasn't defective!

During the London concerts in 1888 (see p. 290 ff.), *The Daily Telegraph* of May 4 noted that Grieg had been soloist in the *A-minor Concerto,* and that his performance really was not sensational; it was not a virtuoso performance. It revealed an artist who was first and foremost a composer, and only secondly a pianist. But the playing was undeniably good, clear, intelligent, and full of expression. *The Times* stated that Grieg played the piano concerto in his own

II. GRIEG AS A PIANIST

In his playing he invested so much of his soul, so much feeling, that he came back to the Green Room entirely exhausted . . . He paced around the room as in a fever. He paid no attention to those standing around, just looked now and then at one or another of them with his childlike, gentle, good-natured glance, in which one could in fact read anxiety. With a weak voice he repeated in German these words: "No, a whole concert! That's too much—far too much. I cannot! I cannot!" (Ernest Closson: *Edvard Grieg et la Musique Scandinave*, p. 32.)

* * *

Likewise we remember on that occasion [his first concert in the Philharmonic Society in St. James's Hall in London, May 3, 1888] Grieg's performance of his piano concerto, a performance that added further beauty to that inherently captivating work. Ah, how feelingly he played the lovely *Adagio*—and as a strong contrast, with what vitality and energy, what rhythmic drive he played the last movement with its free-flowing Nordic melodies. (*Musical Times,* October 1, 1907.)

* * *

There is something supernatural, something ethereal in his touch and in his style. One thing that increased the charm of the playing was that he had wisely included familiar pieces on the program . . . He played everything with the utmost delicacy and an unusually attractive, supple, fine-sounding touch which I have never heard before. In so doing he brought out the unique characteristics of each piece—something that only the composer can accomplish. In particular I was struck by the agility of his left hand, not least in the rendering of a simple melody. In "Erotikon," for example, I have never before heard the "answer" in the left hand played so expressively. (*Musical Courier,* New York, January 1897.)

* * *

As a performer, Grieg is the most original pianist I ever heard. Though his technique has suffered somewhat from the fact that a heavy wagon crushed one of his hands and that he lost the use of one of his lungs in his younger days, he has a way of performing his compositions that is simply unique.

manner; one got the feeling of what the French call "voix de compositeur" (the composer's voice). Both technically and musically his execution was excellent, and his interpretation of the well-known work was a revelation.

After concerts in Paris in December, 1889, the English periodical *Truth* printed a vivid portrayal of Grieg as a performer in which the French correspondent expressed himself in this way: ". . . fair, with a rich growth of hair, graying at the temples. When he emphasizes his *fortissimos* with vigorous movements of his head, this wealth of hair shakes mightily. In his energetic approach he resembles Saint-Saëns—yes, even Rubinstein—and yet he is like only himself. The little great man (for he is a genius) . . . has an extraordinary appearance . . . He walks onto the platform with a determined, self-important bearing; his compositions have set their stamp on him." Several representative assessments of Grieg as a performing pianist are given in the Primary Materials.[11]

As the years passed, Grieg the pianist drifted more and more out of the picture in favor of Grieg the conductor. To be sure, he played his piano pieces and chamber music at public concerts from time to time, and he was Nina's regular accompanist throughout his life; but from the end of the 1880s and on the big concert tours concentrated more on orchestral music. Grieg certainly didn't write many works in this genre, but he remedied this by arranging a number of his songs and piano pieces for orchestra. "The Wounded Heart" and "Last Spring" were the first to be thus transcribed.

Was Grieg a good conductor? Everything suggests that he was. He had no conservatory training as an orchestra leader, but by the late 1860s he had developed his conducting skills in association with both amateur and professional musicians in the orchestras of Oslo and Bergen. These skills now served him well. He did not have Johan Svendsen's natural knack and flexibility—Svendsen, in Grieg's opinion, surpassed both Mengelberg and Nikisch—but the technique he may have lacked with the conductor's baton was compensated by a thorough mastery of the scores.

At concerts he got the orchestral sound to glow in an exceptional manner. Finck, in his biography (pp. 98–99), quotes a striking statement made by Sir George Grove after one of the London concerts in 1888: "A very interesting thing was Grieg's overture last night, and his conducting of it. How he managed to inspire the band as he did and get such nervous thrilling bursts and such charming sentiment out of them I don't know. He looks very like Beethoven in face, I thought, and though he is not so extravagant in his ways of conducting, yet it is not unlike." Countless newspaper reviews also emphasized Grieg's ability to make something of the musical details without losing the larger view.

As a conductor Grieg had a unique ability to transfer the excitement of the musicians on the platform to the audience in the concert hall. His concerts, therefore, became enormous public successes. People felt this "voix de com-

While it lacks the breadth with which the professional virtuoso infuses his works, he offsets this by a most poetic conception of lyric parts and a wonderfully crisp and buoyant execution of the rhythmical passages (Frank van der Stucken to Henry T. Finck, quoted in the latter's biography of Grieg, p. 88.)

12. GRIEG PRAISES NINA AS THE ONLY TRUE INTERPRETER OF HIS SONGS

I don't think I have any greater talent for writing songs than for writing other kinds of music. Why, then, have songs played such a prominent role in my music? Quite simply because I, like other mortals, once in my life was brilliant. And my brilliance was: love. I loved a young woman with a marvelous voice and an equally marvelous gift as an interpreter. This woman became my wife and has been my life companion down to the present day. She has been, I must say, the only true interpreter of my songs. (Letter to H. T. Finck, July 17, 1900.)

13. GRIEG PROTESTS AN INVIDIOUS REVIEW IN STOCKHOLM

Your honorable newspaper has recently carried a review of a concert by my wife and me in Stockholm on December 7. The improper tone and tasteless personal attacks in this review I have never seen the likes of in any respectable newspaper. By way of example I need only cite the following tirade: "As performers both are clearly mere dilettantes, and they certainly don't claim to be anything else either." With your reviewer's kind permission, Mr. Editor: To the contrary, we claim to be artists! Later it is even stated: "In Mr. as well as Mrs. Grieg's outward appearance in front of an audience, we find a certain affectation that obscures the expression of . . ." etc. Now it goes without saying that I never get involved in how the press discusses my art; indeed, I have always found unfriendly reviews—yes, even the sharpest condemnation of my art and of the ideals I am striving for—both interesting and instructive. But when art— for what a true *artist* performs is *art*—is stamped as dilettantism, and when in addition the artists' personal appearance and individual manners before the audience are made the objects of malicious criticism, one must grasp the weapons that the press gives one to protest with contempt such an unworthy concept of the reviewer's task. That the reviewer finds my and my wife's manners affected is simply his opinion. His personal opinion in this respect is not the business of either the public or the art critic. I will not dwell on the lack of chivalry in ridiculing a woman's personal appearance in the concert hall . . . (Article in *Dagligt Allehanda*, December 23, 1876.)

positeur" as a genuine instrument of a message of the spirit, a message from one heart to another.

As we know, Grieg could think of no one who interpreted his songs in a more gripping way than his wife. What does this imply? Her voice was by no means that of a great concert singer, and brilliant virtuosity was not her forte. But Grieg's Romantic music didn't require this either. Its intent was above all to give expression to intimate lyric sentiments, and in this area Nina was at home. Ever since the time of their engagement it had been just her type of voice—a light and bright soprano voice, but one with character as well—that he had in mind when he was composing.[12] On July 17, 1900, he wrote to Finck: "My songs . . . came to life naturally and with a necessity like that of a natural law, and all of them were written for her."

The character of Nina's voice was not at all that of the prima donnas of the glory days of the last part of the nineteenth century, when volume and splendor of voice were decisive for artistic celebrity. For that reason she was often judged unfairly on the basis of those standards. Even in Oslo, where one might reasonably have expected a greater understanding of the distinctive quality in her artistic performances, she had to endure harsh criticism, especially in the early years. This so distressed Grieg that after a concert in Rome in 1884 where Nina's performance was judged on its true merits, he exclaimed in a March 19 letter to Beyer: "It will make me happy that the citizens of Oslo can read about the excitement over Nina's singing; it is a little compensation for what she has suffered in the past from those snakes and trolls, small and large, who don't have the foggiest idea of what constitutes true art . . ." It was at this concert that Nina sang some of Edvard's settings of Ibsen texts, whereupon Ibsen went over to the composer and whispered: "This is true understanding."

In Stockholm the "snakes" had been no less biting. After a December, 1876 concert there by Nina and Edvard, the *Dagligt Allehanda* reviewer wrote most condescendingly about the performance. Grieg became extremely irritated and wrote a furious protest to the newspaper.[13]

Against the background of such unsympathetic appraisals—and of Nina's unique characteristics as an artist—one can well understand why Grieg did not press for an international career for her with big solo concerts. She eventually won major artistic victories both at home and abroad, but generally as the wife of the renowned composer. These factors undoubtedly created friction between two so sensitive artistic natures. Only toward the end of his life did Grieg realize how unfortunate it was that he had failed to promote her as an independent singer.[14]

14. GRIEG'S OWN ESTIMATE OF NINA AS AN ARTIST

She has never done anything to acquire widespread fame. It is perfectly clear to me, however, that this is primarily my fault. I did not understand at first how considerable her artistic talents really were. For me it was so completely natural that she should sing so beautifully, so tellingly—from a full heart and from the innermost depths of the soul . . . [In Leipzig in 1875] I realized how much attention my wife's singing was also capable of awakening among artists outside Scandinavia. (Letter to Finck, July 17, 1900.)

Grieg the conductor, as portrayed by two contemporary caricaturists.

Nina's most outstanding characteristic as a singer lay in her unique ability to "live herself" wholly into the text, to render the most delicate poetic nuances in such a way that not only were the words of the text distinctly articulated but, even more, the artistic intentions behind the words also received an appropriate interpretation. It was just these aspects of her art that so enthralled people of musical insight. At Grieg's request the Danish singer Julius Steenberg, his friend from the Copenhagen period, wrote a statement in October, 1891, about Nina as a singer. This statement, which was to be used in a German biography of Grieg, was right on target. Among other things Steenberg wrote: "What was it that was peculiar to her singing? In a way, she has created her own style. In any case, it was not the conventional—what Wagner called the 'felonious'—type. It was more like an animated dramatic recitative. She struck not only the center of a poem's feeling, but somehow plumbed the depths of individual words so they received a deeper, more distinctive color than one could get from mere reading . . ." It was no accident that Grieg himself spoke of Nina as "the only true interpreter of my songs."

In the *Truth* article quoted earlier, Nina is described so charmingly that one can almost see her on the concert platform: "Mrs. Grieg has a smile and a

15. SINDING PRAISES NINA

Sinding, a strange but I think admirable person—who rarely says anything—took me into a corner and said: "Tell me, why doesn't anyone else sing like that? Yes, why doesn't everyone sing thus? Because basically it cannot be otherwise. It is the only reasonable way." That is brilliantly said, and I will always remember it. (From a letter to Beyer, December 11, 1887.)

16. TCHAIKOVSKY WRITES IN HIS DIARY ABOUT NINA

Now I had the opportunity of learning to appreciate Madame Grieg's many and valuable qualities. In the first place, she proved to be an excellent though not very finished singer; secondly, I have never met a better-informed or more highly cultivated woman, and she is, among other things, an excellent judge of our literature, in which Grieg himself was also deeply interested; and thirdly, I was soon convinced that Madame Grieg was as amiable, as gentle, as childishly simple and without guile as her celebrated husband. (From Tchaikovsky's "Diary of my tour in 1888." Quoted from Rosa Newmarch, *Tchaikovsky: His Life and Works*, p. 191.)

look that somehow invite a friendly reception—and when she sings the Norwegian songs, she is unsurpassed. Has one ever heard a prima donna (Jenny Lind excepted) sing a simple little song or a folk tune in such a natural and unpretentious way? The ordinary singer's stage presence and stereotyped smile almost completely destroy this type of folk music . . . Imagine a concert singer who has scorned all of the usual conventional marks of 'a professional woman artist': no bouquet, no makeup, unconcerned about any wrinkles that she may have, with short-clipped hair, dressed in a high-necked brown silk dress decorated only by a piece of Norwegian silver filigree jewelry at the throat, greeting the audience with a deep, respectful curtsy. Then a glance back to her husband at the piano, and she began. After a few stanzas I had tears in my eyes, for 'Ah! Yes, that is the way it should be' is the way one immediately feels. She penetrates right into one's heart and soul. Her look becomes eloquent, dimples bear witness to a merry piquancy, and the softness, purity, and pathos with which she invests her song surpass all praise. She is completely involved in the song and cares not the slightest about 'Nina Grieg' and how she looks, or about what the public thinks about her little person . . ."

Other characteristic accounts of Nina's singing are given in the Primary Materials.[15,16] They are more reserved than the one in *Truth,* but they give a clear impression of her ability to carry listeners along with her.

The versatility of Nina's artistic talent is evident also in the fact that she was a very able pianist. From her youth and on she was an excellent sight reader, and she and Edvard loved to make music together playing large symphonic works in four-hand arrangements. She has given a humorous account of how they became engaged after playing Schumann's "Spring" symphony together. Now and then they even appeared in concert as duo pianists playing, among other things, the *Norwegian Dances* of Opus 35.

Julius Röntgen was greatly impressed when Nina performed the song cycle, *The Mountain Maid,* "Opus 67," for him at "Troldhaugen" in 1895: "Nina sang and accompanied herself. It was a brilliant performance that made a deep impression . . ." The famous Italian pianist Sgambati also praised her piano playing after a public concert: "In the four-hand playing with her husband, Mrs. Grieg showed that she, too, is a true artist in the fullest sense of the word."

Nina sang little publicly in the last years of Grieg's life. As early as 1895 he wrote somewhat dejectedly to Beyer (letter of October 27): "Now that Nina sings no more I understand for the first time how fortunate I have been in this respect; but now the time is also coming when I, like Diogenes, must look high and low for a person who can continue where she is leaving off."

Nonetheless, from time to time she allowed herself to be talked into performing, even after his death. In both 1909 and 1912 she agreed to sing her husband's songs—accompanying herself—at small recitals at the music conservatory in Manchester. The director there was the Russian violinist Adolph Brodsky, who with his wife had been a member of Grieg's circle of friends ever since the 1880s. After Nina had visited them in 1912 Mrs. Brodsky wrote: "This combination of marvelous energy, depth, and tenderness of feeling is

Edvard and Nina as performing artists. In an article about them in the New York paper Looking-On, *Joachim Reinhard wrote: "Although it is easy to criticize Mrs. Grieg's singing . . . , to this day no other vocal performance has made such an impression on me as hers, and as far as I know everyone who has had the pleasure of hearing her has felt the same . . . As soon as Mrs. Grieg has begun to sing one forgets that one is in a concert hall. We suffer with her, we weep, laugh and rejoice with her from the beginning to the end." (The original hangs in the National Museum in Stockholm)*

the reason she carries her audience away, notwithstanding the fact that her voice has naturally lost some of its freshness and vigor."

We should also acknowledge Nina's considerable gifts as a teacher. Grieg wrote in his diary on March 31, 1906: "It is unbelievable what power she has to *mesmerize* her pupils." During a London visit on June 24 of the same year he described—with obvious enthusiasm—her "great talent in communicating her intentions and mine to others . . ."

It must have been thrilling to see Nina and Edvard together on the concert platform, especially when Grieg's own works were on the program, for then the music received a completely authoritative interpretation. They certainly knew each other through and through, with the result that impulses from the one were immediately picked up and answered by the other. As artists they fully complemented each other, and in their interpretations they preserved throughout their careers the spontaneous genuineness and freshness that are the hallmarks of great performers. It is not surprising that they were concert hall favorites. Indeed, in the entire history of music there is no parallel to such a cooperative effort between two superb musicians: the brilliant composer-performer and the source of his inspiration, his singing wife.

Two New Torsos

In October 1890 Grieg went to Oslo where, in the middle of the month, he gave a solo concert in the Store Sirkus (Big Circus) hall. There was a huge turnout—between two and three thousand people, according to an October 20 letter from Grieg to Jonas Lie. "But I don't think Osloites can yet tolerate true artists among them—*for long*. When we just drop in and then hurry off again, everything is honey and roses. But—but. There is still too much uncivilized coarseness and civilized pettiness here."

In November he went on to Copenhagen, where he remained until the middle of April, 1891. He had been looking forward very much to this opportunity to work for a few months in the Danish capital. Things didn't get off to a very good start, however. He and Nina got a room at the King of Denmark Hotel, where they were accustomed to staying. On November 12, the day after their arrival, Grieg wrote to Beyer: "We came here last evening; I got sick to my stomach during the night, am taking no food today, and am therefore exhausted and out of sorts. The weather is awful. Everything is awful. Under such circumstances it is doubly good to know of a distant but true friendship."

Not much was accomplished. As early as December 9 he was beginning to look forward to summer at "Troldhaugen": "I'm writing these lines out at Feddersen's in Frederiksberg . . . I've been staying in a little attic room here for a couple of weeks, but I don't like it because John Paulsen lives just below me, and from the next level down I hear piano music—even my own music, damn it; it's almost heartless. I must have gotten a lot older, for everything seems changed. Only my old friend Emil Horneman is the same—sensitive, dependable, and brilliant. He is for me in Denmark what you are in Norway! . . . Yes, I'm beginning to look forward to summer."

In a letter dated January 20, 1891, Beyer heard something of what a deadly effect the Copenhagen milieu was having on Grieg, who wanted to go home. "It is a period of decadence and decline. There is nothing inspiring or stimulating. No, give me peaceful nature instead! It speaks more and better than these prattling, petty people. All my ideas become, so to speak, smashed to pieces. I begin and begin, on one thing and another, and suddenly it is as if a barrier has been set up—a barrier that I can't remove no matter how hard I try."

1. ANXIETY ABOUT NOT FOLLOWING THE TRENDS OF THE TIMES

I won't say that I'm afraid of either life or death, but there is one thing I am afraid of: to look at myself and note that I am growing old—that ideas of the younger generation will sail out on expeditions the meaning of which I do not fully comprehend. In a word, I fear the possibility of losing the capacity to feel what is true and great in the outposts of the spirit that move steadily forward throughout one's lifetime. For that reason I have—more now than ever—an instinctive need to know all the nuances that are stirring in the intellectual life [of our time]. If one now allows anything of significance to glide by without having assimilated it—before one knows what is happening it will become a power that one doesn't understand, because one hasn't followed that which is new from the very beginning. To be left lying half forgotten on the road as time marches across one's sinful cadaver—that seems to me the greatest wretchedness that can befall a person. And with how countless many does this not happen? Perhaps with most—but they don't know it and are quite as happy. It is different with the artist: when he becomes a part of the reactionary forces, he is lost. (Letter to Beyer, February 9, 1891.)

2. GRIEG ON THE F-MAJOR QUARTET

. . . that accursed string quartet which constantly lies there unfinished like an old Norwegian cheese. (Letter to Brodsky, December 25, 1895.)

* * *

Perhaps you remember my mentioning an unfinished string quartet? I had also intended to get it done. But these last years have brought so much misery, both physically and spiritually, that I wasn't in the mood to proceed with this cheerful work— quite the opposite of Opus 27. But I hope to find the long-sought tranquility and inclination this summer. (Letter to Henri Hinrichsen, the new director of the Peters firm in Leipzig, February 7, 1903.)

* * *

If only I could at least finish the string quartet for you! (Letter to Brodsky, August 20, 1906.)

A Grieg caricature by the Swedish cartoonist Knut Stangenberg. (Det Kongelige Bibliotek, Copenhagen, Denmark)

His mood was no brighter on February 9: "The music I settle on one day I tear out of my heart the next, for it is not genuine. My ideas are bloodless just as I am, and I am losing confidence in myself. In view of this fact it is of little avail when Dr. Abraham writes that my compositions—the *Peer Gynt Suite,* for example—are being performed in Europe, Asia, Africa, America, and Australia! Therefore: to the mountains, to the mountains! There and there alone is healing." In the same letter he also expressed again the frightening thought that he was getting old. As a matter of fact, he feared that he might end up in the quagmire of reactionism, for then he would be "lost."[1]

What ideas were "smashed to pieces" for him during this period? Principally they had to do with two contemplated large works that he intended to write: a new string quartet and a "peace oratorio" to be written in collaboration with Björnson.

The unfinished String Quartet No. 2 in F Major

Grieg wrote to Beyer from Copenhagen on March 26: "I have written two movements of a string quartet. Of course, it was supposed to have been completely finished down here. But [it isn't]. And I'm going to Oslo in April . . ."

The interruption of progress on the string quartet which occurred at this time proved to be momentous, for Grieg never managed to resume work on it thereafter. The unfinished quartet hung over him like a nightmare for the rest of his life, a continual reminder that he had not been equal to the task.[2]

After Grieg's death in 1907, Nina sent a number of manuscripts to Rönt-

gen to find out if any of them might be suitable for publication. Among these were the two movements of the unfinished quartet. Röntgen replied on October 24 that he had his doubts about this composition. He thought that Grieg would have altered many things in the nearly completed movements, and for that reason he had to take a little time to think about it. At the same time he was working on an article about Grieg for the German periodical *Die Musik,* and on October 30 he asked Mrs. Grieg to approve the manuscript for the article. In the same letter he reported that he had changed his mind about the quartet: "I have studied the first movement of the quartet in great detail. I am quite in love with it. Now I am going to write out the parts, and then at the first opportunity you will hear the piece and enjoy it. Why didn't Edvard ever show us this piece? Then we would surely have gotten him to finish it!" On November 12 he stated explicitly that he wanted to assume responsibility for the publication of the two movements, and that the minor alterations that he would make could be easily accomplished. In the same letter he also gave a delightful account of how the unfinished quartet got its "premiere."[3]

Peters published the two movements in 1908. The first public performance occurred in Copenhagen on January 22 of the same year; the occasion was a Grieg memorial concert consisting entirely of works published after his death.

In the F-major quartet Grieg returned once again to the optimistic, lyrical emotional sphere of the first violin sonata—a youthful work which, it will be recalled, was also in F major. It is especially in the first movement that one senses the composer's retrospective gaze. When comparing the two first movements, one discovers a number of similarities: not only are the key and the time signature identical, but the entire sequence of modulations is the same in both. Even the characteristically Griegian turn to G-flat major appears in the quartet. It is clearly a piece in which Grieg reached a dead end; he was searching for his vanished youth rather than a road into the future.

The first movement is an Allegro in sonata form. An eight-measure introduction leading into the dominant sphere creates tension that is released with the introduction of the principal theme in measure 9:

The secondary theme is in A minor and the closing theme in C major, exactly as in the violin sonata. In the development, motivic materials are moved up chromatically in characteristically Griegian fashion. Rhythmically, the movement is more interesting than the first movement of the violin sonata in that, for example, in some places a distinct $\frac{3}{4}$ rhythm is introduced in contrast to the basic $\frac{6}{8}$ rhythm.

A remarkable example of self-quotation occurs in this movement. At the close of the exposition a phrase appears which—presumably unconsciously—is taken directly from the slow movement of the *A-minor Concerto* (for the sake of comparison the excerpt from the concerto is transposed down a half step):

From 1st movement, Quartet in F Major:

From 2nd movement, A-minor Concerto:

At the close of the movement this phrase appears two more times, now in F major. The recurrence of this little phrase is yet another indication that Grieg was moving in the nostalgic world of his youth while he was working on the quartet. Perhaps the main reason that he never managed to complete this work was precisely the fact that he was unable to free himself from this realm of thought. Or was it the "reaction" he so greatly feared that now appeared in his musical speech?

The second movement is a lengthy piece in *ABA* form, with the *B* section in D major. The subject of the *A* section has a certain resemblance to the introductory measures of the Vinje song "The Forgotten Maid." In the contrasting section one notes Grieg's desire once again to break the rhythmic uniformity through the use of $\frac{2}{4}$ phrases in $\frac{3}{4}$ measures. Here is the thematic beginning of *A:*

Of the third and fourth movements only a few fragments of Grieg's rough draft have been found among his unpublished manuscripts. The fragments are not sufficient to allow a complete reconstruction of these movements.

The first four measures of the third movement are given below. The idea that is introduced is a charming one, and it is a pity that Grieg did not complete the movement. The subject has a certain motivic affinity with measures 3 and 4 of the introduction to the first movement:

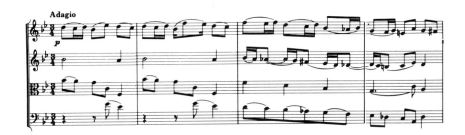

Here, too, are the first six measures of the thematic material that Grieg intended to use in the fourth movement:

In our discussion of the G-minor quartet we made mention of a sketch Grieg had made for the third movement (see p. 229). If we now compare these two examples it is evident that the melodic material is identical, except for the fact that the 1891 version is transposed to F major. What happened can only be explained as follows: as he was working on the F-major quartet in 1891, Grieg found himself in need of a captivating theme for the fourth movement. He then got out the original sketches of the third movement of the G-minor quartet which he had earlier rejected and transposed the music to F major in the hope that it would serve his purpose. About sixty measures are almost identical in the two versions; thereafter they go their separate ways, but in both cases all that remains is some fragments from which it is not possible to reconstruct the entire movements as Grieg may have conceived them. Once again we must say that it is a pity that Grieg did not complete this work, for the thematic material with its *halling* rhythms and other interesting features gives a refreshing impression. Everything was in place, therefore, for a rousing concluding movement to this light-hearted quartet, which would have been a nice counterpart to the dramatic G-minor quartet from the Lofthus period.

It is understandable that the earlier work has thoroughly overshadowed the two completed movements of the F-major quartet, but the almost total neglect of the latter is quite undeserved. As we have tried to show, both movements have many fine qualities both melodically and rhythmically. Moreover, the harmony exhibits a vivacious freshness that is in no way indicative of stagnation in Grieg's development. The expert handling of the instruments is also apparent, with a musical texture that is more lucid than that of Opus 27. This work, though unfinished, is worthy of wider public performance.

Shortly after Easter (1891), after finishing the two movements of the quartet, Grieg left Copenhagen. His immediate destination was Oslo, where he had promised to sit for portraits by two young but noted Norwegian painters—Eilif Petersen and Erik Werenskjold. But he was far too fidgety a person to be a cooperative model; after a short time he reported that he was absolutely "idiotized" by the task of sitting still hour after hour. Thereupon he simply abandoned the project and left the painters in the lurch, apparently unconcerned about whether the portraits could ever be completed. Fortunately, they were completed. Petersen's portrait now hangs in the National Gallery in Oslo, Werenskjold's in the National Museum in Stockholm.

The "Peace Oratorio"—grandly conceived but never completed

After the success of the concert version of *Olav Trygvason*, Grieg wanted to resume the collaboration with Björnson. Realizing that Björnson had no plans to continue the opera project, Grieg wrote enthusiastically from Copenhagen on December 10, 1890: "What do you think of the idea of taking the peace theme, to which music can give added richness and depth, and making it into a Björnson poem—in a kind of cantata form, so it will be suitable for solo voices, choir, and orchestra. It has been my fondest thought in recent years to write a Requiem—a modern Requiem, without dogmatism. But I haven't found a [suitable] text, although I have searched both in secular literature and in the Bible. But when I read the peace talk that you gave in Arbeiderforeningen [the Labor Union Hall], the idea immediately struck me: an apotheosis to peace, that is a Requiem of quite another kind! There need be no lack of contrasts: the great light of peace against the horrors of war! I believe in this idea. Think it over, and if it interests you—then answer."

Björnson replied immediately and discussed in some detail how he thought the idea could be realized. Grieg wrote again on December 19 and suggested the possiblity of using materials from the Old Testament and from the epistles of St. Paul. The fact is, he was reacting negatively to Björnson's "unmusical" words and expressions—for example, "distant factories" and "garrison life." Grieg wanted only "the grandiloquent." The day after Christmas he followed up the idea: "Your vision of a paean of thanks to mankind's benefactors is thoroughly captivating: it is marvelously conceived! I wish you would write it down just as you feel it . . . But the *Requiem* I have dreamed of shall not be only about the great. I want to be able to think about father and mother and friend, about the great and the small, the rich and the poor, who have passed on . . ."

Grieg was delighted—but too soon. On January 8, 1891, he wrote to Björnson: "Your letter yesterday almost made me go crazy! I think that either you overestimate the power of *music*—or else you overestimate mine! I ask but one thing that you don't include too many details. The great simplicity of your text will make it possible for me to succeed. If you in your righteous frenzy try to include everything, I get frightened. When you close factories and banks, and send telegrams (!)—then in that moment I must protest! But now I almost think that you are bribing my imagination so that the astonishment will be all the greater when your noble poem arrives!"

Nina and Edvard Grieg with Karoline and Björnstjerne Björnson. ("Troldhaugen," Bergen, Norway)

Björnson came to Copenhagen, and on Good Friday read his completed poem for a select group including Grieg. Grieg wrote to Dr. Abraham from Oslo on April 20: "I received from Björnson a short time ago an excellent poem entitled 'Peace' which concerns itself only with 'mankind.' When I get home again and am settled down I will start working on it. But it will be a large composition—so for the time being let's not talk about it."

But there would be more talk—between Björnson and Grieg. And unfortunately, the project never went much beyond the talking stage. Grieg just could not move on anything. On June 2 he wrote: "Still, I realize more and more what wonderful things are there in what you have written. But I am an idiot. I am like a cat going around a saucer of hot milk, and can't get going. What I want now lies beyond my reach. When I try to touch it, I fall backwards. I am too clumsy. But it will come. Send me some of your self-confidence. That's what I need." By July 23 he had come no further than to "smell" the text.

Time passed and there was still no peace oratorio from Grieg. Björnson lost patience and in October announced that he was going to publish the text. Grieg wrote on October 27 that he was prepared to give a year of his life to this task, and that it was his intention "to go home in December and get to work in peace and quiet." When Björnson nonetheless reported that the poem would be published (in *Folkeblade*'s Christmas issue of 1891), Grieg wrote on November 6 that in that case it could no longer have the meaning for him that it once had: "The text will lose for me that which is best, that which is inexpressible, that which creates the trembling of enchantment (as it did in *Olav Trygvason*)" In short, the publication of the text would have a paralyzing effect on his creative power. On May 10 of the following year he expressed himself even more sharply in a letter to August Winding: "So far the Björnson text has caused me nothing but vexation, for after his all too hasty publication of the text and the ensuing newspaper accounts, it has lost for me its—yes, what shall I call it—its sacredness, its purity."

What finally resulted from the collaboration on a "Peace Oratorio"? The only thing we know of today is the song "I Loved Him," published after Grieg's death (CW 101, No. 2). The elegiac text has to do with a woman who has lost her beloved—a soldier? It is not a strong text. Grieg's setting is not especially exciting either, though it cannot be considered one of his weakest songs. The harmony is chromatic and typically Griegian. Melodically, however, it sounds like a pale reflection of several of the Vinje songs: the beginning is similar to "The Forgotten Maid" (CW 138, No. 1) and the concluding section resembles the ending of "The Youth" (Opus 33, No. 1).

The deficiency in the 'Peace Oratorio' project—if one can speak of a deficiency in a case like this—was entirely of Grieg's doing. The beginning of the 1890s was a very difficult period for him because of his failing health. It was as if a clammy hand had laid itself upon him and completely squelched the unfolding of his creative power. It was some time before he was willing to admit that the failure was his, but on July 1, 1896, he wrote to Björnson and without circumlocution assumed complete responsibility for what had happened: "Some years ago I imagined that the "Peace Oratorio" lost its attraction for me when you allowed your poem to be published and the press got wind of the fact that I was going to compose it. There is *some* truth in this, for there is something of the mimosa in me. But the main cause lies deeper: I wasn't equal to the task. Partly because the text was more comprehensive than I had anticipated, and particularly because just at that time my health got the serious blow that shook my creative energy to its very roots." Some months later—February 1, 1897—he wrote about the matter again in a more cheerful vein: ". . . but now you have become so lovable that it is almost scary. Good God, say something abusive to me instead! I certainly deserve it, and in view of my sins against you (peace oratorio, etc.) it would feel like a liberation if you really used a bear ['björn'] paw on me."

Happily, however, the year 1891 contained some cheerful things in addition to disappointments.

The first meeting with Gjendine Slaalien

Grieg remained at "Troldhaugen" from May until August, 1891. From Paris he received an unexpected announcement that he had been elected to membership in the French Academy. He wrote to Winding about this on July 4: "I

Kaja Gjendine Slaalien (1872–1972), the peasant woman from Lom whose beautiful singing was the source of "Gjendine's Lullaby" and other folk melodies in Opus 66. Grieg sent her gifts from time to time, and in a thank-you letter dated September 24, 1905, she wrote that the latest gift had "[moved me to] tears in memory of my old tourist friends; not merely friends, but friends who are faithful unto death. I will never forget those enjoyable times in the mountains. This summer I had a visit from Julius Röntgen and his wife Abrahamine. It is nine years since I last saw him, but seeing old acquaintances again is so moving that my heart is agitated long afterwards. I can't describe how happy I become when I get greetings from my old mountain-friends . . . Affectionate greetings from my Halvor and little Thora! And finally from the one who knows you best: warm greetings and best wishes and long life to Edvard Grieg! You are now 60 years old. I read it in the newspapers. Believe me, I devoured every word and carefully read about the honors you received for your good work in the theater. So now, farewell, you and Nina. Hearty greetings!"

Grieg was deeply moved by this greeting. He wrote Beyer on October 25, 1905: "I had a wonderful moment recently. A letter from Gjendine was its cause. To be permitted once again to be soft—really tender-hearted—for that I would gladly give up much that is considered desirable . . . for tears actually wet the paper. What she wrote was so beautiful and genuine. And she included Nina as though she were an old friend. That was so thoughtful. It's marvelous that she thinks I'm an actor."

Gjendine sang her folk melodies well into her 90s and was a living reminder of Grieg at, for example, the Bergen Music Festival. (The photograph was taken by Helge Stenersen in connection with an article about her 100th birthday.)

have recently . . . taken upon my conscience a great sin, one for which certain people in Denmark will never forgive me: I have been elected to membership in the French Academy succeeding Gade. But good God, I certainly can't do anything about it. And the *bread* that I thereby take from the mouths of Danish colleagues they will not begrudge me in any case. But honor? 'Yet, what is honor?' asks Falstaff."

The Röntgen family was to visit Norway that summer (1891), and Grieg set about arranging lodgings for them with the Utnes in Lofthus. On May 28 he wrote to them in Amsterdam with the news that Mr. and Mrs. Röntgen, their two children, and the nursemaid would get three rooms and meals for fourteen Norwegian kroner per day. Grieg, who was accustomed to pinching pennies, added laconically: "I don't think that is exactly cheap."

The Röntgens arrived at Lofthus, and Nina and Edvard visited them in August. Here they laid the final plans for a trip to the Jotunheimen mountains; Beyer was going to join them as well. Röntgen, in his Grieg biography, has given a delightful account of this outing. They traveled by horse and buggy to the Sognefjord, and then by rowboat to Skjolden. "From there," Röntgen wrote, "the path up to Turtagrö is steep. We took a fiddler along, and he played dances for us on that magnificent ride. How appropriate this music was to these surroundings! Grieg listened entranced and continually marked the beat with his head. In his hand he had a glass of port wine from which he gave the fiddler a sip now and then. 'This is Norway,' he said with eyes beaming."

Arrangements were made to ride horses for the last stretch up to Turtagrö. Suddenly they heard shouting from the mountain: it was Beyer, who "in an ebullient Jotunheimen mood" was announcing his arrival to join them. In the evening they visited the shepherd girls, "and after a little hesitation the girls yielded to Beyer's persuasion and agreed to sing for us. Here for the first time I heard Norwegian folk songs in their native setting. What a performance they got! Beyer told about how in the morning, when the cows were milked and the girls sang, he used the back of a cow as a writing table and in that way got the songs 'fresh from the cow.'"

The next day the merry trio continued on toward Mt. Dyrehaugstind, which Röntgen climbed alone because "Grieg didn't feel strong enough to climb to the top." A few days later they went from Turtagrö to Skogadalsböen, with Grieg traveling by horseback part of the time. At the tourist inn they had a truly unforgettable evening. The proprietor's sister-in-law was a nineteen-year-old milkmaid from Lom, Gjendine Slaalien. "The first time we saw her," Röntgen wrote, "she rocked her sister's child in her arms while she sang it to sleep with the beautiful cradle song that Grieg has used in his *Nineteen Norwegian Folk Songs,* Opus 66, under the name of 'Gjendine's Lullaby.' Her singing made a wonderful impression. She sang rhythmically and yet with a natural, free delivery. The music grew steadily slower and softer until it died away completely. She was glad to sing for us, and she knew many melodies . . . Gjendine also played the goat horn, an instrument that has only the first three notes of the minor scale. With these she could produce the most remarkable melodies."

After a jovial evening at the inn they went out into the farmyard "in a fantastic moonlight, and from below could be heard the rushing sound of the river. Gjendine climbed up on a rock and once again sang the cradle song for us. How enchantingly beautiful it sounded! Grieg said to me, 'You are truly a fortunate fellow, for an experience such as this is rare in Norway.'"

After the encounter with Gjendine, Grieg wrote down the lullaby that had made such a strong impression on him and his companions. The following year he received a request from the Viennese music dealer A. I. Gutmann to contribute a composition for a collection of piano pieces which was to be published for a charitable purpose. In response to this request, Grieg harmonized the lullaby for the first time and sent it to Gutmann on May 5, 1892, with the title, "Norwegischer Volkston" [Norwegian Folk Song]. He allowed it to be used for the charitable purpose, but was careful to reserve all other rights for himself. The following year he wrote two new and better harmonizations with the titles "Lullaby from Skogadalsböen" and "Gjendine Sings." The latter differs very little from the final version in Opus 66.

A Demanding Five-Year Period

I. RÖNTGEN'S LETTER OF THANKS
FOR OPUS 54

I have received *my* pieces, and I am writing
to thank you for them. They will be a special souvenir from last summer and a reminder of those unforgettable days in the
Jotunheimen mountains. There is a bit of
yourself and of the Norwegian nation in
each of them, and I think I can actually follow your thoughts in them. The mood of
the first piece, for example, is without a
doubt that of Turtagrö. It conveys a feeling
of utter loneliness. The piece in C major is
very amusing. Here I see you again as you
were when you took such great delight in
the peasant playing his fiddle, and when
one looks around one sees the mountains
and inhales that wonderfully crisp air. "Bell
Ringing"!—a veritable apotheosis of
fifths!—is really quite crazy; something like
this is only an expression of moods, and for
those who don't have a sense for that sort
of thing it obviously will be unintelligible.
(Letter from Röntgen, December 20, 1891.)

The life-giving trip to the Jotunheimen mountains and the meeting with
Gjendine Slaalien in the summer of 1891 greatly strengthened Grieg's desire
and courage to take on new challenges. He had returned from the mountains,
as he optimistically wrote to Dr. Abraham on August 10, "like a new and
better man . . . yes, ten years younger." The best evidence that he had found
himself and was once again ready to produce something worthy of his genius
is the fifth volume of *Lyric Pieces,* Opus 54. He reported that he had had "a lot
of fun" creating the work, and wrote jokingly to Röntgen—to whom he
dedicated it as "a trifling proof" of his warm friendship—that "the last piece
["Bell Ringing"] is absolutely crazy, but in any case you will find here and
there something that isn't." Röntgen's letter of thanks shows that he quickly
felt himself at home in Grieg's world of thought. Between the two friends this
music was from heart to heart.[1]

Opus 54 is without doubt the best of the ten volumes of *Lyric Pieces.* It
surpasses even Opus 43 both in its greater expressiveness and by virtue of a
richer development of the material. Grieg has here reached back to that within
himself which is most original, to a vitality that flows freely and unfettered. It
is as if a sudden rejuvenation has taken place after the stagnation of the
preceding years—but at the same time the music is enriched by the reflection
that comes only with maturity. The melodic vein has suddenly become fresh
and vigorous again. Rhythmically, a kind of "loosening up" is evident in such
things as polyrhythmic passages and more advanced forms of syncopation.
Harmonically, Grieg's imagination expresses itself more subtly and exuberantly than it had for a long time.

Memories of the strong impressions of nature had ignited the creative
spark. "Shepherd's Boy" leads us up to the mountain world where we fill our
lungs with pure and clear air. The extensive use of chromaticism in this piece
fits in naturally with the whole without a trace of Romanticism's jaded salon
style. The finely chiseled "Gangar" is the most striking and successful example
of Grieg's ability to create stylized dances modeled after traditional Norwegian dance forms. It exhibits a singular rhythmic drive and exciting sequences in large dynamic arches.

In "March of the Dwarfs" ("Trolltog"), imaginary inhabitants of the

Jotunheimen mountains swarm about in all their boisterous abandon. In the lyrical midsection it is as if the trolls had been compelled to disappear at sunrise: only the mischievous young trolls carelessly stick their heads out to see what is going on. With "Nocturne" the mystery of night is expressed in muffled sounds, with the aura of mystery further strengthened by unusual rhythmic refinements. The chords are very colorful; the short and agitated midsection is remarkably similar to a passage in Debussy's "Clair de lune," which was composed in the same year. It is strange how the two composers came up with such strikingly similar pictorial and musical ideas quite indepently of each other.

In "Scherzo" Grieg waves his magic wand and takes us back to the atmosphere of "Fairy Dance" in the first volume of lyric pieces (1867). It is the playful, gossamer, fairy world of Mendelssohn that we meet here, but on Norwegian soil. In the moving contrasting section Grieg is at his lyric best.

"Bell Ringing" is a pure study in sound. Harmonically it is in a class by itself for its time—a daring impressionistic experiment. The goal was not melodic beauty. The idea was to recreate an impression of church bells chiming in an almost realistic manner, statically and virtually monotonously:

Two series of parallel fifths, one in the right hand and one in the left, are played off against each other in a syncopated rhythmic pattern; and with the help of the pedal, masses of overtone-laden sound are created which virtually stand up and tremble. Grieg's joking (but perhaps also somewhat apologetic) use of the word "crazy" in connection with this fine piece probably should be viewed in the context of the unflinching consistency with which he carried out the idea. This was music for connoisseurs, but it was the only time he attempted such a thing.

In about 1895 an orchestral version of "Gangar," "March of the Dwarfs," "Nocturne," and "Bell Ringing" was created by the conductor Anton Seidl, who gave it the title *Norwegische Suite.* Seidl sent his arrangement to Grieg from New York in 1903. The following year, after hearing Seidl's arrangement at a rehearsal of the National Theater Orchestra under Johan Halvorsen, Grieg himself set about reorchestrating these four pieces. The result was the *Lyric Suite,* which was published in 1905. In the *Lyric Suite,* however, Grieg replaced the "crazy" and—in his opinion—very radical "Bell Ringing" with his own orchestration of "Shepherd's Boy," which became the first move-

Erik Werenskiold's portrait, painted in Oslo in 1891–92. It was presented to Edvard and Nina as a silver wedding present by music friends in Oslo during the festivities at Troldhaugen on June 11, 1892. It is now in the National Museum in Stockholm, Sweden.

ment. The *Lyric Suite* gives fresh proof of Grieg's flair for orchestral effects, and it has earned a place in the world's concert halls.

After completing Opus 54, Grieg again turned his attention to *Peer Gynt Suite No. 2*, which he had started working on the year before (see further p. 182). It was premiered by the Music Association in Oslo on November 15, 1891, in connection with the celebration of the twenty-fifth anniversary of Grieg's first appearance as a concert performer in that city.

On November 1 he also participated in a stormy meeting of the Student Society, where the issue was whether or not to remove the symbol of the union with Sweden from the Norwegian flag on the Society's building. Grieg took the floor and made a spontaneous plea in favor of a "de-unionized" Norwegian flag: "I think it [the use of a flag containing the union symbol] is as if Norwegians were trampling on old Norway. I think the time has come to ask where our love really lies. In the spirit of this society I venture to ask if we ought not to sing 'Yes, we love with fond devotion' [the first line of Björnson's text for the Norwegian national anthem]." This remark was quoted in the

2. BJÖRNSON PRAISES GRIEG FOR SPEAKING OUT CLEARLY IN THE STUDENT SOCIETY

What you said in the Society—it will live as long as your best songs. It's what I've always said: there is character in that small fellow, character so solid and courageous that he could supply ten Ibsens. There is understanding and participation with respect to our national concern [the Norwegian independence movement]. Many, many thanks! I have the right to say that to you on behalf of thousands, for I know what is felt in Norway regarding this matter. (Letter from Björnson, November 4, 1891.)

3. GRIEG PAYS TRIBUTE TO THE STUDENTS

Many, many thousands of people filled Eidsvoll Square under the flickering torchlight, and standing on the balcony of the hotel I spoke to the young people— these young people whose unabashed belief in life is the thing I want most of all to preserve to my last hour. For one can talk about going around in circles as long as one wants. There is always something new to do. Thoughts will always seek new garb even if there is nothing new under the sun. Yes, if anyone is right it's the young people—and I will say more: I will say that only they are right. Accordingly, if we want the right to life we must devote ourselves to feeling young! (From an incomplete letter to a Danish addressee [J. Steenberg?], November, 1891.)

press, and immediately upon seeing it Björnson sent Grieg an enthusiastic letter of thanks.[2]

A huge jubilee concert was given in his honor on November 23, and he experienced the warm regard that the people of Oslo felt toward him. He stood on the podium like the great victor that he was, and more than two thousand listeners expressed their love and appreciation for him and his music.

That evening he was the guest of honor at a large banquet. One of the speakers was Ibsen, who among other things thanked him because through his marvelous art he had been a spokesman for his—Ibsen's—own work. The two of them, Ibsen said, had mutually complemented each other. The Student Society added luster to the celebration with a brilliant torch-light procession in Grieg's honor. Indeed, the tribute was "like none [he] had ever experienced before." During the procession he stepped out on the balcony of the hotel and gave an extemporaneous speech of tribute to youth.[3]

In the middle of December the Griegs returned to western Norway. Nina wrote to Delius on December 21: "We have had a wonderful trip . . . On the Filefjeld [File mountain] this great eternal solitude, this boundless peace, everything so still, everything frozen. But the sun came and bathed the peaks in gold; they stood there glowing, all those old fellows."

But the happiness experienced on the trip did not last long: shortly after getting home Grieg suffered an influenza attack that sapped his spirits and his desire to work. As previously mentioned, the dampness in the composer's hut at "Troldhaugen" was such that by January of 1892 Grieg had become "crippled with rheumatism" in his feet, and "with that my hut was doomed. I haven't dared to set my foot there since," he wrote in an August 3 letter to Jonas Lie.

The fruit of the winter's labor was a revision of the three orchestral pieces from *Sigurd Jorsalfar*, Opus 56. It was with this rearrangement that the "Homage March" was given an extended trio section and an introductory brass fanfare—music that one does not associate with influenza or rheumatism, but with joy and festivity.

Caricature of Björnstjerne Björnson, signed "AE".

4. GRIEG ON THE MARVELOUS SILVER WEDDING ANNIVERSARY DAY

It was as if a mysterious good fortune guided events that day. We had had a long period of atrocious weather, but on the tenth [June, 1892] it suddenly began to change, and by early evening on the eleventh it was absolutely glorious . . . We stepped into the living room, and it was so filled with gifts we scarcely recognized it. A sea of flowers surrounded us; there stood Frants; outside a chorale was being played in the quiet, sunlit morning; it was such an indescribable moment, one so full of reconciliation for the twenty-five years . . . At 12 o'clock over a hundred well-wishers came . . . In the evening everything was like a fairy tale.

Out in the yard many tables were covered with food, and the guests went at them in the marvelous evening weather (we had eaten dinner with the family at the Beyers'). First came about 150 people (guests), and then at 9:30 came 230 singers with their banners. Then there were songs, speeches, and toasts until late into the night; meanwhile cannons boomed and fireworks. Bengalese lights, and midsummer night bonfires were mirrored in the fjord. It was grand. The fjord teemed with boats, and all the rocks and lookout points were covered with people. The evening trains to Hop had brought more than 5000 people, which is something unprecedented here . . . My friend Holter brought with him from Oslo a big painting (by Werenskiold) as a gift from music friends and a gigantic bearskin from the musicians there. Music friends in Bergen presented us with a beautiful Steinway grand piano . . . We also received about 150 telegrams . . . I played the piano and my wife sang songs which she had sung twenty-five years ago, and never has she sung more beautifully. It was an absolutely unique experience for both of us to perform these songs from the time of our engagement on this day. It was almost too much of a good thing. (Letter to Röntgen, June 19, 1892.)

And there really was to be a celebration: June 11 was the date for the Griegs' silver wedding anniversary. Grieg dreaded this day and "looked forward to the 12th," as he put it. He would have preferred to "crawl off into a mouse hole or something in idyllic solitude," he confided to Winding on June 26. But the actual celebration proved to be one of the most memorable days of his life. "There were two times," he wrote, "when I broke down completely and cried like a child. The first time was in the early morning when, in the most marvelous weather, I walked into my living room and heard the chorale 'A Mighty Fortress Is Our God' being played just outside my window. (Bergen's military music brigade was standing there in formation.) When that happened, both Nina and I were overcome with emotion. Then I recovered again for a while—until I received the priceless album that you sent us [a gift from Danish friends]. Bit by bit as I turned the pages my eyes filled with tears. Finally I said: 'No, I can't stand it!' and I had to slip outside to recover my composure." Grieg sent an even fuller account of the events of the day in a June 19 letter to Röntgen.[4]

The rest of the summer was once again marred by illness, but he improved sufficiently so that he was able to return to Oslo in October. The *Sigurd Jorsalfar* music was premiered November 5. During this stay in Oslo he became better acquainted with Fridtjof Nansen. He wrote to Beyer on October 24: "[Nansen] is much more than just a sportsman or adventurer . . . He is a philosopher worthy of note, and he has a store of knowledge which certainly is rare . . . [He has a] healthy, spontaneous and self-assured nature, yet he is modest and unassuming."

The following month Nina and Edvard went to Copenhagen. After a successful concert there they continued on to Leipzig and then Berlin, where they spent the Christmas holidays with several artist friends: Hans Gude, Iver Holter, Eyvind Alnaes, and Christian Sinding. Returning to Leipzig, Grieg conducted a concert of his own works on February 7, 1893. The program included the piano concerto, with Alexander Siloti as soloist, and the *Peer Gynt Suite No. 2.*

Dr. Abraham had generously invited the Griegs and Sinding to accompany him on a tour to southern Europe. The destination was the city of Menton on the French Riviera, where they remained for the rest of the winter. On an excursion to Monte Carlo, Grieg had the dubious pleasure of hearing "The Death of Aase" in polka tempo (see p. 182), and Sinding—to Dr. Abraham's consternation—made a losing attempt to break the city's casino bank.

In Menton, Grieg's creative urge reawakened, and it is possible that all the pieces in the sixth collection of *Lyric Pieces*, Opus 57, were written there. This seems to be what Grieg was saying in a June 23 letter to Jonas Lie: ". . . I recovered to such an extent that I got the urge to write a volume of piano pieces." Opus 57 is among the weaker of his piano works. In four of the six pieces—"Gade," "Illusion," "Secret," and "She Dances"—it is the cosmopolitan Grieg at work. The melodies are pale and impersonal and the harmonies lack their usual spontaneity. In the remaining two pieces, however—"Vanished Days" and "Homesickness"—Grieg strikes a different note,

5. GRIEG REFLECTS UPON HIS LIFE AT THE APPROACH OF AGE FIFTY

It is simply marvelous here. Endless spruce forests with hidden paths where one can completely forget the whole world . . . I have gotten more fame but less happiness than I dreamt of at that time. And you? You could only reap happiness because you were born to it. Everything you touch results in happiness!—Ah well, I'm coming home soon to find out how you do it—if I can . . . I'm going to turn fifty up here . . . I think some miracle or other has got to occur during these fourteen days. The weather here is as beautiful as can be, and if my health doesn't improve here then it's never going to improve, least of all at "Troldhaugen"—unfortunately. Obviously, I'm going to have to sell it; there's no other way. I have thought about spending next winter in Bergen or Oslo; more than ever before I want Norway, Norway! (Letter to Beyer, June 5, 1893.)

6. GRIEG AND IBSEN MEET AT THE GREFSEN SPA IN OSLO

Ibsen sat deep in thought, solemn and melancholy. But suddenly he cheered up when Grieg, happy as a sunbeam, came up the stairway to the veranda. The two masters clasped each other's hands. They hadn't met for years, and they fired questions and answers back and forth like a couple of boys: Ibsen's thundering bass against Grieg's Bergen soprano. Half seriously, half jokingly they discussed plans for Grieg to write incidental music for Ibsen's play, *The Vikings at Helgeland.* (B. Sontum: "Personal Recollections of Ibsen.")

7. GRIEG BECOMES ILL AT "TVINDEHAUGEN"

Gudbrand Andrisson [Skattebu] was the proprietor there [at "Tvindehaugen"] at that time, and he welcomed us warmly, but he immediately asked us to be very quiet because he had Edvard Grieg lying in one of the rooms wrapped in a wool blanket, or maybe it was even two. Edvard had become ill. (O.K. Ödegaard in *Valdresfolk,* p. 3.)

8. THE JOTUNHEIMEN BEDS EXACT A PRICE

Jotunheimen certainly is beautiful, but it is a pig sty! On the trip home I was suddenly

with folk-like melodies and *springar* rhythms appearing in the midsections of the pieces. Here it is as if the composer's nostalgic memories of the Jotunheimen mountains and Norway's spectacular scenery find expression in fresh music with an unmistakable national tinge.

During the winter on the Riviera, Grieg also wrote a small super-patriotic song for male chorus, "Song of the Flag" (CW 147, text by J. Brun). It was a mere occasional piece that was not published in Grieg's lifetime, but Grieg himself rather liked it.

The original intention was to go to England in the spring—first to give some concerts in London in May, then to go on to Cambridge where Grieg was to receive an honorary doctorate. In April, however, his health was such that he began to have some doubt about whether he ought to take the trip "for the sake of this doctor-humbug." The Griegs headed north instead, going first to Bellaggio on the shore of Lake Como, then to the spa city of Meran in South Tyrol. They stayed in Meran for two weeks, and in the middle of May Grieg finally decided to cancel the trip across the Channel.

They reached Oslo at the end of May, and the doctors there prescribed extended treatment at the Grefsen Baths. Here Grieg spent his fiftieth birthday in complete solitude.[5] A few days later there was a hearty reunion with Ibsen.[6]

Grieg used the time at Grefsen to write a detailed and insightful article on Schumann for the New York periodical, *The Century Illustrated Monthly Magazine.* "People have demanded it of me," he wrote to Beyer on June 24, "and just between you and me I have used the opportunity to say some harsh words to the Wagnerians regarding their obtuseness with respect to Schumann."

On June 25, Grieg left for home by way of the Bandak canal and Haukeli. The Röntgen family came for a visit in July, and Julius and Edvard took a trip to the mountains on horseback while the wives and children remained at "Troldhaugen."

At Turtagrö Grieg wrote down five folk tunes, presumably with the intention of incorporating them in a composition, but he never made use of them. When he came to "Tvindehaugen" he unfortunately became ill and was confined to bed for several days.[7] He wrote to Beyer on August 1: "I can't continue lying here because I can't stand being here (a poor bed, among other things)." Back at "Troldhaugen" a few weeks later he revived his gloomy recollections of life with the bedfellow Jotun-vermin.[8]

Autumn became once again a time for traveling. October found him in Oslo, where he played the new *Lyric Pieces* for the first time, and in November he gave two concerts in Copenhagen. At the first Copenhagen concert, Teresa Carreño played the *A-minor Concerto,* Laura Gundersen recited *Bergliot,* and "The Wounded Heart" and "Last Spring" were performed "with about sixty string players." The second was a charity concert for the dependents of some Jutland fishermen who had perished at sea.

afflicted with a skin condition that almost drove me wild. I can barely control myself as I write these lines. The condition was due to—*the Jotunheimen beds!* I am now going to take a hot bath! (Letter to Röntgen, August 17, 1893.)

One thing that interrupted the normal flow of life at this time was that Nina was hospitalized for several weeks with a serious kidney disease. Grieg wrote to Beyer from Copenhagen on November 24 in a sardonic vein: "I am beginning to be cheerful during the day, but now Nina is coming home so that joy will soon be gone. Yes, my friend, there are many strange truths—for example, the fact that when a man really loves his wife it is mighty good to be away from her for six weeks!" Before she came home, however, he had presented her with two new songs as a gift: "Homeward," Opus 58, No. 1, and "The Mother's Lament," Opus 60, No. 2.

After Nina "got out of the cage," Grieg felt obliged to rent an extra room at the hotel so he could work completely undisturbed and incognito. On December 29 he wrote impishly to Beyer: "So now I have also recovered sufficiently that I can receive visits from elegant ladies. There is one marvelous girl, believe it or not, who has visited me almost daily of late, and she gives me many new songs, some of which do her honor. Yes, long live lyricism and eroticism! Why deny oneself a love affair! I don't go searching for one, but when it comes walking in the door I'm not going to just stand there."

Just who was this "marvelous girl"? It was none other than "Lady Musica"—the muse of inspiration. The result of the visit of this fine lady was "a bunch of new songs with texts by Norwegian poets," Opuses 58, 59, and 60.

From the Paulsen and Krag songs to Seven Children's Songs

Grieg wrote to Iver Holter on January 7, 1894: "I have been so much healthier that I've become a completely young lyricist again. In the course of three weeks I have brought Nina a new song almost every day. It has been a glorious time." Unfortunately, the *Five Songs,* Opus 58, and Six Elegiac Songs, Opus 59—both with texts by John Paulsen—are among his weakest. It is surprising that these banal rhymes, which are almost totally devoid of artistic feeling, could have given him such enthusiasm for work. With the exception of the simple and fervent "To the Motherland" (Opus 58, No. 2), these songs are stylistically vacillating and artistically of no importance. One additional item of interest: in "The Emigrant" (Opus 58, No. 5) the melody, with its hint of the Norwegian *stev* tune, anticipates "Love" from *The Mountain Maid* (Opus 67, No. 5).

Striking proof that Grieg was heavily dependent on textual excellence in his songs is found in the *Five Songs,* Opus 60, with texts by Wilhelm Krag. The mood pictures in Krag's neo-Romanticism inspired him profoundly, and suddenly his melodic lyricism was in full flower. The happy result was an extraordinary display of harmonic invention.

The folk-like melody in "Little Kirsten" has an almost Nordraakian simplicity, related motivically as it is to Nordraak's most beautiful song, "The Tone." In "The Mother's Lament," a tender dirge with a modal tinge, the melodic line is almost recitative-like; meanwhile, the poem's melancholy character is underscored with anguished dissonances. In "On The Water" the melody wraps itself affectionately around the words. It is one of Grieg's most captivating songs and a tasty morsel for all sopranos. If one wishes to speak of charm in connection with Grieg's songs, this one will stand at the top of the list. Its attractiveness is due in large part to its refined chromaticism combined with unexpected cadences and turns to third-related chords.

In the remarkable "A Bird Cried Out" the sounds of nature itself play a role. In one of his sketchbooks Grieg wrote down a motive with the explanation, "Seagull cry heard in the Hardanger fjord," and he made use of this motive in the piano part in both the prelude and postlude of the song (see the excerpt below). The poem describes with concentrated emotion a bird "that cried out so sadly on a gray autumn day," and Grieg has precisely captured its mood in a highly unified song of just fourteen measures. One could scarcely imagine a shorter or more intense setting of the text. It is music that evokes wonderful images, music whose effect on the listener is almost magical. In the first three measures we find one of Grieg's most "impressionistic" series of chords, with parallel seventh chords in stepwise motion. The veiled tonality is retained in the postlude, in which a minor sixth (B-flat) in the bass is added to the sustained D-minor chord. In addition, the sustaining pedal of the piano is to be held continuously while the piercing seagull cry in the right hand is fading ominously away. The concluding measures are given below:

Grieg brought Opus 60 to a rousing conclusion with "Midsummer Eve," a bravura song with an infectious spirit. It is very similar in character to the Opus 49 Drachmann songs "Tell Me Now, Did You See the Lad" and "Kind Greetings, Fair Ladies."

The Wilhelm Krag songs, which were dedicated to the Dutch singer Johannes Messchaert, were premiered in Copenhagen on January 20, 1894. The following week the Griegs came to Leipzig, where they were Dr. Abraham's guests at the city's foremost hotel—"altogether too fine for us peasants," as Nina expressed it. On February 1 Grieg conducted a concert that included the *Sigurd Jorsalfar* music, and this proved to be "the greatest triumph" he had experienced in the Gewandhaus. His success in Munich on

9. CONCERT TRIUMPH IN MUNICH

Last night Norway conquered all around! I haven't witnessed such jubilation since one time in London. Twelve-thirteen-fourteen curtain calls. The audience shouted "Encore!" I conducted the whole concert. But today I am like a rag! (Letter to Wilhelm Hansen, March 10, 1894.)

10. NINA IS HOMESICK

For my part, I am so homesick that I am beside myself these days. I don't dare talk about it, for I will only be made fun of. (Letter to Marie Beyer, April 7, 1894.)

11. GRIEG PREPARES TO RECEIVE AN HONORARY DOCTORATE IN CAMBRIDGE

On Thursday (the 10th) I'll play a comic role in Cambridge. Costume: blue and white surplice, medieval cap. Scene: a festively decorated street. Action: procession through the town. That is how Saint-Saëns described it to me in Paris, and he took part in the same thing last year. How one views such things evidently depends on one's nationality. When I said to Saint-Saëns: "Basically the whole thing must be regarded as a comedy," he replied passionately: "No, not at all; on the contrary, the whole thing is 'serieux' in the highest degree." That sort of public display means something to a Frenchman. (Letter to Beyer, May 6, 1894.)

March 9 was, if possible, even greater. Here he performed his best-known orchestral works, and Oscar Meyer was the soloist in the piano concerto.[9]

After an appearance in Geneva on March 17, the Griegs took an extended holiday at Menton and then went on to Paris. Edvard experienced health problems throughout this time, and both Edvard and Nina felt a great longing for home.[10] The concert at the Châtelet theater in Paris, however, which drew an audience of 3000, was another "victory for Norway." The Colonne Orchestra played, among other things, the *A-minor Concerto*, with Raoul Pugno as soloist. The reviews were mixed—which Grieg attributed to the fact that he hadn't been willing to pay the reviewers a visit beforehand and give them "something else called money." During his stay in Paris he tried in vain to meet Verdi who, however, sent him his calling card. After Verdi's death in 1901, Grieg—who greatly admired his operas—wrote a penetrating memorial article in *Verdens Gang*, Oslo, in which he mentioned in passing that he had preserved the calling card "as a relic."

But Grieg did meet another celebrity whose music was also attractive to him. This was Camille Saint-Saëns, who gave him some idea of what he might expect in the way of ceremony in May when he was to receive an honorary doctorate in Cambridge.[11] Grieg was not overly impressed with the ceremony; the whole affair was "sickeningly laughable," he told Delius two days later. "I didn't laugh, though," he continued, "because I was already sick, and the first thing I had to do as a fresh-baked doctor was—go to a doctor myself."

After a concert in London on May 24, he hastily returned to Oslo for further treatment at the Grefsen Baths. He did not get back to "Troldhaugen" until the end of June.

In late July, at the request of the educator O. A. Gröndahl—the husband of the outstanding piano virtuoso, Agathe Backer Gröndahl—Grieg set about the task of writing music for seven small poems from Nordahl Rolfsen's new primary reader. The reason for the request was that Gröndahl was responsible for selecting the melodies that were to go into the book. Grieg undertook this task willingly; as the work progressed he was gripped by the vigorous texts, and made much more out of them than had originally been planned. The result was that the following year he published them himself under the title *Seven Children's Songs*, Opus 61. The work was dedicated to Nordahl Rolfsen and premiered by Nina in Copenhagen on April 26, 1895.

It has been said that Grieg's Opus 61 comprises the best songs written for children in the nineteenth century, and we agree. Several of them—such as "Farmyard Song," "Good-night Song for Dobbin," "The Norwegian Mountains," and "Hymn of the Fatherland"—have maintained their place in Norway's school song books to the present time. "The Christmas Tree" is one of Norway's most beloved Christmas songs. It is a pity, however, that the two songs which Grieg himself considered the best—"The Ocean" and "Fisherman's Song"—have been the least well received among children. The reason for this obviously is that, owing to their melodic difficulty, they are more at home in the concert hall than in the schoolroom. In the *halling*-like "The Ocean," Grieg uses the augmented fourth in G major (C-sharp); "it must sound like sea salt," Grieg wrote to O. Koppang on September 7, 1895. It was

12. ENTHUSIASM FOR
ORCHESTRATED SONGS

Before the influenza attack I had a great
pleasure that has been with me ever since:
the [Copenhagen] Philharmonic concert
which I conducted. The songs that I had
orchestrated sounded absolutely wonderful.
"Monte Pincio" fine and Mediterranean.
And "Wergeland" as pompous as an old
Scandinavian laudatory poem. What a pity
that, for want of a harp, we can't perform it
at home. (Letter to Beyer, March 29, 1895.)

that very C-sharp that led the German author Richard Stein, in his 1921 biography of Grieg, to make the following bizarre comment: "In No. 1 ('The Ocean') we Germans must take the liberty of changing that distracting C-sharp (the leading tone to the fifth) to a C; even Norwegians must feel that that C-sharp doesn't belong there."

Toward the close of "Good-night Song for Dobbin," to the words "Sleep, my gentle Dobbin," Grieg uses a harmonic device that gives the music a uniquely poetic effect. In four measures of the accompaniment the lowered leading tone (E-flat in F major) results in a gently muffled, coloristic effect. Grieg had previously used the same Mixolydian tinge in 1875 in the last part of "Lullaby. Children's Song from Valdres" (see pp. 172–73).

From a period of ill health abroad to "Wedding Day at Troldhaugen"

In October, 1894, Grieg gave four concerts in Bergen, all of which were well received. At the end of the month he left "Troldhaugen" and went via Oslo to Copenhagen, where he remained for six months. He wrote orchestral accompaniments for six of his songs (CW 148), and these were premiered in March.[12] He had planned to give concerts in Weimar and Berlin in March/April, but he was bothered by illness throughout his stay in Copenhagen and was unable to make the trip to Germany. "Sluggishness, weakness, shortness of breath, lack of energy—these are my major achievements at the moment," he told Beyer on March 29, 1895, after a bout with pneumonia. He had also been invited to join Busoni, Saint-Saëns, Widor, and others as a member of the jury for the Rubinstein competition in Berlin, but had to decline.

Before returning to "Troldhaugen" at the beginning of May, Grieg completed a new work for string orchestra: *Two Nordic Melodies,* Opus 63. Like his other compositions in this genre, the two pieces are exceptionally well done. The first, "In Folk Style," is an arrangement of a little melody that Fredrik Due, the Norwegian-Swedish envoy to France, had sent him after the two had met in Paris the year before. The second piece contains arrangements of two folk melodies from Opus 17, "Cow Call" (No. 22) and "Peasant Dance" (No. 18).

At the same time he was also at work on the seventh volume of *Lyric Pieces,* Opus 62. "Sylph," "Gratitude," and "Phantom" are written in a salon style that is for the most part rather uninteresting, while the charming and melodious "French Serenade" rises somewhat above the commonplace. It is only in "Brooklet" and "Homeward," however, that Grieg returned to the level of the best pieces of Opuses 43 and 54. In the sparkling "Brooklet" he draws upon pure and original sources, and "Homeward" has a pithy, folk-like theme, rhythmic verve, and amusing—almost brazen—chord progressions.

Upon returning to "Troldhaugen" in May, Grieg became enraptured by Arne Garborg's *Haugtussa* poems and immediately began writing music for a considerable number of them (see further p. 339 ff.). In July his closest Danish friends—the Hornemans, the Matthison-Hansens, and the Windings, all of whom he had generously invited to visit western Norway—came to "Trold-haugen." After this visit, unfortunately, there arose a serious disagreement between Grieg and Horneman which, to Grieg's great sorrow, ruined their friendship for life.

In October Grieg went briefly to Oslo and then to Copenhagen enroute to Leipzig where, at Dr. Abraham's invitation, he and Nina planned to spend the winter. In Copenhagen he came in contact with two Danish performing artists: Margrethe Petersen, who was a singer, and her friend, the pianist Bella Edwards. Six letters from Grieg to Bella Edwards—letters written from Leipzig over a two-month period—have recently come to light in the Bergen Public Library. After meeting her in Copenhagen on three different occasions he was, as he wrote in a December 5 letter to her, completely taken with her: "I forget that I am at the noontime of my life; I feel like a lovesick schoolboy who is blissfully giddy over the girl he loves." He begged her to meet him again, but she declined. He ended the correspondence on January 27, 1896, with these words: "I cannot answer your letter without opening up all of the wounds! So just this: Do not write again. Still—since you wish it so: we shall not absolutely sever our relationship! Let us then meet again as friends!"

In Leipzig, moreover, he found himself out of sorts.[13] Nonetheless, he stayed there for about six months. His greatest musical experience at this time was César Franck's oratorio *Les Béatitudes,* which Grieg described as a piece "written by a master so great that, in my opinion, no one now living can measure up to him" (letter to Matthison-Hansen of November 25, 1895). In the middle of January, 1896, Brahms was in Leipzig for a performance of his *Fourth Symphony* by the Gewandhaus Orchestra under Arthur Nikisch, and Grieg renewed his acquaintance with him at that time.[14] They met again a few weeks later in Vienna, where they regularly "taverned together."[15] After the big Grieg concert on March 23, which Brahms also attended, there was celebrating until the early hours of the morning. Grieg spoke so warmly and beautifully of Brahms that everyone was deeply moved. Röntgen wrote later in his book about Grieg (p. 51): "Brahms listened with bowed head, and afterwards he went to Grieg and clasped his hand without saying a word." Grieg nearly missed going to Vienna, however, because just before their scheduled departure Nina suddenly became very ill. On April 2 he wrote to Johan Halvorsen that if Nina had been along "these days would have been among the most beautiful in my life. You should have heard those strings!! And such people—such a city! Happiness, the capacity to get excited, good will, spontaneity. I tell you, they are in a class by themselves."

Nina's illness was far more serious than Grieg had first thought. She was rushed into surgery for what was presumed to be breast cancer, but she was nonetheless able to be present to share with Edvard an especially happy occasion: on April 28, enroute back to Norway, he had the great honor of conducting the Berlin Philharmonic in Copenhagen. The program included his *A-minor Concerto,* with Feruccio Busoni as soloist.

The lengthy stay abroad was followed by a period of peace and quiet at "Troldhaugen." To conserve Nina's strength, Grieg's birthday was celebrated at Lofthus, where relatives and friends were invited to a big celebration.

13. GRIEG IS UNHAPPY IN LEIPZIG

As matters now stand I don't think I'll be here long, for I have become so inflexible down here that I can no longer maintain my own identity in all this Germanness and all this so-called musical life, which in many respects seems to me so worm-eaten. And then there is this: neither sea nor mountain, only coal dust and marshy fog. No: long live Scandinavia! Yes, I'll even be so liberal as to include Sweden! (Letter to Beyer, October 27, 1895.)

14. WITH BRAHMS IN LEIPZIG

Last week we were frequently with Brahms in Leipzig, where he was visiting for a few days, and it was a great pleasure to be together. I don't understand how such a one-sided person as Brahms—one-sided in his greatness, I mean—can appreciate my music which, so far as I can see, goes in a very different direction. But reticent though he is, he let me know that he does appreciate it. His *Fourth Symphony* (in E minor) was performed in the Gewandhaus. It's a work I didn't know before, and its first movement is one of the most beautiful things he has written. (Letter to Beyer, December 31, 1895.)

15. GRIEG MEETS BRAHMS, BRUCKNER, AND DVOŘÁK IN VIENNA

I was with Brahms a great deal. He was jovial and friendly. I can't say the same for Dvořák, with whom, however, I made only a superficial acquaintance. Then I visited old Bruckner, a trembling graybeard, but touchingly childlike. (Letter to Iver Holter, March 28, 1896.)

16. GRIEG MENTIONS SVENDSEN'S
NORWEGIAN RHAPSODIES AS THE
MODEL FOR HIS OWN *SYMPHONIC
DANCES*

"To treat them [folktunes] in such a way
that they can even be used for concert purposes," as you say, is precisely what Johan
Svendsen has done with great mastery in
his *Norwegian Rhapsodies,* and what I have
also tried to do in my *Symphonic Dances.* In
this way the folk tunes merge with one's
own individuality and, after this process has
been completed, become elements in a genuine work of art. (Letter to G. Schjelderup,
October 26, 1905.)

17. THE *SYMPHONIC DANCES* MUST
BE VIEWED AS A WHOLE

To publish the *Symphonic Dances* individually—for such a thing I can't find a German
expression that you would want to hear . . .
If, for example, you published the second
piece, you would thereby ensure that the
whole set would perhaps *never* be played! If
I were ever to perpetrate a symphony, perhaps you would publish the scherzo by itself. Well, why not? In the new century
many Gordian knots from the preceding
century will be untied! In the end man himself will be divided up, and liver and lungs
and heart—each separately—will be offered
for sale! (Letter to Henri Hinrichsen, January 6, 1900.)

Summer and autumn proved to be a productive time, and the results were
noteworthy: Opuses 64–66.

Symphonic Dances, Opus 64, was first written in a piano four hands version
that is dated September 27, 1896. During the autumn Grieg set about or-
chestrating these dances for full orchestra. This took longer than he had
expected, and it appears that the task was not completed until 1898. Opus 64
was dedicated to the pianist Arthur de Greef.

Through his experiences as guest conductor of Europe's leading orchestras
Grieg had acquired greater self-confidence, and he now felt he could venture
into an area that had thus far been Svendsen's exclusive domain: using
Norwegian folktunes as integral parts of large orchestral rhapsodies.[16] In
recognition of Svendsen's pioneering effort in this area, he gave him the
honor of premiering *Symphonic Dances* in Copenhagen on February 4, 1899.

In the four dances Grieg again used material from Lindeman's collection.
"Halling from Valdres" (No. 9 in Lindeman) appears in the first; the *halling*
"The Horse Trader" (No. 548) in the second; "Springar from Aamot" (No.
328) in the third; and "Peasant Song" (No. 443) and "Wedding Tune" (No.
484) in the fourth. Grieg had previously used "Peasant Song" and "Wedding
Tune" in Opus 17 as Nos. 23 and 24, respectively.

It was very important to Grieg that the pieces be played as an organic
whole. In 1900, when Peters wanted to publish the dances singly in a new
edition of Opus 64, he gave the director of the firm a scolding in a very caustic
letter.[17] Shortly thereafter he changed his mind about this, but the dances
never were published individually.

Grieg himself thought highly of the work, but the judgment of history has
not always been so positive. This is due especially to Grieg's tendency in this
opus to pad the material with repetitions and long sequences without any real
development taking place. Grieg himself eventually recognized the tediousness of the many repetitions, and in a letter of January 18, 1900, to the director
of C. F. Peters, he enclosed a memorandum entitled "To the conductor,"
requesting that a number of them be omitted. Grieg's wishes have been
carried out in Vol. 11 of *Edvard Grieg's Complete Works* (1984). What Grieg
lacks in formal inventiveness in the *Symphonic Dances,* however, is counterbalanced by his artistic use of the orchestra. With respect to orchestration, this
is his most richly faceted work. It contains some exquisite subtleties, not least
in the virtuosic use of the winds, especially the brass. The last piece is the most
successful of the four by virtue of Grieg's handling of thematic material, the
harmonic virility, and the brilliant exploitation of orchestral resources.

In a letter to Horneman on September 15, 1896, Grieg wrote: ". . . With all
due respect I must say that I have done nothing except for the so-called 'Lyric
Pieces' that swarm around me like fleas and lice out in the country." The
reference here is to the eighth volume of *Lyric Pieces,* Opus 65, which has
deservedly won great popularity, not least for its value as pedagogical music.
Only one piece—"Salon"—is merely ordinary. "Melancholy" is somewhat
uninteresting melodically—Grieg hammers away no less than eight times on a
motive he had used earlier in "To Spring"—but this is offset by the fact that
harmonically the material is given an advanced, experimental treatment.

"From Early Years" is closely related to "Vanished Days" (Opus 57, No. 1) both thematically and structurally, but is the superior piece by virtue of its more pithy melody.

In two of the pieces—"Peasant's Song" and "Ballad"—Grieg used stylized folk tunes in a natural and engaging manner. "Peasant's Song" also reminds one in some ways of "In My Native Country" (Opus 43, No. 3). The manuscript containing the first draft of "Ballad" also includes three pages of piano sketches for a contemplated orchestral work. "Spring. Symphonic Poem for Orchestra," which was never completed.

Opus 65 is brought to a festive conclusion with "Wedding Day at Troldhaugen." With this piece—more, perhaps, than any other piano piece—Grieg has won the hearts of the world's amateur pianists. It is exceptionally well conceived: it sounds like a bravura piece without demanding great technical skill by the performer. Not least among its virtues is the strongly contrasting midsection, a revelation of the loveliest lyricism inspired by Norwegian nature.

In the original manuscript this piece was called "The Well-wishers are Coming." On July 29, 1896, Mrs. Nancy Giertsen, a close friend of the Grieg family, celebrated her fiftieth birthday. A beautiful congratulatory scroll was created for her to mark the occasion, and on the cover page Grieg wrote the opening of the piece using the title, "The Well-wishers are Coming." The body of the scroll includes the entire piece in the composer's own handwriting. The following year, when Opus 65 was being proofread prior to publication, the piece was given its new and catchier title—one that seems to indicate that it was actually conceived as a resounding memento of that unforgettable silver wedding anniversary day at "Troldhaugen" in 1892.

Back to Original Sources

I. NORWEGIANS ARE BOTH INTROSPECTIVE AND SERIOUS

Yes, Norway! Norway! Let Ibsen say 100 times that it is best to belong to a large nation: I can perhaps agree with him in the practical sense, but not a step further. Because ideally I don't want to belong to any other nation in the world! The older I get the more I feel that I love Norway just because it is so poor, just because in practical matters we are such accursed idiots. Good Lord, anybody can be rich and practical; but not everyone can be *serious* and *introspective!* But it is precisely these two peculiarities that condition the future for our people. These peculiarities loom so large (for me) when I am abroad. For that reason it is doubly pleasant to get away . . . (Letter to Beyer, October 8, 1887.)

On February 3, 1900, Grieg wrote to Johan Halvorsen from Copenhagen: "Although I am currently out of the country, my thoughts are only about Norway and Norwegians, about all our youthful pugnacity up there. Yes, it is like the music of strong triads compared to all the sugary seventh chords down here. The struggle in Norway has to do with spiritual survival; down here they are concerned about trivialities." A few weeks later he returned to the same theme in a letter to Björnson: "Down here people really thrive on 'scoffing.' Scoffing at politics, literature, art, theater scandals, duels. It is one of the good things about us Norwegians that we're not infected by that sort of thing. It just isn't our nature. Quite the contrary. Each year when I go back to Norway I realize more and more the extent to which we are leaden, timid, and fettered. But I'm not complaining, for I know that heaviness is also seriousness—and therein lies our future!"

Thirteen years earlier he had also written about the seriousness and introspection which in his opinion were characteristic of the Norwegians, and which made it "doubly nice" to get away for awhile—from pettiness, narrow-mindedness, and chauvinism.[1]

Indeed, throughout his life he loathed chauvinism. As early as October 26, 1872, he wrote to August Winding: "National pride can be both the most beautiful and the most repulsive thing, but this is certain: it makes people *stupid*." More than twenty-five years later—on February 4, 1898—in connection with the great music festival being held in Bergen, he told Beyer that he wanted to write an article about "What is Norwegian." He elaborated: "When Norwegian music is performed in such a way that it has the effect of strengthening the love of our country, so that people develop a better understanding of our native art, then the effort to achieve this result is dictated by nationalism. This I say from the bottom of my heart . . . Now I'm on my way to sounding ill-tempered, but what actually happens is that when something Norwegian is going to be performed here somebody always comes along and mixes it up with cow-pies and 'bull's mead' and makes it utterly distasteful." Chauvinism, in Grieg's view, had nothing to do with genuine love of country. At about the same time he wrote to Thorvald Lammers: "*You* know that,

2. "COSMOPOLITAN CONFESSION OF FAITH"

Esteemed Mr. Wilhelm Hansen!

In an article entitled "About Nationalistic Compositions" which appeared in your music periodical [*Musikbladet*], you have quoted the views of a Berlin critic on this topic—views that are patently wide open to contradiction. Nonetheless, I shall not take the trouble to act as the defender of nationalistic art in general, for the history of art has taken care of that defense so thoroughly that any further attempt is superfluous. The author of the aforementioned article has, however, tracked down a remark that I made many years ago, a remark that belongs so completely to my very green period that I consider it my duty to disavow it publicly here. The remark to which I refer was this: "We (Nordraak and I) conspired against the Mendelssohn-inspired, effeminate Scandinavianism of Gade, and we set out with enthusiasm on the new road on which the Scandinavian school now finds itself." You will understand that from my present standpoint I cannot acknowledge a declaration which to a greater degree than one might wish expresses mere youthful arrogance. I hardly need to assure you that I am neither so biased as not to have deep respect and admiration for a master such as Gade, nor so superficial as to—as the author of the article put it—"actually claim to be the most nationalistic among the nationalists, the Messiah of Norwegian music." Faced with such an assertion, I dare say that the author lacks the most important qualifications for judging me. If the author had been familiar with my work in its entirety, it would hardly have escaped him that in my later compositions I have moved more and more toward a broader and more universal vision of my own individuality, a vision influenced by the great currents of our time—including those that are cosmopolitan. But—this I willingly admit—never could I bring myself to violently tear up the roots that tie me to my native land.

As I regret that such misleading statements about my art have found their way to a Danish audience, I venture to request a place for these few words in your esteemed periodical. (*Musikbladet*, Copenhagen, October 8, 1889.)

although I hate chauvinism like the plague, in my heart of hearts I am as good a Norwegian as you can find anywhere."

This was the tension in which Grieg lived for so many years. He had a deep love for that which was genuinely Norwegian, but at the same time he had a strong need to reach out, to tear himself loose from that which bound him to a narrow "Norwegianness." So he ran away from it, tried to be European—cosmopolitan—and wrote music in which Norwegianness was nearly eradicated. But then he discovered that this did not lead forward either. Without close contact with the "raw material" of Norway he tended to stagnate. It was when he struggled with the Norwegian "heaviness," when he revealed the "hidden harmonies" of Norwegian folk music, when he built upon its peculiarities and in so doing returned to that which was original and genuine—then it was that he found himself as well. And only then did his art reach a world-wide audience.

Nationalistic dreamer, cosmopolitan, or simply an individualist?

Grieg's dilemma came clearly out in the open in 1889, when he wrote his so-called "cosmopolitan confession of faith." This article, dated September 14, was printed on October 8 in *Musikbladet*, Copenhagen.[2] He protested indignantly against certain remarks of the Berlin critic Alexander Moszkowski that had been quoted in an earlier issue of the paper. Moszkowski had depicted Grieg as a composer who wagered everything on Norwegian nationalism—as if he wanted to be "the virtual Messiah of Norwegian music."

Grieg's strong reaction to Moszkowski's article was principally due to two factors. First, he wanted very much not to be included among those who were opposed to Gade and the Danish music establishment. Even more importantly, he felt the need to distance himself from a view that was current in many circles: that he was in reality a staunch Romantic nationalist who only stole what served his purposes from Norwegian folk music.

To be sure, in the late 1880s he was in a period when he intended to write music with a "wider horizon." In an interview published in the *Pall Mall Gazette* of London on March 20, 1889, he expressed his position thus: "My later works are not so typical of Scandinavian music. I have traveled around and have become more European, more cosmopolitan. These changes occur little by little; we scarcely notice them until suddenly they are there."

Long before this interview, however, he had come out strongly against claims that he deliberately aimed at being "Norwegian" in his music. As early as April 25, 1881, he wrote to his biographer Aimar Grönvold: "In some biographies of Svendsen I have read the remark that for me the national element is the end, whereas for Svendsen it is the means to an end. I will only ask that in the name of truth you speak out against this view. I don't deny the exaggerated Norwegian passion of my youth, but as a modern artist what I am striving for is that which is universal—or, more correctly, that which is

Caricature of Grieg by Olaf Gulbransson. (Photo collection of Det Kongelige Bibliotek, Copenhagen)

individual. If the result is nationalistic it is because the individual is nationalistic, and then it is nothing to be ashamed of."

Here Grieg touched on something essential, both in his own relation to the national element in his music and in our understanding of him as a national composer. For it is altogether too easy to equate that which is simply Griegian and that which is Norwegian. This is a fallacy. Even when Grieg made use of folk music he supplemented it with his own material, particularly in the realm of harmony. When he said that he wanted to bring out the "hidden harmonies" in Norwegian folk music he was obviously speaking metaphorically. These are *his* harmonies and no one else's. One should not say that Grieg's music is typically Norwegian; one should rather say that it is typically Griegian. But because he was Norwegian, and because his music so often was based on the folk music of Norway, his musical language has become virtually synonymous with a purely Norwegian musical feeling. Thus his assertion about the *individual* provides an important clarification: his real goal was not to be Norwegian, but to express his individuality.

Not more than two weeks after the publication of the article in *Musikbladet*, Grieg found it necessary to make a judicious retreat. When the *Olav Trygvason* music was performed in Copenhagen, some critics perceived it as his first attempt to write in a new style in keeping with what he had stated in the article. He felt compelled to respond to this view. In a November 21 letter to the Copenhagen critic Angul Hammerich, he emphasized that *Olav Trygvason* had been written during the 1870s, and that he certainly had a "cosmopolitan" streak in him dating way back to the exaggerated nationalism of his youth. Nonetheless, he wanted an end to the nonsense of having the word "cosmopolitan" used as a point of attack against his music: "I think that just as a human being is both *individual* and *social*, so an artist is both national and cosmopolitan. But he does not always have the opportunity to show both sides equally. I ask you kindly to do whatever you can to prevent the word 'cosmopolitan' being used as a slogan against me, as if it marked a change of direction in my music. For that was never my intention. Indeed, in the [*Musikbladet*] article I explicitly emphasized the presence of *both* elements— the national and the cosmopolitan. Your favorable regard for my music has led me to write this, because I didn't want you to have an incorrect perception of it. Ordinarily as a matter of principle I refrain from delivering such harangues."

In the middle of the 1890s Grieg developed a more relaxed attitude toward national idiosyncrasies. Without inhibitions of any kind, he abandoned all his "cosmopolitan" tendencies and returned to his musical roots—the genuine folk music of Norway. The result was *Nineteen Norwegian Folk Songs*, Opus 66—one of his most successful works in this genre. He drew his inspiration from the same source in the early 1900s in his *Norwegian Peasant Dances*, Opus 72, and *Four Psalms*, Opus 74. Then, in a way, the ring was closed: he had come full circle from the "wild" national enthusiasm of his youth to the mature attitude of his later years. On November 2, 1904, he wrote to Gerhard Schjelderup that in the history of music there is nothing that has proven its vitality "except that which grew out of native soil." He expressed this view even more clearly in an interview in a Berlin paper a few months before his death. He emphasized on this occasion that his path as a composer had to go by way of the folk music of Norway, though he also was at pains to point out that his music nonetheless gave considerable room for personal expression.[3]

It would be difficult to imagine a more beautiful blending of the originality of Norwegian folk tunes and Grieg's own individuality than *Nineteen Norwegian Folk Songs*. The much-traveled composer had "come home" again.

Nineteen Norwegian Folk Songs, Opus 66

Frants Beyer was uniquely important to Grieg not only as his closest friend but also as the immediate source for one of the composer's finest contributions in the area of folk music. The reason is that, with the single exception of "Gjendine's Lullaby," the whole of Opus 66 is based on Beyer's transcriptions of authentic folk tunes. Beyer, in addition to being a gifted amateur composer, had been collecting folk tunes most of his life. Some of the materials he supplied for Grieg's Opus 66 were in fact melodies that he had heard as a child.

During the latter part of July, 1896, Grieg spent nine days as a guest at "Trondsbu," a hunting cabin owned by Beyer's brother-in-law, Börre Giertsen. The cabin was located near Lake Tinnhölen on the Hardangervidda, a barren plateau high in the mountains of south-central Norway. Beyer and Röntgen were also there as well as Giertsen. Here Grieg harmonized a folk tune which Beyer had written down. Grieg presented a fair copy of this arrangement to Mrs. Nancy Giertsen on her fiftieth birthday, with the inscription "29 June, Tinnhölen."

At the beginning of August, Nina and Edvard spent two weeks at Fossli, a tourist hotel located near Vöringsfossen, a large waterfall a few miles east of the village of Eidfjord. The first attempt at harmonizing Beyer's transcription had whetted Grieg's appetite. While at Fossli he received from Beyer two new batches of transcriptions containing a total of fourteen folk tunes. Filled with enthusiasm over the splendid melodies, Grieg threw caution to the wind and gave free rein to his inherently daring harmonic imagination. Upon returning to "Troldhaugen" he received some additional melodies from Beyer, and on September 22 he reported to Röntgen that Opus 66 was finished. During a visit to Leipzig in January, 1897, he personally delivered a fair copy of the manuscript to Dr. Abraham. The collection, naturally enough, was dedicated to Frants Beyer. In the Primary Materials will be found excerpts from three letters in which Grieg, in his characteristic manner, described the work.[4]

Grieg received a total of twenty-two folk tunes from Beyer. He used twenty of these in eighteen arrangements in Opus 66. (In both "Cow Call and Lullaby" [No. 6] and "Lullaby" [No. 17] he made use of two melodies.) The concluding piece in Opus 66 is "Gjendine's Lullaby," which Grieg himself had written down in 1891 (see p. 316). Two original Beyer transcriptions are given below: "Cow Call" (No. 1) and "Lullaby" (one of the two pieces used in No. 17):

3. GRIEG ON THE IMPORTANCE OF THE NATIONAL ELEMENT IN HIS ART

I was educated in the German school. I have studied in Leipzig, and musically speaking am completely German. But then I went to Copenhagen and got acquainted with Gade and Hartmann. It then struck me that I could only develop myself further on a national foundation. It was our Norwegian folk tunes that showed me the way. In Germany the critics treated me badly because I didn't fit into the categories into which composers are commonly placed. In Germany it is often said: "Er norwegert!" [He exaggerates the Norwegianness.] It is true that I create out of the Norwegian folk tunes, but even Mozart and Beethoven would not have become what they did if they had not had the old masters as models. The sublime German folk song was a basis for them, and without such a basis no serious music is possible. This I saw clearly. And in spite of that they say of me: "Er norwegert."

The treasures in our folk tunes are for the most part still unknown. I knew what I was doing when I was twenty years old. But since these treasures have not been collected, there is no one who knows them. That is why it is so careless to say, "Er norwegert." I know very well why my music sounds altogether too national to German ears, but I must also take into consideration the fact that a good deal of my individuality is due to my Germanization. For one doesn't find it among the Scandinavian people. But I believe nonetheless that our people are able to grasp this harmony—indeed, that perhaps it lies there in a mysterious way. As our poets again and again make use of material from the sagas, so also the composer can and must search out the musical sources for his art. (Interview with Grieg in *Berliner Lokal-Anzeiger*, April 4, 1907.)

4. GRIEG'S VIEWS REGARDING *NINETEEN NORWEGIAN FOLK SONGS*

Life is just as strange as folk songs; one doesn't know whether they were conceived in major or minor . . . I spent the afternoons in my room where I harmonized the many folk melodies which Frants had sent me. It was truly festive . . . Some of them are incredibly beautiful. In any case, I have set some hair-raising chord combinations on paper. But by way of excuse, let me say that they weren't created at the piano but in my head. When one has the Vöring Falls nearby, one feels more independent and is more daring than down in the valley. (Letter to Röntgen, August 22. 1896.)

* * *

This summer when I was in the mountains, I got a large number of previously unpublished and unknown folk tunes which are so beautiful that I found it a real joy to arrange them for piano. (Letter to Dr. Abraham, September 22, 1896.)

* * *

How magnificent these heroic ballads are! It is as if the most profound harmonies lie hidden in them, longing for the time when they will see the light of day. In my forthcoming collection of folk songs there are also a few that must be classed as heroic ballads. What should especially interest Norwegians about the collection is that none of the melodies has ever been published before. They were transcribed during the past two years as they were sung by milkmaids and cattlemen in the Jotunheimen mountains. They are characterized by the deepest melancholy, interrupted only now and then by a passing ray of light. (Letter to Agathe Backer Gröndahl, May, 1897.)

The folk tunes varied in a number of ways. Some were old, some of more recent date. They ranged from heroic ballads to popular ditties, vocal dance melodies, cow calls, and lullabies. Most had texts, which Grieg chose to omit. It was an exciting collection of source material. Many of the melodies had a pronounced archaic character resulting from unstable scales and modal passages, and in some the tonality was simply ambiguous. In the second cradle song which Grieg included in "Lullaby" (No. 17), for example, Beyer had indicated that the fourth in G major lay between C and C-sharp. Also, the popular ditties of recent origin had been altered in the style of the folk tradition, thus acquiring a distinctive folk-music flavor.

In his earlier adaptations Grieg himself had selected the melodies he wanted to arrange. This time, however, he was faced with a *fait accompli,* and the challenge that this created undoubtedly had a highly stimulating effect on him. By and large he was faithful to Beyer's transcriptions, but occasionally he deliberately took minor liberties with both notes and rhythms. Moreover, he often used the melodies as material for somewhat longer compositions. In four pieces he employed a contrapuntal technique using the melody as a cantus firmus in the bass or one of the inner voices.

What strikes one most of all about these arrangements is the exceptionally rich harmony. Several of the pieces are very short, but the greatness of the mature master is evident in these as well. Even the simplest folk tunes seem to have elicited the best in him, as in "Cow Call" (No. 1) and "Gjendine's Lullaby" (No. 19). The spectrum of harmonic means is broader than in Grieg's earlier works. A life in "the dream world of the harmonies" had given him the experience that he needed to raise these songs, which were so beautiful in themselves, to still loftier artistic heights. The advanced harmonic means he had developed—such as parallel chords, long series of altered chords, unusual cadences, and veiled tonality—were worked into these arrangements in the most natural manner.

"In Ola Valley, in Ola Lake" (No. 14) stands out as one of Grieg's most impressionistic piano pieces. This splendid folk tune, clad in Grieg's inimitable harmony, made such an impression on the English composer Frederick Delius that he made use of the melody (without acknowledging the source) and colored the material in the spirit of Grieg in what is perhaps his best-known orchestral work, *On Hearing the First Cuckoo in Spring* (1912).

The sound of church bells served as Grieg's starting point in "In Ola Valley, in Ola Lake," just as they had in "Bell Ringing" (Opus 54, No. 6). The text of the song is derived from a legend about a child who has disappeared. In her despair the mother arranges for the parish church bells to be rung, hoping that this will break the power of the underworld. (Note the similarity to the action of Peer Gynt's mother, Aase, at the end of Act I of the Ibsen play.) But the act is in vain: ". . . Öli never found her boy again." Throughout the piece there is a hint of bell sounds which Grieg calls forth in ever new ways; meanwhile the folk tune is interwoven like a thread of fate in the harmonic tapestry.

It is quite possible that all nine of the songs from Lom came from Gjendine Slaalien. In interviews on Radio Norway she reported that Beyer and Grieg had transcribed her melodies during several summers after 1891. Two of these—"A Little Grey Man" (No. 13) and "Tomorrow You Shall Marry Her" (No. 10)—she tape-recorded in 1961 when she was eighty-nine years old. Her version of "A Little Grey Man" is virtually identical to Beyer's transcription. Given below is our transcription of the first stanza of "Gjendine's Lullaby" as she sang it on Radio Norway on June 1, 1951, when she was seventy-nine years old. She had learned the cradle song from her grandmother in Lom. The B in measure 8 and all the F-sharps she sang slightly lower than notated [the words mean: "The child is laid in its cradle, sometimes it cries and sometimes laughs. Sleep now, sleep now in Jesus' name, Jesus watch over the child."]:

The first ten measures of Grieg's final treatment of "Gjendine's Lullaby" as it appears in Opus 66, are given below:

The melodic differences between the two versions, as one can see, are small. The expressiveness in Grieg's simple setting is strengthened by a long pedal point. The harmonic climax is concentrated in measures 9–10—pianissimo. One notices especially Grieg's fine sensitivity in measure 10, where he harmonized the fluctuating leading tone (F-sharp) with an equally ambiguous chord—i.e., one with a flavor of the whole-tone scale. It could hardly have been done more aptly.

Grieg had no intention in Opus 66 of creating a work that would be suitable for the concert hall. Nonetheless, it appears that he wished to invest the collection with a certain internal unity with respect to both use of keys and degree of tension. The pieces seem to be consciously grouped around G as a kind of tonal center. There is a heightening of tension toward the middle of the collection where the pieces are centered around the dominant, and a return to the tonic in the last part. There is also an increase in complexity. The most notable example of this in the first half is in No. 10, and in the second half Nos. 14–18. There then follows a complete relaxation of tension with "Gjendine's Lullaby" in G minor. The *Ballade* in G minor, Opus 24, has much the same construction. The endings of both works also reveal important similarities—melodically, harmonically, and not least with respect to mood.

*Ingebrigt Vik's statue of Edvard Grieg in the
city park in Bergen. It was unveiled September
4, 1917.*

The Garborg Songs

Grieg, brimming with enthusiasm, wrote to Röntgen on June 12, 1895: "During the past few days I have been buried in a most remarkable collection of lyric poetry: it is *Haugtussa* [The Mountain Maid], a book by Arne Garborg that has just been published. It is written in *nynorsk*. It is an absolutely brilliant book in which the music really has already been composed: one has only to write it down." Four days later he wrote to Winding that he had found *Haugtussa* "so full of nature mysticism that I couldn't resist it."

Fifteen years had passed since his last such overpowering encounter with *nynorsk* poetry, and he was immediately entranced by the distinctive quality of the verse and the resonant beauty of the language. The words of this language—so different from the Dano-Norwegian that he had spoken all his life—were thoroughly permeated with music. *Haugtussa,* he wrote to Oscar Meyer on June 7, 1898, was "a masterpiece, full of originality, simplicity, and depth and of an absolutely indescribable richness of color."

Garborg's book, which was published at the beginning of May, 1895, consists of seventy-one poems of which Grieg made use of twenty. As with the Vinje songs of Opus 33, so again with these he wrote the music during a short, hectic period of time—almost as if he were driven by a hunger to be united with the world of Arne Garborg. By June 14 he had completed twelve songs. This is evident from the title page of the earliest manuscript we have of this work; here "Kidlings' Dance" is dated May 27, "Veslemöy. The Young Maiden" May 29, "Love" May 30, and "At the Brook" June 7. The remaining songs are undated in this manuscript; the piano parts for "Blueberry Slope" and "The Tryst" are also incomplete. This manuscript contains the music to just the eight songs which, with some improvements, were published in 1898. The available evidence suggests that the other four that had been completed at this time were "The Sparrow," "Cow Call," "Doomed," and "In the Hayfield" (CW 149, Nos. 1–4). On September 2 Grieg arranged "The Sparrow" for women's chorus (CW 150) and two days later he wrote "Veslemöy is Longing" (CW 149, No. 5). All five of these songs exist in original manuscripts. The two versions of "The Sparrow" are in the Bergen Public Library; the other four manuscripts (in Nina Grieg's hand) are preserved in the Copenhagen Musikhistorisk Museum, which received them as a gift from Nina Grieg. For

1. UNCERTAINTY ABOUT THE SONGS FROM "HAUGTUSSA" AND THEIR FATE

I have been trying to decide how I should organize my *Haugtussa* music, for the text unfortunately creates some obstacles that I still have not overcome. And I don't know anybody in the whole country of Norway who understands these things. (Letter to Matthison-Hansen, September 6, 1895.)

* * *

It is sad to lose oneself in dreams. I've been doing that lately as I write music for *Haugtussa* by Garborg. It's going to be something for voice and orchestra. I'm still not completely sure what form it will take. It is a brilliant book that has moved me deeply. (Letter to Iver Holter, September 10, 1895.)

2. *THE MOUNTAIN MAID* REVIEWED IN THE OSLO PRESS

It is now at least 10–15 years since Grieg wrote his Norwegian songs to texts by A. O. Vinje. Of these we need only mention such songs as "Last Spring," "At Rondane," "The Berry," "The Goal," and several others to remind our readers that they include some of the best of the many beautiful songs that Grieg has given us. They are also an important part of the legacy by which he has secured his national reputation. Since then Grieg's genius has roamed in many directions. Now and then he has also sent a greeting with memories of bygone days. In *The Mountain Maid* he has returned completely to Norway, the home of his youth, and in music reminiscent of his earlier work has created a new group of Norwegian songs that will find their way to everyone who has an ear for the profound and moving spirit that permeates our national music. Such songs as "The Enticement," "The Tryst," "Love," and—most of all, perhaps—the simple and unusually beautiful little song "Veslemöy. The Young Maiden" bear witness that the vein from which they have sprung is fresher and more vigorous than ever before. (*Morgenbladet,* October 23, 1898.)

the most part they appear to be finished and ready for publication, lacking perhaps only the final polishing that the published collection received to good advantage. Also preserved in the Bergen Public Library are some preliminary sketches of "Veslemöy Longing" as well as rough drafts of three additional songs: "Prologue," "Veslemöy Wonders," and "Veslemöy at the Spinning Wheel."

It appears that in 1895 Grieg was unsure about what he should do with the *Haugtussa* material, and that he was toying with the idea of using it in a large orchestral work.[1] He wrote to Beyer from Leipzig in October that he wanted to proceed with *Haugtussa,* but "all of that is a thousand miles away. I don't have the foggiest idea of the mood of that material any more. Yes, surroundings are a delicate spider web, more delicate than one might think."

Surprisingly, Grieg now simply turned away from the *Haugtussa* material without developing it further and without trying to get it published. He wrote to Röntgen on June 20, 1896: "*Haugtussa* slumbers on. I haven't touched it since Christmas when it was sung for you. Of late I have unfortunately been *lyrical,* or perhaps I should say *bestial* [Opus 65]. Can't you cure me of this illness? What I want to compose doesn't get composed, and what I don't want to compose does. A dreadful illness."

Two more years went by before Grieg put the finishing touches on the eight songs that were finally printed as the song cycle, *The Mountain Maid,* Opus 67. The Scandinavian edition was to be published by Wilhelm Hansen of Copenhagen, and in view of the rather substantial differences between *nynorsk* and the standard Dano-Norwegian familiar to most Scandinavians, it was felt that a Danish translation was needed as well. Upon Grieg's recommendation the task of producing this Danish translation was given to John Paulsen, but it was Grieg himself who gave the translation its final form. A German/English version was published by Peters in Leipzig at the same time.

The Mountain Maid was dedicated to Dagmar Möller, a Norwegian-born singer who was pursuing her career in Stockholm. On September 16, 1898, Grieg sent her the first volume to come off the press with the following greeting: "These songs have lain in my desk drawer for over three years because I doubted that they would be understood. But interpreted by you I still have hope."

The first performance of any of the songs occurred a month after their publication, when four of them were sung at a concert in Oslo. The positive review of the songs in *Morgenbladet* on October 23 is fairly representative of the evaluation that they received not only in Norway but in Denmark and Sweden as well.[2] Grieg's misgivings about the negative reaction that they would arouse were totally unwarranted so far as Scandinavia was concerned. In Germany, however, the critics' first evaluation of the cycle was not so agreeable.

The first complete performance of the cycle occurred in Oslo on November 2, 1899, with Eva Nansen and Agathe Backer Gröndahl. Grieg was in Stockholm at the time, where he and Dagmar Möller performed four of the songs on November 7. Arne Garborg attended the Oslo recital, however, and

Dear Edvard Grieg:

So it is in Stockholm that you are wreaking havoc at the moment, Viking that you are. I hope this reaches you there.

I just wanted to tell you that I have now finally heard the *Haugtussa* songs properly sung (at Eva Nansen's concert), and I love them more than I can tell you. It is precisely this deep, soft, subdued character—the music of the underworld—that I in my way have tried to express in words, but that you have really captured. And then suddenly once again blazing sun and the joy of summer, as in the marvelous "Kidlings' Dance." But one of the most enchantingly moving songs of the lot is "At The Brook."

Yes, now I am happy and proud—absolutely disgracefully proud—that you were able to use these verses. Thank you!

Mrs. Nansen sang nicely. I thought she *was* Veslemöy, and I told her so.

Gratefully yours, Arne Garborg.

(Letter dated November 7, 1899.)

was able to rejoice in the fact that it was an overwhelming success. Afterwards he wrote an enthusiastic letter to Grieg expressing his pride over the response his writing had achieved in the musical garb which Grieg had given it.[3] The following week Garborg received an effusive letter of thanks from a very happy Grieg.

That Grieg waited three years before publishing this work—the finest song cycle in the whole corpus of Norwegian music—is undoubtedly due in part to his misgivings about the public acceptance of these *nynorsk* texts. But there was more to it than that. The delay was due equally as much to his realization of the unique emotional climate that permeated these texts—a climate that reflected deep psychological aspects—and to his own perception that the musical language he had adopted was perhaps not so easily accessible to the listener. These songs, he wrote to Oscar Meyer, "are fundamentally different from my earlier ones." But in our opinion the principal reason that he waited so long before getting the cycle ready for publication was that once again, as so often before, he was unsure of his own ability to judge the worth of what he had written. He may have felt—and rightly so—that the twenty songs he had sketched or completed were of uneven quality.

Only after he had carefully weeded and pruned this rich musical garden did the eight flowers that were eventually chosen reveal themselves in all their beauty. Then he was able to write with calm assurance in a March 10, 1898 letter to Thorvald Lammers that these were "the best songs I have written."

Garborg's *Haugtussa* is a richly varied poetic work which nonetheless possesses a high degree of unity. The poems are centered around Veslemöy, the visionary young herd girl from Jaeren, a wilderness area south of Stavanger. She is rejected by her lover, and is trying to escape life's harsh realities and the indifference of those around her. In her visions she comes in contact with nature itself and the powers of the underworld. It is the juxtaposition of these two forces that Grieg chose as the theme for his cycle. The songs alternate between love songs and songs about nature, but are held together by the artist's intuitive sense of their inner coherence.

The cycle begins with "The Enticement," where Veslemöy seems to hear the seductive sounds of the powers of nature who lure her up into the mountain: here she will find a silver spinning wheel on which she will spin a cloak suitable for one who is longing. In the sublime opening measures of the piano part Grieg catches the vague, dream-like mysticism. It is the silver spinning wheel itself with its harp-like sound that enthralls us. What follows is equally magical:

The piano prelude is in F major. The voice part then enters in F minor with a cadence (secondary dominant chord with an added ninth followed by a dominant seventh chord with an added thirteenth) in C minor. The C-minor tonic chord that we expect in measure 9 of the example is not forthcoming. Instead there is a sudden shift to B-flat minor, and the opening phrase is repeated in this key as a melodic rhyme. Then follows a contrasting passage in which the tonality is somewhat vague—almost a mixture of F major and D Aeolian—to the words "Bewitched by your spell, with me you must dwell." This is one of the most impressionistic passages Grieg wrote (it contains, for example, a series of parallel seventh chords in the piano part—"*quasi Arpa*"). At the end of the first stanza we are back in F major as the words "the misty, blue fell" are accompanied by music identical to the prelude. All three stanzas have identical settings, and the piece concludes with a three-measure postlude.

In "Veslemöy. The Young Maiden" Grieg drew one of the most clean-cut portraits of a woman in song literature. He captured the wounded and divided elements in Veslemöy's character in an enchanting way: by placing a simple, innocent melody side by side with an equally simple but refined accompaniment. Veslemöy may indeed display a tranquility with which she imbues "each gesture, each word that is said," but at the same time there is something stirring beneath the surface.

Grieg was very fond of the dominant seventh chord with an added thirteenth. It is worthy of note that in measures 5–6 of the excerpt below he uses—for the first and only time—three such chords in succession. Moreover, the chord progression is related by thirds. This type of progression has been adopted and used so widely in the popular music of the twentieth century that it has become a kind of musical cliché.

In "Blueberry Slope" Veslemöy tells with sly humor what she would do if a bear, a wolf, or a fox were to come. "That splendid boy," too, would get a big smack, "though quite in another fashion." Folk-like elements are especially prominent in this song in both text and melody. The surprises occur primarily in the piano part, notably in the form of unexpected third relationships and some playfully light cascades of sound that pervade all four stanzas.

"The Tryst" depicts the experience of love by alternating between excited anticipation and ecstasy. This song is more elaborate than the first three. Especially at the words "he's come, her handsome lover!" a powerful effect is achieved by means of a genuinely Griegian cadential progression: the dominant seventh chord is followed by the subdominant, not by the tonic. The dynamic range of this song and its concentrated expressiveness make it one of the very best of Grieg's love songs.

In "Love" Veslemöy is reflecting on love, but with her clairvoyant ability to sense what is hidden from others she has a premonition that she will be deceived. In this song Grieg breaks the strophic pattern that he had followed in the first four and uses instead a modified strophic form bordering on the through-composed. The motivic material in the opening stanza, which forms the basis for the entire song, is modeled on the Norwegian *stev*. The very same music, but with different words, is used in the final stanza. The principal key is C major, but in keeping with the division in Veslemöy's personality Grieg deliberately blurs the feeling of tonality with peculiar modal cadences. The midsection of the song consists of variations on the material of the opening stanza, and the first two of these have an unmistakable *springar* character. Here the sense of wavering tonality is heightened as several keys enter briefly. The hectic moods from Veslemöy's meeting with "that splendid boy" are summoned by such a bold series of chords that one cannot help but wonder where it will finally lead. With his unerring sense of harmonic logic, however, Grieg makes everything slide naturally into place.

"Love" is even more painstakingly crafted than "The Tryst," and together with it constitutes the dramatic high point of the entire cycle. It also marks the only case in which Grieg altered the sequence of Garborg's poems: he reversed the order of "Love" and "Kidlings' Dance" in order to create symmetry in the overall structure.

In "Kidlings' Dance" all care is cast aside for a short while. The poet and the composer frolic with almost childish delight, Garborg by inventing funny goat names and Grieg through the use of lively *halling* rhythms and unusual harmonic twists that may hark back to the Norwegian *slaatter*. Especially striking is one brief passage that has a trace of bitonality: A major in the treble staff over a double pedal point in G major (measures 7–8).

"Hurtful Day" reflects the somber gravity of resignation. Veslemöy *has* been deceived: "Hot tears again stream down, her cheeks to sear. Now must she die; she's lost her love so dear." As in "Kidlings' Dance" we are given another purely strophic song with a folk-like flavor. Musically, "Hurtful Day" is a counterpart to "The Tryst," the happy sounds of which are now reflected in gloomy, inward-looking minor. There is also a certain melodic resemblance to one of the other pearls in Norwegian song literature: Halfdan Kjerulf's "Synnöve's Song."

Like the spurned young miller in Schubert's *Die schöne Müllerin*, Veslemöy—in the last song in the cycle—seeks escape and solace in the "soft-swirling brook." With simple but carefully chosen means, Grieg depicts the unceasing flow of the brook. He uses piano figurations and almost impressionistic pedal techniques to create static blocks of sound that are interrupted only at the end of each stanza by Veslemöy's pained, hushed words: "Here will I rest . . . dream . . . remember . . . forget . . . slumber." "At the Brook" is in modified strophic form. John Horton, in his insightful book on Grieg (p. 191), has made an important observation in this connection: "While his general plan here is strophic, Grieg's setting is remarkable for its subtle variations of melodic interval, tonality, meter and tempo and, despite its apparent simplicity, it is one of the most elaborately organized of his compositions."

As Torstein Volden has pointed out, Grieg arranged the cycle in the form of a carefully planned arch. The top of the arch consists of the two love songs that stand in the center: "The Tryst" and "Love." These are supported by a pair of songs—one on each side—that are cheerful and pastoral in nature: "Blueberry Slope" and "Kidlings' Dance." The next pair—"Veslemöy. The Young Maiden" and "Hurtful Day"—are like two portraits whose common element is their melancholy mood. The entire arch rests securely on the nature mysticism of "The Enticement" and "At the Brook."

When we look today at the entire collection of songs from *Haugtussa*— both those published and those not published in Grieg's lifetime—there can be no doubt that the composer chose the best of the lot for Opus 67. Only one of those that he left out might reasonably have been included, and that is "Cow-Call." This is a pure nature idyll in which the voice part is picked up like an echo in the accompaniment. In the manuscript Grieg wrote "cor anglais" (English horn) by the piano part—an indication, perhaps, that he was thinking of the possibility of an orchestral work when he wrote this charming little song. In the piano part at the end of the piece the pastoral mood is further underscored in that Grieg—for the first and only time in any of his songs— used a fragment of an authentic folk melody that he himself had written down. It was the goat's-horn tune that he had heard played by Susanne on the trip to the Jotunheimen mountains in 1886 (see p. 285). Below is a facsimile of the last two systems of the manuscript for "Cow-Call." The melody is completely identical to the example on p. 285 except that it has been transposed from G minor to F-sharp minor. The little phrase in the right hand in the third measure from the end is Grieg's own, and the harmonization is also typically Griegian. Note, for example, the plagal cadence with the major subdominant chord on B as a six-four chord:

The remaining *Haugtussa* songs not included in Opus 67 (which appear in *Edvard Grieg's Complete Works,* Vol. 15) are not of the same caliber.

Music historians sometimes speak disparagingly of Grieg as a "miniaturist." *The Mountain Maid* stands as eloquent proof of the fact that excellence is not a function of length or of demanding and restrictive forms. Great art can equally well be found in that which is small. Here we have eight relatively short songs, mostly in pure strophic form. each of which is a mood picture in which words and music are related to one another in the most intimate way. Yet taken together they constitute a higher, unbreakable unity. For this reason *The Mountain Maid* should, if possible. always be performed as a complete cycle; and it should be judged as a totality, not merely as a collection of individual songs. Only so does the true greatness of this work come fully into view.

*Painting of Grieg by Erik Werenskiold. This
painting now hangs in Grieghallen, Bergen's
lovely new concert hall dedicated in 1978.*

A Century Comes to a Close

Grieg wrote a number of small compositions in the middle of the 1890s in addition to the major works of Opuses 64–67. In 1896 he completed two occasional pieces for male chorus which today are of interest only as curiosities: "Greetings from Kristiania Singers" (CW 151) and "Impromptu for the Grieg Male Chorus in Ft. Dodge, Iowa" (CW 152). That same year he also wrote a little song with a text by Didrik Grönvold: "The Blueberry" (CW 153). The curious occasion for the "Impromptu" was that the director of this Norwegian-American chorus had asked for a composition from Grieg for his group. Björnson hastily wrote a little poem, "Sounds of Norway," which he sent to Grieg on February 29. Grieg set it at once, and on the day it was completed, March 5, he amused himself by replying to Björnson's playfully rhymed letter with some sardonic rhymes of his own.[1]

It was also in 1896 that he wrote an "occasional work" of another kind, and this one he undertook with genuine care and affection: an extensive article on Mozart. It was written in July during a stay at "Trondsbu" on the Hardanger plateau. "Some days it was very cold," he wrote to Horneman on September 15, "and then I crawled into a sleeping bag and wrote a long article which I had promised to prepare for an American periodical." The article, for which he received 1000 French francs, was first published in *The Century Illustrated Monthly Magazine* in November, 1897.

In October and November of 1896, Grieg experienced in Stockholm what he described as "a singular success" and some "marvelous days," with four sold-out choir and orchestra concerts in the Royal Opera House. On November 5 he wrote to Beyer that he was healthier than he had been for many years and, therefore, was "youthful and flexible" and "could give my best both as an artist and as a person . . . And how the orchestra played! Toward the end it

1. BJÖRNSON AND GRIEG EXCHANGE RHYMED LETTERS

(Björnson writes to Grieg):
You to honor, you to cherish,
I myself would gladly perish,
Quick as lightning wrote this down,
Which I send—and don't you frown—
With his note. You'll get no rest
'Till you send to his address
Music—and some verse as well.
Hi to Nina, your sweet belle!

(Grieg replies):
You to honor, you to cherish.
I myself would gladly perish.
I'll respond to your gibBERish
with some verse that's—well, cleVERish.
I think you are plain tiGERish
to demand I deliVERish
an "Impromptu" so feVERish
for Dodge City's NorweGERisch.
Clearly, now, my "I" I'll nourish
with the peacock plumes that flourish
'round you since you insisterish
that I do this task nightmarish.
You should know, my friend so bearish,
your verse has this trait contrarish:
it gives unconventionarish
zeal that, wholly arbitrarish,
makes me spurn tasks customarish.
Your word, though't be antiquarish,
makes all else quite ancillarish.
sets me hopping coronarish,
lest I fail my friend so rare-ish.
Well, old bear (soon centenarish),
let us not be adversarish;

I will act disciplinarish
(I'm not revolutionarish)
and conclude this verse bugbearish:
You to honor, you to cherish!

P.S. Just one question corollarish:
Is it true that in your parish

two young Björnsons (both so fairish)
soon shall wed? Extraordinarish!
We send love complimentarish.
All your children soon binarish!
Greetings warm and debonairish
Both to you and lady fairish,
From E. G. and his—Ninarish! (Ow!)

2. GRIEG'S THOUGHTS UPON HEARING OF BRAHMS'S DEATH

Poor Brahms! No: lucky Brahms! He didn't suffer much, and—he didn't outlive himself. How different the person we call Brahms now suddenly appears to us—more flexible, as it were, than before his death! Now for the first time I see and feel how *whole* he was both as an artist and as a human being as far as I knew him. How glad I am to have been so fortunate as to have known him! (Letter to Röntgen, April 3, 1897.)

3. A SURPRISE AT THE CHORUS REHEARSAL FOR *OLAV TRYGVASON*

When I stepped onto the podium and looked over the large gathering—yes, then my Norwegian heart was stirred: everyone—both the ladies and the men—had small Norwegian (*real* Norwegian! [i.e., not Swedish-Norwegian]) flags on their chests! I had already lifted my baton when I saw this, but I was so moved that I had to lower it again and say a few words. (Letter to O. A. Thommessen, February 21, 1897.)

was as though I was sitting and improvising. The finest, most subtle nuances came off just the way they were supposed to. The orchestra loved me . . ."

On November 1, after the third concert, there was a large banquet for Grieg at the Grand Hotel. Three hundred eminent guests were invited, including Prince Eugen and the famous polar explorer, A. E. Nordenskiöld. In a November 7 letter to Röntgen he reported that he had had the feeling that his trip was a patriotic mission at this time of crisis between the sister countries. During the banquet he gave a talk, concerning which he told Beyer: "I ventured to use that golden opportunity to touch upon the union question. I spoke as a Norwegian, you understand—we had just sung the Norwegian national anthem—and managed to express myself so well—heaven knows how—that people came up to me afterwards to express joy and gratitude."

From Stockholm Grieg went directly to Vienna, arriving on November 15. During the following two months he gave several concerts in Vienna. These included a chamber-music evening on December 16, at which the G-minor quartet was performed, and an orchestra concert on December 19 with Feruccio Busoni as soloist in the piano concerto. A planned appearance in Budapest on December 22 had to be canceled because Grieg came down with a severe case of bronchitis. He reported that it "pained him greatly" to have to decline the opportunity to receive Brahms on three different occasions when the great composer came to visit him. The bronchitis also deprived him of a visit by the "brilliant" Johann Strauss (the younger) and his wife. To Grieg's great joy, however, Brahms, "sick as he was," came to the orchestra concert and participated in the party afterwards. This meeting with Brahms, he reported, "gave my stay in Vienna its greatest value."

Grieg also attended a concert on January 2, 1897, when Brahms received an exceptional ovation following a performance of his string quintet, Opus III. Three months later he was dead.[2]

From Vienna Grieg went to Leipzig, where he remained for a month. In February he went to the Netherlands for an extended concert tour which Röntgen had arranged, including a magnificent concert with the Concertgebouw Orchestra in Amsterdam.[3] A few days later this orchestra, under Willem Mengelberg, gave a concert in his honor. In The Hague, at the conclusion of a concert that he conducted for an audience of 2000 (including two queens), he was awarded the Order of Orange-Nassau. He generally spurned such honors, but he wrote to Dr. Abraham on March 13 that "the medals fit fine in my suitcase. The customs officials at the borders are always extra pleasant when they see them." Röntgen reported that after Grieg had received the French Legion of Honor he dismissed it with the comment: "This honor I share with a whole legion!"

In the middle of March Grieg was in Copenhagen where, for nearly two months, he worked on the orchestration of the *Symphonic Dances*. But on April 10 he wrote to Beyer that "there is a continual hubbub here, and I am so thoroughly bored by all this visiting. Only in the peace of my own home can I accomplish anything . . . I ran into Drachmann on the street here. His atti-

4. GRIEG HAS AN AUDIENCE WITH
QUEEN VICTORIA

I'm not wild about court affairs, as you well
know, but this was something else. The
queen is *sweet*, if one can say this about an
elderly lady. She knew almost the entire
program, *enjoyed* Nina's singing in Norwegian, and asked for more. I played the
"Gavotte" from the *Holberg Suite*. When I
was introduced to her, she said: "I am a
great admirer of your music." Everything
was natural and genuine. She spoke about
Peer Gynt and would have liked to hear
"The Death of Aase" and "Last Spring" for
string orchestra. I declined all meal invitations and went home on the next train.
Nina received a beautiful brooch and I the
Jubilee Medallion. (Letter to Hans Lien
Braekstad, December 6, 1897.)

tude toward me isn't what it used to be, and I don't like the way he's behaving
at all, so I don't go out of my way to see him."

He spent most of the summer at "Troldhaugen," but also took a trip to
Fossli, where he met Röntgen and his second wife, Abrahamine (Mien), who
were on their honeymoon. In the middle of October he set out on a demanding concert tour of Great Britain, giving ten concerts in the space of two
months. "The whole thing is crazy," he wrote to Röntgen on November 19.
"If I get out of this alive I'll surely never do it again."

Early in December he was given the honor of an audience with Queen
Victoria at Windsor castle.[4] He spent the Christmas holidays with Röntgen in
Amsterdam. Immediately after New Year's Day he went to Leipzig, where he
stayed for three months. He received an invitation to conduct six concerts in
Italy but turned it down because of his health, although "the desire was
enormous."

In the autumn of 1897 Grieg had become involved in the planning for a
comprehensive Norwegian music festival that it was hoped might be
launched in connection with a big fishing and industrial exposition to be
held in Bergen the following summer. It was Grieg's fond hope that they
might get Willem Mengelberg and the Concertgebouw Orchestra of Amsterdam to come and show a Norwegian audience how a real orchestra is supposed to sound. It soon became evident, however, that there were many
obstacles in his way that could not easily be overcome. Voices were raised
early on to the effect that a Norwegian music festival should feature Norwegian musicians, and since Bergen at that time did not have a symphony
orchestra of international standard the planning committee decided to invite
the Music Association orchestra from Oslo to participate. The invitation was
in fact sent, but Grieg then withdrew from the committee in protest. He
absolutely *would* have the Dutch orchestra at the festival, no matter what
obligations people might feel toward the Norwegian music establishment.
Nothing was good enough but the very best; all objections to this view were,
in his opinion, only chauvinistic narrow-mindedness. In the April 18 issue of
Aftenposten, Oslo, he published an article in which he stated: "I understand a
music festival to mean a festival whose task it is to perform Norwegian music
as excellently as can possibly be achieved. These compositions will then be
better understood and will enter more deeply into the hearts of the people.
Whether this goal requires Norwegians, Germans, Japanese, or Dutchmen
makes no difference to me. On this opinion I will stand or fall . . ."

He came very close to falling, for his article raised a storm of protest. His
friendship with Iver Holter was broken for a time, and even Frants Beyer felt
constrained to admonish him.

After Grieg pulled out the whole committee was dissolved, and the music
festival was canceled. But then frantic activity began behind the scenes: the
very next morning a new committee was appointed and Grieg was given full
authority to engage the Concertgebouw Orchestra.

Thus the Bergen Music Festival was born, the first such festival to be held
in Norway. It ran from June 26 to July 3, 1898, and it was enormously

5. JOHAN SVENDSEN PUTS MENGELBERG IN HIS PLACE

Personally I found him [Mengelberg] very amiable. I was not at all unwilling to receive practical advice on orchestral matters. But when he—very cautiously, to be sure—wanted to give Svendsen some instruction about how to conduct one thing or another in his own works—Svendsen, who is a hundred times better conductor than Mengelberg—then we got a truly delightful experience. Svendsen gave him a short glance and said something like: "I must say, you have a nice jacket!" (Letter to Röntgen, July 10, 1898.)

6. SICKNESS AS A LESSON ABOUT DEATH

One day I thought I was going to die, and I will never forget how bitterly Nina cried when I said this to her. An illness like that is a good lesson about death. It gives one a larger view of life and disposes one to gentleness. It now seems to me that the greatest happiness is achieved by demanding more of oneself and less of others. (Letter to Beyer, November 19, 1898.)

7. GRIEG CONDUCTS AT THE OPENING OF THE NATIONAL THEATER

So now I am a theater orchestra conductor: I push the button and make the curtain go up and down. This is considerably more difficult to take care of than the music. I had to practice pushing the button with my left hand while conducting with my right. The orchestra is absolutely first rate. Böhn and Lange are very friendly towards me and everybody else is polite. I can't ask for more. (Letter to Beyer, September 1, 1899.)

8. THANK-YOU LETTER TO BJÖRNSON

In these days you have shown me the way . . . The Dreyfus battle was a hard one, that is true, but still—up there with you I got rid of such a heavy load of pessimistic ballast that I think I shall now overcome that sterile self-criticism which, for altogether too long, has hampered my art. (Letter to Björnson, September 14, 1899.)

Thus the Bergen Music Festival was born, the first such festival to be held in Norway. It ran from June 26 to July 3, 1898, and it was enormously successful. The concerts were given in a new hall accommodating about two thousand people. There was a full house every night, and the audiences experienced a unique overview of the best in Norwegian music. The Dutch musicians, under the twenty-seven-year-old Mengelberg, played outstandingly well. Grieg wrote excitedly to Dr. Abraham on July 6: "Everything worked out! I have never heard better performances, not even at the Gewandhaus. Everyone is delighted, and everyone agrees that I was right. Now in both Bergen and Oslo people are saying, 'We *must* have a better orchestra!' That, for me, is the greatest triumph!" The music festival also became the occasion for an entertaining episode involving Mengelberg and Svendsen which is cited in the Primary Materials.[5]

Grieg modestly had kept his own works in the background in order to allow the broadest possible representation of other Norwegian composers—with, however, an absolute demand for only the best of their music. Nonetheless, his critics continued to carp at him for several months after the festival was over. On January 2, 1899, he wrote to Aimar Grönvold that Oslo was full of bile and venom—enough, he said, to "make a witch's brew for a whole generation." Gradually the attacks abated, however, and people began to understand the significance of the contribution he had made to Norwegian music through this comprehensive Bergen festival.

After a mountain trip in August, 1898, Grieg wanted to spend the autumn months working in solitude, and he therefore declined offers to give concerts in Germany, Russia, and America. At the beginning of November he went to Denmark, where he remained for four months. Here he had a very serious bronchitis attack; "a couple more attacks like that would probably be the end of me," he wrote to Beyer.[6] He spent Christmas with a Mr. Neergaard, a friend of many years who owned a castle at Lolland. "Christmas time at a Danish manor such as this is a fascinating new experience," he wrote to Beyer.

Grieg made his last visit to Rome and Naples in March and April of 1899. On April 5 he conducted a large concert in the Eternal City, and afterwards he was summoned to Queen Margherita's box; the queen "lisped some stupid nonsense," he wrote candidly to Dr. Abraham a few days later. He returned to "Troldhaugen" via Leipzig, Copenhagen, and Oslo, arriving near the end of May. In July he once again experienced a powerful impression of nature during a trip to Sunnmöre and Nordfjord.

In September Grieg participated in a gala performance marking the opening of the National Theater in Oslo, where he conducted *Sigurd Jorsalfar*.[7] Björnson also participated in this event, and after it was over he invited Grieg for the first time to visit him at his country home, Aulestad. It was to be an unforgettable week.[8]

What came to dominate the visit to Aulestad was the indignation felt by both Grieg and Björnson over the latest development in the so-called "Dreyfus affair." French army captain Alfred Dreyfus, in a miscarriage of justice motivated in large part by anti-Semitism, had been found guilty in 1894 of treason for allegedly selling military secrets to the Germans. Just at the time of Grieg's visit to Aulestad it was learned that a French military court had reaffirmed Dreyfus's conviction despite substantial evidence that he was inno-

Johan Svendsen, whom Grieg regarded highly both as a conductor and a composer.

cent. Grieg had also just received an invitation from Èdouard Colonne to come to Paris as a guest conductor, and it raised for him an issue of conscience—for as always he found it impossible to separate the artistic realm from the realm of general human experience. With Björnson's strong encouragement he sent the following letter to Colonne: "While I thank you for your kind invitation, I greatly regret to inform you that, in view of the outcome of the Dreyfus case, I cannot agree to come to France at this time. Like all non-Frenchmen, I am so indignant over the contempt with which law and justice are treated in your country that I could not bring myself to perform for a French audience. Forgive me for my inability to feel otherwise and try to understand me."

At the request of Björnson's son-in-law, Albert Langen, Grieg allowed the letter to be published, and within a short time it was widely quoted in the European press. Political prestige was involved in the case, and the French reaction to Grieg's statement was vehement. Grieg received a stream of threatening and derisive letters during the following months. On October 4 he wrote to Colonne again: "Yesterday I received [a letter] addressed to the 'Jewish composer Ed. Grieg.' So it has come to this! I am proud of it! A hurrah for Mendelssohn! Nonetheless, I believe that the impulsive passions of the French people will soon again give way to a reasonable view more in keeping with the 1789 Human Rights proclamation of the French Republic. I hope this primarily for the sake of France, but also for my own sake—so that I can see your beautiful country once more."

Four years were to pass before he set foot on French soil again. When he conducted the Colonne Orchestra in 1903, he felt very strongly that the hatred for him because of his courageous action in 1899 was still alive—not least in the Paris press.

In the autumn of 1899 Grieg gave four successful concerts in Stockholm. Most of the season was spent in Denmark, however, where he gave many concerts in Copenhagen and other parts of the country. At this time he also became acquainted with the talented young Danish composer, Carl Nielsen. It was especially satisfying to him as a friend of the working class that his G-minor quartet, which was performed for an audience of fifteen hundred at a family concert at Copenhagen's Labor Union, was an "enormous success." He wrote to Röntgen on December 22: "Once again I received confirmation of my view. *Here* is where one finds the *best* audiences! To hell with the blasé, bejewelled, so-called fashionable audiences, be they in the Gewandhaus in Leipzig or the Music Society in Copenhagen! No, the unspoiled people are capable of enthusiasm; the others, with rare exceptions, are not."

Nina and Edvard celebrated the turn of the century with friends in Denmark.

Grieg's desire to compose waned for a time during the period 1898–1900. His total production consisted of nine piano pieces, a song ("Ave maris stella," CW 155), and four arrangements. In the summer of 1898 he wrote, among other things, sketches of "White Clouds" and "Gnomes' Procession," both of which are dated August 14. Röntgen edited them and had them published in 1908 together with a third piece, "Wild Dance"—which may date from the same period—under the title *Three Piano Pieces* (CW 154). The compositions are technically demanding, but musically rather insubstantial. Grieg didn't find them worth printing, and Röntgen might have served him better by accepting his judgment in the matter. "White Clouds" (No. 1), which depicts broken clouds in rapid flight, is vacuous; its dominant feature is a series of fluttering figurations in the form of an etude-like "perpetuum mobile." In "Gnomes' Procession" (No. 2) there is a rather interesting Griegian beginning in *halling* rhythms, but through most of the piece the composer only pounds away on the opening motive. The piece closes, however, with a bold impressionistic passage: twenty-one parallel, descending triads in E Dorian. In "Wild Dance" (No. 3), which is stylistically similar to "Gnomes' Procession," Grieg dawdles along with devices that sound vaguely as if they were derived from folk music. The chromaticism is poorly integrated with the rest of the piece and sounds like an inconsistency in style.

It was also during this period that Grieg's ninth and penultimate collection of *Lyric Pieces,* Opus 68, came into being. Sketches for the five last pieces are extant. The datings show that they were written between August 13, 1898 ("At Your Feet") and January 26, 1899 ("Grandmother's Minuet"). "At Your Feet"

9. "EVENING IN THE MOUNTAINS"
THRILLS GRIEG AT A CONCERT IN
AMSTERDAM

In "Evening in the Mountains" I was think-ing of you. It was an absolute mirage. Even I was thrilled. I had seated the oboist far back on the platform so no one could see him. He played so beautifully, so freely, so like an improvisation that when the magnif-icent string orchestra came in it was as if they took their cue from the oboe and the conception was identical. (Letter to Beyer, April 29, 1906.)

and "Valse Mélancolique," with their salon-style clichés, evoke little interest, although the first has a bit of harmonic refinement. The unpretentious "Sail-ors' Song" and "Grandmother's Minuet" are melodically quite attractive. Grieg sent an early version of "Evening in the Mountains" to Beyer with the title "Cow Call" and with the inscription, "Can be thought of as an evening in Utladalen (Skogadalsböen)." It is a pure and sensitive nature impression with echoes of the goat-horn melodies that had so bewitched the two friends on their trip to the Jotunheimen mountains in the summer of 1887 (see p. 285). Oddly enough, Grieg lets the melody speak for itself in the first part of the piece; only in the second part is it harmonized, and then with simple but sophisticated chords.

In 1895 Grieg arranged "Evening in the Mountains" for oboe, horn, and strings, and the charming little "At the Cradle" for strings. These two nicely polished arrangements were subsequently published as *Two Lyric Pieces*, Opus 68.[9]

On the Threshold of a New Age

1. LIFE'S *DIMINUENDO*

In a piece of music one finds not only *crescendo* and *fortissimo*, but *diminuendo* as well. The same things occur in life itself. We have come this far with *crescendo* and *fortissimo*; now it is time for our *diminuendo*. And a *diminuendo can*, in fact, be beautiful. The thought of the coming *pianissimo* is not at all unpleasant to me, but I have the greatest respect for the ugliness of the *diminuendo* (the suffering!). (Letter to Dr. Abraham, September 5, 1900.)

2. GRIEG'S THOUGHTS UPON THE DEATH OF HIS BROTHER

Death leaves a certain mark upon life which in this case, it seems to me, makes it more harmonious and consistent than it was before. How curious! One does not understand the living. One judges them according to one's own assumptions—and, of course, wrongly. Then comes death. And then one understands. Such understanding is a costly purchase. It behooves one to use the time one has left. Use it to judge gently, gently, gently!! (Letter to Julius Steenberg, October, 1901.)

After the turn of the century Grieg's life was increasingly marked by illness. He maintained a nomadic type of existence notwithstanding, and didn't really feel at home anywhere. "For the time being I am still a wanderer and suffer much because of it," he once wrote. Exhausting as the concert tours generally were, they were nonetheless a ray of light in the midst of many dark hours of deep depression. He simply could not get along without the exhilaration that he felt in the presence of an appreciative audience. He often felt ten years younger following a public performance—but after a few days the depression returned once again. Under such circumstances it is understandable that composition was neglected. Remarkably, however, he managed during these years to renew himself in two unique works: *Norwegian Peasant Dances,* Opus 72, and *Four Psalms,* Opus 74.

Grieg had a fairly relaxed attitude toward death. Even during the 1890s he was occupied to some extent with thoughts of life's ending, and even more so during the last years of his life.[1] During his stay in Copenhagen in the winter and spring of 1900 he began drawing up a will, and he exchanged several letters with Beyer regarding various provisions. On March 10 he sent Beyer a draft, the principal provision of which was that after Nina's death the remaining estate should "be used for the development and advancement of the musical life of Bergen." His manuscripts, printed music, letters, and books were to become the property of the Bergen Public Library.

Large sections of Grieg's letters from this period read almost like a series of medical reports. It was not just his physical ailments that he complained about; the normal afflictions of approaching old age also seemed to him a heavy burden to bear. He wrote to Röntgen on February 25, 1901: "To put it bluntly, I've become an old codger. I think that one fine day I'll do like Tristan: end it all. For in reality this is no longer a life." He was greatly affected when his brother John, in a moment of depression, took his own life in October, 1901.[2] But that in the last analysis self-destruction was not for him—and that he himself was aware of this—is evident from a letter he wrote to Matthison-Hansen at the time of John's death: "Yes, it was a *memento mori.* The ring is broken. I will soon go too. That certainly is how I feel. But I would have to be out of my mind for it to happen in the way that John chose." For the rest of his life he considered it a sacred duty to try to make life as happy as possible for his brother's wife and children.

The outward events in Grieg's life during the first five years after the turn of the century can be quickly told. The summers were spent at "Troldhaugen" and on trips to the mountains, the winters in Oslo and Copenhagen and concert tours on the continent. In the middle of April, 1900, he went from Denmark to Oslo, and a month later we find him at "Troldhaugen." He then took a trip to the mountains with Röntgen and a two-week trip to Sunnmöre with Nina and her sister Tony. In the middle of October he began a three-month visit to the "Voksenkollen" sanatorium, which was newly built at that time. "Voksenkollen" was situated in the mountains high above Oslo, and the dry air and beautiful surroundings seemed to him to have a healing effect. He began to think seriously about disposing of "Troldhaugen," and he tried without success to persuade Beyer to move to the eastern part of the country. As late as December, 1904, he was almost tricked into buying a "fashionable little villa in Frognerveien [a street in Oslo]." He realized, however, that this would have been a "colossal blunder." In spite of everything, his ties to "Troldhaugen" and to western Norway were too close to be severed.

Shortly after he came to Copenhagen in January, 1901, he became sick again and was obliged to cancel several concerts abroad. He went home to "Troldhaugen" in May, arriving on the 17th—Norway's Independence Day—and remained there until December. Winter at "Troldhaugen" was more than he could tolerate, however, so he moved to Bergen for a month. At the end of January, 1902, he was in Oslo enroute to Copenhagen, but for some reason or other was not present at the premiere of a new staging of *Peer Gynt* at the National Theater. In April he felt strong enough to fulfill a promise to participate in an all-Grieg concert in Warsaw, Poland, with Teresa Carreño as soloist in the *A-minor Concerto*. He later remembered the visit to Warsaw as "a beautiful dream, but a dream come true," as he wrote to Beyer on April 28. He continued: "I got a reception such as I have received before only on that first visit to London. But what far surpassed London was the incessant increase in the excitement . . . Out on the streets . . . constant ovations with all kinds of strange sounds and shouts. It reminded me a little bit of Ole Bull in Bergen in the old days!"

It was not far, however, from "the beautiful dream" to the harsh realities of life. In a letter to Röntgen dated the very same day, he wrote about the oppressive political situation in Poland: "One cannot speak about political matters here, but I have gotten a vivid impression of how the Poles seek and find recompense for their political misery in art."

By the middle of May he was back at "Troldhaugen." July was spent at Vestre Slidre, a valley in central Norway. After two concerts in Bergen in November, he went to Oslo to participate in the "uniquely wonderful and magnificent" festivities in connection with the celebration of Björnson's seventieth birthday on December 8. Three days later he and Nina performed songs from Opuses 61 and 67 at a benefit concert. Grieg reported to Beyer that 3000 people paid a few öre each to get in, and that they responded to the performance with wild enthusiasm. "There is something wonderfully moving about making music for the lower class. They have an immediacy that the higher classes have lost. We raised over 1400 kroner for the unemployed workers. Today we are happy."

Honors and triumphs at home and abroad

The first part of 1903 was an eventful time for Grieg. It began quietly enough in Oslo, where he spent January and February resting at "Voksenkollen." In March he journeyed via Copenhagen to Prague, where he was given a welcome worthy of a king.[3] He interpreted the audience's reaction as recognition and admiration, but even more as affection for him and his art—and for Norway. He wrote to O. A. Thommessen on March 28: "You can't imagine how Norway and Norwegianness have been buzzing in the ears of people in the Bohemian countries during these days. During my stay in Prague my works have been played in all of the larger cities just to show how glad they are that I am in the vicinity."

Like Björnson, Grieg was almost a symbol for the Czech national consciousness. He felt this so strongly that after the concert on March 27 he could not refrain from giving a little improvised speech. He commented later that "Nina's criticism probably is correct: 'Everything could have been absolutely wonderful if only you had kept your mouth shut!'" Grieg was in fact quite concerned about how the press would react to his speech, as is evident from a letter he wrote to his second cousin, John Grieg, on March 23: "Now I'll probably get a real tongue-lashing in Germany, although I didn't really talk politics: all I did was mention the word 'fatherland.'"

The soloist in the *A-minor Concerto* was Teresa Carreño's daughter, Teresita. She "roams brilliantly over the keyboard like a wildcat," he wrote to Beyer on April 1, "but there is poetry in everything she does. There was also a little singer by the name of Magda Dvořák, a daughter of the composer. She sang with ardor, but in Czech—which made things a bit tough for me. I enjoyed having a little time with Dvořák. He is, to put it mildly, a character. But he was amiable enough." After Dvořák's death the following year Grieg sent a letter of condolence to his daughter, who then wrote to Grieg: "Your visit to Prague will always be among the most beautiful moments of my life, and it makes me so happy that you have remembered me. My father always talked about you with the greatest affection, and the sound of your name is dear to us."

From Prague, Grieg went to Warsaw by way of Berlin, traveling by "luxury train, as a first-class passenger!" After successful performances in Warsaw he went to Paris, where he had been invited to conduct the Colonne Orchestra on April 19. It was like walking into the lion's den, for his courageous stand with respect to the Dreyfus affair just four years earlier (see p. 351) had by no means been forgotten by the French chauvinists. He had received letters warning that he could expect a beating if he ever dared to show his face in the French capital again.

Grieg has given a number of pithy and humorous descriptions of his

(see p. 351)

3. OVATIONS IN PRAGUE

And when the "Homage March" from *Sigurd Jorsalfar* was finished, the pathway from the podium was filled with people who came with bouquets and wreaths as big as a mill wheel, and on a silk cushion under a glass cover there was a silver wreath. And as I rode home crowds of people ran beside the carriage; sometimes I had to stand up and sometimes, like a king, wave greetings first to one side, then the other. (Letter to Börre Giertsen, April 1, 1903.)

Nina and Edvard at Voksenkollen in 1903. (Photo collection of Universitetsbiblioteket in Bergen)

4. DEBUSSY COMMENTS ON THE A-MINOR CONCERTO

Apropos, has anyone noticed how people from Scandinavia become unbearable when they try to be like south Europeans? The end of this concerto, which is reminiscent of Leoncavallo, is a striking example of this. The piano "puts on airs," if I may put it so. And the orchestra follows with such an effusive outpouring of color that one could almost have a sunstroke. But Mme. Carreño has great talent—much greater than Grieg, for example, who in my opinion abuses his Norwegian birthright. (Debussy in *Gil Blas,* March 16, 1903.)

5. DEBUSSY COMMENTS ON THE COLONNE CONCERT

One is tempted to overlook the fact that the concert, which began with an imitation of Schumann and ended with something worthy of [the music-hall] Excelsior, was not especially original. The piano was handled in a completely traditional way, and besides—I never have understood why it is interrupted here and there by trumpets of war. They generally indicate that a little "cantabile"—where one is supposed to swoon—is about to begin. (Trumpets—their innocence is being violated!) . . .

How melodious are the two *Elegiac Melodies* for strings. One notes, especially in the second, the influence of Massenet (albeit without the characteristic sensual excitement that causes one to love it almost perversely). With Grieg, the whole thing is stretched out like those all-day suckers one can buy at country fairs—the kind that often have the clerk's fingerprints on them—which, apparently, is absolutely essential to their success? These two melodies follow the same formula that Grieg has used successfully before. They begin with an innocent little phrase that is going to be our companion for the remainder of the piece. Along the way it runs into some lush chords with which it covers its nakedness. Thereupon the whole thing is moved up a floor or so—muted, of course—and then it comes back down in a series of deceptive cadences. Finally there is a deadly boring ritardando, and then we are supposed to

swoon all over again. Afterwards we sit there with a bizarre and charming taste in our mouths—as of pink candy filled with snow . . .

To tell the truth, the best part of the afternoon was *Peer Gynt,* the orchestral suite that Grieg wrote for Ibsen's drama. Here the ideas are charming, the rhythms were precise, and it has a genuine Norwegian stamp. The handling of the orchestra is also

stormy reception by the French public. He was clearly in high spirits when he wrote to John Grieg on April 20: "Yes, it was fun. I've never seen anything like it, and I tell you truly that if I had received the invitation [to come here] *after* Jaurès had reawakened the passions surrounding the Dreyfus affair I wouldn't have accepted it. But now I couldn't back out without looking like a coward. The press had already urged people to demonstrate—indeed, in a meaner way than I had anticipated. At the beginning of the concert a small group among the 3500 people present greeted me with boos and catcalls, so I quite calmly put the baton down, left the podium and just stood and waited. When it sounded like it was about over I mounted the podium again, but then it started anew. This time, however, it was I who made music. I didn't hesitate a second, but made an energetic signal to the orchestra to begin—fortissimo, fortunately! And once I managed to begin, I had the upper hand. Moreover, everybody else in the audience was on my side, and the police—three times the usual number for a concert—threw these *paid* troublemakers out of the hall."

The letter continues: "The concert itself was one great crescendo, and it ended with the most tremendous ovations. It was a triumph in every way. The orchestra played magnificently! When Nina and I got into the carriage that was to take us to our hotel, it was surrounded by a cordon of police. I felt like a Cromwell or Emperor so-and-so. The newspapers today are furious about my triumph and are as mean as possible. There is only one person—the composer Gabriel Fauré in *Le Figaro*—who has shown a noble heart. Yes, what strange people! Just think that the very same critic in *Le Temps* who a few years ago praised me to the skies now chides me for the *same* things he previously commended! Another critic insinuates that I was well paid for risking a visit to Paris. He concludes by saying: 'A few omnibuses filled with riffraff awaited Grieg at the end of the concert to escort him to Gare du Nord with his waistcoat *better lined* than by all that fur that he needs up in the fjords.' If only it were true! But unfortunately the hotel and the trip gobble it all up. That and more."

It was easy enough for Grieg to ignore the poison darts of ordinary critics, but he was hurt by the remarks of Claude Debussy. A full month before Grieg's Paris concert, Debussy had used the occasion of a Lamoureux concert to launch an attack on Grieg.[4] After the Colonne concert, in a long article in the periodical *Gil Blas,* he made it painfully clear that he had not forgotten Grieg's public statement regarding the Dreyfus affair.[5] It should be noted that Debussy's vicious sarcasms were written shortly before the Dreyfus case was

more balanced; excessively superficial effects are replaced by imaginative ideas . . .

It is regrettable that Grieg's visit to Paris has not taught us anything new about his art. He is and will remain a noble musician when he assimilates his country's folk music . . . Apart from this he is nothing more than a clever musician, one who is more concerned about mere effects than true art. (Debussy in *Gil Blas,* April, 1903.)

6. GRIEG COMMENTS
ON DEBUSSY'S ART

I am in the fortunate position of being not only independent of his judgment, but also able to consider his music with approbation. It has been very interesting for me to read through his three *Nocturnes*. Considerable talent as well as unusual inventiveness are expressed there, and I am very grateful to you for giving me an opportunity to become acquainted with this work. I hope to be able to have it performed in Scandinavia. With respect to *Pelléas et Mélisande* I will not presume to make a judgment merely on the basis of the piano score. I hope to hear the opera in Berlin. Obviously I see in this work as well the deep seriousness that inspires this artist. It is precisely this seriousness—which he mistakenly claims to be absent from *my* music—that attracts me to him and that I myself strive for in my work. (Letter to Michael Calvocoressi, May 2, 1903.)

* * *

To get acquainted with Debussy certainly was, for a connoisseur like me, to discover a truly tasty morsel. He spins a brilliant web of orchestral sound [in *L'aprés-midi d'un Faune*]. Wonderful harmony, completely nontraditional but genuinely felt—albeit overdone. As experiments of an individual whose training and experience have brought him to this point, these things seem to me remarkable in the highest degree. But they must not establish a school along these lines. Unfortunately it is undoubtedly going to happen anyway, for what we have here is something that the copy-cat composers can imitate. (Diary entry, December 8, 1906.)

to be reviewed once again—a process that in 1906 finally led to a finding of Dreyfus's complete innocence and the restitution of his civil rights.

Grieg was not the only composer to feel the sting of Debussy's sarcasm. In published articles the Frenchman frequently made derisive comments about other composers both living and dead, including Beethoven, Berlioz, Wagner, César Franck, and Richard Strauss. What chiefly upset Grieg was that Debussy misrepresented the facts, both with respect to what he had said about the Dreyfus affair in the Colonne letter of 1899 and regarding what had actually happened at the concert. Debussy claimed that some Norwegian hotheads had caused the disturbance at the concert, and that they had been "escorted to the banks of the Seine to cool off." Moreover, Grieg was pained to think that a fellow composer for whom he had such high regard could stoop to such ignoble pronouncements about his compositions.

Grieg made mention of his indignation over Debussy's article in a May 2 letter to the Paris critic Michael Calvocoressi: "I am astonished at the tone that he as an artist presumes to adopt with respect to a colleague. Naturally I also regret the total lack of understanding of my art that he reveals in his review—but this is not the main point. No, the main point was and is his venomous and disrespectful tone. A true artist should in general seek a high moral plane and show respect for the views of other serious people and artists . . . It is totally unworthy of a talented artist such as Debussy to knowingly state an untruth in order to malign a colleague." Later in the same letter Grieg offered his evaluation of Debussy's compositions.[6] It should be acknowledged, however, that Debussy expressed deep respect for Grieg's ability as a conductor: "He conducts the orchestra with an incredible precision and great power, and he emphasizes all of the subtleties with tireless care."

It appears that in his later years Debussy changed his estimate of Grieg as a composer. Thus in 1914—in a program consisting otherwise of only his own works—he played the piano in one of Grieg's violin sonatas with Arthur Hartmann as the violinist. At about the same time he wrote approvingly of some of Grieg's arrangements of folk songs, the *Album for Male Voices,* Opus 30 (see p. 232).

Grieg summed up his thoughts upon leaving Paris in a May 13 letter to Röntgen (written from Leipzig): "I was glad to say farewell to France, and especially Paris. It is sad that I left with the impression that Paris is a city of phonies. Everything: social relations, art, politics—is phony!"

In contrast to the cool reception that he had gotten in France, back in Bergen he was given an exceedingly warm tribute on the occasion of his sixtieth birthday on June 15. Everybody did everything possible to show him how much he was loved by his countrymen. Many costly gifts were given, eulogistic speeches were made, and about five hundred letters and telegrams streamed in from near and far. The National Theater Orchestra and its conductor, Johan Halvorsen, came from Oslo to add their luster to the occasion.

In good old-fashioned Norwegian style, the festivities lasted for three entire days. On the 15th there was a large reception at "Troldhaugen," and in the evening a banquet at the Grand Hotel. There were also special concerts;

Björnson and Grieg at "Troldhaugen" in 1903 on the occasion of Grieg's sixtieth birthday. ("Troldhaugen," Bergen, Norway)

Grieg himself conducted the *In Autumn* overture at one of them. An open-air concert, a trip to the top of Mt. Flöyen for the orchestra from Oslo, and more receptions were some of the other highlights.

The banquet was attended by a representative group of men and women from Norway and abroad. *Bergens Tidende*, which published a special Grieg edition a few days later, concluded by stating that it was a celebration "carried along by an atmosphere and enthusiasm completely worthy of the great master who on this occasion was to receive the greetings and tribute of his native city and country. Not least because of Björnson's marvelous speech, it had an aura of splendor that will not be soon forgotten by those who had the opportunity to be there." Björnson picked up some of the major threads in the history of Norway. Norwegians, he said, often lack the ability to set long-range goals, but Grieg was one of those who had been able to take a longer view and had built a foundation on which others could build yet further. Grieg's music, he said, was as Norwegian as Norway's landscape, and had, like nothing else, brought Norway into homes the world over: "Yes," he said to Grieg, "what you have won for us out there is nice, but it is nothing compared with what you have won for us here at home by taking our most noble and lofty sentiments and giving them back to us so transfigured and so close to perfection as you have been able to do. And finally: I say this because I truly believe it, that if one will measure the stature of a great man one must consider not only what he has done but also what he has *made it possible for others to do.*"

Grieg himself made many speeches—for Norway, for Björnson, Halvorsen, Lammers, Röntgen, and in memory of Ole Bull. He also spoke from the balcony to all the members of the song societies in Bergen who had come together to pay tribute to him in song: "May this [your coming together] be a symbol of Norway's unification, for we are not yet a united people. But we have—as in 1814 [when Norway gained its independence from Denmark]—shown that we can be that. Let that Norway that comes together live. That is what we want, and that is what we need! Long live Norway!"

After it was all over, Grieg—happy and in high spirits—wrote to John Paulsen: "Yes, those Bergensians are born party-givers. I wish you had been here! You would have enjoyed the bright and happy atmosphere that hovered over the city as it basked in the summer sun—and the same atmosphere hovered also over Björnson's weighty speech, which he with his great oratorical ability delivered with enormous effect." He went on to say that during the party at the top of Mt. Flöyen, Björnson, in his typical manner, had given an impromtu speech based on the public notice: "Don't spit on the floor." Norwegians, Björnson had said, know how to spit—and far, too. "Don't spit on others, don't spit on art and science, don't spit on those who think differently—don't spit on the floor!" He concluded his talk with a toast for tolerance—a theme that was dear to Grieg, who had always urged that understanding of the views of others is of the greatest importance in both life and art.

The remainder of that summer was not a good time for Grieg. He suffered greatly from insomnia, and this led to mental disorientation. He did not spend a single day in his composer's hut, and a trip to Maristuen on Mt. Filefjell at the beginning of August only made him worse. He finally had himself admitted to the hospital in Bergen under the care of his friend, Dr. Klaus Hanssen. It appears that what he needed most of all was to get some rest.

In the latter part of September he traveled to Trondheim and then to Oslo. Right after Christmas he and Nina went to Aulestad again to visit the Björnsons for three weeks. Once more they had a great time together: "Björnson is in a class by himself," Grieg wrote to Beyer on January 4. "And he has that ability to stimulate others. I have become a new person up here. Nina doesn't recognize me. I am letting the lighter side of my being prevail. And if only you knew how good it feels!"

In March he left on another concert tour to Sweden, with performances in both Stockholm and Gothenburg. He did not get back to "Troldhaugen" until the end of May.

In the summer of 1904, the German Emperor Wilhelm II anchored his yacht "Hohenzollern" in the Bergen harbor. Grieg was invited to have breakfast with him at the home of the German consul, where everything under the sun was discussed: ". . . poetry, painting, religion, socialism, and God knows what. Fortunately he was just a man and not an emperor. I was therefore able—very tactfully, of course—to express my views openly," Grieg wrote to Henri Hinrichsen on July 21. The ship's forty-member orchestra played the music to *Sigurd Jorsalfar* and *Peer Gynt,* and Wilhelm II—who was knowledgeable about music—was interested in hearing Grieg's own comments on the music. Grieg himself played the minuet from the piano sonata and "Wedding Day at Troldhaugen."

The following evening Grieg was invited to dinner aboard the "Hohenzollern." After dinner the orchestra played out on the open deck, to the pleasure of both the invited guests and the people in the hundreds of boats that crowded around the yacht. Grieg felt very much at ease in the emperor's company on this occasion, for he remembered well the Germans' aid to the victims of the catastrophic fire in the Norwegian city of Aalesund earlier that year. He characterized Wilhelm II as "a most unusual human being, a remarkable mixture of enormous energy, great self-confidence, and genuine goodness." Around New Year's Day of the following year he also received this telegram from the emperor: "To the Scandinavian composer whose music I have always enjoyed, I send my sincere good wishes for the new year and for new creative activity."

Grieg gave two concerts with the National Theater Orchestra in Oslo in October, 1904. The renowned actress Johanne Dybwad performed in *Bergliot,* and Grieg was delighted. "She is entrancing," he reported to Matthison-Hansen after the dress rehearsal. "She enters into the music in such a way that the delicate relationship between the music and the performer is never broken for an instant." Two evening song recitals with Ellen Gulbranson, however, failed to win the response he had hoped for from either the audience or the press. The reason probably was that he had chosen to introduce some of his newest songs, and people were not familiar with them.

In other respects the autumn of 1904 was a quiet one for Grieg, except for a controversy between Björnson and Knut Hamsun in which Grieg also got involved. Hamsun, who was later to win a Nobel Prize for literature himself, had attacked Björnson for his position regarding Norway's relationship to Sweden, and at the same time had insinuated that Björnson had—as Grieg put it—"purchased the Nobel prize with his so-called change of political stance." Grieg considered Hamsun's attack unfair and unfounded, and showed his support for his friend in the form of an open letter to Björnson that appeared in *Verdens Gang* on December 7.

Immediately after Christmas Grieg moved from Hotel Westminster in Oslo to the prestigious Hotel Phoenix in Copenhagen, where he settled down to rest for nearly five months.

The last songs and Lyric Pieces

Grieg wrote to H. T. Finck in 1900 as follows: "When I write songs, my principal goal is not to write *music* but to do justice to the *poet*'s most intimate intentions. My task is to allow the text to speak—indeed, to allow it to speak in an amplified form. If I have accomplished this, then the music is also successful. Otherwise it is not, though it be ever so beautiful." In view of this conviction regarding the supremacy of the text, one can readily understand why it was so essential for Grieg to have worthy texts in order to do his best work as a song writer. The proof of this is to be found in his settings of the best Norwegian lyric poetry of his day, culminating in the *Haugtussa* cycle. After producing this full-fledged work it appears almost as if he was afraid to come to grips with Norwegian poetry ever again, for all of his later songs are settings of non-Norwegian texts.

Around the turn of the century Grieg experienced a sudden burst of enthusiasm for Danish poetry, and during his stay in Copenhagen in 1900 he wrote the ten songs of Opuses 69–70 to texts by Otto Benzon. It strikes us as almost incomprehensible that he would have anything to do with these trifles, nearly all of which are simply dull and banal. Only two of the ten are on a somewhat higher plane: "Snail, Snail!" and "Summer Night." It is also somewhat surprising to learn that Grieg himself thought well of them: after their initial performance in Copenhagen on March 23, 1901, he wrote to Robert Henriques: "According to the unanimous judgment of the critics, my new songs are of no significance. And here I even thought that they marked a kind of forward step! And that I had a fairly well developed sense of self-criticism!" He went on to say that, after the poor reception the critics had given his G-minor quartet after its first performance in Leipzig, he had wanted to burn the manuscript. "But time has vindicated me. I hope that it will do the same with these songs."

In this case, however, Grieg's vaunted self-criticism must have failed him, for in many of the songs the music is not much better than Benzon's mediocre texts. One can faintly recognize Grieg in some of them, but largely in the form of overused melodic and harmonic stereotypes. The "forward step" to which

Grieg alluded can be found only in the ambitious concepts that he tried to employ in several of them. The sphere of the tender, intimate song, where he was so at home, is here abandoned in favor of a more grandiose vocal display. These songs absolutely cry out for an orchestral accompaniment. Occasionally Grieg managed, in spite of the texts, to write some pleasing music. "A Boat on the Waves Is Rocking" is rather attractive. "Eros" starts out with quite a bit of spontaneity, but unfortunately the overall impression is considerably weakened by an insipid series of chromatic sequences in the midsection. These two, however, have a verve reminiscent of some of the songs of Richard Strauss.

The best of the ten Benzon songs is the beautiful and simple mood picture, "Summer Night," which is devoid of the bravura character that marks most of the others. The style here is similar in many ways to that of Hugo Wolf, a composer whom Grieg greatly admired.

Grieg also wrote music for an English text by Otto Benzon, "To a Devil" (CW 157). It was not published in Grieg's lifetime. Here he succeeded in capturing the flavor of British folk songs in a merry, rousing melody with fresh and original chord progressions. He also came upon a Norwegian translation of a Kipling poem, "Gentlemen-Rankers" (CW 158), in *Verdens Gang*. He was struck by the "repugnantly jaunty mood" of the poem, its abhorrence of war and everything at all chauvinistic. His setting of this text is quite powerful, but both it and the insignificant "Yuletide Cradle Song" (CW 101, No. 5) were filed away in Grieg's desk drawer. The latter, as well as "The Hunter" (CW 101, No. 6), which dates from 1905, was published in 1908 in a volume of posthumous songs. With "The Hunter," a rather trite setting of a German text, Grieg rounded off his song production as he harked back to the German style that he had used forty years earlier in "Hunting Song" (Opus 4).

Grieg's last volume of *Lyric Pieces,* Opus 71, was written in the first half of 1901. Five of the seven pieces have manuscript dates showing that they were written between June 4 ("Gone") and June 25 ("Remembrances"), while "Summer's Eve" and "Puck" evidently were written earlier. Opus 71 was dedicated to Röntgen's second wife, Mien (Abrahamine). With this volume, which is of consistently fine quality, Grieg brought his ten volumes of small pieces for piano to a worthy conclusion. In "Summer's Eve" and "Peace of the Woods" he created musical pictures of scenes in nature with fine sensitivity. "Puck," with its mischievous, frolicking harmony, and "Halling"—a virtuoso piece if there ever was one—are among the most genuinely Norwegian pieces Grieg wrote. The volume is framed by melodious and nostalgic mood pieces: "Once Upon a Time," "Gone," and "Remembrances." "Once Upon a Time" is a kind of Norwegian-Swedish fraternizing, inasmuch as the first part ("in Swedish folk-tune style") is related to the Swedish song "Ack Värmeland, du sköna" while the middle part is a stylized Norwegian *springar.* In "Remembrances" Grieg transformed the very first of his *Lyric Pieces*—"Arietta," Opus 12, No. 1—into a lovely waltz. In so doing he concluded nearly forty years of writing in this genre by reminding us in a touching and delightful way of the time of his youth.

From Hardanger fiddle to piano: Norwegian Peasant Dances. *Opus 72*

7. THE OLD *SLAATER* MUST BE SAVED FOR POSTERITY

As I am an older national Hardanger fiddler and have carefully learned to play like the good old fiddlers Myllarguten, Hovar Giböen, and Hans Helaas [Hellos] from Böe, I have long pondered deeply whether they [the old dance tunes] cannot be played from [written] notes and not be buried with the artist, I therefore venture to send you a few lines since from newspapers and reports I have heard that you are our country's greatest musician, if you have any interest in such a thing, I have great admiration for beautiful music, I come from a musical family, I started to play violin when I was ten years old and got instruction from my grandfather . . . (Letter from Knut Dahle to Grieg, April 8, 1888. Many words are misspelled in the original.)

We now turn to an important development in Grieg's life that began, in a way, many years earlier. In the spring of 1888 Grieg had received a touching, unsolicited letter from Knut Johannessen Dahle of Vestfjorddalen in Tinn. This well-known fiddler from Telemark had, in his younger years, learned to play the Hardanger fiddle from Myllarguten—the most illustrious Norwegian fiddler of all time—and others. He mentioned in the letter that he had often skied forty miles to "rehearse all the fingering" with Myllarguten. Now he thought it was time to get the old dances written down. The letter sounded as if it came from someone who knew what he was talking about. The handwriting was firm and beautiful, and the peculiar orthography showed that he had done his utmost to express himself in the (to him) unfamiliar Dano-Norwegian form of the language.[7]

Grieg's enthusiasm for Hardanger-fiddle music had been kindled as early as the middle 1860s, first by Ole Bull and later by Ola Mosafinn. In 1888 he also met Sjur Helgeland at a concert that Helgeland gave in Bergen, and visited him in Voss several times over the years. The communication from Knut Dahle had captured Grieg's interest. He wrote back and proposed a visit to Dahle at some mutually agreeable time. On June 10 of the same year he suggested to Beyer that perhaps the two of them could take the trip together. They actually started out for Telemark, but "unforeseen circumstances forced us to give up the trip," Grieg later told Johan Halvorsen (letter of October 18, 1901).

Dahle, however, did not give up. On August 8, 1890, he wrote Grieg again: "Your welcome letter to me from Bergen I have read through many, many times and thought 'is it possible that he will ever come here' and 'no, he certainly will never come, he has so much to do abroad.'" Dahle then sug-

Knut Johannessen Dahle (1834–1921). He wrote to Grieg on October 25, 1901: "Please accept my photograph. I now wear a full beard so I look much different than I used to." It is clear that his stay in Oslo in 1901, when Johan Halvorsen wrote down seventeen of his slaatter, whetted his appetite, for on August 22, 1902, he wrote to Grieg: "I intend to reimburse you for what you paid for my hotel in Oslo—or if you would like more of my slaatter I will take care of the expenses myself. I have at least twenty more that are just as good as the ones you got." Another Oslo trip never took place, however. Dahle continued as a fiddler far into his 80s. In addition, he recorded some of his slaatter on wax cylinders, and these recordings still exist. Dahle also managed to teach many of his slaatter to two of his grandsons, Johannes and Gunnar, who not only have kept the material alive but have also taught it to new generations of fiddlers. (Universitetsbiblioteket of Bergen, Norway)

8. GRIEG ASKS JOHAN HALVORSEN
FOR ASSISTANCE

It is clearer to me now than at that time
that *only a violinist with Norwegian emotional
makeup, one who is capable of transcribing,*
can accomplish the task at hand. It really is
crazy that the Storting [Norwegian Parlia-
ment] pays people who are not violinists to
collect folk songs, since these people can't
transcribe the instrumental dance tunes—
which are at least as important as the songs
and just as numerous. What is to be done?
To get Myllarguten's *slaatter* written down,
that is the task that can't be postponed for a
single day, for Knut Dahle is an old man. I
would prefer that *you* undertake the
task . . . Just think: if you did this, and if I
then set the *slaatter* for piano, and if in this
way we made them world-famous through
Peters—right under the noses of our *un-na-
tional* National Parliament! (Letter to
Halvorsen, October 18, 1901.)

gested that he could just as well come to Oslo, but "I am, as usual, short of
money." November 16 he sent off two more letters, but as far as we know he
got no response from Grieg. In fact, eleven years passed before anything
happened.

In the meantime, Dahle had spent four years in America. During most of
this time he was in Decorah, Iowa, where he had a son who was a shoemaker.
He had returned to Norway after the death of his son in 1900. The following
year he wrote to Grieg in Bergen (October 11, 1901) that some of his dances,
especially those that he had gotten from Myllarguten, had been transcribed in
America (probably by a professor of music at Luther College in Decorah).
"But," he wrote, "I would like it so much better if a composer here would do
the same and transcribe them, I am now the only one left who learned them
from Myllarguten—I still have the letter I got from you many years ago, when
I am gone the dances will also be gone, those now being played are entirely
different."

Somewhat dejectedly, Dahle asked Grieg if he could find someone else to
transcribe the dances if he himself was not interested. Now Grieg responded
in earnest. On October 18 he wrote Dahle that he would immediately set
things in motion to get the dance tunes written down. The same day he
approached Johan Halvorsen and asked him to undertake the job.[8]

Three days later Halvorsen replied: "I will transcribe those dance tunes
with pleasure and enthusiasm! I have wanted to do this for many years. Send
Knut Dahle here without delay! I assume that he is the right person to use for
this purpose."

On October 31 Dahle confirmed that he would be glad to come to Oslo and
would stay there as long as Halvorsen needed him. He mentioned that "[all
the] dance tunes that have names and legends associated with them I will
carefully explain as they have been explained to me."

On November 4 Grieg sent 100 kroner to Dahle. He wrote to Halvorsen
telling him of this and went on to say: "Will you now please tell me your
impression of him as quickly as possible, so that I can get moving to scrape up
what he needs for an extended stay if this should be necessary. If only he
proves to be the right man! In any case, it's high time to save the pieces."

So Knut Dahle finally came to Oslo. In the course of a few weeks Halvorsen managed to get the dance tunes down on paper, and in two enthusiastic
letters to Grieg he wrote of the joy he had experienced in doing it and his
good impression of Dahle. The feeling evidently was mutual, for on November 30—two days after returning home—Dahle wrote to Grieg: "Halvorsen
is a master violinist, I haven't heard his equal, I hope that you will be satisfied
with my dance tunes."

They were satisfied—indeed, very satisfied. There were seventeen dance
tunes in all, which Halvorsen sent to Bergen on December 3 with these words:
"Dear Grieg! I send herewith the results of Knut Dahle's stay in Oslo. I hope
you find something you can use. I have tried to write down everything as
accurately as possible. There is no end of repetitions, but that is easy enough
to correct. With regard to the tonality: there is an oddity in that *G-sharp* is
nearly always used (in the beginning of the D-major dances). G comes only

9. GRIEG ON THE *SLAATTER*

The past fourteen days I have been busy with Knut Dahle and Halvorsen's folk tunes. It interests me greatly, but it is a hellish job. Why? Well, I have become more critical than before in the interests of maintaining a unified style. In this case there is also a difficulty that I didn't have to deal with in working with the Lindeman materials, and that is to decide what should be retained of the original violin notation with respect to the lower part. And now, since the original will be published at the same time as my arrangement, I will no doubt provoke the German critics. As a matter of fact, in this connection I have been thinking of writing a preface in which I explain my views on these matters. This will give a better understanding of what I have and have not desired and will, I hope, disarm to some extent those who might wish to attack me. There are a couple of dance tunes that you will love. How easy it would be to rob them of their fragrance! (Letter to Beyer, September 2, 1902.)

* * *

[Halvorsen], to put it briefly, has performed the very complicated task of transcribing in a sensitive and comprehending—yes, an absolutely masterful—manner. And that has great significance, for it is my intention to have the originals published by Peters at the same time as my arrangements. This will be the first time that Norwegian *slaatter* are being published in the original version, and it will undoubtedly be interesting and exciting news for violinists. (Letter to Röntgen, September 5, 1902.)

* * *

They are so genuine and so buoyantly giddy and wild with touching undercurrents here and there, that I am just happy they were rescued in time. I sent the fiddler to Halvorsen, who transcribed them in their original form. It is quite different from Lindeman's collection, where one never knows what is original and what is Lindeman. I shall now see to it that the originals are printed at the same time as my free arrangements, so one can see which is which. It is a great pity that we don't have a body of primary source material. (Letter to Iver Holter, September 15, 1902.)

* * *

Working out the verbal part of this manuscript was very difficult. I must earnestly request that you correct errors in my German. Since cultural history plays such a central role in this matter, I regard the Preface and all the comments as indispensable. Although my individuality is clearly expressed in these piano arrangements—indeed, perhaps more clearly than many

toward the end (on the lower strings). For my part, I think *G-sharp* is fresh and fun, whereas G would sound dull. Then there are the trills and the appoggiaturas and *Nachschlags*. These ornaments, together with the rhythm, are the adornment and soul of the dance tunes. They are often produced merely with a vibration of the hand, in which case they sound like a kind of 'quivering.' An exception is the trill on the open A string, which sounds clear and fresh. I noted that even the most 'devilish' appoggiaturas and trills did not detract in any way from the rhythmic lines of the dances. I am practicing every day on the Hardanger fiddle and have acquired a fair degree of 'authenticity.' A fiddle like this clucks and shrieks and 'whines' and quivers. And it can sound so beautiful—in Myllarguten's bridal march, for example. Of the *gangars* I think 'The Skuldal Bride' takes the prize. I should certainly get hold of Sjur Helgeland, Ole Moe, and all the others now that I have begun with this."

Grieg responded enthusiastically on December 6: "This is quite some Saturday night, dear Halvorsen. Outdoors there is raging a southerly gale that shakes the house, not to mention a veritable deluge pouring down from the heavens. But here in the house it is cozy and comfortable. I have just received your dance tunes and finished reading through them, and I am absolutely chortling with delight. But at the same time I am mad as hops about not being a violinist. How I hate that conservatory in Leipzig!—But to the matter at hand: this 'oddity' that you speak of with respect to the use of *G-sharp* in D major was the thing that drove me out of my mind in 1871. Naturally I stole it immediately for use in my *Pictures from Folk Life*. This phenomenon is something for the musicologist. The augmented fourth can also be heard in the peasants' songs. It is a holdover from one old scale or another. But which? It is hard to believe that no one among us has taken an interest in the study of our national music when we have such rich sources in our folk music—for those who have ears to hear with, hearts to feel with, and the knowledge to transcribe them. At the moment it seems to me that it would be a sin to arrange the dance tunes for piano. But that sin I probably will commit sooner or later. It is too tempting. Many thanks for your work. It has given me great pleasure, and the future will show that you have done more than that. I can't really do anything with them until next summer. Would you like for me, at the proper time, to try to get Peters to publish both your work and mine?"

Not until August of 1902 was Grieg in a position to devote himself to arranging the dances—a task that was to occupy him for the next six months. Grieg was not well versed in the Hardanger-fiddle dance tune tradition, and it gave him enormous satisfaction to feel that, with sure instinct, he had mastered the great challenge that he faced in arranging this unique material for piano. In the Primary Materials will be found a series of characteristic statements by Grieg about the *Norwegian Peasant Dances*.[9]

Grieg insisted on having Halvorsen's original transcriptions published

would wish—I am well aware that you would have preferred an original work from me. That certainly will come. Just give me a little better health! (Letter to Henri Hinrichsen, February 28, 1903.)

10. PERCY GRAINGER'S
IDEAL INTERPRETATION

I had to become sixty-four years old to hear Norwegian piano music interpreted so understandingly and brilliantly. The way he plays the *Norwegian Peasant Dances* and folk-song arrangements, he breaks new ground for himself, for me, and for Norway. And then this enchanting, natural, profound, serious, and childlike naturalness! What a joy to gain a young friend with such qualities! (Diary entry, July 27, 1907.)

contemporaneously with his own arrangements, because these were of considerable interest both artistically and scientifically. This bold demand was grudgingly accepted by the Peters publishing firm. Moreover, Grieg's unconventional work was stylistically far off the beaten track. It was strictly his established reputation that convinced the firm's director, Henri Hinrichsen, to publish the work in 1903. Interestingly enough, it was dedicated to a German musicologist, Professor Hermann Kretzschmar.

Grieg also found it pedagogically desirable to add a preface in which he explained the principles that he had used as a basis for his arrangements. For the sake of cultural history he also included the legends which, according to Knut Dahle, were associated with three of the tunes: "Halling from the Fairy Hill" (No. 4), "Myllarguten's Bridal March" (No. 8), and "The Maidens from Kivledal" (No. 16).

Peters elected to risk only a small print run in the first edition, and it was necessary to reissue the work just a year later. Grieg used the opportunity to incorporate a large number of improvements in the music, and it is in this revised form that *Norwegian Peasant Dances* is known today.

How was this pioneering work regarded by Grieg's contemporaries? Grieg himself was deeply disappointed at the lack of positive response after playing six of the pieces at a concert in Oslo on March 21, 1906. That evening he wrote in his diary: "Nina thought that I had *never* played so well . . . What hurt me was that the *slaatter* didn't strike home as they should have. I played them with all the affection and magic that I could muster. But—where my evolution as a composer has led me, I don't have my own people with me, and that is hard to bear. Here they are forever expecting me to write in the style of my early works, which time and again are praised at the expense of my recent ones. But—I must not let that hinder me. I hope that I can continue to develop as long as I live. That is my fondest wish. The understanding of the general public will come in due course."

Six days later the concert, at cut-rate ticket prices, was repeated at Oslo's biggest auditorium (Calmeyergatens Misjonshus). "Here nearly 3000 people acclaimed those *slaatter* which had achieved only limited success the previous time. All things considered, the solicitude of this audience was far greater and more genuine."

There were few Norwegian pianists during Grieg's lifetime who ventured to perform Opus 72. It was all the more exciting for him, therefore, when a brilliantly gifted young Australian pianist, Percy Grainger, immediately understood the greatness of the work and recreated it in his own spirit.[10] In the years that followed it was Grainger who introduced the *Norwegian Peasant Dances* to the rest of the world.

Equally encouraging was the information Grieg received regarding the reception of Opus 72 in France. He wrote to Hinrichsen on June 29, 1906: "And in Paris—according to what Halvorsen has told me—the *Norwegian Peasant Dances* have been discovered by some young musicians, and they are wild about 'le nouveau [the new] Grieg.' I mention this to you because it really has pleased me. Young people: they really are the future."

It was not for young Frenchmen that the new Grieg came to have the

Edvard and Nina at about the time he was working on Norwegian Peasant Dances. *Nina had an ear ailment at that time that concerned him greatly. On January 20, 1903, he wrote to Beyer, "I wish so much that I could say that things are going better here at home. But unfortunately: Now I too am beginning to have my doubts! I fear for her hearing. The result of the treatment of these doctor-idiots—specialists and non-specialists alike—is of late—and daily—increasing deafness. It is hopeless. I feel like crying as I write this. Think what music means for Nina, think what it means for the whole of our life together . . . God knows whether these Norwegians are not too brutal for such a delicate art as ear treatment . . . 'I could shoot them!' as my pious and gentle father always said." (Troldhaugen, Bergen)*

greatest significance, however, but for a Hungarian: Béla Bartók. Paris was the center for the musical avant-garde at this time, and the ambitious and brilliant young Hungarian went there as well. It is highly likely that here, in about 1910, he became acquainted with Grieg's Opus 72, for as early as 1911—in his article "Instrumental Folklore in Hungary"—he referred to Norwegian *slaetter* and Romanian *joc* as typical instrumental folk dances. That Bartók employed the distinctively Norwegian word *slaatt* at this early date can in our opinion be explained only on the assumption that he was familiar with Grieg's *Norwegian Peasant Dances*. Moreover, in a series of later articles he frequently pointed to Grieg as one of the forerunners of nationalism in music. According to Andor Foldes, he also used Grieg's piano music extensively as teaching material for his own students.

Bartók's interest in Norwegian folk music also manifested itself in a very concrete way: in the summer of 1912, on the advice of Delius, he took a four-week trip to Norway. His travels took him all the way up to Lofoten, and his son, Béla, Jr., reports that while there his father bought a very special souvenir of his trip to Grieg's homeland: a Hardanger fiddle.

It is evident that Grieg's accomplishments with the Norwegian *slaatter*, both as historical research and as artistic creations, had an impact on Bartók's own work. It gave further impetus to his search for that which is genuine in folk music, and to his effort to give adequate expression to this music in arrangements of the highest artistic quality. As with Grieg, characteristics derived from folk music played a prominent role in Bartók's own compositions.

Halvorsen was a concert violinist who had no background in folk music. It is not surprising, then, that he encountered many difficulties in the process of transcribing the Dahle *slaatter*, but he succeeded amazingly well. It is immediately evident that what we have before us is truly indigenous Hardanger-fiddle music: the distinctive two-part texture, the rich ornamentation, the characteristic phrasing patterns—they are all there. In his comments Halvorsen also exhibits a clear understanding of the subtleties in the playing of such music. Indeed, he became so entranced by the music that he procured a Hardanger fiddle for himself in order to study the material as profoundly as possible.

The special *springar* rhythm of the Telemark *slaatter* is not captured in Halvorsen's notation—or, for that matter, in any other similar transcriptions either. The problem is that the beat lengths are supposed to be of varying duration—with the third beat always the shortest—and there is no way to accommodate this peculiarity in the standard system of music notation. Somewhat more problematic are the misplaced bar lines in some of the *springar*s—in Nos. 2 and 13, for example. The result is that in Halvorsen's—and thereby also in Grieg's—transcriptions, what should have been the third beat of the measure becomes the first beat instead. This is no problem for one who already "has the Telemark rhythm in his blood"; such a one can easily play the dances from Halvorsen's transcriptions. But in the piano arrangements it becomes more evident that the rhythm is distorted, because here the downbeat is normally stressed much more than the other beats.

Grieg's *Norwegian Peasant Dances* represent his most thoroughgoing attempt to directly convert folk-music material into a form suitable for the concert hall. It is brilliantly done, but for a fiddler who has the sounds and rhythms of the *slaatter* in his blood, the result of such a conversion is to place these dance tunes in a completely different musical world. The *slaatter* are created out of small motives that are repeated and modified and linked together. Monotony is avoided through ingenious phrasing, melody, rhythm, and harmony. It is this constant variation, often improvised, of tiny elements that gives the *slaatt* its vitality. Such variation is very difficult to reproduce on the piano.

Grieg was well aware of the problems. In the preface to the Peters edition of *Norwegian Peasant Dances* he wrote: "My object in arranging the music for the piano was to raise these works of the people to an artistic level, by giving them what I might call a style of musical concord, or bringing them under a system of harmony. Naturally, many of the little embellishments, characteristic of the peasant's fiddle and of their peculiar manner of bowing, cannot be reproduced on the piano, and were accordingly omitted. On the other hand, by virtue of its manifold dynamic and rhythmic qualities, the piano affords the great advantage of enabling us to avoid a monotonous uniformity, by varying the harmony of repeated passages or parts. I have endeavored to make myself clear in the lines set forth, in fact, to obtain a definite form. The few passages in which I considered myself authorized as an artist, to add to, or work out the given motives, will easily be found, on comparing my arrangement with the original, written down by Johan Halvorsen, in a manner reliable even for research work, and published by the same firm."

As often happened when Grieg worked with folk-music materials, he did not slavishly follow the original notation. He altered the melodies now and then, and also moved the motives up and down in various octaves. He also added preludes, interludes, and postludes, and occasionally he extended some of the *slaatter* by developing some of the motives. The most radical examples of this are the *hallings*, "Halling from the Fairy Hill" (No. 4) and "Rötnams-Knut" (No. 7). In both of these a slow, contrasting section in a minor key—using motivic materials from the *slaatter* in augmented note values—is introduced over expressive, chromatically colored chords. He had used this same technique in earlier folk-music arrangements in Opuses 30 and 35.

Grieg created variety by making imaginative use of the piano's possibilites. He managed with remarkable success to convey the distinctive sounds of the Hardanger fiddle within the limitations of his own instrument. The flavor of the gently vibrating sympathetic strings, which also strengthens the richness of the fiddle's overtones, is recreated with great finesse. This is achieved by devices such as sustained tones, pedal-point effects, and not least by the subtle use of the sustaining pedal of the piano.

In accordance with Halvorsen's transcriptions, which are generally in two voices, the ornamentation in the piano part is predominantly given to the right hand. As one would expect in a piano adaptation, however, the melody is set in relief by lines in contrary motion and by counter-rhythms in the inner voices and in the bass, occasionally with a linear stamp. Among the striking

*Grieg wrote to Beyer on January 20, 1903:
"[Gustav] Vigeland has modeled a bust of me.
Neither bad nor good, I think; but more good
than bad." ("Troldhaugen," Bergen, Norway)*

features of the collection are the numerous subtleties within each individual piece and the richness of contrast among the various pieces.

In its basic conception, Opus 72 is concert music of high quality. In order to do justice to the work it is not enough that the performers have a brilliant technique: these pieces require a deep insight into the very essence of the *slaatter*. It was precisely this latter aspect that impressed Grieg so strongly in Percy Grainger's interpretation of the work.

The characteristic that aroused the greatest contemporary reaction, both positively and negatively, was the unusual and uncompromising harmonization in these pieces. As late as 1921, Richard Stein—a German biographer of Grieg who was usually enthusiastic about his compositions—could not tolerate the boldness of the harmonic language. He wrote: ". . . in many of the dances (Nos. 4, 7, 13, and 15) there are shrill dissonances that are almost unbearable on the piano. These unfortunate results may be attributed to the fact that this time Grieg wanted to let diatonicism predominate" (p. 152).

It cannot be denied that to Grieg's contemporaries the harmonies sounded rather harsh. In fidelity to the character of the *slaatter*, Grieg consciously chose a method of expression in which dissonances are particularly prominent. Alongside the gentle major seconds and minor sevenths, the music absolutely crackles when the parts collide to form minor seconds, major sevenths, and augmented fourths. The dissonances often accumulate in blocks of sound in which pedal points and sustained tones play important roles.

Aside from Nos. 2, 9, and 10, Grieg built all the *slaatter* in the form of a kind of arch. The peak of intensity and dissonance occurs toward the middle, and there is a gradual relaxation of tension thereafter.

Grieg's *slaatter*, strongly dissonant as they are in many places, point beyond the harmonic conventions of his time. They approach the style that is primarily associated with Béla Bartók, i.e., barbarism. (The name comes from his 1911 piano piece "Allegro barbaro.") Barbarism, however, is characterized not only by the unorthodox juxtaposition of dissonances but also by a certain "primitivism." The thirds of chords are omitted; open fifths remain. Fifths and fourths may also be superimposed. Grieg had employed this technique earlier, but it is much more prominent in Opus 72. In addition, like Bartók and the other devotees of barbarism, he incorporated here an unusual rhythmic vitality. At times the piano is used almost as a percussion instrument: the rhythm is literally "pounding."

Harshness is not the only quality that characterizes the *Norwegian Peasant Dances,* however. There are also sections with a charming softness marked by sophisticated chord progressions that must undoubtedly have sounded fascinating to the young French impressionists.

There is one piece in the collection—"Myllarguten's Bridal March" (No. 8)—that is in a class by itself. It reveals an impressionistic harmonic vocabulary of great subtlety. Legend has it that the march was composed by Myllarguten when his beloved, Kari, forsook him to marry another. It is not, therefore, a happy wedding march of the traditional sort. Rather, it resembles a deeply melancholy funeral march in which Myllarguten, with incomparable beauty and tenderness, plays out his sorrow in the sunny key of A major. Here the strings of the brilliant fiddler created sympathetic vibrations in Grieg's innermost soul, and the result was a piece that stands as one of his supreme achievements for piano. The first two lines of the bridal march are given below:

Grieg and Politics

Norway's dramatic year of destiny—1905—was, paradoxically, one of the most quiet years of Grieg's Life with respect to travel and compositional work. It began with a five-month stay at Hotel Phoenix in Copenhagen during which he was, however, ill much of the time. He was treated by five doctors, but—as he wrote in a March 7 letter to Beyer—"None of them has managed to—I almost said: to take my life. They never were good enough for that."

He left Denmark on May 27 and was in Oslo for a few days before returning to "Troldhaugen" on June 5. He was there until September 20, whereupon he returned to Oslo and remained there for the rest of the year. During the Christmas holidays he was hospitalized.

He composed very little during that year. On August 29 he wrote to Matthison-Hansen that he just couldn't seem to get his strength and that he felt "100 years old, at the very least." He had worked as hard as he could under the circumstances, but the whole of what he had been able to produce was "so small that you need a magnifying glass to see it: it is only a collection of piano pieces to cast into the jaws of Mammon. This will be bait for Peters in Leipzig to get them to publish two orchestral scores without protesting [Opuses 51 and 54]. But with this [composition] I have realized for the first time that I have grown old . . . There are some Norwegian pieces in between—a couple of years old—that I like, but I really haven't put my heart into the rest of them."

Grieg was referring here to *Moods,* Opus 73, and his judgment of it is correct. The quality is uneven, and it is indeed the two pieces inspired by folk music that stand out. In "Folk Tune from Valdres," which originally (No. 254 in Lindeman's collection) was a goat-horn melody, Grieg slightly modified Lindeman's transcription. He also provided the melodies with exquisite harmonic dress both in this piece and in the somewhat modal "Mountain Tune." A bit of the authentic Grieg shows through also in "Night Ride" and "Resignation." In the latter, which was originally written in Röntgen's autograph album with the title "Sehnsucht nach Julius" [Longing for Julius], Grieg gave a handsome greeting to his best foreign friend. The remaining pieces—"Scherzo-Impromptu," "Homage to Chopin," and "The Students' Serenade"—are euphonious but somewhat routine pastiches.

Photograph of Grieg taken some time after 1900, perhaps as late as 1905. This photo was used by the German painter Herrmann as the basis for the portrait reproduced on p. 373. (Gyldendal, Oslo)

Freedom is the struggle for freedom

Grieg was socially conscious and politically engaged throughout his adult life, and it is therefore not surprising that the ideals of the French Revolution—liberty, equality, fraternity—were always dear to him. The political crisis of 1905, when Norway and Sweden very nearly went to war over Norway's demand that the Swedish-Norwegian Union be dissolved, served as a stimulus to Grieg to further clarify his political views. We shall follow the events of the time as he experienced them, but to get a more complete picture of his democratic views we must look also at some of his earlier political actions and pronouncements.

As early as the 1860s he reacted against the gross inequities of the society of his day, and his hatred of social injustice, lust for power, and snobbery were

1. AN UNWILLING VISIT WITH THE DANISH QUEEN LOUISE

I have greetings to you from Gade . . . He was here yesterday and sat for a long time. We got into politics. He had a message from the queen that she wished to see me. When I told him that I unfortunately couldn't accept the invitation because as an arch-republican I would be acting insincerely in going to the palace, he got pretty hot under the collar and insisted that it would be very discourteous to decline. So he finally got me to go up there on the condition that he would go along, and as a result I have had a big hangover for several days. (Letter to Winding, July 22, 1875.)

Portrait by the German artist, A. Herrmann

established during this time. He always sympathized with the weak rather than the strong. A laudable feature in his character was his willingness to place himself and his art at the service of people who were suffering—for example, the victims of natural catastrophes, fires, or unemployment. He gave many concerts for such purposes.

As a fervent believer in a non-monarchical form of government, he developed at an early age a deep aversion to anything related to royalty.[1] The court and nobility seemed to him to be the epitome of snobbery. He wrote to Matthison-Hansen on March 27, 1885: "Do you ever see Svendsen or does he spend all his time with the royal court and people with silk gloves? It's a good thing that there are various tastes in the world. I think it is healthier to do as you do: to associate with Bach and Handel. Indeed, they are the people who become greater each year that one lives." When he himself was decorated with orders and other symbols of honor, it rarely elicited from him more than a smile. But his aversion to royalty diminished with the years, not least as he had an opportunity to observe the human qualities of the royal personages with whom he had contact. Nonetheless, upon the death of Queen Victoria in 1901 he flatly refused a request from England to write a coronation march for King Edward VII.

Grieg perceived himself as a political radical, thanks not least to the influence of Björnson. In 1873, for example, Björnson sent him a jovial exhortation to vote for the Liberal Party: "N.B. See to it that there is a good vote in Söndre Bergenhus [the county in which Bergen was located], you rascal!" Grieg replied on June 17: "I hope you are satisfied with my parliamentary vote: red Sverdrupians!" (Sverdrup was the leader of the Liberal Party.) Some years after the Paris Commune of 1871, while vacationing at August Winding's summer home outside Copenhagen, he jokingly "[raised] the [French] republicans' red banner on a broomstick . . . in an outburst of excitement." He did it, he said, as evidence of his "redness."

In later years, when the political and social situation became truly perilous, there was bitter seriousness in his statements on these topics. Upon the death of Emperor Wilhelm I in 1888, he foresaw a coming upheaval in Germany and wrote to Beyer from Leipzig on March 21: "The revolution against the great iron oppression will come in this country . . . but it will happen only when people cry out in despair, for it is unbelievable how servile and well-tamed the populace is." He was enraged at the abuse of the common people by the upper classes. In a letter to Dr. Abraham on September 30, 1898, he intimated that some day the "unenlightened masses" would take the power in their own hands: "There *will* come another time. By blood or intelligence? I hope by the latter." The following year, as we know, he got involved in the Dreyfus affair fully aware of the risk he was taking.

Grieg attempted to stay informed about the political events of his day. He was acutely aware of the general turmoil in Russia after the turn of the century and felt aggrieved at the Russian attack on Japan, and he reacted violently against the tyranny and imperialism of the czars. On behalf of artists everywhere he felt ashamed that they talked of culture and civilization while people were being slaughtered, and in no uncertain terms he refused invitations to

Björnson and Grieg at about the time of the political crisis that resulted in Norway's independence. This is one of the few photographs we have in which Grieg is smiling. On May 16, 1907, Grieg wrote to Björnson, "Well, dear Björnson, I daresay that the 'thank you' that I send you now is more sincere than ever before. From a gratitude born of youthful enthusiasm it has become a gratitude imbued with understanding, with conviction. The years have ripened me, made me deeper, more substantial. May you feel that everything in me that is good is gathered together in this 'thank you'!" (Troldhaugen, Bergen)

give concerts in Russia. In this connection he emphasized that the human and the artistic spheres cannot be divided. "One must *first* be a human being. All true art grows out of that which is truly human," he wrote in a letter to Alexander Siloti on October 29, 1904. On April 26 of the following year, referring to the massacre of demonstrators in St. Petersburg, he stated to Adolph Brodsky: "We Norwegians never kiss! But I would willingly make an exception for all of the wretched, persecuted Russian people. I wish that I could place a bomb under the Russian government and administration, starting with the czar! They are the worst criminals of our time!"

Despite his outspoken radicalism, Grieg would not identify himself with any definite party. He stated his position on this matter in a letter to John Paulsen on June 3, 1881: "Kristiania [Oslo] is nothing but one big insane asylum. And then all this party-puffery in Norway! No, the older I get the more I say to myself: not conservative, not liberal—but both. Not subjective, not objective, but both. Not realist, not idealist, but both. The one extreme must include the other within itself."

The only system of government he could accept was a parliamentary democracy, and it was a great joy for him when such a government was established in Norway in 1884. "Now it will also be possible to live in Norway," he wrote to Ravnkilde on July 21 of that year. He continued: "It is a wonderful time for those who, like me, believe in progress. Let us hope the struggle will continue, for without a struggle for freedom life isn't worth a pickled herring. But the hatred and the pettiness will diminish, and then there will be room for other interests. It is just this that has been unhealthy about our politics—that it has extinguished interest in everything that didn't rally 'round the party's banner."

2. GRIEG AND BJÖRNSON ARE TOGETHER AT "A GREAT TIME"

Björnson came alone to visit us, and he sat and talked about everything under the sun. I wish that every word could have been recorded, for I don't think there is much slag mixed in with the infinity of beauty and deep, genuine human feelings that characterize everything that comes from his mouth when we sit and talk in this way. And then politics and the close connection between him and what has now taken place. I call this a great time. (Letter to Beyer, November 2, 1903.)

3. FEAR OF IMMINENT WAR

Should the Swedes commit the monstrous crime of attacking us, it will be a terrible time. You are absolutely right: we would then fight like the Japanese—fanatically, and to the last man. What is truly frightening about the situation is becoming clearer all the time: Norway is a modern country, whereas Sweden is still in the Middle Ages. Thus a collision is inevitable. Here the people govern themselves; Sweden is governed by a few noblemen with archaic views who work in secret. Everything now depends on whether or not the king will be forced to abdicate. If he does not step down, peace will probably prevail, but otherwise—? (Letter to Henri Hinrichsen, June 25, 1905.)

Caricature of Björnstjerne Björnson.

The relationship with Sweden became more and more strained in the 1890s as the dissolution of the Swedish-Norwegian Union became increasingly inevitable. As early as July 4, 1892, he expressed his irate attitude toward the Swedish court in a letter to Iver Holter: "These damned Bernadottes! When the time comes I'll take part in throwing them out." Four years later he struck another tone, however, for he realized that negotiation was the only way out of the impasse. The previous year he had been "too furiously indignant to be able to give [his] art away to the Swedes," he wrote to Lammers on March 6, 1896, but now he had "done an about-face." He felt that by giving concerts in Stockholm he could perform "a national mission" and be a bridge builder between the two countries (see further p. 348). He would soon discover, however, that such a position was hard for some Norwegian chauvinists to swallow.

After the turn of the century Grieg found himself increasingly in agreement with Björnson's political ideas.[2] During the first four months of 1905, as the union crisis moved toward its climax, he followed events with intense interest during his illness in Copenhagen. Prime Minister Christian Michelsen's view that negotiation with Sweden was the only reasonable course met strong opposition in certain circles in Norway; indeed, there were some who wanted him replaced. The world-famous explorer Fridtjof Nansen, who was a national hero in Norway, was being discussed as a possible candidate for the position of prime minister. That elicited a strong reaction from Grieg. He wrote sarcastically to editor O. A. Thommessen in *Verdens Gang* March 1, 1905: "I am a great admirer of Nansen. But I would rather have prime minister Thommessen than prime minister Nansen! Yes, 1000 times rather. And if dilettantism is really going to be the order of the day in Norway, why not prime minister Grieg? He isn't as stupid as you think."

In a March 6 letter to Björnson, Grieg—who wholeheartedly supported his fellow townsman Michelsen—thundered against the warmongers in Norway: "There are evil powers on the loose. powers of brutality and negativity! We must hate them both. To goad the young people to war and to scorn, that is a disgrace in these days. It is the old Norwegian contentiousness and vindictiveness rampant again."

In Grieg's opinion, a major obstacle to a peaceful solution was the aggressive attitude taken by Crown Prince Gustaf: "The Crown Prince's letter appears to be a calamity. But it has contributed mightily to unification. This Crown Prince Regent is our worst enemy, and there is no hope for Norway until we get rid of him."

During the decisive proceedings in Parliament Grieg stayed in Oslo, where all the important events were taking place. On June 7, however, when Norway declared its independence from Sweden, he was on the boat to Bergen. He immediately sent a congratulatory telegram to Michelsen.

The danger of war now became acute. The Norwegian army, ready for combat, stood at the Swedish border. Grieg feared the worst, and wrote of the catastrophe that seemed about to occur in a June 25 letter to Henri Hinrichsen.[3] In Sweden, the resentment over Norway's action manifested itself in a most grotesque way. During concerts in Strömstad, the audience responded

4. GRIEG EXPRESSES THANKS TO CHRISTIAN MICHELSEN

Let me be one of the first to wish you good luck and to thank you as warmly as any Norwegian can! You know better than I how much work and self-denial were put into this Karlstad Convention. But as a modern man I would say only this, that twice as many boundary fortresses would not have been too much of a sacrifice for Norway's independence. My instincts tell me to rejoice, for the spirit of the future and of progress hovers over this accomplishment. (Letter to Christian Michelsen, September 25, 1905.)

5. HUMILIATION MUST NOT BREED VINDICTIVENESS

We have been thoroughly *humiliated*. The cultural level in Sweden is so low that the Swedes really wanted to humiliate Norway, quite simply to punish us as one punishes naughty children . . . Sweden has only itself to thank for Norway's course of action. It is therefore stupid and ludicrous to want to take revenge. Chauvinism leads only to stupidity; I hope that the stupidity latent in every nation will not in this situation break out in Norway. (Letter to Henri Hinrichsen, September 26, 1905.)

to Grieg's works with boos and cat calls. He had to decline an invitation to conduct two concerts in Helsinki in September because, according to an August 29 letter to Matthison-Hansen, he could not travel through Sweden without risking maltreatment and deportation from the country. "Isn't it incredible? They won't perform Björnson's plays, and my music is greeted with hisses and demonstrations. Here in Norway all Swedes are treated with elaborate courtesy. I think this shows clearly who has the bad conscience and who has the good one!"

In September, when the Karlstad negotiations entered their decisive phase, Grieg thought that perhaps, with his international position, he again had a mission to perform—as a mediator. At the request of some of his friends he addressed telegrams to Emperor Wilhelm II and King Edward VII requesting that they intervene to prevent an outbreak of war. He received no response from either of them, however.

In Karlstad, reason eventually prevailed and war was averted. Shortly after the agreement was signed on September 23, Grieg sent an effusive letter of thanks to Michelsen.[4] The very next day, however, in a letter to Henri Hinrichsen, he gave a more sober assessment of the agreement and pointed out the conditions that he found humiliating for the Norwegian people.[5]

Before the plebiscite in November to determine whether there was to be a republic in Norway, Grieg saw that a continued monarchy was the only reasonable course in the situation in which the country found itself. He indicated this to G. Schjelderup on October 26: "And I think that as much as I love the idea of a republic, I do not doubt for a moment that *at present* a monarchy is required. Only that can save us from the inevitable economic and political misery . . . It is to be hoped, then, that by the end of November we will have a king and queen and, with that, the peace that is so sorely needed in our country."

The plebiscite, by a large majority, endorsed the idea of a monarchy, and by November 25 a former Danish prince and his English wife—King Haakon and Queen Maud—had set foot on Norwegian soil. The elaborate welcoming ceremonies had their artistic culmination in a festival performance of *Sigurd Jorsalfar* at the National Theater on November 28. When the curtain fell, both Björnson and Grieg were called to the royal box. That same evening Grieg began the diary that he kept until four days before his death—the most valuable personal document we have from the last two years of his life. In this first entry (November 28) he wrote enthusiastically about the royal couple: "The king and queen received us with the greatest kindness. If they are as unpretentious and straightforward as they here appeared to be, then we may dare to hope for a democratic monarchy . . . This first meeting with free Norway's first king and queen struck me as something beautiful and meaningful, and for that reason I choose this day to start my long-intended diary."

Four days after the festival performance, Grieg again met the king and queen at a banquet given by Prime Minister Michelsen: "The royal couple once again appeared unpretentious and straightforward. But parties like that are an abomination to me in their unspeakable tediousness and superficial, meaningless emptiness. And then the formality. These people should take lessons from the royal couple."

As a part of the celebration in honor of the royal couple, the Music Association gave a festive concert at which Grieg conducted *Land Sighting*. The rehearsals had sorely taxed his strength: "Is this the beginning of the end? Perhaps a bit of exertion at the rehearsal was too much for me. I hope for the sake of all the others that I can manage it this evening. I myself no longer have any ambition. Only the artistic satisfaction of knowing that it was a good performance . . ."

But the predominant feeling at this time was a deep joy over the happy resolution of Norway's political crisis. His December 12 letter to Beyer is jubilant: "When I go up Slottsbakken [the slope leading to the royal palace] I remain standing and fall to daydreaming—about the royal banner that waves so magnificently up at the palace, about the sentries, about the lively, pleasant motion going on all around me. This has really become a warmer and more pleasant place to be. I am—as I think you are, basically—a believer in a republican form of government and have been ever since my youth; but I also do not doubt for a moment that, in view of the circumstances, the right choice has been made. And not only that, but also that we have been so unspeakably fortunate."

In Grieg's diary entry on New Year's Eve it is as if he was able to sum up in beautiful words the gratitude of all his countrymen: "Now the year 1905—the great year—goes to rest, and I part from it with deep gratitude because I experienced it! And yet: without the youthful dreams which this year has made real my art would not have had its proper background. The longings have placed their stamp upon my music. Had the 7th of June come in my youth, then what? No, it is good as it is. The lifelong struggle has been the greatest good fortune both for the individual and for the nation. Freedom is: the struggle for freedom!"

Grieg and Religion

1. GENEROSITY TO BEYER

It was a heart-rending letter! I cried like a child! . . . No, it just cannot be allowed to happen! For here I sit and I am saying [to quote one of Brorson's hymns]: "O my Sulamit! All that I have is also yours!" And at this moment I have more than I need. Must I tell you, dear Frants, that everything I own is at your disposal! It would make me unhappy if you did not take me up on this—indeed, I'm afraid I would think less of you than I always have . . . If you finally decide that you absolutely must sell "Naesset"—well, then one of two things will happen: either I will also sell "Trold-haugen" or else I will be at the auction when "Naesset" is sold! (Letter to Beyer, January 29, 1888.)

2. CHARITY IS CONCEALED EGOTISM

Dear friends! I really haven't done anything for you at all. On the contrary, I have been pleasing myself now and then. That's all. I thoroughly disagree with Georg Brandes, who considers love to be "making others happy!" Poppycock! Love is making oneself happy. That is the big secret that Christianity will not admit: that egotism lurks even in love—inasmuch as it gives satisfaction and a feeling of happiness. But for this reason egotism, too—viewed from an ideal perspective—is a good thing. At least when it is presented undisguised and not—like margarine. (Letter to Matthison-Hansen, June 29, 1904.)

Grieg had many opportunities to think about the fundamental problems of life during his periods of illness, and much of what he had to say on the subject of religion was in fact written from his sickbed. Just a week before his death, in a letter to the Swiss theologian Louis Monastier-Schroeder, he wrote these words: "Pure science? As a means it is excellent, but as an end—at least for me—it is completely unsatisfying. I must retain the concept of God, even if this altogether too often comes in conflict with the concept of prayer." But what, exactly, was Grieg's concept of God? And where did he stand with respect to the basic questions of human existence?

He regarded the ethical precepts of the Sermon on the Mount as a lodestar for life and everyday conduct. He was a genuinely good person who lived out his philosophy of life in concrete acts of charity. There are countless examples of his deep concern for the welfare of others, and this frequently found expression in concrete acts of assistance. It is moving to learn, for example, that in the winter of 1888, when his friend Beyer was in danger of losing his home, Grieg offered to share with him everything he owned to help him through the crisis.[1]

So far as possible, Grieg kept his charitable acts a secret. In 1904, when he gave the Matthison-Hansen family a large gift of money, he disguised his good deed by writing a humorous note attributing it to self-interest.[2]

Another beautiful expression of his generosity was the many charitable concerts that he gave through the years. Family members, too, were the special beneficiaries of his concern—not least his parents-in-law, who had not always shown much confidence in him. But more distant relatives also benefitted from time to time from his generous disposition. Grieg's strong sense of duty occasionally came into conflict with his integrity as a creative artist, and now and then he felt disheartened by the importunity and greed of some people.

In his heart Grieg was a religious person. He grew up in a Christian home where "correct belief" was of central importance. The childhood faith that he took with him from this milieu he retained in a more or less uncritical form until well into the 1870s. During this time he regarded the atheistic currents of the day as utterly unworthy of belief. After his father's death in 1875 he

3. SOME ASPECTS OF GRIEG'S RELIGIOUS VIEWS

Even if I do not hold precisely the same beliefs that you do, I nonetheless believe fully and firmly in the same spirit of love: everything is created for a good purpose, and love has never revealed itself so fully as through Him whose birth we now are about to celebrate. Therefore I, like you, rejoice at the coming of Christmas, and wish only for the strength to struggle to acquire just one tiny spark of that spirit of love that Christ made to shine forth in his life. (Letter to J. A. B. Christie, December 14, 1881.)

* * *

I believe in humanity, and I believe in God, and I still believe that the God who created human beings intends something good for them. Otherwise I wouldn't want to live for another moment . . . (Letter to J. A. B. Christie, January 30, 1888.)

* * *

Whether one believes in God, Satan, and Christ as well as the Holy Spirit and the Virgin Mary, in Mohammed or in Nothing, it is nonetheless the case . . . that the mystery of death cannot be argued out of existence. This is the mystery for which I have wanted to find a suitable expression. This is also the mystery concerning which one finds in the Old Testament passages which—in both content and style—are of absolutely gripping intensity and power. This is the case, for example, in the Psalms of David, especially where the subject is the transitory nature of life. I find less of what I am seeking with regard to complete devotion in the idea of death linked to a belief in universal love, whether there is an afterlife or not. For this—to be safe and secure—is of no interest to me whatsoever. Atheists and dogmatic Christians are equally foreign to me. (Letter to Björnson, Christmas Day, 1890.)

4. INDIVIDUALITY MUST NOT BE OPPOSED

When I have finished reading what you write about the individuality that is to be opposed, I find that it sounds nice but there is no substance in it, for this question quickly presses itself upon me in all its unlimited enormity: In which cases shall individuality be opposed and which not? For I trust that we agree that it shall and ought not *always* to be opposed. To fight against individuality is one of Christianity's basic principles, and in our time it has become a catch phrase of the clergy leading straight to hell—away from all truth and freedom of spirit. You can't expect people to say to themselves: in this situation I shall act according to what I feel is the truth, in another case not. One should certainly examine one's motives before one acts, that is true, but if I insist that every person should act according to what *I* regard as right, and if it is on this principle that I judge people's actions, then I am being unreasonable. To be sure, most people are unreasonable in just this way, but such unreasonableness is at root medieval and is based on ignorance and narrow-mindedness. (Letter to Beyer, July 29, 1883.)

mentioned that the dogmas may be whatever they will, but "the thought of immortality I must have! Without that everything is nothing." (See quotation on p. 199.)

It is evident that a short time thereafter Grieg struggled through a serious religious crisis that completely destroyed the beliefs of his childhood. When he characterized the Lofthus period as his "hard, spiritual struggle," it is easy to believe that the struggle had to do not only with marital and artistic problems but also with religious doubt and torment. During this period he had some searching conversations with his distant relative, Rev. Johann A. B. Christie, who was himself no stranger to religious doubt. Grieg came to feel more and more that the dogmas of orthodoxy were a strait jacket that inhibited the free development of the intellect. He no longer regarded Jesus as the son of God but, rather, as "a remarkable seer" and an authentic ideal for the independent modern human being to follow. This led him to a concept of God that left no room for Christ. In the Primary Materials will be found excerpts from several letters which express Grieg's views on various important questions of life philosophy.[3,4]

In Grieg's acute crisis of 1883, it is obvious that he could not accept the Christian idea of a struggle with the sinful self, and he fiercely defended himself when Beyer chided him for his self-centered attitude. There were, for Grieg, two concerns here that were in conflict. On the one side was the artistic nature that necessarily had to have a strong sprinkling of egotism to be able to develop itself fully; on the other side was the command to "love thy neighbor as thyself." He felt this conflict very deeply, and it is the crux of what he wrote to Rev. Christie on this occasion.

Grieg returned to the same theme three months later, but by then his tone had become milder. After his triumphs in Weimar (see p. 241), where he had experienced art's power to "free and ennoble," he wrote to Beyer (October 17): "Never have I felt stronger than I did yesterday that you cannot separate the artist from the human being. If the sun shines upon the artist, the best human qualities—the urge to the good and the true—awaken. Those things are naturally present in every individual who strives for them, but there are moments when one makes a solemn vow to oneself to aim high and forsake egotism. I am sure that you have known such moments. What makes them so wonderful and so authentic is that the vow is voluntary, not coerced as in all of the ecclesiastical rites. In such moments it is as if one no longer had a body, but hovered in space like one who had already entered the realm of the blessed."

Grieg eventually broke completely with organized Christianity as repre-

5. ATTACKS ON CHRISTIANITY

I am now beginning to understand that we have only *one* enemy, but it is an implacable one which, as things unfortunately are, it is our inescapable duty to arm ourselves against. It is sad that all that money can't rather be used to enlighten the country so as to clear the air of that damned pietism that paralyzes the common sense of the people. Pietism and the Swedes—let us take up arms and be on guard against both. (Letter to Jonas Lie, August 3, 1897.)

* * *

All these clergymen who stifle every good aspiration among us! There is just one thing that we all should do: get out of the state church, this lizard that in addition to its complete impotence has nothing but a poisonous stinger to sting with. There is something in me that could make me into a criminal if I didn't choose to get out of the way of this creature. You stand in the middle of the road and say: Go ahead, sting! I can't do that. But I admire you who can do it. (Letter to Björnson, July 10, 1897.)

* * *

[As Cato said to the Roman senate]: "It is my opinion that Carthage ought to be destroyed." And my Carthage is in fact the clergymen. I can't swallow them. I vomit them up again and can never get rid of their repulsive, greasy, and nauseating taste. They sprawl all over everything. (Letter to Beyer, March 27, 1902.)

sented by both the state church and the narrow-minded form of pietism. His statements about both groups are unusually crass, at times offensive.[5] He never revealed the underlying cause of this strong aversion, but in any case it contrasted sharply with the spirit of love that he himself defended on the basis of his concept of God.

As the seeking person that he was, Grieg longed to find a firm anchor for his faith, a reference point that satisfied both his religious feelings and his intellectual questioning. During a visit to Birmingham, England in August of 1888 he found a group of like believers in a religious fellowship in which he felt at home: the Unitarians. Their belief in the one true God included at the same time an abandonment of a number of central Christian dogmas, above all the divinity of Christ. This was the position to which Grieg's own religious questioning had taken him, and he was attracted by the way in which the Unitarians practiced their faith. Their charitable disposition, unselfish way of life, and broad-minded view of culture were in complete agreement with ideals that had now also become his own.

The leader of the Unitarian movement in England, a Rev. Brooke—who had himself been an Anglican priest—made an especially strong impression on Grieg. On a visit to London the following year he expressed his admiration for Mr. Brooke in a March 16 letter to Beyer: "A large, wonderful, radiant person, full of fire and strength. We talked about this and that: about the Unitarian faith and socialism, about Ibsen and Björnson, also a bit about politics . . . and I dare say that he felt exactly as I do about these things."

Grieg held to his Unitarian faith for the rest of his life. In the letter to Monastier-Schroeder cited earlier (written, it will be recalled, on his deathbed) he said further: "During a visit to England in 1888 I was taken by the Unitarian views, and in the nineteen years that have passed since then I have held to them. All the sectarian forms of religion that I have been exposed to since have not succeeded in making any impression on me." Nina Grieg came to share her husband's views on these matters.

It appears that Grieg little by little abandoned the idea of a personal God. He combined the belief in God with an idealization of nature, a pantheistic view that has no connection with any particular religion. God is the creator of the world and permeates all of nature, not as a personal being but as the primal power in the universe. For Grieg there obviously was something comforting in the idea that nature is good in itself and that "everything happens for the best," as he often optimistically expressed it.

After a visit with Björnson in 1906, Grieg made this entry in his diary (November 1): "As a Unitarian I am close to Björnson, but his concept of God is not altogether clear to me. Primal power, fine. But to be able to see a great love behind the inexorable manifestations of this primal power—cause and effect, manifestations which often look for all the world like the work of an evil demon—that is of prime importance. It is the great divide that separates many free-minded, truth-seeking people."

The feeling of oneness with nature was expressed in an especially beautiful way in a letter to Beyer of August 4, 1905: "But nature itself? I stood before it in silent respect and awe as if before God himself. You did the same, it is true, but for me the feeling of awe extinguished all other feelings. To be sure: I revere science's demand for clarity. But the sphere of the supernatural attracts me nonetheless—yes, right down to the present day. I don't think there is any contradiction in this. Although [they are] different spheres, science and the transcendent do not necessarily interfere with each other."

The last composition: Four Psalms, *Opus 74*

Christian poetry rarely awakened a response in Grieg. It appears that he refused to set texts which he could not wholeheartedly endorse, and the result was that prior to 1906 he had dealt with only three religious songs. Two of them—"Fairest among Women" and "The Great White Host"—were in *Album for Male Voices,* Opus 30, Nos. 9 and 10 respectively. The third was "Ave Maris Stella," CW 155 and CW 156, No. 2.

In the summer of 1906 he undertook a continuation of the *Album for Male Voices,* but this time he chose mixed chorus with baritone solo as his medium.[6] The result was *Four Psalms,* Opus 74, one of the most significant sacred choral works of the late Romantic period. But it is not correct to say—as some have said—that these *Psalms* reflect Grieg's own religious beliefs. It was impossible for him to agree with texts such as "Jesus Christ Our Lord Is Risen" and "God's Son Hath Set Me Free." Nina Grieg was undoubtedly correct when she stated to Percy Grainger on February 5, 1929: "The *Psalms* were not a reflection of what one calls 'religiosity.' Grieg was very far from being orthodox."

Grieg was mainly attracted by the unusually beautiful Norwegian folk melodies associated with this religious poetry from the Baroque era. He mentioned this on several occasions as the work proceeded. He completed three of the Psalms at "Troldhaugen" during the summer; the fourth, "How

6. GRIEG ON HIS *FOUR PSALMS*

Once again I am sitting alone in my little hut and am busily at work on a continuation of the *Album for Male Voices.* It is a project in which I am very interested. There are some beautiful and singular melodies among them, melodies in which old Catholic and folk elements are blended together. The folk elements are not at all as they appear in the [Danish] versions. In other words: the dissonances that you miss there are not lacking here. (Letter to Röntgen, August 15, 1906.)

* * *

Completed three Psalms for mixed choir and solo voices, free arrangements of Lindeman's Norwegian folk songs. They are so beautiful, these melodies, that they deserve to be preserved in an artistic form. These little pieces are the only things my wretched health has permitted me to write during the summer months. This feeling: "I could, but I can't"—it's depressing. I am fighting in vain against the odds and soon, I believe, must give up completely. (Diary entry, September 15, 1906.)

* * *

I am sitting here with a stirring Psalm in A minor that I am setting for mixed chorus. I have a work room in the hotel and am feeling like a better human being. (Letter to Röntgen, November 21, 1906.)

The Rev. J. A. B. Christie, Grieg's close friend and confidante with respect to religious questions. "Four Psalms," Opus 74, was dedicated to him. (Photo collection of Universitetsbiblioteket in Oslo)

Fair Is Thy Face," which was placed first in the published version, was written at the Hotel Westminster in Oslo in November. This stunningly beautiful piece was to be the last thing he would write.

It was once again Lindeman's *Aeldre og nyere norske Fjeldmelodier* (Nos. 376, 138, 327, and 326) that served as the starting point for Grieg's "free arrangements." Here and there he slightly altered Lindeman's version of the melodies and, as so often before, he expanded the simple arrangements to give them new dimensions.

In three of the four *Psalms*—the exception being the quiet, meditative "Jesus Christ Our Lord Is Risen"—there is an urgent intensity to the music. One notes, for example, a series of utterly ecstatic outbursts. Grieg here paints the text with powerful strokes using great dynamic arches, increasing melodic intensity, and colorful chord progressions that were most unusual in the church music of the time. As in all his vocal works, Grieg reveals here an ideal sense of prosody. To a greater extent than in his earlier choral works, the handling of the choir is marked by a rich display of sound and significant technical demands. The choral parts are well-adapted to the voices throughout the *Psalms*. This applies both to the two homophonic pieces—"Jesus Christ Our Lord Is Risen" and "In Heav'n Above"—and to the more intricately crafted and partly polyphonic "How Fair Is Thy Face" and "God's Son Hath Set Me Free."

Stylistically, the pieces range from "Jesus Christ Our Lord Is Risen" to "God's Son Hath Set Me Free." The former has an intentional archaic stamp established at the outset by the Dorian-tinged melismatic melody. The archaism is further accentuated by the responsive singing between the soloist and the choir throughout the piece.

At the opposite extreme, "God's Son Hath Set Me Free" shows Grieg's most radical side. The midsection is based on something uniquely daring in Grieg's harmony: a bitonal juxtaposition in which the soloist sings the folk tune in B-flat major while the choral part (sung by a small male chorus or quartet) is in B-flat minor. With this Grieg clearly intended to illustrate the freed man's confident refusal of the world's constant temptations: "No, I have been purchased at too great a price to play sin's game of chance." The powers of light (the soloist's B-flat major) contend with the powers of darkness (the choir's B-flat minor). Grieg never allows the major and minor thirds (D/D-flat) to sound simultaneously. The overall effect is a kind of neutralization of the major/minor genders. A significant feature in this connection are sharp cross-relations between thirds (D/D-flat), sixths (G/G-flat) and sevenths (A/A-flat). Thus, in the fourth measure of the following example there is a cross-relation between the soloist's note A-natural and the basses' A-flat. The linear texture also reinforces the dissonant character:

The release occurs when the opening theme is repeated as the choir shouts in triumphant B-flat major: "My heart is filled with cheer, death holds for me no fear." At the very end the sense of triumph is further strengthened by a luxuriant unfolding of sound in a remarkable and daring series of luminous triads sung fortissimo by the full choir.

Fifteen years earlier, Grieg had expressed to Beyer his anxiety about becoming old and no longer being able to be a musical pioneer together with the younger composers (see p. 307). Now, at the beginning of the new century and in his sixties, he had demonstrated with the *Norwegian Peasant Dances* and *Four Psalms* an admirable will to create something truly new. Despite failing health, his ability to compose and his gift for concentration were still alive and well. These two works are among the most sparkling and unconventional ever written by a Norwegian composer. They point toward the future.

With *Four Psalms* Grieg wrote the final cadence to his creative work. For one last time he had given beautiful expression to his "intimations of the hidden harmonies in our folk tunes." A composer could scarcely desire a more beautiful swan song.

Grieg felt that his long stay in Oslo in 1905–06 was like living in a "half-barbaric country." People were so stubbornly conservative in their musical tastes that they wouldn't even attend the concert when Halvorsen conducted Richard Strauss's *Death and Transfiguration*. "If I had to *work* here," he wrote to Beyer on January 14, 1906, "I'd go out of my mind." For peace and quiet, however, Oslo was the ideal place for him.

In April of 1906 he left on another tour—to Copenhagen, Berlin, Leipzig, Prague, Amsterdam, London, and Hamburg. He was uncertain about how it would go, as is clear from his diary entry of March 19: "Will this journey be my last? And will my life end out there? Vague premonitions hover around me."

In Leipzig on April 11 he recorded six piano pieces on the "Phonola," a recording technique wherein the music was transferred to a perforated paper roll (the "Welte-Mignon" system). Grieg was impressed by the technical quality of these recordings, which were superior in every way to those he had made two or three years earlier. Grieg's "Phonola" recordings are still in existence.

At the concert in Prague on April 16 he was applauded as never before. He finally went so far as to don his overcoat before going out on stage to accept the last round of applause. Only then would the audience let him go. His reunion with the Concertgebouw Orchestra was equally cordial. After the concert on April 27 he wrote in his diary: "Again and again I must say with

7. GRIEG TELLS KING HAAKON ABOUT HIS VISIT TO BUCKINGHAM PALACE

Had the unpleasant task of delivering greetings from King Edward and Queen Alexandra to the Norwegian royal couple. We were received at two o'clock by both the king and queen. As before, they were both very friendly and straightforward; but when the conversation got around to art—music—there was hell to pay. When the king asserted that King Edward loves music, I couldn't refrain from saying that it must be a peculiar kind of love, for I had nearly caused a scandal at Buckingham Palace because the king sat and talked aloud to Nansen while I was playing—so much so that twice I had to stop playing. Thereupon the king [Haakon] said aloud those divine and characteristic words: "Yes, but King Edward is the kind of person who can very well listen to music and carry on a conversation at the same time!" But then I couldn't contain myself any longer and I blurted out: "Well, I don't care whether he is the king of England or an ordinary man, but that is bad manners and I can't accept it. There are some things I absolutely will not do because of respect for my art." Then the king made a movement like a jumping jack and with a smile turned the conversation to other matters. (Diary entry, June 12, 1906.)

Vinje: 'I got better than I deserved!' . . . A lucky star shone over the entire concert." At a chamber-music concert on May 2 he was joined by Pablo Casals in a performance of the cello sonata, Opus 36. He described Casals as "incomparable, a *great,* great artist for whom the composition is No. 1 and the artist is No. 2."

There were full concerts in London on May 17 and 24. After the latter Grieg wrote excitedly in his diary about "wonderful Percy Grainger, who turned pages for me at the concert, and whom I love as if he were a young woman. It is a dangerous thing to be greatly admired, but when one admires in return as I do here it all evens out. I've never met anyone who *understands* me as he does. And he is from Australia. So what are those esteemed critics talking about when they criticize my music on grounds that it is too Norwegian? It is just stupidity and ignorance, nothing more." The meeting with Grainger was the beginning of a friendship that brought great joy to Grieg during the last year of his life.

May 29 marked the festive conferral of an honorary doctorate at Oxford University. He also had an audience with the British royal couple, from whom he took a personal greeting to King Haakon.[7]

Home once again, he noted in his diary on July 12: "Wonderful, comforting sleep! Rejuvenating! I love my 'Troldhaugen' as never before." But by July 31 the tone had completely changed: "No, 'Troldhaugen'—oh, western Norway is a costly love for me, for it is taking my life. But—western Norway gave me life, zeal, the desire to recreate it in music. The gift has been only a loan. I must repay it when the time comes."

At the end of September he returned to Oslo, where he stayed at the Hotel Westminster for nearly six months. He was extremely vexed that the National Theater disgraced itself by playing Franz Lehar's popular operetta *The Merry Widow:* "Miserable!" he wrote angrily in his diary. But he enjoyed the quiet evening hours with Nina, hours that they spent reading aloud and in heart-to-heart conversation. Nina gave a beautiful description of these evenings in a December 14 letter to Anna Brodsky: "I am so happy during these evening hours, when after the day's work . . . we sit quietly and securely together and sense the warm mood that pervades the room. We read aloud, engage in a bit of intimate conversation—in short, we are ourselves. It is the best time of the day. Therefore we get to bed too late, for we can't bring ourselves to allow these lovely evenings to end."

Grieg at Oxford on May 29, 1906, after receiving an honorary doctorate. In his diary he wrote: "I was created a 'dr. honoris causa' with all due ceremony. With Falstaff I must ask: What is honor? I preferred the ceremony in Cambridge; somehow it was more festive, although here there were also speeches in Latin and gold-embroidered gowns and tasselled mortar-boards." (Universitetsbiblioteket of Bergen, Norway)

Grieg in Kiel, Germany, in April, 1907.
(Troldhaugen, Bergen)

Forward, Ever Forward, Toward Nothing— Or Something More!

On December 31, 1906, in a letter to Röntgen, Grieg attempted to look ahead to the new year—which, unknown to him, was to be the last year of his life. He wrote: "But as long as one lives, the rule must be 'hold your head high' and 'forward, ever forward, toward nothing—or something more!'" The thought of death was his daily companion at this time, but he suppressed it with his indomitable will to live. Despite rapidly waning strength, he drove himself during the winter of 1907 to undertake new and exhausting tasks.

On January 12 he conducted the *A-minor Concerto* in Oslo. On March 6 he played the *Norwegian Dances,* Opus 35, with Röntgen and accompanied Nina in some of his songs. Nina considered it a risky undertaking on her part, but according to Grieg's diary it went well. "We wanted to do everything, everything for Julius," he wrote. "As an encore she sang 'Kidlings' Dance,' and when the enthusiastic applause continued she concluded with 'Moonlit Forest' [Opus 18, No. 1]—old youth! But the listeners made it evident that it was youth that won out!!" Grieg also arranged a big party for forty-two guests at Cafe Engebret in honor of his faithful Dutch friend, who had won the hearts of all both as an artist and as a person.

The following week he went to Denmark for the first concerts of what was to be his last journey abroad. In Copenhagen he attended Carl Nielsen's opera *Mascarade,* which was not altogether to his liking. He made the following comments in his diary on March 19: "Often I find, as it were, surrogates for music, things that are the products of pure intellect. But just as often there are great lines and music that is truly felt. And a mastery, a singular technique that surprises one."

On April 7 there was a concert in Munich, but the high point of the tour was the concerts in Berlin April 12 and 14. The Schiller Theater, with a capacity of 3000, had been sold out far in advance. The critics were only lukewarm—indeed, they were almost indifferent—but Grieg was acclaimed by the general public as never before. During this stay in Berlin he met three fellow composers: Saint-Saëns ("he still had not forgotten Dreyfus!"), the more amiable Massenet, and Richard Strauss. Grieg, who earlier had been moved to tears by Strauss's *Death and Transfiguration,* got the shock of his life when he attended the latter's opera *Salomè*. He wrote in his diary on April 15:

"What shall I say? As music this work is an impossibility, and decadence is in full swing. It is the triumph of technique over spirit. I grant that the technique is often brilliant, but what has become of imagination, the very foundation of music? The piece lasted nearly two hours—and it felt like seven. I got more cacophony than I could stomach."

Grieg tied up another important thread from his youth during this trip to Berlin: he visited the cemetery where Rikard Nordraak was buried and laid a laurel wreath upon his grave. His diary contains a gripping account of his feelings as he stood near the remains of the friend of his youth (see p. 97).

After an appearance in Kiel on April 26—the last public concert of his life—he returned to Denmark. He remained there for six weeks, during which time he sought help for his worsening health at Finsen's electric light baths. Neither this nor a stay at the Skodsborg sanatorium resulted in any apparent improvement. Nor did he really want to spend all this time in Denmark, for as early as April 28 he wrote to Lammers: ". . . then there is this thing called my Norwegian heart that longs mightily for the Norwegian spring! With Vinje I ask: 'Do you think this might be the last?'" A week later he shared his melancholy sentiments with Röntgen: "The Adagio time has come. I suddenly feel two thousand years old and do not even have a desire to compose! I want only to get rest, rest!"

Summer at "Troldhaugen" was painful and difficult—so much so that it is absolutely heartrending to read his diary from this period. July 13 he wrote: "Ten sad days that have convinced me that I am going downhill faster than I had thought. The shortness of breath is increasing despite fourteen days of massage; my brain and my digestion together are putting me in a state that could drive me crazy—anything, but not that. Would that I had the means to just quietly sleep away into that eternal sleep when the time comes that I just can't stand this any longer. Although—I would probably lack the courage. I am not among those who consider suicide an expression of cowardice. To the contrary. I have the greatest admiration for the courage that I feel I myself do not have."

Visits by Röntgen and Grainger in the latter part of July were rays of light in the midst of these dark days. After their departure, however, his health became steadily worse. Nina reported that he almost never was able to sleep because he could not breathe properly. Whenever he was on the verge of falling asleep he would sit up because of the feeling that he was about to choke. On August 25 he wrote in his diary, "The 6th–25th has been pure suffering. Shortness of breath and sleeplessness increasing. We spent the 20th, 21st, and 22nd with Beyers and Elisabeth [his sister] at Voss. I hoped that the inland climate would allow me to sleep. But no, only in a very general way will I say that I am feeling better. We had a calm, warm, sunny day—the *only* such day in the whole summer, I think—and I felt that that was what I needed. But the next day it poured down again, and so it has continued. Last evening (the 24th) Klaus Hanssen and his wife came to see us, and oddly enough they came at exactly the same time as my new masseur, Mr. Olsen, who was going to give me massages and 'packs' à la Skodsborg. Klaus examined me with the greatest care and stayed with me for the entire treatment. The upshot is that the

Nina and Edvard with Percy Grainger and Julius Röntgen at "Troldhaugen on July 26, 1907. The following day Grieg wrote: ". . . so I had the great pleasure of bringing these two splendid people together, knowing that they would understand each other. A horizon such as Julius has is rare . . . And now this fascinating, unaffected, profound, serious, and child-like nature [Grainger]! What a joy to win such a friend!"

Röntgen wrote to Nina on September 13: "Do you know what Edvard said to me when we went to the station? He said: 'We won't see each other again; the end is near for me now!' It made me feel so indescribably sad. It was well that I didn't have any idea of how soon his words would be fulfilled. But we had some wonderful days together this summer, and it is wonderful to think that he left us when he was in full command of his mental powers." (Universitetsbiblioteket of Oslo, Norway)

massages are to be discontinued, since they are hard on the nerves. The packs are to be continued, however, as they did me some good and made it possible for me to get a little sleep, at least in the first part of the night. Today 25th miserable after breakfast, don't know why, it must be the strain of the massage last evening."

Thereafter the diary is silent for a week. On August 27 Grieg was admitted to the hospital. He went home to "Troldhaugen" on August 31, and on that date made his last diary entry. It is gripping in its restraint: "Spent 27th–30th at the hospital in Bergen under Klaus Hanssen's observation. Illness unfortunately got steadily worse. The first night was without sleep, the second and third I slept on [the drug] Kloral. Today 31st everything impossible, as Isopral didn't help at all, so I lay awake almost the entire time. The whole situation is most depressing. Nonetheless we ought to prepare for the trip overland [to Oslo] on the 3rd. I've got to get away from this climate, though the trip to England at this time appears to me more than doubtful."

With an almost unfathomable strength of will, Grieg set about practicing the *Lyric Pieces* that he was supposed to play at the music festival in Leeds. Nina wrote about this in a letter to Monastier-Schroeder on September 29: "I paced back and forth and marveled. Finally I went over to him and said, 'You

1. GRIEG'S LAST BOW

It was evident that Grieg was very weak. During the night I had to prop him up with pillows. It was because of his breathing. Most of the night I was alone with him. He asked me to sit by the bed and hold his hand. He suffered terribly during his sleeplessness. Once he dozed off. Then I went over to the window and took out my bag of sandwiches to have something to eat. But suddenly the sick man noticed that he was alone. "Take the sandwiches with you and come here," he said as he groped for my hands.

The next day Dr. Klaus Hanssen, the medical director, came and ordered him admitted to the hospital. I myself slept during the day, but went to be with him again that evening. Grieg's room was on the second floor. It was a private room. Mrs. Grieg and her sister, Tony Hagerup, had gotten a room in another building where the head nurse lived. Late that evening Dr. Klaus Hanssen came to see Grieg again. They were close friends, those two. Klaus Hanssen comforted Grieg by saying that the night didn't have to be so bad. "I will give you a shot," he said. "Do you think I can stand it?" Grieg asked—and these were to be his last words. "I will be careful, Vardo," the doctor replied. When he left he squeezed both Grieg's hand and mine.

Grieg soon fell into a doze, and as the night wore on I realized that his life was about to ebb out. I wanted to go out in the corridor and get a nurse, and Mrs. Grieg also needed to be advised that the end was near. Suddenly something remarkable occurred, something that I will never forget. Grieg sat up in bed—augustly, as it were—and made a deep, courteous bow. It was not merely an involuntary movement of some kind. I had no doubt whatsoever that it was a real bow, exactly like those that artists make when they bow to the audience. Then he sank quietly back on the pillow and lay there, motionless. When the others came in, none of them was absolutely sure that he really was dead. There was nothing to indicate the actual moment of his passing. (Clara Sofie Jensen in an interview with Hans Jörgen Hurum in *Aftenposten*, September 3, 1958.)

are really two persons.' Then he replied quietly and sadly, 'No, I am just one, but I am a fighter.'"

On Sunday, September 1, Klaus Hanssen and the Beyers were at "Troldhaugen" for dinner. They all tried to persuade Grieg to give up the trip to England, but he wouldn't hear of it: "These concerts will give me strength," he said.

The following day Beyer was shocked at how sick and miserable his friend was, but Grieg insisted on proceeding with the trip anyway. Accompanied by the Beyers, Nina and Edvard drove into Bergen. The plan was to stay at Hotel Norge until they were ready to leave on their trip. Grieg visited his tailor to arrange for proper clothing for the trip. The following morning, however, the state of his health had become so problematic that Klaus Hanssen forbade him to proceed with his travel plans and ordered him admitted to the hospital. That evening Beyer visited him, and later reported: "When I took his hand to bid him farewell, he scarcely had strength enough to ask me to greet my wife."

The doctors were aware that there was no longer any hope of saving his life. Grieg, who also realized that the end was near, said, "So this is to be my fate."

Clara Sofie Jensen, the nurse who attended him the last two days of his life—including the night at the hotel and the following hours at the hospital—gave a detailed account of the last hours of Grieg's life.[1] Shortly after midnight on September 4 he drifted off into a coma. Nina was called, but by the time she arrived he was gone.

Dr. P. H. Lie, who wrote the coroner's report, concluded that the direct cause of death was heart failure caused by an advanced state of emphysema in the right lung. The other lung, it will be remembered, had not functioned since his youth. After the autopsy Klaus Hanssen pointed out how remarkable it was that Grieg had been able to survive as long as he did with such a serious illness. It was due solely to his indomitable will.

The funeral was an extraordinary public event. Telegrams of condolence streamed in from all over the world—from friends and colleagues, from kings and emperors. Röntgen and Brodsky came from abroad to honor their friend; Brodsky also played in the orchestra that Halvorsen conducted at the funeral service in Kunstindustrimuseet [the Industrial Arts Museum]. After the lovely sound of "Last Spring" had died away, Klaus Hanssen gave a touching memorial address. He emphasized the unity between the man and the artist whom everyone had learned to love. "I am not thinking now of his great intelligence and sparkling wit. I am thinking rather of the most fundamental features of his character: his sense of justice that did not allow the slightest place for a spirit of compromise, his great conscientiousness and high standards that allowed no place for indifference, his faithful mind and his warm heart."

A large male chorus conducted by Ingolf Schiött sang "The Great White Host," and after the laying of wreaths the orchestra played the *Funeral March for Rikard Nordraak*. Grieg had actually carried a copy of the latter piece with him on his last concert tours in case he should die abroad.

As the funeral procession began, a military band from Bergen played

Grieg looking out over Bergen from Lövstak-
ken, one of the seven mountains surrounding
the city. He wrote to Jonas Lee in 1888, "The
mountainous terrain of western Norway con-
tinually draws me back with irresistible power.
It is as if they still had so very much to tell me."
(Gyldendal, Oslo)

Chopin's "Funeral March." Tens of thousands joined the procession. Hundreds of clubs and other groups marched with their banners held high. Schools and business places were closed. Everyone joined in to pay their final respects to Bergen's and Norway's great native son.

At the crematorium the Reverend Carl Konow gave a brief speech before conducting the committal ceremony.

Beyer, who had assumed responsibility for the preparation of the permanent burial site in the cliff at "Troldhaugen," wrote to Nina on April 7 of the following year: "So now Edvard's ashes have come to their final resting place . . . I placed the urn in the grotto, and then the stone was placed in front of it. A blackbird was singing in the spruce trees overhead. The sun was setting behind gold-rimmed clouds, casting its last beams across the water and upon Edvard's name . . ."

Artistic Views and Stylistic Characteristics

Throughout his life Edvard Grieg regarded himself as a pioneer in the Norwegian milieu, with respect to both his world of ideas and his understanding of his task as a musician. As early as the 1860s he was aware of his vocation as a composer. He wanted to create music that united strictly personal elements with national characteristics. Mounting the barricades as a champion of new ideas in the narrow artistic world of Norway was a demanding task but one that gave him a sense of inner satisfaction, a feeling of fulfilling a mission that was his alone.

Grieg's was a composite nature. In many respects he was a true child of Romanticism, yet he was also a down-to-earth realist with both feet on the ground. Moreover, on many subjects he held quite radical views. He was always open to progressive ideas, a characteristic that found expression in both word and deed.

Grieg had a flair for writing and was eager to articulate his strongly held views. His esthetics—i.e., his understanding and experience of art—found frequent expression in articles and other contributions to newspapers and periodicals. Most importantly, his views on these matters were expressed in many of the thousands of letters that he sent to friends and colleagues over the years. He had a special knack of stating his thoughts in concise, almost epigrammatic terms and phrases that often appear to be spontaneous but in fact were carefully considered. Much of what he wrote is so brilliantly and poetically worded that it will stand comparison with the finest commentaries on music in the nineteenth century. It is also interesting to observe how his esthetic views are reflected in his compositions.

Unfortunately, Grieg's views on music were expressed in bits and pieces in many different places, and no one to date has attempted to bring these elements together into a single unified picture. In the present book we have made every effort to show the versatility of Grieg the man and the artist, and we have endeavored from time to time to penetrate into his world of ideas. In this concluding chapter we shall try to gather together the most important strands of his thought so as to present a concentrated picture of his philosophy of art, not least in connection with the music he created.

Photo of Grieg by one Herr Bieber, a Berlin photographer. (Photo collection of Det Kongelige Bibliotek, Copenhagen)

The lot of the Norwegian artist

Grieg's love for Norway and its spectacular scenery was virtually boundless. He wrote to Frants Beyer from Leipzig on March 10, 1890: ". . . embracing Norway is my supreme delight, and I do so every day in my thoughts. No great spirit can one love so completely and purely as nature!" Art, for him, was indissolubly linked with nature, as he stated in another letter to Beyer (December 17, 1895): "Art—the best of art—and nature never disappoint; indeed, they are the *only* things that do not disappoint. You and I have, of course, talked about this truth, but it shines ever more brightly the older I get."

There was a great paradox in Grieg's life: when he was home he was always yearning for the pulsating life of the continent, but when he was abroad he felt a nagging urge to return to Norway. He was constantly drawn to "the majestic scenery at home, which more than anything else is akin to great art," as he wrote in a letter to Johan Halvorsen on January 26, 1897.

Both Grieg's esthetics and his music are rooted in his love of country and his experience of nature. As early as 1875—in a February 21 letter to Björnson—he was perfectly clear about his vocation as a national composer: "To write music depicting Norwegian scenery, the life of the people, the country's history, and folk poetry," he wrote, "appears to me to be a calling in which I feel I could achieve something."

What he did achieve, with this as his starting point, is unique, for it was through his art that music lovers all over the world got their first glimpse of Norway's indigenous culture. Meanwhile, for his own countrymen his music has become the quintessence of that which is distinctively national—indeed, to such an extent that they often make the mistake of equating that which is Norwegian with that which is genuinely Griegian.

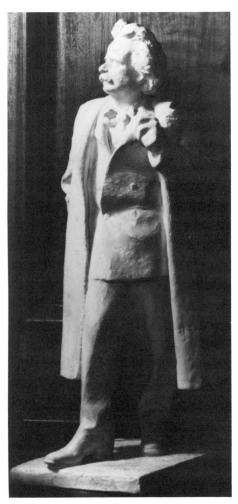

One of the many plaster models that Ingebrigt Vik made in preparation for her statue of Grieg. (Troldhaugen, Bergen)

Grieg's contribution to the musical arrangements of his country's folk tunes set the pattern for many other composers both in Norway and elsewhere. Today, to be sure, one can question his idea that such music needs to be "ennobled" through artistic refinement in order to show to full advantage—as if folk art were little more than a body of raw material that in itself was of interest mainly for research. Such a view was in harmony with the Romantic outlook of Grieg's day, but it is far removed from that of our own. On the other hand, it must be admitted that it is precisely Grieg's "ennobling"—that is to say, his artistic treatment of folk music—that deserves most of the credit for bringing it into public view and making it accessible in circles that would otherwise never have had an opportunity to enjoy its unique beauty.

Grieg undoubtedly shared the elitist views of his contemporaries that art is exclusive and artists are the ones who set the standards. Because of his democratic turn of mind, however, he felt an inner urge to build a bridge between the world of artistic elitism and the common man. On August 27, 1886, after hearing Wagner's *Parsifal,* he wrote to Beyer: "How strange that art is so aristocratic, that out of the whole family of man only an infinitely small minority is capable of understanding its mysteries. Just imagine if *everyone* could experience this beauty! It would mean 'the new heaven and the new earth, wherein blessedness dwells!'" Now and again he experienced the great joy of being a bridge builder himself, and it was far more satisfying to him to feel the spontaneous appreciation of his listeners at a cut-rate concert for working people than to receive the polite applause of a "genteel" audience.

Grieg's bridge-building activity and his desire to get away from artistic elitism required a rather strong emphasis on the national element. He realized full well, however, that abroad he was sometimes identified with a narrow-minded chauvinism, and he reacted vehemently against this. Toward the end of the 1880s, therefore, he felt the need to issue his "cosmopolitan credo," in which he rightly protested that his music, despite its undeniable Norwegianness, rises above narrowly national limits. True art, he said, knows no boundaries. Nonetheless, he considered his major task to be that of championing the cause of his own people in words and music. On October 18, 1888, writing to Jonas Lie, he stated: "[The Norwegian artist] has a glorious calling, and I would not exchange it for anything in the world."

Music as the beneficent power that ennobles minds and customs

With his exalted ethical attitude toward a number of life's questions, it was imperative for Grieg to insist on the ennobling power of music. During a visit to his Dutch friend Julius Röntgen, he wrote in his diary (April 25, 1906): "This home is filled with music, whether anyone is actually making music or not. Here music has become the beneficent power that ennobles minds and customs." In his view of art the ethical factor was supreme: the task of music was to elevate and enrich.

The concept of the *ideal* was central in Grieg's thought. In connection with some performances of contemporary music in Oslo, he wrote (in a letter to August Winding) as early as January 3, 1872: "I can tell you I have quite a burden resting on my weak shoulders—the task of arousing an awareness of the ideal in music. But it is wonderful to have a mission in life, and that I have. It demands a willingness to make sacrifices, that's for sure, but then there are moments when I experience a truly radiant joy."

Grieg's concept of the ideal involves merging the personal and the national, but it also connotes a number of elements of universal character: genuineness, truth, naturalness and naïveté (a term that for Grieg had positive associations), clarity, inspiration, depth of feeling, yearning, richness of mood, imagination, development. In his opinion, in order for art to cause the human mind to resonate, all these elements had to be united as the components of a balanced whole. When he discussed these things, he generally avoided associating them with his own compositions and their inherent qualities. Since they were absolutely essential to him, however, it is obvious that they also inspired his own endeavors as a creative musician. They became, in fact, the very basis for the integrity that marks his work.

Integrity—being honest with oneself and others—was for Grieg one of the most important moral imperatives for an artist and his work of art. That which was emotionally and stylistically insincere was as repugnant to him as the idea of a composer copying the musical ideas of another. On October 23, 1904, he wrote to Julius Steenberg: "In the last analysis there is only *one* source of riches, and there the ideals are one's *own*. It is a great mistake to think that one can use those of other people—as so many do." The pressing need to continually create something new and original pursued him all his life. He evidently was speaking from the depths of his being when he wrote to Röntgen on May 3, 1904: "In recent years I have constantly asked myself the question: what is this thing called originality, this thing called newness? It is *not* the most important thing, for the most important thing is *truth*—truth of feeling."

It would be unreasonable not to include the criterion of integrity in any discussion of Grieg's attitude toward such Classical-Romantic musical forms as the symphony, the concerto, the string quartet, and the sonata. As we have pointed out in our analyses, he often experimented boldly and deftly with the formal elements, and it is simply incorrect to say that he was lacking in technique in this respect—even though he himself sometimes made statements to that effect. He mastered the problems of form on his own terms; the *A-minor Concerto,* the G-minor quartet, and the five sonatas are ample proof of this.

The desire to continue composing large-scale works endured throughout his life. Nonetheless, his writing in the larger forms ended abruptly at the end of the 1880s right after the completion of one of his most important compositions, the *Violin Sonata in C minor.* There were many reasons for this. Outwardly he blamed it on his declining health, which resulted in flagging inspiration and ability to concentrate. Closely related to this was his escape into strenuous concertizing—which, to be sure, satisfied his need for international recognition, but also took a heavy toll of his physical and emotional resources. The most important reason, however, was in our opinion something different from all of these.

Traditional musical forms had served as his starting point, but as he developed he discovered that his personal style could no longer be cast in the old moulds. If he were to continue on these lines, he would be caught up in a sterile formalism with a false musical content. The reason that the unfinished F-major quartet of 1891 gave him a bad conscience for more than fifteen years was that he was unable to come to terms with the problematic situation to which his artistic bent and temperament had led him. One manifestation of this unresolved problem was the conflict between cosmopolitan ideas and his innate Norwegianness, a conflict that he was not able to resolve within the confines of the larger musical forms.

During his last period he did come to terms with this reality, but restricted his compositional work to the smaller forms. It was at this stage, almost exclusively in compositions with a national background, that his inspiration was fresh and spontaneous, for only in these compositions could he be completely honest with himself.

Grieg's special talent was such that it was precisely in small piano pieces, songs, and short orchestral works—preferably with some connection to folk-music idioms—that he himself experienced the greatest satisfaction. The simple and concise—which nonetheless allow room for formal nuances of a most delicate kind—are embodied in these genres, and with such works he aroused a powerful response in his listeners. Here he felt himself completely in harmony with that which is natural and "naïve". As early as November 15, 1876, he asked John Paulsen: "And how goes it with 'naïvete'? Has Ibsen sent it packing? . . . For let me tell you: It is the most beautiful thing an artist possesses."

In Grieg's opinion, that which was simple and natural was too often unjustly overlooked or frankly disparaged by the critics. The broader listening public, on the other hand, had an intuitive ability to appreciate it without allowing themselves to be duped by the know-it-all attitude of the pundits. In a March 6, 1866 letter to Ravnkilde he wrote: "The great public, in my opinion, is not as stupid as it is sometimes taken to be, but has fine and well-developed instincts."

The inability of some critics to understand these aspects of Grieg has occasionally resulted in a warped view of his work. His preference for the smaller musical forms, for example, has persuaded some critics condescendingly to dismiss him as a "mere miniaturist." Such an evaluation reveals a failure to realize that greatness is often manifest in that which is simple. Grieg referred to this in an interview with Arthur M. Abell in 1907 as reported by Abell in his book, *Talks with Great Composers* (p. 211): "I make no pretensions of being in the class with Bach, Mozart, and Beethoven. Their works are eternal, while I wrote for my day and generation . . . Liszt once said of Thalberg: 'His province is the smaller forms, but in this he is great.' That saying could be applied to me as a composer."

Grieg was by no means always sure of himself, however. There were times

1. NORWEGIAN MUSIC COMPARED WITH GERMAN MUSIC

We [Norwegians] have always loved that which is clear and to the point; even our daily speech is clear and precise. We strive for a similar clarity and precision in our art. Notwithstanding the boundless admiration that we have for German art and the depth of its brilliant products, it is hard for us to get excited about some of its modern expressions, which we often find heavy and somewhat ponderous. (Interview in *Signale,* Leipzig, April 1907, as quoted in Schjelderup & Niemann: *Edvard Grieg,* p. 195.)

* * *

German art now—especially, perhaps, that designed to be performed—is either *school* art or *guts* art! Neither achieves a high, clear level and both, therefore, have a bad smell—like that of a schoolroom or an anatomy dissecting room. A kingdom for a dram of aquavit! (Letter to Johan Halvorsen, January 26, 1897.)

2. ENTHUSIASM FOR RUSSIAN MUSIC

. . . Russian art—which I regard as so significant because of its grand conception, richness of color, and advanced technique—can never be taken away from me. I carry it in my heart with endless gratitude. (Letter to A. Siloti, September 25, 1902.)

when he overestimated something that he had written and allowed it to be published even though it was not up to his usual standards. At other times he was unreasonably critical of his own work, to such an extent that compositions clearly deserving publication were tucked away in his desk drawer and left to gather dust. In later years he identified his self-criticism as one of the main reasons why he composed so little. Writing to Frederick Delius on January 12, 1896, he said of this trait: "It erodes every idea like poison, until at last nothing remains of it."

Towards the end of his life he became more and more skeptical of the idea that the success of the moment could be taken as a gauge of the value of his music. He emphasized this point in a letter to Beyer on October 18, 1904: "When I consider the so-called 'success of the moment,' then the only thing I can believe in is that which remains fresh despite the passing of time. I know perfectly well that no matter how much of a soft spot I may have in my heart for some piece that I have written, it still doesn't amount to anything if it lacks this quality. And then, it's important ruthlessly to kill one's own ego."

Grieg's critical stance found expression not least in his strong aversion to any form of striving for mere effect. This, in his view, was incompatible with true art both in the creative sphere and in the concert hall. Music containing cheap effects does not deserve to exist. In his own compositions he consciously tried to avoid all external bravura. There are, of course, a number of virtuoso passages—for example, in the *A-minor Concerto* and the G-minor *Ballade*. These, however, do not sound at all as if they were merely "tacked on" to the composition. They have musical substance. This is precisely what he found lacking in many of Richard Strauss's works, which he characterized as "hunting for sensation," "legerdemain with orchestra," and "brilliance shorn of music." He was equally critical of what he perceived as stilted and specious in much other new German music.[1] Max Reger was the subject of particular disapproval. His music, Grieg said, is "leaden constipation, nothing else. It is outrageous to observe how some composers elbow their way [to the fore] at the expense of others of a more healthy nature." (Diary entry, May 8, 1906.)

Grieg was much more attracted to contemporary French music and even more to Russian music.[2] Mimi Segal Daitz, in an interesting article written in 1978, has shed new light on his relations to French composers in connection with a visit by the French musician Pierre Onfroy de Bréville to "Troldhaugen" in 1887. Her article includes excerpts from de Bréville's diary recording his conversations with Grieg as well as her own comments on this new material.

Grieg's relationship with performing artists, particularly female singers, was by no means all honey and roses. He was capable of getting extremely angry when they exalted themselves to the detriment of the music and condescendingly presumed to "improve" what the composer had written. Nor did he have much respect for the exaggerated rubato playing characteristic of the late Romantic period. Writing to Röntgen on April 29, 1901, he said: "It is remarkable that the most talented performers of our age fall victim to the terrible 'rubato influenza.' Rubinstein never did anything like that. Nor did

Liszt. 'Sensation' is a serpent that threatens to devour great, genuine, noble art! Everyone conspires together—violinists, pianists, singers, and especially conductors. That damned 'Let's improve what the composer has written.'" Those are strong words, and they are particularly surprising in view of the fact that the recordings we have of Grieg's own playing make it clear that he himself was no stranger to a fairly liberal use of rubato!

Grieg believed that so far as possible performers should observe the intentions of the composer; he even emphasized, as we have seen, the importance of fingering in editions of his piano music. Nonetheless, he did not desire absolute uniformity of interpretation, as is evident from a remark he made to Percy Grainger in 1906: "You don't play it exactly as I intended it, but for heaven's sake don't make any changes, for I love interpretations with an individual touch." Within certain limits, in fact, he was willing to allow truly great artists complete freedom. He felt that Grainger, for example, had the unusual ability as a performer to elevate that which he played from the merely national to the universal level. But the truest art, in Grieg's view, came to full fruition when the composer's innermost feelings awakened a similar response in the performer. To the singer Dagmar Möller he wrote on November 4, 1896: "You must strive to convey *all* that the soul [of the composer] has breathed into the notes; there is no art beyond that of the lifeblood."

Art as "the excess of yearning that cannot express itself in life or in any other way"

Grieg tended to work by fits and starts in short periods of intense concentration. He was essentially a creature of moods, entirely dependent on inspiration. His imagination could only be set on fire when kindled by the creative spark of the moment. But, as he wrote to G. Schjelderup on July 10, 1902, as long as a wave of inspiration of this kind—"the most beautiful thing in an artist's life"—continued, one could "raise oneself above everything, above absolutely all the tribulations of life. And people call that egotism! It is the most unselfish condition in a human life. Completely absorbed in sheer ideas."

Grieg often spoke of inspiration, and his sources of inspiration were highly varied ranging from nature, poetry, and history to human life in all its diversity. His whole output testifies to the way in which mankind's destiny is reflected in music. National, political and religious ideas—which we have dealt with in some detail in earlier chapters—were interwoven with his intense sensitivity to nature.

For Grieg as a creative artist, yearning and depth of feeling were of decisive importance. Art is really "the excess of yearning that cannot find expression in life or in any other way," he wrote to Beyer on October 27, 1886. To compose without feeling would only result in arid music. "An artist must live his life in accordance with his best feelings, even though they rend his whole life," he wrote to Jonas Lie (October 18, 1888).

Closely associated with the life of the emotions was his penchant for the mysteries of art and music. Music in its essence is inscrutable; when he spoke about naturalness, clarity, and so on he was referring primarily to the outward musical language that is evident to all. When the content of music—the inner meaning of a piece—was to be explained, he appealed to the irrational element. This is how he expressed it to Beyer on August 4, 1905: "In my case, mysticism has always prevented exultation from getting the upper hand . . . Admittedly, I love the scientific quest for clarity; but the mystical element nevertheless draws me on—yes, to this very day." In the presence of the mystical, the inscrutable, the intellect must yield to imagination.

It was in his piano music that Grieg allowed freest rein to his imagination—especially the *Lyric Pieces,* many of which have highly picturesque titles. He never really composed "program music" in the sense that the music was supposed to follow a prescribed external course. On the other hand, a typical Romantic attitude is evident in the titles given to many of his piano compositions all the way from Opus 12 (1866) to Opus 73 (1905). What we have here is "mood music," often in the form of impressions of nature, but never an attempt to create a musical "illustration" of nature. Grieg simply built on the tradition of Schumann's "character pieces." The titles, in most cases, were added after the music was written. When it was time to give a piece a title, Grieg tried to put himself in the place of a listener: the mood evoked by the music decided the choice of title, and not vice versa. It is equally clear, however, that once the pieces had been given their names the composer deliberately led performing artist and listener alike along definite paths of experience. In so doing he laid the groundwork for a programmatic view of these works.

In the incidental music we find, not surprisingly, several typical examples of purely descriptive music, particularly in *Peer Gynt.* In the original version this music was carefully linked to the drama on the stage. When this music is removed from the theatrical setting and performed in the concert hall, however—as in the *Peer Gynt* suites—it obviously retains a programmatic flavor that is sometimes very strong. This is the case, for example, in "Stormy Evening on the Sea."

Grieg clearly had a considerable aptitude for orchestration. His orchestral works are sonorous and imaginative, yet the scoring is temperate and well balanced. Strangely enough, however, he seems to have suffered from an inferiority complex precisely in this field. There appear to have been two reasons for this: the inadequate training in orchestration that he received at Leipzig, and the almost paralyzing respect he had as early as the 1860s for Johan Svendsen's innate talent as an orchestrator.

When Grieg set a song text his imagination was influenced by the basic character of the text, by the situation described, and by the coloring of the language. Poetic quality was the decisive factor for such a sensitive artist. Fine poetry inspired him to produce his very best, whereas inferior texts rarely fostered music of lasting value.

In his songs it was not the detailed depiction of individual words that primarily interested him, and rarely did he assign the interpretation of the poem to an independent accompaniment. The essential thing for Grieg was to capture the underlying mood of the text in a melodious vocal line supported by expressive harmonies. Thus he did not hesitate to arrange some of his best-known songs for string orchestra, and in Opuses 41 and 52 he transformed some of them into typical character pieces for piano.

The songs of a people were for Grieg a reflection of their very souls, and the authenticity that we sense in his music is due in large part to his close identification with his own countrymen. He emphasized that the spirit of Norway's music hovered over everything he had written, though he took serious exception to the suggestion that in his art songs he had *imitated* folk songs. This actually occurred only once, viz. in "Solveig's Song."

Grieg's finest songs often owe their inspiration to the simple genuineness of their texts—frequently texts with a national strain. For that reason the strophic form came very naturally to him. Occasionally he made effective use of a peculiar Norwegian song pattern, the so-called *nystev*. However, he also demonstrated his mastery of the modified strophic and through-composed forms in a number of fine songs.

As a writer of songs Grieg was more akin to Brahms than to Schubert and Schumann. Like Brahms, he preferred the strophic form with the musical emphasis on the melodic line. In view of this, it is rather surprising to find him writing in a letter to Ravnkilde on July 21, 1884: "My eyes have really been opened to Brahms's significance as a composer of songs, despite the fact that I consider him too much the musician and too little the poet. A symphonist and musician and nothing else. But if one is going to set a text, one really ought to pay attention to the words."

Although Grieg's song production reveals a markedly lyrical strain, he was capable—when the text called for it—of writing songs of a more dramatic or declamatory nature. "The Soldier" (CW 100, No. 5) and "A Bird Cried Out" (Op. 60, No. 4) are examples of such songs. In "A Swan" (Op. 25, No. 2) and "Beside the Stream" (Op. 33, No. 5) he explored the borderland between the lyrical and the dramatic.

In his basic orientation as a composer Grieg, like Brahms, leaned toward the classical. Imagination was held in check by a concern for clarity and restraint in such a way as to avoid exaggeration. But as a child of Romanticism he was, of course, a person of deep feeling, prone to varying moods: "The artist is *flexible,*" he wrote to Monastier-Schroeder on August 22, 1903, "and his task is to give artistic expression to *contrary views.*"

Salient features of Grieg's style

In Grieg's music the tension between contrasts erupts in brilliant flashes. The conflicts are incorporated into his work as esthetic factors, emotionally and formally. In sonata movements, for example, the abrupt switches between principal and secondary themes or groups of themes are characteristic and entirely intentional. He disliked subtle transitions, the absence of which in his compositions is a feature of his style for which he is often criticized even today.

In two chamber-music works—the *Violin Sonata in G Major* and the *String Quartet in G Minor*—the effect of these contrasts is vividly felt. Nonetheless, the sense of unity is preserved both in the individual movements and in each composition as a whole. The source of unity is an underlying cyclical idea: most of the thematic material is, in fact, rooted in the same soil. In the string quartet this root is fairly obvious, but in the sonata it appears that Grieg deliberately tried to conceal it precisely in order to emphasize the contrasts. There is, however, an obscure motivic-thematic thread which can be unraveled only through a detailed musical analysis.

If we consider the *Lyric Pieces,* we are struck by the alternation in character between the various sections: the dramatic against the lyrical, the rapid against the slow, major key versus minor key, and so on. Yet the music does not seem episodic; on the contrary, these works generally possess a rounded, natural, and uncontrived wholeness. This is due not least to the fact that in this genre, too, Grieg frequently attempted to create links in motives and themes between the various sections. The middle section, for example, might be built on an augmentation or a diminution of the theme of the first section, perhaps in a parallel or relative key.

Grieg's ebullient imagination and intense contrasts are less evident, however, in rhythm and counterpoint. In the area of rhythm he was much closer to the Viennese classicists than to, for example, Schumann and Brahms. He generally adhered to regular, established metrical patterns; one looks in vain in Grieg's works for the delicate variation in rhythmic play, not least in the inner parts, that was characteristic of the latter composers. The marked rhythms of Norwegian folk music frequently emerge—sometimes in a very striking way, as in the last movement of the *A-minor Concerto.* It would be incorrect to say, however, that Grieg pointed the way forward to a liberation from the tyranny of the bar line. This was carried out by such composers as Stravinsky and Bartók who, like Grieg, were strongly influenced by the folk music of their native countries.

As a composer Grieg had a decided preference for homophonic rather than polyphonic texture. The paradigmatic Grieg composition consists of a melody in the top part supported by chords underneath. Only rarely did he venture into the realm of polyphony. In such cases it was usually only for simple attempts at imitation which then, for no apparent reason, were abruptly brought to a conclusion. This happens, for example, in the last movement of the F-major violin sonata. The contrapuntal passages in the third movement of the G-minor string quartet constitute the most sophisticated examples of Grieg's polyphonic writing. On the whole, Grieg appears to have placed little emphasis on the individual life of the inner parts. When the lower voices—particularly the bass—move chromatically, this is occasioned by the harmonic context rather than by a desire for individual part-writing.

It was Grieg's hope that in his world of ideas and in his music he would be capable of retaining the vigor and freshness of youth. He was constantly on guard against tendencies to stagnate and lapse into the past. Gerhard Schjelderup, in his 1903 book on Grieg (pp. 155–56), quotes from a letter in which Grieg asserted this point of view: "I fully admit that we are living in a culturally 'thin' age, but those of us who are now growing old must not forget to stay abreast of the best of everything that our young contemporaries are seeking. We should not live only in the ideals of our own youth. I don't believe for a minute in that old nonsense about being true to the ideals of one's youth . . . If that were so, there would obviously be no progress. What has given me the greatest happiness in life has been the feeling of having conquered just a tiny little bit of an ideal *loftier* than those of my youth. Good Lord, the whole business is, after all, a struggle in search of truth. How, then, could one possibly remain rooted in 'the ideals of one's teens'? I love Schumann, but not as I did at the age of seventeen. I love Wagner, but not as I did at the age of twenty-seven. The love one has for art, as for a woman, changes character but doesn't thereby become less beautiful. Perhaps just the opposite. Wine improves with age. Don't get out of sorts just because you don't feel as you did when you were seventeen years old, provided your feelings are honest and true."

One area in which Grieg reached an ideal much loftier than that of his youth was that of harmony. Here his ingenious and radical approach found a substantial outlet, and it is not too much to say that he became one of the pioneers leading to the revision of harmonic concepts in the twentieth century.

Grieg had a rare ability to create music that appealed to the public taste without having recourse to facile clichés. His progressive bent was such, however, that he was never afraid to depart radically from the beaten path. Now and then even he had the feeling that what he had written was shocking—indeed, sometimes downright "crazy," as he said of his "Bell Ringing."

From childhood the realm of harmony was his "dream world," and here his imagination had free play. The years at the Leipzig conservatory gave him a good grounding in German Romanticism, but the maturing process in Copenhagen, during which he became truly familiar with Scandinavian—and especially Norwegian—music, proved decisive for his continued growth. It might safely be said that by the mid-1860s he had found his own unique style as a harmonist.

While as a melodist Grieg showed a marked preference for diatonicism, as a harmonist he was fascinated by the potential afforded by chromaticism. In chordal progressions he explored the chromatic style in new, ingenious, and captivating ways. He did not go as far as Wagner in *Tristan and Isolde* in the direction of virtually breaking the fetters of the strictly functional harmonic system, but he contributed in other ways to a moving of the frontiers of harmony that has been effected in modern music.

The basis for Grieg's harmony was functional tonality. But a number of harmonic flights of fancy—extended chromatic passages, the avoidance of traditional cadences, the use of unconventional chord progressions, abrupt changes of key, etc.—often result in long passages in which the tonality becomes vague, ambiguous, and cursory. Another distinctive feature of his style was the integration of modal scale material, both melodically and harmonically, into otherwise functional progressions. It is as though this enabled him to wave his magic wand over the music.

The use of modality to add tonal color was not unique to Grieg; a number of other national composers of the Romantic period employed it as well. The point of departure for all of them was their national folk music, both vocal and instrumental. In Grieg's compositions, features derived from Norwegian folk dances played on national instruments—the Hardanger fiddle and the *lang-leik*—were incorporated into his harmonic style. There are, for example, pungent dissonances resulting from the use of internal and external pedal points. This also explains to some extent why his harmony is so replete with seconds, sevenths, and augmented fourths. The supply of dissonant chords seems almost inexhaustible. A predilection for triads with an added major seventh, particularly on the tonic or subdominant, is highly characteristic. But Grieg was also fond of ninth, eleventh, and thirteenth chords which he often distributed in new and unexpected ways. The dissonance acquired a special value of its own as a means of tonal coloration—for example, with chains of dissonant chords, sometimes in parallel motion as well. Occasionally he even concluded a composition on an unresolved dissonance with the aid of the pedal. To treat dissonance in this way—giving it a life of its own, so to speak—illustrates Arnold Schönberg's striking statement that in reality dissonances are nothing but remote consonances.

Grieg was one of the boldest harmonists of his day, but with his oft-expressed aversion for exaggeration and superficial effects he never engaged in experimentation merely for its own sake. In his development as a harmonist we find two trends. One points in the direction of increased refinement, with an emphasis on shading and sophistication foreshadowing the supple art of Impressionism. The other, which is linked to indigenous Norwegian folk music, moves toward that which is sharp and craggy and almost untamed—toward what is sometimes called "barbarism."

Investigations have shown that several aspects of Grieg's harmony anticipated features of the Impressionists, and it is indisputable that he was an important influence on the work of Claude Debussy and Maurice Ravel. While Debussy was reluctant to admit any debt to his predecessors, Ravel on one occasion declared that he had not written a single work that had not been influenced by Grieg. A statement of this kind must obviously be received with a certain amount of reservation, but Percy Grainger expressed a similar view in an article on Grieg written in 1943. He made reference to a conversation between Delius and Ravel, in which the English composer maintained that "modern French music is simply Grieg plus the prelude to the third act of *Tristan.*" Ravel replied: "You are right. We have always been most unjust towards Grieg."

With regard to barbarism, it should be mentioned that one finds instances of harsh and jarring harmonies even in some of Grieg's early works. The boldest examples of this appear, however, in *Norwegian Peasant Dances,* Opus 72. The work, which was perceived as being typical of "the new Grieg," got an enthusiastic response among the avant-gardists in Paris. We also have evi-

Nina wrote to Sophus Andersen on March 14, 1923: "First and foremost, he was a good and honorable person—that was most important to him—and then the good, genuine artist. He was a friend of humanity." (Universitetsbiblioteket of Oslo, Norway)

dence that Béla Bartók was familiar with these piano adaptations of Hardanger-fiddle tunes. When it is stated that folk music is one of the bases for the renewal of music in the twentieth century, it is due in no small measure to Grieg's contribution.

If we consider Grieg's harmonic style in a wider perspective, we are struck by his unerring ability to create a synthesis out of the most diverse elements which fit together so well to form a unified whole. Herein lies one of the keys to an understanding of his stature as a major composer.

* * *

We have endeavored to trace the close relationship between Grieg's life and his art, for, in his view, life and art are warp and woof of the same fabric. He regarded music as an inseparable part of human existence because he considered emotional expression just as essential as intellectual unfolding. We have, so far as possible, allowed the composer to speak for himself. In this spirit—and in accordance with the title given to our book—we shall let Grieg have the final word. In a letter of November 14, 1886, to his Danish friend Gottfred Matthison-Hansen, he wrote that he found it difficult to distinguish the artistic from the human: the man and the artist, he said, "cohere to the very highest degree."

Appendixes and Indexes

Glossary of Norwegian Terms

The following Norwegian terms, for which there are no adequate English equivalents, are used without translation in this book. They appear in italics in the body of the text.

gangar: a Norwegian folk dance ("walking dance"); a folk-dance tune in $\frac{6}{8}$ time (or in $\frac{2}{4}$ with triplets) used for such a dance.

halling: a vigorous Norwegian folk dance, most often performed as a male solo dance; a folk-dance tune in $\frac{2}{4}$ time used for such a dance.

kulokk: the most prominent and complex type of Scandinavian herding music. Part of a communicative system for the control of livestock, it is composed of a broad spectrum of musical expressions (speech, speech song, calls, vocalizing, singing) to comply with a still greater variety of "day rhythm" functions: humming when close to the animal during milking, soft calling and singing when leading the herd out in the morning, directing it during the day with alternately soft and loud sounds, calming it in moments of fear and stress, frightening wild animals away from it, and, not least of all, from a considerable distance and with astonishingly high-pitched and effective voice production, calling it home in the evening. Despite its functional nature, the *kulokk* had and has an undeniable esthetic value, with great room for improvisation and personal expression.

langleik: an ancient stringed instrument of the zither type, with one fretted melody string and three to seven drone strings; still played in the Valdres region.

nynorsk: "New Norwegian"—a second form of the Norwegian language derived from local dialects.

nystev: new *stev*. See *stev*.

slaatt: a Norwegian dance tune of instrumental character.

springar: a lively Norwegian folk dance; a folk-dance tune in $\frac{3}{4}$ time used for such a dance. In western Norway performed as if notated in $\frac{1}{4}$ time. In the valleys of central Norway the three beats in each measure are of unequal duration. In Telemark, for example, they are long–medium–short, while in Valdres they are short–long–medium.

springdans: same as *springar,* but the term is mainly used outside the regions where the Hardanger fiddle is commonly played.

stev: a type of mono-strophic folk poetry in specific metrical patterns ("old *stev*" or "new *stev*"), sung to traditional and mostly very old *stev* tunes. Still practiced in the Telemark and Setesdal regions of Norway.

Catalog of Works with Thematic Incipits

The Catalog of Works is in two parts. The first part contains all of the compositions to which Grieg gave opus numbers (1–74), presented in the order that he thereby assigned to them. The second part contains the compositions to which no opus numbers were assigned, including many that were not published during the composer's lifetime. In this part we use the numbers 100–162. The numbering in this part, which is our own, is chronological except for a few collections that were published after Grieg's death and that include works from several different years. In the body of the text we use the symbol CW when referring to a composition in this second group. Thus CW 105, for example, means "Catalog of Works listing 105."

The Catalog of Works gives for each composition the following information: the title; for vocal works, the first line of the text (in the original language) as well as the name of the author of the text; the beginning of the first melodic line—or, in the case of compositions with several movements, the principal theme of each movement; the year of composition; the year in which the composition was first published, and the name of the publisher. We include also a number of cross-references in the cases where Grieg himself had rearranged earlier works and given them—or, in some cases, neglected to give them—new opus numbers.

The symbol GGA in this listing denotes *Edvard Grieg's Complete Works*, the twenty-volume edition of Grieg's works currently being issued by C. F. Peters (Frankfurt).

Compositions with Opus numbers

Opus 1. Four Piano Pieces. Comp. 1861. 1st pub. 1863–64 (Peters, Leipzig).

No.1. *Allegro con leggerezza*

No.2. *Non allegro e molto espressivo*

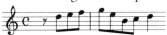

No.3. *Mazurka*

Con grazia

No.4. *Allegretto con moto*

Opus 2. Four Songs. For alto voice and piano. Comp. 1861. 1st pub. 1863–64 (Peters, Leipzig).

No.1. *The Maid of the Mill* (Chamisso)

Andante serioso

Die Müh-le, die dreht ih-re Flü-gel

No.2. *Closely Wrapped in Misty Billows* (Heine)

Presto impetuoso

Ein-ge-hüllt in grau-e Wol-ken

No.3. *I Stood Before Her Portrait* (Heine)

Un poco lento

Ich stand in dun-keln Träu-men

No.4. What Shall I Say? (Chamisso)

Andante espressivo

Mein Aug' ist trüb', mein Mund ist stumm

Opus 3. Poetic Tone Pictures. For piano. Comp. 1863. 1st pub. 1864 (Chr. E. Horneman, Copenhagen).

No.1. *Allegro ma non troppo*

No.2. *Allegro cantabile*

No.3. *Con moto*

No.4. *Andante con sentimento*

No.5. *Allegro moderato*

No.6. *Allegro scherzando*

Opus 4. Six Songs. For alto voice and piano. Comp. 1863–64. 1st pub. 1864 (Horneman & Erslev, Copenhagen).

No.1. *The Orphan* (Chamisso)

Andante moderato e doloroso

Sie ha-ben mich ge-heiss-en

No.2. *Morning Dew* (Chamisso)

Animato

Wir woll-ten mit Ko-sen und Lie-ben

No.3. *Parting* (Heine)

Allegretto serioso

Das gel-be Laub er-zit-tert

No.4. *Hunting Song* (Uhland)

Presto con brio

Kein' bess'-re Lust in die-ser Zeit

No.5. *The Old Song* (Heine)

Allegretto semplice

Es war ein al-ter Kö-nig

No.6. *Where Have They Gone?* (Heine)

Allegro molto agitato

Es ragt ins Meer der Ru-nen-stein

Opus 5. Melodies of the Heart. Texts by H. C. Andersen. For voice and piano. Comp. 1864–65. 1st pub. 1865 (Chr. E. Horneman, Copenhagen). (No. 1 also appears in CW 133 as No. 95. No. 2 also pub. for piano as Op. 52, No. 3. No. 3 also pub. for piano as Op. 41, No. 3. See also CW 133, No. 71.)

No.1. *Two Brown Eyes*

Allegretto con grazia

To bru-ne øj-ne jeg ny-lig så

No.2. *The Poet's Heart*

Allegro molto ed agitato

Du fat-ter ej bøl-ger-nes e-vi-ge gang

No.3. *I Love But Thee*

Quasi andante

Min tan-kes tan-ke e-ne du er vor-den

No.4. *My Mind Is Like a Mountain Steep*

Allegro molto

Min tan-ke er et mæg-tigt fjeld

Opus 6. Humoresques. For piano. Comp. 1865. 1st pub. 1865 (Horneman & Erslev, Copenhagen).

No.1. *Tempo di Valse*

No.2. *Tempo di Menuetto ed energico*

No.3. *Allegretto con grazia*

No.4. *Allegro alla burla*

Opus 7. Piano Sonata in E Minor. Comp. 1865. 1st pub. 1866 (Breitkopf & Härtel, Leipzig).

1st movement: *Allegro moderato*

2nd movement: *Andante molto*

3rd movement: *Alla Menuetto*

4th movement: *Finale. Molto allegro*

Opus 8. Violin Sonata No. 1 in F Major. Comp. 1865. 1st pub. 1866 (Peters, Leipzig).

1st movement: *Allegro con brio*

2nd movement: *Allegretto quasi Andantino*

3rd movement: *Allegro molto vivace*

Opus 9. Songs and Ballads. Texts by A. Munch. For voice and piano. Comp. 1863–66. 1st pub. 1866 (Horneman & Erslev, Copenhagen). (No. 2 also pub. for piano as Op. 41, No. 1).

No.1. *The Harp*

Et sagn nu meg dra-ges til min-ne

No.2. *Cradle Song*

Sov min sønn, o slum-re søtt

No.3. *Sunset*

Nu da-ler so-len sak-te ned

No.4. *Outward Bound*

Det var en dem-ren-de som-mer-natt

Opus 10. Four Songs. Texts by Chr. Winther. For voice and piano. Comp. 1864–66. 1st pub. 1866 (Chr. E. Horneman, Copenhagen).

No.1. *Thanks*
Allegretto tranquillo

Jeg tak-ker dig for hver en stund

No.2. *Woodland Song*
Allegretto

Der sad en fugl på bø-ge-kvist

No.3. *Song of the Flowers*
Con grazia

Fra vin-ter-ens kul-de vi kom-mer her-ind

No.4. *Song on the Mountain*
Poco Andante

I af-ten ens glands mon glø-de

Opus 11. In Autumn. (A Fantasy for piano four hands). Comp. 1866. 1st pub. 1867 (Abraham Hirsch, Stockholm). Revised and arranged for symphony orchestra as **Concert Overture** 1887. 1st pub. in latter form 1888 (Peters, Leipzig).

Un poco Andante

Opus 12. Lyric Pieces I. For piano. Comp. 1864(?)–67. 1st pub. 1867 (Chr. E. Horneman, Copenhagen). (No. 8 also arr. for male chorus a cappella with Björnson's text "Onward! Onward!" Pub. in Johan D. Behrens's *Samling af flerstemmige Mandssange* [Collection of Part Songs for Male Voices], fifth series, No. 479, Oslo. Cf. CW 133, No. 17.)

No.1. *Arietta*
Poco Andante e sostenuto

No.2. *Waltz*
Allegro moderato

No.3. *Watchman's Song*
Molto Andante e semplice

No.4. *Fairy Dance*
Molto allegro e sempre staccato

No.5. *Folk Song*
Con moto

No.6. *Norwegian*
Presto marcato

No.7. *Album Leaf*
Allegretto e dolce

No.8. *National Song*
Maestoso

Opus 13. Violin Sonata No. 2 in G Major. Comp. 1867. 1st pub. 1871 (Breitkopf & Härtel, Leipzig).

1st movement:
A. *Lento doloroso*

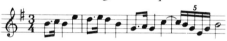

B. *Allegro vivace*

2nd movement: *Allegretto tranquillo*

3rd movement: *Allegro animato*

Opus 14. Two Symphonic Pieces. Arrangement for piano four hands of 2nd and 3rd movements from *Symphony in C minor.* Cf. CW 112. Comp. 1864. 1st pub. 1869 (Horneman & Erslev, Copenhagen).

1st movement: *Adagio cantabile*

2nd movement: *Allegro energico*

Opus 15. Four Songs. For voice and piano. Comp. 1864–68. 1st pub. 1868 (Horneman & Erslev, Copenhagen). (No. 1 also pub. for piano as Op. 41, No. 2, and for female chorus, pub. in *GGA*, Vol. 20. Cf. CW 133, No. 8. Nos. 2 and 4 also pub. for piano as Op. 52, Nos. 5 and 1.)

No.1. *Margaret's Cradle Song*, from *The Pretenders* (Ibsen)

Nu løf-tes laft og lof-te

No.2. *Love* (H. C. Andersen)

Se, so - len blus-ser så el - skovs - rød

No.3. *Folk song from Langeland* (H. C. Andersen)

Hun har mig glemt, min sorg hun ej se!

No.4. *A Mother's Grief* (Ibsen)

Så du ham, min lil - le dreng

Opus 16. Piano Concerto in A Minor.
Comp. 1868. 1st pub. 1872 (E. W. Fritzsch, Leipzig).

1st movement: *Allegro moderato*

A.

B.

2nd movement: *Adagio*

3rd movement: *Allegro moderato molto e marcato*

Opus 17. Twenty-five Norwegian Folk Songs and Dances ("arranged for piano"); in the Peters edition the collection is called *25 nordische Tänze und Volksweisen.* Melodies from L. M. Lindeman's collection. Comp. 1869. 1st pub. 1870 (C. Rabe–W. Harloff, Bergen).
(Nos. 18 and 22 also pub. for string orchestra as Op. 63, No. 2. Nos. 23 and 24 were also used in Op. 64, No. 4.)

No.1. *Springar*

No.2. *The Swain*

No.3. *Springar*

No.4. *Nils Tallefjorden*

No.5. *Dance from Jölster*

No.6. *Wedding Tune*

No.7. *Halling*

No.8. *The Pig*

No.9. *Religious Song*

No.10. *The Wooer's Song*

No.11. *Heroic Ballad*

No.12. *Solfager and the Snake King*

No.13. *Wedding March*

No.14. *I Sing with a Sorrowful Heart*

No.15. *Last Saturday Evening*

No.16. *I Know a Little Maiden*

No.17. *The Gadfly and the Fly*

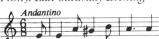

No.18. *Peasant Dance*

No.19. *Hölje Dale*

No.20. *Halling*

No.21. *The Woman from Setesdal*

No.22. *Cow Call*

No.23. *Peasant Song*

No.24. *Wedding Tune*

No.25. *The Ravens' Wedding*

Opus 18. Nine Songs. For mezzo soprano/ baritone and piano. Comp. 1865–69. 1st pub. 1869 (Horneman & Erslev, Copenhagen). (No. 1 also appears in CW 133, No. 90. No. 2 also pub. for piano as Op. 41, No. 4. No. 6 also appears in CW 133, No. 38. No. 9 also appears in CW 133, No. 113. No. 9 also arr. for male chorus a cappella and baritone solo.)

No.1. *Moonlit Forest* (H. C. Andersen)

Min sø - de brud, min un - ge viv

No.2. *My Darling is as White as Snow* (H. C. Andersen)

Hun er så hvid, min hjer - tens kjær

No.3. *The Poet's Farewell* (H. C. Andersen)

Løft mig kun bort, du   stær - ke død

No.4. *Autumn Storms* (Chr. Richardt)

No.5. *Poesy* (H. C. Andersen)

No.6. *The Young Birch Tree* (Jörgen Moe)

No.7. *The Cottage* (H. C. Andersen)

No.8. *The Rosebud* (H. C. Andersen)

No.9. *Serenade for Welhaven* (Björnson)

Opus 19. Pictures from Folk Life. For piano. Comp. 1869–71. 1st pub. 1872 (Horneman & Erslev [S. A. E. Hagen], Copenhagen). (No. 2 also pub. for piano four hands [Peters, Leipzig]).

No.1. *In the Mountains*

No.2. *Bridal Procession*

No.3. *From the Carnival*

Opus 20. Before a Southern Convent. Two pieces from Björnson's *Arnljot Gelline.* Comp. 1871. 1st pub. for piano in 1871 (Horneman & Erslev, Copenhagen). Revised orchestral score pub. 1890 (Peters, Leipzig).

No.1. *Who Knocks So Late at the Cloister Door?* For sop. and alto voices with orchestra.

No.2. *From Guilt, from Sin, to God Come In.* For four-part female chorus and orchestra.

Opus 21. Four Songs. Texts by B. Björnson. For voice and piano. Comp. 1870–72. 1st pub. 1873 (Chr E. Horneman, Copenhagen). (No. 1 also arr. for string orchestra as Op. 53, No. 2, and for piano as Op. 52, No. 2. Cf. CW 133, No. 150. No. 3 also pub. for piano as Op. 41, No. 6).

No.1. *The First Meeting*

No.2. *Good Morning!*

No.3. *To Springtime my Song I'm Singing*

No.4. *Say What You Will*

Opus 22. Sigurd Jorsalfar. Eight pieces of incidental music written for Björnson's play. Comp. 1872. 1st pub. for piano in 1874 (C. C. Lose, Copenhagen). (Nos. 1, 2, and 4 also pub. for piano four hands [Lose, 1874]. Cf. adaptation of Nos. 1, 2, and 4 for orchestra in Op. 56, 1892. Full score in *GGA*, Vol. 19 (1988).

No.1. *Introduction* to Act 1.

No.2. *Borghild's Dream.* Introduction and Melodrama.

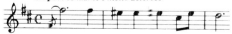

No.3. *At the Matching Game.* March (Introduction to Act 2). For orchestra. (Originally composed for violin and piano in 1867 under the title "Gavotte," and pub. separately as Op. 22, No. 2 and as Op. 56, No. 1.)

No.4. *Northland Folk* (end of Act 2). For tenor solo, male chorus and orchestra.

No.5. *Homage March* (Act 3). For orchestra.

No.6. *Interlude I.*

No.7. *Interlude II.*

No.8. *The King's Song* (Act 3). For tenor solo, male chorus and orchestra.

Opus 23. Peer Gynt. Twenty-six pieces of incidental music written for Ibsen's play. Comp. 1874–75, revised 1885, 1887–88, 1890–92 and 1901–02. 1st pub. in part 1876 (Lose, Copenhagen). Orchestral score arr. by Johan Halvorsen pub. 1908 (Peters). Cf. Op. 46 and Op. 55. (Nos. 12, 15, 16, 19, and 26 also pub. for piano. No. 19 also pub. as Op. 52, No. 4. Nos. 1, 4, 8, 9, 12, 13, 15, 16, and 21 also pub. for piano four hands. Nos. 17, 19, and 26 also pub. for voice and piano. Nos. 19 and 26 also pub. for voice and orchestra = CW 148, Nos. 1 and 2.) Complete score in *GGA*, Vol. 18 (1987).

ACT 1:

No.1. *At the Wedding* (Prelude to Act I). For orchestra.

No.2. *Halling* (2nd and 3rd scenes). For solo violin. (Also used in Op. 47, No. 4.)

Allegretto

No.3. *Springar* (3rd scene). For solo violin.

Allegro moderato

ACT II:

No.4. *The Abduction of the Bride.* Ingrid's Lament (Prelude to Act II). For orchestra.

Allegro furioso

No.5. *Peer Gynt and the Herd Girls* (3rd scene). Song and melodrama.

Allegro marcato

Trond i Val - fjel - let, Trond i Val - fjel - let

No.6. *Peer Gynt and the Woman in Green* (Introduction to the 5th scene). For orchestra.

No.7. *Peer Gynt: "You can tell great men by the style of their mounts!"* (End of the 5th scene).

Presto

No.8. *In the Hall of the Mountain King* (6th scene). For orchestra and chorus.

Alla marcia e molto marcato

No.9. *Dance of the Mountain King's Daughter* (6th scene). For orchestra.

Allegretto alla burla

No.10. *Peer Gynt Hunted by the Trolls* (6th scene). Melodrama.

Presto

No.11. *Peer Gynt and the Böyg* (7th scene). Melodrama and chorus.

Andante

Gi svar!

ACT III:

No.12. *The Death of Aase* (Prelude to Act III and in the 4th scene). For orchestra.

Andante doloroso

ACT IV:

No.13. *Morning Mood* (Prelude to Act IV). For orchestra.

Allegretto pastorale

No.14. *The Thief and the Receiver* (5th scene). For two bass voices and orchestra.

Presto

Lan - ser - nes tun - ger

No.15. *Arabian Dance* (6th scene). For orchestra.

Allegretto vivace

No.16. *Anitra's Dance* (6th scene). For orchestra.

Tempo di Mazurka

No.17. *Peer Gynt's Serenade* (7th scene). For baritone solo and orchestra.

Poco Andante

Jeg steng - te for mitt pa - ra - dis

No.18. *Peer Gynt and Anitra* (8th scene). Melodrama.

Allegro vivace

No.19. *Solveig's Song* (10th scene). For soprano solo and orchestra.

Un poco Andante

Kan - skje vil der gå bå - de vin - ter og vår

No.20. *Peer Gynt at the Statue of Memnon* (Introduction to the 11th scene).

Largo

ACT V:

No.21. *Peer Gynt's Homecoming.* Stormy Evening on the Sea (Prelude to Act V). For orchestra.

Allegro agitato

No.22. *The Shipwreck* (Close of the 1st scene). For orchestra.

No.23. *Solveig Sings in the Hut* (5th scene). For soprano solo and string orchestra.

Andante

Nu er her stel - let til pin - se - kveld

No.24. *Night Scene* (6th scene). Melodrama.

Un poco Allegro

No.25. *Whitsun Hymn: "Oh Blessed Morning"* (10th scene). For mixed chorus a cappella.

Vel - sig - ne - de mor - gen

No.26. *Solveig's Cradle Song* (10th scene). For soprano solo with orchestra.

Lento

Sov du, dy - res - te gut - ten min!

Opus 24. Ballade in G Minor (*Ballade in the Form of Variations on a Norwegian Melody*). For piano. Based on the folktune "The Northland Peasantry" from Valdres, borrowed from L. M. Lindeman's collection. Comp. 1875–76. 1st pub. 1876 (Peters, Leipzig).

Andante espressivo

Opus 25. Six Songs. Texts by Henrik Ibsen. For voice and piano. Comp. 1876. 1st pub. 1876 (C. C. Lose, Copenhagen). (No. 2 also pub. for voice and orchestra = CW 148, No. 4).

No.1. *Fiddlers*

Til hen - ne stod mi - ne tan - ker

No.2. *A Swan*

Min hvi - te sva - ne

No.3. *Album Lines*

Jeg kal - te deg mitt lyk - ke - bud

No.4. *With a Water Lily*

Se __, Ma - ri - e hva jeg brin - ger

No.5. *Departed!*

De sis - te gjes - ter vi fulg - te til grin - den

No.6. *A Bird-Song*

Vi gikk en dei - lig vår - dag

Opus 26. Five Songs. Texts by John Paulsen. For voice and piano. Comp. 1876. 1st pub. 1876 (Lose, Copenhagen).

No.1. *Hope*

Molto vivace

Jeg kun - ne jub - le for al - le vin - de

No.2. *I Walked One Balmy Summer Eve*

Allegretto

Jeg rei - ste en dei - lig som - mer - kveld

No.3. *You Whispered That You Loved Me*

Allegro agitato

I ha - ven her du hvi - sket

No.4. *The First Primrose*

Allegretto dolcissimo

Du vår - ens mil - de, skjøn - ne barn

No.5. *Autumn Thoughts*

Andante

Si, hu - sker du i som - mer

Opus 27. String Quartet No. 1 in G Minor. Comp. 1877—78. 1st pub. 1879 (E. W. Fritzsch, Leipzig).

1st movement:
A. *Un poco Andante*

B. *Allegro molto ed agitato*

2nd movement: *Romanze*

Andantino

3rd movement: *Intermezzo*

Allegro molto marcato

4th movement: *Finale*

A. *Lento*

B. *Presto al saltarello*

Opus 28. Album Leaves. For piano. Comp. 1864—78. 1st pub. 1878 (Carl Warmuth, Oslo).

No.1. *Allegro con moto* (1864)

No.2. *Allegretto espressivo* (1874)

No.3. *Vivace* (1876)

No.4. *Andantino serioso* (1878)

Opus 29. Improvisations on Two Norwegian Folk Songs. For piano. Comp. 1878. 1st pub. 1878 (Carl Warmuth, Oslo).

No.1. *Andante*

No.2. *Allegretto con moto*

Opus 30. Album for Male Voices. Arrangements for soli and male chorus a cappella of pieces from L. M. Lindeman's collection. Comp. 1877—78. 1st pub. 1878 (Carl Warmuth, Oslo).

No.1. *I Lay Down So Late*

Jeg lag - de meg så sil - de

No.2. *Children's Song*

Allegretto scherzando

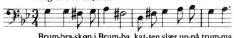

Brum-bra-skøn i Brum-ba, kat-ten slær up-på trum-ma

No.3. *Little Torö*

Andante espressivo

Du va - set - tø seg på lil - jan - kvist

No.4. *Kvaalin's Halling*

Molto moderato

Sut - tam, su - de - li - ta lut - tam, lut - tam

No.5. *It Is the Greatest Foolishness*

Un poco Andante

Dæ æ den stør - ste dår - le - heit

No.6. *Springar*

Allegretto scherzando

Går e ut ein kveld

No.7. *Young Ole*

Andante serioso

Han O - le han tjen - te i kon - ning-gens gård,

No.8. *Halling*

Allegro molto

Ha du 'kji hop - pa, so hop - pa du væl no

No.9. *Fairest Among Women*

Moderato

Dej - lig - ste blandt kvin - der

No.10. *The Great White Host*

Andante religioso

Den sto - re hvi - de flok vi se

No.11. *The Gypsy Lad*

Vivace

Den ti e skuld' te Kungs - ru å fri

No.12. *Rötnams-Knut*

Allegretto vivace

Røt - nams - Knut e kåt å mjuk

Opus 31. Land Sighting (Björnson). For baritone, male chorus, and harmonium/organ. Comp. 1872. 1st pub. in Joh. D. Behrens's *Sangbog for Mandssangforeninger*

(Song Book for Men's Singing Clubs), Vol. VI, No. 55, Oslo. Revised and arr. for baritone, male chorus, and orchestra 1881 (Peters). Also pub. as piano transcription.

Og det var O - lav Tryg - va - son

Opus 32. The Mountain Thrall. For baritone, string orchestra, and two horns. Comp. 1877–78. 1st pub. 1882 (Wilhelm Hansen, Copenhagen). The text comes from M. B. Landstad's *Norske Folkeviser* (Norwegian Folk Poetry), 1853.

Eg for vilt i ve - du - sko - gin

Opus 33. Twelve Songs to Poems by A. O. Vinje. For voice and piano. Comp. 1873–80. 1st pub. 1881 (Wilhelm Hansen, Copenhagen). (Nos. 2 and 3 also pub. for string orchestra = Op. 34, Nos. 1 and 2. No. 2 also pub. for voice and orchestra = CW 148, No. 5. No. 12 also pub. for string orchestra as Op. 53, No. 1. No. 7 also pub. for piano as Op. 52, No. 6).

No.1. *The Youth*

Du fe - rer vidt og du vert trøytt

No.2. *Last Spring*

En - no ein gong fekk eg vet - ren å sjå

No.3. *The Wounded Heart*

Mitt hjar - ta hev vo - re i li - vets strid

No.4. *The Berry*

Ty - te - bæ - ret up - på tu - va

No.5. *Beside the Stream*

Du skog! som bøy - gjer deg i - mot

No.6. *A Vision*

Ei jen - te eg såg som gjor - de meg fjåg

No.7. *The Old Mother*

Du gam - le mor, du sli - ter arm

No.8. *The First Thing*

Det fyr - ste du hev å gje - ra, mann

No.9. *At Rondane*

No ser eg at - ter sli - ke fjell og da - lar

No.10. *A Piece on Friendship*

Tro __ ei ven - ner

No.11. *Faith*

Guds ri - ke er eit fre - dens ri - ke

No.12. *The Goal*

Ve - gen vi - ta, på vill - stig ven - da

Opus 34. Two Elegiac Melodies. Arrangement for string orchestra of Op. 33, Nos. 2 and 3. Comp. 1880. 1st pub. 1881 (Peters, Leipzig). Also pub. for solo piano and for piano four hands (Peters, 1887).

No.1. *The Wounded Heart*

No.2. *Last Spring*

Opus 35. Norwegian Dances. For piano four hands. Comp. 1880. 1st pub. 1881 (Peters, Leipzig). Also pub. for solo piano (Peters, 1887).

No.1. *Allegro marcato*

No.2. *Allegretto tranquillo e grazioso*

No.3. *Allegro moderato alla marcia*

No.4. *Allegro molto—Presto e con brio*

Opus 36. Cello Sonata in A Minor. Comp. 1883. 1st pub. 1883 (Peters, Leipzig).

1st movement: *Allegro agitato*

2nd movement: *Andante molto tranquillo*

3rd movement:
A. *Allegro*

B. *Allegro molto e marcato*

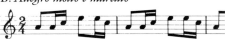

Opus 37. Waltz Caprices. For piano four hands. Comp. 1883. 1st pub. 1883 (Peters, Leipzig). Also pub. for solo piano (Peters, 1887).

No.1. *Tempo di Valse moderato*

No.2. *Tempo di Valse*

Opus 38. Lyric Pieces II. For piano. Comp. 1883. 1st pub. 1883 (Peters, Leipzig).

No.1. *Cradle Song*

No.2. *Folk Song*

No.3. *Melody*

No.4. *Halling*

No.5. *Springar*

Allegro giocoso

No.6. *Elegy*

Allegretto semplice

No.7. *Waltz*

Poco Allegro

No.8. *Canon*

Allegretto con moto

Opus 39. Six Songs (Older and Newer).

For voice and piano. Comp. 1869–84. 1st pub. 1884 (Wilhelm Hansen, Copenhagen). (No. 1 also pub. for voice and orchestra = CW 148, No. 3. No. 5 also pub. for mixed chorus = CW 156, No. 1).

No.1. *From Monte Pincio* (Björnson)

Poco Andante

Af-te-nen kom-mer, so-len står rød

No.2. *Hidden Love* (Björnson)

Lento

Han tverr o-ver ben-ke-ne hang

No.3. *Upon a Grassy Hillside* (J. Lie)

Allegro

I li-en høyt der - op-pe

No.4. *Among Roses* (Kr. Janson)

Allegretto

I ha-gen sat mod'-ri med bar-net på fang

No.5. *At the Grave of a Young Wife* (O. P. Monrad)

Lento

Blek-net, blek-net

No.6. *Hearing a Song or Carol* (N. Rolfsen)

Allegro agitato

Hø-rer jeg san-gen klin-ge

Opus 40. Holberg Suite.
For piano. Comp. 1884. 1st pub. 1885 (Wilhelm Hansen, Copenhagen). Arr. for string orchestra 1885. 1st pub. 1885 (Peters, Leipzig).

1st movement: *Preludium*

Allegro vivace

2nd movement: *Sarabande*

Andante espressivo

3rd movement: *Gavotte*

Allegretto

4th movement: *Air*

Andante religioso

5th movement: *Rigaudon*

Allegro con brio

Opus 41. Transcriptions of Original Songs I.
For piano. Comp. 1884. 1st pub. 1885 (Peters, Leipzig).

No.1. *Cradle Song* (Op. 9, No. 2)

Allegretto dolcroso

No.2. *Little Haakon* (Margaret's Cradle Song, Op. 15, No. 1)

Andante e ber. tenuto

No.3. *I Love Thee* (Op. 5, No. 3)

Andante

No.4. *She Is So White* (Op. 18, No. 2)

Poco Allegretto e semplice

No.5. *The Princess* (no Opus number; see CW 126)

Allegretto

No.6. *To Spring* (Op. 21, No. 3)

Allegro vivace

Opus 42. Bergliot (Björnson). Melodrama
with orchestra. Comp. 1871. Revised and orchestrated 1885. 1st pub. 1887 (Peters,

Leipzig). Also pub. in piano transcription (Peters, 1887).

Allegro moderato e maestoso

Opus 43. Lyric Pieces III.
For piano. Comp. 1886. 1st pub. 1886 (Peters, Leipzig).

No.1. *Butterfly*

Allegretto grazioso

No.2. *Solitary Traveller*

Allegretto semplice

No.3. *In My Native Country*

Poco Andante

No.4. *Little Bird*

Allegro leggiero

No.5. *Erotikon*

Lento molto

No.6. *To Spring*

Allegro appassionato

Opus 44. Reminiscences from Mountain and Fjord.
Texts by Holger Drachmann. For voice and piano. Comp. 1886. 1st pub. 1886 (Wilhelm Hansen, Copenhagen).

No.1. *Prologue*

Andante molto

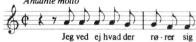

Jeg ved ej hvad der rø-rer sig

No.2. *Johanne*

Allegretto con moto e semplice

En fil-le-hyt-te var dit bo

No.3. *Ragnhild*

Allegro giocoso

Å, der var en jen-te

No.4. *Ingeborg*

Allegro moderato un poco marcato

Din hånd er bar-ket, In-ge-bjørg

No.5. *Ragna*

No.6. *Epilogue*

Opus 45. Violin Sonata No. 3 in C Minor. Comp. 1886–87. 1st pub. 1887 (Peters, Leipzig).

1st movement: *Allegro molto ed appassionato*

2nd movement: *Allegretto espressivo alla romanza*

3rd movement: *Allegro animato*

Opus 46. Peer Gynt Suite No. 1. Arrangements for orchestra of Op. 23, 1887–88. 1st pub. 1888 (Peters, Leipzig). Also pub. for solo piano and for piano four hands (Peters, 1888).

No.1. *Morning Mood* (Op. 23, No. 13)

No.2. *The Death of Aase* (Op. 23, No. 12)

No.3. *Anitra's Dance* (Op. 23, No. 16)

No.4. *In the Hall of the Mountain King* (Op. 23, No. 8)

Opus 47. Lyric Pieces IV. For piano. Comp. 1885–88. 1st pub. 1888 (Peters, Leipzig).

No.1. *Waltz-Impromptu*

No.2. *Album Leaf*

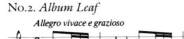

No.3. *Melody*

No.4. *Halling*

No.5. *Melancholy*

No.6. *Springar*

No.7. *Elegy*

Opus 48. Six Songs. For voice and piano. Comp. 1884 and 1889. 1st pub. 1889 (Peters, Leipzig).

No.1. *Greeting* (Heine)

No.2. *One Day, O Heart of Mine* (Geibel)

No.3. *The Way of the World* (Uhland)

No.4. *The Nightingale's Secret* (W. von der Vogelweide)

No.5. *The Time of Roses* (Bodenstedt)

No.6. *A Dream*

Opus 49. Six Songs. Texts by H. Drachmann. For voice and piano. Comp. 1886 and 1889. 1st pub. 1889 (Peters, Leipzig).

No.1. *Tell Me Now, Did You See the Lad*

No.2. *Rocking, Rocking on Gentle Waves*

No.3. *Kind Greetings, Fair Ladies*

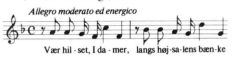

No.4. *Now Is Evening Light and Long*

No.5. *Christmas Snow*

No.6. *Spring Showers*

Opus 50. Scenes from "Olav Trygvason." For mixed chorus, soli, and orchestra. Incidental music to a play by B. Björnson. Comp. 1873; revised and orchestrated 1888. 1st pub. 1888 (piano excerpt, Peters, Leipzig). Orchestral score 1890 (Peters). (Nos. 2 and 6 arranged for piano and pub. as "Prayer" and "Temple Dance" [Peters, 1893].)

1st Scene:

No.1. *Concealed in the Many Enticing Names.* For soli with chorus and orchestra.

No. 2. *You, Coming Out of Urd's Well.* For chorus and orchestra.

2nd Scene:

No.3. *Evil Man's Evil Genius.* For alto solo with chorus and orchestra.

On - de manns on - de vet - ter

No.4. *Thank You for Speaking.* For chorus and orchestra.

Takk! Takk! Takk at I tal - te

3rd Scene:

No.5. *Give All Gods a Toast of Joy.* For chorus and orchestra.

Gi al - le gu - der gam-mens og gle-des-skål

No.6. *All Goddesses.* For chorus and orchestra.

Al - le a - syn - jer æt - ler vi yd-myk bønn

No.7. *The Eternal Religon of the Ases.* For chorus and orchestra.

E - vi - ge a-sa-tro, alt li - vet el-sker du!

Opus 51. Old Norwegian Melody with Variations. For two pianos. Comp. 1890. 1st pub. 1890 (Peters). Revised and arranged for orchestra 1900–05. 1st pub. 1906 (Peters). The variations are based on a folk tune from Hallingdal, "Sjugurd and the Troll Bride" (Cf. CW 125). The orchestral version is somewhat abbreviated.

Opus 52. Transcriptions of original Songs II. For piano. Comp. 1890. 1st pub. 1890 (Peters, Leipzig).

No.1. *A Mother's Grief* (Op. 15, No. 4)

No.2. *The First Meeting* (Op. 21, No. 1)

No.3. *The Poet's Heart* (Op. 5, No. 2)

No.4. *Solveig's Song* (Op. 23, No. 19)

No 5. *Love* (Op. 15, No. 2)

No.6. *The Old Mother* (Op. 33, No. 7)

Opus 53. Two Melodies for String Orchestra. Comp. 1890. 1st pub. 1891 (Peters, Leipzig). Arrangements of original songs. Also pub. for piano (Peters, 1891).

No.1. *Norwegian* ("The Goal" Op. 33, No. 12)

No.2. *The First Meeting* (Op. 21, No. 1)

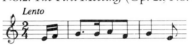

Opus 54. Lyric Pieces V. For piano. Comp. 1891. 1st pub. 1891 (Peters, Leipzig). (Nos. 1–4 also arranged for orchestra as *Lyric Suite* (Peters, 1905).

No.1. *Shepherd's Boy*

No.2. *Gangar*

No.3. *March of the Dwarfs*

No.4. *Nocturne*

No 5. *Scherzo*

No.6. *Bell Ringing*

Opus 55. Peer Gynt Suite No. 2. Arrangement for orchestra of Op. 23, 1890–92. 1st pub. 1893 (Peters, Leipzig). Also pub. for solo piano and for piano four hands (Peters, 1893).

No.1. *The Abduction of the Bride. Ingrid's Lament* (Op. 23, No. 4)

No.2. *Arabian Dance* (Op. 23, No. 15)

No.3. *Peer Gynt's Homecoming. Stormy Evening on the Sea* (Op. 23, No. 21)

No.4. *Solveig's Song* (Op. 23, No. 19)

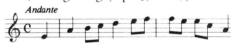

Opus 56. Three Orchestral Pieces from "Sigurd Jorsalfar." Arrangement of Op. 22, 1892. 1st pub. 1893 (Peters, Leipzig). Also pub. for solo piano and for piano four hands (Peters, 1893).

No.1. *Prelude: In the King's Hall* (Op. 22, No. 2)

No.2. *Intermezzo: Borghild's Dream* (Op. 22, No. 1)

No.3. *Homage March* (Op. 22, No. 4)

Opus 57. Lyric Pieces VI. For piano. Comp. 1893. 1st pub. 1893 (Peters) in two volumes.

No.1. *Vanished Days*

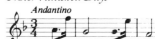

No.2. *Gade*

Allegro grazioso

No.3. *Illusion*

Allegro serioso

No.4. *Secret*

Andante espressivo

No.5. *She Dances*

Tempo di Valse

No.6. *Homesickness*

Andante

Opus 58. Five Songs. Texts by John Paulsen. For voice and piano. Comp. 1893–94. 1st pub. 1894 (Wilhelm Hansen, Copenhagen). (No. 3 also pub. for voice and orchestra = CW 148, No. 6).

No.1. *Homeward*

Andantino un poco marcato

Jeg stod på dek - ket   og jeg så

No.2. *To the Motherland*

Molto Andante ed espressivo

Du er min mor,   jeg el - sker deg

No.3. *Henrik Wergeland*

Andante solenne

Van-drer jeg i gran-sko-gen stil - le

No.4. *The Shepherdess*

Allegretto leggiero

Det duf - tet av gran og det ljo - met fra fjell

No.5. *The Emigrant*

Poco Andante

Nu visst det vå - res i Nor-ges da - ler

Opus 59. Six Elegiac Songs. Texts by John Paulsen. For voice and piano. Comp. 1893–94. 1st pub. 1894 (Wilhelm Hansen, Copenhagen).

No.1. *Autumn Farewell*

Molto Andante

Når lø - vet fal - ler trett fra sko - gens kro - ner

No.2. *The Pine Tree*

Allegretto tranquillamente

På Nor - ges nak - ne fjel - le

No.3. *To Her (I)*

Poco Andante

Du er den un - ge vår

No.4. *To Her (II)*

Poco Andante

Hvor-for svøm - mer ditt øy - e

No.5. *Good-bye*

Poco Andante

En sva - ne strøk mot syd

No.6. *Your Eyes Are Closed Forever*

Allegretto serioso

Nu hvi - ler du i jor - den

Opus 60. Five Songs. Texts by Wilhelm Krag. For voice and piano. Comp. 1893–94. 1st pub. 1894 (Wilhelm Hansen, Copenhagen).

No.1. *Little Kirsten*

Andantino molto tranquillo

Li - ten Kir - sten hun satt så sil - de

No.2. *The Mother's Lament*

Molto Andante

Gret - chen lig - ger i ki - ste

No.3. *On The Water*

Allegretto grazioso

Vill - gjess, vill - gjess i hvi - te flok - ker

No.4. *A Bird Cried Out*

Lentamente

Der skrek en fugl o - ver ø - de hav

No.5. *Midsummer Eve*

Allegro risoluto e marcato

Og jeg vil ha meg en sil - ke-vest

Opus 61. Seven Children's Songs. Songs to texts from Nordahl Rolfsen's reader. For voice and piano. Comp. 1894. 1st pub. 1895 (Brödrene Hals, Oslo).

No.1. *The Ocean* (Rolfsen)

Allegro molto marcato

Skjær og ø! Hav og sjø

No.2. *The Christmas Tree* (J. Krohn)

Andantino semplice

Du grøn - ne glit - ren - de tre, god-dag!

No.3. *Farmyard Song* (Björnson)

Allegro leggiero

Kom buk - ken til gut - ten

No.4. *Fisherman's Song* (Petter Dass)

Presto con brio

Det hen - der vel of - te

No.5. *Good-night Song for Dobbin* (Rolfsen)

Allegretto

Fo - la, fo - la Blak - ken!

No.6. *The Norwegian Mountains* (Rolfsen)

Allegretto

I - fall du føl - ger meg o - ver hei - en

No.7. *Hymn of the Fatherland* (Runeberg with Rolfsen)

Andante religioso

Du Her - re, som er sterk og stor

Opus 62. Lyric Pieces VII. For piano. Comp. 1895. 1st pub. 1895 (Peters, Leipzig).

No.1. *Sylph*

Allegretto con moto

No.2. *Gratitude*

Allegretto semplice

No.3. *French Serenade*

Andantino grazioso

No.4. *Brooklet*

Allegro leggiero

No.5. *Phantom*

Poco Andante e espressivo

No.6. *Homeward*

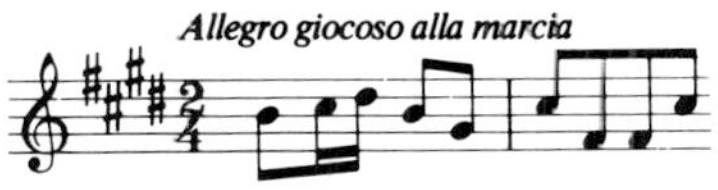
Allegro giocoso alla marcia

Opus 63. Two Nordic Melodies. Arrangements for string orchestra, 1895. 1st pub. 1895 (Peters, Leipzig). Also pub. for solo piano and for piano four hands (Peters, 1895 and 1896).

No.1. *In Folk Style* (melody by Fredrik Due).

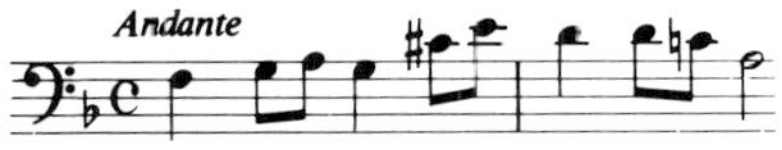
Andante

No.2. *Cow Call and Peasant Dance* (Cf. Op. 17, Nos. 22 and 18).

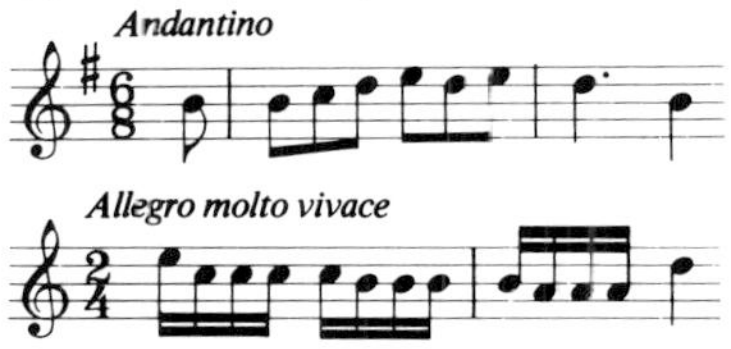
Andantino
Allegro molto vivace

Opus 64. Symphonic Dances. For orchestra. Comp. 1896–98. 1st pub. 1898 (Peters, Leipzig). Orig. pub. for piano four hands (Peters, 1897).

No.1. *Allegro moderato e marcato*

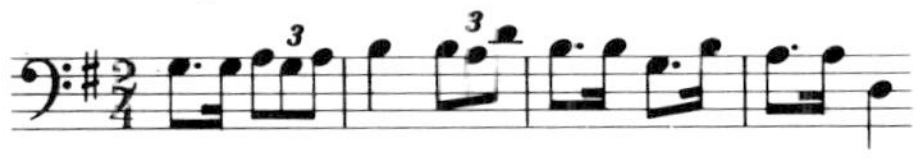

No.2. *Allegretto grazioso*

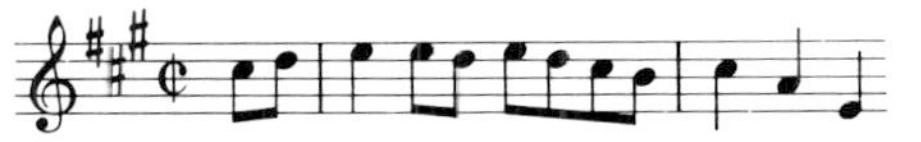

No.3. *Allegro giocoso*

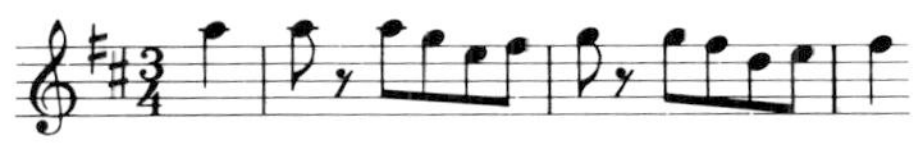

No.4. *Andante. Allegro risoluto*

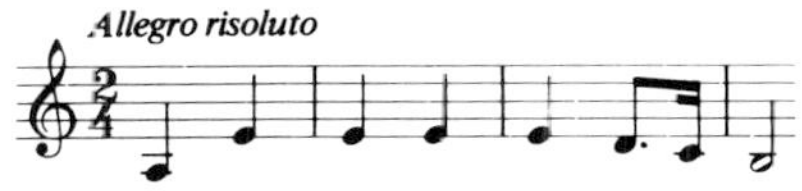
Allegro risoluto

Opus 65. Lyric Pieces VIII. For piano. Comp. 1896. 1st pub. 1897 (Peters, Leipzig).

No.1. *From Early Years*

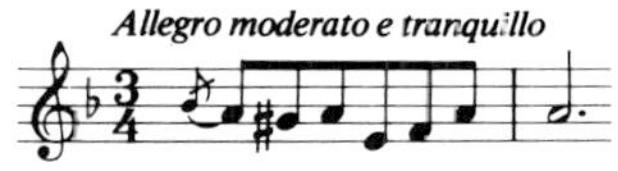
Allegro moderato e tranquillo

No.2. *Peasant's Song*

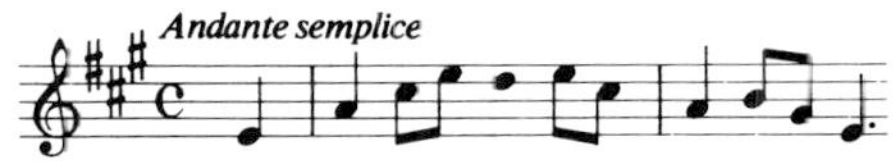
Andante semplice

No.3. *Melancholy*

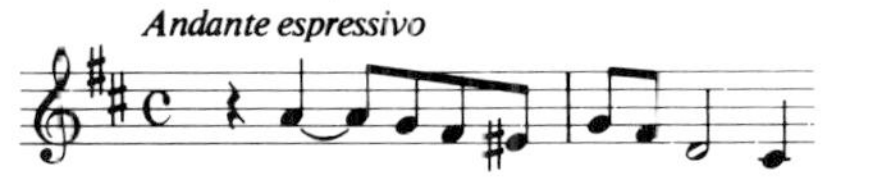
Andante espressivo

No.4. *Salon*

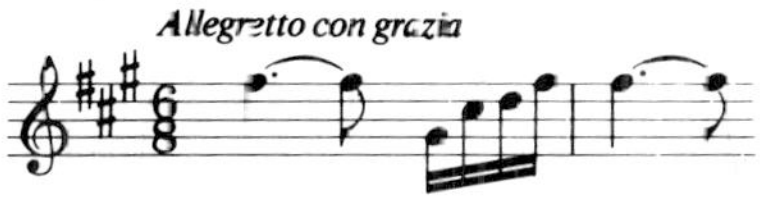
Allegretto con grazia

No.5. *Ballad*

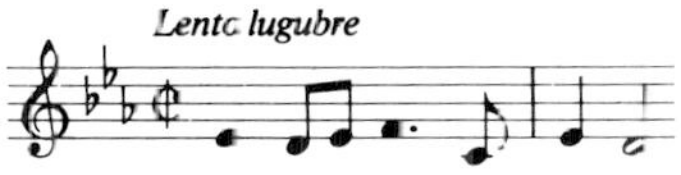
Lento lugubre

No.6. *Wedding Day at Troldhaugen* (This piece was originally called "The Well-wishers are Coming." It was given the new title during the correction of printer's proofs.)

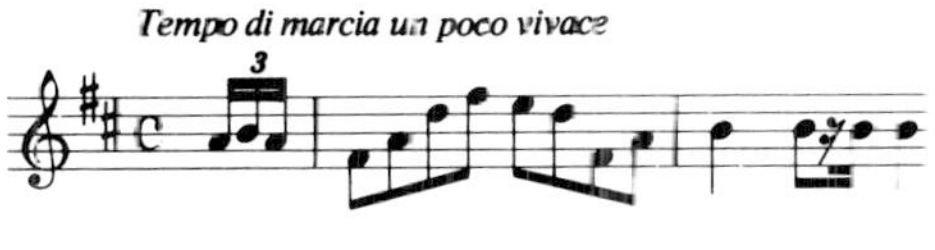
Tempo di marcia un poco vivace

Opus 66. Nineteen Norwegian Folk Songs. For piano. Comp. 1896. 1st pub. 1897 (Peters, Leipzig).

No.1. *Cow Call* (from Lom)

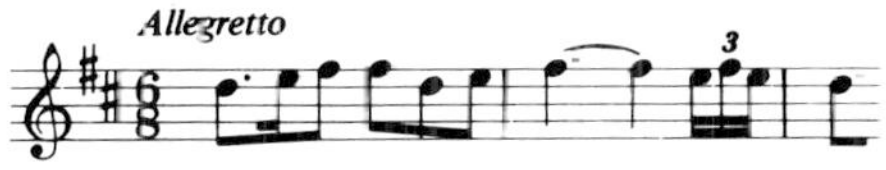
Allegretto

No.2. *It Is the Greatest Foolishness* (from Sunnmöre)

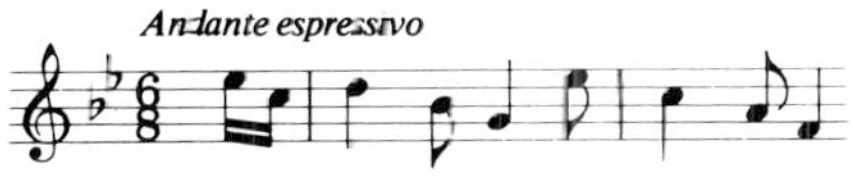
Andante espressivo

No.3. *A King Ruled in the East* (from Sogn)

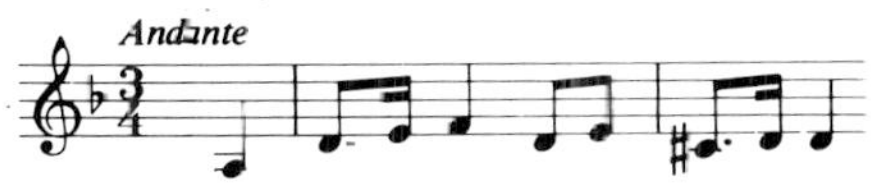
Andante

No.4. *The Siri Dale Song* (from Aardal in Sogn)

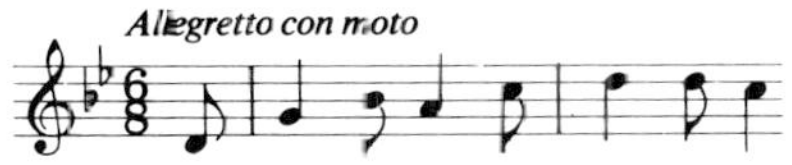
Allegretto con moto

No.5. *It Was in My Youth* (from Luster in Sogn)

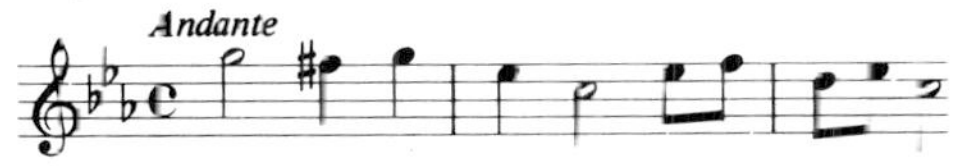
Andante

No.6. *Cow Call and Lullaby* (from Luster in Sogn)

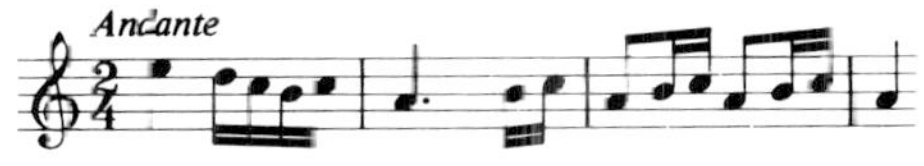
Andante

No.7. *Lullaby* (from Ryfylke)

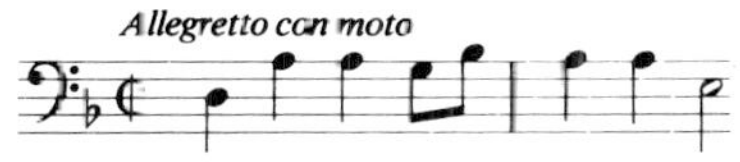
Allegretto con moto

No.8. *Cow Call* (from Lom)

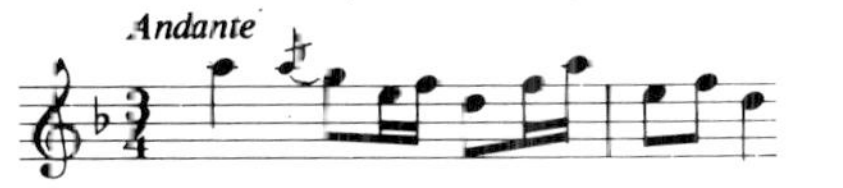
Andante

No.9. *Small Was the Lad* (from Östre Slidre)

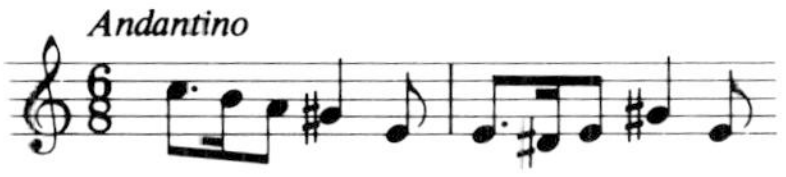
Andantino

No.10. *Tomorrow You Shall Marry Her* (from Lom)

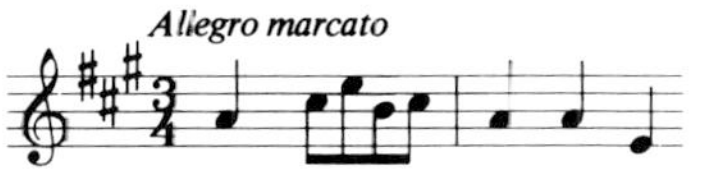
Allegro marcato

No.11. *There Stood Two Girls* (from Lom)

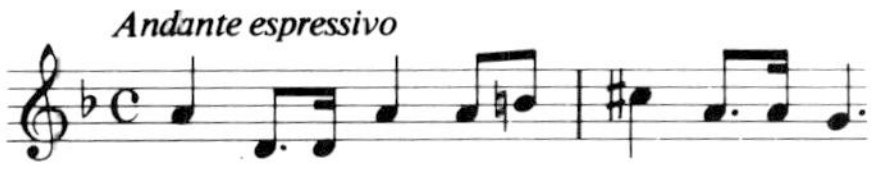
Andante espressivo

No.12. *Ranveig* (from Lom)

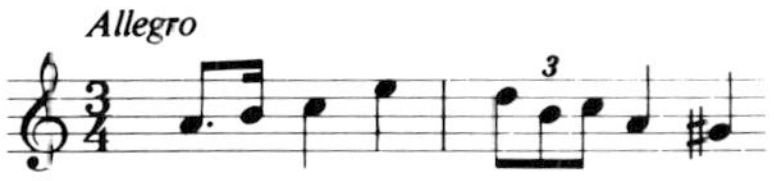
Allegro

No.13. *A Little Grey Man* (from Lom)

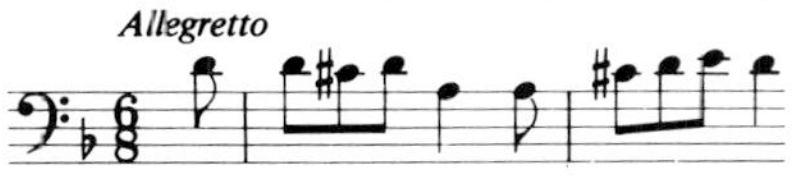
Allegretto

No.14. *In Ola Valley, in Ola Lake* (from Östre Slidre)

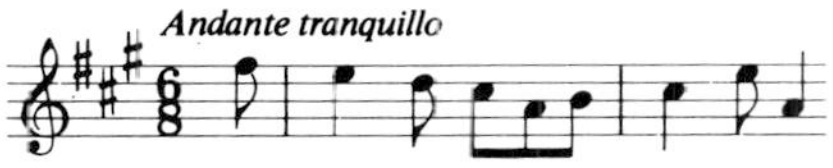
Andante tranquillo

No.15. *Lullaby* (from Lom)

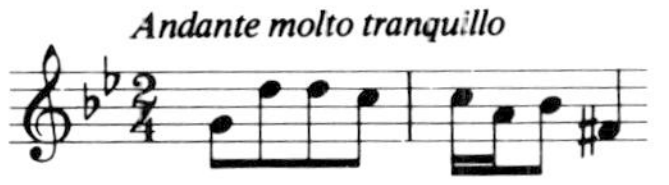
Andante molto tranquillo

No.16. *Little Astrid* (from Lom)

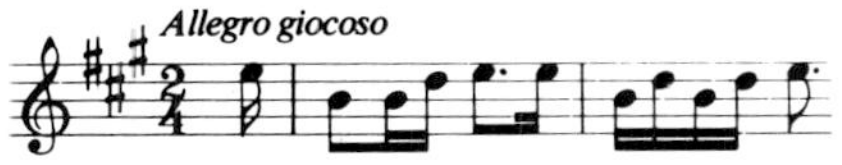
Allegro giocoso

No.17. *Lullaby* (from Turtagrö in Sogn)

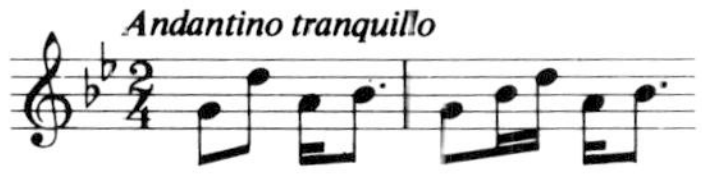
Andantino tranquillo

No.18. *I Wander Deep in Thought* (from Turtagrö in Sogn)

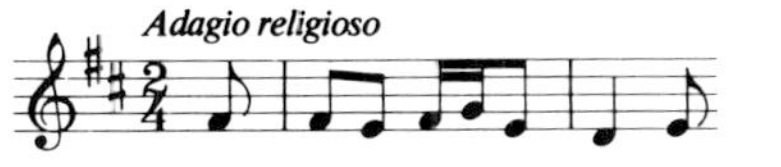
Adagio religioso

No.19. *Gjendine's Lullaby* (from Lom)

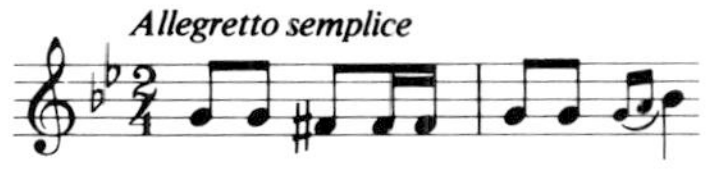
Allegretto semplice

Opus 67. The Mountain Maid. Texts by Arne Garborg. For voice and piano. Comp. 1895–98. 1st pub. 1898 (Wilhelm Hansen, Copenhagen).

No.1. *The Enticement*

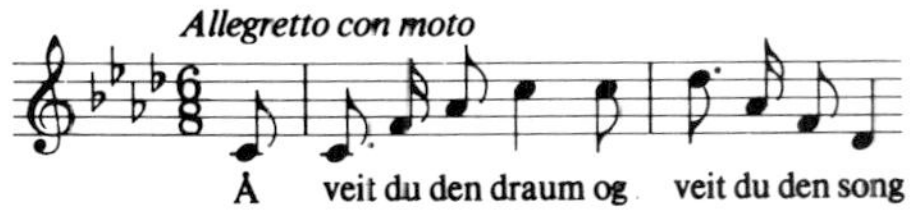
Allegretto con moto
Å veit du den draum og veit du den song

No.2. *Veslemöy. The Young Maiden*

Allegretto molto espressivo

Ho er ma - ger og myrk og mjå

No.3. *Blueberry Slope*

Vivace

Nei sjå, kor det blå - nar her!

No.4. *The Tryst*

Andante espressivo

Ho sit ein sun - dag leng-tan-de i li

No.5. *Love*

Allegretto con moto

Den gal - ne gu - ten min hug hev då - ra

No.6. *Kidlings' Dance*

Allegretto vivace e marcato

Å hipp og hop - pe og tipp og top - pe

No.7. *Hurtful Day*

Andante espressivo

Ho rek - nar dag og stund og sei - ne kveld

No.8. *At the Brook*

Allegro moderato

Du sur - lan - de bekk

Opus 68. Lyric Pieces IX. For piano. Comp. 1898–99. 1st pub. 1899 (Peters).

Nos. 4 and 5 also pub. for orchestra (Peters, 1900).

No.1. *Sailors' Song*

Allegro vivace e marcato

No.2. *Grandmother's Minuet*

Allegretto grazioso e leggierissimo

No.3. *At Your Feet*

Poco Andante e molto espressivo

No.4. *Evening in the Mountains*

Andante espressivo

No.5. *At the Cradle*

Allegretto tranquillamente

No.6. *Valse Mélancolique*

Tempo di Valse tranquillo

Opus 69. Five Songs. Texts by Otto Benzon. For voice and piano. Comp. 1900. 1st pub. 1900 (Wilhelm Hansen, Copenhagen).

No.1. *A Boat on the Waves Is Rocking*

Allegro grazioso

Der gyn - ger en båd på bøl - ge

No.2. *To My Son*

Allegretto espressivo

Min kæ - re lil - le gent - le - man

No.3. *At Mother's Grave*

Lento Funèbre

Sov nu sødt, du lil - le mor

No.4. *Snail, Snail!*

Allegro non troppo

Snegl, snegl! Kom ud af dit hus!

No.5. *Dreams*

Allegretto con moto

Mit alt var du ble - vet

Opus 70. Five Songs. Texts by Otto Benzon. For voice and piano. Comp. 1900. 1st pub. 1900 (Wilhelm Hansen, Copenhagen).

No.1. *Eros*

Andante

Hør mig, I kø - li - ge hjer - ter i nord

No.2. *A Life of Longing*

Allegro molto agitato

Jeg hav - de be - talt, hvad jeg skyld - te

No.3. *Summer Night*

Andantino con moto

Var det ej ny - lig, so-len sank ned

No.4. *Walk With Care*

Allegretto espressivo

Se dig for, når du væl - ger din vej

No.5. *A Poet's Song*

Allegro con spirito

Der er jo de som er ho'de kun

Opus 71. Lyric Pieces X. For piano. Comp. 1901. 1st pub. 1901 (Peters, Leipzig).

No.1. *Once Upon a Time*

Andante con moto

No.2. *Summer's Eve*

Allegretto tranquillamente

No.3. *Puck*

Allegro molto

No.4. *Peace of the Woods*

Lento

No.5. *Halling*

Allegro molto

No.6. *Gone*

Andante doloroso

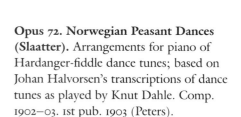

No.7. *Remembrances*

Tempo di Valse

Opus 72. Norwegian Peasant Dances (Slaatter). Arrangements for piano of Hardanger-fiddle dance tunes; based on Johan Halvorsen's transcriptions of dance tunes as played by Knut Dahle. Comp. 1902–03. 1st pub. 1903 (Peters).

No.1. *Giböen's Bridal March*

Marcia

No.2. *John Vaestafae's Springar*

Allegro moderato

No.3. *Bridal March from Telemark*
Alla marcia

No.4. *Halling from the Fairy Hill*
Moderato

No.5. *The Prillar from Os Parish.* Springar
Allegro

No.6. *Myllarguten's Gangar*
Allegretto e marcato

No.7. *Rötnams-Knut.* Halling
Allegro moderato, ma vivace

No.8. *Myllarguten's Bridal March*
Allegretto grazioso

No.9. *Nils Rekve's Halling*
Maestoso

No.10. *Knut Luraasen's Halling I*
Moderato

No.11. *Knut Luraasen's Halling II*
Allegretto tranquillo

No.12. *Myllarguten's Springar*
Allegro

No.13. *Haavar Giböen's Dream at the Oterholt Bridge.* Springar
Allegro

No.14. *The Goblins' Bridal Procession at Vossevangen.* Gangar
Allegretto

No.15. *The Skuldal Bride.* Gangar
Allegro maestoso e marcato

No.16. *The Maidens from Kivledal.* Springar from Seljord
Allegro moderato

No.17. *The Maidens from Kivledal.* Gangar
Allegretto marcato

Opus 73. Moods. For piano. Comp. 1901–05. 1st pub. 1905 (Peters, Leipzig).

No.1. *Resignation*
Allegretto con moto

No.2. *Scherzo-Impromptu*
Allegro capriccioso

No.3. *Night Ride*
Allegro misterioso

No.4. *Folk Tune from Valdres*
Andante pastorale

No 5. *Homage to Chopin*
Allegro agitato

No.6. *The Students' Serenade*
Andante espressivo

No.7. *Mountain Tune*
Allegretto semplice

Opus 74. Four Psalms. For mixed chorus a cappella with baritone solo. Arrangements of four old Norwegian hymn tunes. Melodies from L. M. Lindeman's collection. Comp. 1906. 1st pub. 1907 (Peters, Leipzig).

No.1. *How Fair is Thy Face* (Brorson)
Un poco Allegro

Hvad est du dog skjøn

No.2. *God's Son Hath Set Me Free* (Brorson)
Allegretto animato

Guds Søn har gjort mig fri

No.3. *Jesus Christ Our Lord Is Risen* (Thomissön)
Lento

Je-sus Kri-stus er op-fa-ren

No.4. *In Heav'n Above* (Laurentii)
Andantino

I Him-me-len, i Him-me-len,

Compositions without Opus numbers

CW 100. Posthumous Songs I. For voice and piano. Comp. 1865–67. 1st pub. 1908 (Wilhelm Hansen, Copenhagen, and Peters, Leipzig). No. 2 pub. separately 1896 (Nordiske, Copenhagen).

No.1. *The Fair-haired Maid* (Björnson). 1867

Jeg el·sker deg, du blon·de pi·ke

No.2. *My Little Bird* (H. C. Andersen). 1865

Min lil·le fugl, hvor fly·ver du

No.3. *I Love You, Dear* (Caralis = Caspara Preetzmann). 1865

Dig el·sker jeg, dig el·sker jeg!

No.4. *Tears* (H. C. Andersen). 1865

Mit hjer·te er en him·mel grå

No.5. *The Soldier* (H. C. Andersen). 1865

Med dæm·pe·de hvirv·ler trom·mer·ne gå

CW 101. Posthumous Songs II. For voice and piano. Comp. 1873–1905. 1st pub. 1908 (Wilhelm Hansen, Copenhagen, and Peters, Leipzig).

No.1. *On the Ruins of Hamar Cathedral* (Vinje). 1880

Vi står og syn·ger på Ha·mars grav

No.2. *I Loved Him.* From the unfinished "Peace Oratorio" (Björnson). 1891 (?)

Jeg el·sket, el·sket u·ten ord

No.3. *A Simple Song* (Drachmann). 1889

Når tro·fast, varm og re·de·lig

No.4. *Sighs* (Björnson). 1873

Af·ten·so·lens hyg·ge

No.5. *Yuletide Cradle Song* (Langsted). 1900

Du har så blød en vug·ge·seng

No.6. *The Hunter* (W. Schulz). 1905

Die Mor·gen·sonn' die Vög·lein weckt

CW 102. Larvik's Polka. For piano. Comp. 1858. Pub. in *GGA*, Vol. 20.

CW 103. Three Piano Pieces. Manuscript is in the handwriting of Benedicte Grieg. Comp. 1858. Included in CW 105.

No.1. *Longing* (= CW 105, No. 2)

No.2. *Allegro con moto* (= CW 105, No. 6)

No.3. *Allegro assai* (= CW 105, No. 5)

CW 104. Nine Children's Pieces. For piano. Bears the inscription "To Miss Ludovisca Riis, September 6, 1859 from the composer. Leipzig 7/28/59." The outside of the wrapper has German text plus the words "Op. 17"[!]. Comp. 1858–59. Included in CW 105.

No.1. *Andante quasi allegretto* (= CW 105, No. 4)

No.2. *Pearls* (= CW 105, No. 9)

No.3. *By Gellert's Grave* (= CW 105, No. 10)

No.4. *Prayer* (= CW 105, No. 19)

No.5. *Loss* (= CW 105, No. 21)

No.6. *Fifth Birthday* (= CW 105, No. 18)

No.7. *Allegretto con moto* (= CW 105, No. 13)

No.8. *Scherzo. Allegro assai, quasi presto* (= CW 105, No. 16)

No.9. *A Dream* (= CW 105, No. 7)

CW 105. Short Pieces for Piano. Manuscript bears the inscription "To be destroyed after my death. Must never be printed." Comp. 1858–59. Pub. in *GGA*, Vol. 20.

No.1. *Allegro agitato*

No.2. *Longing. Allegro desiderio*

No.3. *Molto allegro vivace*

No.4. *Andante quasi allegretto*

No.5. *Allegro assai*

No.6. *Allegro con moto*

No.7. *A Dream. Andante quasi allegretto*

No.8. *Allegro assai*

No.9. *Pearls. Andante moderato*

No.10. *By Gellert's Grave. Andante con gravita*

No.11. *Vivace*

No.12. *Preludium. Largo con estro poetica*

No.13. *Allegretto con moto*

No.14. *Allegretto con moto*

No.15. *Two-part Preludium. Con passione*

No.16. *Scherzo. Allegro assai, quasi presto*

No.17. *Molto adagio religioso*

No.18. *Fifth Birthday. Allegro molto*

No.19. *Prayer. Andante moderato*

No.20. *Allegro vivace*

No.21. *Loss. Andante moderato*

No.22. *Gently, not too fast*

No.23. *Assai allegro furioso*

CW 106. Look to the Sea (Geibel). For voice and piano. Comp. 1859. Pub. in *GGA*, Vol. 15 (1989).

CW 107. Three Piano Pieces. Comp. 1860. Printed in facsimile in *Norsk Musikkgransk-ning. Aarbok 1951–53.*

No.1. *Allegro agitato*

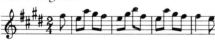

No.2. *Allegretto*

No.3. *Allegro molto e vivace, quasi presto*

CW 108. The Singing Congregation (Grundtvig). For alto voice and piano. Comp. 1860. Pub. in *GGA*, Vol. 15 (1988).

Allegretto non troppo

Guds me - nig - hed syng for vor Ska-ber i løn

CW 109. Fugue in F Minor. For string quartet. Comp. 1861. Pub. in *GGA*, Vol. 9 (1978).

Allegro con fuoco

CW 110. Dona nobis pacem. Fugue for mixed chorus a cappella. Comp. 1862. Pub. in *GGA*, Vol. 17 (1985).

Andante espressivo

Do - na no - bis pa - cem

CW 111. Four Songs for Male Voices. For male chorus a cappella. Comp. 1863. Pub. in *GGA*, Vol. 17 (1985).

No.1. *Norwegian War Song* (H. Wergeland)

Raskt

I søn - ner av fjel - let, av sjø - en den blå!

No.2. *Fredriksborg* (Chr. Richardt)

Noe langsomt

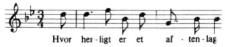

Skjøn - ne, sunk - ne Fred - riks - borg,

No.3. *Student Life* (Chr. Richardt)

Hvor her - ligt er et af - ten - lag

No.4. *The Late Rose* (A. Munch)

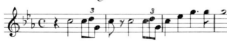

Du yn - di - ge ro - se, vi blom - strer du nu?

CW 112. Symphony in C Minor. Comp. 1863–64. 2nd and 3rd movements pub. for piano four hands 1869 (as Op. 14). Full score pub. in *GGA*, Vol. 11 (1984).

1st movement: *Allegro molto*

2nd moveme

3rd movemer

Allegro en.

4th movement: *Finale*

Allegro molto vivace

CW 113. Denmark (H. C. Andersen). For mixed chorus and piano. Comp. 1864. Pub. in *GGA*, Vol. 17 (1985).

Moderato

End - nu er ej Dan - mark en kæm - pe-grav

CW 114. Devoutest of Maidens (C. Groth). For voice and piano. Comp. 1864. Pub. in *GGA*, Vol. 15 (1989).

Allegretto

Til kir - ken hun van-drer så stil - le og from

CW 115. Clara's Song, from *Courting on Helgoland* (B. Feddersen). For voice and piano. Comp. 1864. Pub. in *GGA*, Vol. 15 (1989).

Allegro con moto

CW 116. Agitato. For piano. Comp. 1865. Pub. in *GGA*, Vol. 20.

CW 117. Funeral March for Rikard Nor-draak. For piano. Comp. 1866. 1st pub. 1866 (Chr. E. Horneman, Copenhagen). Also arranged for large wind ensemble with percussion 1867, rev. and pub. 1899. (Peters, Leipzig).

CW 118. Intermezzo. For cello and piano. Comp. 1866. Pub. in *GGA*, Vol. 8 (1979).

Allegretto tranquillo

CW 119. Little Lad (Kr. Janson). For voice and piano. Comp. 1866. Pub. in *GGA*, Vol. 15 (1989).

Allegretto

Ves - le gut sit på tu - va

CW 120. The Bear Hunter (Jörgen Moe). For male chorus a cappella. Comp. 1867. 1st pub. in Joh. D. Behrens's *Samling af* *flerstemmige Mandssange* [Collection of Part Songs for Male Voices], 5th series, No. 455 (Oslo). Cf. CW 133, No. 57.

Nu står gra - nen stak - ket med sne

CW 121. Evening Mood (Jörgen Moe). For male chorus a cappella. Comp. 1867. 1st pub. in Joh. D. Behrens's *Samling af flerstemmige Mandssange* [Collection of Part Songs for Male Voices], 5th series, No. 454 (Oslo).

Nu syn - ker af - te - nen sak - te ned

CW 122. Election Song (Björnson). For male chorus a cappella. Comp. 1893. 1st pub. 1894 (Brödrene Hals, Oslo). Also pub. for voice and piano by the same publisher.

Hva si - er de dog om deg

CW 123. Cantata for the Unveiling of the W.F.K. Christie Monument, May 17, 1868 (A. Munch). For male chorus and horns. Comp. 1868. Pub. in *GGA*, Vol. 16 (1985).

Before the unveiling:

Vår - stor - mer gikk o - ver fe - dre - ne - lan - det

After the unveiling:

Vi hans å - syn at - ter sku - er

CW 124. Norwegian Sailors' Song (Björnson). For male chorus a cappella. Comp. 1869–70. 1st pub. in Joh. D. Behrens's *Sangbog for Mandssangforeninger* [Song Book for Men's Singing Clubs], Vol. VI, No. 15 (Oslo). Cf. CW 133, No. 14.

Den nor - ske sjø - mann er

CW 125. The Odalisque (Carl Bruun). For voice and piano. Comp. 1870. 1st pub. 1872 (Chr. E. Horneman, Copenhagen).

Nu syn - ker so - len i A - si - ens da - le

CW 126. The Princess (Björnson). Comp. 1871. 1st pub. 1871 (Immanuel Rees, Copenhagen). Also pub. for piano as Op. 41, No. 5.

Prin - ses - sen satt høyt i sitt jom - fru-bur

CW 127. At J.S. Welhaven's Grave (Jörgen Moe). For male chorus a cappella. Comp. 1873. 1st pub. in Joh. D. Behrens's *Firstemmig Mands-Sangbog* [Four-part Songs for Men's Voices], Vol. VII, No. 8 (Oslo).

Stil - le nu! Sak - te to - nen gyn - ger

CW 128. The White and Red, Red Roses (Björnson). For voice and piano. Comp. 1873. Pub. in *GGA*, Vol. 15 (1989).

Den hvi - te, rø - de ro - se

CW 129. Four Occasional Songs.

No.1. *To Christian Tönsberg* (J. Bögh). For voice and piano. Comp. 1873. Pub in *GGA*, Vol. 15 (1989).

Du sit - ter i min - nets lund

No.2. *For L. M. Lindeman's Silver Wedding Anniversary* (V. Nicolajsen). For voice and piano. Comp. 1873. Pub. in *GGA*, Vol. 15 (1989).

No.3. *Morning Prayer* (Fredrik Gjertsen). For voice and piano. Comp. 1875. Pub. in *Nordisk illustreret Börneblad*, Vol. 3, No. 5, December 1875 (Copenhagen).

I ditt dy - re - ba - re navn

No.4. *Beneath the Christmas Tree* (N. Rolfsen). For voice and piano. Comp. 1885. 1st pub. (as a contribution) in

Illustreret Tidende for Börn, Vol. 1, 1885–86 (Bergen).

Vi løf - tet din rot!

CW 130. Cantata for Karl Hals (Björnson). For tenor, female chorus, mixed chorus, and piano. Comp. 1873. 1st pub. in *GGA*, Vol. 17 (1985).

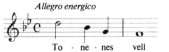

To - ne - nes vell

CW 131. Chorus for the Supporters of Freedom in Scandinavia (Björnson). For male chorus a cappella. Comp. 1874. Pub. in *Dansk Folketidende*, July 24, 1874 (Copenhagen).

For - ak - tet av de sto - re

CW 132. At the Halfdan Kjerulf Statue (A. Munch). Comp. 1874. 1st pub. in Joh. D. Behrens's *Sangbog for Mands-sangforeninger* [Song Book for Men's Singing Clubs], Vol. VI, Nos. 73 and 74 (Oslo).

Before the unveiling. For tenor solo and male chorus a cappella.

I to - ne - strøm - mens fyl - de

After the unveiling. For male chorus a cappella.

Dek - ket er fal - det, som slø - ret

CW 133. Norway's Melodies. Arranged for piano with accompanying texts. 152 numbers in all. Comp. 1874–75. 1st pub. 1875 (E. Wagner, Copenhagen). In 1878 the collection became the property of Wilhelm Hansen, which issued several printings, but Grieg was first identified as the editor of the collection in the 1910 edition. In the first edition Grieg identified the following numbers as his own arrangements of folk tunes:

No.6. *Springar* (from Vinje)

No.22. *Halling* (from Österdal)

No.45. *Springar* (from Numedal)

No.59. *Lullaby* (children's song from Valdres)

No.125. *Sjugurd and the Troll Bride* (from Hallingdal)

Arrangements of Original Compositions:

No.8. *Margaret's Cradle Song* (Op. 15, No. 1)

No.14. *Norwegian Sailors' Song* (CW 124)

No.17. *Onward* (Op. 12, No. 8)

No.38. *The Young Birch Tree* (Op. 18, No. 6)

No.57. *The Bear Hunter* (CW 120)

No.71. *I Love But Thee* (Op. 5, No. 3)

No.90. *Wood Wandering* (= "Moonlit Forest," Op. 18, No. 1)

No.95. *Two Brown Eyes* (Op. 5, No. 1)

No.113. *Serenade for Welhaven* (Op. 18, No. 9)

No.150. *The First Meeting* (Op. 21, No. 1)

CW 134. Six Norwegian Mountain Melodies. For piano. 1st pub. 1886 (Wilhelm Hansen. Copenhagen). A revised edition of the six folk-tune arrangements in CW 133 which Grieg had identified as his own.

No.1. *Springar* (from Numedal [No. 45])

No.2. *Lullaby* (from Valdres [No. 59])

No.3. *Springar* (from Vinje [No. 6])

No.4. *Sjugurd and the Troll Bride* (from Hallingdal [No. 125])

No.5. *Halling* (from Österdal [No. 22])

No.6. *The Lad and the Lass in the Cow-Shed Loft* (No. 126)

CW 135. Mozart Piano Sonatas with a Freely Composed Second Piano Part. Comp. 1877. 1st pub. 1879–80 (E. W. Fritzsch, Leipzig).

No.1. F major (No. 1 in the Peters edition, K. 533)

No.2. C minor with preceding "Fantasy" (No. 18 in the Peters edition, K. 475)

No.3. C major (No. 15 in the Peters edition, K. 545)

No.4. G major (No. 14 in the Peters edition, K. 283)

CW 136A. Inga Litamor. For baritone and male chorus a cappella. Comp. 1877–78 (?). Pub. in *GGA*, Vol. 17 (1985).

CW 136B. Album Leaf. For piano. 1st pub. 1878 (C. Warmuth, Oslo).

CW 137. Andante con moto. Trio movement in C minor for piano, violin, and cello. Comp. 1878. Pub. in *GGA*, Vol. 9 (1978).

CW 138. Vinje Songs not included in Opus 33. For voice and piano. Comp. 1880. Cf. CW 161, No. 1. Pub. in *GGA*, Vol. 15 (1989).

No.1. *The Forgotten Maid*

No.2. *The Young Woman*

CW 139. My Finest Thought (Olaf Lofthus). For male chorus a cappella. Comp. 1881. 1st pub. in Joh. D. Behrens's *Firstemmig Kor- og Kvartet-Sangbog for Mandsstemmer* [Four-part Chorus and Quartet Song Book for Male Voices], Vol. VIII, No. 4 (Oslo).

CW 140. Our Watchword (Olaf Lofthus). For male chorus a cappella. 1st pub. in Joh. D. Behrens's *Firstemmig Kor- og Kvartet-Sangbog for Mandsstemmer*, Vol. VIII, No. 19 (Oslo).

CW 141. A Greeting to the Singers (Sigvald Skavlan). For male chorus a cappella. Comp. 1883. 1st pub. in Joh. D. Behrens's *Firstemmig Mands-Sangbog* [Four-part Songs for Male Voices]. Vol. VII, No. 97 (Oslo).

CW 142. Piano Concerto in B Minor (fragments). Outlines of 1st and 3rd movements only. Comp. 1883. Printed in *Die Musik*, 1907–08 (Berlin).

1st movement:

3rd movement:

CW 143. Holberg Cantata ("Cantata for the unveiling of the Holberg monument December 3, 1884. Words by Nordahl Rolfsen"). Comp. 1884. 1st pub. 1884 (lithograph). For baritone solo and male chorus a cappella.

Before the unveiling:

No.1. *Allegro con brio*

No.2. *Molto andante*

No.3. *Allegro molto vivace*

After the unveiling:

No.4. *Allegro moderato e maestoso*

CW 144. Easter Song (A. Böttger). For voice and piano. Comp. 1889. 1st pub. 1904 (Peters, Leipzig).

Die Glo-cken läu-ten das O-stern ein

CW 145. You Often Fix Your Gaze (Drachmann). For voice and piano. Comp. 1889. Pub. in *GGA*, Vol. 15 (1989).

Du ret-ter tidt dit ø-je par

CW 146. String Quartet No. 2 in F Major. Comp. 1891, but not completed. The two first movements were prepared for publication by Julius Röntgen in 1908 (Peters).

1st movement:

2nd movement:

3rd movement: Sketches only; pub. in *GGA*, Vol. 9 (1978).

4th movement: Sketches only; pub. in *GGA*, Vol. 9 (1978).

CW 147. Song of the Flag (Johan Brun). For male chorus a cappella. Comp. 1893. Pub. in *GGA*, Vol. 17 (1985).

Fram, nord-menn, fram un-der flag-get!

CW 148. Six Songs with Orchestra. Orchestrated 1894–95. 1st pub. 1895–96 (Peters).

No.1. *Solveig's Song* (Op. 23, No. 19).

No.2. *Solveig's Cradle Song* (Op. 23, No. 26, short version).

No.3. *From Monte Pincio* (Op. 39, No. 1).

No.4. *A Swan* (Op. 25, No. 2)

No.5. *Last Spring* (Op. 33, No. 2)

No.6. *Henrik Wergeland* (Op. 58, No. 3)

CW 149. Garborg Songs not included in Opus 67. For voice and piano. Comp. 1895. Pub. in *GGA*, Vol. 15 (1989).

No.1. *The Sparrow* (Cf. CW 150).

Små - spor - ven gjeng i tu - net

No.2. *Cow-Call*

Å, ky-ri mi ve-ne, å ky-ri mi!

No.3. *Doomed*

Eg hev som vig-de Mam-mons træl

No.4. *In the Hayfield*

No ljå-en han syng på den saf-ti-ge voll

No.5. *Veslemöy Longing*

No stend ho stel-ler i kjø-ken-krå, ho mor!

CW 150. The Sparrow (Garborg). For 3-part female chorus and piano. Comp. 1895. (Cf. CW 149, No. 1). Pub. in *GGA*, Vol. 17 (1985).

Små - spor - ven gjeng i tu - net

CW 151. Greetings from Kristiania Singers (Jonas Lie). For baritone solo and male chorus a cappella. Comp. 1896. 1st pub. 1896 (Brödrene Hals, Oslo).

Nu pin-sens klok-ker run-ger

CW 152. Impromptu for the "Grieg Male Chorus" in Ft. Dodge, Iowa (Björnson). Comp. 1896. Printed in facsimile in *Bergens Tidende* Nov. 24, 1959.

Nor-ske to-ner, nor-ske to-ner

CW 153. The Blueberry (D. Grönvold). For voice and piano. Comp. 1896. 1st pub. in *GGA*, Vol. 15 (1989).

På tu-net gikk små-gut-ten

CW 154. Three Piano Pieces. Comp. 1898. 1st pub. 1908 (Peters, Leipzig). Prepared for publication by Julius Röntgen.

No.1. *White Clouds*

No.2. *Gnomes' Procession*

No.3. *Wild Dance*

CW 155. Ave maris stella (Thor Lange). For voice and piano. Comp. 1893. 1st pub. 1893 (C. J. Kihl & Langkjaer, Copenhagen). Also pub. for mixed chorus = CW 156, No. 2.

Hill deg, ha-vets stjer-ne

CW 156. Two Religious Choral Songs. Comp. 1899. 1st pub. 1900 (Wilhelm Hansen, Copenhagen). For mixed chorus a cappella.

No.1. *At the Grave of a Young Wife* (Op. 39, No. 5).

No.2. *Ave maris stella* (CW 155).

CW 157. To a Devil (O. Benzon). For voice and piano. Comp. 1900. Pub. in *GGA*, Vol. 15 (1989).

I tell you, if an an-gel

CW 158. Gentlemen-Rankers (R. Kipling). For voice and piano. Comp. 1900. 1st pub. in *GGA*, Vol. 15 (1989).

Til de tap-tes le-gi-o-ner

CW 159. To Ole Bull (Welhaven). For male chorus a cappella. Comp. 1901. 1st pub. in *GGA*, Vol. 17 (1985).

Allegretto tranquillo

Hvor søtt å fav-nes av aft-nens fred

CW 160. National Song (John Paulsen). For voice and piano. Year of composition unknown. 1st pub. in *Nye Melodier*, Copen-

hagen 1894, entitled "Syttendemaisang" (Song for the Seventeenth of May).

Andante

En hyt-te sim-pelt tjel-det

CW 161. Westerly Wind (Jonas Dahl). For male chorus a cappella. Year of composition unknown. 1st pub. by Carl Sander (un-dated).

Ve-stan-vær! Ve-stan-vær! Ve-stan-vær!

CW 162. Fragments of a Piano Quintet. Year of composition unknown. 1st pub. in *GGA*, Vol. 9 (1978).

Principal theme:

Secondary theme:

Compositions arranged according to genre

In addition to the foregoing two-part Catalog of Works we give here an overview of Grieg's works arranged according to the genre to which each composition can be assigned. Grieg's own arrangements are included in this listing, but not arrangements of his works by others. Numbers 1–74 are opus numbers; numbers 100–162 indicate compositions to which Grieg did not assign opus numbers.

Piano

1 Four Piano Pieces
3 Poetic Tone Pictures
6 Humoresques
7 Piano Sonata in E Minor
12 Lyric Pieces I
16 Piano Concerto in A Minor
17 Twenty-five Norwegian Folk Songs and Dances
19 Pictures from Folk Life
23 Peer Gynt: Nos. 12, 15, 16, 19, and 26
24 Ballade in G Minor
28 Album Leaves
29 Improvisations on Two Norwegian Folk Songs
34 Two Elegiac Melodies
35 Norwegian Dances
37 Waltz Caprices
38 Lyric Pieces II
40 Holberg Suite
41 Transcriptions of Original Songs I
43 Lyric Pieces III
46 Peer Gynt Suite No. 1
47 Lyric Pieces IV
50 Scenes from "Olav Trygvason"
52 Transcriptions of Original Songs II
53 Two Melodies for String Orchestra
54 Lyric Pieces V

55 Peer Gynt Suite No. 2
56 Three Orchestral Pieces from "Sigurd Jorsalfar"
57 Lyric Pieces VI
62 Lyric Pieces VII
63 Two Nordic Melodies
65 Lyric Pieces VIII
66 Nineteen Norwegian Folk Songs
68 Lyric Pieces IX
71 Lyric Pieces X
72 Norwegian Peasant Dances
73 Moods
* * *
102 Larvik's polka
103 Three Piano Pieces
104 Nine Children's Pieces
105 Short Pieces for Piano
107 Three Piano Pieces
116 Agitato
117 Funeral March for Rikard Nordraak
133 Norway's Melodies
134 Six Norwegian Mountain Melodies
136B Album Leaf
142 Piano Concerto in B Minor (fragments)
154 Three Piano Pieces

Piano Four Hands

11 In Autumn
14 Two Symphonic Pieces
19 Pictures from Folk Life
22 Sigurd Jorsalfar: Nos. 1, 2 and 4
23 Peer Gynt: Nos. 1, 4, 8, 9, 12, 13, 15, 16 and 21
34 Two Elegiac Melodies
35 Norwegian Dances
37 Waltz Caprices
46 Peer Gynt Suite No. 1

55 Peer Gynt Suite No. 2
56 Three Orchestral Pieces from "Sigurd Jorsalfar"
63 Two Nordic Melodies
64 Symphonic Dances

Two Pianos

51 Old Norwegian Melody with Variations
* * *
135 Mozart's Piano Sonatas with a Freely Composed Second Piano Part

Violin and Piano

8 Violin Sonata No. 1 in F Major
13 Violin Sonata No. 2 in G Major
22 Sigurd Jorsalfar: No. 3, "At the Matching Game," originally "Gavotte." Also published as Opus 56, No. 1
45 Violin Sonata No. 3 in C Minor

Cello and Piano

36 Cello Sonata in A Minor
* * *
118 Intermezzo

Piano Trio

137 Andante con moto

String Quartet

27 String Quartet No. 1 in G Minor
* * *
109 Fugue in F Minor
146 String Quartet No. 2 in F Major (unfinished)

Piano Quintet

162 Fragments of a Piano Quintet

Bibliography

Abell, Arthur M. *Talks with Great Composers*. Garmisch-Partenkirchen, 1964.

Abraham, Gerald (ed.). *Edvard Grieg. A Symposium*. London, 1948.

Anker, Öyvind (ed.). "Tre Grieg-brev til Björnson." *Norsk musikliv*, 1943.

———. "Knut Dale—Edv. Grieg—Johan Halvorsen. En brevveksling." *Norsk musikkgranskning. Aarbok 1943–46*, Oslo, 1947.

Asafjev, Boris I. *Grieg*. Moscow & Leningrad, 1948.

Bain, Robert. *The Clans and Tartans of Scotland*. London & Glasgow, new edition 1953.

Bartók, Béla. "Instrumental folklore i Ungarn" (A hangszeres zene folkloreja Magyarozágon). *Zeneközlöny*, Budapest, 1911.

Bartók, Béla, Jr. "Béla Bartók i Norge." *Norsk musikktidsskrift*, 1978.

Bauer, W. "Die Harmonik in den Werken von Edvard Grieg." Unpublished doctoral dissertation, Vienna, 1931.

Benestad, Finn. *Johannes Haarklou. Mannen og verket*. Oslo, 1961.

———. "Noen notater om Edvard Griegs ufullendte strykekvartett i F-dur." *Festskrift Gunnar Heerup*, Egtved, 1973.

———. "Et ukjent Grieg-brev om strykekvartetten i g-moll." *Norsk musikktidsskrift*, 1973.

Berg, Adolph and Haakon Mosby. *Musikselskabet Harmonien 1765–1945*. Bergen, 1949.

Berg, Sigurd (ed.). "Nogle breve fra Edvard Grieg til Niels Ravnkilde." *Ord och bild*, 1947.

Bergen Offentlige Bibliotek (ed unknown): *Katalog over Grieg-utstillingen 22. mai–7. juni, 1952*. Bergen, 1962.

Beyer, Marie. Unpublished manuscript from 1924 concerning Grieg's correspondence with Frants Beyer. In Norwegian. National Archive, Oslo.

Beyer, Marie (ed.). *Breve fra Edvard Grieg til Frants Beyer 1872–1907*. Oslo, 1923.

Bindingsbö, Gunnar. "Fraa hardingfele til klaver. Ein klangstudie i Halvorsen: 'Slaatter' og Grieg: 'Slaatter op. 72.'" Unpublished M.A. thesis, University of Oslo, 1963.

Björkvold, Jon-Roar. "Peter Tsjaikovskij og Edvard Grieg—en kontakt mellom to aandsfrender." *Studia Musicologica Norvegica 2*, Oslo, 1976.

Björndal, Arne. *Ole Bull og norsk folkemusikk*. Oslo, 1940.

———. *Norsk folkemusikk*. Bergen, 1952.

———. "Edvard Grieg og folkemusikken." *Bergens Tidende*, May 30 and June 1, 1953.

Böe, Finn. *Trekk av Edvard Griegs personlighet*. Oslo, 1949.

Breithaupt, R.M. "Edvard Grieg." *Die Musik*, 1903.

Brodsky, Adolph. "Ein Besuch bei Grieg." *Musical World*, 1907.

Brodsky, Anna. *Recollections of a Russian Home*. London, 1904.

Capellen, Georg. *Die Freiheit oder Unfreiheit der Töne und Intervalle . . . Grieg-Analysen als Bestätigungsnachweis und Wegweiser der neuen Musiktheorie*. Leipzig, 1904.

Cederblad, Johanne Grieg. *Sangen om Norge*. Oslo, 1948.

Cherbuliez, Antoine-V. *E. Grieg. Leben und Werk*. Zurich, 1947.

Christie. W.H.C. *Slaegten Christie i Norge*. Bergen, 1909.

Closson, Ernest. *Edvard Grieg et la Musique Scandinave.* Paris, 1897.

Cuypers, Jules. *Grieg.* Haarlem, 1948.

Daitz, Mimi Segal. "Grieg and Bréville: 'Nous parlons alors de la jeune école francaise . . .'" *19th Century Music,* Vol. I, No. 3, Davis, California, 1978.

Dale, Kathleen. "Edvard Grieg's Pianoforte Music." *Music and Letters,* 1943.

——. "Grieg Discoveries." *Monthly Musical Record,* 1954.

Day, L. A. *Grieg.* New York, 1945.

Desmond, Asta. "Grieg's Songs." *Music and Letters,* 1943.

Dolinescu, Elisabeta. *Edvard Grieg.* Bucharest, 1964.

Eggen, Erik. "Grieg og Nordraak." *Syn og Segn,* 1912.

——. "Grieg og Skotland." *Musik,* Copenhagen, 1921.

Eide, L. W., Book Printers, Bergen (editor unknown): *Edvard Grieg* (a collection of articles in English). Bergen, 1953.

Eriksen, Asbjörn Ö. "Griegs mest impresjonistiske romanse." *Norsk musikk-tidsskrift,* 1976.

Fabricius, Lars Börge. *Traek af dansk musiklivs historie.* Copenhagen, 1975.

Feddersen, Benjamin J. "Fra Griegs Ungdom." *Illustreret Tidende,* Copenhagen, 1899.

Fellerer, Karl Gustav. *Edvard Grieg.* Potsdam, 1942.

——. "H. Cleve und E. Grieg." *Festschrift Friedrich Blume.* Kassel, 1963.

Festspillene i Bergen (editor unknown): *Katalog over Grieg-materiale utstilt i Bergens Kunstforening 1953.* Bergen, 1953.

Finck, Henry T. *Edvard Grieg.* New York, 1906. New and enlarged edition, New York, 1909.

——. *Grieg and his Music.* New York, 1929.

Findejsen, N. F. *Edvard Grieg.* Moscow, 1908.

Fischer, Kurt von. *Griegs Harmonik und die nordländische Folklore.* Bern and Leipzig, 1938.

Fischer, Trygve. "Den instrumentale viseform hos Grieg." *Norsk musikkgransk-ning. Aarbok 1942,* Oslo, 1943.

Foerster, Josef B. *Edvard Hagerup Grieg.* Prague, 1890.

Fog, Dan. *Grieg-Katalog* (in Danish and German). Copenhagen, 1980.

Foss, Hubert. "Edvard Hagerup Grieg." *The Heritage of Music.* Oxford, 1951.

Freiheiter, I. Jerzy. *Harmonica Edwarda Griega.* Lwow (Lemberg), 1931. Published in an abbreviated form by Erik Eggen in *Tonekunst,* Oslo, 1932.

Gaukstad, Öystein. "Edvard Grieg 1843–1943. En bibliografi." *Norsk musikk-kgranskning. Aarbok 1942,* Oslo, 1943.

——. "Temaet i Griegs ballade." *Norsk musikktidsskrift,* 1964.

——. "'Mig tyckis at Verden er underlig.'" *Norsk musikktidsskrift,* 1967.

——. "Edvard Grieg og Adolf Brodsky." *Norsk musikktidsskrift,* 1967.

——. *Toner fra Valdres.* Leira, 1973.

Gaukstad, Öystein (ed.). *Edvard Grieg, Artikler og taler.* Oslo, 1957.

Geijer, Gösta. "Grieg som romanskomponist." *Svensk musiktidning,* 1887.

Göllner, K. "Die Vokalmusik Norwegens als Grundlage des Schaffens Edvard Griegs." Unpublished doctoral dissertation, Vienna, 1940.

Grainger, Percy Aldridge. "Personal Recollections of Grieg." *Musical Times,* 1907.

——. "Personal Recollections of Edvard Grieg." *The Etude,* 1943.

——. "Grieg's Last Opus." *Hinrichsen's Musical Year Book,* London, 1952.

Grieg, J. Russell. "Grieg and his Scottish Ancestry." *Hinrichsen's Musical Year Book,* London, 1952.

Greni, Liv. *Rikard Nordraak.* Oslo, 1942.

——. "Grieg og folkemusikken." *Syn og segn,* 1954.

Grieg, Edvard. *Complete Works,* Vol. 1–20 (C. F. Peters, Frankfurt/London/New York).

I. INSTRUMENTAL MUSIC
Solo Piano:
1. Lyric Pieces I–X (ed. Dag Schjelderup-Ebbe)
2. Other Original Compositions (ed. Dag Schjelderup-Ebbe)
3. Arrangements of Norwegian Folk Music (ed. Dag Schjelderup-Ebbe)
4. Arrangements of Own Works (ed. Dag Schjelderup-Ebbe)

Piano Four Hands:
5. Original Compositions and Arrangements of Own Works (ed. Rune Andersen)
6. Dramatic Music (ed. Nils Grinde)

Two Pianos:
7. Original Compositions and Arrangements (ed. Arvid Vollsnes)

Chamber Music:
8. Sonatas for Violin and Piano, Sonata for Cello and Piano (ed. Finn Benestad)
9. String Quartets, Other Chamber Music, Arrangements of Own Works for Chamber Orchestra (ed. Finn Benestad)

Orchestra:
10. Piano Concerto in A Minor (ed. Kjell Skyllstad)
11. Original Compositions (ed. Finn Benestad and Gunnar Rugstad)
12. Suites for Orchestra (ed. Finn Benestad and Dag Schjelderup-Ebbe)
13. Arrangements of Own Works and Compositions without Opus Numbers (ed. Gunnar Rugstad)

II. VOCAL MUSIC
Songs with Piano Accompaniment:
14. Songs Op. 2–49 (ed. Dan Fog and Nils Grinde)
15. Songs Op. 58–70 and songs without Opus Numbers (ed. Dan Fog and Nils Grinde)

Vocal Compositions with Orchestra:
16. Original Compositions and Arrangements of Own Works (ed. Hans Magne Graesvold)

Unaccompanied Choral Music
17. Original Compositions and Arrangements of Own Works (ed. Dan Fog)

III. DRAMATIC MUSIC
18. Peer Gynt (ed. Finn Benestad)
19. Other Original Compositions (ed. Finn Benestad)

IV. APPENDIX
20. Addenda and Corrigenda (ed. Finn Benestad and Dag Schjelderup-Ebbe)

——. *Artikler og taler.* Edited by Öystein Gaukstad. Oslo, 1957.

——. *Breve fra Edvard Grieg til Frants Beyer 1872–1907.* Edited by Marie Beyer. Oslo, 1923.

——. *Breve fra Grieg. Et Udvalg ved Gunnar Hauch.* Copenhagen, 1922.

——. *Briefe an die Verleger der Edition Peters 1866–1907.* Edited by Elsa von Zschinsky-Troxler. Leipzig, 1932.

——. Diaries from 1865–66 and 1905–1907 (unpublished) in the Bergen Public Library.

——. *Essays and Articles*. Edited by Bjarne Kortsen as *Grieg the Writer*, Vol. 1, Bergen, 1973.

——. *Griegs brev til Frants Beyer*. Edited by Bjarne Kortsen. Bergen, 1973.

——. "Komposten." *Norden. Illustreret skandinavisk Revue*. Copenhagen, 1886.

——. Letters to Aimar Grönvold. *Samtiden*, 1927.

——. Letters to Alexander and Gesine Grieg. *Samtiden*, 1892.

——. *Letters to His Friend Frants Beyer*. Edited by Bjarne Kortsen as *Grieg the Writer*, Vol. 2. Bergen, 1973.

——. Letters to [publisher] John Grieg. Edited by Sigurd Grieg. *Norsk musikkgranskning. Aarbok 1943–46*, Oslo, 1947.

——. Letters to Knut Dahle and Johan Halvorsen. Edited by Öyvind Anker. *Norsk musikkgranskning. Aarbok 1943–46*, Oslo, 1947.

——. Letters to Niels Ravnkilde. Edited by Sigurd Berg. *Ord och Bild*, 1947.

——. Letters to Oscar Meyer. *Die Musik*, 1908.

——. Letters to Tor Aulin. Edited by Bo Wallner. *Ord och Bild.*, 1957.

——. "Min första suksess." *Artikler og taler* (ed. Öystein Gaukstad). Oslo, 1957.

——. "Tre Grieg-brev til Björnson." Edited by Öyvind Anker. *Norsk musikkliv*, 1943.

Grieg, Edvard and Nina Grieg. Letter to Louis Monastier-Schroeder. *Norsk musikkgranskning. Aarbok 1943–46*, Oslo, 1947.

Grieg, Sigurd (ed.). "Brever fra Edv. Grieg til John Grieg" [the publisher]. *Norsk musikkgranskning. Aarbok 1943–46*, Oslo, 1947.

Grinde, Nils. *Norsk musikkhistorie*, third ed. Oslo, 1981.

Grönvold, Hans Aimar. *Norske musikere*. Kristiania (Oslo), 1883.

Gröttum, Kaare I. "En studie i Griegs harmonikk. Klanglige saertrekk i op. 17 og 66. En analyse og sammenlikning." Unpublished M.A. thesis, University of Oslo, 1968.

Gurvin, Olav. "Rikard Nordraaks musikk og dei nasjonale föresetnadene for han i kunstmusikken." *Syn og Segn*, 1942.

——. "Three Compositions from Edvard Grieg's Youth." *Norsk musikkgranskning. Aarbok 1951–53*, Oslo, 1953.

Haarklou, Johannes. *Musikfesten i Bergen*. Kristiania (Oslo), 1898.

——. "Erindringer om Grieg." *Ekko*, May 2, 1908.

Halvorsen, Johan. Unpublished papers. Collected by R. Grieg Halvorsen. University Library, Oslo.

Hauch, Gunnar (ed.). *Breve fra Grieg*. Copenhagen, 1922.

Hille, Ragnar. "Edvard Grieg: 'Ballade' op. 24. Et bidrag til en analyse." Unpublished M.A. thesis, University of Oslo, 1965.

Horton, John. *Grieg*. London, 1950.

——. "Grieg's Slaatter for Pianoforte." *Music and Letters*, 1945.

——. "Ibsen, Grieg, and Peer Gynt." *Music and Letters*, 1945.

——. *Scandinavian Music. A Short History*. London, 1963.

——. *Grieg* (The Master Musicians Series). London, 1974.

Huldt-Nyström, Hampus. *Fra munkekor til symfoniorkester. Musikken i det gamle Christiania og i Oslo*. Oslo, 1969.

Hurum, Hans Jörgen. *I Edvard Griegs verden*. Oslo, 1959.

Jappe, Nanna (ed.). "Rikard Nordraak-brev." *Norsk musikkgranskning. Aarbok 1937*. Oslo. 1937.

Jong, J. de. "Een Noorweegsch componist: Edvard Grieg." *De Tijdspiegel*, Haag (The Hague), 1881. Published in a Norwegian translation in *Bergensposten*, May 29, June 2, June 3, and June 5, 1881.

Jordan, Sverre. *Edvard Grieg. En oversikt over hans liv og verker*. Bergen, 1954. (*Supplement I*. Bergen, 1959.)

Josephson, Ludvig. *Ett och annat om Henrik Ibsen och Christiania Theater*. Stockholm, 1898.

Kortsen, Bjarne. *Zur Genesis von Edvard Griegs g-Moll Streichquartett, Op. 27*. West Berlin, 1967.

——. "Grieg's String Quartet and Robert Heckmann." *Music and Letters*, 1968.

——. *Four Unknown Cantatas by Edvard Grieg*. Bergen, 1972.

Kortsen, Bjarne (ed.). *Griegs brev til Frants Beyer*. Bergen, 1973.

——. *Grieg the Writer*: Vol. 1: *Essays and Articles*; Vol. 2: *Letters to his Friend Frants Beyer*. Bergen, 1973.

Kremlev, I. *Edvard Grieg*. Moscow, 1958.

Kühn, A. "R. Wagners Vermächtnis. Musikalische Betrachtungen an der Hand von E. Griegs 'Olav Trygvason.'" *Schweizerische Musikzeitung*, 1894.

La Mara (Maria Lipsius). "Edvard Grieg." *C. F. Peters Grieg-Katalog*, Leipzig, 1898.

Lee, E. Markham. *Grieg*. London, 1928.

Levasjeva, Olga E. *Edvard Grieg. Otsjerk sjisni i tvortsjeva*. Moscow, 1962.

Lindgren, Adolf L. "Edvard Grieg." *Svensk musiktidning*, 1892.

Linge, Ola. *Ole Bull*. Oslo, 1953.

Linge, Tormod. "Det tematisk-motivske förlöp og samspillet i Griegs fiolinsonater." Unpublished M.A. thesis, University of Oslo, 1972.

Mason, Daniel Gregory. *From Grieg to Brahms*. New York, 1902.

——. "Grieg and his Idiosyncrasies." *The Musician*, 1907.

Mathisen, Oddvin. "Fire etterlatte, men fullstendige 'Haugtussasanger' av Edvard Grieg." *Norsk musikktidskrift*, 1973.

Midböe, Hans. *Peer Gynt. Teatret og tiden I–II*. Oslo, 1976–78.

Moe, Wladimir (ed.). *Rikard Nordraak. Hans efterlatte breve*. Oslo, 1921.

Monastier-Schroeder, Louis. *Edvard Grieg*. Lausanne, 1897.

Monrad Johansen, David. *Edvard Grieg*. Oslo, 1934. English trans. by Madge Robertson. Princeton, 1938.

Mortensen, Tore. "Greigs harmoniske stil i strykekvartettene med saerlig henblikk paa impresjonistiske trekk." Unpublished M.A. thesis, University of Oslo, 1970.

Mowinckel, Laila. "Grieg og Debussy." *Norsk musikktidskrift*, 1973.

Musalevskij, V. *Edvard Grieg*. Leningrad, 1936.

Nagelhus, Lorents Aa. "Stoff og stiltrekk fra norsk folkemusikk i Edvard Griegs instrumentalverker." Unpublished M.A. thesis, Norges laererhögskole, Trondheim, 1972.

Newmarch, Rosa. *Tchaikowsky: His Life and Works*. London, 1908.

Niemann, Walter. "Kjerulf und Grieg." *Die nordische Klaviermusik*. Leipzig, 1918.

Nilsen, Halkild. *Kirke- og skoleforhold i Bergen i biskop Jacob Neumanns tid*. Oslo, 1948.

Nordraak, Rikard. *Hans efterlatte breve*. Edited by Wladimir Moe. Oslo, 1921.

Ödegaard, Ola K. "Minner." *Valdresfolk*. Risör, 1919.

Orr, Charles Wilfred. "Grieg's Songs." *Monthly Musical Record*, 1938.

Paulsen, John. *Mine Erindringer*. Copenhagen, 1900.
———. *Samliv med Ibsen* (first volume). Copenhagen and Kristiania (Oslo), 1906.
———. *Billeder fra Bergen*. Kristiania (Oslo), 1908.
———. *Reisen til Monaco*. Kristiania (Oslo), 1909.
———. *Samliv med Ibsen* (second volume). Kristiania (Oslo), 1913.
Peters, Wilhelm. "Grieg the Man." *Illustrated Monthly Magazine*, 1907.
Platzhoff-Lejeune, Eduard. "Aus Briefen Edvard Griegs an einen Schweizer." *Die Musik*, 1907.

Reznicek, Ladislav. "Grieg og Foerster." *Norsk musikktidsskrift*, 1970.
———. *Edvard Grieg og tsjekkisk kultur*. Oslo, 1975.
Rokseth, Yvonne. *Grieg*. Paris, 1933.
Röntgen, Abrahamine (ed.). *Brieven van Julius Röntgen*. Amsterdam, 1934.
Röntgen, Julius. "Edvard Griegs musikalischer Nachlass." *Die Musik*, 1907.
———. *Edvard Grieg*. Second edition, Haag, 1930.
———. *Brieven van Julius Röntgen*. Edited by Abrahamine Röntgen. Amsterdam, 1934.

Sandbakken, Arild. "Modulasjoner og andre former for tonalitetsforandringer i Griegs lyriske stykker for klaver." Unpublished M.A. thesis, University of Oslo, 1967.
Sandvik, Ole Mörk. "L. M. Lindeman og Edvard Grieg." *Kirke og kultur*, 1922.
———. "Det religiöse i Griegs musikk." *Gamle spor. Festskrift til Lyder Brun*. Oslo, 1922.
———. "L. M. Lindeman og Edvard Grieg i deres forhold til norsk folkemusikk." *Syn og Segn*, 1922.
———. "Edvard Grieg und die norwegische Volksmusik." *D. F. Scheurleer Gedenkboek*. Haag, 1925.
———. "Griegs melodikk." *Norsk musikkgranskning. Aarbok 1942*. Oslo, 1943.
———. "Korkomponisten Grieg." *Norsk musikkliv*, 1943.

———. "Nordiske musikkblade." *Norsk musikkgranskning. Aarbok 1943–46*. Oslo, 1947.
Sandvik, Ole Mörk and Gerhard Schjelderup. *Norges Musikhistorie*. Oslo, 1921.
Sawyer, F. "The Tendencies of Modern Harmony as Exemplified in the works of Dvořák and Grieg." *Proceedings of the Musical Association*. London, 1895–96.
Schjelderup, Gerhard R. *Edvard Grieg og hans Vaerker*. Copenhagen, 1903.
———. "Grieg und sein Einfluss auf die Entwicklung der Musik." *Die Musik*, 1932.
Schjelderup, Gerhard and Walter Niemann. *Ed. Grieg. Biographie und Würdigung seiner Werke*. Leipzig, 1908.
Schjelderup-Ebbe, Dag. *A Study of Grieg's Harmony: With Special Reference to his Contributions to Musical Impressionism*. Oslo, 1953.
———. "Grieg och folktonen." *Musikrevy*, 1957.
———. "En ukjent artikkel om Nordraak av Grieg." *Aftenposten*, July 5, 1961.
———. "Neue Ansichten über die früheste Periode Edvard Griegs." *Dansk Aarbog for Musikforskning*. Copenhagen, 1961.
———. *Edvard Grieg 1858–1867*. Oslo, 1964.
———. "Sibelius og Norge." *Suomen Musiikin Vuosikirja 1964–65*. Helsinki, 1965.
Sirnes, Egil. "Edvard Griegs '4 Salmer,' op. 74. Karakteristiske trekk ved form og harmonikk." Unpublished M.A. thesis, University of Oslo, 1968.
Sjögren, Emil. "Edvard Grieg. Naagra erinringar." *Ord och Bild*, 1907.
Skyllstad, Kjell. "Edvard Grieg: Konsert i a-moll." Unpublished M.A. thesis, University of Oslo, 1960.
———. "Theories of Musical Form as Taught at the Leipzig Conservatory in Relation to the Musical Training of Edvard Grieg." *Studia Musicologica Norvegica 1*. Oslo, 1968.
———. "Thematic Structure in Relation to Form in Edvard Grieg's Cyclic Works." *Studia Musicologica Norvegica 3*. Oslo, 1977.
Sontum, B. "Personal Recollections of Ibsen." *The Bookman*. New York, 1913.
Stein, Richard H. *Grieg. Eine Biographie*. Berlin & Leipzig, 1921.
Steinsfjord, Eigil. "Analyse av Edvard Grieg: Lyriske stykker op. 71." Unpublished M.A. thesis, University of Oslo, 1972.
de Stoecklin, Paul. *Grieg*. Paris, 1926.
Stölen, Arnfinn. "Debussys stryke-kvartett i g-moll op. 10 og ei jamföring mellom

denne og Griegs strykekvartett i g-moll op. 27." Unpublished M.A. thesis, University of Oslo, 1968.
Storaas, Reidar. "Edvard Grieg og J. A. B. Christie." *Hardanger*. Nordheimsund, 1964.
Svendsen, Arne R. "Edvard Griegs Vinjesanger." Unpublished M.A. thesis, University of Oslo, 1971.

Tchaikovsky, Peter I. *Life and Works* (ed. by Rosa Newmarch). London, 1908.
Törnblom, Folke H. *Grieg*. Stockholm, 1943.
Torsteinson, Sigmund. *Troldhaugen. Nina og Edvard Griegs hjem*. Fourth edition, Oslo, 1959.
———. *Femti aar med Troldhaugen*. Oslo, 1978.
Traedal, Trygve. "Harmoniske saertrekk i Griegs Slaatter op. 72." Unpublished M.A. thesis, University of Oslo, 1972.
Tveitt, Geirr. "Edvard Grieg og norsk Folkemusikk." *Dansk Musiktidsskrift*, 1943.

Volden, Torstein. "Studier i Edvard Griegs Haugtussasanger med saerlig henblikk paa sangenes opprinnelse og paa forholdet mellom poesi og musikk." Unpublished M.A. thesis, University of Oslo, 1967.
Vorosjilov, H. *Edvard Grieg*. St. Petersburg, 1898.
Vos, A.C. *Het leven van Edvard Grieg*. Haag (The Hague), 1951.

Walker, Ernest. "Edvard Grieg." *Music and Letters*, 1938.
Wallner, Bo (ed.). "Edvard Griegs brev till Tor Aulin." *Ord och Bild*, 1957.
Weismann, A. "Grieg als Liederkomponist." *Zeitschrift für Musik*, 1932.
van Westrhene, P. A. *Edvard Grieg*. Haarlem, 1897.

Zeitschrift der Internationalen Musikgesellschaft, Hefte 6. 1906.
Zschinsky-Troxler, Elsa von (ed.). *Edvard Grieg. Briefe an die Verleger der Edition Peters 1866–1907*. Leipzig, 1932.

Index of Compositions

Italics denote a composition containing discrete movements. The titles of all other compositions, including titled elements of larger works, are in quotation marks. Arabic numbers refer to the main text. Arabic numbers followed by an asterisk refer to primary materials or text accompanying an illustration.

General Index